program
budgeting
and
benefit-cost
analysis

HARLEY H. HINRICHS
*United States Naval Academy
and the University of Maryland*

GRAEME M. TAYLOR
*Management Analysis Center, Inc.
Washington, D. C.
and the University of Maryland*

program budgeting and benefit-cost analysis

CASES, TEXT
and READINGS

GOODYEAR PUBLISHING CO., INC.,
PACIFIC PALISADES, CALIFORNIA

program budgeting and benefit-cost analysis
CASES, TEXT and READINGS
by
HARLEY H. HINRICHS
GRAEME M. TAYLOR

*To the
Members and Staff of the
Joint Economic Committee of the
United States Congress*

© 1969 by Goodyear Publishing Company, Inc.
Pacific Palisades, California

Library of Congress Catalog Card Number: 70–83541

Printed in the United States of America

Current Printing:
10 9 8 7 6 5 4

preface

Revolutions are often not recognized until they are over. Not so today. The twentieth century has seen the rise of the public (government) sector to unprecedented size and scope as well as more widespread systematic analysis of the use of these greatly increased resources. The day is past when government activities were so limited that policy-executors and policy-makers (ultimately the electorate) could safely ignore the efficiency of government operations. Likewise, economic models could concentrate on the private sector and pass off the public sector with a shrug. Public Finance as an academic subject would have been more appropriately titled Public Taxation.

Today the revolution is with us. Government expenditures in the United States by 1970 will be *treble* the entire Gross National Product reached in 1940. Expenditure analysis is no longer an academic exercise (even a belated one).* Some 90,000 units of government in the United States—ranging from sewer districts to the federal government itself—are now seeking to discover, learn, and teach what there is to know about the systematic analysis of public expenditures. Universities and government agencies have rapidly established courses to organize this learning process. What is known and being discovered about expenditure analysis is recent and growing. Hence, the current search for texts, resource materials, reference works, and supplementary readings. This volume incorporates much of the best of what is known, recent, and vital to acquiring a grasp of the fundamentals of this new wave of public expenditure analysis. We believe it offers one answer in the search.

Analyzing government expenditures involves more than mere theory—or mere practice. Answers are being developed in both academia and in the confines of government agencies. Teaching and learning this analytic process or, more grandiloquently, this philosophic and scientific approach means more than under-

---

* It took more than a hundred years after Dupuit's classic paper (1844) on the utility of public works before serious public sector analysis was exhumed from its unwatered grave. Non-academic concern with benefits was almost exclusively limited to river and harbor projects (The River and Harbor Act of 1902) and later water resource problems (such as in the Flood Control Act of 1936 and later measures).

standing new theories, rules, procedures, and vocabulary. It involves a judicious combination of formal discipline (such as mathematics and logic), social sciences (such as political science and economics), and management arts and practices. Hence the combination in this book of theory, cases, and readings: theory for the foundation; cases to test and apply theory, to learn by doing; and finally, readings to explore new issues and thinking on the frontiers of this rapidly evolving area of concern and study.

This book is designed for a diverse, tool-seeking, and policy-oriented audience. Government policymakers, technicians, and consultants as well as professors, graduate and upper-level undergraduate students should find the contents relevant and useful. In a university or college this book will be useful as a text for courses in program budgeting, benefit-cost analysis, public expenditure criteria and analysis, and government investment project analysis; it should also be useful as a text or as a collection of supplementary readings for courses in public sector economics, government finance and expenditures, public finance, public administration, and even in business administration courses touching on management of public enterprises and public utilities. More specific use for this book may be found in federal, state and local agency courses concerned with the systematic analysis of public expenditures and with the initiation and refinement of planning-programming-budgeting (PPB) systems. As evidenced by the keen interest of the Joint Economic Committee of the United States Congress, numerous state legislatures, city and county councils, and legislative members and their staffs should also find the comprehensive treatment of benefit-cost analysis presented here as virtually required reading if this revolution in public expenditures is to be understood and properly managed.

This book is organized so as to present a logical sequence for understanding benefit-cost analysis. It begins by asking "Why Benefit-Cost Analysis?" This introduction states the rationale of benefit-cost analysis, what it is and what it is not. Then a simple but comprehensive primer of benefit-cost theory is outlined to alert the reader to the broader, conceptual framework of economic theory: ends, means, rules of the game, externalities, and measurement problems compounded by differences in time and the risks and uncertainties of such ends and means. Following this introductory setting of the stage, theory, readings, and cases are presented: the concept of a program budget, the design of a program structure, determining objectives, criteria, and output measures.

At the core rests an extensive treatment of program analysis itself. This includes capital budgeting, model-building, assumptions and constraints, decision rules, estimating market demand in the public sector, externalities and incommensurables, multiple objectives, time, risk, and uncertainty, systems analysis, problem formulation, price incentives, and finally—having now progressed to levels of greater sophistication and complexity—comprehensive program evaluation, monitoring, control, and the multiple purposes of budget systems. To round out the volume as a self-contained text, appendices provide present value tables (to aid in the case solutions) and an extensive bibliography of articles, books, and cases.

The contents comprise a variety of new articles and surveys designed solely for this book, edited reprints of important articles (some of which are inaccessible or out of print, others published as recently as 1968), and fifteen cases from diverse settings, ranging from the Peace Corps to the Forest Service, from the Post Office to the Office of Economic Opportunity, from disease control to controlling airport congestion. Eleven of these cases were prepared by Management Analysis Center, Inc. under government contract for use by the Civil Service Commission and the Bureau of the Budget; the remaining four cases were specifically developed for this book by graduate students (all government officials) under the supervision of the editors; each case was classroom-tested and subsequently revised to enhance its teachability and instructional value. This is the first appearance of a collection of cases of this nature.

Contributions have been drawn from a variety of authorities including the former Director of the Bureau of the Budget, Charles L. Schultze, and the former Secretary of Defense, Robert S. McNamara, both of whom have pioneered the introduction of program analysis of a more sophisticated style in the federal government. Other authors and contributors include an expert on state and local programs (Harry P. Hatry), the former head of the Program Evaluation Staff of the Bureau of the Budget (John Haldi), the Director of PPB Training for the Civil Service Commission (Chester Wright), authorities in the field of systematic analysis and program budgeting (Alain Enthoven, Henry Rowen, James Schlesinger, and Allen Schick), and leading academic economists (Arthur Smithies, William Baumol, and Jacob Stockfisch). The legislative viewpoint is represented by extracts from reports of the Comptroller General (Elmer B. Staats) and the Joint Economic Committee.

The editors of this book are both teachers and practitioners of benefit-cost analysis. Harley H. Hinrichs has taught graduate public finance theory courses, including benefit-cost analysis, at the Universities of Wisconsin and Maryland (both classes included selected federal officials in the PPB training program) as well as having taught at Harvard University, El Colegio de Mexico, Kabul University (Afghanistan), and Purdue University; he has also worked as a fiscal economist for both the executive (Office of the Secretary of the Treasury) and the legislative (Joint Economic Committee) branches of the federal government as well as for international organizations and foreign and state governments.

Graeme M. Taylor, vice president of Management Analysis Center, Inc., heads the Washington office of the firm, an organization actively involved in management education and the application of techniques of systematic analysis to problems of industry and government. He has had extensive experience in the case-method of instruction, both at the University of Maryland and through courses he has developed for numerous federal, state, and local legislative and executive groups. In 1967 he was invited by the University of Maryland and the Bureau of the Budget to design a new case-method graduate course in benefit-cost analysis. This course, Economics 237, formed part of the federal government's extended program in systematic analysis offered at Maryland in 1967–1968. The editors taught the course jointly, and "tested" the contents of this volume under class conditions.

Thanks are due to many: to Professor Dudley Dillard, chairman of the

Economics Department at the University of Maryland, for his cooperation and support in establishing the new course; to the contributors to this book, especially for editorial advice on the use of their articles by Charles Schultze, Arthur Smithies, John Haldi, Allen Schick, and Harry Hatry; to the many government agencies and officials who generously provided material, data, and advice during the development of the cases; and above all, to the student members (including government officials) of Economics 237 at the University of Maryland who prepared, debated, and revised their own and other cases, many of which appear in this book. Their names deserve to be recorded:

Mark Adelman, Gerard Beaulieu, Robert Creller, James Cudney, Robert Dougan, Robert Dunker, Jr., Allan Fehr, Jr., John Flory, Joseph Goodwin, William Grodowitz, Donald Hartman, Billy Hinkle, Stephen Lejko, Herbert Mars, James Mason, Jr., Kenneth McConoughey, Michael McKay, Edmund Perry, Thomas Ronzetti, Mohammed Safa, Frank Santini, John Scanlon, Robert Stansberry, Lowell Sturgill, Frank Urabeck, and Mable Warnecke

We are especially indebted to the Joint Economic Committee, its chairman Senator William Proxmire, its Staff Executive Director John R. Stark, Research Director James W. Knowles, and Staff Economist Daniel J. Edwards for their dedicated efforts to focus on the PPB System in recent years. Their studies, hearings, and reports have been an exceedingly useful contribution in this area. We are grateful for their permission to reprint relevant excerpts in this book.

The eleven cases prepared by Management Analysis Center, Inc. were written under the supervision of three members of the faculty of the Harvard Graduate School of Business Administration—Professors Charles J. Christenson, Warren A. Law, and Richard F. Vancil. Our thanks go to these men, not only for their efforts in pioneering the application of the case-method of instruction to government PPB training programs on behalf of the U. S. Civil Service Commission, but also for their cooperation and assistance in making it possible to include these cases in this volume. We are deeply appreciative of the leadership and counsel of officials of both the Civil Service Commission and the Bureau of the Budget who initiated and guided the case development project which produced the set of cases from which the eleven included here were selected. We would particularly like to recognize the contributions to this effort of William Medina, Chester Wright, John Haldi, and David Page.

Generous logistical support was provided by Management Analysis Center, Inc. (both in Washington and Cambridge, Massachusetts), and untiring administrative devotion was graciously given by Elizabeth Butt. Early interest and inspiration for this book can be credited to Al Goodyear, president of Goodyear Publishing Company.

HARLEY H. HINRICHS
GRAEME M. TAYLOR

Washington, D. C.

table of contents

PART

I

the resource allocation framework

PART

II

objectives criteria and output measures

program analysis

PART

conclusion

INTRODUCTION

Why Benefit-Cost Analysis?

By
CHARLES L. SCHULTZE

Much has been published on PPB. Learned articles have treated it sometimes as the greatest thing since the invention of the wheel. Other articles attack it, either as a naive attempt to quantify and computerize the imponderable, or as an arrogant effort on the part of latter-day technocrats to usurp the decision-making function in a political democracy.

PPB is neither. It *is* a means of *helping* responsible officials make decisions. It is *not* a mechanical substitute for the good judgment, political wisdom and leadership of those officials.

The need for PPB, along the lines we are trying to establish, stems from two sources:

First, the resources of the government are always less than we need to accomplish all the good and useful things that we would like to do. Therefore, among competing claims on resources, we must choose those which contribute most to our national objectives, and we must execute our choices effectively and efficiently in order to free scarce resources for other good and useful things.

Second, government programs rarely have an automatic regulator that tells us when an activity has ceased to be productive or could be made more efficient, or should be displaced by another activity. In private business, society relies upon profits and competition to furnish the needed incentives and discipline and to provide a feedback on the quality of decisions. The system is imperfect, but basically sound in the private sector—it is virtually nonexistent in the government sector. In government, we must find another tool for making *choices* which resource scarcity forces upon us.

Now to say that wise choice ultimately depends on good judgment is not the same thing as saying that good judgment *alone* makes for wise choices. Forced to choose among irrelevant alternatives, on the basis of misleading facts, and without the benefit of solid analysis, even the best judgment can do little but grope intuitively in the

This introductory paper places benefit-cost analysis in the perspective of the Planning-Programming-Budgeting (PPB) System. Edited excerpts are from a statement by the former Director, Bureau of the Budget, before the Subcommittee on National Security and International Operations of the Committee on Government Operations, U.S. Senate, 90th Congress, 1st Session, August 23, 1967.

dark. PPB is a means to improve the decision-making process, in order to assist the final judgment, not to supplant it.

While I realize that the major outlines of PPB are familiar to you, let me summarize briefly its five major elements, as I see them, and then concentrate in some detail on several general aspects of PPB.

I ask your indulgence to spend some time on this general treatment, before turning to the national security and foreign affairs areas, because there are several features of PPB which have plagued understanding of it for some time. I would like to try to clear the air on these matters.

THE NATURE OF THE PPB SYSTEM

As the *first* step PPB calls for a careful specification and analysis of basic program objectives in each major area of governmental activity. The key to this part of the operation is forcing federal agencies to back away from the particular program they are carrying on at the moment and to look at their objectives. What are they really trying to accomplish? The objective of our intercity highway program, for example, is *not* to build highways. Highways are useful only as they serve a higher objective, namely transporting people and goods effectively and efficiently and safely. Once this is accepted as an objective, it then becomes possible to analyze aviation, railroads and highways to determine the most effective network of transportation. But so long as we think of the ultimate objective of the highway program as simply laying concrete, this comparison of different transportation systems is impossible.

At the same time, while we want to view our objectives broadly we are not helped at all by stating them too broadly. Highways or transportation, for example, generally may contribute to the good life and to national unity, but to take these as our sole stated objectives does not tell us much, if anything, useful about the desirable rate of highway building, the character of the highways, their locations, or their relations to other elements of our transportation system. In the case of highways, we want a specification of objectives broader than "laying concrete" but narrower than "improving our national life." As a matter of fact, there is a constant interaction between the decision process and our knowledge of our true objectives. Often, the more we learn about *how* to reach an objective, the more clearly we begin to understand the objective itself.

The *second* step, under the PPB system, is to analyze insofar as possible, the *output* of a given program in terms of the objectives initially specified in the first step. Again, for example, in the case of highways, we must ask not primarily how many miles of concrete are laid, but more fundamentally what the program produces in terms of swifter, safer, less-congested travel—how many hours of travel time are eliminated, how many accidents are prevented.

The *third* step is to measure the *total costs* of the program, not just for one year, but over at least several years ahead. In this year's budget, for example, $10 million in budget funds are requested for the Atomic Energy Commission to design a 200 billion electron volt atom-smasher. But the total cost of constructing this machine will amount to $250 million or more. We have commonly had some estimate of the total capital cost in mind when we have embarked on construction projects. This has not happened systematically, however. And we can't stop here. Once the machine is built, the annual operating costs will run $50 to $100 million per year. This is not to say that because of these costs we should decide to abandon the project. But it does mean that we should be aware of all the costs when we make the initial $10 million decision, not just the capital costs but the follow on operating costs as well. Or, to cite the highway example again, in deciding to build an expressway through a downtown area we must take into account not only the cost of the expressway, but also the cost of relocating the displaced residents and, in a qualitative sense, the effects of the freeway on the areas through which it is to run.

All of this sounds obvious. Yet, too often large federal investment decisions have been made on the basis of the first-year costs alone—or made without taking into account all of the indirect associated costs.

The *fourth* and crucial step is to analyze *alternatives,* seeking those which have the greatest effectiveness in achieving the basic objectives specified in the first step or which achieve those objectives at the least cost. In the highway case, for example, we should be comparing the effectiveness of additions or improvements to highways with that of additions or improvements to aviation and railroads as a means of providing safe and efficient transportation. This does not mean that we pick only one. Of course, we should not. But we do need to decide, at least roughly, which

combination of alternatives is the preferred one.

By this process we hope to induce federal agencies to consider particular programs not as ends in themselves—to be perpetuated without challenge or question. Rather, they must be viewed as means to higher objectives and subjected to competition with alternative and perhaps more effective programs. It is this competition among alternatives which is crucial as a means of testing the effectiveness and economy of existing and proposed programs.

The *fifth* and final element of this approach is establishing this method and these analytic techniques throughout the government in a *systematic* way, so that, over time, more and more budgetary decisions can be subjected to this kind of rigorous analysis.

Merely writing up academic papers is not enough. The analysis has to be an integral part of the budgetary decisions. The programming concept is the critical link that relates planning to budgeting, converting planning from paper exercise to an important part of the decision process.

SOME SPECIAL CONSIDERATIONS

There are several aspects of this system which warrant special attention, in part because they have been subject to some criticism. Let me elaborate briefly on two of those aspects.

Multi-year programs

PPB, particularly as it is presented in brief summaries and—I must admit—as we first conceived it, puts heavy stress on *forward programming*—on laying out for five or ten years ahead a program of action in each major area of federal activity, be it highway construction, foreign assistance, or aid to elementary education.

Clearly, one cannot address the problem of the urban ghetto solely in terms of what can be done in a single fiscal year. If we restrict ourselves to such a narrow outlook, we will simply be rushing around putting band-aids on festering wounds. We cannot attack the problem of water supplies for the arid sections of the nation solely in terms of individual projects, or a slate of public works authorizations for a single year. Nor can we deal with problems of rising medical costs and scarcity of medical manpower by devising a series of one-year programs. After all, it takes 10 to 14 years to turn a high school graduate into a doctor. And a P.L. 480 program which ignored the long-run necessity to increase food production in the developing countries could, as we have begun to realize, do more harm than good.

A reasonable decision-making process must, therefore, provide the decision-maker with a perspective longer than a single year. Ad hoc solutions are often extremely valuable. But in dealing with deep-rooted problems pure "ad hocery" can become a destructive force rather than a tool for good. And so PPB lays great stress on forward planning as an essential aid to decision-making.

But here we come up against a dilemma. When the chips are down, no President, no Cabinet officer or Budget Director—or Congress for that matter—is really willing to commit himself in advance to decisions in 1967 about the specific level of Federal programs in 1970 or 1972. Nor should

he be. There is nothing inherent, for example, in the nature of a P.L. 480 program which requires us to decide this year how much food aid we should provide in 1971 or 1972. The Elementary and Secondary Education Act —for which we have requested $1.6 billion in 1968—could be funded at several very different levels in 1971, depending on the fiscal situation, competing needs, and our evaluation of the merits of the program at that time. Some of our programs are frankly experimental, and we want to examine the results before we *commit* to full scale activities—even though for *planning* purposes, we might assume a full-scale commitment. In other words, for most programs, our decisions today do not necessarily bind us to a particular level of those programs several years ahead. And there is no use pretending that we need make these decisions before we have to—indeed, making such decisions prematurely would be harmful.

At the same time, *some* of the decisions about this year's budget *do* imply legal or moral commitments about future budgetary levels. In the example I noted earlier, this year's decision about the 200 Bev accelerator clearly implies specific capital and operating outlays for many years to come.

A decision to shift the mix of airlift vs sealift in transporting and supplying our conventional forces abroad, carries with it a whole series of implications about future budgetary levels. It is essential that we know, program by program and, at least roughly, for the budget as a whole, what costs we are firmly committed to next year from this year's budget decisions. Unless we know this, we can find ourselves unknowingly foreclosing future options by current decisions.

How do we sort out realistically this tangle of conflicting needs and problems with respect to multi-year planning and budget figures? We have begun to approach it as follows.

Each Federal agency, for each of its major programs, is asked to present and evaluate those programs in terms of long-run objectives. To the fullest extent possible, programs are to be analyzed and this year's budget request justified in the context of forward planning toward basic targets.

But these long-run plans are not to be considered *commitments* on the part of the agency head. As you might expect, the sum total of all the forward plans of all federal agencies tends to exceed, by far, any reasonable projection of available resources. Consequently, the acceptance or rejection of this year's budget request is *not* to be considered an acceptance or rejection by the President of future plans. Rather, the forward planning is a means of evaluating current decisions in the context of a comprehensive analysis of problems and alternative solutions. It is an aid to current decision-making, not a premature commitment to future decisions.

At the same time agencies will be required to specify the future-year budgetary consequences of current decisions. For example, HEW may present a program for assisting the construction of medical schools in the context, say, of increasing the supply of doctors 35 percent by 1975. Analysis of the rationale behind the 1975 target and knowledge of the future budgetary costs of reaching it are an aid to making current decisions. But

the program, within reason, can be accelerated or decelerated in succeeding years as conditions require. Hence, acceptance of *this year's* program implies no commitment about the specific rate of progress toward the target in later years. The future year costs of reaching the target are treated as planning aids, not immutable decisions. On the other hand, if the particular program for medical school construction envisaged entering into advance five-year commitments to match medical schools' own construction outlays with federal funds, then we would insist on having an estimate of the federal costs over the full five years. For in this case, the current year's decisions will definitely commit the expenditure of federal funds over five years—there would be no options left open, on the downward side at least. And these kinds of future year estimates, we must have.

In short, then, we are encouraging multi-year *planning;* we do *not* consider the forward years' part of the plan as a decision or commitment, except where current decisions bind us to future year outlays.

Mathematics, statistics, computers and the decision process

While our approach to the PPB in the past may, perhaps, legitimately be criticized for lack of precision about forward planning, there is another frequently heard criticism of PPB which stems, I believe, from a straight misconception as to what PPB is all about.

This criticism takes a number of forms. But basically it charges that PPB and cost-effectiveness analysis set up a bias in decision-making: by concentrating on the cost accounting elements of an issue and ignoring those human factors and intangibles which cannot be quantified; or, conversely, by naively attempting to put numbers on these essentially imponderable elements, thereby misleading the decision-maker.

Often this criticism is expressed in terms of an attack on PPB for trying to "computerize" what is essentially a political and judgmental process. Or sometimes it is expressed in terms of "not letting the statisticians and cost accountants take over."

I might interpolate, Mr. Chairman, that on the basis of my experience in government, which is limited, I will admit, this fear of the statisticians and analysts taking over ranks about 28th on my list of fears, perhaps just below my fear of being eaten alive by piranhas. I have many fears of government, and this is not one of them so far.

Quite frankly, Mr. Chairman, these kinds of criticisms—however sincere—reflect a complete misunderstanding of the issue. And sometimes they simply reflect chagrin that particular pet projects do not show up well under the light of cost-effectiveness analysis.

PPB *does* call for systematic analysis of program proposals and decisions, concentrating upon those decisions which have budgetary consequences. But systematic analysis does not have to be and is not co-extensive with quantitative analysis. The word "analyze" does not, in any man's dictionary, have the same meaning as the words "quantify" or "measure," although analysis often includes measurement.

Systematic analysis is an aid to policy debate. Too often these debates revolve around a simple list of pros and cons. There are no means of making progress in the debate, since participants simply repeat, in different words, their original positions. Systematic analysis is designed to improve this process by:

Uncovering the irrelevant issues.

Identifying the specific assumptions and factual bases upon which alternative recommendations rest, and,

Tracing out the knowable consequences and costs of each alternative.

By this means, systematic analysis is designed to narrow the debate, to focus it on the important issues, and— I underline and stress this—to separate those points about which the judgments of reasonable men can disagree from those which are demonstrably true or false.

Now such analysis often does, and must, involve quantitative estimates. Most of our decisions—in fact, all of our budgetary decisions—willy-nilly involve quantitative consideration. For example, take the question of how many doctors to train and how much aid to give to medical schools. We can debate this simply in terms of arguing more or less budget dollars for the program. Alternatively, we can calculate the current and projected ratio of doctors to population, examine the relationship between the doctor/population ratio and various indices of health, review the distribution of doctors throughout various areas in the nation, estimate the costs of training doctors, and a host of similar factors. We cannot, of course, measure precisely, or even close to precisely, the national advantages to be gained from a program of aid to medical schools, nor can we account for all of the costs. But we can isolate, in a quantitative form, a number of the key elements involved in the program. The debate then can proceed in terms of weighing fairly specifically the advantages the nation gains from alternative increases in the supply of doctors against the costs of achieving each alternative.

Handled properly, a well constructed numerical estimate can be worth a thousand words. And, in PPB, we seek to encourage quantitative estimates, as part of the systematic analysis of budgetary issues.

But this, most emphatically, does not mean that quantitative estimates are the only elements of systematic analysis. The latter is far broader than the former. Human factors and intangible elements in a decision must not be ignored. And that which cannot reasonably be measured should not be.

In short, Mr. Chairman, PPB does not represent an attempt to "computerize" decision-making or to measure the immeasurable or to ignore the intangible. It merely seeks to subject to systematic analysis both the tangible and the intangible elements of a program decision.

PROSPECTS AND PROBLEMS

Let me turn to our prospects for PPB and some of the problems we are facing.

As you know, it was two years ago this month when the President instructed that PPB be installed in all major civilian agencies. Not surprisingly, the application of PPB to 21 agencies so far (36 agencies ultimately) dealing with a variety of national problems, has resulted in great differences in technique and result. Performance so far has been spotty,

with great disparities between agencies and between constituent parts of agencies. This is due in part to differences in the extent to which agencies have worked out means of adapting and using PPB, and in part to the difficulty of the substantive questions involved.

From each agency we are requiring this year three formal kinds of submissions:

1. A *Program Memorandum* for each of its major program categories. These memoranda:

Contain the major recommendations of the agency head for the coming budget;

Identify the major issues involved in the recommendations, in terms of a selection from among alternative choices;

Explain the basis for the recommended choice among those alternatives.

Realistically, we cannot yet expect that every choice be backed up by a full analytic approach. Analytic staffs are just being developed in many cases; and there are thousands of issues. But we have required that where the analytic base is lacking, the Program Memorandum at least contain a clear statement of the reasons which were employed in choosing the particular recommendations involved.

2. *Special studies* of individual issues. These studies, addressed to issues of particular importance, form the analytic background for many of the recommendations in the Program Memorandum. Work on these studies should be a year-round affair, not something confined to the few weeks or months before the budget is developed.

3. A *Program and Financial Plan* which lays out in tabular form the costs and, wherever possible, the outputs of agency programs. This is a multi-year table. For future years, the entries show the future-year implications of present decisions—i.e., they do not reflect future decisions but only the future consequences of present decisions.

Some of the major problems we face are:

Maintaining a schedule that will permit PPB material to be used in the development of the budget. One of our problems here is the crowding together of the analytic discussion of major issues and the detailed budgetary decisions which follow out major program decisions. Ideally, we would like to schedule this so that we first make major program decisions and then translate them into detailed budget issues, but, given the human frailties of the agency and Budget Bureau staffs involved, the decisions tend to get crowded together. It is a massive problem to sort them out, because we must do all of it in three or four months. This is a real problem and we have not licked it yet;

Linking broad program analysis to the budgetary decision process in terms of detailed appropriation requests: HEW alone, for example, has 116 separate appropriations;

Securing appropriations for, and developing, experienced PPB staffs appropriately placed within the agencies to improve the quality of their planning processes;

The difficulty of obtaining relevant data;

The problem of defining program benefits in concrete and specific ways;

The application of PPB to programs which require participation by federal, state and local governments;

Finally, convincing harassed and skeptical agency officials of the utility of PPB in their operation.

The list of problems is formidable, but I believe we are making progress. The Program Memoranda this year appear to be more useful than last, in terms of form and focus, if not in terms of analytic content. I think that a number of the documents this year will at least provide useful summaries of program strategy.

I look forward to substantial improvements next year in terms of schedule, understanding of the role and desired character of the Program Memoranda, and perhaps more important, in terms of their analytic content. Analytic staffs have been assembled and have had a chance to shake down; a number of data collection efforts and long term study efforts should reach fruition; and we are learning how to state program issues in a way that facilitates analysis and comparison. We have not yet by any means achieved my expectations for the system. That is partly because I have such high expectations for it.

Ultimately I expect we will realize those expectations.

Government Decision Making and the Theory of Benefit-Cost Analysis: A Primer

By
HARLEY H. HINRICHS

INTRODUCTION: THE STUFF OF REALITY AND THE NATURE OF DECISION MAKING

In the beginning, there was stuff: bits and pieces of phenomena. Man, by his very nature, has tried ever since to organize this stuff both in his mind and in his acts. This organization of stuff is called science. It serves to explain the past and to help predict the future. To do this man is forced to simplify reality—abstract from it, put it into boxes or categories, to infer relationships and to make decisions assuming these relationships will hold. This is the basis of decision making.

Ever since the Garden of Eden man has been concerned with allocation problems, the problems created by scarce means and unlimited ends. Then it was allocating four fig leaves between two people; now it is spending billions of dollars to pacify millions of people.

In theory the problem is simple; it is difficult only in practice. In theory, say in a simple nondimensional world of no time, no space, no uncertainties, one merely decides what he wants (specifies ends), measures them (quantifies benefits), and then uses his limited means to achieve the greatest possible value of his wants (benefits). In a more complex world the means

become budgets so that one merely has to maximize the benefits (once specified and quantified) for any given set of inputs (specified and quantified costs). This may be called Problem Type I: maximize benefits, given costs, e.g., build the highest pyramid with a given number of bricks.

A different allocation problem is

This simple primer is designed for the upper-level undergraduate and/or government decision makers who have long since passed through the portals of academe or who have not had extensive training in economics. As a primer, it is a "first lesson" that presumes little or no previous exposure to the subject matter. For more advanced surveys (upon which this primer leans heavily) see Otto Eckstein, "A Survey of the Theory of Public Expenditure Criteria," in *Public Finances: Needs, Sources, and Utilization*, National Bureau of Economic Research (Princeton: Princeton University Press, 1961), pp. 439–494; and A. R. Prest and R. Turvey, "Cost-Benefit Analysis: A Survey," *Economic Journal*, December, 1965, pp. 683–735, and also reprinted in *Surveys of Economic Theory*, Vol. III: Resource Allocation (New York: Macmillan and St. Martin's Press, 1966). The Prest and Turvey survey includes a 90-item bibliography. For ease in reading and fluidity in style this paper has been shorn of most of its footnotes; thus, readers who have more serious research intents are advised to refer to the Prest-Turvey bibliography which underlies this paper. The author is grateful to the following for their comments on earlier drafts of this paper: A. R. Prest, Chester Wright, Graeme Taylor, Wade Sewell, and Nancy MacIvor Hinrichs.

Problem Type II: minimize costs to achieve any given level of benefits (often called "cost-effectiveness" analysis). Problem Type III becomes more sticky when both benefits and costs may vary. This type of problem requires solving for the optimal size of the public sector (à la Samuelson), which reverts the original problem back to one of Type II. Given production possibilities in the widest possible scope, the name of the game is still scarce means. But keeping in mind a separate Type III problem for less-than-global solutions allows the decision maker to see how sensitive outputs are to marginal changes in inputs and vice versa.

This is all elementary. If one knows the data of any of these problems (i.e., the benefits and costs), the solution is nothing new but merely another name for what one already has. Consequents are buried within antecedents; inferences are drawn logically, not created *de novo*. Thus, the crux of all benefit-cost problems lies in a statement of the problem, for if one knows the problem, one already has the solution (given free computer time). What then is the problem(s)? It is deciding:

1. What do you want? (Specify ends/benefits.)

2. How do you measure these wants? (Quantify, if possible, these benefits in dollar terms so that different benefits may be compared against each other and against the costs of attaining them.)

3. What does it cost? (Specify which costs are to be counted; in a more meaningful sense these costs represent other benefits foregone.)

4. How do you measure these costs? (Quantify, if possible, in dollar terms to allow comparisons.)

5. What are the rules of the game

you are playing? (Specify the constraints.) What do you assume as untouchable and/or unchangeable in reaching a solution? That is, what solutions otherwise optimal must be discarded because they break the rules that you or others impose?

6. Can you ignore the externalities? (As everything causes—or is related to —everything else, you have by necessity excluded some inputs (costs) and outputs (benefits) from your earlier analysis simply to arrive at some conclusion; now you must decide if these excluded phenomena really make no difference in your analysis.)

These are the core questions. We have excluded further questions as to the political strategy of getting legislative or other bodies to accept your (the technician's) solution as well as management-administrative techniques to implement the solution, once adopted. Let us then explore the theoretical issues within each of these questions, but subsequently ordered in the more traditional fashion of (1) the objective function, (2) constraints, (3) externalities, (4) time, and (5) risk and uncertainty.[1] The latter two categories interject the time and uncertainty problem into measuring costs and benefits. When neither costs nor benefits are simultaneous and certain, then one must deal with comparing dollars of cost and benefit at different times (and thus values) and at different (known and/or unknown) probabilities of occurring.

THE OBJECTIVE FUNCTION

What do you want? That is, what do you value? What are the benefits you desire—among all other possible bene-

---

[1] This is the organizational structure of Otto Eckstein, *op. cit.*

fits? Do you, in fact, wish to "maximize" these benefits? (Some, perhaps following Herbert Simon, may wish simply not to rock the boat and thus "satisfice" rather than "maximize.") In theory the answer is simple: by all means, let's maximize welfare,[2] happiness, ultimate satisfaction, or what have you. All ends may be transformed into merely means towards this ultimate end. The only problem is attaching numerical values (say dollars or even utiles) to this ultimate end and then comparing such values among different people with different tastes. Even if we could quantify Nirvana, we would still have to specify more precisely what we wanted. We have four choices:

1. Ignore societies, groups, regions; attach value only to individuals (thus junking organic theories of the state), and maximize:

$$W = W(W_1, \ldots, W_n). \quad (W = \text{welfare})$$

Thus given this maximand, there remain three other questions for any policy decision to change the status quo, and therefore move toward maximizing welfare. (A change in welfare being: $\Delta W = \Delta W(\Delta W_1, \ldots, \Delta W_n)$

2. Play the game "Everybody wins." That is, move the pieces in the game of life so that all individuals gain in welfare, i.e.,

$$\Delta W_i > 0 \quad \text{for all } i.$$

3. Play the game "Somebody wins, nobody loses." (Movement toward Pareto Optimality.) That is, move the

pieces so that at least one individual gains and nobody is worse off, i.e.,

$$\Delta W_i \geqq 0 \quad \text{for all } i.$$

4. Play the game "The winners outweigh the losers." That is, move the pieces so that there is a *net* gain, the gains outweigh the losses. This results in a further decision being required. Do you measure at prices before the move (Kaldor), after the move (Hicks), or both (Scitovsky)?

Even after these four relatively easy decisions are made, one must find proxies for "welfare." Do we choose as the appropriate stand-in "income," "consumption," "probable income or consumption," "probable present (or terminal) value of a future stream of income and/or consumption"?

The game most economists and policymakers prefer seems to be Game 4, such as in the Trade Expansion Act of 1962, whereby the gains to the winners (consumers and exporters) are considered to outweigh the losses to the losers (import-substitute industries and their workers) with compensation—adjustment assistance—to be made in theory if not in practice.[3] The proxy most often used for welfare seems to be per capita income, or in more sophisticated analyses, the present value of an expected future stream of income for the individuals affected by a policy decision (for example farmers affected by an irrigation project). Secondary benefits (for example pecuniary spillovers or windfall profits) are generally excluded. For example the benefits of irrigation projects may be determined by computing the value

---

[2] Welfare as used in this paper should not be confused with the meaning of welfare in the expression "health, education and welfare" or "social welfare work" but is restricted to the more technical economists' definition concerned with individuals' subjective sense of satisfaction and/or the achievement of preferences.

[3] See Harley H. Hinrichs, "A Benefit-Cost Analysis of the Removal of Import Quotas on the Stainless Steel Flatware Industry," *Hearings* (Washington, D.C.: U.S. Tariff Commission, May 23, 1967).

of the increase in grain output (less increased farmers' costs) but would exclude the increased profits of the railroads in hauling the grain.

Other types of objectives

When the world is not so simple as to see goals in terms of "maximizing goodies" or "minimizing baddies," when uncertainties and incommensurabilities may prevail, objectives and/or criteria may be quite different from the conventional sort. In a series of possible outcomes one may wish to opt for (1) a maximin criterion: maximize the minimum possible gain regardless of what moves you or others may make, e.g., in U. S. defense strategy the choice of offensive and defensive weapons quite often is premised on achieving some "assured destructive capability" (or minimum effective deterrent) rather than, say, maximizing happiness; (2) a minimax criterion: minimize the maximum regret possible regardless of what moves you or others may make, e.g., in U. S. civil defense, expenditures may be allocated on the basis of preserving a functioning government and in minimizing loss of lives and property, or in another example, infantry tactics are often based on the enemy's capabilities rather than his suspected intentions as a way to minimize loss to your own forces if you guessed wrongly about his intentions. There are a host of other possible objectives or criteria one may use (be it in preventing riots or reducing flood damage); the major point here for the student of government decision making is that to know what you want is the critical first step in knowing what you must do.

Pitfalls in setting objectives

Among the many possible pitfalls in setting objectives, four are worth noting here:

(1) REGARDING MEANS AS ENDS. Obviously one cannot use as the ultimate end happiness or satisfaction (if indeed this is the ultimate end) for every problem. One is always involved in choosing a penultimate or prior end which is one of many means to a further end. The issue is how far back should one go in selecting ends or objectives for a particular area? In education, for example, one may achieve distorted results if one goes too far back and selects suboptimal objectives that may be technologically uncertain as to the accomplishment of some more ultimate end. Maximizing teacher/pupil ratios, or maximizing classroom space per pupil, or maximizing teachers' salaries (all subject, of course, to some budget constraint) may or may not "maximize education" per budget. This suboptimizing may involve trying to achieve inputs or means which may or may not be the correct or most efficient ones in achieving ends or outputs (if outputs could be measured, such as by scores on final examinations, or admissions to more advanced schools, or streams of future earnings, or marginal contributions to the growth of both the quality and quantity of GNP). Thus one must take care to focus not on means as ends, but on ends as ends: consumers don't eat fertilizer, they eat food.

(2) NOT REGARDING MEANS AS ENDS. Paradoxical with the first extreme above of focusing on means as ends (maximizing fertilizer instead of food),

the second classic *faux pas* is *not* to consider a means an end when indeed it is. In many areas of life it is the process which is highly valued in and of itself rather than any set of finite goals as such. In justice and politics one has foremost examples. Effective law is not a legal system that fills the jails or maximizes convictions per dollar or maximizes fines per conviction; it is instead a system which guarantees a due process wherein rights are preserved. Likewise in the political arena, the means toward reaching group decisions through democratic processes, free assembly, free speech, voting rights, and so on, may be valued as more important than the outcome. As in the case of justice, one may not have a certain way of knowing if a man is guilty or innocent, or right or wrong for the presidency, or if a foreign policy should or should not be adopted; one can only say that the decision was reached in accordance with the previously adopted consensus as to how such decisions are to be made. Thus, in such areas the student of government decision making has to determine if the rules of the game are more ultimate ends than the outcomes of the game.

(3) TO MEASURE IS TO KNOW BUT NOT NECESSARILY THE RIGHT THING. Quantification in and of itself is at the very core of science. However, improperly used it may lead to distorted results in the art and science of government decision making. All decision making models must simplify; a one-to-one map is of no use. But it is here that the danger lurks. The science part of the art and science of decision making has a built-in and justified bias toward including these variables (both means and ends) which can be quantified. This is all to

the good unless the nonquantifiable variables excluded do in fact make a difference; if the critical means or ends are nonquantified or nonquantifiable, then superficial precision with numbers within the analysis may be irrelevant to the solution. Indeed, many ends— beauty, love, freedom, justice, wisdom —may be obscured by a myoptic fetish-like preoccupation with first-glance numbers.

(4) ONE OBJECTIVE MAY BE NOT TO REVEAL OBJECTIVES. Certain times and places, be they political coalitions or ideologically-fragmented groups, may not be well suited for spelling out precise objectives or even trying to agree on objectives. Passing an education bill in the Congress might involve different groups with different motives. Preventing national or even world civil wars may involve obscuring objectives which may be changing or changeable. Pragmatism may take precedence over ideological motives if jobs are to be done. Thus, the student of government decision making must not always assume that obscure and obfuscated objectives are totally lacking in function. Many times objectives are uncertain, changing, conflicting; this may not be the time for total inaction but instead a time of discovering and discussing objectives in the very process of moving in a general direction. Objectives often are a result of a feed-back process in getting the job underway and in working toward broader goals.

CONSTRAINTS

Having settled upon some set of objectives or objective function, the next logical step is to see what limits its achievement. In the broadest sense limited resources are the prime constraint. This is the economic aspect of the problem: allocating finite resources to achieve a maximum of an infinite array of objectives. Following Eckstein's survey article previously mentioned, constraints can be categorized as follows:

1. PHYSICAL CONSTRAINTS: Given technologies and production possibilities, there are limits as to what can be achieved. Blood cannot be squeezed from stones nor gold congealed from lead, at least not yet.

2. LEGAL CONSTRAINTS: Laws, property rights, international conventions, agency rulings, and so on can reduce any list of feasible solutions. It takes time and due process to build superhighways through peoples' living rooms; it often takes legislative, executive, and judicial action for rules to be made or to be broken.

3. ADMINISTRATIVE CONSTRAINTS: Programs to be implemented require people to be hired, trained, and put to the task. Devising utopian tax systems, for example, for less developed countries may be unrealistic without means to administer them.

4. DISTRIBUTIONAL CONSTRAINTS: Development programs may be limited by the distribution of income generated: by regions, income classes, generations.

5. POLITICAL CONSTRAINTS: The process of decision making itself is costly, time consuming and often frustrating; solutions in theory may not be realizable in the practical politics of the moment. Planning political impossibilities may be an interesting avocation for philosophers but not a promising profession for programmers.

5. FINANCIAL OR BUDGET CONSTRAINTS: Resource scarcity is translated into monetary and budget scarcity. Most problems thus devolve into suboptimization problems where budget levels get set for governments, departments and agencies and one is limited to the less-then-optimal task of maximizing benefits with a fixed budget. Of course, many interesting analyses can flow from marginal benefits to be gained or lost from minor ups and downs in budget levels, but for most people at most times there is a financial ceiling which finally limits program expansion. In a wider sense financial constraints include not only domestic currency limits but also limits on foreign exchange.

6. TRADITIONAL, SOCIAL, AND RELIGIOUS CONSTRAINTS: Social customs, mores, values all tend to preclude options and possible action.

For the student of government decision making the proper use of constraints is critical. To ignore constraints to solution making is to depart from the real world; to regard all solutions except one as blocked by some constraint is to remove the problem from analysis. In this latter extreme certain constraints might be transformed into variables so that there is at least a choice as to which constraints might be relaxed and with what results.

EXTERNALITIES

In making maps or models some things are left in, some left out. This is in the very nature of classification and of model building. Phenomena are put into boxes or classes. Items in the same class are there because of a certain quality; other characteristics they may have are assumed to make no difference for the purposes of the analysis. Likewise a number of boxes or categories are enclosed within the "big box"—the model or system of ends and means being considered. Items excluded are different from those included and their exclusion is assumed to make no difference to the solution. Thus the crucial test of many models rests on two tests: (1) are phenomena within classes in the model or the "big box" categorized so that their "alike- ness" within a class swamps any differences they may possess, thus distorting the analysis? For example, is it safe to lump together money costs of inputs (all converted at official exchange rates) irrespective of the origin of the inputs (say, from foreign countries demanding dollars instead of Afghanis, or money wages paid to otherwise employed skilled workers as compared to money wages for otherwise unemployed unskilled workers who might be used or trained)? (2) are phenomena outside of classes and outside the model so different as to be indifferent to the results you desire? For example, should one ignore in government development projects such considerations as the rate of reinvestment by the beneficiaries of the projects—or even the rate of population increase by such beneficiaries?

The philosophic underpinnings of Western science are keyed to sorting phenomena between boxes, deciding if they are in or out of some box. In Aristotelian terms, a thing is either A or non-A. In computer language (based on binary systems), a thing is either 0 or 1. In the simple calculus of market- oriented profit-maximization, a decision counts only as it raises or lowers profits, social gains and losses being excluded. Internalities concern themselves with *quid pro quo's* between two parties; externalities concern themselves with third parties getting in the same transaction some *quo's* for which no *quid's* are paid. That is, in the Pigovian sense, A in rendering a paid service to B also serves (or disserves) C for which no payment is made. In government decision making such external effects, often better called spill- overs or repercussion effects, may be important to arriving at optimal solutions. The initial decision as to which effects to internalize must be checked at the end of analysis so that any externalities that do make a difference can be internalized.

This is a difficult but necessary in- gredient in any analysis. Even though everything may be related to every- thing else, analysis is premised on the view that some things are more im- portant than other things. In the Aristotelian world of Western science the some things are in, the other things are out. In the Miletan world-view, the world is one category: things are not in boxes but in process. In the West Man A steps into River A; in the Miletan world, in the language of Heraclitus, "The same man cannot step into the same river twice," as both the man and the river are changing. To arrive at solutions one must simplify reality and assume the Aristotelian world, but to make certain that the solution is correct one must not forget the Miletan world. The externalities may be important. For example, river valley development à la T.V.A. may be a proper govern- ment program for an underdeveloped region in one place at one time, but not so at other places, say, Helmand Valley in Afghanistan, at other times.

What are some of these external effects to be considered, especially when one moves from the private sector which maximizes private profits and consumer satisfaction to the public sector which is concerned with social benefits and social costs?

External effects may be outlined as follows:

1. Production-to-production: an activity by one producer affects the output of other producers, e.g., the water pumped from one mine affects other nearby mines.

2. Production-to-consumption: an activity by one producer affects consumers, e.g., noise and pollution.

3. Consumption-to-consumption: an activity by one consumer affects other consumers, e.g., radio noise in a public park.

4. Consumption-to-production: an activity by one consumer affects producers, e.g., hunting through crops.

In public sector decision-making repercussions often excluded from the analysis but which may be important at a final glance may include a range of considerations: physical interdependencies (e.g., upstream storage reservoirs affecting downstream projects), population effects, local or national unemployment, savings and reinvestment ratios in different sectors, large changes in inputs and outputs, social overhead costs, long-term investment decisions (trading off short-run allocative efficiency for long-run investment patterns), manpower needs and human capital effects, changing human attitudes (in determining industrial versus agricultural investments), balance of payments considerations, use of shadow wage, interest, and foreign exchange rates, backward and forward linkage in capital projects, local market and price structures (monopoly and monopsony problems), and so on. Again the test for the government decision maker is to go beyond the initial analysis and conclusions for a second thought, to see if the exclusions do not upset the abstracted results. In certain cases, such as the inclusion of reactions in an antiballistic missile program, second thoughts have been quite influential in the spending (or non-spending) of vast sums of Federal funds.

TIME: INTEREST RATES

Thus far we have simplified benefit-cost analysis to that of a certain, timeless world. Objectives are ascertained and quantified, in dollars usually; constraints, including costs, are ascertained and quantified. Thus the achievement of our objectives becomes limited by scarcity and the list of feasible solutions shrinks; but if any feasible solutions remain, we do arrive at a definite solution to our Type I—maximize benefits—or Type II—minimize costs—problem. To arrive at this point and to reach a definite solution we have abstracted from reality only a partial selection of objectives and constraints, assuming the internalities were the critical variables and that the externalities will not make any significant difference to our decision making process.

Now enter time. We have already abstracted the bits and pieces of phenomena (benefits and costs) into dollar boxes. But in a world of time a dollar is not a dollar is not a dollar. A dollar has a specific value only at a specific date. (We assume money is in banks and not in the ground.) Thus, a dollar yesterday is equal to $1.05 today, at 5% interest per day, and $1.1025 tomorrow. Likewise a dollar tomorrow is worth only 95¢ today. A dollar's value becomes a function of time.

Our previous analysis took the stuff of reality and put it into homogeneous boxes of benefit dollars and cost dollars so we could compare and decide. Now our homogeneity and means of comparison again disappears as dollars are no longer equal to dollars. We must not only get the stuff of reality into dollar boxes but dollar boxes of the same date. This forces another decision: which date? Present Value (telescope all dated dollar values to the present date) or Terminal Value (turn the telescope around and convert all dated dollar values to say dollar values at the end of some project or time horizon). Remember again, the ultimate criterion for selection among spending choices (investment projects) is to maximize $(B - C)$ at some date. That is, to achieve the highest amount of net benefits at either a present or future date. Use of an internal rate of return criterion achieves an optimum and thus can be equated to this other criterion only under certain conditions.[4]

Thus the crux of decision making is comparison, and the crux of comparison is getting stuff into homogeneous

boxes. Apples cannot objectively be compared to pears; it becomes a matter of subjective taste rather than objective science. But if we abstract apples and pears into fruit boxes, then we may assume that one fruit equals another fruit. But then to avoid dangers of green or over-ripe fruit, we must get fruit of the same date of ripeness. Then we can decide: two ripe fruits are better than one on the basis of our decision making criterion that more is better than less.

Timing benefit streams: time preference

Consumption now is preferred to consumption later; a bird in the hand is worth two in some certain future bush. But at what rate do we discount future birds? Or what length of time equates the bird in the hand with the the two in the bush? Do we accept the rate of individuals' time preference expressed by market rates of interest, say 5%, as for risk-free, long-term government bonds? Do we use a lower "social" rate, say 3%, including considerations for unborn generations, or do we assume that short-sighted individuals should not judge for society because of their "defective telescopic faculty" (Pigou)? Do we accept a view of interdependence among individuals' choice making so that one's own preference is partly determined by other choices or by mutually determined or autocratically chosen rates of time preference? What we really have is not one rate but a schedule of rates depending on a host of factors: the amounts of present and future goodies involved (with or without assumptions as to diminishing marginal utility of income or goodies), the rate of growth of these goodies, and the

---

[4] Where projects are not interdependent or mutually exclusive, where starting dates are given, where no constraints (budgets) are operative, where the reinvestment rate is the same as the internal rate of return, where benefit and cost streams do not fluctuate wildly over time. See Prest and Turvey, *op. cit.*; also J. Hirshleifer, "On the Theory of Optimal Investment Decision," *Journal of Political Economy*, August, 1958, pp. 329–352.

expected life spans of individuals and societies to consume these goodies. The nature of the choice itself among rates has to be determined: by people voting with dollars in the market place or by ballots in the polling booth. Economists have no set answer except that rates determined by imperfect capital markets and reflecting private instead of social interests are not the only (or best) rates to use.

Timing cost streams: opportunity cost of capital

Costs for economists are measured in terms of opportunities foregone. Spending $100 million in the public sector means that there is $100 million less spent in the private sector on either investment or consumption goods, assuming fully employed resources. If resources are not fully employed, government spending merely reduces enforced leisure, i.e., unemployment. Thus, the opportunity cost of capital is really a set of schedules reflecting different rates of return from alternative uses of different amounts of capital. *If* the goal or benefits desired is rapidly growing GNP, then the equalization principle would prevail in that resources earning say 15% in U.S. manufacturing would be clearly misallocated if they were shifted to government investment projects producing a stream of benefits at an annual rate of only 4%. If the resources are garnered by tax dollars instead of bond dollars, then, following Eckstein, one might measure the incidence of the chosen tax among income groups to gauge increased borrowing costs, reduced investment yields, reduced consumption values, and so on. The critical test hinges on exactly what

opportunities are foregone. The issue is not totally resolved, but there appears to be a growing consensus for much higher interest rates (10–15%) in judging government investment projects than previously used.

Summing up: a guide to action

1. For the decision maker the first operational issue is: do interest rates make a difference in making any decision? Thus, one might see how sensitive decisions are to differing interest rates, say 5–10–15%. Some economists have found that there is not much difference within a range of 4–8%.

2. For social welfare projects (health, education, urban renewal, and so on) that are not justified by high interest rates (10–15%) it may be that the error is not in the use of a high interest rate but in the failure to include enough of the externalities or indirect benefits.

3. For certain public sector spending it may be more effective to convert the analysis to Type II (cost-effectiveness: finding least-cost solutions) problems, where it is assumed the benefits are chosen by public will or social values, rather than attempting to measure the benefits relative to a stream of future private consumption or GNP.

4. When there is a fixed budget over time, there is no opportunity cost of capital; however a social discount rate should still be used to equate intertemporal lumps of benefits.

5. For state and local policy makers, or any case involving sub-optimization, the Machiavellian manager would be acting less than rationally if he did not use his borrowing costs, for instance

tax-exempt municipal bond rates. He might well assume that in this imperfect world of third bests his low borrowing rate reflects a national policy that prefers him to control greater resource allocation than would be possible at a higher "truer" discount rate. On the other hand national policy makers such as those in the Bureau of the Budget or on the Joint Economic Committee of the U.S. Congress would be concerned that such sub-optimizing resource allocators are given the right signals, i.e., discount rates.

6. Interest rates usually are important but there may be no one correct rate. The one or ones to use depend upon the changing times, capital productivity, objectives, benefits and costs included and excluded in the analysis, and the level of optimization. Once more the answer rests on the initial determination as to how badly one wants consumption or investment, now or later, in the public or the private sector.

RISK AND UNCERTAINTY

Finally, in our simple conceptual framework of benefit-cost analysis, we leave the model of a certain world. The decision maker has specified and quantified his benefits and costs. If they occur in different time periods, he has converted the dollar values into dollars at the same time. However, streams of dollar benefits and costs are not simple points in time; instead, they are probability distributions of points in time. If he knows these probability distributions (the amount of risk involved), he can alter the values of these expected dollars by their chance of actually occurring. Worse yet, if he doesn't know the probability distribution over time, he is faced with uncertainty and must deal with it. How does he do this?

1. If these streams of benefits and costs are irregular, he may allow for uncertainty by adjusting the annual levels of benefits and costs. He might again try a sensitivity analysis to see how far wrong he can be in his expected values and still have the proper decision. He might set ranges of maximum and minimum values for his benefits and costs; he might know the limits of the ranges but not the probability distributions within them. He might throw in contingency allowances to cover errors or to overcome some downward or upward bias in the analysis. He might change his objective from one of simple maximization to other strategies such as maximin or minimax or others as mentioned earlier. He might build the bridge or elevator twice or ten times stronger than historical or normally expected stresses.

2. If the uncertainty or risk is a strictly compounding function of time, the decision maker might simply add a premium on the discount rate.

3. If the risk or uncertainty is thought to be illusive only after some time period, then the decision-maker may wish to compare alterative programs within a more limited time period. One may thus set terminal dates by which to standardize the analysis of different projects such as dams or buildings.

A FINAL WORD

This brief primer of government decision making and the theory of benefit-cost analysis has provided only the conceptual framework—the set of boxes—with which the analyst will be concerned. These five boxes—objectives, constraints, externalities, time, and risk and uncertainty—are the places to sort out the stuff of reality. They affect all decisions. But the right decisions are the ones that have embodied good sorting rather than simply a mechanical adding up of the benefits and costs once they are sorted.

the resource
allocation framework

This section deals with development of the governmental unit's program structure—the format for presentation of budgetary information under the PPB System. The significance of the conceptual design of the program structure in a text on benefit-cost analysis lies in the use of the program structure as (a) the analytic framework within which analyses of public programs will henceforth be largely performed, and (b) the decision-making framework for the allocation of resources to programs.

The introductory paper by Chester Wright develops the concept of the program budget and discusses the analytic usefulness of the program structure. Graeme Taylor then examines the process of designing the program structure, with examples drawn from all levels of government—federal, state, local, and individual agency. Part I concludes with two cases. "Post Office Department" is a vehicle for discussion of the major conceptual and practical difficulties encountered by a federal agency as it sets about the task of establishing its program structure. "Federal Communications Commission," in addition to posing the open-ended question of what structure should be adopted by the FCC, also introduces the student to the problem of choosing appropriate output measures of public programs, a topic which is developed in detail in Part II.

The Concept of a Program Budget

By
CHESTER WRIGHT

Planning, Programming, Budgeting as a management system had its birth in the Department of Defense under Secretary McNamara. It is perhaps typical of Mr. McNamara that when the system was initiated in Defense it didn't have a name. It was not called operation splendor or any other such honorific. This was very likely because the Secretary did not consider it a thing requiring a name, but merely the way an intelligent man would go about conducting the world's largest business.

The civilian agencies of the Federal Government have had two years' experience in trying to apply the Planning, Programming, Budgeting approach. We have found that what is required is an approach that is similar to, but not the same as, the Defense system. We have also found that in many ways the task of installing the system has been more difficult than in Defense. We are pleased that state and local governments are starting to develop systems of their own. We suspect that they will find that what is required is similar to, but different from, the Federal efforts and that in many respects their job will be harder. Having survived the past two years, we have a strong humanitarian instinct to spare others some of the worst of our problems.

I would like to be sure that while investigating the philosophy and methodology of PPBS, we do not lose sight of the basic meaning and purpose that the system serves. PPBS is a system for assisting choice related to the use of resources. It does not make choices. It does not even reduce decision to the selection of one clearly correct course of action. Quite the contrary, it has the built-in objective of expanding available alternatives. It does, however, have the faculty of making the ingredients of choice and the probable consequences of alternatives extraordinarily clear. Central to this process of illuminating choice is the necessity for a program budget.

Before coming to grips with the central issue of a program budget, it might help to examine briefly the complete budgeting system. Stated baldly, PPBS

Chester Wright is Director, Financial Management and PPB Training Center, Bureau of Training, U.S. Civil Service Commission. This address was presented before the National Association of State Budget Officers Conference, September 1967, Lexington, Kentucky.

is the application of price and allocation theory to decisions regarding the
production of public goods. As such, it
promptly gets involved in considerations traditionally reserved for a market system. For example, PPBS is concerned with the demand for those
goods and services supplied by government action; that is, through the public sector of the economy.

The larger industries in the private
sector are becoming quite expert at
accurately predicting the demand
curves for their goods. Even the auto
manufacturers, who have locked themselves into a statistically difficult one-
year cycle, are left with a remarkably
small number of unsold cars at the end
of the year. And even though marginal
price and production adjustments may
be required, the whole process is a
marvel of efficiency.

We cannot claim anything like this
sort of expertise in determining the
demand for public goods. Indeed, we
are unaccustomed to thinking in anything like these terms. The demand for
public goods has traditionally been expressed second-hand through the political process. Even there, the difference between what one person or party
was offering in relation to another was
generally vague, often deliberately so.
In fact, the seeker for public office who
tended to be specific about the goods
and services he proposed to provide
was frequently accused of "buying
votes." A curious concept.

PPBS proposes that governments are
in the business of providing goods and
services to the people whose creature
they are. Thus, legislative bodies are
purchasing agents for the people, procuring for them those things which they
desire to purchase and consume in

common and providing value in return
for foregone private consumption as
represented by taxes. Executive departments of government, then, are producers of goods, charged with producing those goods and services which
cannot or should not be purchased directly by the individual consumer from
the private market place.

This view of the functions of the
divisions of government in no sense
reduces the importance of these activities. One of the services that people
generally expect to receive from government is what our ancestors rather
aptly called domestic tranquillity. Now,
our legislative purchasing agents may
determine that their customers are not
sufficiently tranquil. They may choose
to purchase more police, more parks,
or more job training programs, or some
combination of these. Their choice is
not simple and there is little question
that the amount of tranquillity received
per dollar spent is going to depend in
part on the aptness of their selection.

The tranquillity per dollar ratio is
going to depend further on the efficiency of the management of each of
the alternative tranquilizers. The extra
police may be trained for riot control
or community action. They may concentrate on apprehending gamblers or
on patrolling dark streets. The parks
may be bird sanctuaries or playgrounds. The job training programs
may train janitors or auto mechanics.
All of these may be done poorly or
well, depending on the skill and abilities of their respective managers. But
the crucial point is that we not confuse
activity with objective. Only to the
extent that the purchasers and producers remember that what is being
bought and sold is not bird sanctuaries

nor apprehended gamblers, but domestic tranquillity, is the public going to be satisfied. They gave up something in the confident expectation of getting something which they valued higher. If a citizen who has supported a tax increase, expecting that more police will make him secure in his person, gets knocked on the head one night and then reads in the following day's paper that fifteen crap shooters have been arrested, he is going to be unhappy. He has a right to be. He has been cheated.

The problems generated by this concept are extreme. Not the least of these is the near perfect elasticity of many public goods. Public recreation, for example, will apparently be consumed in any amount it is provided, with consumption tapering off only when facilities become grossly overcrowded. This is true because in recreation the immediate consumer is aware of a cost quite different from those that concern public officials. The consumer's view of cost is his time, the expense and inconvenience associated with travel from his home to the recreation site, plus any user fee. If the facility is badly overcrowded, his apparent costs have not changed, but the product—recreation—has been adulterated. He may choose not to consume the offered product, thus giving a false appearance of a leveling off of demand.

Even if, like the auto industry, we were able to predict accurately the demand for public goods, we would still be confronted with questions of how much to produce and even whether we should produce at all. PPBS can answer neither of these questions; however, it can provide data regarding the costs and relative benefits of various productive undertakings. In addition, through its basic market orientation it can make the political apparatus aware of shifting demands to which it may or may not wish to respond. Most states hold a monopoly on betting on horses. Two have recently decided that if their citizens wanted to play the numbers, they would run the game. PPBS provides the sort of specific information that can enable the public official to engage in a meaningful dialogue with the citizens he serves. But it can only do this from the basic foundation of a program budget, as we will see shortly.

Let me assure you that I am well aware that a frank and open exchange between governed and governing may not be welcome everywhere. The utter openness, the complete candor of PPBS analysis, may be highly disruptive of the political process as it has developed over a great many years. The kind of information which PPBS provides was not available in the past, even if those in authority had wished to reveal it. There is a very real question as to how much the people want to know. But, once the sort of information that PPBS can produce becomes available, to withhold deliberately it could be construed to be a conspiracy against the people.

It seems probable that it is a lot easier to make decisions in a heterogeneous democratic society when the exact nature of the decisions are shrouded in generalities. What is going to happen when we know the exact nature of our decisions, who is going to profit and who is going to suffer, and by exactly how much? Can our particular brand of democracy survive the impact of explicitness? I don't know. But I suspect we are all going to find out.

Supply and demand considerations are relevant only in relation to specific price information. It has been next to impossible for a concerned citizen to find the real price of public goods. This is hardly surprising since public officials were, by and large, little better informed. The fact is that administrative budgets do not provide reliable information regarding the cost of specific goods. In some areas we have been under the unfortunate illusion that we have good cost data when we do not. We frequently find published comparisons of the cost per capita of educating elementary school children. Newspapers will publish the amount of money that County "X" spends per child in relation to County "Y," and draw odious comparisons. The clear indication being that if one school system spends more, its system is necessarily better. The assumption here is that "one year of attendance at an elementary school by one child" is a sufficient definition of product. But what follows is worse, for a market definition of value is assumed without the further necessary conditions for a market value system.

To examine this question further: In a market economy, the value of a good is the price that a fully informed consumer is willing to pay for that good in preference to all others. To be more precise, it is the consumption he is willing to forego in order to consume that particular good. In the school system example the conditions of choice and, more particularly, of comparative information are so conspicuously lacking as to render current cost and value considerations meaningless. PPBS, then, is concerned with a much more detailed assessment of cost, of value,

and of alternatives than are most present systems.

By indirection we have arrived at the central activity of PPBS. Through analysis we are attempting to establish a market system of choice for the production of public goods. We have not attempted to supplant the political process for decision making. We have simply made the decision making process at once broader and more explicit. To the politics of choice we have added the economics of choice.

Under the theoretical umbrella of economics there is room for a broad range of empirically derived techniques including the entire range of mathematical and statistical analysis as well as the machine centered technology generally referred to as management science. This has led to a certain unfortunate amount of confusion in cases where one or more of these independent techniques is identified as PPBS. An analogy to economic theory and practice may help to make these relationships clear. An economist can draw supply and demand curves forever without the need for information about the market. However, if he wishes to derive accurate curves of a future market condition, he is going to need every bit of information he can lay his hands on, including not only information produced by mathematical and statistical analysis but the products of industrial engineering and perhaps sociology as well. This does not mean that industrial engineering is a part of economics. It does mean that the economist is going to be hard put to provide information of value to a manufacturer without drawing on either industrial engineers or on the same body of skills which they employ. By the same token cost accounting or automated management information systems are not part of PPBS in a theoretical sense, but the PPBS analyst is going to find it hard to provide useful information for management decision making without inputs from these and a host of similar information producing techniques. PPBS is not so much a body of techniques as it is a viewpoint. It is the view that the majority of governmental activity has to do with the allocation of resources. And that, as such, governmental activity should be the subject of economic analysis.

The entire range of management science is completely compatible with the PPBS viewpoint. Indeed, as I have indicated, the serious analysis of problems of the scope confronting modern society is possible only through the data-handling potentials of electronic data processing equipment.

With the foregoing for a background we can proceed directly to a consideration of the nature and value of a program budget. Perhaps the best approach to understanding a program budget is to consider how to go about constructing one.

The development of a program budget starts with the identification of final products. For a governmental entity it means identifying those goods and services that are distributed among the people the government serves. After all the final products of government have been identified, the second step is to aggregate the products into categories representing the areas of social welfare which they support. (It is possible to reverse the procedure, but for state and local governments particularly the suggested procedure may have real benefits.)

When the process is complete, most states would find that they are providing the following broad categories of services: law and order (or, as it was called earlier, "domestic tranquillity"); education; recreation; economic growth and stability; and general welfare. Each of these program categories will be supported by a long list of elements— that is, identifiable units of goods or services distributed directly to the public.

The foregoing represents a sizable effort, but the task is far from complete. It is an axiom of program budgeting that the budget should facilitate the process of comparing alternative methods of obtaining objectives. Now, it may fall to the lot of Government that in a world plagued by scarce resources choices may have to be made between law and order on the one hand and education on the other. But these sorts of gross comparisons are not adequate for decision making. Far more frequently the decision maker is faced with choices between alternative means for achieving a single objective. A program budget must support these as well as the broader decisions. Within the program of law and order one might wish to choose between community action and patrol cars, prisons and delinquent children counseling service. Therefore, a careful selection of program sub-categories is required in order that the choice maker may be confronted with genuine, valid alternatives.

At this point one would have four or five broad categories representing the major goals of a society which are to be served by government action. These are divided into program sub-categories which permit direct comparison of alternative methods of obtaining objectives. These are further divided into program elements which are quantifiable units of government output. One has a program budget, with a lot left over.

What is left over are those goods which are consumed in the production of final outputs. In a productivity equation they would be classed as purchased intermediate products. These include government personnel offices, most data processing activities, and a host of similar support services. The reason these activities are not considered as outputs should be obvious— they are not consumed directly by the customer but are merely a contributor to the cost of the product. To consider them separately in some framework of cost and benefits is analogous to an auto manufacturer quoting separate prices for all the major components of the auto he presents for sale.

The concept presents little difficulty except where these activities exist as separate organizations with separate budgets, providing their services "free" to the other organizations which require them. The result is likely to be inefficient use of resources and false pricing of the final product.

The first of these difficulties results from a classic economic principle: Resources improperly priced below the market value will be inefficiently utilized. The most common example is the inefficient use of manpower by armies supplied by cheap draftee labor.

The false pricing position is supported by the economists' homily, "there is no such thing as a free lunch." If a state official is attempting to decide between alternatives for providing law and order, he might consider a specially trained riot control unit and im-

proved communication equipment. Now, if he determined that all other things were equal, relative costs might become a decisive factor. Suppose that the costs were nearly the same, but that one choice had a heavy element of personnel services and the other did not. If the decision maker receives the services of the personnel organization "free"—if these services do not appear on his budget—he is very likely to consider that they are in fact free and not enter them into his calculus. The result is a bigger bill to the taxpayer for the same service.

It is vitally important, then, that intermediate products not be included in a program budget as a final product, but they must be included as a cost of final products.

When all this has been accomplished, then one has a program budget —a budget which makes explicit the goals and objectives of a society and which makes possible direct comparison of the economic consequences of alternative means of obtaining those objectives. In addition one has a budget which informs the consumer of the nature, quality, and amount of goods with which he is provided and the complete cost, both in total and by item, of these goods.

The usefulness of a program budget can be examined by considering its relation to two particular modes of analysis; systems analysis and marginal analysis.

Systems analysis is the most democratic of intellectual endeavors, taking unto itself any method that proves useful. This fine impartiality blesses systems analysis with the same problems of definition that confused PPBS. However, systems analysis can be fairly accurately described by its three essential characteristics: one, its completeness; two, its concern for environmental considerations; and, three, its adherence to scientific methodology. Systems analysis, then, is the process of identifying the significant elements of a problem and describing, preferably quantitatively, their relationships —all of this within the context of the problem environment. The analysis must process the three essential characteristics of the scientific method. That is, it must have internal logical consistency, explicitness, and objectivity.

Systems analysis is a fairly recent phenomenon, not because the process was not understood before but because of the functional impossibility of manipulating without computing machinery the data involved in a real world system.

Once the machinery became available, we discovered that our mathematical constructs were not as complete as we had assumed in the absence of any opportunity to test them. We were further confounded by the discovery that even the most elegant of our mathematical concepts described a most limited world. To make the results of systems studies valuable as well as interesting, it has been necessary to approach them from a multi-discipline viewpoint. Lawyers and economists, physicians and mathematicians, have had to sit down together and try to communicate to each other detailed information from their professions. This is a process that has sometimes proven most distressing to all concerned.

The important thing, however, is that systems analyses are being conducted and they are providing better and better results.

A preliminary and vital step in systems analysis is to define the system. This definition must be inclusive of all those elements that interact on one another in some sort of first order causative relationship; and since all the world relates to itself in some fashion, it must exclude those factors which are not among what Pareto would call "the vital few." To err on one side is to produce an essentially meaningless study, one which does not consider relevant factors. The other extreme produces a mass of interacting details that even present technology cannot manage.

Once constructed, a program budget performs this important definitive function. The categories of a program budget are major governmental systems. For smaller studies the sub-categories are sub-systems. There is no need to go through a massive sorting process prior to each study. There is no problem of communication between the producers or users of analysis as to the boundaries of the system being analyzed.

I must emphasize again that PPBS is a system for assisting choice. The function of systems analysis in this process is to bring order to the overwhelming deluge of detail that tends to drown the decision maker in data. Systems analysis has the ability to pull this data into focus so that significant considerations stand out clearly; and most important of all, so that the total costs and total expected benefits associated with each alternative are sharply displayed.

There is no guarantee in all this that the choice maker is going to choose an alternative of which you or I would approve. There are factors of judgement, even of political necessity, that have no place in an analytic study, but which, nonetheless, are going to exert a powerful influence on public officials. The system is not foolproof. Foolish men will make foolish choices no matter what. PPBS is predicated on the faith that most men are rational and given better information, will make better choices.

A second area of analysis where a program budget is essential is marginal analysis. Marginal analysis has long been a standard part of the repertoire of a successful business man. Stated precisely, marginal analysis determines the total additional cost of producing a single additional unit of output. The term is frequently given a somewhat looser meaning when what is considered is the effect on unit production and/or product quality of "small" increases or decreases in the total amount of dollars available for productive effort.

In the area of public expenditure a great deal of attention is given to questions regarding starting new programs as well as in those rare instances when old programs are considered for disestablishment. These sorts of decisions, however, form a fractional percentage of the total number or importance of decisions which confront the public official. Decisions on marginal investment, on the other hand, are an almost daily occurrence. They are, almost without exception, made on the basis of inadequate or incomplete economic data. It would be a rare public official who could predict the effect on distributed output of a 5 per cent increase or decrease in program funds. He would be even harder put to provide accurate cost predictions for a proposed increase in distributed output.

Marginal analysis applied to the program category "education" could prove a valuable instrument in budgeting and planning. Both fixed and variable costs in an education program are easily identifiable and reasonably susceptible of analysis. Marginal costs of education, at any given product quality, tend to rise very slowly up to a point. That point is the one at which a large incremental investment in capital equipment is required. This produces a rather sharp increase in total costs with marginal costs taking a steep dip until they start to rise again. Those responsible for the program category "education" should be in possession of information regarding the slope of the marginal cost curves as well as of total cost curves, including the points of sudden discontinuity caused by heavy capital investment.

Given a market system, or any system that is concerned with costs in relation to benefit, decisions regarding the appropriate level of investment are focused at the margin. Considering investment in terms of the additional return in relation to additional costs will produce a different answer than simple considerations of average costs, whether these be average costs-per-student-year, or any similar system.

Any attempt to develop marginal cost data for an educational system will highlight the inadequacies of both present product definitions and of short cycle budgets. It has been a great many years since we measured a man's education in terms of the number of years of school he had completed; so, measuring the number of students times days or years does not seem adequate. In fact, judging from the amount of attention given the "drop-out problem," we do not consider that we have produced an educational product until a student has completed high school. This is the first product that, in practice, we are willing to accept as final.

School systems generally produce at least two readily identifiable primary products: the high school graduate who intends to enter the workforce and the high school graduate who intends to enter college and eventually become the product of the second stage of the educational process. It is likely that the marginal cost of these two primary school products will vary.

Armed with marginal cost data coupled with demograph and sociological information, school administrators can engage in meaningful long-range planning—planning, one might hope, relatively free of the hysteria that surrounds so much of the present discussion of school budgeting.

A word of caution is necessary regarding our crude product definitions. We are talking about distributed output. A manufacturer does not count as output items which are defective and unusable. They are, however, part of the cost of production. In the same sense a school system should count as products of its college preparatory program only those students actually accepted by accredited colleges. By the same token those students who are produced for immediate entry into the workforce should be measured only if employed, or at an absolute minimum, fully employable without further instruction. With time these definitions could be further refined into broad categories of the excellence of the colleges to which students are admitted, for example, or in the other case, salary range or social desirability of initial employment.

These definitions of product shed a different light on costs. A large capital investment in better plant or equipment might substantially increase the number of students who are employed on graduation. This could very well have the effect of lowering the marginal product cost. Similarly, better labs or libraries, while adding to total costs, once again might have the effect of lowering marginal costs as measured against the increased number of students accepted by accredited colleges.

Marginal analysis could prove equally meaningful in many other areas of governmental services: e.g., mental health, correctional systems, fire protection. Marginal analysis is performed along product lines. To be useful these product lines must be clearly delineated and the final product must be specifically identifiable. One must have, in short, a program budget.

In practically every area of analytic endeavor applied to questions relating to the planning of governmental activities, a well developed program budget is a vital necessity. Enormously powerful and complex techniques such as input-output analysis await only the development of program budgets to become the servants of the government executive. The examples of systems analysis and marginal analysis thus are meant to be indicative of the analytic usefulness of program budgeting. They by no means exhaust present possibilities. Time and experience can be expected to unfold many more.

In summary I can state that a program budget is a necessary precondition for a planning, programming, budgeting system. The program categories are the articles in an economic covenant between a people and their government. The sub-categories not only illuminate the process of decision making, they go far toward defining the character of government. The program budget is a potent instrument for communication and an intellectual superstructure without which analysis becomes futile.

Designing the Program Structure

By
GRAEME M. TAYLOR

An organization's program structure has two primary uses—first, as a format for the presentation of budgetary information and, second, as a framework within which resource allocation decisions are made. A program structure can be designed for any organization, including hospitals, schools and universities, non-profit foundations, and business firms. This paper will, however, be concerned primarily with the principles governing the design of the program structure for a unit of government.

In October, 1965, the Federal Government directed the major agencies of the executive branch to design their own individual program structures, subject to review by the Bureau of the Budget but with minimal official guidance in the form of design criteria. State and local governments, on the other hand, have largely tended to set forth "statewide" or "city-wide" program structures, at least at the highest levels of program aggregation, requesting that the individual agencies of the government design their program structures to conform with the government-wide structure. In a few instances the government's central staff agencies, usually the Budget Office or the Planning Office, have themselves designed the complete program structure. As might be expected, therefore, inspection of the program structures adopted by various units of government reveals quite startling differences in interpretation of the concept of a program structure, depending on the degree to which overall guidance was given initially by the responsible central staff agency.

FEDERAL GUIDELINES

The initial instructions to the heads of federal agencies concerning the design of program structures were contained

The author is indebted to Allen Schick, of The Brookings Institution, and G. William Helm, of Management Analysis Center, Inc., for their helpful comments on earlier drafts of this paper.

in Bulletin 66-3, issued by the Bureau of the Budget on October 12, 1965. Section 5 of that directive reads as follows:

a. An early and essential step for each agency is the determination of a series of output oriented categories which, together, cover the total work of the agency. These will serve as a basic framework for the planning, programming, and budgeting processes (including work on systems analysis, reporting, evaluation of accomplishments, and other aspects of management) and for relating these processes to each other. The following principles should guide the development of such output categories.

(1) *Program categories* are groupings of agency programs (or activities or operations) which serve the same broad objective (or mission) or which have generally similar objectives. Succinct captions or headings describing the objective should be applied to each such grouping. Obviously, each program category will contain programs which are complementary or are close substitutes in relation to the objectives to be attained. For example, a broad program objective is improvement of higher education. This could be a *program category*, and as such would contain Federal programs aiding undergraduate, graduate and vocational education, including construction of facilities, as well as such auxiliary Federal activities as library support and relevant research programs. For purposes of illustration and to aid understanding, Exhibit 2 shows some program structures as they might be applied to two organizational units within different agencies; the same approach, of course, applies to the agency as a whole. (See below)

(2) *Program subcategories* are subdivisions which should be established within each program category, combining agency programs (or activities or operations) on the basis of narrower objectives contrib-

uting directly to the broad objectives for the program category as a whole. Thus, in the example given above, improvement of engineering and science and of language training could be two program subcategories within the program category of improvement of higher education.

(3) *Program elements* are usually subdivisions of program sub-categories and comprise the specific products (i.e., the goods and services) that contribute to the agency's objectives. Each program element is an integrated activity which combines personnel, other services, equipment and facilities. An example of a program element expressed in terms of the objectives served would be the number of teachers to be trained in using new mathematics.

b. The program structure will not necessarily reflect organization structure. It will be appropriate and desirable in many cases to have the basic program categories cut across bureau lines to facilitate comparisons and suggest possible trade-offs among elements which are close substitutes. It is also desirable to develop program formats which facilitate comparisons across agency lines (e.g., in urban transportation and in recreation).

c. Basic research activities may not be and frequently are not mission or output oriented. Whenever this is the case, such activities should be identified as a separate program category or subcategory as appropriate. However, applied research and development is usually associated with a specific program objective and should be included in the same program category as the other activities related to that objective.

d. To facilitate top level review, the number of program categories should be limited. For example, a Cabinet Department should have as many as 15 program categories in only a rare and exceptional case.

e. Program categories should not be restricted by the present appropriation pattern or budget activity structure. (Eventually, however, it may be necessary and desirable for the "Program by Activity" portion of the schedules in the Budget Appendix to be brought into line with the program structure developed according to this Bulletin.)

To illustrate the concept of the program structure, Exhibit 2 of Bulletin 66-3 presented examples drawn from the Coast Guard and the Forest Service. The Coast Guard example is shown below:

COAST GUARD

Present Appropriation Structure

GENERAL AND SPECIFIC FUNDS:

Operating expenses
Acquisition, construction and improvements
Retired pay
Reserve training

INTRAGOVERNMENT FUNDS:

Coast Guard Supply Fund
Coast Guard Yard Fund

Present Activity Schedule

Vessel Operations
Aviation Operations
Shore Stations and Aids
  Operations
Repair and Supply Facilities
Training and Recruiting
  Facilities
Administration and Operational
  Control
Other Military Personnel
  Expense
Supporting Programs

Proposed Program Structure

Search and Rescue
Aids to Navigation
Law Enforcement

Military Readiness
Merchant Marine Safety
Oceanography and Other
  Operations
Supporting Services

Following the initial experience with the introduction of planning-programming-budgeting (PPB) in the major civilian agencies, the Bureau of the Budget revised its official instructions and issued Bulletin 68-2 on July 18, 1967. Section 5 of that bulletin, shown below, is noteworthy for three reasons. First, the usefulness of the program structure as an analytic framework was stressed. Second, the maximum recommended number of program categories was revised from fifteen to ten. And third, for the first time in official print there appeared a reference to the intention of the Bureau to "fit agency program structures into a Government-wide structure."

(5) *Program structure.* The program structure groups the activities of an agency into a set of program categories that facilitates analytic comparisons of the costs and effectiveness of alternative programs. Individual program categories establish the scope of the related Program Memorandum. The program categories should, therefore, be chosen so far as possible to permit a self-contained analysis of programs with common outputs or with common objectives.

a. The program categories used in each agency should provide a suitable framework for considering and resolving the major questions of mission and scale of operations which are the proper subject of decision at the highest level within the agency and within the Executive Office of the President. These program categories will not necessarily be consistent with appropriation categories or with organizational structures.

b. Normally, an agency will have between five and ten major program categories. Most program categories will contain one or more subordinate levels, called subcategories and program elements. Some of the subcategories and program elements will complement others within the same main category. Some may be competitive with others.

c. Each agency is responsible for proposing its own program structure and for reviewing it regularly and proposing its amendment where appropriate. The Bureau of the Budget should be consulted with respect to program structure and its approval obtained for changes therein.

d. The Bureau of the Budget will provide leadership in seeking to fit agency program structures into a Government-wide structure. As progress is made in this effort, agencies may be asked to adjust their structures to permit achieving a comprehensive and compatible structural pattern across agency lines.

On April 12, 1968, the Bureau of the Budget issued its third PPB instruction—Bulletin 68-9. Section 4 of this Bulletin contained revised guidelines for the development of agency program structures. The nature of program elements, treatment of support and indirect activities, the decision-making intent of the program structure, and the intention of the Bureau to develop a government-wide program structure were all discussed in more detail than in the previous bulletins. Excerpts from Section 4 of Bulletin 68-9 follow:

c. *Program elements.* A program element covers agency activities related directly to the production of a discrete agency output, or group of related outputs. Agency activities which contribute directly to the output should be included in the program element, even though they may be conducted within different organizations, or financed from different appropriations. Thus, program elements are the basic units of the program structure.

Program elements have these characteristics: (1) they should produce clearly-definable outputs, which are quantified wherever possible; (2) wherever feasible, the output of a program element should be an agency end-product—not an intermediate product that supports another element; and (3) the inputs of a program element should vary with changes in the level of output, but not necessarily proportionally.

d. *Treatment of support and indirect activities.* In dealing with the costs of support and indirect activities, arbitrary allocations which are made solely for the purpose of distributing all costs should be avoided. Allocations should be made only where they contribute to better decisions.

When supervisory and support operations (such as comptroller, personnel and administrative service operations) are completely involved in a single program element, they should be reflected in that element.

In many situations, however, such operations may support two or more program elements. In such cases, the costs of the supervisory or support activities should be distributed to each supported program element—if there is a reasonable basis for doing so, and if those costs may be expected to vary reasonably in line with trends in each of the program elements involved.

Where there is no reasonable basis for allocating such activities, or where allocation would not contribute to more effective decision-making in budget review, these activities should be reflected in appropriate separate classifications within the program structure.

e. *Adaptation of program structure to decision-making needs.* There are many instances where the program structure, if it is to facilitate decision-making, must cut across organization lines, appropriations, and other classifications. Pursuit of absolute uniformity and consistency in development of a program structure will, however, be counter-productive in some instances in terms of the major objective of PPB: the improvement of the basis for decision-making.

For example, there are cases where a specific target group is an important focus of decision-making, while the services provided to the group would normally fall within several different classifications of the program structure. This would apply, for example, to a group of refugees who are furnished health, education, and other services, but where decisions in the Executive Branch are in fact made in terms of this group of refugees as a whole. In such a case, all activities concerning the group should be reflected in one unique program element within the subcategory and category predominantly involved, unless this would produce significant distortions in the basis for decision-making in the other part of the program structure.

A second example involves certain overhead and support activities or administrative expense items, which may be technically allocable among various program elements under guidelines furnished above. In some instances, these costs are large collectively, but distributed among many program elements, are not a significant factor in decisions regarding those program elements. Where this is true, and where decision-makers in the Executive Branch must focus at some point upon the costs in total, it is better to segregate them within the program structure, rather than allocating them.

As a third example, excessive fragmentation of appropriations and organizations should be avoided. For example, if about 80 percent of an appropriation or the costs of an organization would fall within one part of the program structure,

the entire amount should be so allocated unless this would cause significant distortions in the basis for analysis and decision-making. Further, there is usually little to be gained by spreading very small appropriations or small parts of an appropriation within the program structure. Normally, they should be allocated in total to that element into which the costs predominantly fall.

Agencies should review their structure in light of these criteria. In addition, Bureau representatives will advise individual agencies of a number of specific instances where the program structure should be modified in accordance with the foregoing.

f. *Relationship to other classifications.* As part of its effort in the review of program structures in individual agencies, the Bureau will continue to work toward development of a Government-wide program structure. As this effort progresses, agencies will be asked to adjust their structures to produce a comprehensive and compatible pattern across agency lines.

To facilitate the translation of program decisions and related data into the classifications used in the budget, it is desirable to bring program and appropriation structures into as close a relationship as possible. In refinement of the PPB system, the aim is to interrelate, to the maximum extent, the functional classification employed in the budget, the agency program structures, and the appropriation activity classifications in the budget. Attention should be given to changes in structures which will contribute to this objective.

STATE AND LOCAL GOVERNMENT GUIDELINES

The approach adopted by most of the state, city and county governments that are installing PPB differs markedly from the federal approach. For example, the design of the program structure for one large eastern city proceeded as follows.

The first two levels of the program structure were designed by the responsible central staff agency, in this case the city's Operating Budget Department. After revision and approval by the three top city officials, the two-level city-wide program structure (labelled "Programs" and "Sub-Programs") was sent to individual agency heads with a request that they fit the activities of their agency into the overall structure, grouped according to "Program Elements." The following major programs were chosen for the city (the numbers in parenthesis show the number of sub-programs identified):

    I. Community Development (6)
    II. Transportation (4)
    III. Judiciary and Law Enforcement (5)
    IV. Conservation of Health (3)
    V. Public Education (2)
    VI. Cultural and Recreational (1)
    VII. Improvement of General Welfare (7)
    VIII. Services to Property (4)
    IX. General Management and Support (8)

Statements of goals and descriptions were provided for each program and sub-program to assist agency heads in determining the most appropriate location for their various activities.

This procedure resulted in a three-level program structure for the entire city government, grouped according to a hierarchy of goals. For example, Program III, labelled "Judiciary and Law Enforcement," consisted of all city activities which contributed to the stated goal: "To prevent and suppress crime; to apprehend criminals; to investigate and prosecute crime; to support a complete Court System; and to confine, control, and rehabilitate all persons committed to Prisons and Detention Centers." (Other program goal statements were not so precise; the goal for Program I—Community Development—read as follows: "To improve the physical and economic condition of the City.") The sub-programs of Program III were labelled:

Crime Prevention
Patrol and Apprehension
Criminal Prosecution
Judiciary and Court Administration
Detention and Rehabilitation

The goal for the Crime Prevention Sub-Program was: "To reduce and prevent crime by means of control of juvenile delinquency, professional counseling of crime-disposed families, and professional social work with young people; by the improvement of relations between police and the community; by educational programs; and by research into the causes of crime and recommending corrective action."

Three separate agencies responded with program elements contributing to the goal of the Crime Prevention Sub-Program:

Youth Conservation Services (Public Welfare Department)
Community Group Liaison (Police Department)
Law Enforcement Planning Council (Finance Department)

The goal of the Youth Conservation Services Program Element was: "To reduce and prevent crime by the prevention and control of juvenile delinquency; through professional counseling to hard-core families; by directing pre-delinquents into constructive activity through referral committees; by discouraging school drop-outs by providing a work experience for boys in conjunction with the school system and by the control of gangs."

Sixteen departments in all contributed to the accomplishment of the goal of the Judiciary and Law Enforcement Program through activities grouped in twenty-seven separate program elements.

The central staff agency of a large eastern state government, following the federal example, initially embarked on the task of designing the program structure by asking each individual agency to devise its own structure. The result was somewhat less than satisfactory, with the individual structures submitted reflecting a wide disparity of views as to what constituted a program structure; many agencies simply followed organizational lines. The central staff responded by issuing new guidelines in which (a) the output-oriented nature of the ideal program structure was emphasized, and (b) a suggested two-level statewide program structure was outlined. Agencies were asked to devise internal two-level program structures which would fit beneath the proposed statewide structure.

Another state government has promulgated the following program structure as the basis for farther subdivision by individual state agencies:

1. Improve the Standard of Living for All the People
   1. Remove social and economic barriers

2. Development of economic environment
3. Unassignable support

2. Provide Opportunities for Formal Education
   1. Preschool
   2. Elementary and secondary
   3. Higher education
   4. Continuing education

3. Improve the Health of All the People
   1. Physical health
   2. Mental health
   3. Environmental health
   4. Unassignable support
   5. Unassignable research and planning

4. Provide Adequate Transportation
   1. Water transport
   2. Air transport
   3. Urban transit
   4. Motor vehicle transport
   5. Unassignable research and planning
   6. Unassignable support

5. Provide a Satisfactory Physical Environment
   1. Water supply
   2. Land development
   3. Waste disposal
   4. Conservation and beautification
   5. Drainage and flood control
   (6. Environmental health—included under program category 3)
   7. Unassignable support

6. Provide Cultural and Recreational Opportunities
   1. Build and operate facilities
   2. Conduct cultural and recreational programs
   3. Unassignable research and planning
   4. Unassignable support

7. Safeguard the Individual, His Rights and His Property
   1. Crime prevention and control
   2. Traffic law enforcement

3. Adjudicate civil disputes
4. Fire prevention and control
5. Disaster prevention and control
   —natural and man-made
6. Control standards of service
7. Unassignable support

8. Contribute to the Attainment of National Goals
   1. Other
   2. Unassignable support

9. General Administration and Support
   1. General government management
   2. Comprehensive planning
   3. Unassignable financial services
   4. Unassignable purchasing and property management
   5. Unassignable personal services
   6. Unassignable EDP
   7. Unassignable legal services
   8. Legislature
   9. Other

In addition to the unstructured method which characterizes the approach of the federal government and the early efforts of some state and local governments, and the government-wide format or structured approach which has been adopted by many state and local governments, there remains what might be described as the *ex cathedra* approach embraced by a few jurisdictions. The *ex cathedra* approach has a certain appeal. Intransigent Commissioners or Department Heads do not have to be cajoled into cooperating in what, to many, must seem an academic exercise; uniformity and consistency will be assured; time can be saved. For the *ex cathedra* approach involves the preparation of the complete program structure for the entire jurisdiction, in all its pyramidal symmetry, by the central staff agency working alone. The success of this approach, however, presupposes an omniscient central staff. Moreover, it violates one of the few cardinal rules that can confidently be given for program structure design, namely that line managers should participate in the process.

FACTORS INFLUENCING THE DESIGN OF THE PROGRAM STRUCTURE

Many factors influence the manner in which a jurisdiction sets about the task of installing a planning-programming-budgeting system. These same factors affect particularly the program structure design phase. Let us first consider the major factors affecting the choice of *approach,* which may be summarized as follows:

1. The understanding of, sympathy for, and commitment to the principles of PPB on the part of the chief executive of the jurisdiction (president, governor, mayor or city manager, county executive)

2. The personality and management philosophy of the chief executive.

3. The size and organizational structure of the jurisdiction; the number of agencies and commissions reporting to the chief executive; the degree of autonomy prevailing.

4. Constitutional powers (particularly with respect to budget-making) vested in the chief executive.

5. The ability, size, organizational location, and prestige of the responsible central staff agency.

Once an overall approach has been selected, be it structured, unstructured, or *ex cathedra,* other factors will inevitably influence the response of individual agencies. Some important influences would undoubtedly include at least the following:

1. The clarity, precision, and specificity of any guidelines issued by central staff.
2. The perceptions by individual agency heads of the degree to which the chief executive is backing the effort.
3. The understanding of, sympathy for, and commitment to the principles of PPB on the part of the agency head.
4. The personality and management philosophy of the agency head.
5. The existing size and organizational structure of the agency; the number of separate bureaus or divisions involved; the degree of centralization or decentralization both geographically and in terms of lower-level autonomy.
6. The nature of the mission, or missions, of the agency.
7. The homogeneity or lack thereof in the agency's problem mix; the degree to which agency problems are stable or in flux.
8. The range of the agency's activities.
9. Relations between bureaus or divisions within the agency.
10. Inertia and tradition.
11. Political popularity of the agency's programs; the personal interest of the chief executive in aspects of the agency's programs.
12. Characteristics of the agency's existing data systems (Financial accounting, cost accounting, work measurement, performance monitoring, management information, etc.)

13. Appropriations structure
14. Structure of allotments, apportionments, etc.
15. Statutory obligations of the agency.
16. Relationship of the agency with key legislators.
17. The nature of the agency's clientele groups.
18. Reporting requirements of other levels of government (both superior and subordinate).
19. Existence of, and relations with, competitive agencies within the jurisdiction.
20. The ability, size, organizational location, and prestige of the responsible staff within the agency.

STEPS IN DESIGNING THE PROGRAM STRUCTURE

In considering the actual process of designing the program structure, our perspective will be that of the agency head. We will assume that general guidance has been given in the form of a statement of broad program categories for the jurisdiction as a whole.

Usually the central staff agency will have indicated the number of structural levels desired for central reporting purposes. If not, the first task is to choose the number of levels—normally two or three, resulting in a total of three or four levels, including the broad category level suggested by central staff. The PPB system, as it applies to the civilian agencies of the federal government, was conceived *primarily* as a tool to assist agency heads, the budget director and the president in making broad strategic decisions. Since this is also the intent of those state and local governments presently installing PPB, it can be concluded that, for any jurisdiction-wide PPB system, no more than three or four levels should be employed. More than four levels would tend to clutter the program structure with excessive detail, thus reducing the utility of the system as a convenient aid to strategic planning. (There is no reason why, for internal planning purposes, the agency should not adopt a greater number of levels, if this would prove useful to top management within the agency.)

Once the number of levels has been determined, the agency must formulate statements of its objectives, select categories, and prepare descriptive statements for each component of the structure. These three steps actually comprise an *iterative* process of continuous redefinition and clarification, but for convenience they will be discussed as if they were separate, sequential steps.

The first step is to define the agency's objectives. Arthur Smithies makes the following pertinent observations: [1]

National goals do not emerge fully blown from the head of Minerva. They are the result of decisions reached during the political process. But in reaching decisions, politicians can be more or less informed by objective evidence, quantitative or qualitative, concerning the social, economic, and political consequences of pursuing such goals. A fundamental assumption of PPB is that they should be so informed.

Furthermore, goals should be formulated with due regard for their feasibility, which depends on the economic resources

available to the country—most generally on its potential GNP. For example, the U.S. can regard universal social security as a goal; India cannot afford to do so. Uruguay does establish such goals, but cannot afford them.

Even goals that are feasible in this sense cannot be pursued to the fullest extent desired. We do not in fact provide social security for everyone. We do not avoid all highway accidents. Nor do we defend the country against all external threats. Compromises must be made among them, in order to achieve a total program that will best serve the national interest.

Moreover, the extent to which goals can be pursued depends on the efficiency with which each is pursued. A major component of efficiency is resource cost. Consequently, another major objective of PPB is to ensure that any level of activity will be achieved at minimum economic cost.

PPB is thus concerned with the determination of goals, with assessment of their relative importance to society, and with the allocation of resources to their attainment.

In order to avoid semantic confusion it must be emphasized that the statements of objectives required for program structure design are not the same as statements of objectives required for analytic purposes. For example, a statement such as: "To reduce the incidence of infant mortality in Jurisdiction X" (Type A) would constitute an acceptable statement of an objective appropriate for, say, a sub-category grouping of activities within a health agency. On the other hand, a statement such as: "to reduce the incidence of infant mortality in Jurisdiction X from its present rate of four times the national average to twice the national average within five years" (Type B)

---

[1] Arthur Smithies, *Outline for Discussion,* unpublished mimeograph prepared for a PPB Seminar conducted by Management Analysis Center, Inc., July/August, 1966.

would be an appropriate statement of a target, the desirability (or cost-effectiveness) of which, given available resources, must pass the acid test of analysis. One of the primary purposes of PPB is, of course, to assist decision-makers in converting Type A statements into Type B—to translate broad statements of purpose into clear program objectives that are analytically based and operationally useful. The program structure should provide the optimum framework for this conversion process.

The task of formulating precise but non-quantitative statements of objectives as the first step in designing the program structure is not easy and must be approached with due care. It is often helpful to pose the question: "What are we really trying to accomplish, and for whom?" One of the objectives of a public employment service, for example, might be stated: "To assist the unemployed in securing satisfactory jobs appropriate to their abilities." (Sub-objectives might be concerned with accomplishing the above for specific target groups including, perhaps, disadvantaged versus relatively skilled workers, or residents of urban ghettos versus the rural unemployed.) The objective of a public employment service is *not* "To interview, test, counsel and place unemployed persons in jobs." This statement focuses on process, rather than mission; it emphasizes the activity schedule of the agency rather than its ultimate purpose.

Following the establishment of a structure of objectives and sub-objectives, the next step in our iterative process is to group the activities of our agency according to the sub-objectives

to which they contribute. (Here we are assuming that we are constructing a three-level program structure.) Each separate activity thus identified in the program structure is usually known as a "program element."

The task of designing the program structure is completed by the preparation of labels and descriptive statements for each component of the structure, thus clarifying the intended scope, coverage, and content of each component.

It must be emphasized once again that the above three steps are not to be performed sequentially. For example, initial preparation of tentative descriptive statements for categories and sub-categories will amplify the category and sub-category titles (which are themselves usually to be thought of as shorthand labels derived from the statements of objectives and sub-objectives), and hence will assist in determining which activities (elements) should be placed within each sub-category. Sometimes it will not be possible to formulate precise statements of objectives and particularly sub-objectives (hence delineating categories and sub-categories) until the activity schedule of the agency has been examined in detail.

In designing a program structure it will often be useful to ask not only the question "what are we really trying to accomplish, and for whom?", but also "what are we currently doing and for whom?" Thus, viewing the structure both from the top (objectives) down and from the bottom (activities) up will be helpful.

One of the most crucial choices in designing a three-level agency program structure is the selection of the subcategories which, in our model, is virtually synonomous with selection of sub-objectives. The problem which faces the program-structure designer is that there are many possible ways of sub-dividing an objective. The cardinal rule to be observed in making the choice is to consider which particular dimension of the objective is of most concern to the agency head and the chief executive. This principle derives from one of the primary reasons for designing the structure in the first place: namely, to facilitate allocation of scarce resources among competing programs. Allocation implies choice. The program structure should therefore be designed to illuminate choice, or "surface trade-off opportunities," in the jargon of the trade. This in turn implies that we should select that dimension of the objective within which important choices are most frequent or significant.

By "dimension" we mean such possible classification schemes as the following:

Geographical region
Age group
Sex
Race
Income level
Urban vs. rural
Narrower objectives

For example, the decision-maker in a particular jurisdiction might be more interested in a display of data concerning a crime prevention program arranged by age-group (e.g., juvenile versus adult) rather than by geographic region or race or income level. His decision-making requirements will not necessarily be the same as his counterparts in other jurisdictions. Of course, our decision-maker will most probably wish to see program data displayed according to a variety of different dimensions. His second preference can constitute the dimension in which the program elements are chosen while other displays would require special tabulations.

No individual program structure can possibly satisfy the desires of everyone for all types of information displays for all purposes.[2] A choice has to be made as to the optimal dimension within which the display will be of most significance and utility to the decision-makers.

There are some general principles, however, which can assist in the choice of sub-categories.[3]

(1) The more administrative flexibility or discretion possessed by the decision-maker in a particular program area, the larger will be the appropriate *number* of sub-categories.

(2) The sub-categories should reflect the higher levels of decision-making powers possessed only by top management, rather than powers delegated to lower-level managers. For example, let us suppose that a Manpower Agency conducts two programs, "Training" and "Placement," which are administered regionally; let us also suppose that the Regional Directors have complete discretionary authority to allocate funds between these two programs, subject only to an overall budgetary constraint determined by the Agency Head. It might make more

---

[2] Allen Schick's paper on "Multipurpose Budget Systems" (on page 358) amplifies this point.
[3] The author acknowledges his debt to John Haldi for many of the ideas here presented.

sense in this example to use the various Regions as the sub-categories of the Manpower Program Category (rather than "Training" and "Placement"), since only the Agency Head can allocate funds among Regions. "Training" and "Placement" would then comprise the elements for each Regional sub-category.

(3) By viewing the structure "from the bottom up," the designer of the program structure can help identify appropriate sub-category classifications by identifying "natural groupings" of program elements. These clusters of program elements will most frequently be distinguished by identifying competing or complementary programs. "Competing" programs are close substitutes for each other as alternative means of achieving an objective. For example, juvenile counseling services and police patrol cars could be regarded as alternative and hence, given scarce resources, competing means of preventing crime. The activities of the homicide squad, however, might more logically be considered under the heading of "detection of crime and apprehension of criminals." "Complementary" programs are those which form a closely related system, wherein an increase in consumption in one will usually lead to a corresponding increase in the others. For example, an increase in activities related to criminal prosecution would probably lead to an increase in the activities of the prison system.

Many of the twenty factors, which we suggested in a previous section of this paper influence the design of the program structure, have their most significant impact on the choice of sub-categories.

SOME CAVEATS

It is suggested that excessive effort to attain purity should not be expended on the design of the program structure. As we have indicated, it is quite possible to design a variety of logical structures for a single agency, particularly at the sub-category level. Reasonable men of good judgment can consequently be expected to hold legitimate differences of opinion on the optimal design. Rather than indulge in interminable philosophic discussions about the proper dimensional classification of sub-categories or the choice of the sub-category to which a particular program element belongs, the design team's efforts should be directed toward achieving a logical and reasonably consistent whole.

It is essential that top agency management be involved in the design process, particularly in the selection and definition of categories and sub-categories. A top management decision-making apparatus that is constructed without the active understanding and involvement of the top managers will have little practical utility. If they do participate actively, top managers may discover that the design process itself yields remarkable insights into the workings of the organization.

The result of the design effort will almost certainly not be the perfect structure, nor should it be expected to endure immutably for all time. It will not satisfy all the needs of all its users, but it must be remembered that the program structure is not the agency's only format for information display. The program structure says nothing about the worth or benefits of program elements nor about the desirability of the objectives which underpin the structure, nor does it provide a magical algorithm for resource allocation. It aims to be nothing more than a format for presentation and a framework for analysis.

But if the structure is not used analytically, it will remain a lifeless skeleton, rattling dustily in some obscure closet, a mocking reminder of the futility of expecting to transform *vin ordinaire* into vintage claret simply by changing decanters. The mere act of recasting an agency's budget in program structure terms has no intrinsic virtue, other than providing an educational and often salutary experience for those involved in the design of the structure and marginally increasing the informational value of the budget document. The act itself will represent at best a rather trivial manipulation of data, a sort of budgetary legerdemain.

A good program structure can be used rather in the manner of the Periodic Table of elements, as an orderly array to trigger systematic thinking about programs.

IMPORTANCE OF PROGRAM STRUCTURE DESIGN

The mistaken notion is frequently held that an important effect of the choice of a particular program structure is a subsequent change in the organization structure of the government or individual agency. This arises from comparisons of organization and program structures; apparent anomalies or conflicts can usually be readily detected. Adoption of a program structure which differs from the existing organization structure does not, however, automat-

ically mean that the organization structure is wrong and must be changed. Although in some cases the organization structure may indeed be poorly conceived, in very few cases has it been changed due to the adoption of a program structure.

There is a logic to the manner in which an agency or government is organized and managed which is different from the logic of planning. We still have an Army, Navy, and Air Force, despite the fact that the Secretary of Defense makes his major planning (resource allocation) decisions within the framework of the program structure—strategic forces, general purpose forces, etc.

Occasionally, however, a logical program structure design reveals or highlights weaknesses in an organization structure which are truly organizational weaknesses, and not simply apparent (and illusory) incompatibilities with the program structure. The U. S. Department of Labor, for example, has been steadily developing its organization structure for the past fifteen years or so along program lines. The adoption of a program structure by the Labor Department under the PPB System merely served to emphasize the organizational advantages of continuing this process.

The significant effect of the choice of a particular program structure, therefore, will not be found in changes in the formal organization structure; they will be found in shifts in the *informal* organization structure. They will manifest themselves in shifts in the power structure, changes in the manner in which resource allocation decisions are made and, possibly, significant alterations in the emphasis placed on particular programs. The magnitude and nature of these effects will depend on the degree to which PPB is aggressively used to make budgetary decisions. These effects have, of course, been most marked in the Department of Defense.

An illustration of the degree to which the choice of a particular program structure could have really significant effects on the *modus operandi* of a government is suggested by Thomas Schelling in a discussion of PPB and foreign affairs: [4]

The point is that the basic program package is not Peace Corps, financial aid, military aid, agricultural surpluses, propaganda, or diplomatic representation; the basic package is the country.

Maybe somebody can think of a better package. But what we are presently struggling for in our budgetary procedures is an identification of the objectives or "outputs" toward which our programs are supposed to be oriented. Just getting recognition that the country, rather than the agency or program, is the basic unit of analysis would be a heroic step. After that the people with specialized analytic talents, with schemes for the orderly collection of data, and with professional training in PPBS can go to work. The first step toward PPBS is officially identifying program packages; and that step has not yet been taken.

To say that the basic program package in foreign affairs is the individual country can provoke either of two objections —that it is wrong, or that to say so is trivial. Those who object that it is wrong do not worry me; I share their discontent with the country as the basic pack-

age, but do not believe they can identify a better package, and in the end we shall, equally discontent, settle on the individual country as the least unsatisfactory basic package for foreign affairs budgeting.

Anyone who says that the individual country is so obviously the basic package that in saying so I have said nothing, is plain wrong. What I have said is trivial as far as analytical budgeting is concerned; but bureaucratically it is revolutionary. Charles Schultze is a sensible and responsible man; that does not mean he is not revolutionary, only that he makes his revolution slowly, carefully, and responsibly. The revolution is in considering all programs for a country together, rather than all countries for a program together. It is examining what the United States does with respect to Greece, Thailand, Brazil, India, or Nigeria, rather than what the United States does with aid, Peace Corps, agricultural surpluses, military assistance, and propaganda. This is revolutionary not just because somebody would be looking at the totality of U.S. programs with respect to a particular country all together, relating them to the same set of objectives, comparing them with respect to their effectiveness, demanding that the same set of objectives be acknowledged in the consideration of each program, eliminating inconsistency and reducing duplication. Nor is it that, once the basic country packages are identified, countries would be compared with each other as claimants for U.S. resources and U.S. attention.

No, what would be revolutionary is that somebody or some agency has to do this, and it has to be decided who or which agency would do it. (It also has to be decided whether the Congress wants this done; and that may depend on who does it.)

Of course, Professor Schelling is discussing a situation involving the creation of a sort of government-wide

[4] Thomas Schelling, *PPBS and Foreign Affairs,* memorandum prepared for the Subcommittee on National Security and International Operations of the Senate Committee on Governmental Operations, January, 1968.

program category labelled "Foreign Affairs." His arguments and questions apply with equal force to every other sphere of federal activity—health, education, transportation, law enforcement, welfare, natural resources, economic development, science and technology, and general government (to name some possible categories). His use of the word "revolutionary" is appropriate if we contemplate the ultimate establishment of a government-wide program structure. In the meantime the effects he envisions have been less than revolutionary in that the ramifications of the adoption of particular program structures have been confined, internally, to individual departments.

This is not to say that certain departments of the federal government have not experienced significant effects, albeit less than revolutionary, through the adoption of particular program structures. The Departments of Labor and the Interior, among others, have designated individual assistant secre-taries to monitor each program category, even though all component programs in the secretaries' categories are not necessarily within their organizational jurisdiction. If this arrangement is properly utilized, hopefully these departments will reduce considerably program inconsistency and duplication.

The potential for revolutionary effects as a result of the adoption and use of a logical, meaningful program structure is much greater in the case of state and local governments—and more imminent. Since those states, cities, and counties that are implementing PPB have largely tended to adopt the government-wide approach to program structure design, it follows that they will soon face the need to choose between making overall budgetary decisions on the more rational basis revealed by their program structures or, as before, along organizational lines. Their choice may determine the rationality of public expenditure decision-making for many years to come.

CASE

1

POST OFFICE DEPARTMENT

CHOICE AMONG COMPETING PROGRAM STRUCTURES

"The Mail Must Go Through." This had been the simple and traditional cry of the Post Office since 1789, the date of its establishment by Congress. The slogan was more likely to convey a picture of a Pony express rider fighting off Indians or robbers than a system of men and equipment capable of carrying 72 billion pieces (12 billion pounds) of mail in 1965.

Although never formally revised, the Post Office's slogan had changed in practice due to Congress' wish and a changing environment. "The mail must go through with varying degrees of speed at varying rates (depending on the class of mail), efficiently (610,079 man years required in 1965) and privately." Only when a strike or natural disaster threatened mail service did the public realize the magnitude of the Post Office's task.

Some miscellaneous statistics gave an indication of the scope of operations. In 1789 the Federal Postmaster General supervised a service embracing 75 postmasters and two thousand miles of postroads. In 1965 there were over 40,000 postmasters. During its

history the Department had developed a deep tradition of public service.

Arthur E. Summerfield, Postmaster General from 1953 to 1960, presented some interesting facts about the Post Office in his book, *U.S. Mail*.[1] He observed the loyalty of Postmaster Beardsley of North Lansing, New York who served under twenty Presidents and remained at his post for 75 years. He presented Abraham Lincoln, Postmaster, Salem, Illinois as a sign of the Department's integrity. The Department's dependability was highlighted

This case was prepared with the cooperation of the United States Post Office Department by James N. Kelly under the supervision of Richard F. Vancil, Associate Professor of Business Administration, Harvard University, on behalf of the Office of Career Development, U.S. Civil Service Commission. The case is intended for class discussion only, and certain names and facts may have been changed which, while avoiding the disclosure of confidential information, do not materially lessen the value of the case for educational purposes. This case is not intended to represent either effective or ineffective handling of an administrative situation, nor does it purport to be a statement of policy by the agency involved.

[1] Arthur E. Summerfield, *U.S. Mail* (New York: Holt, Rinehart and Winston, 1960).

when the Hope Diamond was sent safely from New York to Washington by regular first-class mail.

Mr. Summerfield also pointed out the change in the economics of postal service during its long history. "In 1800 it cost six cents to send a single-sheet letter sixty miles (two sheets cost twelve cents, etc.) at a time when Delmonico's fashionable restaurant in New York served a full-course dinner for twelve cents."

SERVICES OF THE
POST OFFICE DEPARTMENT

The original purpose of the Postal System, to provide "the best means of establishing posts for conveying letters and intelligence through the continent," was confirmed by the Postal Policy Act of 1958 which also stated that "The Postal Establishment was created to unite more closely the American people, to promote the general welfare, and to advance the national economy." As described in the Government Organization Manual, the Post Office had also been "extended and expanded into a nationwide network of services and facilities for communicating intelligence, disseminating information, advancing education and culture, and distributing articles of commerce and industry."

These general purposes of the Postal System were translated into specific services to be performed by the Post Office by Congressional legislation. In 1965 the Post Office was authorized and instructed by Congress to conduct twenty-three services for the public and government. A complete list of these services, with the revenue and expense allocated to each service for F. Y. 1965, is presented as Exhibit 1.

First, second, third, and fourth class mail were the most important postal services, representing 88 per cent of total revenue and 86 per cent of total costs. First class mail alone accounted for 50 per cent of total revenue and 37 per cent of total cost. These four services were defined by Congress as follows:

First class mail—Written communication (including typewritten) in the form of envelopes, flats or rolls.

Second class mail—Newspapers, magazines, or other periodicals approved by the Post Office as time-valued material.

Third class mail—Advertising, circulars, packages less than one pound, and other material not included under first, second or fourth class mail.

Fourth class mail—Parcel post and books, packages over one pound.

Congress alone sets rates for first, second, and third class mail. In the Postal Policy Act of 1958, however, Congress had left the rate-setting authority for parcel post and other special services with the Postmaster General, who traditionally exercised this responsibility. The Act also provided that a portion of the losses incurred by the Post Office in processing certain categories of second, third, and fourth class mail and all special services were in the public interest and automatically approved by Congress as "Public Service Losses." The magnitude and distribution of "Public Services Losses" is shown in Exhibit 1. After deducting "Public Service Losses," the Post Office incurred a deficit of $277 million out of a total operating budget of $5,275 million in fiscal year 1965.

ORGANIZATION AND MANAGEMENT

In order to provide Congress and the Postmaster General with information on the revenues and costs attributable to each class of mail the Department produced the Cost Ascertainment Report, one of several information systems maintained by the Department. The Cost Ascertainment Division in the Bureau of Finance and Administration was in charge of preparing the report which was usually completed six months after the close of a fiscal year. During one week in each quarter the Cost Ascertainment Division performed statistical tests of revenue, expense, and volume at approximately 500 post offices. These tests were utilized to allocate the revenue received and the full costs of operating the system to the 23 Postal Service categories. The system was oriented toward obtaining reliable statistical measures upon which to apportion costs and revenues, rather than toward determining the nature of expenses (fixed versus variable) incurred by the Post Office.

Although Congress received, reviewed, and acted upon financial information by service category, appropriations were made to the Department on a different basis. The primary Postal appropriation categories and amounts for fiscal 1965 were (in thousands):

Administration and regional operation	$ 85,941
Research development and engineering	17,956
Operations	4,241,059
Transportation	588,524
Facilities	199,476
Plant and equipment	75,000
Grand Total	$5,207,956

A detailed description of the budget submissions and changes for fiscal year 1965 is presented as Exhibit 2.

The relationship between funds budgeted and funds spent was the subject of a second information system. This study, called the Operating and Financial Report, was produced for each of 13 accounting periods during the fiscal year by the Assistant Comptroller for Accounting within the Bureau of Finance and Administration. The report also contained information about volume of mail, aggregate revenue received, productivity, and Postal employment. Organization of the report, however, centered around the appropriation categories of the Department, shown on page 59.

Organization of the Department was also closely aligned with appropriation categories. An organization chart is presented as Exhibit 3. The Department was organized on a parallel basis from the headquarters to regional offices to the local post offices. Headquarters contained ten bureaus and offices, the largest one being the Bureau of Operations (F. Y. 1965 appropriation $4.2 billion). Administrative authority for field operations was transferred from the Postmaster General to 15 Regional Directors (under the Office of Regional Administration). Each regional office contained divisions paralleling the headquarters organization which received functional guidance from its headquarters counterpart and administrative guidance from the Regional Director. The larger post offices contained the same organizational divisions and maintained a similar functional-administrative relationship with the regional organization.

Because the Bureau of Operations received just over 81 per cent of the Department's appropriation in fiscal year 1965, the Bureau's organization and measurement system were extremely important. The bulk of this appropriation was for mail handlers and clerks ($1,881 million) and collection and delivery carriers ($1,617 million). In total these accounted for over 80 per cent of the Bureau of Operations budget. These two types of personnel handled a majority of the Post Office functions of collecting mail, receiving mail, providing mail window and special service, sorting mail, transferring mail, and delivering mail.

Measuring the efficiency of the Post Office operating functions was the primary purpose of the Work Measurement System. This system was operated by the Bureau of Operations with the assistance of the Bureau of Finance and Administration. The system was in constant operation at the nation's largest post offices. A statement of the purpose, elements, and responsibilities of the system is presented as Exhibit 4. Work measurement was primarily oriented toward establishing standards and reporting productivity for the processing functions of the Post Office.

The cost and productivity of carriers required to collect and deliver the mail varied widely depending upon population and geographic conditions. For this reason collection and delivery routes (and the resulting carrier expense) were reviewed yearly by a special inspection and were therefore not of primary concern in the Work Measurement System. Rather, the system concentrated upon the processing functions performed in relation to the clerk-mail handler hours required. A report relating pieces processed to hours spent at the largest seventy-five post offices was prepared at the end of the thirteen accounting periods. The major statistics contained in the report are listed in Exhibit 5. The Work Measurement report presented a summary of total hours and total pieces. More detailed data was available, however, because the system gathered statistics by major work stations within the post office.

A small number of post offices produced a large share of the Department's volume, revenue, and costs. For instance, in fiscal year 1965 the revenue of the Department was distributed as follows:

Cumulative Number of Offices	% of Total Offices	Cumulative Total Revenue (millions)	% of Total Revenue
23	.1%	$1,453	34%
69	.2	2,077	49
321	1	2,867	68
611	2	3,187	76
1,311	4	3,531	84
2,526	7	3,783	90
4,437	13	3,957	94
7,190	21	4,072	95
11,287	33	4,148	98
24,252	71	4,217	99
34,040	100	4,228	100

For this reason the Work Measurement Report covering the largest 75 offices, prepared at the end of each accounting period, was presumed to give an accurate indication of changes in the Postal volume and productivity.

INTRODUCTION OF PPB

Planning, Programming and Budgeting was introduced to the Post Office Department in a memorandum dated October 19, 1965 from the Deputy Postmaster General (D.P.M.G.) and distributed to all of the bureaus and offices above the field organization, as indicated on Exhibit 3. In addition, copies of the memorandum were issued to the Special Assistant to the Postmaster General for Public Information and the Special Assistant to the Postmaster General for Policy and Projects, two positions within the office of the Postmaster General.

The three main elements of the October 19, 1965 memorandum were as follows:

1. The President announced on August 25 that he has asked all Departments and Agencies of the Federal government to install a planning-programming-budgeting system. On October 12 the Bureau of the Budget issued a bulletin implementing the President's directive. While we are now engaged in preparing a draft of the instructions for establishing the programming portion of this system in the Post Office Department, which will be circulated for comment when ready, we must take immediate action to meet the first major deadline of the Bureau on November 1.

2. Attached (Exhibit 6) is a preliminary version of the Post Office Department program objectives (or program categories) derived from the submissions of Bureaus and Offices last July. Also attached [2] is a summary of some briefing charts which should be used as guides with respect to the way in which we organize to accomplish the programming function in the Department, and with respect to the dates we will attempt to meet pending the issuance of more formal instructions.

3. Each addressee should review the attached summary of program objectives with particular attention to the first three pages. The Department must decide on its major program categories and submit them to the Bureau of the Budget by November 1. I expect we will have to live with these categories for some time so careful attention of the top staff to their formulation is extremely important. Please make your comments with respect to program categories to me, by close of business October 26.

Analysis of the responses to the memorandum was assigned by the D.P.M.G. to the Bureau of Finance and Administration. It was this bureau's responsibility to summarize the comments received from other bureaus and offices and to make final recommendations to the Program Review Task Force, headed by the D.P.M.G., regarding the final Post Office program categories.

The response to the D.P.M.G.'s memorandum by the Special Assistant to the Postmaster General for Policy and Projects took exception to the preliminary version of program categories and proposed that the Post Office program categories should be constructed in line with the missions of the Department, rather than the activities conducted to achieve the missions. The missions were viewed by the Special Assistant as fulfilling the four major

---

[2] Not reproduced in this case.

responsibilities given to the Post Office by Congress:

1. The delivery of private correspondence.
2. The delivery of periodical publications.
3. The delivery of direct mail advertising material.
4. The delivery of merchandise.

These responsibilities corresponded almost exactly with the four existing classes of mail. The Special Assistant maintained that, because these classes of mail each had different service requirements, rate structures, and costs, they were really the "products" of the Departments activities and therefore should be used as the Department's primary program categories. Adopting such a product-oriented program structure was felt to be "more meaningful than a series of separate measurements by function," because the "public evaluates our effectiveness" by product performance, not by functional performance (acceptance, transportation, delivery, etc.). The entire memorandum submitted by the Special Assistant to the Postmaster General for Policy and Projects is presented as Exhibit 7.

On November 19, 1965 the Bureau of Finance and Administration issued its summary of the alternatives submitted by the various bureaus and offices and also its recommended structure for Post Office categories and subcategories. The Bureau did not support the suggestion made by the Special Assistant for Policy and Projects that the program categories should reflect the "products" of the post office—classes of mail. The reasons given for not adopting the class of mail approach were:

1. The prime product of the Post Office was collection and delivery of mail which was independent of class of mail.
2. A primary breakdown by class of mail would tend to fractionate programs which should be considered on a broader basis.
3. Obtaining information by class of mail would be expensive and difficult. The cost ascertainment system does provide information by class of mail sufficient for rate purposes.

On November 27, 1965 the program categories recommended by the Bureau of Finance and Administration were forwarded to the Bureau of the Budget by the Postmaster General for the Bureau's comments. In addition, suggestions of output measures for the program sub-categories were attached to the recommended categories and sub-categories. Excerpts from the Postmaster General's submission to the Bureau of the Budget is attached as Exhibit 8.

At the same time as the initial program categories were submitted, the Postmaster General indicated to the Bureau of the Budget Director that he was very interested in finding a highly qualified and experienced individual to direct the new Office of Planning. The Director pledged the support of the Budget Bureau in finding such an individual and also indicated that the new man, when selected, could continue the development of the final program categories for the Post Office.

Communication regarding the Post Office Department's program categories continued on December 1, 1966 with the issuance of another memorandum from the Policy and Projects Special Assistant to the Bureau of Finance and Administration. This memorandum is excerpted in Exhibit 9. Two subjects were raised in this new memorandum. First, it was suggested that the categories recommended by the Bureau would be more meaningful if the subcategories "Collection" and "Processing" were replaced with the three subcategories of "Acceptance," "Distribution," and "Transfer." Detailed reasons for this suggestion were presented in the memorandum. The second subject of the memorandum concerned "the value of, and the cost of, reporting functional (i.e., sub-category) data by class of mail."

On December 10, 1965 the Bureau of Finance and Administration again summarized program category suggestions received after their November 19th memorandum. This memorandum repeated the Bureau's objections to "class of mail" categories, attached recommendations received from other bureaus and offices, and recommended a new, slightly revised, program structure. This memorandum from the Bureau of Finance and Administration to the Deputy Postmaster General is excerpted in Exhibit 10.

At the end of December 1965 the Bureau of the Budget notified the Postmaster General that they had found someone to act as temporary Director of the Office of Planning until a permanent man was located. They suggested that a prominent economist, then a consultant to BOB, be appointed as Acting Director. The Postmaster General agreed that such an arrangement would be very satisfactory and asked the economist to start immediately,

even though formal announcement of his position would take some time.

THE MEETING ON JANUARY 15, 1966

After reviewing the historical development of Post Office program categories, one of the Planning Director's first actions was to request that members of the Policy and Projects (Policy) staff and Bureau of Finance and Administration (Finance) staff meet with him in the near future. This meeting was held on January 15, 1966 with Messrs. Norm Samelson [3] and Allen South representing the Bureau of Finance and Administration and Messrs. David Cannom and Don Erman present from the Policy and Projects Special Assistant's staff. A summary of the discussions which took place at this meeting follows:

DIRECTOR OF PLANNING:

I've called this meeting primarily for my own benefit. As you know, Post Office operations are brand new to me and I'm trying to gain an understanding of the nature of the Department.

At the same time, I think that time pressure dictates that we all work to reach a final agreement on the composition of program categories in the Department. Our program memoranda are due at BOB on May 1st. That doesn't leave much time for their preparation, much less for any further theoretical discussions concerning the categories.

Although I haven't gone as far as locking the doors and keeping you here until an agreement is reached, I am going to ask that you come up with a

---

[3] Names changed.

compromise structure by the end of January.

I've read all of the background material on the subject and thus would like to limit discussion to new observations concerning the appropriate program structure and also suggestions for resolving the different viewpoints expressed.

NORM SAMELSON:
(Finance)

Perhaps one of the dangers of PPBS is that it encourages everyone to dwell on the theoretical. I agree our past discussions have been fun, but now let's concentrate on getting the job done.

Let me try and summarize the thinking behind our suggested categories (let's call them the functional categories) in a slightly different way. Our orientation is toward the management of the Department. We feel the basic purpose of the program structure is to maximize the effectiveness of management after the installation of a program structure. It would serve no useful purpose if a structure were developed which represented a theoretically ideal distribution of functions if program managers could not effectively manage the programs to which they were assigned.

In this regard, we feel a structure orientated toward class of mail is unmanageable. The Post Office is not managed by class of mail. The revenue received from various classes of mail is incidental to the management process. Setting rates is a Congressional matter and does not influence how we manage the mails. Management is concerned with functions of collecting and distributing the mail, regardless of class or rates.

DON ERMAN:
(Policy)

Norm, I hate to get dramatic, but please excuse me while I conjure up the spirit of old Ben Franklin. I'm sure that Ben would support me that we must be concerned with the effectiveness, the quality, of our service to the public. This is not done now in any explicit manner and I think this is the real opportunity presented to the Post Office by PPBS. Only by taking a systems approach, rather than functional approach, to mail service can we judge our present effectiveness and plan for future improvement. We should concentrate on our 'product line,' the classes of mail.

AL SOUTH:
(Finance)

I can see only two reasons for establishing categories by class of mail. The first is to establish rates and I think we can eliminate that one due to the existence of the Cost Ascertainment System which is designed especially for that purpose. The second is to measure the quality of our service to the public and examine alternatives for improving that service. In an agency such as the State Department this ability to measure the effectiveness of alternatives to achieve missions is important. However, in the Post Office the missions are obvious, clear and quite easily measured without establishing a new information system.

The Post Office's primary concern must be with the efficiency of its operations. If the effectiveness of our service declines the public will tell us through their actions. If the effectiveness of the State Department missions declines it would be far more difficult to determine.

DAVE CANNOM:
(Policy)
If all agencies followed your reasoning no one would attempt to adopt missions for their program categories. If the Post Office, whose goals are quite explicit, can make an argument that "the efficiency of an activity is more important than its effectiveness to the accomplishment of the Department's goals," can't the State Department make an even better argument?

AL SOUTH:
(Finance)
No. I'd say that when goals are quite explicit and readily measured it is quite logical to be more concerned with efficiency than effectiveness or quality.

DIRECTOR OF PLANNING:
Is this at all connected with who is judging the Post Office's performance, Congress, the mailer, or the Post Office itself? Is the output of the Department the same to all of these groups?

NORM SAMELSON:
(Finance)
Yes, it is. The Post Office really only has three outputs. One is special services which are more or less by-products of the mail service. The second is mail with preferential treatment and the third is mail with non-preferential treatment. Even though there are a total of 23 rate categories, in reality, Congress, the mailer, and the Post Office look at mail in only these three ways.

DON ERMAN:
(Policy)
That's an excellent point, Norm. What does that mean for the program categories?

DAVE CANNOM:
(Policy)
Yes, doesn't that mean that we ought to view Post Office functions in light of these three outputs?

Also, don't you feel your latest set of suggested categories is still a little too organizationally oriented? Category I, Collection, Processing, and Delivery of Mail is almost all the Bureau of Operations. Category II, other Postal Services, takes in the remaining Bureau of Operations activities plus the Postal Inspector. Category III, Postal Support Activities, encompasses the remaining Bureaus. This really doesn't represent the functions of the Post Office.

DIRECTOR OF PLANNING:
These last comments have brought out an interesting point. There seem to be three different ways of looking at activities. Who is doing it? What are they doing? Why are they doing it? At the 'who' level we're talking about the organization and the way in which dollars are spent. At the 'what' level we are concerned with functions and how efficient they are. At the 'why' level we are interested in missions and how effectively they are being accomplished. What combination of these approaches is most appropriate for the program structure of the Post Office Department?

QUESTIONS

Summarize and evaluate the arguments presented in the memoranda in Exhibits 7 through 10. Which program structure would you recommend?

EXHIBIT 1

POST OFFICE DEPARTMENT

Apportioned Revenues and Expenses Fiscal Year 1965 (all amounts in millions)

Postal Services	Apportioned Revenue	Apportioned Costs	Public Service Loss	Revenue (Under) Over Costs
First class	$2,193	$1,965	—	$ 228
Domestic airmail				
Letters and cards	168	153		15
Parcel post	75	45		30
Second class	134	524	$165	(225)
Third class	650	999	87	(262)
Fourth class	701	846	64	(81)
International mail				
Surface	64	85	—	(21)
Airmail	76	62	—	14
Air parcel post	12	11	—	1
Penalty	117	97	—	20
Franked	7	7	—	—
Free for blind	—	3	3	—
Registry	33	47	14	—
Certified	11	15	4	—
Insurance	29	35	6	—
Collect on delivery	13	26	13	—
Special delivery	34	59	25	—
Stamped envelopes	15	20	5	—
Money order	59	72	13	—
Postal savings	3	3	—	—
Box rents	34	30	(4)	—
Non-postal services	45	66	21	—
Unassignable	8	8	—	—
Public service costs	—	99	99	—
Grand Total	$4,481	$5,277	$515	$(281)

Source: Cost Ascertainment Report, Fiscal Year 1965

EXHIBIT 2

POST OFFICE DEPARTMENT

Appropriations for Fiscal Year 1965 (in thousands)

	Administration and Regional Operation	Research, Development, and Engineering	Operations	Transportation	Facilities	Plant and Equipment	Total
To Bureau of Budget, Oct. 3, 1963	$89,200	$17,300	$4,088,000	$607,800	$209,000	$137,000	$5,148,300
Amendment to Bureau of Budget, Oct. 15, 1963	+32				+170	+905	+1,107
Appropriation transfer request	−1,245		−100		+1,069	+276	
Adjusted request	87,987	17,300	4,087,900	607,800	210,239	138,181	5,149,407
Bureau of Budget reduction	−1,532	−4,300	−53,000	−6,800	−5,170	−47,905	−188,707
To Congress	86,455	13,000	4,034,900	601,000	205,069	90,276	5,030,700
Administrative reduction House Document 240, Mar. 9, 1964[1]	−500		−12,200				−12,700
House reduction	−455	−1,000	−2,700	−6,000	−5,069	−1,276	−16,500
Senate restoration				+3,000	−2,000		+1,000
Conference action				−1,500	+1,000		−500
Public Law 88–392, Aug. 1, 1964	85,500	12,000	4,020,000	596,500	199,000	89,000	5,002,000
Fund transfer, Aug. 21, 1964[2]				+3,000		−3,000	
Unobligated balance forwarded, Sept. 10, 1964[3]		+5,956					+5,956
Fund transfer, Jan. 5, 1965[4]			+7,000	−7,476	+476		
Supplemental Public Law 89–16, Apr. 30, 1965							
Legislative transfer[4]	+1,951		+4,059			−6,000	
Additional funds[4]			+200,000				+200,000
Fund transfer, May 21, 1965[5]	−1,500		+10,000	−3,500		−5,000	
Total appropriation	$85,941	$17,956	$4,241,059	$588,524	$199,476	$ 75,000	$5,207,956

[1] Post Office Department revision.
[2] To replace part of funds cut by Congress.
[3] No-year appropriation from 1964.
[4] Increased pay costs.
[5] Increased pay costs and additional operating funds.

EXHIBIT 3

POST OFFICE DEPARTMENT

Post Office Department Organization Chart

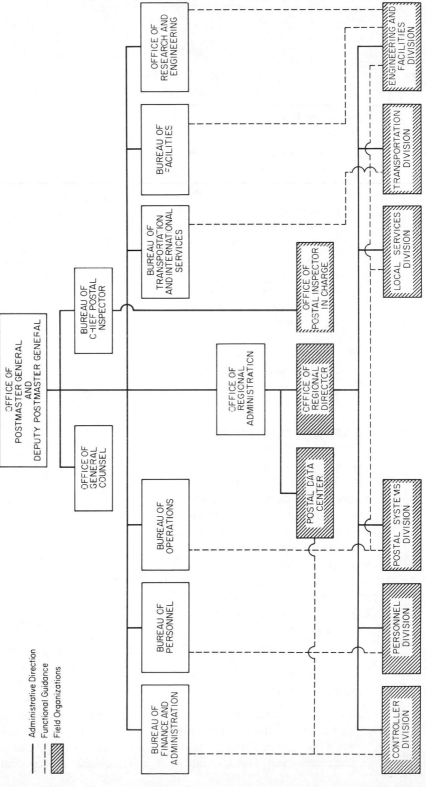

Administrative Direction
Functional Guidance
Field Organizations

59

EXHIBIT 4

POST OFFICE DEPARTMENT

Extracts from Post Office Document Describing the Work Measurement System

---

*1.1 Purpose of Work Measurement
System*

THE WORK MEASUREMENT SYS-
TEM IS DESIGNED TO:

a. Furnish postal management
with essential information on
the relationship between mail
processed and man-hours used
to process that mail.
b. Provide means for judicious
use of personnel so that the
cost of operating post offices
is kept within budgetary limitations.
c. Provide postmasters with reliable data to assist in managing post offices more efficiently.

*1.2 Qualification Criteria for Part I
and Part II Offices*

AS THE NEEDS OF THE SERVICE
REQUIRE, THE BUREAU OF OPERA-
TIONS WILL DETERMINE ANNU-
ALLY THOSE OFFICES WHICH WILL
REPORT UNDER THE PROVISIONS
OF PART I AND PART II. THIS
DETERMINATION WILL BE DIS-
SEMINATED TO ALL REGIONAL
DIRECTORS SUFFICIENTLY IN AD-
VANCE OF THE BEGINNING OF
EACH FISCAL YEAR.

1.3 Basic Elements of System

THE WORK MEASUREMENT SYS-
TEM CONSISTS OF:

a. The development and application of local standards for
work performed in mail-handling activities. The standards

referred to in this Handbook
are developed by means of
accepted engineering practices
and techniques.
b. The recording of mail volume
counts for the various categories of mail processed. These
records consist of basic volume
forms, located at predetermined mail measuring points.
c. The recording of man-hours
expended in processing mail,
and the man-hours expended
in other than mail-handling
activities, such as training,
office work, etc.
d. The preparation of adequate
reports for the postmaster and
his staff, reflecting performance in mail-handling activities
and man-hours expended in
non-mail-handling operations.
e. The measurement of individual distributor's performance.

*1.4 Departmental and Regional
Responsibilities*

.41 *The Bureau of Operations* has
primary responsibility for the
installation, operation and administration of Work Measurement Systems in post
offices.
.42 *The Bureau of Finance* is responsible (a) for the preparation and analysis of recurring
reports and special reports required by other bureaus; (b)
for providing the necessary
technical guidance to the regional offices and chief ac-

countants, or other designated post office personnel, for the accumulation of data, preparation of reports and interpretative analyses; (c) for developing mail count procedures, and monitoring mail volume and manhour recording and reporting for procedural compliance and accuracy.

.43 *The Office of Research and Engineering,* with appropriate bureau liaison, will develop Work Measurement Systems.

.44 *The Bureau of Personnel* is responsible for coordinating procedures affecting labor-management relations Headquarters. The special assistant for employee relations has this responsibility in each region. Employee organizations will be kept advised of any changes to the system subsequent to its installation at the local level.

.45 *The Director, postal systems division,* is responsible for overall administration and management of the Work Measurement System in each region. Based on the controller's analysis and interpretation of WMS data, the director, postal systems division, will undertake to correct unfavorable conditions disclosed and will initiate operational improvements indicated to be necessary by the analyses, or from on-site observations and other experience sources.

.46 *The regional controller* is responsible for reviewing and approving methods of preparing required reports; for analyzing and interpreting Work Measurement System data developed at Post Offices; and for preparing all Work Measurement System reports for use by regional or Headquarters' staff.

EXHIBIT 5

POST OFFICE DEPARTMENT

Work Measurement System Accounting Period Operating Summary

Productivity

PIECE HANDLINGS

Index (LDS) or % Change from Base
　　Current
　　Year-to-Date
Hours Changed From Base This Report Saved $ or Lost

FIRST HANDLING PIECES

Per Mail Processing Hour

% Change Same Period Last Year (SPLY)
Per Total Clerk-Mail Handler Hour

Mail Processing

TOTAL HOURS

% CHANGE SPLY

Support Hours

HOURS

% CHANGE SPLY

EXHIBIT 5—Continued

Total Clerk-Mail Handler Hours	*Other Work Hours*
HOURS	TOTAL CITY CARRIER
% CHANGE SPLY	Hours % Change from SPLY
CUMULATIVE DIFFERENCE COMPARED TO SPLY	TOTAL SUPERVISOR
	Hours % Change from SPLY
First Handling Pieces	GRAND TOTAL
PIECES PROCESSED	Hours
% CHANGE SPLY	% Change from SPLY

EXHIBIT 6

POST OFFICE DEPARTMENT

Preliminary Program Categories (October 19, 1965)

A possible program structure (based on Bureau- and Office-submitted objectives and goals) might be:

Collection and Delivery of Mail
Collection and Safeguarding of Postal Revenue
Sale and Payment of Money Orders
Operation of the Postal Savings System
Enforcing Postal Laws and Regulations
Providing Services to other Government Agencies
    Let's look at this system in more detail—

Collection and Delivery might be further subdivided into:

Collection
Processing and Distribution
Transportation between cities in the United States
Transportation between the United

States & other Countries
Delivery
Providing Special Mail Services, i.e.,
    Parcel Post
    Special Delivery
    Registered Mail
    COD
    Self-Service Postal Units etc.

Looking at "Processing and Distribution" we might have certain inputs with their supporting programs such as:

PROVIDING SPACE

Programs: Post Offices
         Air Mail Facilities
         Truck Terminals
             and Transfer
             Offices
         Highway Post
             Offices
         Railroad Post
             Offices

PROVIDING PERSONNEL

   Programs: Pay for clerks
                Pay for Contract
                Services in
                Terminals
            New employment

to reduce over-time
Overtime compensation for substitutes

EXHIBIT 7

POST OFFICE DEPARTMENT

October 26, 1965

Subject: Planning-Programming-Budgeting in Post Office Department

From: Special Assistant to the Postmaster General for Policy and Projects

To: Deputy Postmaster General:

We have examined the Bureau of Finance preliminary suggestions for establishing Planning-Programming-Budgeting in the Post Office Department, and find two areas where our viewpoints do not fully coincide.

Organization—The major responsibility for the new system should, we believe, reside in a central staff reporting to the Postmaster General or his Deputy.

This appears to be the intent of Bureau of the Budget Bulletin 66-3:

"each agency will . . . establish an adequate central staff for analysis, planning and programming."
"Planning-Programming-Budgeting activities are functionally linked but it is not essential that they be located in the same office so long as they are well coordinated. However, it is important that the head of the central analytic staff be directly responsible to the head of the agency or his deputy."

In a recent exchange of letters on the subject, Mr. Gronouski and Mr. Schultze agreed that this function should be directed from an Office of Plans and Programs on the staff of the Postmaster General.

There are several important areas in which there seems to be full agreement:

1. Planning should be directed from the Office of the Postmaster General.
2. Budgeting should remain in the Bureau of Finance.
3. Each Bureau has planning and budgeting responsibilities and should formalize them organizationally.
4. The entire program has great potential value but requires the cooperation and support of all Bureaus if it is to succeed.

Certain other organization questions, however, are yet to be resolved, among them:

EXHIBIT 7—Continued

A. should programming be closer organizationally to *planning* or to *budgeting?*
B. should the central planning office concern itself only with long range studies ("the fifty cities still on the drawing boards") or with the five-year program?
C. where should the systems analysis work—essential to developing actionable alternatives—be done?
D. should such analysis be concerned with items for next year's budget?
E. should program evaluation for the Department be centered in the Postmaster General's Office or in a Division of a Bureau?

We view the new system less as an improved budgeting technique than as a structure through which top management sets the direction of the Post Office, directs its operations, obtains the 'real' costs of programs, and observes program successes and shortcomings.

The Program Structure—Bulletin 66-3 describes the program structure as a

"series of output categories which, taken together, cover the total work of the agency. These will serve as a basic framework for the planning, programming and budgeting processes (including work on systems analysis, reporting, evaluation of accomplishments, and other aspects of management), and for relating the processes to each other."

The program structure should show the principal missions of the Post Office, the resources devoted to each, and provide for each a physical measure of performance to indicate the extent to which each program is achieving its goals. It should be established, we suggest, not by compiling a list of what each Bureau reports as its Bureau's goals, but by an analysis of postal missions and activities to determine the objectives of the Post Office as a government agency. An attempt at such an analysis follows.

The mission of the Post Office is to deliver the nation's mail. This broad objective is accomplished through a number of activities directly related to moving the mail (acceptance, distribution, transfer, transportation and delivery); a series of supporting activities needed to maintain the postal establishment (training, maintenance, inspection, record-keeping, administration, etc.); and several investment programs intended to improve future-year effectiveness or efficiency (construction, research and development). To a minor extent our resources are used on certain non-postal activities (money orders and postal savings) and in certain convenience tasks for other government agencies (sale of migratory bird stamps, alien registration, etc.). Since all of these last activities add up to approximately 2% of our costs, they should be introduced into the basic program format as a miscellaneous category.

The basic tasks of the postal establishment are thus seen to be those primary functions involved in moving the mail. But are these tasks the missions of the Post Office? Is the Post Office in business to collect mail, to distribute it, and so on, or does it have a further end-purpose, a *mission* which may be more properly used as the output category?

Congress has entrusted to the Post Office four major responsibilities:

A. the delivery of private correspondence
B. the delivery of periodical publications
C. the delivery of direct mail advertising material
D. the delivery of merchandise

Each of these can be considered a distinct program coinciding almost exactly with the existing classes of mail. The classes of mail have differing service requirements, different rate structures, different unit costs of handling. In sum these four 'products' constitute a statement of the missions of the Post Office.

The "physical measure of performance" which is an important element to each program under planning-programming-budgeting is readily defined: it is the service provided each class of mail.

For example, for first class mail there are at present these standards of service we expect to provide:

1. ABCD local mail—same day delivery
2. other local, metropolitan area and short-range surface mail —next day delivery
3. air mail—next day delivery
4. other surface mail—2–5 days, depending upon distance.

(After 1967 groups 3 and 4 will merge with a next-day service goal.)

For each group the service actually being provided can be readily determined by service test sampling, an inexpensive measurement independent of the process being tested. The measure of performance (after 1967) thus becomes the percentage of mail receiving next-day delivery.

This method constitutes a "system check" of the entire postal process and is far more meaningful than a series of separate measurements by function. It is also the same measure by which the public evaluates our effectiveness. Measurement of objectives by function (e.g. distribution efficiency) remains as an effective internal technique for management control, but our performance measurement cannot stop there.

Recommended Program Structure

We suggest that the following program structure be considered for the Post Office Department:

Principal Program #1
–First Class Mail

Principal Program #2
–Second Class Mail

Principal Program #3
–Third Class Mail

Principal Program #4
–Fourth Class Mail

Miscellaneous

Support Program #1
–Postal Administration

Support Program #2
–Inspection

Support Program #3
–Training

Support Program #4
–Record-keeping

Support Program #5
–Maintenance

Support Program #6
–Customer Services

EXHIBIT 7—Continued

Support Program #7
    —Occupancy
Investment Program #1
    —Construction of Facilities
Investment Program #2
    —Research and Development

In addition to Program costs, the costs of mail processing functions (acceptance, distribution, etc.) should be reported through the information system since certain of these (e.g. delivery) are managed along functional rather than program lines.

The costs of support and investment programs should be collected and examined separately from direct costs since these programs have their own objectives, performance measurements, and management control channels. Furthermore, their costs do not vary with mail volume, but rather with management objectives. For control purposes, investment decisions or program evaluation, management will want to examine direct and indirect costs separately. On the other hand, for rate-making, or for determining fully allocated program costs, all support and investment expenses must be apportioned to a specific class of mail. Some support costs relate inherently to a single mail service (e.g., maintenance of parcel sorting machines) while others are in the general overhead categories (e.g., postmaster salaries).

Conclusion

The Post Office is unique among government agencies, and what works well for another agency may not be the final answer for us. There is no doubt that the new system is a management tool of great potential value, but much further study will be needed before the many questions raised by such a radically new approach can be answered.

Whatever organizational management or program structure is finally chosen, we are anxious to participate actively and helpfully in the administration of this system. I would be happy to arrange for a more detailed presentation of our point of view for your consideration.

EXHIBIT 8

POST OFFICE DEPARTMENT

November 19, 1965

Subject: Program Categories
From: Bureau of Finance and
            Administration
To: Deputy Postmaster General

Attached is a revised structure for program categories and subcate-gories for the Department. I believe these are as good as we can devise at this time, and recommended that they be used to fulfill our requirements to provide the Bureau of the Budget with our program category structure. I am summarizing below what we have considered to be the major alternatives offered by various Bureaus and Offices (their comments are also attached) together with our comment on why we have not incorporated them into this structure.

The Special Assistant to the Postmaster General for Policy and Projects recommended that we establish program categories for first, second, third and fourth class mail. Their proposal was advanced as being the best way of looking at the Department's programs from a service point of view. There are three principal reasons why we believe the Department should not adopt the proposal at this time:

a. Our prime product should be viewed as a collection and delivery service which is not dependent on class of mail.

b. We believe that most program elements which we will wish to review or compare will cut-across classes of mail, but can usually be considered in relation to collection, processing, delivery, etc. Therefore, a primary breakdown by class of mail would tend to fractionate programs which should be considered on a broader basis.

c. The information systems, e.g., revisions to the accounting system, etc., required to back-up information by class of mail would be very expensive and very difficult to obtain particularly in the time frame we must work within. It should be noted that the cost ascertainment system does provide information by class of mail sufficient for rate purposes.

We intend to keep this proposal in mind and try to develop information by class of mail within the system whenever this is possible.

The Office of Regional Administration suggested a proposal which would have made program categories synonymous with organization. While much of their proposal is very helpful in developing an overall system, we cannot adopt an organizational approach and meet the objectives of the programming system. The organizations of the Department are not oriented toward outputs. In addition, one of the benefits of the system is its ability to cut-across ordinary organizational lines. We believe, however, that it is important to be able to take the information by programs and summarize it both by existing organizational and appropriation categories and will include such a capability in the programming system.

*   *   *   *   *

Therefore, we recommend that the Program Review Task Force consider adopting the program categories and subcategories that we have established in the attached. While in some cases the Bureaus and Offices feel strongly on these points, in general we believe that everyone in the Department is approaching the problem of establishing a program structure in a cooperative and open-minded manner, has recognized that the final structure cannot please everyone, and has exhibited a willingness to cooperate in whatever structure is introduced.

Attachments:

EXHIBIT 8—Continued

REVISED PROGRAM CATEGORY STRUCTURE

Program Category I—Collection and Delivery of Mail

PROGRAM SUBCATEGORIES:

Collection
Processing
Transportation
Delivery
Special Services

Program Category II—Non-Mail Service

PROGRAM SUBCATEGORIES:

Assist monetary exchanges
Operate a savings system
Collect and safeguard postal revenues

Enforce postal laws and regulations
Support other Government Programs

Program Category III—Supporting Activities

PROGRAM SUBCATEGORIES:

Management and direction
Provide and maintain a work force
Budgeting and accounting
Provide space, equipment, and supplies
Conduct research and development
Management information systems

EXHIBIT 9

POST OFFICE DEPARTMENT

December 1, 1965

Subject: Program Budgeting

From: Special Assistant to the Postmaster General for Policy and Projects

To: Bureau of Finance and Administration

The Bureau of Finance proposal for a program format appears to us to be an excellent document, the product of careful research and analysis. The suggestions we will make in this paper are an attempt to make even more useful a programming system which already promises to be a significant improvement over the present management information system. The grouping of postal work centers into functional categories, as the Bureau of Finance suggests, should transform the accounting system into a valuable management tool even without further refinement.

Class-of-Mail Reporting

As you know, the chief divergence of opinion between the Bureau of Finance and our staff centers about the value of, and the cost of, reporting functional (i.e., subcategory) data by class of mail.

We remain convinced that it would be highly valuable to have current information on the costs incurred in handling each class of mail.

Much of the attention of top postal management is directed to problems relating to a specific class of mail: the Priority Mail program, ABCD, and airlift, for example, have to do with first class mail. Scheduled Service, damage prevention, detached mail unit policy and certification affect only fourth class mail. The examination of policy alternatives would be easier and more accurate if financial information by the four classes of mail were available on a current basis.

Furthermore, the effect of mechanizing or changing our practices in other ways could be observed quantitatively if system-wide costs were collected by class of mail.

Beyond its value as a planning and control device, we urge a class-of-mail approach because our service to the public must, in the final analysis, be considered by class of mail. The ultimate measure of our effectiveness, as a Department, is how long it takes us to deliver letters, and magazines, and circulars, and parcels. The peripheral activities we perform pale to insignificance beside the question of how well we perform our primary role. Since service analysis is a class-of-mail measure, we are led to suggest that it would be valuable to collect costs on the same basis, to determine how trends in service could relate to trends in costs, and to institute a service-oriented basis for our planning and programming system.

The difficulty of relying on the Cost Ascertainment Report for this data is twofold: the annual Cost Ascertainment Report apportions, as it must, to each class of mail the full cost of all supporting activities. This is indispensable for rate-making. For planning purposes, however, it is necessary to know the marginal costs of each class of mail. These can be determined only by examining our direct costs separately from our indirect costs.

The care with which the apportionment of indirect costs must be made and the highly refined techniques which must be used result in a long interval between the time costs are incurred and the time they are presented in a form useful to management. This time lag is a serious impediment to the use of Cost Ascertainment as a management tool.

By reporting direct costs for each class of mail on a current basis, the new information system could permit management to analyze postal programs in the same manner that businesses analyze their operations —on a current basis, by product line.

The Cost of Class-of-Mail Reporting

The principal issue over collecting costs by class of mail, however, concerns not the value of the data but the cost of getting it.

Some of our work centers are devoted exclusively to one class of mail—parcel post distribution, for example, or letter distribution at certain times of the day. There is little difficulty in preserving these costs by class of mail. Many postal costs, however, are joint costs. Since a high level of precision is *not* needed for planning purposes, statistical samples of mail mix at work centers can be used to determine the ratios to apply to total work center costs.

In its proposal, the Bureau of

EXHIBIT 9—Continued

Finance considers "Collection" to be a subcategory separate from "Delivery" even though the same truck and driver are often used for both functions. The apportionment of cost between two separate functions is a well-established cost accounting practice. The possibility of a 2% error in that apportionment need not concern us: for planning purposes it is close enough. The driver's paycheck is based on a ledger account and will be exact. It is important, we suggest, to distinguish among our audit and payroll accounts which must be exact, our functional subcategories which can be more approximate, and our totals for planning purposes which need not be nearly as precise.

There is obviously much work to be done before a comprehensive postal accounting system is perfected. Apportionments will be relied upon heavily, especially at first. For smaller offices, class-of-mail reporting may never be practical—instead, their total direct costs would be apportioned based on tests made in typical offices in a class.

The routine problems in any cost accounting system should not prevent us, however, from providing for a class-of-mail tag on costs coming up through the new accounting system. Many of these costs are readily identifiable now by mail class; others will be apportioned grossly at first but with greater precision as time goes on.

A system such as we suggest would eliminate the need for the many one-shot studies which now must be made for special purposes. Special studies add to the paperwork burden of supervisors and postmasters, and lack the validity of a continuously operating system. In a special cost study where there is no need to balance total costs, we find the recurring problem of 'paper' savings which frequently never materialize in the account books.

We recognize that this approach raises many questions which have not yet been answered to everyone's satisfaction.

I am sure you agree, however, that despite the pressure of external deadlines the importance of the program format warrants an exhaustive review before a final decision is made. We would welcome the opportunity to present our views to the Program Advisory Committee.

EXHIBIT 10

POST OFFICE DEPARTMENT

December 10, 1965

Subject: Program Categories and Subcategories

From: Bureau of Finance and Administration

To: Deputy Postmaster General

Attached is a newly revised structure for program categories and subcategories for consideration by the Program Advisory Committee. This is the same structure forwarded to the Bureau of the Budget on November 27, and the structure we asked the Bureaus and Offices to comment on by December 1. However, there have been some changes in titles suggested by Bureaus and Offices which we have incorporated. Several changes have been recommended by Bureaus and Offices which you may wish the Program Advisory Committee to consider.

The Special Assistant to the Postmaster General for Policy and Projects has recommended that we consider a structure based upon class of mail, and has asked for an opportunity to present his proposal. He bases the proposal on the following considerations:

A. Many of the Department's problems are best looked at in terms of class of mail.

B. Service is best considered in terms of class of mail.

C. Statistical information techniques coupled with minor sacrifices in precision will enable us to produce the desired information at a reasonable cost.

As we indicated in our memorandum of November 19, on this subject, we do not believe the Department should adopt this proposal at this time because:

A. Our prime product should be viewed as a "collection and delivery service" which is not dependent on class of mail.

B. We believe that most program elements which the Program Advisory Committee will wish to review or compare will cut-across classes of mail, and a primary breakdown by class of mail would tend to fractionate program elements which should be considered on a broader basis.

C. The changes in present information systems will be expensive and will be very difficult to make in the time required.

It should also be noted that class of mail is both an arbitrary and an unstable grouping.

CASE

2

FEDERAL COMMUNICATIONS COMMISSION

PROGRAM STRUCTURE AND OUTPUT MEASURE

Following the introduction of the Planning-Programming-Budgeting System throughout the Federal Government in August, 1965, Peter Martin, a member of the staff of the Executive Director of the Federal Communications Commission (FCC), was given the task of drafting a preliminary design of the FCC's PPB System. Mr. Martin was instructed to concentrate initially on selecting a recommended program structure, with appropriate output measures, for the Commission.

As a first step, Mr. Martin asked his assistant, John MacLean, to prepare a staff paper summarizing for him the organization and activities of the FCC. The remainder of this case consists of Mr. MacLean's report.

INTRODUCTION

The expanding uses of electronic communications, now extending to satellites above the earth, are evidenced in increased responsibilities and problems of the Federal Communications Commission in regulating the host of non-governmental radio facilities which now operate close to six million fixed, portable and mobile transmitters.

Early control over communications was shared by the Interstate Commerce Commission, the Department of Commerce and various other agencies and bureaus until 1934 when their many functions were consolidated into the Federal Communications Commission by the Communications Act of 1934. The Commission was created "as an independent agency for the purpose of regulating interstate and foreign commerce in communication by wire

This case was prepared by Herbert B. Mars under the supervision of Graeme M. Taylor. The case is based on published sources, particularly the FCC Annual Report for 1966. The situation described in the case is, however, hypothetical. The case is intended for class discussion only, and certain names and facts may have been changed, which, while avoiding the disclosure of confidential information, do not materially lessen the value of the case for educational purposes. This case is not intended to represent either effective or ineffective handling of an administrative situation, nor does it purport to be a statement of policy by the agency involved.

and radio so as to make available, so far as possible, to all the people of the United States a rapid, efficient, nation-wide and worldwide wire and radio communication service with adequate facilities at reasonable charges, for the purpose of the national defense, for the purpose of promoting safety of life and property through the use of wire and radio communication, and for the purpose of securing a more effective execution of this policy by centralizing authority heretofore granted by law to several agencies and by granting addi-tional authority with respect to inter-state and foreign commerce in wire and radio communication. . . ."

OPERATION OF THE FCC

The FCC is administered by seven commissioners who are appointed by the President with the consent of, and subject to confirmation by, the Senate. All policy determinations are made by the Commissioners acting as a body, with authority also delegated to groups of commissioners acting as committees, to commissioners acting individually and to staff units. The Commission functions through eleven bureaus and offices whose work is coordinated and expedited by an executive director. The agency employs about 1450 per-sons, and of a total budget (1966) of approximately seventeen million dol-lars, about fifteen million dollars is for personnel compensation and benefits. The agency is organized on a functional basis with four operating bureaus. The organization chart of the FCC is pre-sented as Exhibit 1. Exhibit 2 shows the agency's budget for Fiscal Year 1966. Distribution of personnel be-tween the various bureaus and offices is

shown in Exhibit 3. Exhibits 4, 5 and 6 display various workload data for three of the operating bureaus.

FIELD ENGINEERING BUREAU

The Field Engineering Bureau is the largest of the four operating bureaus employing almost one-quarter of the agency personnel. Among its responsi-bilities are the enforcement of laws and regulations, the resolution of radio in-terference, the examination and licens-ing of radio operators, the processing of applications pertaining to painting, marking and placement of antenna towers, and furnishing direction-finding aid in connection with ships and air-craft in distress, including locating of returning spacecraft in our space pro-grams. It has twenty-four district of-fices and operates a network of eighteen monitoring stations.

It is required to resolve cases of in-terference between and within services every day of the year. Interference is produced by technical difficulties (the result of equipment malfunction, com-ponent failure or faulty adjustment) or operational deficiency stemming from failure of the human element to comply with the regulations. Among the major enforcement tools are the monitoring stations. Despite great efforts made with limited manpower and facilities, noncompliance with the rules is wide-spread and has increased with the up-surge in use of Class D Citizens Band Radio. Interference with radio com-munication services results in approxi-mately 38,000 calls annually to field engineering offices requiring investiga-tion of the cause and taking action to eliminate it. Diverse equipment such as automatic garage-opener receivers can cause interference and have affected air communication and navigation.

The bureau composes tests for six grades of commercial operating licenses. Nearly every facet of its work requires the use of specialized electronic equipment which generally is not available from commercial sources and must be designed and constructed through the agency's own resources.

COMMON CARRIER BUREAU

A communications common carrier is one whose services are open to public hire for handling interstate or foreign communications by electrical means. Broadcast stations are not deemed common carriers. The bureau exerts regulatory controls over telephone and telegraph companies, prescribing the forms and records to be kept and requiring that they file monthly and annual reports giving specified financial and operating information. The common carriers file tariff schedules with the Commission which are subject to review and regulation. The rates to be used in determining the depreciation charges to be included under operating expenses is set by the agency. The Communications Satellite Corporation is subject to the same controls as other common carriers and its financing and procurement of equipment and services is subject to control by the agency.

SAFETY AND SPECIAL RADIO SERVICES BUREAU

The nation's radio and TV broadcast stations are few in number compared to the vast array of other types of radio stations that perform services that are almost as varied as they are numerous.

They embrace the use of radio by boats and aircraft; by rail and motor carriers; by local governments; by amateurs interested in the radio art; by industry, public utilities and other business; by individuals for private convenience; by agencies concerned with police and fire protection; and for national defense and other emergency services. At the end of Fiscal Year 1966, over 1.6 million licensees operated more than 5.6 million fixed, portable and mobile transmitters.

The bureau's Legal, Advisory and Enforcement Division activities have been increasing with more than half of its time spent on stations in the Citizens Radio Service. License revocation proceedings have been increasing and monetary forfeitures have been applied because of willful and repeated violations of rules and regulations.

BROADCAST BUREAU

The major activities in the general regulation of broadcasting have two phases. The first phase deals with the allocation of spectrum space to the different types of broadcast services in accordance with international agreements, the Communications Act and other domestic laws affecting broadcasting. The second phase directly concerns individual stations and embraces applications to build and operate; assignment of frequencies, power, operating time and call letters; inspection of equipment and engineering aspects of operation; passing on transfers and assignments of facilities; modifying permits and renewing licenses; reviewing the service of a particular station to determine if it has been operating in the public interest; licensing operators of transmitters, and otherwise discharging domestic regulatory responsibilities.

Stations are licensed to serve the public interest, convenience and necessity, and normally are licensed for a three-year period. The overall performance of each station is periodically reviewed to determine whether it has lived up to its promises and obligations.

In addition to its regulation of general radio and television broadcasting affairs, including programming, censorship and free speech, advertising, and equal time opportunities in political broadcasts, the agency must decide policy questions concerning subscription TV, educational broadcasting (both radio and TV), and technical problems such as color TV systems.

CATV systems have been considered by some to be outside the jurisdiction of the agency as they are not considered broadcasting and technically are not in the category of common carriers. Legislation has been proposed to bring all such systems within the control of the commission.

SUPPORTING OFFICES

The four operating bureaus are supported by seven office activities. The activities of all eleven bureaus and offices are controlled, directed, coordinated and expedited through the office of the Executive Director. Concentrated in this office are the Personnel Budget and Fiscal, Data Processing, Office Services, Management Information and Emergency Communications functions.

The Office of Hearing Examiners is responsible for presiding at hearings and issuing initial decisions. A total of 665 cases were designated for hearing during fiscal 1966, of which 368 involved safety and special services (revocation of licenses as well as applications) and 180 were for broadcast activities and facilities. During the fiscal year 1966, 468 orders and memoranda opinions were issued. The Office of Opinions and Review drafts decisions for and at the direction of the Commission as a body. The Review Board was established to act on certain adjudicatory cases and to hear appeals from rulings and decisions of the hearing examiners.

Much of the work of the Commission involves application and interpretation of existing legislation, proposals for new legislation and enforcement of rules and regulations including litigation that may be required. The Office of the General Counsel is responsible for carrying out these functions.

MISCELLANEOUS OPERATIONS

As part of its effort to promote a more effective use of the radio spectrum, the Commission encourages scientific investigation in basic research and practical development of radio communication techniques through the Experimental Radio Services. Authorizations are granted to all classes of experimenters, from grade school students working on small projects to large commercial laboratories engaged in the most advanced pursuits.

The Commission is also responsible for determining the acceptability of transmitting equipment for licensing in most of the radio services. Type Acceptance is one procedure used with the objective of improving spectrum utilization by limiting duplication of effort in the various Commission bureaus concerned with licensing radio equipment.

Certain specific types of equipment receive approval only upon successful completion of tests in the Commission's laboratory. (This procedure differs from Type Acceptance which is based upon manufacturers' reports of their own tests.) One class of devices requiring such testing consists of those which unintentionally emit radio waves that may interfere with radio or TV communications, such as diathermy and ultrasonic equipment. Equipment required for safety on shipboard or monitors used in AM, FM or TV broadcast stations are also required to be tested for approval.

The Commission operates a laboratory near Laurel, Md., where it conducts studies of radio systems and equipment, including the standardization of apparatus and measuring methods. Evaluations are made as to the effects of propagation on systems. The laboratory also makes experimental studies of monitoring and measuring techniques to enable the Commission to cope with problems created by the continuing increase in the number of radio stations. It modifies and calibrates the equipment used by the field enforcement units and tests equipment on request of other governmental agencies.

OBSERVATIONS

The design of a program structure for any agency is a difficult matter. I submit it is particularly difficult for a regulatory agency such as the FCC. Do we choose our program categories accord-ing to our organization structure, our broad missions, or the major functions we perform? As I see it, the FCC is in an intermediate position between inputs (i.e., our budget) and ultimate benefits to society. The actual users of the radio spectrum produce benefits, e.g., communication of intelligence, convenience, promotion of safety, etc., but the activities of the FCC themselves do not. Our role is limited to regulating the activities of the producers of ultimate benefits. Perhaps we could design our program structure according to the types of our "clients"—common carriers, commercial broadcasters, amateur radio enthusiasts, etc. This approach would suggest a structure closely parallel to our organizational structure.

Regarding the choice of output measures, I suspect that we may have to use workload data. Much of our work, of course, is prescribed by law and by regulation, with little room for discretion. Therefore, efficiency in performing our prescribed tasks is important, perhaps more important than attempting to measure ultimate benefits to society over which we actually have little control. I suggest that our choice of output measures therefore be made with a view to facilitating top management review of our operating efficiency.

QUESTIONS

As Mr. Martin, review Mr. MacLean's report. Based on the information presented in the report, how would you define the objectives of the FCC? What program categories and subcategories would you select for the FCC? What output measures would be appropriate?

EXHIBIT 1

FEDERAL COMMUNICATIONS COMMISSION

Organization Chart—June, 1966

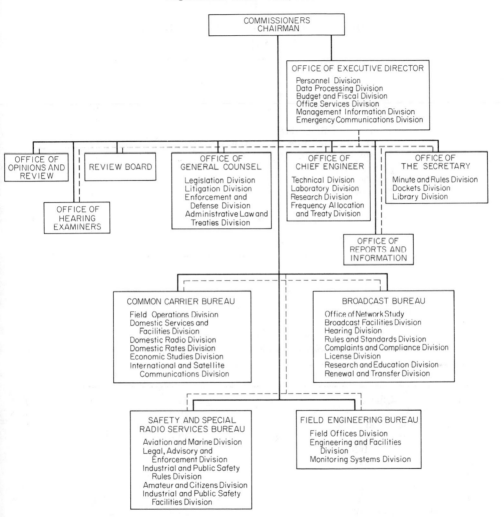

EXHIBIT 2

FEDERAL COMMUNICATIONS COMMISSION

Budget for Fiscal Year 1966

Budget Item	Amount
Personnel compensation	$14,192,179
Personnel benefits	1,022,974
Travel	244,995
Transportation of things	62,009
Rents, communications, and utility services	428,057
Printing and reproduction	234,544
Other services	318,281
Supplies and materials	234,422
Equipment	547,251
Land and structures	51,452
Insurance claims and indemnities	1,811
Total amount	$17,337,975

EXHIBIT 3

FEDERAL COMMUNICATIONS COMMISSION

Personnel Distribution—1966 (Man-Years)

Office Where Employed	Washington	Field	Total
Commissioner's Offices	47.1	0	47.1
Review Board	30.5	0	30.5
Office of Opinions and Review	15.6	0	15.6
Office of Hearing Examiners	32.6	0	32.6
Office of Reports and Information	4.9	0	4.9
Office of Executive Director	167.1	14.3	181.4
Office of Secretary	35.7	0	35.7
Office of General Counsel	46.1	0	46.1
Office of Chief Engineer	74.6	18.0	92.6
Common Carrier Bureau	133.9	25.7	159.6
Safety and Special Radio Services Bureau	148.2	16.5	164.7
Broadcast Bureau	251.6	0	251.6
Field Engineering Bureau	63.2	333.1	396.3
Total	1,051.1	407.6	1,458.7

EXHIBIT 4

FEDERAL COMMUNICATIONS COMMISSION

Common Carrier Applications—Fiscal Year 1966

Class	Pending June 30, 1965	Received	Disposed of	Pending June 30, 1966
Radio facilities:				
New and changed facilities:				
Domestic	1,760	7,245	7,228	1,775
Overseas	2	61	63	—
Renewal of license		6,775	2,868	3,907
Total radio facilities	1,762	14,081	10,159	5,682
Wire facilities:				
Telephone extensions	13	367	377	3
Telegraph extensions	2	102	96	8
Telephone reductions		6	6	
Telegraph reductions	86	500	513	73
Total wire facilities	101	975	992	84
Miscellaneous:	4	31	31	4
Grand total	1,865	15,087	11,182	5,770

EXHIBIT 5

FEDERAL COMMUNICATIONS COMMISSION

Number of Broadcast Authorizations

Class	Fiscal 1965	Fiscal 1966	Increase or Decrease
Commercial AM	4,097	4,153	56
Commercial TV	689	735	46
TV translators and boosters	2,023	2,187	164
Community antenna relay	0	1	1
Educational TV	125	144	19
Instructional TV fixed	33	53	20
Experimental TV	25	21	(4)
Auxiliary TV	1,688	1,847	159
Commercial FM	1,565	1,744	179
Educational FM	272	302	30
International	3	3	0
Developmental	5	7	2
Remote pickup	7,748	8,587	839
Studio transmitter linkup and relay	143	184	41
Low-power (cueing)	128	157	29
Total	18,544	20,125	1,581

EXHIBIT 6

FEDERAL COMMUNICATIONS COMMISSION

Applications for Stations—Safety and Special Radio Services

Class of Station	Fiscal 1965	Fiscal 1966	Increase or Decrease
Aviation services	45,023	44,523	(500)
Marine services	40,376	44,359	3,983
Public safety services	21,109	24,757	3,648
Industrial services	49,281	50,340	1,059
Land transportation services	7,038	6,696	(342)
Amateur and disaster services	121,571	110,425	(11,146)
Citizens	210,325	223,845	13,520
Total safety & special services	494,723	504,945	10,222

PART

objectives, criteria, and output measures

This section deals with three interwoven topics—formulation of program objectives; development of analytical effectiveness criteria to judge achievement of these objectives; and choice of measures for reporting various program parameters.

Henry Rowen's introductory paper discusses the difficulty of formulating explicit statements of program objectives, then emphasizes the need to generate imaginative alternatives as an essential first step in analysis. A brief discussion of the problems of measuring each alternative's costs and benefits is followed by an examination of three current social problems that demand deep analysis—race, public order and health. Harry Hatry's paper represents, in the author's words, ". . . a first attempt at identifying specific criteria (i.e., measures of effectiveness) for use in evaluating alternative proposals for programs for carrying out major state and local governmental functions." Although primarily concerned with the problems of state and local governments, the principles developed by Mr. Hatry have widespread application at all levels of government.

The "Peace Corps" case provides an opportunity to relate program objectives, program structure, and analytic effectiveness criteria in a situation where all three are at issue. The "Bureau of the Census" case introduces the further complication of devising appropriate workload measures for management control purposes, and raises the question of the relationship between measures used in internal agency reports and the measures appropriate for PPB requirements.

Objectives, Alternatives, Costs, and Effectiveness

By
HENRY ROWEN

. . . The essential aspects of PPB are—

A careful specification and a systematic analysis of objectives;

A search for the relevant alternatives, the different ways of achieving the objectives;

An estimate of the total costs of each alternative—both direct and indirect costs, both initial costs and those to which the alternative commits us for future years, both dollar costs and those costs that cannot be measured in dollar terms;

An estimate of the effectiveness of each alternative, of how close it comes to satisfying the objective;

A comparison and analysis of the alternatives, seeking that combination of alternatives that promises the greatest effectiveness, for given resources, in achieving the objectives.

Now let me mention a few things that PPB is *not*.

PPB is *not* a substitute for the experience, the intuition, and the judgment of the decisionmaker. On the contrary, its aim is to sharpen that intuition and judgment by stating problems more precisely, by discovering new alternatives, and by making explicit the comparison among alternatives.

PPB is *not* decisionmaking by computer. In the first place, decisions will continue to come, as they should, from the political process, influenced by value judgments, from the pressures coming from the various interested parties as well as from the process of systematic analysis. PPB, through such systematic analysis, seeks to aid the policy debate by being clearer and more explicit about objectives and assumptions and facts, by trying to distinguish relevant issues from irrelevant ones, and by tracing out the costs and consequences of the alternatives, to the extent these are knowable.

PPB is *not* a computer operation, though computers may be helpful from time to time. Nor can the thinking that must underlie well worked-out plans be produced by machine-like analysts.

From *The Planning–Programming–Budgeting System: Progress and Potentials* (Hearings before the Subcommittee on Economy in Government of the Joint Economic Committee, Congress of the United States, 90th Congress, 1st Session, U.S. Government Printing Office, Washington, D.C., 1967). Henry Rowen is president of the RAND Corporation, Santa Monica, California.

Most problems of importance are simply not susceptible of solution merely by highly abstract mathematical or economic techniques, though these may contribute to solution of important parts of the problem. In any case, a good analyst should be able to explain his study and its results to the decision-maker, in clear language, free of jargon.

PPB and systematic analysis are *not* limited to cost-accounting, to economic considerations in the narrow sense; PPB should *not* neglect a wide range of human factors but it should *not* attempt, naively, to measure those factors that are really unmeasureable. Wherever relevant, quantitative estimates are to be encouraged. But good systematic analysis does *not* try to assign numbers to every element of a problem, does *not* ignore the intangible, does *not* rule out subjective evaluation and the appropriate use of judgment, as long as these are made explicit. Good systematic analysis does *not* neglect questions of values. On the contrary, the very name "cost-benefit analysis" reminds us that the question of *who* benefits and *whom does it cost* is a question involving values as well as analysis.

Now let me turn to a few comments about the analytic elements of PPB—objectives, alternatives, costs, and effectiveness.

If PPB led to nothing more than each agency re-examining its objectives, then PPB would be a useful system. Objectives of government programs are often stated in such vague and nonoperational terms as to be little more than home-and-mother platitudes. At the other extreme, they are sometimes stated in such narrow and conventional terms as to rule out any consideration of relevant alternatives. For example, the objective of the inter-city highway program is not merely to lay concrete. Nor is the objective of an educational problem the attaining of a given pupil-teacher ratio. Nor should improvements in the nation's health be confused with attaining a given ratio of hospital beds per thousand of population. Again, the stated and publicized objectives of a program may be different from the real, operational objectives; good systematic analysis will push behind the overt objectives to deal with deeper ones.

In some problems the objective is clearly defined and agreed upon. For example, the inventory policy of a school system should be designed with the objective of minimizing stock outages for a given cost. There are not complex issues of objectives or of measurement in this instance.

But in many cases the problem of stating wisely the objective is not at all simple. In health care, for example, is the objective really to keep patient-day costs at a certain level, or to take so many chest X-rays a year, and so on? Shouldn't our primary concern be with the social and economic costs of death, or with the value, the significance, the quality of life? Shouldn't the goals of education concern achievement in the standard subjects, learning in special subjects, an improved ability to reason, to be creative, arousal of the sense of wonder, the development of social poise, the improvement of mental and physical health, and the custodial care and civilized taming of the young?

In such complex subjects as these there is a danger that poor work will reduce the multiple, incommensurable, and conflicting goals to a single objective that admits of easy measurement: for example, the loss to gross national product occasioned by deaths from heart attacks, or the test scores showing scholastic performance in basic subjects. But the risks of selecting the wrong goals are minimized if it is required that the analysis be clear and explicit, that it be open and subject to review and criticism, and that it be exposed to competitive analysis.

Since my subject is future developments in PPB, and in systematic analysis which is at the heart of PPB, I note that we need to improve our ability to deal with problems in which objectives are not simple. This, like other needed improvements, will come through doing analysis, exposing it to criticism, and learning to do it better.

In this connection we need to do several things concurrently: we need to take seriously the need for analysis, not just at the Federal Executive level, but also in the Congress, and at the state and local level throughout the country; we need to establish planning and analytic groups wherever an adequate supply of talent exists to make this possible; doing this means that we need more people trained in the necessary skills and methods to do good planning and analysis.

Next, a few comments on the second element of PPB that I listed above—alternatives. A vital element is a clear and objective presentation of alternatives. A planning document that does not present and compare alternative ways of achieving the objectives is a document that merely tries to make a case for a predetermined position.

The alternative means of achieving the objectives may not be obvious substitutes, and it may be an important achievement of the analyst to show that there are additional alternatives that had not been recognized.

For example, our ability to support military forces abroad can be accomplished by the use of airlift, or sealift, or prestocking supplies at foreign bases. Or through a combination of these techniques, which might differ from region to region or differ by type of commodity being supplied. Or a new alternative might be invented—as it has—in the system which combines sealift with prestocking by having loaded ships kept on station abroad.

Again, the educational level may be raised by a variety of alternatives—increase in student participation, research and development in education, including the building of model facilities, improvements in the professional staff and in administration, the addition of new equipment, the reorganization of instruction, adult retraining, education in the home, education of the disadvantaged, and other categories of alternatives. Each of these categories, in turn, involves many alternatives. For example, student participation can be increased through loan funds, work-study programs in industry, educational leaves, starting public school at a younger age, new patterns of continued schooling aimed at the dropouts, and many others.

In the field of health there are the obvious alternatives of improved medical education, both for doctors and for auxiliary personnel, community education, expanded research, support of specialized services such as centers for diagnosis and treatment of specific diseases. But there are additional alternatives that are relevant to the problems of national health: an attack upon infant mortality in slums and rural regions, reduction in accidents and homicides, physical education programs, problems of diet, of smoking, continual preventive care, and others.

It is important that these problems be looked at in a context sufficiently broad that many relevant alternatives are compared. This means looking at not only the comparison of alternatives that happen to be around but the *invention of new ones* if the available ones are not satisfactory.

Initially the effort devoted to PPB has had to deal largely with questions of format and structure and the phasing of procedures into the budgetary cycle. In the future, the effort should be devoted increasingly to better analysis, to being more inventive, more imaginative at designing useful alternatives that will achieve the goals of our social programs.

The third element consists of costs. The costs of a given alternative are the resources that can no longer be used for other purposes, the opportunities that this alternative precludes. The PPB analysts often prefer to speak not of *cost analysis* but rather of *resource analysis* in order to remind us that dollar cost is only a convenient and not always adequate common denominator by which we can aggregate the many and varied physical quantities and activities that use resources. For example, we may be "costing" a system that calls for many highly skilled personnel or for large quantities of a scarce commodity. In the long run we may be able to supply these requirements by spending dollars now, but in the short run we may have to give these items special treatment.

The relevant costs cannot usually be gotten by pricing out a system described by a detailed set of concrete specifications. Often we are considering future activities, concrete specifications are not available, and these activities take place in a future whose principal characteristic is uncertainty. And this uncertainty should be treated explicitly. The time-phasing of needed resources should be treated. And all of the appropriate costs should be taken into account—whether or not they are a charge to a particular budget. For example, depending on the purpose of the analysis, meaningful costs of education include the direct operating costs, the capital resource costs, miscellaneous expenses to students and parents, and the foregone earnings of students while in school. The costs of putting an expressway through a city include not only the initial and maintenance costs of the expressway, but also the costs of taxes foregone, the economic and social costs of relocating the displaced residents, the smog generated by additional travel, and all the other social costs involved.

Finally, the concepts, the methods, and the analytical techniques used in a cost analysis will depend upon the context of the problem and the decisions that may be affected by the analysis. For example, in your own personal accounting, how you amortize the cost of your automobile depends on the decisions to be affected by your accounting —choice of limousine or compact, trade in after one year or ten, ride or walk.

In addition to the economic costs, there are, as we have seen, social costs that must be dealt with—for example, in the military, the effect on morale within a service, or the political costs of inconvenience and irritation to an ally. These may not be measured numerically, but they should be recognized clearly and explicitly.

The last item in the list above of the essential analytic elements of PPB was effectiveness—or benefits, or utility, as you prefer. I have a few comments on this subject.

We need better ways of estimating the benefits of proposed programs. Benefits are hard to measure well, especially in the case of new and untried programs. Moreover, I have suggested that benefits are often not adequately expressed by simple mechanical measures of output, like the number of acres reclaimed or number of cases brought to trial. Many important benefits can't be quantified easily—or at all. But numbers can tell us a great deal. Mortality rates, school dropout rates, real income levels, unemployment figures— all these can help us estimate what a proposed program will attempt to accomplish.

Much of the future work leading to the improvement of PPB needs to concentrate on the problems of measuring and analyzing benefits. What should we measure? Which benefits accrue to which people and at what future times —which of these are relevant for a given problem? How can we better handle the mixture of outputs of a program, outputs that are measured in incommensurable terms? I have no quick and easy solution to propose to getting this work done. The only answer I have is a slow and hard one: get as many good people as possible working systematically and continually on the most urgent problems and give them enough time.

We have been discussing the subject of systematic analysis—the elements involved in carrying it out, some of the difficulties involved, and some prospects for future developments. Let us turn now to some of the areas in which we need badly to do better.

Many of our society's most urgent problems are inadequately understood and, therefore, inadequately coped with by us. Despite our nation's wealth, and our willingness to allocate much of this wealth to public purposes, our performance falls far short of what we should be able to attain as the world's most advanced nation in the level of education, technical skills, and administrative competence.

Our shortcomings are of two kinds: one is substantive. It is an inadequate identification, definition, and analysis of important issues of society and of the alternative choices open to us. These issues usually involve many variables—economic, technical, social— that interact in complicated ways. The other is institutional. Our governments don't make adequate use of the individual talents and organizational skills we possess.

What is needed is more systematic and continuing work on our central concerns, work that is carried out in ways that can help illuminate and improve our social choices.

Out of the long list of social problems that we could discuss here—race, education, poverty, and so on—I choose three as examples of subjects that need deeper analysis: race, public order, and health.

Race

The general situation of the Negro is now recognized to be our key domestic political problem. Most of the others are closely linked to it. Thus the poverty problem is to a considerable extent a Negro one. The U.S. ranks relatively low on a number of indicators of health because of the high incidence of morbidity among Negroes. Urban crime is concentrated in the ghetto slums of our large cities. Negroes also have high rates of mental illness, of alcoholism, and of family break-up. The breakdown of the urban public school has been located disproportionately among Negroes.

The heart of this problem has been located by some observers in the Negro culture, family, and social structure generally. In a real sense, it is comparable to the problems of development in many underdeveloped countries. Both in sections of the "third world" and in the Negro community, there is a self-sustaining negative cycle which preserves elements which are strongly resistant to modernization or social developments. These inhibit their ability to take advantage of opportunities when they occur.

Other observers stress the "low level trap" aspects of Negro life, a life constrained by housing segregation, high unemployment, poor schools, inadequate transportation.

Since the Supreme Court's desegregation decision in 1954, and the growth of the civil rights movement, efforts to improve the situation of the Negro have emphasized an attack on inadequate education through desegregation, Head Start programs, and adult vocational and other forms of education. The results to date are pessimistic. Desegregation has failed in a number of ways. Most Negro children do not attend desegregated schools. Integration has

been followed by tipping, the fleeing of the whites to private schools or other neighborhoods. It is important to analyze the conditions under which tipping has taken place, to locate those schools which have not tipped and to find out why they have not.

More disastrous, however, has been the inability of Negroes to succeed in integrated schools. The Coleman Report, the most comprehensive study of the effects of integration, suggests that integration may actually have hurt many Negroes, while it helped others. The optimum conditions for improvement seem to be attendance by middle-class Negro youth in predominantly white schools. Inadequately prepared and motivated Negro children placed among whites often do worse. Thus, the problem is pushed towards finding ways of preparing Negro youth to function adequately in good integrated schools.

Headstart also has not proved to be a panacea. Initially, Negro children exposed to intensive educational "therapy" seem to improve in learning capacity and educational motivation. However, when placed in regular public schools, most such children seem to revert downward in ability and motivation.

The third educational suggestion involves upgrading the ghetto schools through pouring in more resources to make Negro schools the best in the country. As yet, for obvious political and financial reasons, little has been done. But there is as yet no evidence that any one school in the country which is primarily Negro does a good job, as measured by the results.

The upshot has been the conclusion that reformers have asked too much of the school system. The school cannot be expected to make up for inadequate cultural background, for a family and neighborhood environment which often negates the values of the school. The Negro family and community, as the Moynihan Report argues, is the crux of the matter. Here too, we find pessimistic research findings.

The larger culture which defines the Negro as inferior, which exposes him to a white dominated world on television, in the press, the movies, the employment structure, also contributes to the negative self image of the Negro.

Although these findings are not beyond question, it seems clear that a program of social experimentation is called for. Various suggestions have been offered:

(1) Provide more jobs. It is being argued that unemployment in the ghettos is much higher than the already high level officially reported. Public work and tax incentives to industry have been proposed. These will be expensive. How much will they help? If it is too late to change the motivations of Negro adults, it is still necessary to place them in socially respectable roles for humane reasons and to give more stability to the Negro family, to give children fathers they can respect. The one agency which can do this for poor Negroes is the government. Is it possible to find forms of employment for this group which will not be stigmatized?

(2) One possible way to deal with the problem of the Negro community, family, culture, etc., is to create an elite group of integrated boarding schools. Testing the efficacy of such an experiment would, of course, take a number of years. It would be worth looking into the achievements of the small groups of Negro youth who have been attending good private schools during the past few years. The Russians have used boarding schools for war orphans and their experience is worth examining.

(3) We have no real evidence on the ways in which special local schools have succeeded. How well do Negro children do in Catholic parochial schools which have a different sense of discipline and authority structure than other integrated schools?

(4) Incentives—The most readily available incentive is economic. To what extent can behavior and attitudes be changed by economic incentives? If Negro children do badly in school because of a lack of motivation, an understanding of an adequate means—ends relationship between work in school and ultimate payoff if they lack the capacity for deferred gratification, can this be short-cut by paying them for doing well? Can similar techniques work with adolescents and adults? Are adequate jobs with incentive systems in which men are paid more and promoted quickly for conforming to the work ethic enough to break through negative motivations?

We want to know a great deal about the success stories among Negroes. Those children who are doing well in school should be studied intensively, as should successful Negro adults. Are there any communities, schools, religious denominations, members of political groups, who have done much better than others?

David McClelland, the Harvard psychologist, who initiated research in the sources of variation in "achievement motivation" argues that it is possible to change such motivation through courses. Can this be done with lower-class American Negroes? The kind of research we need requires the collaboration of psychologists like McClelland, of sociologists interested in education and social mobility, of sociologists and anthropologists concerned with value systems, of specialists on family structure, of psychiatrists and psychologists interested in personality formation, of students of incentive systems, and the like. Such research should be of different sets of factors on behavior. At the moment, students of the Negro problem cannot supply answers to questions concerning where the government and other agencies should place their resources.

Public order

The widespread and intense riots of the summer of this year have made public order the most urgent political issue in the country. The surprising intensity and rapid spread of the riots is testimony to the widespread lack of understanding of the attitudes of the Negro community and of the role violence could play in the Negro community.

The President's Advisory Commission on Civil Disorders now is setting about the task of finding out why riots occur in some cities and not in others; why some individuals break the law and others in similar circumstances do not; the effects of police-community relations on the probability of a riot happening or spreading; who takes part in riots; who suffers; what government programs have been most helpful? Although surveys on earlier riots, for example in Watts, give some insights, it will not be easy for the Commission to get answers to these questions, for much of the basic work has not been done.

The riots are an extreme form of deviant behavior that clearly needs better understanding. Even apart from the riots there has been growing public concern about crime. The fact of public concern about crime is incontrovertible; what is less clear is how much crime there is and how to prevent it. With the work of the National Crime Commission we have the beginning of a systematic approach to understanding the causes of crime and ways of reducing it.

It is clear that far too little work has been done in most areas relating to public order, except perhaps in those dealing with purely legal questions, and this lack has been a major handicap in devising strategies to meet the crime problem. Crime and delinquency until very recently were unfashionable stepchildren of the law, sociology, and social sciences. This subject has enjoyed low status and attracted few first-rate people and little research money. To some extent this situation has changed, but the result of several generations of neglect is that there are few good workers and only very fragmentary sound work. For example, the Crime Commission Report in 1967 continues to rely on the empirical and observational studies of the Chicago School of the Twenties to show the relationship of the city slum and crime.

Statistical description of the incidence of criminal behavior and of the operation of agencies of justice is generally poor. Economic analysis of the costs of crime and the operation of illicit economies is unavailable. Legal research has tended to view problems in isolation. Rarely have empirical or sociological studies been made of the actual workings of the criminal justice institutions, of their effect on the persons involved, of their success, or of other practical issues. Relatively few studies have drawn on talents from a broad range of disciplines to study criminal problems.

There are two broad classes of questions to be examined. One is the effect of the social environment on the incidence of crime: education, jobs, family structure. This environment is partially susceptible to change and one class of policy issues is the effect of specific changes on crime. The other is the operation of the criminal justice system in terms of both its efficiency and its fairness.

One issue is the definition of crime. This issue becomes clouded when the concept of criminality is used outside the area of violence and to enforce moral or economic order, or to deal with medical problems or administrative violations.

Another is the criminal law process viewed as a decision system, some of it formal and some of it very informal and not readily observable. Thus, law enforcement officers exercise broad discretion—police reaction to events in the street and the decision to arrest; prosecutorial decisions whether to charge, what charge to file, and guilty plea negotiations; judge and jury discretion whether to convict and what sentence to impose; and finally, the many decisions made by correctional authorities in dealing with the convicted offender. How can we measure how the system in fact operates when most cases are disposed of informally? What would be the impact of policy guidance as to how discretion should be exercised and of other checks on the way these decisions are made? How can we better select and train the persons who make such decisions? What kinds of procedures and information can help in making these decisions?

Another aspect is the relationship between public perceptions, particularly the sense of fear and insecurity and the attitude toward offenders, and the reality of crime. Consider the effects of these public perceptions on the quality of social life in the city, upon the definitions of crime, upon tolerable methods for dealing with offenders, and upon the opportunities that are available for the reintegration of offenders into society. Consider the effect of the perceived high incidence of violent crime on the flight from the inner city. How can a community be led to accept the presence of a halfway house or a center for treating addicts in its neighborhood? How can the public be encouraged to employ persons with police records?

The economics of crime. What does the nation spend on security, including law enforcement agencies, private policing, locks and alarms, and insurance? What is the loss from theft, bodily injury? Consider the role of insurance companies and their capacity to distribute the costs of crime as well as to encourage adequate security by property owners. What is the place of deviant systems (e.g., professional crime, the fencing of stolen goods, employee theft, shoplifting, commercial fraud) in the nation's total economic structure? Consider the collateral economic effects of crime on small business, movement to the suburbs, and its impact on the economic squeeze on big city governments.

There are other questions including the applications of technology to public order, but this list should suffice to indicate some of the analytic needs.

Health

As individuals and as governments, we have been devoting increasing energies, concern, and resources to the attainment of good health. Because health care has been equated largely to medical care, the greatest emphasis has been on improving medical care.

In recent years there has been a remarkable rise in national expenditures on health care services and supplies from $17 billion in 1955 to $37 billion in 1965. If these trends continue, health care services in 1975 will account for 7 percent of our total national production—implying a national health care budget of around $90 billion.

The nation has purchased far less than one would expect with these resources. As measured by the only index of health for which reliable statistics exist, and one of the major objectives of improved care, life expectancy, there has been a barely perceptible improvement in the last decade. Nor have we reached an "upper limit" of life expectancy. Among countries for which good statistics are available, the United States ranks thirty-seventh on the basis of remaining lifetime for men at age 40, and at age 10 the life expectancy of males is 4.5 years less than that of those in the leading country (Norway).

This experience raises the question of whether our emphasis on medical care as the principal means to improved health is appropriate. A major policy issue is whether there are more productive ways to increase health levels than simply by increasing the inputs of medical care. Answering this question will require research to provide a better understanding of the relationships to health of nutrition, environment, occupational factors, etc.

In any case, medical care will continue to be the largest and most important component of the health budget. And the need for improvement in the medical care system is apparent. The present system has overburdened practitioners who cannot spend sufficient time with their patients; physicians whose actual medical practice deviates significantly from current best practice; patients treated in a hospital when they could equally well be treated on an outpatient basis; hospitals whose high costs are not justified by the extent or effectiveness of the services they provide; persons with serious medical conditions who cannot gain good access to medical care. These problems are increasing rather than diminishing as medicine grows in complexity, physician-specialization becomes dominant, and hospital insurance covers an increasingly large number of people.

It is quite clear that the traditional patterns of medical practice and hospital organization are becoming increasingly obsolescent. But these traditions are so deeply embedded in our society that they will not be changed until the cost of this obsolescence is irrefutably documented. Such documentation should be a major objective of a research program, since the fragmentary evidence now available indicates that the cost in terms of dollars and lives is high: Studies have found wide variations in the quality of medical practice conducted both inside and outside of hospitals and in the costs of care provided. Studies of hospitalization rates for Federal employees indicate that perhaps as many as one-third of the hospitalizations paid by the Blue Cross-Blue Shield were not medically justified.

Still another major problem area relates to the provision of care to the poor. The federally supported Medicaid program is one approach to solving this problem, but many barriers other than finances impede the access of the indigents to good medical care. The problem is to devise new programs and policies that will move us in the right direction—and will do so within the constraints imposed by the nature and history of our health institutions and professions.

These comments are made by way of example, to suggest a longer list of areas of social concern that are in need of concentrated work.

In all of these areas the problem is not so much lack of knowledge as lack of knowledge relevant to policy; not so much lack of technique, as lack of technique for analyzing policy questions; and not so much lack of skills, as lack of skilled people working together on these problems. What must be found is some way to harness our knowledge of social processes, to sharpen our process of analysis, and to involve and train good people in methods of structuring and solving complex policy questions.

These problem areas are, in large part, the concerns of government at all levels. But they lack the means for tackling these problems effectively. At the Federal level few Departments have an analytic capacity of any consequence. They generally lack the ability to identify problems with precision, see that relevant data are collected, policy alternatives formulated, valid experiments run, existing programs evaluated. Even the simplest fact, such as finding out how many able-bodied males in this country are supported by welfare, has taken many months for a high official to acquire. Straightforward data on health care, education, ghetto jobs, housing, are often inadequate. The more complex question, "What is really being accomplished by these programs?" is rarely addressed in depth.

As the current hearings of this Subcommittee show, actions have been taken by the President within the past two years to introduce more systematic methods of analysis of objectives and programs throughout the Federal Government. I suspect that the hearings will also show that while progress has been made in some agencies, little has happened in many. The future will undoubtedly see an improvement in the performance of government agencies in conducting systematic analysis.

Finally a question of great importance is the extent to which the Congress has available to it the data and analyses it needs in order to discharge its responsibilities. Most of what it needs it should be able to get from Government agencies. But a good case can be made for the Congress having available to it an improved analytic capability of its own. How this might be provided is a matter on which I am not prepared to comment. It does seem to be a suitable subject for investigation by the Congress.

Criteria for Evaluation in Planning State and Local Programs

By

HARRY P. HATRY

This paper aims at clarifying and developing some of the fundamental concepts of the approach to governmental program planning commonly included under the term "planning-programming-budgeting (PPB)" system. This paper represents a first attempt at identifying specific criteria (i.e., measures of effectiveness) for use in evaluating alternative proposals for programs for carrying out major State and local governmental functions.

To date there has been little written that attempts to identify specific criteria useful for government program analysis. This paper discusses the criteria problem and makes the rash attempt to identify meaningful criteria in the hope that it will stimulate further efforts both within individual governments and by professionals outside governments who are experienced in analytical techniques. The list of criteria provided here is far from being either exhaustive or definitive.

It is to be emphasized that for individual program analyses, considerable effort will still need to be applied to the determination of evaluation criteria appropriate to the specific problem. The list of criteria contained in . . . this paper can be used as a starting point.

The emphasis in this paper is on nonmonetary criteria where the author feels the greatest effort is needed in State and local government program analyses.

The author wishes to express his appreciation to the following persons for their time spent in reviewing early drafts of this paper and for their most helpful suggestions: Alan J. Goldman, of the National Bureau of Standards; Prof. Jesse Burkhead, of Syracuse University; Joel Posner, of the International City Managers Association; Nestor Terleckyj, of the U.S. Bureau of the Budget; and John F. Cotton, of the State-Local Finances Project.

In order to place the material in this report in clearer perspective the nature of planning-programming-budgeting systems is summarized.[1]

A study paper published by the Subcommittee on Intergovernmental Relations of the Committee on Government Operations, U.S. Senate, U.S. Government Printing Office, Washington, D.C., July 21, 1967. Harry P. Hatry, formerly Deputy Director, State-Local Finances Project, The George Washington University, is now with the Urban Institute.

[1] This summary is drawn from Harry P. Hatry and John F. Cotton, "Program Planning for State, County, and City," State-Local Finances Project, George Washington University, January, 1967.

PPB systems are aimed at helping management make better decisions on the allocation of resources among alternative ways to attain government objectives. Its essence is the development and presentation of relevant information as to the full implications—the costs and benefits—of the major alternative courses of action.

PPB systems do not examine many aspects of government management. Such problems as budget implementation, the assessment and improvement of the work-efficiency of operation units, manpower selection, and the cost control of current operations are outside PPB. Cost accounting and non-fiscal performance reporting systems are very important in providing basic data required for PPB analyses (as well as for fiscal accounting and management control purposes); however, such systems are usually considered to be complementary to PPB rather than being directly part of it.

PPB systems hope to minimize the amount of piecemeal, fragmented, and last minute program evaluation which tends to occur under present planning and budgeting practices.

There is actually little new in the individual concepts of PPB. The concepts of program and performance budgeting with their orientation toward workload data and toward program rather than object classification (such as personnel, equipment, and so forth) have been applied by a number of governments since at least 1949, when the Hoover Commission strongly recommended their use. The analytical methods, such as marginal analysis and cost-benefit analysis, are familiar tools of economic analysis. What is new is the combination of a number of concepts into a package and the systematic application of the package in total to government planning.

MAJOR CHARACTERISTICS

The primary distinctive characteristics of PPB are:

1. It calls for an identification of the fundamental objectives of the government.

2. It requires explicit consideration of future year implications.

3. It calls for systematic analysis of alternative ways of meeting the governmental objectives. This characteristic is the crux of PPB. The selection of the appropriate criteria for the evaluation of each alternative against relevant objectives is the subject of the main body of this report.

Note that the terms "PPB" and "program budgeting" as traditionally used are not equivalent. Typically the term "program budgeting" has been limited to budgeting systems emphasizing categorizations by programs without explicit provision for the systematic analysis and multiyear perspective of PPB.

MAJOR COMPONENTS OF A PPB SYSTEM

A PPB system typically has the following components:

1. An across-the-board governmental program structure. One of the first steps performed in instituting PPB is the identification, at least tentatively, of the government's basic objectives. Based upon these, the government's activities are grouped into categories, which aim at grouping together activities (regardless of organizational placement) that contribute toward the same objectives. An abbreviated example of a PPB program structure is shown in the appendix. [Not shown.]

2. A multiyear program and financial plan. At any given point in time there should exist an approved multiyear plan which uses the program structure categories discussed above. The plan is in two major parts. The first part is the "financial plan." All pertinent costs are considered—including capital costs as well as noncapital costs, and associated support costs (such as employee benefits, associated vehicle and building maintenance costs) as well as direct costs. Major associated external revenues should be identified where appropriate and the expected net cost to the jurisdiction indicated. The program, or output part of the plan, should contain the major measures which indicate to the users of the plan the scope and magnitude of the approved programs. Five years in addition to the current fiscal year has typically been selected for presentation in these multiyear plans.

3. Program analyses. The systematic identification and analysis of alternative ways to achieve government objectives is the cornerstone of PPB.

The analysis of a program issue should result in the identification and documentation of—

(1) The fundamental governmental objectives involved;

(2) The major feasible alternatives;

(3) For each alternative the best available estimates of the total program costs for each year considered;

(4) For each alternative the best available estimates of the benefits (and/or "penalties") relevant to the objectives for each year considered;

(5) The major assumptions and uncertainties associated with the alternatives; and

(6) The impact of proposed programs on other programs, other agencies, other levels of government, and on private organizations.

The presentation and discussion of alternatives and of the costs and benefits of each goes considerably beyond the scope of typical budget justification material which describes specific budget funding requests and goes beyond the scope of material generally included in physical planning studies.

To be most useful, the analysis should indicate preferred program mixes at different funding levels since specific funding levels should seldom be chosen without explicit consideration of the change in costs and benefits (i.e., the "marginal" costs and benefits) in going from one level to another.

The analysis process should not ignore the political and legislative constraints that are relevant. The analysis should seek to optimize resource allocation within these constraints. However, analysis also should be used to indicate the potential penalties arising from them. This will provide information to government decisionmakers suggesting how worth while it might be to try to overcome these constraints. In the short run these may indeed be firm constraints; for the long run, however, changes may be possible.

This type of analysis places emphasis

on the preparation of quantitative information, but when this information is not available, qualitative materials should be included to place the issues in proper perspective.

In PPB, analysis can take many different forms and can be done at many levels of refinement. However, it is useful to distinguish two levels—a less-refined, less-rigorous analysis, and "in-depth" analysis. Each is briefly described below.

Less "rigorous" analysis.—This level of analysis is very likely, at least initially, to be the most prevalent. Where in-depth studies are not attempted or prove of slight use, a considerably improved understanding of program alternatives can be achieved through less-rigorous, less-refined analysis. A great deal can be achieved for resource allocation problems through the identification and examination of the six elements listed above.

Although these elements are also essential for in-depth studies, their investigation even without the more rigorous analytical tools can provide considerable illumination.

Much of the real gain from existing PPB systems has probably been derived from the "dialog"—the questioning and response—among the decision makers, the proposal makers, and the program analysts. Much of the relevant analytical work done thus far in government PPB systems has resulted not from very sophisticated, technical analyses, but from penetrating questioning and the improved perspective obtained on the issues by applying this less rigorous level of analysis.

"In-depth" analysis.—A fully implemented PPB system should provide for the preparation of in-depth studies, often referred to as cost-benefit studies —also sometimes called cost-effectiveness or cost-utility analyses. These studies draw heavily upon the analytical tools of the professional disciplines, including mathematics, economics, operations research, engineering, and the computer sciences. They also seek the six elements listed above, but with a much closer examination. The studies attempt to identify, quantitatively to the extent possible, the cost and benefit implications of the range of feasible alternatives.

Cost-benefit analyses can seldom provide complete answers. They are intended primarily to provide information to decisionmakers concerning the major tradeoffs and implications existing among the alternatives considered. This information would then be available for use by decisionmakers, along with any other information available— e.g., that pertaining to political, psychological, and other factors which may not have been included in the cost-benefit study.

Program analysis, at either level, is not easy. It is still true that program analysis (or whatever it may be called) is still as much an art as a science. Probably the most important limitations on the undertaking of meaningful analyses are:

(1) Problems in defining the real objectives;

(2) The presence of multiple, incommensurable benefits;

(3) Inadequacies of data relevant to the analysis, including information as to what effect each alternative course of action will have on the objectives as well as information describing where we are today; and

(4) Difficulties in considering a time stream of costs and benefits and not simply the evaluation of costs and benefits for a single point in time.

4. Program updating procedure. PPB requires explicit provision for the revision and updating of resource decisions. The system must be responsive to changing needs and changing information. The latest multiyear program and financial plan can form the "base" from which proposals for program changes can be made.

CONCLUSION

PPB potentially can help State and local governments deal with public problems ahead of time, in a comprehensive manner, and can place in much improved perspective the principal issues on resource allocation. The visibility of relevant information (on costs and benefits of pertinent alternatives) provided by PPB is the key element.

There are considerable difficulties and potential misuses that can occur. Certainly, too much should not be expected of the system. It should never be expected that PPB will be able to give definitive answers, but rather considerably improved information pertinent to resource allocation and program selection decisions.

An integrated PPB system is designed to provide information that is so vital to decisionmaking in our complex governmental structure. It is primarily a tool for high level decisionmaking, it will not be worth while unless the high level management understands it, wants it, and uses it.

THE CRITERIA PROBLEM

A major part of a program planning process is the attempt to estimate the contribution that each alternative program, or mix of programs, makes toward meeting fundamental governmental objectives. For the purpose of this paper, the terms "goals," "aims," "purposes," "missions," or "functions" may be substituted for "objectives." The need for evaluation criteria arises because funds and physical resources are scarce; there are not enough available to satisfy all needs and proposals. (The term "measures of effectiveness" is sometimes used by analysts instead of "criteria.") Thus the problem of choice arises, and evaluation of proposals is needed to make the best use of available resources. To perform this evaluation, it is necessary to identify specific criteria that can be used to evaluate performance against the governmental objectives.[2] For example, if a governmental objective such as "to reduce crime" was identified, then it would be appropriate to use crime rates as the major criterion (but not necessarily the only criterion) for evaluating activities aiming at these objectives. That is, in comparisons between various proposals, each proposal's effect upon the anticipated future crime rates would need to be estimated.

---

[2] The term "output measure" is also occasionally used instead of "criteria." However, when "output measure" is used, it often is used to encompass not only program evaluation criteria (the subject of this paper) but also indicators of the size of programs such as the number of cases handled, the number of fire stations, policemen, teachers, hospital beds, etc., which though of considerable interest are not major evaluation criteria in the sense used in this paper.

As the example indicates, the selection of criteria depends upon the objectives that are formulated. Also the process of selecting the criteria will often suggest the need for revision of the objectives. Thus, the establishing of objectives and criteria are interacting processes. In this paper, the emphasis is on criteria; objectives are discussed and presented only briefly. Ideally, a thorough discussion of State and local government objectives would be undertaken first.

An important characteristic of both "objectives" and "criteria" as used in this paper is that they are intended to be "end" oriented rather than "means" oriented. That is, they are intended to reflect what is ultimately desired to be accomplished and for whom, not ways to accomplish such objectives. For example, the phrase, "to disperse cultural facilities rather than concentrating them in a single locality" is a means "to provide adequate cultural opportunities to all." Use of the former phrase as the statement of objective rather than the latter would lead to somewhat different criteria, such as "the number of cultural facilities." Program analysis would better compare dispersal programs with centralized programs as alternative means to providing adequate cultural opportunities.

Also, the concept of objectives as used in this paper avoids inclusion of specific numerical magnitudes. For example, a statement of objectives such as "to reduce crime rates 10 percent" should be avoided. For program analysis it is seldom appropriate to prespecify magnitudes. The specific amount of improvement that should be sought should generally not be determined until after the alternatives have been evaluated as to the costs and benefits of each and after these tradeoffs are understood.

The criteria for program analyses ideally should have the following general properties:

(1) Each criterion should be relevant and important to the specific problem for which it is to be used. (This will depend upon the fundamental objectives to be satisfied.)

(2) Together the criteria used for a specific problem should consider all major effects relative to the objectives. Enough criteria should be evaluated to cover all major effects. The use of insufficient criteria can be very misleading. For example, programs to improve housing conditions should in general consider not only the number of acres of slums removed but also the effects upon the persons removed (perhaps by including a second criterion: the number of persons still living in substandard dwelling units).

Although it would make the evaluation considerably easier to have only one criterion, or at least very few criteria, the important thing is to avoid excluding major considerations from an analysis.

As indicated in the previous example, probably any single objective, if emphasized too much without considering other needs, could lead to excesses and result in even worse conditions. Other examples are: sole consideration of safety in moving traffic could result in excessive trip delay times; in the law enforcement area, sole concentration on crime rates might lead to programs that result in excess control of individual movement.

With all the criteria expressed in terms of one unit (such as the dollar) or two units (such as the dollar and some nonmonetary unit), neat, analytically optimizable solutions would usually be possible. However, forcing the analysis into oversimplified forms may hide many major considerations. Use of multiple evaluation criteria seems, in general, to be unavoidable.

(3) Each of the criteria ideally should be capable of meaningful quantification. This involves two major problems. The first is the measurement of the current and historical magnitudes of each of the criteria. This measurement is needed to give a clear picture of the magnitude of the problem, to determine how well the jurisdiction is actually doing toward meeting its objectives, and to provide a basis for making projections into the future. For the housing example used above we would want to be able to measure how many acres of slums and how many people living in substandard dwelling units there currently are, and how many were living in such units previously.

The second problem is the estimation of the future magnitudes for these criteria for each of the alternative programs being considered. Projecting into the future is always hazardous. One of the most, if not the most, difficult problems in program analysis is the estimation of the effects on the criteria of the various courses of action. Historical data are important both for measuring progress and for making inferences as to what has caused any changes that have occurred. This latter information is very important for preparing estimates of the effects of future courses of action.

In practice, it is very difficult, and probably impossible, to meet perfectly all three of these ideal properties of criteria. The list of criteria on pages 114 to 119 . . . is a first attempt to identify the major criteria that are likely to be pertinent for governmental programs. An explicit attempt has been made to make the list conform with the first two properties (that is, relevancy and coverage) given above for ideal criteria. However, the list is certainly far from definitive in either depth or coverage. It is also somewhat idealistic; the analysts' ability to estimate meaningfully the effects of alternative programs upon the criteria (the third property given above) will undoubtedly be limited in many instances—particularly with current information systems.

On occasion, it may be necessary to utilize purely qualitative measures such as, "In reducing crime, alternative A is more effective than alternative B but less effective than C." This ranking procedure might be partially quantified by having experts apply their judgments to some type of ranking scale. This would result in such a result as, "In reducing crime, alternative A has a value of 80 on the specially prepared ranking scale, B has a value of 65 and C a value of 85."

Thus in practice, even though criteria are not completely capable of being satisfactorily quantified, criteria that have the other two properties may still be useful.

The list of criteria . . . is hoped to be a reasonable starting point from which individual governments would develop a sound set of criteria appropriate to their own specific problems and governmental objectives. Many of these criteria are already in use. For an individual problem, the analysts will need to determine the specific criteria appropriate to that problem. The list . . . may help to suggest the appropriate ones. Each interested reader is encouraged to think through and work out what he feels to be an improved list.

With few exceptions, only nonmonetary criteria are listed in this paper. It is assumed that, in general, all problems will need to consider the actual monetary effects of each alternative course of action proposed. That is, one objective in all problems will be to keep monetary costs as low as possible for any level of program effectiveness aimed for. However, it is a premise of this paper that in the past too much emphasis has been placed upon attempting to translate all program effects into dollar terms. It is true that if this could be done meaningfully, the evaluation of alternative and final program selection would be eased considerably since the quantitative evaluations would all be expressed in the same unit—the dollar.

Realistically most governmental problems involve major objectives of a nondollar nature. Not only is it very difficult for analysts to assign dollar "values" to such nondollar objectives, but it is also questionable whether it would be desirable even if it could be done. Thus, questions of the value of such effects as reducing death rates, reducing illness incidences and severities, improving housing conditions, and increasing recreational opportunities should not become simply a problem of estimating the dollar values of these things.

The analysts should rather concentrate upon the estimation and presentation, for each alternative, of full information as to the actual dollar effects and the effects upon the nonmonetary criteria. This is the primary function of program analysis—and of "cost-effectiveness," "cost-benefit," "cost-utility," or "systems analysis," terms which for the purpose of this paper are all assumed to be equivalent. Attempts to force the criteria into commensurability are in most cases not worth much effort. It should be left to the decisionmakers to provide the value judgments needed to make the final program decisions.[3]

DISCUSSION AND QUALIFICATIONS

The illustrative criteria which follow on pages 114 to 119 are subject to a number of substantial qualifications and warnings; these are discussed below.

Criteria must relate to governmental objectives

As has been already indicated, the problem of selecting the appropriate criteria is dependent upon the problem of specifying objectives correctly. Thus, for a traffic-control problem, if the

---

[3] However, if the analysts can uncover some clues as to the worth that the jurisdiction's public does assign to such nonmonetary criteria, this information should also be provided to the decisionmakers (but not substituted for the basic information on the nonmonetary effects) to assist them in making their judgments. For example, various surveys of the public might give some information as to the degree to which persons currently might be willing to exchange money for changes in the nonmonetary criteria magnitudes. Highway tolls, for example, do indicate that the persons still using the highway are willing to pay at least the price of the toll for the advantages provided by the highway over alternate routes.

problem had originally been stated solely in terms of "reducing the number of traffic accidents," and if the analysts had limited themselves solely to this objective, the only criterion would have been the number of traffic accidents. Alternatives which, for example, restricted traffic flow such as by slowing down traffic considerably, would still tend to be the most "cost effective" since the rapidity of traffic movement was not implied in the statement of objectives and therefore was not included in the criteria.

For each major program area identified in the list, a brief statement is first given which summarizes the assumed objectives of the major program area. The criteria listed for the major program area should ideally provide a specific basis on which to evaluate the contribution that each alternative course of action makes to these objectives. If the reader prefers different statements of objectives, he is also likely to be led to somewhat different criteria.[4]

The specific objectives of a jurisdiction also depend upon the jurisdiction's own concept of the extent of the government's role in each program area. In many instances, there are likely to be considerable differences of opinion as to the proper role of the government. However, in general, such functions as law enforcement, fire protection, and water supply are usually assumed to

be primarily governmental functions. Such other functions, however, as health, intellectual development, job opportunities, and leisure-time opportunities may rely heavily upon private sectors. Nevertheless, governments do have some role in most of these, usually at least having a part in helping the "needy" to reach certain minimum standards.

A related problem is that of the many and periodically changing ways in which government's role is divided among the various levels of government such as among city, county, State, and National, and, of increasing importance, special regional organizations.

The specific role played by the government in each individual jurisdiction must be considered in selection of the appropriate criteria.

In this paper no consideration is given to the question of "national objectives" such as national prestige and national security. It would seem that for State and local governments such issues, though of considerable interest, are peripheral to these governments' functions.

State and local governments, however, must, of course, be concerned with the notions of individual liberty, privacy, freedom of choice, and democratic processes. The degree to which each program option may impinge upon these individual rights and processes should, of course, be considered in a complete evaluation.

There are different "levels" of criteria

One of the major difficulties in specifying criteria is that there are many different levels of criteria. The specific

---

[4] Persons with different perspectives, different cultures, would probably develop a different set of objectives—thereby implying somewhat different criteria. For example, the caveman would probably insist upon a major program area entitled "Food Supply," and one labeled "Mate Procurement." (The latter would be a tough one for State and local governments.)

criteria that are appropriate will depend upon the specific problem at hand.

At the highest level we might say that all government programs aim at contributing "to the maintenance and improvement of the well-being of humanity." This overall objective is too general; it is very difficult to measure, is vague, and is not very useful for analysis. The objectives and related criteria presented in the list on pages 114 to 119 are at a lower level. However, they are intended to provide the major criteria that should preferably be used in governmental program analyses. These criteria may still be at too high a level for many problems.

Thus, for example, if we are concerned with examining the desirable size and nature of public health nursing services, it is likely to be very difficult to relate some of these services directly to mortality rates, morbidity rates, or days of restricted activity. Preferably, estimates would be made of the effect of alternative levels and mixes of public health nursing services and other types of health service alternatives on each of these criteria. However, because of the difficulty in linking the nursing service programs to these criteria, it may be necessary to use some "indirect," "proxy," or "substitute" criteria. One expedient might be simply to estimate the caseload that can be handled by each public health nursing service program proposed.

Another example: For the objective, "to prevent (deter) crime," judging accused persons can be considered one of the pertinent types of activity. "Judging" itself can be said to have the following subobjectives:

(a) To be fair.
(b) To be swift.

(c) For the guilty, to provide appropriate sentence (neither excessive nor overly lenient).

Alternative programs for "judging" could each be compared through criteria that reflected these subobjectives. Nevertheless, the crucial question would remain as to what extent meeting these criteria to various degrees would deter crime.

Such subcriteria as are indicated in these two examples are not included in the list on pages 114 to 119, but may often be necessary for individual analyses.

Unfortunately, "program size" indicators such as discussed in the public health nursing example (i.e., caseload) tell little about the important effects, e.g., the effects upon community health that the program achieves. Presentation of only this information to the decisionmakers leaves it completely to the decisionmakers to make subjective judgments as to the effects of the service. Presentation of the costs and the program size indicator for each alternative is better than nothing, but leaves much to be desired.

It should be recognized that, in most cases, at least some information can be obtained relating programs to the major criteria. For example, it may well be possible to examine current and past records of the jurisdiction and other jurisdictions and to relate to some extent the more fundamental health criteria to program size; inferences would then be made as to the probable future effects of the newly proposed programs. A second approach is to conduct experiments (controlled as much as is practical) in which characteristics other than those investigated are similar from one group to another.

Pertinent information would be kept about these groups, and inferences subsequently would be drawn as to the effects of the program characteristics.

Such information gathering does, of course, cost money. Also, the experimental approach may take a long time before useful results become available —possibly too long for the immediate problem but still useful if similar problems are expected to be of concern when the results do become available. In the absence of analytical techniques that identify the best approach to given objectives, the jurisdiction probably can afford to (and indeed may have to) experiment to some extent.

The point is that the program analyst should not be quick to accept lower level criteria such as program size indicators as the only criteria on which he can obtain information.

Criteria are grouped under seven major program areas

The criteria presented on pages 114 to 119 are grouped under each of seven "major program areas":

(a) Personal safety.

(b) Health.

(c) Intellectual development and personal enrichment.

(d) Satisfactory home and community environment.

(e) Economic satisfaction and satisfactory work opportunities.

(f) Satisfactory leisure-time opportunities.

(g) Transportation-communication-location.

Together, these major program areas are intended to encompass the great majority of the activities of a governmental jurisdiction. Though many such classifications could be made, these appear to be a reasonable set for discussion of criteria for evaluation of governmental programs. . . .

Many, if not most, analyses will at least initially concentrate upon but one part of one of these major program areas. In some of these analyses it may be necessary to utilize lower level criteria. For example, for an issue raised on manpower training programs the criterion "percent of enrollees satisfactorily completing the training program" might be appropriate. However, as already noted above unqualified use of such a lower level criterion for program selection could be misleading. The more fundamental problem of government relevant to manpower training is to get unemployed (or underemployed) persons satisfactorily employed and self-sufficient. The mere fact of graduation from a training program does not mean reduced unemployment. Employment and earning criteria, even if not feasible to use directly as criteria, should be recognized as being more truly the objectives of manpower training.

Most program-oriented categorizations of governmental programs (called program structures in PPB systems) will also contain a major category for general government activities. This will include such activities as the government's financial, legal, and legislative activities. No criteria are included in the list for these activities. The viewpoint of this paper is that these general government activities are primarily supporting services to the other, primary, government functions. That is, these activities are not themselves aimed at achieving fundamental governmental purposes.[5]

More than one criterion will frequently be needed for individual problems

For each of the seven major program areas, several criteria are listed. In some cases there is some overlap and redundancy. However, for the most part, each of the criteria contains some potentially important aspect that is not contained in the other criteria. As has been already noted, the evaluation of program alternatives would be eased considerably if all criteria were commensurable, i.e., expressed in some common unit such as "dollars." However, practically speaking, few major program issues can be meaningfully evaluated solely in terms of a single criterion.[6] The analysts should concentrate upon providing as full and accurate information as possible as to the effects of each program alternative on each of the criteria, leaving it to the decisionmakers to weight the criteria.[7]

---

[5] The point, however, can be made that these activities do contribute to the fundamental function of providing "democracy."

[6] However, frequently it may be reasonable to concentrate the analysis on one key, non-monetary criterion, and treat the other criteria as study constraints or as relatively minor considerations. Even in these instances, however, two criteria, one monetary and the other nonmonetary, will need to be explicitly evaluated. As has been indicated, forcing a dollar value on a nonmonetary criterion does not in general seem a good practice.

[7] A technique occasionally used with multiple criteria is to have experts in the specific field estimate the relative weights of each criterion. By applying the prechosen weights, the multiple criteria can be combined into one index thus permitting a ranking on the same scale of all the alternatives. As with

Though the list of criteria is divided into major program areas, this is not meant to imply that all program analysis problems will necessarily fall into one major program area, and only one. On the contrary, major governmental problems will frequently spill over into more than one program area. For example, mass transit system proposals could have significant impact on many if not all of the listed major program areas: Traffic safety is directly affected by the substitution of a mass-transit system for individual automobiles; an inexpensive mass-transit system might permit low-income workers to consider job opportunities further away than they can currently afford; families who wished to live further out in the country might be able to do so with a convenient, rapid, inexpensive transit system; recreational opportunities previously too far away and too expensive to reach might be opened to certain segments of the public; individual health and intellectual development might be furthered (indirectly) by the combination of the preceding effects; certain penalties could also occur, such as the transit system having an adverse effect on the physical attractiveness and living conditions of the areas where it

---

attempts to translate all nonmonetary criteria into monetary units, such a practice can too easily be misleading. It is the author's belief that if the analysts believe that the resulting information is meaningful, it may be provided to the decisionmaker, but the basic information as to each program alternative's effect upon each of the individual criteria before any weights are applied should always be provided so that meaningful information is not obscured.

is constructed; air pollution and noise effects would also occur.

Another example is that of education programs that in addition to contributing to individual intellectual development also lead to improved employability and reduction in unemployment.

Thus, specific programs may simultaneously have many complex and interacting effects on many program areas and many criteria.

It is important in program analyses to attempt to consider and evaluate all such effects to the extent that they might be important to the decision-making process.

It will be necessary to distinguish "target groups"

An important aspect of program evaluation is the identification of the specific population groups that receive benefits (or penalties) from each program proposed. Though not specifically included in the list, it will often be appropriate to break down further certain of the criteria into subcriteria in order to distinguish specific clientele, or "target groups." For many issues a government will be interested in distinguishing the effects of alternative programs on specific population groups identified by such characteristics as age, sex, race, income, family size, education, occupation, geographical location, special handicaps, etc. For example: For many health issues, distinctions by age, income level, family size, etc., may be required to evaluate the effects of various health programs on each category within such groups. Another example: It will probably be necessary for many law-enforcement

issues to distinguish crimes committed by adults from those by juveniles.

Though neither the objectives nor the illustrative criteria . . . explicitly single out "equal opportunity" objectives the use of target groups in the criteria will provide information on such objectives.

Criteria need to be thoroughly defined

No attempt is made in this paper to define the listed criteria. However, when utilizing criteria it is important to have clear, thorough definitions. In almost all cases, misinterpretations (often subtle ones) can occur if complete definitions are not provided. For example, for major types of crimes it is necessary to define each type of crime, e.g., does "larceny" include thefts of automobiles and bicycles; does it include thefts of any magnitude or only those beyond a specific dollar value? Another example: What is meant by "restricted activity" when the number of days of restricted activity for health reasons per person per year is to be estimated? Again, how is "poverty" defined when the number of persons and families in the jurisdiction's "poverty population" is estimated? Or, what is meant by "substandard" when dwelling units are evaluated?

Definitions should generally specify such things as who is involved, how, what time period is to be covered by the criteria, what geographical location is included, etc. For example, for measuring restricted activity due to health reasons, it is necessary to know—

(a) What specifically is meant by "restricted activity"?

(b) Whether the whole population

of the jurisdiction is involved or some specific segment such as "all males between the ages of 16 and 21 living in the North Smithtown" section of the city.

(c) Whether the magnitudes are to be on a "per person per year" basis or on some other.

Some attention should also be given to the influence of time which may affect the definitions. For example, wherever a dollar figure is involved in defining a criterion, price-level changes over time may alter the meaning. For example, if "larceny" is defined to include only thefts over $50 at current price levels, price-level rises will automatically bring more thefts into the category even though there is no change in the total number of thefts of each type. Explicit provision will be needed for adjustments of the criterion, based upon price-level changes. Another type of change over time that may occur is change in the jurisdiction's boundaries, possibly requiring adjustments to make compatible the magnitudes assigned to the criteria for different years.

Criteria can be expressed in different forms

Given that a certain factor is considered sufficiently important to be included as an evaluation criterion, there frequently will be a variety of forms in which the criteria can be expressed. Five such choices are noted below:

(a) Both "absolute" numbers and rates are called for by the criteria included in the list. Absolute numbers by themselves can present a misrepresentation of the situation. For example, the total number of various crimes or of traffic accidents, though, of course, of interest in themselves, do not reflect the associated levels of activity. Crime rates and traffic accident rates (the latter related to the volume of traffic) will give improved perspectives as to what is happening in those areas. Both forms are probably needed by the decisionmakers.

(b) Some of the criteria listed below call for "averages"; for example, "average waiting time for the use of certain recreational facilities." In such cases, the analysts will frequently also need to consider the distribution of waiting times as well as the average. There is danger that if only the average is considered, important information may be ignored. For example, the average waiting time throughout the week on a city's golf courses may be 15 minutes, which, if it were applicable at all times, would probably be quite acceptable to the city's golfers. However, the distribution of waiting times for specific times of the week might show prolonged, perhaps several-hour, waits during certain hours of the weekends, probably causing considerable annoyance among golfers and suggesting the need for corrective action. Use of only the overall average would hide the pertinent information.

In the list [beginning on page 114] the dangers of the use of averages for waiting times of recreational facilities have been reduced considerably by requiring the calculation of the averages for specific key periods.

Wherever "averages" are considered for use in criteria, consideration should be given to the possibly important information that such criteria hide.

(c) In many instances it will be desirable to compare the magnitudes for the criteria with the magnitudes existing in other, similar jurisdictions, both the current magnitudes and those estimated for the future. For example, local crime rates may be compared with those of other parts of the country (perhaps by using the FBI's uniform crime reports).

The relative conditions, such as displayed by the ratios of the jurisdiction's own crime rates to those of the Nation, or some segment of it, could be used as criteria. It may also be of interest to compare health, education, recreation, unemployment, and housing conditions to conditions elsewhere.

Care should be taken to ascertain that the figures are really comparable since definitions and reporting systems can differ substantially. For example, the crime reports referred to above have been criticized for lack of uniformity.

Too much concentration on "what the other fellow is doing" is not desirable; the absolute forms of the criteria (for example, the total amount of crime in the government's own jurisdiction) should not be neglected.[8]

The list of criteria . . . does not specifically include comparisons with other jurisdictions. As appropriate, the

[8] It is also to be noted that the mere fact that the projected magnitudes for a criterion indicate a retrogressing situation (either relative to other jurisdictions or even relative to earlier years within the jurisdiction) does not in itself necessarily indicate that the jurisdiction's programs are poor. External conditions outside the control of the jurisdiction (such as a significant shift in the characteristics of the population due to inmigration or the entry of a new disease virus from outside) can cause the retrogression. Selection of program alternatives should be made as to which alternative is best relative to the others; i.e., which minimizes the adverse situation, even though none of the alternatives is estimated to cause an absolute improvement in the conditions.

criteria could readily be modified to reflect such comparisons.

(d) Certain criteria can be displayed either as the "total number" of something or as a "reduction (or increase) in the number" of this thing. For example, "total number of accidents from cause X" could also be shown as "reduction of the total number of accidents from cause X." The use of the term "reduction" implies that there is a base from which the alternatives are measured. When alternative courses of action are being compared, the "reduction" is simply the difference between the base and the number resulting from the alternative.

The "reduction" form is the more direct way of showing effects but does not indicate the level still existing. In the list of criteria below both forms are sometimes shown.

(e) Certain of the individual criteria might be combined in various ways to form a new, single criterion. For example, for health programs the "number of sick days" might be multiplied by the severity index (if there is one) to give a "severity-sick-days index." This procedure is sometimes followed in order to reduce the number of criteria for analytical simplification. The list of criteria . . . does not include examples of these combined criteria.

Estimates of the criteria magnitudes
are needed for each year of the plan

Another aspect of the criteria problem arises from the necessity in program analysis to consider program impacts on each year for several years in the future. Though various pressures usually act to emphasize current and near future needs, good governmental planning obviously requires consideration of the longer range needs. In preparing its plan of action, a government needs to assure that the plan would provide desired goods and services in each year of the plan.

Different alternative courses of action will affect different years in different ways. One mix of programs may, for example, result in greater benefits for the near future, while another mix of programs might emphasize current investments that are expected to produce superior benefits in later years. Therefore, in deciding among courses of actions the magnitude of each criterion for each year is an important consideration.

The weighting of the importance of each particular year of the plan will probably be the province of the decisionmakers rather than the analysts. The main job of the analysts will be to provide as complete and accurate information as possible as to the nature and phasing of the program impacts, leaving it to the decisionmakers' judgments for the final weightings of one year versus another.

A monetary criterion is always needed

The one common criterion in all problems of choosing among alternative programs is the monetary (i.e., dollar) effects of each alternative. This criterion is not repeated for each major program area in the list of criteria given below, but should be assumed to be pertinent in each case. Primarily nonmonetary criteria are included in the list. In a few cases a monetary criterion seemed to be necessary as a proxy to reflect important social factors, and these are included in the list.

The term "monetary criterion" as used here refers to the actual dollar changes that would occur (for each alternative program mix as compared to some base)—but not including dollar values imputed to nonmonetary things. These dollar changes, whether affecting the government's own financial picture or that of other sectors of the economy, should be considered in the evaluation. Effects on the various sectors, as well as on the various clientele groups, should be identified separately so that the decisionmakers have a clear perspective of the impacts.

Theoretically, all of the nonmonetary criteria listed below could be translated into dollar values by estimating, in some manner, the dollar "worth" to the government (or to some other specified group) of changes in the magnitudes of each of the criteria. For example, it might be estimated that the population of the jurisdiction would be willing to pay x dollars to reduce the number of criminal homicides per year from Y to Z. It is, however, a premise of this paper that such translations present some almost insurmountable obstacles (at least with the current state of the art of program analysis) and at best will represent the judgment of one limited group of persons at one point in time. Therefore, it is always desirable to display the values for the specific nondollar criteria, such as those listed [on pages 114 to 119] so that the actual decisionmakers have full information with which to make their own judgments. Information that attempts to estimate the dollar "value" to specified target groups for changes in the nondollar criteria can also be presented to the decisionmakers if the analysts believe such information to be useful. For those who insist upon translating all units into dollar terms, the list of criteria might at least be a guide to the major factors to which dollar values have to be attached.[9]

The monetary criteria can be very complex

Before we leave the subject of the monetary criteria as applied to program evaluation, the complexity of these criteria should be noted. The monetary effects of a program alternative can be of many types. These effects include the following elements (note that the term "cost" refers only to dollar costs):

PROGRAM COSTS. These are the governmental costs that are incurred in

---

[9] Occasionally, the criterion "added future earnings" is used to estimate the value of increasing life expectancy and the value of reducing illness. If this criterion is used alone or predominantly, the evaluation can be misleading. For example, elderly persons or others out of the labor market are at a significant disadvantage, as are housewives (depending upon the amount imputed as their "earnings"). The use of future earnings seems to imply that such factors as growth in "GNP" are the fundamental objectives whereas the value of merely increasing GNP (without, for example, considering per capita GNP and the standard of living) would not seem to be the critical issue in our current society. A very pertinent question is: How does the loss of the individual affect the individual and the remaining population? We know how it affects the individual—and the significant effect is not a monetary one. How it affects the remaining population is a very complex question. Individual population groups, such as those close to the decedents, the taxpayers, the insurance-paying public, the businessmen who lose the decedents' spending power, etc., are each affected in different ways. For a more extensive discussion of these points see the Schelling reference listed in the bibliography.

undertaking the activities called for by the program. These costs include the various administrative and other support-type costs as well as those directly incurred.

PROGRAM MONETARY EFFECTS WITHIN THE GOVERNMENT. As a result of the activities called for by the program, certain government costs may be increased or decreased. For example, a slum-clearance program might in future years result in reductions in fire and crime protection services for the cleared area; on the other hand it might lead to increased demand for park and recreation services. A slum-clearance program would also have some effect upon the tax base of the jurisdiction.

PROGRAM MONETARY EFFECTS OUTSIDE THE GOVERNMENT. Many of the monetary effects of governmental programs will occur outside the jurisdiction, perhaps affecting the private sector of the economy or other jurisdictions. Changes in transportation systems or in housing, for example, will have considerable effect on many types of businesses in the area. Such effects may be important in many kinds of studies. Governments are generally interested, for example, in monetary measures of gross business and income in relation to persons and businesses within their jurisdictions. Specific examples of such economic measures include: manufacturing value added, retail and wholesale sales, amount of bank deposits, and industrial capital expenditures. (However, it should also be recognized that too much emphasis can be placed upon such measures. For example, attracting businesses into the area though increasing total sales and total earnings, could also adversely affect the overall physical attractiveness of the community.) Another example of effects upon the private sector is the effect upon insurance rates of illness, fire, and crime prevention programs.

It is not desirable to add all of these dollar effects [i.e., (a) plus (b) plus (c)] to yield one overall monetary impact. The impact on each sector should be presented to avoid obscuring pertinent considerations.

It will not always be clear whether an item is a "program cost" or a "program monetary effect." (Other terms that have been used to distinguish these are "direct versus indirect" and "primary versus secondary.") However, the important thing is not the classification but the identification and consideration of these monetary effects if significant to the program at hand.[10]

Another major problem in handling monetary changes is the time pattern associated with the cash flow. As discussed above, the time pattern is of importance to a government. The use of a "discount" (i.e., interest) rate to translate actual net dollar flow (after consideration of both in-flows or out-flows) into a single "present value" is frequently recommended. This discounting procedure has the advantage of—

(a) Reducing the complexity of evaluation by replacing the several dollar figures (i.e., one for each year of the time period) by one number, the present value.

(b) Reflecting the time value of money in the sense that, in general, money this year is worth more than the same amount of money next year since potentially it can be put to work now and grow into a larger sum by next year.[11]

Unfortunately, however, despite the well-grounded economic basis for discounting (as the procedure is commonly called), there are some difficulties and drawbacks such as the following:

(a) First, there is considerable disagreement over the appropriate discount rate to be used. The range usually debated appears to be 4 to 10 percent. The rate chosen can have a significant effect upon the results if, for example, the competing programs have major differences in their expenditure patterns. Nevertheless, uncertainty as to the appropriate rate is not sufficient reason to avoid discounting.

(b) A more important concern to governments is found in the practical constraints in their annual funding capabilities. Major fluctuations in revenue needs from one year to the next may present insurmountable difficulties. It seems, therefore, that whether or not discounting is deemed appropriate, the actual (i.e., unadjusted by the discount rate) time-phased dollar flows should be shown to the decisionmakers. In addition, the discounted present values of the alternatives can be provided

---

[10] Arguments as to whether such cost reductions should be considered as an offset to total costs or as an addition to "benefits" is important if cost-benefit ratios are being used as the primary evaluation criterion; however, reliance on such ratios is not good practice. The question as to whether to consider such cost reductions as belonging on the cost or benefit side should not affect a decision.

[11] Discounting is partly a substitute for the explicit consideration of all effects; that is, if the before-and-after sides of all facets of the economy were explicitly included, this procedure would directly show the time value of the money, and advantage (b) would not apply.

(perhaps for more than one discount rate). This suggested procedure applies to monetary flows both inside and outside the government.

In most cases, the use of discounting will probably be of secondary concern relative to the many other problems of program analysis.

Nevertheless, as a practical matter, governmental decisionmakers are likely to have strong time preferences as to funding requirements of their jurisdictions and need to be shown the time-phased monetary implications of the alternative courses of actions.

As has already been noted, the purpose of this discussion has been to indicate the scope and complexity potentially involved with the monetary criterion. Most of the remainder of this paper is directed at nonmonetary criteria.

The criteria are not intended for use in organizational evaluations

The criteria discussed in this paper are not intended for the purpose of measuring the efficiency of the administrative organizations of a government (such as the police or fire department). The measurement of day-to-day operational performance, though important, is not the subject of this paper.[12] The

---

[12] Though some of the criteria discussed in this paper probably could be used in the measurement of organizational performance, they would seldom by themselves be adequate for that purpose. The criteria in this paper are probably too aggregative: seldom will one government department or agency have full control over these criteria. More specific and more directly related criteria (for example, the average time that it takes to get the firetrucks away from the station after an alarm is received, the number of public assistance cases handled per caseworker per month, etc.) are needed to measure organizational efficiency. Such meas-

criteria in this paper are intended for the purpose of evaluating proposed program alternatives, not of evaluating staffs' or departments' current operating efficiency.

Measurements of program size are also needed but not as evaluation criteria

Governments that install a formal planning-programming-budgeting system, in addition to undertaking individual program analyses, will probably also prepare a multiyear program and financial plan. One of the main parts of this plan is an "output plan," a presentation that indicates the estimated outputs obtainable from the program plan for each year covered by the plan. At first glance, it might appear that the outputs contained in these output plans should be the evaluation criteria, the measures of effectiveness, utilized in the program analyses—such as those discussed and presented in this paper. In practice, however, the "outputs" contained in the formal multiyear plan will probably have to be somewhat different. They are more likely to be measurements that indicate the magnitude or size of the program rather than its effectiveness. "Effectiveness" is too intricate a subject to present simply as a string of numbers not accompanied by evaluative comments. However, certain common and fairly clearly understood effectiveness measures such as crime and accident rates would probably be appropriate and desirable for inclusion in the formal output plan. In any case, measurements indicating the magnitude of each program (for ex-

---

ures are useful in program analysis as planning factors from which estimates of overall program costs and effectiveness are built up, but are not the fundamental criteria sought for program evaluation purposes.

ample, the number of persons treated in public hospitals, the number of miles of highway, the number of acres of playgrounds, etc.) will be information useful to readers of the government's formal multiyear program and financial plan.

This paper does not attempt to list the program-size measures that might be appropriate for use in a multiyear program and financial plan.

Criteria for government-citizen relations may be desirable

For many of the services which a government provides to its citizens, the pleasantness, courtesy, quietness (e.g., in the case of waste collection), etc., involved in the provision of the service are factors in the overall quality of the service. To some extent these factors are more a problem of operational performance than of program planning. Nevertheless, to the extent to which program planning is involved (for example, a proposal to provide training of policemen on police-citizen relations would be a program-planning problem), these factors need to be considered. Generally, however, they will be secondary to the fundamental purposes of the service. While measures for these factors are not presented in the illustrative criteria below, it may be appropriate for a particular jurisdiction to include such criteria for certain of its analyses.

Uncertainties and political considerations are additional evaluation factors

In addition to such nonmonetary criteria as are presented [on pages 114 to 119], and the various monetary benefits and costs, other considerations enter into final program decisions. Such factors as the amounts of uncertainty and risks involved (which should be indicated and quantified in the analysis to the extent practicable) and various political considerations may also play important parts in the final decisions. These factors can also be considered evaluation criteria and should not be ignored. Wherever possible they should be discussed, and quantified to the extent practicable, in the analysis.[13]

Criteria frequently will be difficult to measure

As has already been indicated, it will undoubtedly be extremely difficult to get good historical information on many of these criteria and to make good estimates of the future magnitudes of the criteria for the various program alternatives.[14] In some of these cases, information systems can be feasibly developed to provide improved information in the future. In cases where this appears impossible, it will still be desirable to make crude estimates— based upon judgment if nothing else.

As already noted, at the very least, alternatives can be ranked on each criterion or, a more complex technique, experts can be asked to assign a

---

[13] Note that good analysis in general will not make a decisionmaker's job easier. In fact to the extent that it provides him with additional considerations that previously were hidden, good analysis can actually make his job harder. Good analysis should, however, provide him with considerably improved information on which to base his decisions.

[14] For some criteria, it may be that "reported" data is known to be incomplete. In such cases, estimates of the unreported cases should also be made if this is at all possible. If not, the analysis or the definition of the criteria should at least make clear the omission. Examples of such unreported data are the incidences of various illnesses and of unreported crimes.

value to each criterion for each alternative based upon an arbitrary scale (for example, 1 to 10). Public opinion polls, using appropriate sampling techniques, can be used to obtain information on various "intangible" criteria (though there are many difficulties in such polls). Even this information will often be helpful. If even qualitative estimates cannot reasonably be made, substitute criteria will be necessary.

It is to be emphasized that even though an important evaluation criterion resists quantification, this does not mean it should be ignored in the analysis. Relevant qualitative information should be provided; or at the very least the inability to say anything meaningful about the criterion should be clearly pointed out along with its possible implications. The decisionmakers will then at least be alerted to the problem.

Intangibles will always be with us

The decisionmaker will inevitably be faced with major intangibles. In addition to the difficulties discussed above certain important aspects of governmental (and perhaps personal) objectives are bound to be omitted from the criteria that are quantified or discussed qualitatively. Since even the type of criteria presented here falls short of indicating ultimate "value" or "utility," and even if all the listed criteria could be satisfactorily quantified, intangibles would still remain. For example, though the number of families living in "substandard" dwelling units is a tangible figure, the "value" of reducing this number by various amounts is primarily intangible.

Most often the governmental executives will have to make these judgments

themselves. There also will be times when such intangible issues should be put before the legislative branch or directly before the voters.

Program analysis, with the use of such criteria as are contained here, can only aim at improving the relevant information on the issue at hand. It does not need to, nor can it, provide the definitive answers on program selections.

ILLUSTRATIVE LIST OF CRITERIA FOR THE EVALUATION OF PROPOSED PROGRAMS [15]

I. PERSONAL SAFETY [16]

Objective: To reduce the amount and effects of external harm to individuals and in general to maintain an atmosphere of personal security from external events.

A. Law Enforcement

Objective: To reduce the amount and effects of crime and in general to maintain an atmosphere of personal security from criminal behavior. (To some persons the punishment of criminals may be an important objective in itself as well a means to deter further crimes.)

------

[15] This is only a partial outline of programs analyzed by Mr. Hatry. See the original study paper cited earlier for criteria regarding housing, employment, recreation, and transportation programs.

[16] Criteria for personal safety are here presented for two subcategories: "Law Enforcement" and "Fire Prevention and Firefighting." Other subcategories could be identified such as "Traffic Safety" (in this paper relevant criteria for traffic issues are included under major program area VII) and "Protection From Natural and Manmade Disasters." The appendix illustrates the particular subcategories that might be included under this, as well as the other, major program areas. [Not shown.]

1. Annual number of offenses for each major class of crime (or reduction from the base in the number of crimes).

2. Crime rates, as for example, the number per 1,000 inhabitants per year, for each major class of crime.

3. Crime rate index that includes all offenses of a particular type (e.g., "crimes of violence" or "crimes against property"), perhaps weighted as to seriousness of each class of offense.

4. Number and percent of populace committing "criminal" acts during the year. (This is a less common way to express the magnitude of the crime problem; it is criminal oriented rather than "crime oriented.")

5. Annual value of property lost (adjusted for price-level changes). This value might also be expressed as a percent of the total property value in the community.

6. An index of overall community "feeling of security" from crime, perhaps based on public opinion polls and/or opinions of experts.

7. Percent of reported crimes cleared by arrest and "assignment of guilt" by a court.

8. Average time between occurrence of a crime and the apprehension of the criminal.[17]

9. Number of apparently justified complaints of police excesses by private citizens, perhaps as adjudged by the police review board.

10. Number of persons subse-

quently found to be innocent who were punished and/or simply arrested.

NOTES

(a) Criteria 1 through 6 are criteria for the evaluation of crime-prevention programs. Criteria 7 and 8 are aimed at evaluating crime control after crimes have occurred (i.e., when crime prevention has failed). Criteria 9 and 10 and to some extent 6 aim at the avoidance of law-enforcement practices that themselves have an adverse effect upon personal safety. Criterion 6 and to some extent 8 aim at indicating the presence of a fearful, insecure atmosphere in the locality.

(b) Some argue that the primary function of criminal apprehension and punishment is to prevent future crimes; and, therefore, that criteria 7 and 8 would not be sufficiently "end oriented," but rather "means" oriented, and would not be included in the list.

(c) For many analyses it would probably be appropriate to distinguish crime activity by the type of criminal, including such characteristics as age, sex, family income, etc. (juvenile delinquency is an obvious subcategory).

B. Fire Prevention and Firefighting

Objective: To reduce the number of fires and loss due to fires.

1. Annual number of fires of various magnitudes (to be defined).

2. Fire rates, for example, number per 10,000 inhabitants per year.

3. Annual dollar value of property loss due to fire (adjusted for price level changes).

4. Annual dollar value of property lost due to fire per $1 million of total property value in the locality.

5. Annual number of persons

---

[17] A major purpose of criterion 8 as used in this list is to reflect the psychological reduction in anxiety due to the length of this time period. Note that it is not the purpose of this or any of these criteria to evaluate the efficiency of the police organization.

killed or injured to various degrees of seriousness due to fires.

6. Reduction in number of fires, in injuries, in lives lost, and in dollars of property loss from the base. (These are primarily different forms of criteria 1, 3, and 5 and can be substituted for them.) This reduction might in part be obtained by, for example, drawing inferences from the number of fire code violations (by type) found.[18]

7. Average time required to put out fires from the time they were first observed, for various classes of fires.

NOTES

(*a*) Criteria 1 through 6 are intended for evaluation of fire prevention programs. Criteria 7 and to some extent 3, 4, and 5 can reflect the results of programs which aim at the control of fires after they have started. Criterion 7 also is a proxy for the anxiety related to duration of fires.

(*b*) It may be appropriate to distinguish among geographical areas within the jurisdiction.

II. HEALTH

Objective: To provide for the physical and mental health of the citizenry, including reduction of the number,

length, and severity of illnesses and disabilities.

1. Incidence of illness and prevalence (number and rates).[19] (Armed Forces rates of rejection for health reasons of persons from the jurisdiction could be used as a partial criterion.)

2. Annual mortality rates by major cause and for total population.[20]

3. Life expectancy by age groups.

4. Average number of days of restricted activity, bed confinement, and medically attended days per person per year. (Such terms as "restricted activity" need to be clearly and thoroughly defined. Also, probably more than one level of severity of illness should be identified.)

5. Average number of workdays per person lost due to illness per year.

6. Total and per capita number of school days lost owing to illness per year.

7. Number of illnesses prevented, deaths averted, and restricted-activity days averted per year as compared with the base. This is primarily a different form of such criteria as 1 through 6.

8. Average number of days of restricted activity, of bed confinement and of medically attended days per illness per year.

9. Number and percent of patients "cured" (of specific types of illnesses and various degrees of cure).

10. Some measure of the average

---

[18] From current data on the violations found, estimates could be prepared of the number of additional violations that would be found and corrected if more fire-code inspectors were added. However, the more important (that is, the higher level) criterion is not the number of violations found and corrected but the reduction in the number of fires and in the loss of lives and property. To get to this higher level criterion, estimates would have to be made of the consequences of not finding and correcting such violations. This footnote is included to indicate the kinds of inferences that are likely to be needed in program analyses. Similar situations can be identified for many of the other criteria presented in this list.

[19] Here and in the following material the term "illness" is also intended to cover disability and impairments.

[20] Suicide rates should be included; these are likely to provide some indication of the overall mental health of the community. Note that reducing mortality from certain causes would presumably increase mortality from other causes. Life expectancy, criterion 3, is thus a more important overall criterion.

degree of pain and suffering per illness. (Though there seems to be no such measure currently in use, some rough index of pain and suffering could probably be developed.)

11. Some measure, perhaps from a sampling of experts and of patients, as to the average amount of unpleasantness (including consideration of the environment in the care area) associated with the care and cure of illnesses.

12. Number or percent of persons with aftereffects, of different degrees, after "cure."

13. Number or percent of persons needing but unable to afford "appropriate health care"—both before receiving public assistance and after including any public assistance received.

14. Number or percent of persons needing but unable to receive "appropriate health care" because of insufficient facilities or services.

15. Some measure of the overall "vigor," the positive health, of the populace, rather than simply the absence of illness—such as "the average per capita energy capacity." Meaningful measures are needed.

NOTES

(a) A number of subobjectives can be identified for this major program area. Those subobjectives and the criteria that attempt to measure each are as follows:

1. Prevention of illness—criteria 1 through 7.

2. "Cure" of patient when illness occurs including reduction of its duration—criteria 1 through 9.

3. Reduction of unpleasantness, suffering, anxiety, etc., associated with illness—criteria 10 and 11.

4. Reduction of aftereffects—criterion 12.

5. Making necessary health care available to the "needy"—criteria 13 and 14.

Note, however, that during consideration of the overall problem of health, these subobjectives will often compete with each other. For example, with limited funds, they might be applied to programs aimed primarily at preventing an illness or at reducing its severity (or at some mix of these programs). Also note that criteria 1 through 7 are affected by programs that are directed at curing illnesses as well as those directed at preventing them.

(b) The criteria can be defined to distinguish among specific types of illnesses as well as to consider the aggregate effect on individuals of all possible illnesses. For certain problems the incidence of a specific disease may be of concern, whereas for other problems the incidence of illness per person per year, regardless of specific disease, might be the appropriate criterion. One such breakdown which is very likely to be desirable distinguishes mental health from physical health, though even here there will be interactions.

(c) Note that such common measures as "hospital-bed capacity" or "utilization rates of available medical facilities" are not included above since these are not fundamental indicators of the effectiveness of health programs.

(d) As with most of the major program areas, program analyses will need to consider the contributions of other sectors, including private institutions and activities undertaken by other jurisdictions.

(e) The role of governmental jurisdictions may emphasize health services for certain specific target groups such as the needy, and the very young. Therefore, it will frequently be appropriate to distinguish target groups by such characteristics as family income, race, family size, and age group.

(*f*) To further focus on the positive side of health, in addition to the use of criterion 15, such criteria as 4 might be replaced by such criteria as "average number of healthy days (appropriately defined) per person per year."

III. INTELLECTUAL DEVELOPMENT

Objective: To provide satisfactory opportunities for intellectual development to the citizenry. See also notes (*b*) and (*c*) below.

1. Annual number and percent of persons satisfactorily completing various numbers of years of schooling.

2. Annual number and percent of dropouts at various educational levels.

3. Annual number and percent of each age group enrolled in educational institutions.

4. "Intellectual development attainment" measures, such as performance on various standardized achievement tests at different ages and educational levels.[21] Major educational areas, for example, reading skills, reasoning skills, and general knowledge, might be measured.

5. Performance on the achievement tests indicated in criterion 4 as related to intelligence tests (to indicate attainment relative to capacity).

6. Annual number and percent of students continuing their education at post-high-school educational institutions.

7. Participation in selected cultural and civic activities (and perhaps the number of persons who read newspapers, or at least certain parts of them).

NOTES

(*a*) Criteria 1, 2, and 3 emphasize quantity of formal education received. Criteria 4, 5, 6, and 7 attempt to indicate the quality of education received. Since formal education is not the only means to intellectual development, criteria such as 4, 5, and 7, when various age groups are considered, should be applied to persons regardless of whether they are in school or not or how much formal education they have had. Criterion 6 also provides some information as to the success of education to stimulate intellectual curiosity. None of the criteria provides much help in measuring the development of individual creativity, if it can indeed be developed.

(*b*) Education not only affects intellectual development but also social development. The above criteria (with the minor exception of 7) fail to measure such things as "social adjustment," "responsible citizenship," and increased "personal pleasure." Such criteria as crime rates, juvenile delinquency rates, including school vandalism, etc., such as are used for major program area I, "personal safety," might be used to draw inferences on certain aspects of social adjustment.

(*c*) "Education" clearly may be a means to other ends (for example, to lower crime rates) as well as an end in itself. In fact some persons may consider education to be primarily a means to increase future dollar earnings and therefore would consider the above criteria solely as proxy measures for

---

[21] Armed Forces rejection rates—for intelligence reasons—of persons from the jurisdiction could be used to provide a partial measure.

getting at earnings. If so, education programs would better be considered under major program area V, "economic satisfaction and satisfactory work opportunity for the individual." The perspective here is that education and, more broadly, intellectual development, has more than economic value to individuals and society, and is, therefore, an important end in itself. The objectives: to increase earnings, to increase job opportunities and job satisfaction, and to supply needed scarce skills are, in the categorization used in this paper, considered under major program area V. Education programs are some of the means to these ends and in this role would need to be considered in performing such program analyses.

(*d*) To estimate quality of formal education, frequently such "proxy" indicators are used as "annual expenditures per student," "professional-student ratios," "number of professionals with advanced degrees," "teacher salary levels," etc. These are less direct, lower level criteria than those given above, but nevertheless may be of some use if qualified sufficiently.

(*e*) The role of government in intellectual development varies considerably among jurisdictions.

(*f*) It will frequently be appropriate to distinguish target groups by such characteristics as: race, family income level, family size, and sex.

CASE

3

PEACE CORPS

PROGRAM STRUCTURE, OBJECTIVES, AND EVALUATION CRITERIA

In the summer of 1967 Mr. Lincoln Vernon, analyst in the Peace Corps' Office of the Director of Planning and Program Review, was a member of a study group whose task was to evaluate the Peace Corps' PPB System. Mr. Vernon had been asked to focus particularly on recommending improved output measures which could be related to the program structure, and to

consider how Peace Corps personnel could best establish tangible goals and then measure the degree of achievement of these goals.

This case was prepared with the cooperation of the Peace Corps by Graeme M. Taylor under the supervision of Warren A. Law, Professor of Business Administration, Harvard University, on behalf of the Bureau of the Budget. The case is intended for class discussion only, and certain names and facts

MISSION AND ORGANIZATION
OF THE PEACE CORPS

The Peace Corps was created by Executive Order on March 1, 1961; the first volunteers were trained and sent to their overseas assignments during the summer of 1961. In September, 1961 Congress passed the Peace Corps Act, which declared that the purpose of the Peace Corps was to "promote world peace and friendship by making available to interested countries and areas men and women of the United States qualified for service abroad and willing to serve, under conditions of hardship if necessary, to help the peoples of such countries and areas in meeting their needs for trained manpower, and to help promote a better understanding of the American people on the part of the peoples served and better understanding of other peoples on the part of the American people."

The Peace Corps was to be an independent agency within the Department of State. Overseas, all Peace Corps personnel in a host country, including the country director, were to be responsible to the United States ambassador. The organization of the Peace Corps in July, 1967 is shown in Exhibit 1. As of June 30, 1967 the Peace Corps had 3,057 volunteers undergoing training, and 11,895 volunteers serving in 53 countries and one U. S. trust territory. A summary of the

may have been changed which, while avoiding the disclosure of confidential information, do not materially lessen the value of the case for educational purposes. This case is not intended to represent either effective or ineffective handling of an administrative situation, nor does it purport to be a statement of policy by the agency involved.

number of volunteers serving in Latin American countries is shown in Exhibit 2. In fiscal year 1962 the Peace Corps budget was $30 million; by 1967 it had risen to $110 million. Administrative costs as a percentage of the total budget dropped from 32% in 1962 to 20% in 1967, and the average annual cost per volunteer dropped from $9,074 in 1963 to $7,400 in 1967.

Unlike other foreign assistance programs of the U. S. government, the Peace Corps' method of operation was based on personal relationships between individual volunteers and citizens of the host country. The unique flavor of the Peace Corps way of doing things is perhaps captured in the following extracts from the Peace Corps' Annual Report for 1966:

In 1961, the Peace Corps took the drab concept of public service and gave it dash. It was high adventure with higher purpose, a blow against the chauvinism of the 50's, a disarming, fresh approach to international relations. It appealed equally to the gambling instincts and social consciousness of youth, and to the forgotten idealism of older generations.

If the early Peace Corps was more of an approach than a solution, no one seemed to mind. In a world beset by ambiguity and chronic mistrust, it had the ring of truth and that was enough.

Today, five years later, it is not nearly enough. The Peace Corps is a victim of its own innovations. Once the child prodigy of public service, it must now skip quickly over adolescence and become a responsible adult in a world it helped to sophisticate.

Within the Peace Corps in 1967 there was a growing emphasis on the significance of the third "legislative goal" stated in the Peace Corps Act:

... (to promote) a better understanding of other peoples on the part of the American People.

It had been recognized that Peace Corps training and service not only "promoted a better understanding of other peoples" on the part of the returning volunteer, but also helped mold the character of the volunteer. Hence, the increased ability of the returning volunteer to make a contribution to society in the United States was recognized as a significant output of the Peace Corps program.

As of June, 1966, the returned Peace Corps volunteers were occupied as follows:

Continuing education:	2,739 volunteers
Teaching:	1,363 "
Federal, State and Local Government:	1,145 "
Business and non-profit organizations:	792 "
Extended Peace Corps Service:	530 "
Housewife:	301 "
Other:	187 "

THE PEACE CORPS' PPB SYSTEM

On March 14, 1966, the Peace Corps' Director of the Office of Planning and Program Review (OPP) issued a memorandum to all field representatives describing the Peace Corps' Planning-Programming-Budgeting System. The program structure consisted of five program categories:

1. Program Direction and Support
2. Food Supply
3. Education
4. Health and Sanitation
5. Public and Private Institutions

A detailed breakdown of the program structure is shown in Exhibit 3. A separate Program Memorandum (PM) was to be prepared for each host country.

It was suggested that the PM be structured around answers to the following questions:

1. What are the major problems facing your country in the next five years?
2. Which of these problems, or which elements of these problems, lend themselves to volunteer programs— Peace Corps or other?
3. What goals can the Peace Corps in your country set for itself in relation to these pressing issues?
4. What alternative programs would achieve these goals?
5. How do these alternative approaches compare in terms of cost effectiveness and host country interest?
6. Which program alternatives are best?

Each PM was expected to conclude with a table projecting the five-year estimated number of Volunteers required for each program subcategory.

The full text of the memorandum's discussion of question number 3 is given below:

Consideration should be given to the reasonable alternatives available in selecting goals and some explanation offered as to why you selected the goal or goals you did. The goals should be stated with enough precision so that there is some basis for assessing progress over a reasonable period of time, although they need not necessarily be attainable by 1971. They can be general ("to help the government expand its agriculture extension service"), or, hopefully, expressed in quantitative terms ("to provide agricultural extension services to 10,000 farmers in the northeast"). The system however does not require that programs be distorted by selecting those goals and programs which are quantifiable simply because they are quantifiable. While goals set should be responsive to the problems of the country and not to PPBS quantification desiderata, they should be stated to permit assessment of progress made toward the goals you set.

In discussing question number 4, the memorandum gave the following caveat:

In assessing alternative approaches you must, of course, consider host country priorities and programs in each problem area, including programs assisted by public and private assistance agencies or foundations. Host country requests will obviously be the principal governing factor for program allocations in 1967 and even 1968. In your longer range analysis, however, you may assume that we can convince host governments of our effectiveness in activities not open to us or which we have never undertaken.

The memorandum recognized that:

...forecasting in most countries is at best informed but hazardous guesswork, especially for Peace Corps programs. The limitations of such projections without host country participation is recognized. What is wanted in the material required for the system is the best judgment of each Peace Corps country director about the future of the country and of the Peace Corps in that country. To the extent that the country director has developed the kind of continuing exchanges with host country nationals which shape his judgments, so much the better. The program forecasts will need to be reviewed and revised often to reflect host country conditions and requests. Throughout your analysis, your knowledge of host country plans, priorities, and problems should be brought to bear.

Included in the discussion of question number 5 were the following comments on

Each alternative program category should be compared in terms of capability of achieving goals which you set. If you set maximum production of teachers as your goal in the primary schools, it is quite likely that by adding 500 teacher trainers, 100% of the children would be eventually affected. On the other hand, if the Peace Corps sent 500 primary teachers, they would be in only one of every thirty primary schools. If you set some other goal, thirty primary schools may be precisely the geographic areas or may have precisely the demonstration effect your goal requires.

The discussion of question number 6 follows:

Your analysis and comparison of alternative programs should permit you to select, on the basis of cost-effectiveness, the most promising programs and to indicate an order of priority among your program choices. These priorities (or minimum size projects) should be clear enough to serve as guidelines when cuts in the program become necessary because of Volunteer input or other limitations.

To illustrate the types of "output measures" that might be used, the memorandum concluded with a table listing possible output measures for the three legislative goals by Program Category and Sub-Category. This table is reproduced as Exhibit 3.

After the country directors had responded to OPP's request for Program Memoranda, the following letter was sent to the field by the Director of OPP on November 22, 1966:

The Peace Corps Planning-Programming-Budgeting System is well under way. A Program Memorandum, including your individual country papers, has been given to the Budget Bureau and is serving as the basis for a Summer Program Plan made up of your highest-priority projects. The Peace Corps has an improved sense of direction and involvement with the most critical problems of the developing world.

The next step in making the System even more valuable is to sharpen our description of what we are trying to do and to begin collecting information that indicates our progress. Measurement of what happens as a result of a Peace Corps project is not easy, but it is important that we begin trying to do it, for only this way can the full significance of Peace Corps work be recognized, by us or anyone else.

The Regional Offices and OPP are working together to develop a set of possible indicators and method for systematically collecting information about them. Some suggested measures were also included in the March 14, 1966, draft instruction on preparation of Country Program Memoranda.

The purpose of this letter is to involve you in this effort. We are asking you to select *one* project which has been in country for at least eight months and to go through the steps necessary to produce meaningful information about performance. We want to find out whether this can be done and, if it can, the least burdensome and most useful ways of doing it.

Pick a project for which you had a specific goal or goals in mind. State what they are and then select one *or more* indices which you think give some indication of progress in relation to these goals. Try to keep them simple and clear, so that the person collecting the information knows what to look for. There is no intention to develop an elaborate system of measurements with exhaustive questionnaires. We hope you can help us come up with information that yields a few meaningful figures with a minimum of collection difficulties.

The gathering of information should involve Volunteers as much as possible. You may be able to find other sources of information as well. Volunteers may be able to provide information from general observation and their daily work (e.g. number of pupils taught, number of farmers raising chickens) or they may have to explore further (e.g., number of Volunteer-trained mechanics who have found work, number of clubs now functioning independently). We want to find out how Volunteers feel about taking a look at Peace Corps and what kinds of information can be collected without detriment to their work.

A brief note setting forth the goals, measurement criteria and summarized information should then be sent to your Regional Director. Any explanations, criticisms and suggestions will be helpful. The results of your efforts will determine the manner in which we proceed with our efforts to appraise Peace Corps performance.

Since we have no previously established guides to what may be expected of a project, the information you furnish will not be used in cost-benefit analysis or for invidious comparisons. It will be helpful to us, and hopefully to you, in getting a more realistic idea of what can be expected to happen in future projects of like intent.

We would hope to have your replies within a month after you receive this letter.

On February 15, 1967, the Director of OPP sent a memorandum to the field outlining instructions for submission of PM's for the 1968–1972 planning period. Part of the text of this memorandum is given below:

The first memoranda have given us some ideas which should make the revisions even more useful, without creating additional work. The revised program memorandum will be an effort to refine further and to make more explicit your reasons for choosing a particular program strategy over available alternatives. There will be more discussion of your reasons for arriving at projected total strength and distribution with less review of broad critical problems and conceivable but unlikely alternatives. It will also include a section relating your program projections to staff and other costs, so that Peace Corps can build up budget requirements directly from anticipated field programs. This should improve our ability to provide you with all of the elements needed for the success of your program.

The revised program memorandum should be in narrative form as before, answering similar questions briefly and informatively. A copy of last year's instruction is included to refresh your recollection, but the revision should use the following format:

1. *In which critical problem areas facing your country do you propose that the Peace Corps assist and in what order of priority do you rank them?*

General discussion of the major problems facing your country may be omitted and it will be assumed that you have reviewed these problems and determined which of them lend themselves to Volunteer programs. Your analysis should be concentrated on describing the problems, and the elements of them, to which you give priority for Peace Corps work and your reasons for electing these priorities. Discussion of priorities should include data and comment on seriousness and extent of problems, host country interest and ability to do something about them, and your appraisal of the significance of Peace Corps participation for assisting in their solutions. If your choice of priority is based upon certain assumptions about the kinds of people or material assistance that Peace Corps or others may provide, that should be clearly stated, so that your program may benefit from new developments. (For example, 'If Peace Corps could supply 300 math/science teachers, instead of generalists, the problems of education would be our highest priority.' If Peace Corps does get more math/science teachers, your true priority can be honored.)

Countries for which no program memorandum has yet been written should follow the previous instruction. This will allow country directors to present the broad discussion of critical problems and Peace Corps alternatives which is particularly useful in initial memoranda. The previous instruction should be modified to provide for use of June 30th dates in the five-year forecast and should include the table and discussion of staff and cost projections which are described at the end of this memorandum.

Where a program memorandum has already been done, the discussion and analysis of problem priorities should refer to the earlier memorandum and may, in many cases, be no more than an updating and refinement of it. Where country conditions have changed substantially or Peace Corps programming has deviated from original projections, detailed explanation should be given.

In your discussion, after indicating the problem areas in which you propose to involve the Peace Corps, please set forth the broad goals or objectives of Peace Corps involvement. The purpose of the discussion is to explain as clearly as possible what you think the Peace Corps ought to be doing in your country and why. It should be noted, however, that, *if* goals are broadly stated (e.g., 'to increase social development,' 'to transform the rural areas'), you should then define what these goals mean in relation to specific problem areas, such as agriculture, education, and economic activity. (Thus, 'The broad goal of increasing social development involves Peace Corps in agriculture because . . . the broad goal of transforming the rural areas involves Peace Corps in health work because . . .').

Many country directors have preferred to choose broader goals rather than limiting focus to the critical problem areas offered in the earlier instruction. There are advantages to concentrating on one or two priority problem areas, but your country program goals may be stated more broadly if you wish.

While you may start at any level of abstraction you choose, your statement of goals should be refined to a point that permits you and others to assess the progress that may be made by individual Peace Corps projects directed toward these goals. Your broad statement of goals and objectives should also be refined sufficiently to permit *project* alternatives to be placed in the program structure categories:

Food Supply (the problem of hunger)
Education (the problem of ignorance)
Health and Sanitation (the problem of sickness and disease)
Public and Private Institutions (the problem of nation building)
Other problems

2. *Consideration of alternatives.*

This section is no longer expected to be a review of all program possibilities you can think of. It is, rather, intended to be your justification for choosing the preferred alternative projects which you will include in your five-year forecast. To do this effectively will require some discussion of your reasons for rejecting obvious alternatives which initially would seem to be equally effective for reaching your goals. If your choice of alternatives is limited by host country priorities and programs or determined by particular host country conditions, your conclusion and the reasons for it should be stated. Discussion of preferred alternatives should make very clear the unique capacity of Peace Corps for performing the chosen tasks or the advantages of Peace Corps participation over alternative approaches.

In considering alternatives, you should weigh carefully the costs of a particular project against the benefits or results likely to follow from it. Do not reject an alternative simply because of cost, if you feel that impact will far exceed that of lower cost projects. The Peace Corps is prepared to experiment with longer training, additional material or staff support, and other added costs where justified.

After you have chosen your preferred alternatives and discussed their order or priority, explain how the goals of each are related to your broad program goals *and the means by which results in each alternative would be measured.* We are not looking for project targets (e.g., 'As a result of this project 3500 farmers will adopt _____ technique of wheat cultivation and increase wheat yield by 8%'), but rather the terms in which results can be appraised (e.g., 'The results of this project will be measured, in part, by the number of individual farmers adopting _____ technique of wheat cultivation and the percentage change in wheat yields among farmers with whom Volunteers work, etc. . . .').

Once again, it would be helpful to know if your selection of a project is due to some assumption about the kind of Volunteers Peace Corps can provide, since this is subject to some variation. For example, Peace Corps will be experimenting this summer with a number of degree programs that offer potential for dramatically increasing our supplies of certain specialties.

The narrative portion of your revised program memorandum should conclude with a discussion of the factors affecting the total country program strength reflected in your five-year forecast. Include in your discussion the constraints resulting from host country positions, your ideas on saturation, absence of host country support or structure, and any other considerations you think relevant.

In addition, point out any limitations placed on your total program by shortages of skilled Volunteers in different categories. You need make no specific assumption regarding worldwide Peace Corps Volunteer numbers, since recent experience indicates possibilities for wide variation in individual country totals independent of the worldwide total. Do not hesitate to project a doubling or more of your present strength if that is what you think optimum program effectiveness requires. You may assume that any reduction from the total you project will be taken from the areas to which you give lowest priority.

Your revised program memorandum should continue with a program forecast table projecting your estimate of Volunteers requested for the program activities you choose over the period 1968–1972. Your 1968 figures should reflect all projects actually approved for implementation at the time of your revision. The categories and activities have not been changed. The test of classification is now 'in which program category does the project seek to implement country goals?' If, for example, you propose what is apparently a food supply project to achieve what is primarily a nation-building purpose, the project should be placed in the food supply category. It represents an alternative for achieving the goal of nation-building and your choice of it should be explained in terms of that goal.

The absence of output measurement tables from the revised program memoranda is deliberate. The need for measurement of performance will be met by installation of a routine data collection procedure, which we hope to initiate before June 1. The procedure will be based on replies received to our request for an initial measurement effort and will be adaptable to your situation and requirements. References to measurement in the revised program memoranda may be limited to the explanations made, in choosing your preferred alternative projects, of how project success in progressing toward goals is to be determined. Individual project descriptions submitted for Program Plan cycles can then be used to provide more detailed statements of suggested output measures.

THE PROGRAM MEMORANDUM FOR LATINIA

Mr. Vernon had before him the Program Memorandum submitted by the Peace Corps director for the South American country of Latinia. After listing the basic problems facing Latinia, the PM went on to state the goals of the Peace Corps in Latinia in the areas of rural development, education, urban development, and industrial development. The rural development goals were stated as follows:

Overall goal: To increase the quantity and quality of local food production and consumption and to strengthen the capabilities and increase the commitment of Latinian agencies involved specifically in agricultural development.

Particular projects and goals: (a) General agricultural and home economics work with the agricultural extension service to provide technical assistance in agriculture and home economics, especially in the mountain regions where there is a great need for technical aid and craft services and a severe shortage of extension workers. (b) Technical assistance work through the extension service and the Latinian Institute of Cooperatives with already existing agricultural cooperatives, to teach better management procedures and to strengthen the cooperative movement as a means of food production and the dissemination of technical assistance; this work will focus on coastal areas. (c) Youth work through the extension service to strengthen the activities of Latinia's 4H Clubs in programs of food production, information dissemination, and leadership training; this work will focus on the mountain regions.

In addition to these larger projects, there will be an experimental program in rural education, working through rural community schools, to undertake commercial projects in food production and agricultural extension.

The PM also contained a section discussing choice of indices for evaluation of program effectiveness, a brief portion of which is reproduced below:

Indices for Evaluation of Project Effectiveness

Although quantitative indicators are not totally valid representations of the effects or effectiveness of Peace Corps programs, quantitative assessment will be used to supplement staff and Volunteers' thinking and to introduce rigor in program approaches.

Two major limitations to accurate quantitative measurement are:

1) The lack of staff time, proficiency and resources to devise and implement the rigorous research and evaluation procedures necessary for valid measurement.

2) The dangers of "spoiling" the Volunteers' responses to assessment devices through the frequent application of questionnaires, interviews, etc. to the same persons.

Measurement of the change is a sophisticated scientific process which is expensive, time consuming and requires expert personnel.

The following schema of variables will be assessed for each project using Volunteer questionnaires and reporting by the associate representatives.

A. Rural Development—Food Production
   1. Agricultural Extension
      a) Process Goals
         1) Number of individual farmers assisted by Volunteers on a regular basis (one contact/week)
         2) Number of Cooperatives assisted by Volunteers on a regular basis.
         3) Number of 4H Clubs assisted by Volunteers on a regular basis.
         4) Number of new permanent relationships established between extension service personnel and farmers as a result of Volunteer effort.
         5) Number of improvements in use of fertilizers, seeds, machinery or other technological methods introduced to number of farmers on a permanent basis.

End goals
1) Increases in total production by assisted farmers.
2) Increases in yield (prod./hectare) of assisted farmers.
3) Increases in income of assisted farmers.

THE CORNELL EVALUATION STUDY OF PEACE CORPS PROGRAMS IN PERU

The Cornell Peru Project of the Department of Anthropology, Cornell University, had performed a study titled "Measurement of Peace Corps Program Impact in the Peruvian Andes." The 329-page study, published in January, 1966, was described in the Peace Corps 1966 Annual Report as follows:

It reports on a two-year study by a group of anthropologists from Cornell University.

Fifty Peace Corps Volunteers were put under a social science microscope from the time they entered training in the summer of 1962 to the time they completed service; the 15 communities where they worked were assessed before, during and after their tours.

The report states that the Peace Corps program in the Peruvian Andes did achieve a measurable impact—communities with Peace Corps Volunteers developed nearly three times as fast as those without.

Peace Corps' first Director, Sargent Shriver, viewed the report as being of 'great practical and historical significance.'

'For the first time,' said Shriver, 'we have objective, scientific validation of the successes Peace Corps Volunteers are registering in the field of community development. It is hard, demanding work in isolated areas under sometimes difficult and frustrating conditions, but the report shows that the Volunteers have been successful even beyond our initial hopes.'

Dr. Henry F. Dobyns, one of the Cornell research team leaders, describing the report's findings, said that in the field of community development 'results are normally computed over the course of decades . . . (but) these Volunteers produced measurable results in two years. Some would consider this progress incredible.'

The following extracts from the Cornell report describe the design and findings of the research project.

The Peruvian National Plan for Integrating the Aboriginal Population requested Peace Corps Volunteers for each of four Departmental [1] Integration Programs. Volunteers were recruited, trained, and assigned to the PNIPA for these four area programs. The settlements affected by these programs could be, therefore, considered as 'experimental' communities in terms of research design. These populations would be subjected to the stimulus of Peace Corps Volunteer activities. A certain quantity of data about each of these communities was already available, moreover, to provide measures of their condition and characteristics before they were affected by Peace Corps Volunteers. The members of the Cornell Peru Project could hope, then, to measure the amount of change the presence of Volunteers in these settlements produced, by studying their condition and characteristics after the Volunteers completed their assignments and left, and comparing these with the pre-Peace Corps program situation.

The members of the Cornell Peru Project could not expect that the changes Peace Corps Volunteers might bring about in these particular communities where the Peruvian government was conducting Indian integration programs would go on without regard and completely independently of changes occurring simultaneously in the other communities that make up the Peruvian nation. As social scientists, the members of the Cornell Peru Project recognized that local settlements

---

[1] Department: like the French "Département," a Peruvian Department was the largest governmental unit within the country.

in modern national states are subject to many and varied influences. In order to complete a truly comparative design, therefore, the Cornell Peru Project planned to select more or less matched communities which would serve for comparison to the 'experimental' communities benefitting from Peace Corps programs. By definition, the comparative communities would be settlements where no Peace Corps Volunteers were assigned during the period of Peace Corps activity in the 'experimental' communities. . . .

The four anthropologists actively engaged in collecting field data for this study developed a one hundred point scale of social structure that permits the direct comparison of the relative degree of socio-economic differentiation in Peruvian settlements.

In selecting the indices included in this scale, its authors deliberately sought measures that would place the Peruvian national capital, Lima, at 100 on this scale. The city is both the largest population agglomerate in Peru, with over 2,000,000 inhabitants, and by far the most differentiated Peruvian city in terms of commerce, finance, industry, the arts and sciences, and government.

In structuring the scale in this way, its authors consciously limited the universality of application of this particular scale to other national societies. The continuum employed for Peruvian analysis cannot be utilized without modification for the direct comparison of communities in the United States, for example. The major metropolitan area in the United States, New York, is not the national capital of the country, for one thing, so that the specific continuum here employed would not apply to this condition without qualification. The situation in the United Kingdom where London is both the national capital and the major metropolis is much more parallel to the Peruvian national structure. There are a number of other nations where this population dominance of the national capital city does also obtain—Mexico, Argentina, France, Italy, Chile, Venezuela, Japan.

In developing the hundred item scale that follows, its authors proceeded to select indices that seemed to them relevant in terms of their accumulated experience in Peruvian research.

SCALE OF SOCIAL STRUCTURE OF PERUVIAN SETTLEMENTS

Governmental Structure

1. National Capital—seat of Congress, chief executive, and principal national appellate court.
2. Department capital—seat of a Prefect, analog of a state in Mexico or the United States.
3. Provincial capital—seat of a Subprefect, analog of a county in the United States.
4. District Capital—seat of registrar of vital statistics, and the smallest official unit of national government. The *Alcalde* (principal administrative officer) may or may not reside in the district capital.
5. Police protection—defined as having a resident policeman of the *Guardia Civil,* the national militarized police force.
6. Government buildings other than those specified in other categories (e.g., community headquarters, customs sheds, military or naval barracks).
7. Public Charity Society (Sociedad de Beneficencia Publica) a public assistance and welfare agency endowed with land, often manors with serfs bound to them.
8. Community land ownership—parks, central square, streets, commons, etc.
9. Municipal police force, independent of national police.

Educational Structure

10. Graduate level university instruction.
11. University level instruction, including normal schools.
12. Secondary level instruction, defined here as complete, e.g., five years.
13. Primary level instruction, defined here as five grades.
14. Literates—one or more literate residents (% if known).
15. Primary school graduates—one or more residents (% if known).
16. Secondary school graduates—one or more such residents (% if known).
17. University graduates—one or more such residents (% if known).
18. Agricultural extension services.

Religious Structure

19. Seat of archbishop or cardinal.
20. Diocesan seat with cathedral and resident bishop.
21. Parish headquarters, with resident parish priest.
22. Church or chapel building.
23. Protestant chapel and congregation.
24. Religious lay voluntary associations that are permanent and formally organized, other than congregations.

Basic Community Services

25. Electricity—electric power plant, public lighting, household service.
26. Market—public marketing area, supervised and housed in public building.
27. Water supply, piped into public taps and/or houses.
28. Canal irrigation works.
29. Public square—improved (e.g., concrete walks, trees, shrubs, fountains, etc.).
30. Paved or cobbled streets.
31. Garbage collection and disposal.
32. Swimming pool.
33. Public school pupil-feeding program.
34. Welfare program (such as Caritas).
35. Intra-city bus, colectivo, taxi service.
36. Sports field.

37. Cemetery.
38. Public library, or sectarian or private.
39. Museum—public or private (number per 1,000 population if known).

Communications

40. Airport and regular flights.
41. Railway.
42. Highway—a vehicular road that is passable.
43. Post Office.
44. Telegraphic service.
45. Telephonic service.
46. Interprovincial tramp truck service and scheduled truckers.
47. Interprovincial bus service.

Health Services

48. Medical service—settlement receives regular visits by doctor.
49. Resident physician (or number per thousand inhabitants).
50. Hospital.
51. Resident nurse(s).
52. Medical post.

Mass Media

53. Daily newspaper—published in settlement.
54. Weekly newspaper locally published.
55. Weekly, bimonthly or monthly magazines published.
56. Radio station.
57. Television station.
58. Book publishing industry.
59. Newspaper reading—metropolitan newspapers are delivered and read **regularly.**
60. Banking institutions—main offices, branches, agencies.
61. Credit unions, including housing co-operatives, loan associations, finance companies.

Industrial Structure

62. Construction industry with specialized skills (e.g., mason, tile factory).
63. Processing industry—soda water, mineral water, canneries, brewery, cordage mill, match factory, vegeta-

ble oil mill, soap factory, furniture factory.

64. Clothing industry—textiles, shoes, hats, etc.
65. Metallurgical industry—extraction, processing, manufacture (e.g., railway shops, machine manufacture).
66. Pharmaceutical industry.
67. Chemical industry (e.g., caustic soda).

Commercial Recreation

68. Moving picture theaters.
69. Legitimate theaters.
70. Concert band or orchestra (European instruments)—professional full-time musicians.
71. Bull-ring or stadium.
72. Indoor recreation (e.g., billiards, night clubs, bowling alleys, shooting galleries, skating rinks, gymnasiums.

Commercial Differentiation

73. Fair, regularly held.
74. General retail stores.
75. Specialized stores—wholesalers.
76. Specialized stores—groceries.
77. Specialized stores—clothing (e.g., hat, shoe, tailor, underwear, tie).
78. Specialized stores—department.
79. Specialized stores—pharmacies.
80. Specialized stores—hardware.
81. Specialized stores—garage, gasoline station.
82. Specialized stores—automobile dealer.
83. Specialized stores—glass (e.g., plate, window, picture, glasswares).
84. Specialized stores—book or magazine.
85. Specialized stores—home appliances (e.g., radio, sewing machine, refrigerator, stove, record player).
86. Specialized stores—agricultural supplies (e.g., seed, fertilizer, implements, tractors).
87. Specialized stores—photographic.
88. Specialized stores—bakeries.
89. Specialized services—insurance.
90. Specialized services—undertaking.
91. Specialized services—barbers and beauticians.
92. Specialized services—hotels, including inns and pensions.
93. Specialized services—restaurants and drinking establishments (bars, taverns, soda parlors).
94. Locally owned trucks and other motor vehicles.
95. Cooperative (producers' or consumers').
96. Skilled commercial handicraft production.

Other

97. Settlement is a target of migration.
98. Cosmopolitanism—foreign colony or colonies.
99. Social clubs, either purely local or multi-settlement (e.g., Masons, country club, Rotary, Lions, provincial).
100. Sports clubs.

In making use of this hundred point scale, we have sought to introduce the time dimension in order to attempt to demonstrate graphically what changes occurred in the settlements where Peace Corps volunteers were assigned during the years 1962–1964. We have dated as many as possible of the beginnings of the hundred traits listed above in each of the settlements under study. In some cases, a particular trait has been dated as begun in a given community prior to 1864, or it has proved impossible to date a trait. In such cases, these traits are arbitrarily assigned to the settlement as of 1864, at the beginning of the century of development including the two years of Peace Corps volunteer program activity under analysis at its termination.

Table 1 lists the scores of both the 'experimental' settlements where Peace Corps volunteers worked, and the comparison settlements where Peruvian life went ahead during 1962–1964 without the presence of volunteers. The 1962 and 1964 scores are presented to indicate volunteer impact in 'experimental' settlements, and the normal rate of improvement in other Peruvian settlements during the period.

The rank order of Peruvian communities expressed in Table 1 indicates that our one hundred point scale of social structure indeed serves to distinguish between various types of settlements. Three Departmental capital cities range from ninety to eighty-five per cent of the complexity or differentiation of the national capital city in terms of this relatively simplistic scale. Three provincial capitals rank from eighty-two to sixty-six per cent of the national capital's differentiation, while District capitals vary from sixty-seven and one-half per cent to as low as sixteen per cent in the case of a geographically isolated town in northern Lima Department.

The rural Peruvian town or village that is not even a District capital, and has not been the target of some governmental or other external change program typically shows less than one-fourth the differentiation of the national capital on this scale. The populations that have been the targets of development programs, such as those of Cuyo Chico and Vicos, show an impressively high degree of differentiation that reflects program accomplishments in changing these originally Indian populations in the direction of integration into Peruvian national culture.

Conclusions

The first general conclusion to be stated is that the Peace Corps program in the Peruvian Andes did achieve a measurable impact upon its target communities. This conclusion is the more

TABLE 1

SCALE OF SOCIAL STRUCTURE SCORES OF PEACE CORPS AFFECTED AND COMPARISON SETTLEMENTS IN PERU IN 1962–1964

Settlement	1962	1964	Settlement	1962	1964
Lima—nc	100	100	Huasta		34
Huancayo—sc	90		Pararin*—dc	25	28
Chimbote		88	Aquia—dc		28
Puno*—sc	85	85	Vicos*	23	25
Huaraz*—sc	85	85	Mita*	18	25
Caraz—pc	82	82	Guyo Chico*	20	23
Yungay—pc	76	76	Chaquicocha		23
Chiquian—dc		67.5	Parquin		21
Recuay—pc		66	Ichu*	17	21
Carhuaz*—pc	63.5	64.5	Huancollusco*	17	21
Paramonga		64.5	Chijnaya*	0	21
Huallanca		56	Picoy		20
Huaylas—dc		55	Chinchera	19	19
Paucartambo—dc	46.5	48.5	Accopata		18
Chucuito*—dc	45	47	Chuichin		18
Moche—dc		46.5	Caroas		17
Viru—dc		46	Jucul—dc		16
Marcara—dc		44.5	Mayobamba		14
Pucara—dc		41	Camicachi*	11	11
Taraco*—dc	37.5	38.5	Recuayhuanca*	7	9
Mito—dc		36			

* Peace Corps volunteer affected settlements.

remarkable because the investment of social assets in a pioneering program of this sort normally must be assessed in a complex social context calculated to include several years during which effects rise and spread. The Peruvian volunteers thus fulfilled one of the three missions defined for the Peace Corps by the Congress in establishing the organization, by contributing to the development of a critical country in the South American region that is one key to the future course of world history.

In an attempt to measure Peace Corps program impact in the Peruvian Andes objectively, the Cornell Peru Project undertook to establish, albeit roughly, a base rate of institutional change and increasing complexity for rural settlements in the area. Members of the research staff conducted a series of studies of communities where Peace Corps volunteers were not assigned, with the goal of discovering the base rate of increasing scale in the Peruvian highlands during the period 1962–1964.

The data from which the base rate of rural settlement scale increase during the 1962–1964 period has been calculated are summarized in Table 2. The base rate of scale increase turns out to have been 0.6 point per settlement per year. It will be noted that this base rate was achieved by equal local community development inputs, and local action combined with Peruvian government agency reinforcements.

Parallel data on rate of scale increase in the settlements where Peace Corps volunteers worked are summarized in Table 3. The sample of such settlements is 15, three times the size of the comparison settlement sample. The gross rate of scale increase turns out to be 1.67 points per settlement per year. This rate of social scale increase in the communities where Peace Corps volunteers worked is two and four-fifths times as rapid as the base rate for settlements where there were no volunteers.

The nature of our scale of social structure is such that it differentiates between less complex communities better than between the more complex urban type settlements in Peru. A realistic differentiation between Lima, Arequipa, Trujillo, Cuzco, Huancayo, and other large cities in Peru would require us to employ quantitative comparisons within the various categories in our scale. We would, for example, need to compare not whether these cities have one or more banks, as the scale does in its present simple form, but to compare the number of banks

TABLE 2

BASE RATE OF SOCIAL STRUCTURE SCALE INCREASE IN FIVE RURAL PERUVIAN COMMUNITIES NOT AFFECTED BY PEACE CORPS VOLUNTEER ACTIVITIES DURING 1962–1964

| | | No. Scale Points Added by | | |
| | 1962 | Local Action | With Govt. | 1964 |
Community	Score	Only	Agency	Score
Carcas	18	0	0	18
Accopata	16	1	1	18
Mito	34	0	1	35
Chaquicocha	20	0	1	21
Paucartambo	46.5	1	1	48.5
5	134.5	2	4	140.5

TABLE 3

RATE OF SOCIAL STRUCTURE SCALE INCREASE IN FIFTEEN PERUVIAN
SETTLEMENTS AFFECTED BY PEACE CORPS VOLUNTEER ACTIVITIES
DURING 1962–1964

Settlement	1962 Score	1964 Score	Scale Increase Points	Annual Rate
Recuayhuanca	7	9	2	1.0
Mita	17	24	7	3.5
Carhuaz	63.5	64.5	1	0.5
Vicos	23	25	2	1.0
Huaraz	85	85	0	0
Pararin	25	28	3	1.5
Cuyo Chico	20	23	3	1.5
Cuzco	93	93	0	0
Taraco	37.5	38.5	1	0.5
Huancollusco	17	21	4	2.0
Camicachi	11	11	0	0
Chucuito	45	47	2	1.0
Ichu	17	21	4	2.0
Chijnaya	0	21	21	10.5
Puno	85	85	0	0
15	546	596	50	1.67

functioning in the various cities. This more complex form of analysis is probably unnecessary for the purposes of the present analysis. It is mentioned here to point out that the types of institutional changes that a Peace Corps volunteer is likely to be able to bring about in a Peruvian city are qualitatively different from those that volunteers can bring about in simply organized rural areas. It seems reasonable therefore to eliminate from our comparison for purposes of more accurate evaluation, the three departmental capitals included in our sample of settlements affected by Peace Corps volunteers. While these cities were affected by volunteers, they were not affected in the same way as less complex settlements, nor are they matched by a departmental capital in our sample of comparison communities.

Eliminating Puno, Cuzco, and Huraz from our sample of volunteer affected settlements leaves us with 12 such An-

dean communities and the same amount of social scale increase. For these 12 highland communities where volunteers achieved institutional changes, therefore, the rate of scale increase turns out to be 2.1 points per community per year. This is a rate nearly 3½ times (actually 3.47) as rapid as that established for the comparison community sample.

Extracts from some of the detailed discussions of individual communities follow:

Vicos gained one point on our scale of social structure with the arrival of the volunteers in October of 1962, and another with the formation of the local credit union by a National Agrarian University staff member in 1963. . . .

As a result of the combined efforts of A. E. R.,[2] and the people of Mita, rein-

---

[2] A. E. R. was a farmer from Mita who acted as community leader.

forced by the U.S. AID/Peru Special Projects Program, and three Peace Corps Volunteers, Mita scored significantly higher on our scale of social structure late in 1964 than it had in 1962. The inhabitants of Mita led by A.E.R. themselves added four scale points by purchasing locally owned trucks in 1962, recovering communal land in 1963, which placed them on interprovincial bus routes, and enabled them to organize production cooperatives. One volunteer provided advice and some technical assistance in the last mentioned endeavor. He also set up the first athletic equipment in Mita, and another volunteer started the pupil feeding program in 1963. U.S. AID/Peru's Special Projects Program also provided books for the Mita Library in 1962. (These seven innovations gave Mita a seven-point increase in its 1964 score over its 1962 score.)

As the result of Penny's efforts, Ichu bettered its ranking on the integration scale by two points, through her work with the medical post. Preston laid the groundwork for another increase in the scale by assisting the fishermen in starting a small producer's cooperative, although this had not, in fact, come into being at the time he left Peru. He did, however, bring agricultural extension service to the area where it was lacking previously. Not only did he perform this function, but also he was instrumental in introducing the representatives of the Agricultural Development Bank to the area.

Perry was able to bring to Huancollusco or to encourage its inhabitants to build or to organize for themselves four of the items in our scale of structural complexity. This represented a 23.5% increase in structural scale in Huancollusco in a few months in 1963, and a rise from 17 to 21 points in our scale. This calculation ignores the scale point Perry temporarily provided to Huancollusco by residing there and establishing a foreign colony by his presence. It considers only the permanent gains made by Huancollusco. (The four items were a barber's shop, a circulating library, a sports club, and a consumers' cooperative.)

QUESTIONS

1. As Mr. Vernon, prepare a critique of the various OPP instructions regarding PPB quoted in the case, particularly (a) those concerned with the definition of goals, and (b) the choice of output measures listed in Exhibit 3.

2. Do you think that the methodology of the Cornell Peru Project study outlined in the case is appropriate for the measurement of the achievement of Peace Corps goals?

3. Prepare to discuss in general the relationships between the Peace Corps' missions, program structure, choice of output measures, and its methods of establishing goals and measuring goal achievement.

EXHIBIT 1

PEACE CORPS

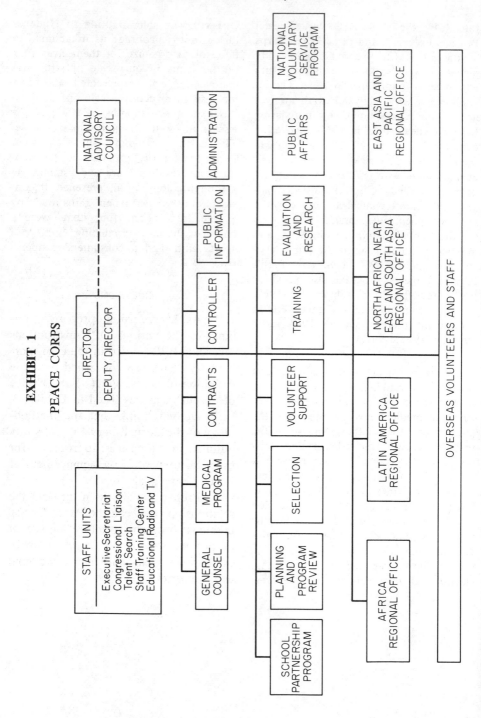

EXHIBIT 2

PEACE CORPS

Peace Corps Volunteers in Latin America *

	FIVE YEAR SUMMARY: VOLUNTEERS IN COUNTRY AT END OF FISCAL YEAR					
	1962	1963	1964	1965	1966	Totals**
Brazil	43	168	210	548	639	989
Chile	45	99	106	294	397	617
Colombia	103	229	561	544	506	1,329
El Salvador	25	21	46	55	51	132
Jamaica	38	32	62	77	70	163
St. Lucia	15	14	17	5	16	53
Venezuela	5	83	117	265	292	570
Bolivia		112	125	220	266	533
British Honduras		33	18	49	33	91
Costa Rica		26	63	61	107	192
Dominican Republic		144	171	85	101	347
Ecuador		156	236	309	211	681
Guatemala		27	105	83	69	191
Honduras		27	44	103	107	177
Panama		28	75	133	196	288
Peru		285	293	379	301	940
Uruguay			18	4	48	68
Barbados					29	29

**Total individual Volunteers now serving or having served in host country since 1961.

"The largest of all Peace Corps regions (some 8,500 Volunteers have served in Central and South America since 1961) added two more nations to its list this year: Guyana (formerly British Guiana) and Paraguay; the first Volunteers will arrive during the coming year. Heart of programs in all 20 countries is community development, which takes many forms but has only one basic goal: create sense of identity, promote idea of self-help."

Activities of Peace Corps Volunteers in Latin America during 1966:

Community Development:	1,819 Volunteers	
Education:	695	"
Public Health:	532	"
Agriculture:	330	"
Other:	2	"

*Source: Peace Corps Annual Report for 1966.

EXHIBIT 3

PEACE CORPS

Peace Corps Program Structures and Measures of Output

Country:_____	OUTPUT MEASUREMENT ESTIMATES		
	First Legislative Goal	Second Legislative Goal	Third Legislative Goal

Program Direction and Support:

A. Direction	None	None	None
B. Support	None	None	None

Food Supply (The problem of hunger) ·

A. General Farming/Agriculture Extension/Livestock, Dairy Poultry/Fisheries	Number of service contacts	Total number of foreigners who gain knowledge of America from Volunteers	Number of RPCVs
B. Farm related public works (irrigation, water, land clearing)	Area affected		
C. Cooperatives (producer coops, marketing, credit unions)	Number of farmers affected		
D. Nutrition, Home Arts, School Lunch	Number of persons affected		
E. Community Action/Agriculture	Number of persons affected		

Education (The problem of ignorance):

A. Elementary		Total number of foreigners who gain knowledge of America from Volunteers	Number of RPCVs
B. Secondary			
1. English			
2. TEFL, TESL			
3. Math/Sci.			
4. Phys. Ed.			
5. History, geography			
C. University			
1. Physical and Biological Sciences	Number of students taught		
2. English			
3. Social Sciences			
4. Humanities			
5. Other			
D. Teacher Training			
1. Education			
2. Content (see Sec. Ed.)			

EXHIBIT 3—*Continued*

	OUTPUT MEASUREMENT ESTIMATES		
Country:_____	First Legislative Goal	Second Legislative Goal	Third Legislative Goal
E. Other/Adult			
1. Literacy	Number of stu-	Total number of	Number of
2. Vocational	dents taught	foreigners who	RPCVs
3. Phys. Ed.		gain knowledge	
4. Handicapped		of America from	
5. Educational TV		Volunteers	
6. Headstart			
Health and Sanitation (The problem of sickness and disease):			
A. Preventive Health	Population served		
B. Medical Care (curative)	Number of pa-tient encounters		
C. Health Education	Number of per-sons affected		
D. Laboratory Technicians	None		
E. Health Related Public Works	None		
F. Community Action/Health	Number of per-sons affected		
Public and Private Institutions (The problem of nation building):			
A. Architecture, City Planning	None		
B. Surveying	Amount of proj-ect area surveyed		Number of RPCVs
C. Public Administration and Law	None	Total number of	
D. Non-agricultural coops, Small Business Counseling, Credit Unions and Savings and Loans	Number of per-sons affected	foreigners who gain knowledge of America from Volunteers	
E. Rural Community Development	Population affected		
F. Urban Community Development	Population affected		

C A S E

4

BUREAU OF THE CENSUS

WORKLOAD AND OUTPUT MEASURES FOR THE
FOREIGN TRADE PROGRAM

The Foreign Trade Program, a program element in FY 1966 of the Department of Commerce PPB Program Category No. III, "National Demographic and Economic Statistical Services," is a major ongoing activity of the Bureau of the Census. Under legal sanction and through the cooperation of the Customs Bureau, Department of the Treasury, import and export declarations are collected in Customs Offices and copies forwarded to Census for statistical compilations that result in a series of regularly published foreign trade reports.

The law requires that declarations be filed with Customs by authorized agents to report on all commodities entering or leaving the United States. There may be several items or articles included on a declaration, listing different commodities contained in a shipment. The heading of a declaration form would include such data as: point of origin of shipment, date of shipment, name of firm or individual transporting goods, name and address of consignor, point of destination for shipment, estimated entry date, name and address of consignee, ultimate destination of shipment, and if waterborne, the name of the vessel carrying shipment. The remainder of the form would deal with information about the specific items in the shipment, giving information such as the following: description of the item, unit of measure, quantity, shipping weight, estimated dollar value, and standard commodity classification code (from coding manuals). Several different forms are used to differentiate imports, exports, air cargo, vessel cargo, other forms of transportation, and to indicate warehouse storage goods, immediate consumption goods, intermediate products, and raw materials.

These data are compiled for the preparation of statistical reports, largely monthly, with cumulative year-

This case was prepared by Michael S. McKay under the supervision of Graeme M. Taylor. The case is intended for class discussion only, and certain names and facts may have been changed which, while avoiding the disclosure of confidential information, do not materially lessen the value of the case for educational purposes. This case is not intended to represent either effective or ineffective handling of an administrative situation, nor does it purport to be a statement of policy by the agency involved.

to-date figures included. Information is shown on imports and exports of merchandise in a variety of formats. Detail is provided as to commodities shipped, country of origin or destination, and trade through the various U. S. customs districts. Breakdowns by vessel and air transportation, with dollar value and shipping weight, and total vessel shipments by port of lading and flag (or registry) of vessel are provided. United States trade with Puerto Rico and with the U. S. possessions is summarized in a regular report, while another gives the highlights of U. S. import and export activity. There are eight major monthly reports produced from current trade information, several special reports, and a variety of reference works containing past years' data.

Other tabulations are prepared regularly from Census records for government agencies and private firms. In addition requests for special tabulations are accepted from individuals or firms as well as from the government. For example, if a regularly published Census report contains detail that is too highly aggregated or grouped in a manner not useful to a customer, he can request a special tabulation of certain categories of information. The customer may be interested, for example, in more detail about a specific commodity class, a port, or customs district.

Requests that concern confidential information or that would give unfair business advantage to the requestor are not accepted. Customers are charged the full cost of producing these tabulations. The regularly scheduled reports have priority, and the number of special tabulations prepared depends upon the availability of staff and facilities

and upon the nature of the Census records.

The various compilations of the Foreign Trade Program constitute the official U. S. statistics on the import and export of all types of merchandise and their method of transportation, including import and export of gold and silver. Commodity classifications used match those of the tariff schedules and are comparable for the most part with the classifications used by other countries. The information prepared by Census is used extensively by the government for planning and policy purposes, besides providing valuable statistics for business and research organizations.

Decisions made as to the report formats for publishing take into consideration the needs of the users, and the Bureau, working with the Department of Commerce, has the responsibility of keeping abreast of these needs. Advisory committees with representatives from both the private and public sectors are consulted as to specific decisions of this type. If it is determined that a special tabulation being prepared is of general interest, its availability is advertised in publications and catalogs. The subject matter specialists in the Census Bureau and in the Department of Commerce maintain contact with customers through attendance at conferences, handling customer correspondence, and meetings with individual users.

CENSUS BUREAU OPERATIONS— FOREIGN TRADE PROGRAM

The Foreign Trade documents sent by Customs to the Census Bureau account for all reported foreign trade of commodities involving the United States and its possessions. The documents, which are sequentially numbered for control purposes, are checked in to establish those entries for the monthly statistical periods and to assure receipt of all current documents. The absence of only a few documents could be critical if the missing entries were to consist of some large or unusual transactions.

Editing and coding of documents is then performed, either on all forms or on a sample basis, depending on the statistical plan in use. (Not all documents can be processed due to the large monthly volume and the consequent high cost and time-consuming processing requirements. Among those sampled are import documents with all items under $100 in value.) The coding of documents, performed directly on the forms, is to facilitate the keypunching operation that follows this clerical processing. In order for the data to be easily and accurately prepared on punch cards certain conversions must be made from the written or typed word. Where possible, within the capability of the clerical and professional staff, corrections are made to erroneous entries and obvious omissions completed. When this is not feasible, contact is made with the appropriate business or government agency involved in the transaction for the needed information. A sample verification procedure based on quality control plans is carried out to assure the quality of the basic data prior to key punching.

After the selected documents have been punched, verified, and corrections made, the punch cards are converted to magnetic tape for computer process-ing. A series of computer programs are used to edit, compute, and arrange the data into the desired formats for the reports. High-speed printer paper, on which the output is printed, serves as the camera copy for printing.

PERFORMANCE REVIEW FOR
OPERATING PROGRAMS—PROP

The Census Bureau conducts an internal management reporting system known as PROP—Performance Review for Operating Programs. Objectives of PROP are to report progress of the Bureau's programs on a timely basis and to compare the results with annual operational work plans. Operational work plans are detailed planning documents showing periodic workload and cost estimates prepared by each participating division and approved by the Budget Division. They serve as the detailed back-up to the official budget requests. Planned and actual summary information are compared monthly for individual divisions and at the Bureau level, and significant variances are highlighted for investigation. The Foreign Trade Program was the first program to be covered by the PROP system.

Tied into PROP is the Bureau's work measurement system, through which incentive awards are paid to employees for high levels of productivity combined with high quality. Work measurement is largely confined to repetitive clerical operations.

The reporting structure used for PROP requires that distinct work units be described for individual assignments (tasks), for groupings of these assignments (operations), for the next highest level of aggregation (sub-projects), and for division and Bureau summaries (projects and programs). Each program is made up of two or more projects, which in turn are subdivided into their component operations, which are made up of tasks.

The PROP reports are prepared in several formats for each division for a variety of time periods (ranging from weekly to annual reports) and for different organizational levels (unit, section, branch, and division). A separate report form is submitted for every Census employee each week, showing the assignments worked on during the period. These report forms are the source of the PROP reports. Using the standardized six-digit organizational coding structure (two digits each for unit and/or section, branch, and division) and the ten-digit assignment coding scheme (four for project and two each for sub-project, operation, and task), it is possible to provide great detail from the individual worker level to aggregate program summaries.

WORKLOAD MEASURES

Before instituting the PROP system, it was necessary to establish appropriate workload measures that would be useful to the various levels of management. There were four primary divisions of the Bureau involved in the regular operations of the Foreign Trade Program in FY 1966: Economic Operations, Data Processing Systems, Administrative Service, and Foreign Trade.

In the Economic Operations Division, where the documents were first received, edited, coded, control established, and where the computer programming and systems analysis was done, different workload measures were established according to the specific tasks and operations being performed, as in all the divisions. The one workload measure chosen for the division as a whole, against which to relate total costs of the Foreign Trade Program, was the number of *documents processed*. The workload total consisted of only those documents that were edited and coded, since the remaining documents were selected out and filed away early in the processing stage. All Foreign Trade costs of the division were grouped to arrive at a unit cost per document processed.

The Data Processing Systems Division, which performed the keypunching and the computer processing, selected *cards punched* as its program workload measure. This total consisted of the number of cards punched from documents, the number of these verified, and the number which had to be correction punched. An advantage of this definition of cards punched was that it provided an overall total of cards actually run through the keypunch and verifier equipment.

Most of the contribution to the program of the remaining two divisions, Administrative Service and Foreign Trade, was of a professional nature; this was considered to be more difficult to relate to a general workload measure. For the clerical area of Administrative Service, dealing with the final preparation of the copy for printing, the number of pages prepared might have constituted a useful measure; however, the division summary work unit selected was *man hours worked*. Activities such as layout, design, printing planning, consultation, and contracting for printing did not fit meaningfully in terms of pages prepared.

The Foreign Trade Division, consisting largely of subject-matter specialists, also chose *man hours worked* as its measure, since its work primarily involved planning, analysis, research, public contact, and consultation. Certain sections within the division did record document counts for those problem referrals from the clerical processing operation, but this was done for internal management purposes only and the document counts were not significant.

These individual division program workload measures were designed to provide top division management with good summary information for evaluation and control purposes. How valuable a man-hours total was to the Foreign Trade Division at the program level might be questionable, but at the project, operation, and task levels it was useful. Lower level PROP reports were essential for management below the division chief.

The work measurement program, using individual production standards for the most part (group or unit standards were used infrequently), required specific work units for reporting of individual assignments. Examples of such work units were documents coded, batches of documents checked in, pages of listings reviewed, cards punched, verified, or corrected, and problem documents referred for review. These work units were aggregated by task and by operation and were used to compute mechanically performances of employees against production standards for the clerical operations. A unit supervisor was more concerned with the specific tasks and operations performed in his unit than with division and bureau summaries and was responsible for knowing what each of his

employees was accomplishing, and how well, in relation to the production standards in effect. PROP reports were thus designed to provide each level of management with appropriate information on a timely basis.

Although most of the non-clerical work was reported in terms of manhours worked by task and operation, the recording of the codes provided valuable information as to the specific work being done by each employee. This type of information was further extended, for example, in the computer programming areas to reveal, through still another set of codes, what programs were being developed, the stages of development, the computer languages being used, and the general types of programs. The aim was to reach a point where a complete cost history would be available for separate computer runs, from planning, programming, and testing, through the production of the final tabulation.

Detail was helpful in the identification of problems, so that if a summary report seemed to show some difficulty arising, it would be possible to go down the ladder of detail for an analysis. The availability of this detail, either on printed reports or stored on tape for printing if needed, also served as a planning and cost estimating tool.

The overall Census Bureau summary PROP reports used the *documents processed* measure for the Foreign Trade Program, the same unit used in the Economic Operations Division summary. It was felt that, since document workload fluctuations could be directly related to costs, and since past years' records were available in the same unit of measure, documents processed would be the most advantageous choice. The entire program was aggregated at the Bureau level on a monthly basis, cumulative for the fiscal year, showing total cost, total workload, percentage performances for measured work, and unit costs for each project in the program and for the program as a whole. Each individual participating division was shown separately, with its own workload figures, for each project in the program, building to the final Bureau summary. The planning figures were contrasted with actual figures for the workload, cost, performance, and unit cost categories, with variances computed and shown. Exhibit 2 is an example of the monthly table for a project.

OUTPUT MEASURES FOR PPB REPORTING PURPOSES

A program summary of this type provided the highest level of reporting in the system, but there was a need for the selection of an output measure for the program element in the departmental PPB structure. The objective of the Foreign Trade Program was to meet the need for official U. S. statistics on the import and export of all types of merchandise and the method of transportation used for the transactions. The statistics were of necessity to be of high quality and to be published on a timely basis. The output measure selected for this PPB element was the number of Foreign Trade *reports published*. It was felt that this was the most tangible and unambiguous measure, since it did represent the

final product of the basic program. The unpublished reports and special tabulations were considered to be by-products of the primary output. Some of the shortcomings of the chosen output measure were the variations in length of the reports, the differences in the amount of work and cost involved in preparing the different reports, and the mixture of old with new data in the reports.

QUESTIONS

1. Based on the material presented, would you agree that the PPB output measure of "reports published" is the best available measure to use? What other measures would seem reasonable to consider?

2. Do you think that the "reports published" measure would be useful in comparing alternative procedures within the Foreign Trade Program? What apparent alternatives do you see?

3. How do you explain the use of two different program level measures, one for PPB and one for the internal reporting system? Or, do you feel that the same measure should be used for both? Why?

4. Prepare to discuss the differences between output measures, workload measures, benefit measures, and measures designed to evaluate employee performance.

5. How would you change the measurement system used by the Bureau of the Census as described in this case?

EXHIBIT 1

BUREAU OF THE CENSUS

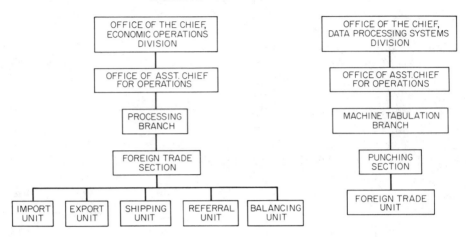

EXHIBIT 2

BUREAU OF THE CENSUS

Facsimile of Bureau Level PROP Summary Report

PROP TABLE SIX A—MONTH OF JANUARY, 1966   FOREIGN TRADE PROGRAM

Division	W/unit	Workload			Cost			Performance			Unit Cost		
		Plan	Actual	Var.	Plan	Actual	Var.	Plan	Actual	Var.	Plan	Actual	Var.
F.T.	M/hrs.	—	—	—	—	—	—	—	—	—	—	—	—
Ad. Svc.	M/hrs.	—	—	—	—	—	—	—	—	—	—	—	—
E.O.D.	Docs.	—	—	—	—	—	—	—	—	—	—	—	—
D.P.S.D.	Cards	—	—	—	—	—	—	—	—	—	—	—	—
Totals	Docs.	—	—	—	—	—	—	—	—	—	—	—	—

PART
III

program analysis

This part of the book contains a series of readings laying the theoretical foundation for the study and discussion of the cases that follow. John Haldi's introductory paper outlines the role that analysis can play in the evaluation of both existing and proposed public programs. Alain Enthoven discusses the concepts and application of the systems analysis approach. Robert McNamara's statement describes a series of analyses of important defense systems—NIKE-X, Damage Limiting programs, manned bombers, air-launched missiles, manned interceptors, and airline aircraft. Arthur Smithies, in an original paper, introduces the use of an input-output matrix into program budgeting for systems analysis. There follows a selection of three papers on the choice of the appropriate discount rate for use in analyzing public programs by Jacob Stockfish, William Baumol, and Elmer B. Staats, the latter consisting of a report prepared by the Comptroller-General following a survey of the use of discounting in the federal government.

Following the readings are eleven cases, each offering the student an opportunity to develop his analytical skill by attempting to answer the questions listed at the end of each case. Although practically all the cases were selected as vehicles for the application of *several* concepts or techniques, they have been arranged in roughly ascending order of difficulty according to the *major* topics illustrated by each case as indicated in the table of contents.

The Role of Analysis

JOHN HALDI

Probably the most important component of the PPB system, the most difficult to initiate, and the most difficult part to gain acceptance of in the Government, is systematic analysis of Government programs. Unfortunately, the application of analysis to Government programs has become somewhat controversial and because of this I would like to define briefly what I mean and what I think others associated with PPB mean by *systematic analysis.*

Systematic analysis is often associated with quantitative analysis. However, it is by *no* means coextensive with quantitative analysis. The word "analyze" does not have the same meaning as the words "quantify" or "measure," although analysis often includes measurement. Let us be more specific and examine the steps involved in a good systematic analysis of a Government program.

First, the analysis should start by *defining program objectives.* "Objectives" include statements about—

What the program is trying to accomplish;

How the planned program accomplishments fit in with what other

Government agencies or private business firms are doing in the same area;

Who the program aims to reach—that is, the target group or clientele group of the program.

Statements of program objectives should be made after analyzing the relevant laws, congressional resolutions, and Presidential commitments. These usually embody somewhat broad and abstract statements of general goals, such as "Improve the health of American Indians on Reservations" or "Make American Indians as healthy as the general population," and proceed to somewhat more precise objectives, such as "Reduce infant mortality on Indian Reservations to the same rate that occurs in the general population by, say, 1972." Once formulated from a "legal" background, program objectives need

From The Planning–Programming–Budgeting System: Progress and Potentials (Hearings before the Subcommittee on Economy in Government of the Joint Economic Committee, Congress of the United States, 90th Congress, 1st Session, U.S. Government Printing Office, Washington, D.C., 1967). John Haldi is former Chief, Program Evaluation Staff, Bureau of the Budget.

to be examined very carefully to make sure that they are acceptable—politically acceptable, economically acceptable, technologically feasible, acceptable to common sense, and so on.[1]

Formulation of a good, consistent set of program objectives is not nearly so easy as it may appear. It requires a considerable amount of hard thought process, and there are a number of pitfalls to beware of. But these details are not of concern here. One other point worth mentioning, though, is that computers and mathematical models are definitely *not* required in the formulation of program objectives. What is required is an attempt to be as precise as possible about what programs are doing, or what they are supposed to be doing, and not stop short and be content with statements like "Supply a little bit to every citizen who needs it," or "Assist underprivileged groups," or "Improve national prestige."

Statements of our national goals are clearly a vital part of the process of systematic analysis. If formulated too broadly, like "A better life for all citizens," they are not meaningful guides

to the hard program choices and decisions which must be made each year. If formulated too narrowly, however, like "Build concrete freeways" (instead of a broader transportation objective), they will overly restrict meaningful choices. Because of the importance of having good, rather precise statements of our national goals, the Joint Economic Committee should give serious consideration to holding hearings on the subject. This is one area of PPB where congressional leadership should definitely be provided.

Second, after an acceptable set of program objectives has been set down, alternative means of reaching these objectives should be identified. To return to the example from the Bureau of Indian Affairs, if one immediate objective for Indian health is reduction of infant mortality, there are obviously several alternative programs which will help to accomplish this:

Prenatal care programs;
Postnatal care programs;
Training of subprofessional medical personnel; and
Building of clinics.

Just to start the analysis. A most important aspect of this part of systematic analysis is to search *imaginatively* for better alternative means of accomplishing program objectives. To search *imaginatively* one must be *critical.* That is, one must examine sharply the existing way of doing things, with an open mind. The person who is to analyze *cannot* be dedicated to the existing way of doing things. Identification with existing programs almost inevitably leads to little more than defensiveness and rationalizations for the existing state of affairs. Moreover,

---

[1] Government agencies customarily have a rather difficult time stating their program objectives with any sort of reasonable precision. Whether they realize it or not, however, existing programs always contain certain "objectives" implicitly. For example, whom is the program reaching and whom is it not reaching? What is the program accomplishing and what is it not accomplishing? When put down in black and white the answers to these questions may not be what one would like to see, but nevertheless these facts exist for every program. Systematic analysis is merely a discipline that brings one face-to-face with hard and unpleasant issues like these. In a *partial* way, good systematic analysis can help impose on Government managers a helpful discipline which is similar to that imposed on businessmen by the forces of competition.

creative program alternatives do *not* come from computers or mathematical models. They come from creative individuals, 100 percent of the time.

Third, the alternatives which result from the search process need to be screened and weighed against one another, in terms of cost and in terms of the extent to which they contribute to achieving the program objectives. This is the step that has often been referred to as "cost-effectiveness analysis." This, of course, is what any rational person does when he makes a major personal expenditure decision, such as buying a house or a car. And it has been done by men for literally thousands of years. However, objections to such analysis are raised on a variety of grounds:

Computers are said to be replacing "judgment";

Intangibles are said to be omitted from the calculation;

It is sometimes claimed that there are attempts to quantify the non-quantifiable; or

Costs are said to be given too much emphasis.

Quite frankly, Mr. Chairman, these kinds of criticisms—however sincere —reflect a complete lack of understanding. Sometimes they simply reflect chagrin that particular pet projects do not show up well under the light of cost-effectiveness analysis. For, if you remove the cost aspect from cost-effectiveness analysis, then you are left with "effectiveness at any price whatsoever." And this is scarcely an acceptable approach to decision-making. Suppose you were buying a house. There are many intangibles which must be considered: the quality of the school system, the friendliness of the

neighbors, playmates for your children, etc. Still, you don't buy a house without also considering such measurable factors as the price of the house, or the distance, time and cost to get to work.

It would be uncandid of me to claim that *all* cost-effectiveness studies were perfect or even represent good analysis. Programs are complex, cost estimates that must extend over many years are subject to a considerable amount of uncertainty, analysts are human, and to be human is to err. All analyses should be subject to careful review and criticism. But it is one thing to attack a specific study as being incomplete, and quite another to denigrate a whole approach just because conclusions differ.

Good systematic analysis does not replace the decision-maker, but is an aid to him. When confronted by complex issues, diverse opinions, and alternative ways to go, it helps him zero in on his final decision by—

Uncovering irrelevant issues;

Pinpointing crucial assumptions and facts which underlie alternative recommendations; and

Tracing out the knowable consequences and costs of each alternative.

Then with the best possible knowledge of what is knowable and quantifiable about the decision, he can use informed judgment and experience to take into account the intangible and unquantified aspects of the problem.

Systematic analysis of Government programs does not represent some brand new set of intellectual tools developed by the Department of Defense or the Bureau of the Budget, but rather it is an amalgamation of the skills and disciplines that are constantly evolving and improving in many fields:

Mathematics and statistics;
Economics;
Operations research;
Management science; and
Computer technology.

Along with others. Perhaps it is worth noting that every one of these topics is now *required* subject matter in virtually *every* Graduate School of Business in the United States. To say that systematic analysis is "wrong" is to say that, first, all the researchers and teachers in these fields are "wrong," and, second, decisions should be made almost "at random," without the benefit of available knowledge.

Let us now return to the role of analysis. For the sake of this discussion, it will be useful to consider the areas where analysis can be useful in two categories:

1. Evaluation of existing, ongoing programs.
2. Study of new proposals—either new programs or changes in existing programs.

PROGRAM EVALUATION

Government programs take a number of different forms, but to narrow the discussion let us distinguish between grant programs and Government administered programs. By this classification I mean to include under "Government administered programs" all programs which do not make grants or loans. In other words, I am talking about programs where Government agencies have considerable room for managerial initiative, because they do indeed manage the program. In the civilian area such programs account an-

nually for tens of billions of dollars of expenditure. These programs include a wide variety of activities, such as—

Operate the world's largest hospital system and provide care for several hundred thousands of patients annually (VA);
Operate the world's largest postal system;
Maintain and regulate the Nation's air space by planning, installing and operating air traffic control towers, instrument landing systems, radar and a host of other aids to air navigation (DOT);
Make and sell geologic charts of the entire United States (Interior) as well as charts of all territorial waters surrounding the United States (Commerce);
Grow and cut one-fourth of all commercial timber in the United States (Agriculture);
Plan, develop, and operate outdoor recreational areas for millions of people;
Plan, research and build spacecraft (NASA) and nuclear reactors (AEC);
Train the underprivileged (OEO and other agencies).

It seems a virtual certainty that not only will the Government continue to operate and manage such programs, but in the future their number and scope may well expand. To narrow the discussion, let us focus attention on the role of analysis in evaluating these Government administered programs.

It is fundamental, of course, that Government programs need to be well managed, and that the money and resources appropriated to these need to be guided by correct decisions. Annually, thousands upon thousands of decisions need to be made, such as—

When and where to build new airport towers?

What maps to make?

What timber to cut?

Briefly stated, my arguments linking analysis to systematic evaluation of these decisions are:

1. Many decisions are governed in large part by *criteria* found in agency manuals.

2. These criteria are usually technical in nature, and Congress delegates to agencies authority to establish and change most of these criteria.

3. Bureaucratic agencies characteristically display a deep-rooted *bias,* which might be termed a "professional" bias, a "fundamentalist" bias, or a "program advocate's" bias. This bias is pervasive and predictable.

4. The ultimate effect of these biases is to spend money on projects which are frequently not effective and are not necessary.

5. The loser when this occurs is the taxpayer.

6. In a governmental system built on checks and balances, we currently have no check or counterbalance to argue the case for the general taxpayer.

7. Systematic analysis, originating in the right places, can provide a highly desirable counterbalance to the existing biases.

8. Congress should originate or at least evaluate critically such analysis.

Criteria governing expenditures

The criteria, rules, or guidelines found in the manuals of all Government agencies cover virtually every area of Government activity. These criteria tend to be all-pervasive, and together they help regulate annual expenditures of billions of dollars. For example, guidelines govern investment in all sorts of facilities, ranging from relatively expensive projects such as dams or air traffic control towers, to relatively inexpensive projects or items such as fish ladders, boundary markers or stream measuring devices. Other investment criteria determine such things as the size and approved construction standards of interstate highways, timber seeding and planting in National Forests, or the quality of information contained in maps and charts. And, once an investment has been made in a facility, still other criteria are used to determine the level of operations at the facility.

Regional and field offices usually rely heavily on their agency manual and the criteria contained in it when making plans and submitting budget proposals. Thus the aggregate impact of these criteria is quite extensive.

Since criteria like those cited here are so numerous, and so technical, Congress delegates to agencies the authority to establish and change them. The right of congressional review is of course reserved, but as a practical matter it can be exercised only rarely. New or changed criteria are usually generated within an agency by routine coordination of proposals through all cognizant or interested branches of the agency. But because the total money involved is so great, two important questions which should be asked are—

What conscious or unconscious motivations govern the agencies when they write their criteria? and

What assurance does Congress have that these criteria lead to desirable decisions?

Agency biases

At the bureau level many Government agencies tend to be dominated by one profession. For example, the following list associating bureaus and professions should contain no surprises.

Bureau	Profession
Geologic Survey	Geologists
Weather Bureau	Meteorologists
Office of Education	Educators
Bureau of Commercial Fish	Biologists
Public Health Service	Physicians
Bureau of Public Roads	Engineers

Since some departments are made of several diverse bureaus, they are not associated with any one profession. In other agencies, however, a single profession tends to be predominant throughout. For example, the entire Justice Department and Atomic Energy Commission are dominated by lawyers and physicists, respectively.

Because bureaus are so frequently dominated by a single profession, there is a tendency for what might be called *professional biases* to be reflected in the criteria which a bureau generates to help govern its various expenditures. These biases generally result in favoring those things which are either professionally interesting or professionally exacting. As one might expect, the economic impact of this frequently is to spend money on projects which are not

necessary and which yield predictably few benefits to any clientele group.[2]

The list of uneconomic activities that can conceivably result from this sort of bias is almost unending. Just for the sake of concrete illustration, it is possible to have—

Instrument landing systems installed at airports where bad weather virtually never occurs;

Expensive water pollution control devices installed where less expensive alternatives are available;

Wilderness areas mapped or charted to an unwarranted degree of accuracy;

Stream flow measured at intervals too frequent for any useful purpose;

Multiple fish ladders built where single fish ladders would suffice; or

Trees planted on low-value land while high-value land remains unplanted; and so on.

The potential for program evaluation

Where appropriate checks and balances have been built into our Government, they seem to work reasonably well. At present, however, there would seem to

---

[2] Unless, perhaps, the Government employees concerned receive some benefit. But this is not meant to imply that Government employees derive personal benefits in any immoral or dishonest way. People with professional biases often resemble *fundamentalists,* or people to whom things like trees, maps, weather observations, or miles of freeways become end objects to be desired in and of themselves. Bureaucratic biases have recently been studied in much more detail by Anthony Downs, *Inside Bureaucracy* (Boston: Little Brown & Co., 1967). Instead of the term *fundamentalist,* Downs classifies most bureaucrats as either *zealots* or *advocates.*

be no effective check on the tendency of Government bureaus to engage in uneconomic activities. GAO audits can be useful in preventing fraud or dishonesty and in seeing that activities operate at minimum cost, but even the best accounting audits will not show where wrong programs are being operated or where wrong program alternatives were chosen. One should keep in mind that it is quite possible for an agency to operate wrong programs very efficiently. Accounting audits are not designed to make this sort of managerial appraisal, and it would be grossly unfair to criticize them for doing so.

Subjecting programs to analytic evaluation of the type described earlier is one way to attempt to control unnecessary program expenditures such as those alluded to earlier. It is not possible, of course, to analyze every aspect of every program. But for each agency it is possible to select those programs which consume the greatest amount of money and subject them to a critical evaluation.

Program evaluation should attempt to ascertain in as measurable a way as possible whether programs are achieving their objectives, and whether there exist even more worthwhile objectives which should be considered in lieu of existing objectives. Rigorous analysis of this sort could help subject Government programs to the sort of discipline that competition forces on private business firms when they review their earnings and question whether there exist changes in products or services which their customers would welcome.

But just as competition is not a pressure which all businessmen welcome, so rigorous program evaluation is not welcome in all Government bureaus.

Good analysis involves hard work, and it can be a thankless task if its message falls only on deaf ears. In order to have a worthwhile impact on programs, analysis or evaluation *must be properly sponsored and motivated.* This is why the initial Bureau of the Budget instructions implementing PPB required that the head of the analytic staff report directly to the head of the agency or his immediate deputy. And also for this reason, Congress should consider originating its own analysis to act as a check on the work done in agencies. If it is not possible for Congress to sponsor such analysis, then it should at least evaluate the analysis done by agencies. This would provide an important and worthwhile stimulus to the PPB effort.

The term "new proposals" is intended to include major new projects, new programs, and extensive changes in existing programs. As the population grows, as our environment changes, and as the Government turns its attention from one complex social problem to another—problems such as air and water pollution, crime prevention, traffic congestion, depressed areas, education of the poor and underprivileged, poverty, and others—and if we think ahead over some future period such as the next 5, 10, or 20 years, it seems virtually inevitable that a number of new Government programs will be initiated. Nor should we restrict our thinking only to new problem areas, for under the impact of changing techniques and shifting population some of our existing programs will tend to grow obsolete and will have to take new directions.

Each new program, or shift in an existing program, will be aimed at achieving one or more of our evolving national goals. There will always be a number of alternative ways to achieve any specified objective, and planning for these new programs should include a systematic search for the best of the available alternatives. It was chiefly to facilitate the earlier discussion, of course, that evaluation of existing programs was treated separately from the generating of proposals or ideas for future changes and improvements. In fact, however, these two are closely linked. For out of careful, critical study of the past often come the best ideas for constructive changes.

As new ideas are generated—from evaluation of existing programs, from people outside the Government, or from whatever source—the better ones will need to be sifted out. This will require good cost estimates, study of probable effectiveness, using the best techniques available, and considerable thought given to questions such as: What can go wrong? In other words, new ideas and proposals should be subjected to systematic analysis, especially where they involve the expenditure of billions of dollars, or even hundreds of millions. From this process can come some of the best and most defensible proposals for new programs and new legislation.

We all recognize, of course, that we have with us at all times an intellectual thought process generating new ideas and, through debate and discussion, a sifting out of these ideas. This process occurs at our universities and colleges, in the public press, on the floor of our legislatures, and elsewhere. From our universities each year come a number of penetrating studies pertaining to public issues. From all this activity, and because of the public spirit of most

of these people, when important issues are being considered the Government has available to it many of the experts in the country, if it so chooses.

But we should not be complacent, either. We must also ask: Are we getting *all* the studies that we need? And are they the sort of studies that we need for the budget decisions which we face each year? On the basis of my experience, I believe the answer to both questions is an emphatic *no*. The Government has many programs, consuming in aggregate billions of dollars annually, which are not being adequately studied and which are not likely to be so studied if we wait for outside investigators to somehow develop an independent interest. Only a few of the studies done by independent investigators tend to be strictly pertinent to those decisions which have to be made at budget time.[3] For example, it is not common practice for an academic study either to cost out alternative approaches or to present alternative possibilities in the manner needed for program management of budget decisions.[4] Hence, unless the Government commissions such studies to be made they are not likely to be forthcoming. In their ab-

---

[3] This is not meant in any way to be a criticism of academic studies. In general, there is no reason why students of public programs should be motivated to develop such presentations.

[4] Cost estimating for complex program proposals can be a profession in itself. There are a number of good reasons why one should not expect good cost estimates in academic-type studies: (a) Cost estimate techniques may not be within the competence of the investigator, (b) outside investigators usually don't have sufficient data, (c) cost-estimating is time-consuming, hard work and usually has little relevance to academic publication, which unfortunately is often the principal goal of many writers.

sence we will have to continue making budget decisions involving billions of dollars with a considerable dearth of information—information that could be obtained at a relatively small cost.

PPB was, of course, initiated in order to help overcome this weakness. Looking ahead, we can foresee a day when all agencies will have an analytic staff, and will have in-depth studies forthcoming from these staffs on a regular basis. As we approach this state of affairs, some of the previous caveats concerning evaluation ought to be kept in mind. Recalling succinctly, analysts are human, and their work is not and should not be above criticism. We should consider building into our system some checks and balances on the output from these analytic staffs. There are probably a number of ways in which this can be done, but the best check on an analytic study that I know of is another study of the same problem. Then, if there are critical differences, they should be "debated" before congressional committees.

The Systems Analysis Approach

By
ALAIN C. ENTHOVEN

There is a great deal that might be said about the Systems Analysis approach. In this statement, I would like to pick out a few of the aspects that seem to me to be especially relevant and to make these points largely by the use of excerpts from *A Modern Design for Defense Decision*.[1]

In my statement, I would like to expand on the following points:

(1) Systems Analysis is a reasoned approach to problems of decision, accurately described as "quantitative common sense."

(2) Systems Analysis is an application of scientific method, using that term in its broadest sense.

(3) There are limitations in the application of Systems Analysis, although these have often been overstated.

(4) In 1961, the Defense planning and budgeting system had to be changed to permit the application of Systems Analysis.

(5) Systems Analysis is a regular working contributor to the annual Defense decision-making cycle.

---

[1] Industrial College of the Armed Forces. *A Modern Design for Defense Decision— A McNamara-Hitch-Enthoven Anthology*, edited by Samuel A. Tucker, Washington, D.C., 1966.

Presentation prepared for the Special Subcommittee on the Utilization of Scientific Manpower, Senate Labor and Public Welfare Committee, 89th Congress, 2nd Session, U.S. Government Printing Office, Washington, D.C., May 17, 1966. Alain C. Enthoven is Assistant Secretary of Defense, Systems Analysis.

(6) Two necessary conditions for the successful application of Systems Analysis as a working part of an operating organization are that it be used by decision-makers, and that it be fed with ideas by a broadly based interdisciplinary research program.

(7) Systems Analysis can be applied to the problems of State and local government, including programs for social welfare.

SYSTEMS ANALYSIS APPROACH

Systems Analysis is nothing more than quantitative or enlightened common sense aided by modern analytical methods. What we seek to do in the systems analysis approach to problems is to examine an objective in its broadest sense, including its reasonableness or appropriateness from a national policy point of view, and then develop for the responsible decision-maker information that will best help him to select the preferred way of achieving it. This process of selection requires that we first identify alternative ways of achieving the objective and then estimate, in quantitative terms, the benefits (effectiveness) to be derived from, and the costs of, each alternative. Those aspects of the problem that cannot easily be quantified are explicitly stated. In principle, we strive to identify the alternative that yields a specified degree of effectiveness for the least cost or, what is the same thing, the greatest effectiveness for a given cost. In essence, it is a way of dealing with the basic economic problem—how best to use our limited national resources. So much for what systems analysis is. A few words on what it is not.

Systems Analysis is not synonymous with the application of computers.

There is no essential connection between the two. Certainly the development of the former in no way depends on the latter. Some researchers, working within the limits of the systems analysis approach, try to do their analyses by means of large-scale computer simulations. Actually, the computer simulation approach so far has not been particularly fruitful as a method of weapon systems analysis. However, the potential advantages offered by high-speed electronic computers are very great. One of the primary advantages of the computer to the systems analysis function is to permit us to examine a much larger number of alternatives in a shorter period of time than would be otherwise possible. This is especially important in the case of very complex and interrelated systems where hand calculations would limit the time available for the more important work of analysis. I intend to try to exploit more fully the potential of high speed computers. But I would like to make it clear that I view the computer as a mechanical aid in my work and not as the substance of my work.

Moreover, systems analysis is not mysterious or occult. It is not performed with the help of a mysterious black box. A good systems analyst should be able to give a clear nontechnical explanation of his methods and results to the responsible decision-makers.

APPLICATION OF THE SCIENTIFIC METHOD

I would like now to turn to what I believe are some of the basic characteristics of the Systems Analysis method. Systems Analysis is at once eclectic and unique. It is not physics, engineering, mathematics, economics, political science or military operations and yet it involves elements of all of the above disciplines. But regardless of its make-up, the art of Systems Analysis—and it is an art—like the art of medicine, must be based on the scientific method, using this term in its broadest sense.

What are the relevant characteristics of scientific method as applied to the problem of choosing strategies and selecting weapon systems, or, for that matter, to the analysis of any problem of public policy involving allocation of the nation's scarce resources. I would like to answer this by quoting a passage from an address I gave before the Naval War College in 1963.

"First, the method of science is an open, explicit, verifiable self-correcting process. It combines logic and empirical evidence. The method and tradition of science require that scientific results be openly arrived at in such a way that any other scientist can retrace the same steps and get the same result. Applying this to weapon systems and to strategy would require that all calculations, assumptions, empirical data, and judgments be described in the analysis in such a way that they can be subjected to checking, testing, criticism, debate, discussion, and possible refutation. Of course, neither science nor systems analysis is infallible. But infallibility is not being claimed; it would be worse than unscientific to do so. However, scientific method does have a self-correcting character that helps to guard science from persistence in error in the long run.

"Second, scientific method is objective. Although personalities doubtless play an important part in the life of the Physics profession, the science itself does not depend upon personalities or vested interest. The truth of a scientific proposition is established by logical and empirical methods common to the profession as a whole. The young and inexperienced scientist can challenge the results of an older and more experienced one, or an obscure scientist can challenge the findings of a Nobel Prize winner, and the profession will evaluate the results on the basis of methods quite independent of the authority of the contenders, and will establish what is the correct conclusion. In other words, the result is established on the objective quality of the Physics and not on the reputations of the persons involved. * * *

"Third, in scientific method in the broadest sense, each hypothesis is tested and verified by methods appropriate to the hypothesis in question. Some are tested and verified logically, some experimentally, some historically, etc. Some sciences, of course, can reproduce experiments cheaply and they tend to emphasize experiment. This is notably the case with the Physical Sciences. In others, particularly some branches of Medicine and the Social Sciences, one cannot experiment readily, if at all, and the detailed analysis of available historical data is most appropriate. In this respect, they resemble Military Science very closely. In choosing weapon systems some experimentation is possible but a great deal of analysis is also required. In fact, in the development of weapon system analysis, one is more handicapped than in most of the sciences, for fully realistic tests come only at infrequent intervals in war, while the development of new weapon systems also takes place in peacetime. But this argues for better analysis and more heavy reliance on analysis where fully relevant experience is not generally available.

"Fourth, quantitative aspects are treated quantitatively. This is not to say that all matters can be reduced to numbers; or even that most can be, or that the most important aspects can be. It is merely to say that the appropriate method for dealing with some aspects of problems of choice of weapon systems and strategies requires numbers. Nonquantitative judgment is simply not enough. What is at issue here really is not numbers or computers versus words or judgments. The real issue is one of clarity of understanding and expression. * * *

"Numbers are a part of our language. Where a quantitative matter is being discussed, the greatest clarity of thought is achieved by using numbers instead of by avoiding them, *even when uncertainties are present*. This is not to rule out judgment and insight. Rather, it is to say that judgments and insights need, like everything else, to be expressed with clarity if they are to be useful.

"Let me emphasize the point about uncertainties. Many people seem to feel that quantitative analysis is **not** possible if there are any uncertainties. But this view is incorrect. In fact there is substantial literature on the logic of decision-making under uncertainty going back at least as far as Pascal, Bernoulli, and Bayes in the 17th and 18th centuries. Moreover, there are simple practical techniques for dealing with uncertainty which make it possible to do analyses that point up the uncertainties for the decision-maker and indicate their significance. In fact, rather than conceal uncertainties, a good analysis will bring them out and clarify them. If it is a question of uncertainties about quantitative matters such as operational factors, it is generally useful to examine the available evidence and determine the bounds of the uncertainty. In many of our analyses for the Secretary of Defense, we carry three estimates through the calculations: an 'optimistic' a 'pessimistic,' and a 'best' or single most likely estimate. If there are uncertainties about context, at least one can run the calculations on the basis of several alternative assumptions so that the decision-maker can see how the outcome varies with the assumptions."

THE LIMITATIONS OF SYSTEMS ANALYSIS

I have frequently been asked about the shortcomings and limitations of the Systems Analysis approach. Let me refer to an article I wrote for the Naval Review, 1965, reprinted in *A Modern Design for Defense Decision*.

"What's wrong with systems analysis? What are its particular limitations and biases? One criticism I have heard is that emphasis on quantitative analysis risks ignoring those factors that cannot be reduced to numbers, or at least overemphasizing those that can.

"Suppose, for example, that the problem is to choose between two alternative ways of destroying a certain set of targets. The less costly way is to base short-range missiles on the territory of an ally; the more costly way is to cover the targets with long-range missiles based in the United States. But suppose basing the missiles on the ally's territory would lead to political difficulties, to the embarrassment and possible fall of a friendly government. How does one take account of such political aspects in a quantitative analysis? The answer is that one doesn't. There is no way of "grinding in" the potential political difficulties of an ally. The most the analysis can do is to make clear to the decision-maker the differences in cost and effectiveness between the two approaches so that he can make an informed judgment about their weight in relation to the political problems.

"I would not want to deny that there is potential danger here, even though there is nothing about the systems analysis approach that prevents an assessment of the political or other non-quantitative factors from being included in the staff work. I am confident that the top-level leaders of the Department of Defense who use systems analyses as one of their sources of information are careful to give balanced consideration to all factors, whether quantitative or not.

"Another criticism sometimes made is that application of the 'flat of the curve' argument to force or performance requirements may lead people to ignore the decisiveness of a narrow edge in superior performance. There is a danger here if an unwary analyst confuses *performance* and *effectiveness*. There is no question but that, in some cases, a narrow edge in performance may have a very great impact on effectiveness. The performance advantage of the Japanese Zero fighter over American aircraft at the beginning of World War II is a good case in point. But there are other cases in which even a substantial increase in performance, purchased at a high price, may have a small impact on effectiveness. For example, many Navy aviators believe that under today's conditions, a sub-

stantial speed advantage in attack aircraft may mean rather little in terms of increased effectiveness. It is easy to confuse performance and effectiveness. But this mistake is clearly not peculiar to the systems analysis approach. The only way to avoid it, and to relate performance to effectiveness properly, is with the help of good analysis.

"Next, it is argued that the system analysis approach may be biased against the new and in favor of the old. I am sometimes concerned that our analyses may be subject to such bias, but I think that the method of open explicit analysis is much less likely to be so biased than is reliance on judgment or intuition or experience unsupported by analysis. The reason for the bias is that we all tend to compare the old and the new in the current mission that happens to have been optimized for the old. * * *

"Finally, sometimes it is said that systems analyses oversimplify complex problems. Of course, we have to simplify the complex problems we face; no one could possibly understand most problems of modern weapon systems and strategy in all their complexity. And it is a natural human failing to oversimplify. But I believe the facts are that the systems analysis approach is much less prone to oversimplification than any alternative approach. For it is part of systems analysis to bring to bear all of the best of modern analytical techniques for organizing data and summarizing clearly its most relevant aspects. Moreover, reliance on the method of open, explicit analysis is our best guarantee against persistence in harmful oversimplification. For if I must lay out clearly all of my assumptions, objectives, factors, and calculations, my critics can see what I have done and point out where I have oversimplified, if indeed I have done so. But if I am allowed to keep it all in my head and appeal to experience or judgment, others have no way of knowing whether or not I have oversimplified the problem."

INTRODUCTION OF SYSTEMS ANALYSIS IN THE DEFENSE DEPARTMENT

Although Systems Analysis is a reasonable and straightforward concept, it was not an easy one to implement in the Department of Defense. In conducting a sound cost-effectiveness study you must be able to associate both the benefits and costs with the alternatives to be examined. The Defense management system as it existed five years ago did not permit this. Assistant Secretary Hitch described the problems he encountered as follows:

"In 1961, the chief, in fact the Secretary's only systematic and comprehensive vehicle for the allocation of resources in the Defense Department, was the annual budget. For the task which it was being asked to perform, it was deficient in several respects. The budget focused on the financial problems of a single upcoming fiscal year, thereby discouraging adequate consideration of decisions whose near term dollar impact was slight but whose impact in later years was very large, to the point of becoming an important constraint on Defense managers. The structure of the budget, which portrays the Defense program in terms of broad functional purposes (e.g., personnel, procurement and construction) and organizational components also limited its usefulness as a management tool.

Rational military strategies and force requirements have to be planned and expressed in terms of the final products of the military program such as numbers of combat ready divisions and deployed missiles, rather than in terms of the basic resource ingredients of the budget. Moreover, in the Department of Defense at that time there was an almost complete dichotomy between military planning, which was long range, expressed in terms of outputs, and performed by military planners in the Joint Staff and the Military Departments; and budgeting, which was short range, expressed in terms of inputs, and performed by the Comptroller organization.

"It was to bridge the gap between these two functions that we designed and installed the 'programming' system. By linking military planning and budgeting in a unified planning-programming-budgeting decision-making process we are able to produce a single departmentwide blueprint for the future known as the 'Five Year Force Structure and Financial Program.' The program projects not only the military forces needed to meet the requirements of our long-range military plans but also the personnel, equipment, supplies and installations required to support them. In addition, the program projects the full costs of these resources, thereby permitting responsible decision-makers to assure themselves that the program they are planning is financially feasible and is providing a sound basis for the development of our annual budget requests to Congress.

"The Five Year Program is organized by forces and weapon systems grouped by mission. At the broadest level of aggregation, there are ten major military programs—the Strategic Retaliatory Forces, the Continental Air and Missile Defense Forces, the General Purpose Forces, Airlift and Sealift Forces, and Research and Development Program, etc. These major military programs are made up of subaggregations. These, in turn, are made up of 'program elements' which we consider the basic building blocks as well as the decision-making level of the programming process. A 'program element' is an integrated force or activity—a combination of men, equipment and facilities whose effectiveness can be directly related to national security objectives. The B-52 bomber force, together with all of the supplies, bases, weapons, and manpower needed to make it militarily effective is such a program element. Other examples would be attack carriers or infantry divisions. There are in all about 1,000 program elements. Groupings of program elements are based on a common mission or set of purposes, with elements either complementing each other or being close substitutes which should be considered together when making major program decisions."

The Programming System thus allows the reader to see at a glance how much of the Department of Defense Budget is going to strategic retaliatory forces and how much of that is going to each of the major weapon systems included in that category. This is clearly a far more meaningful way of subdividing the Defense Budget from the point of view of determining its overall shape. But even more importantly, the Programming System permits us to relate both benefits and costs to the forces and activities that must be compared

and planned. This feature is essential to any agency that hopes to apply the Systems Analysis approach to its problems.

THE WORK OF SYSTEMS ANALYSIS

The primary function of Systems Analysis in the Pentagon is to assist the Secretary of Defense by developing information that will be useful to him in making key decisions on force levels and resource requirements. For this reason the work of the staff is tied very closely to the annual Defense decision-making cycle which is based on detailed continuing requirements studies. Carefully formulated, detailed analytical studies are basic to sound decisions on force and resource requirements. We develop each year a program of studies that we believe should be conducted during the coming year. These proposed studies are submitted to the Secretary who reviews them, decides which ones he feels are required, and requests the Joint Chiefs of Staff and the Service Secretaries to have their staffs conduct them. My staff works closely with the groups that are actually conducting the studies to advise them on methodology, selecting assumptions, and to insure that the study is focused on the questions the Secretary feels need answering. When the studies are completed and submitted to the Secretary we assist him by reviewing them, indicating weaknesses, summarizing them for his use, etc.

The completed studies normally serve as the basis for proposed changes to the Five Year Defense Program. These changes may be submitted by one of the Military Departments or by the Joint Chiefs of Staff. Proposed changes to the Force Structure are then reviewed in depth by the staff of the Office of the Secretary of Defense. We in Systems Analysis emphasize "cost-effectiveness" studies of the proposals, comparing each with the previously approved force and other alternative ways to accomplish the mission. The Secretary then makes tentative decisions on the Force Structure. These tentative decisions are reviewed by the Joint Chiefs of Staff and the Military Departments, who have the opportunity to make further recommendations. After further discussions with his principal military and civilian advisers, the Secretary of Defense makes his final decisions, and these decisions serve as the basis for the annual budget. The budget is reviewed by the Secretary in the fall of each year and, of course, submitted to Congress in January. By this point we are well into the next cycle and new requirements studies are being initiated.

Throughout the decision-making cycle, Systems Analysis emphasizes integration of the various elements of the defense program and focuses on the broad national security objectives. This should be a primary objective of any Systems Analysis staff, at the Federal, State, or local governmental level, as it is an area in which most government organizations are weak. This was particularly true in Defense five years ago.

A 1961 organization chart of the Department of Defense would show the advisers to the Secretary of Defense on forces and military strategy, the Joint Chiefs of Staff; the adviser on research and engineering matters, the Director of Research and Engineering; the adviser on financial matters,

the Comptroller; the adviser on production matters, the Assistant Secretary for Supply and Logistics; the adviser on international matters, the Assistant Secretary for International Security Affairs; etc. Each adviser was concerned primarily with his own specialty rather than the Defense program in its entirety. The Secretary of Defense, virtually alone, was expected to integrate all of these diverse facets personally and to do so without systematic assistance.

The Programming System was developed to provide one mechanism for integrating the diverse parts of the Defense program, especially to integrate force planning with budgeting and support programs. The Systems Analysis Office was established to gather and display information associated with these different areas in a manner that would show the Secretary of Defense how the pieces fit together. Its work cuts across these various specialties. Of course, the information that we provide the Secretary of Defense is only one of many inputs available to him, and the integrating functions that we perform in no way reduce the very great importance the Secretary attaches to the advice and information provided by the Joint Chiefs of Staff and his other civilian advisers.

SOME IMPORTANT PRECONDITIONS FOR SUCCESS

Two conditions seem to me to be necessary to the successful development and functioning of a Systems Analysis group within a policy making organization. The first is that the responsible decision-makers make use of Systems Analysis and take it seriously.

Without this, the professional personnel will recognize in time that their work is not influencing the course of events and their motivation is likely to be destroyed. By using Systems Analysis and taking it seriously, I do not mean that the decision-makers must accept the results of the analyses uncritically or that they must rely exclusively on the Systems Analysis input. Far from it. Every analysis must be based on many assumptions, and a responsible decision-maker may not choose to accept the assumptions that his analysts have made. What is important is that the analyses be given a fair hearing and be acted upon if they successfully stand up under reasonable debate and criticism; or, if they are not acted upon, that the analysts are told why so that they can correct their work in the future. The analysts must have this "feedback" from the decision-makers if they are to know which issues are considered relevant or significant, which objectives the decision-makers wish to pursue, and which assumptions appear to them to be plausible. A Systems Analysis capability installed as "window dressing" is not likely to develop into a good one.

The second necessary condition is that the Systems Analysis operation be fed with ideas growing out of a broadly based interdisciplinary research program. A research program is necessary in order to develop analytical tools, to define criteria and objectives for programs, and to invent new alternatives for achieving the objectives. Certainly, in Defense, the research program must be interdisciplinary, because the scope and complexity of Defense problems is too great to be encompassed with any single discipline. I am sure that this would also be true of Systems Analysis applied to major social problems outside of Defense.

One practical implication of this is that, generally speaking, research funds in these fields are likely to be better spent supporting research institutes containing groups of scholars from a variety of relevant disciplines oriented toward the problems, rather than on individual scholars who are more likely to be oriented toward the exercise of their academic specialties.

SYSTEMS ANALYSIS
NON-DEFENSE APPLICATIONS

Finally, let me repeat my conviction that Systems Analysis can be applied fruitfully to social problems. I feel certain that good analysis can assist in the design, development and consideration of alternative approaches to education, health, urban transportation, justice and crime prevention, natural resources, environmental pollution and numerous other problems. In fact, there is already a great deal of useful research going on in these areas.

It is often suggested that these problem areas will be resistant to systematic analysis because they do not lend themselves to quantification. In commenting on that, I would like to point out that we, in the Defense Department, also have our own imponderables to deal with. We try to measure those things that are measurable, and insofar as possible, to define those things which are not, leaving to the responsible decision-makers the job of making the difficult judgments about the imponderables. It has been our experience that in those areas most difficult to quantify, years of research and the application of a good deal of ingenuity will often yield ways of measuring and making comparisons that were not available at the outset.

Ultimately, policy decisions will be based on judgments about relative values, the likelihood of uncertain future events, which risks we should and should not run, et cetera. But, in De-fense, and in these other areas as well, good analysis can do a great deal to sharpen the issues, clarify the alternatives available to the decision-makers, and narrow substantially the range of uncertainty, thus freeing the responsible officials to concentrate their attention on the crucial judgments.

The Analysis of Nuclear Defense: The Ultimate Case

BY
ROBERT S. McNAMARA

DEPLOYMENT OF NIKE-X FOR DEFENSE OF OUR CITIES AGAINST A SOVIET ATTACK [1]

What is involved here is an analysis of the contribution the NIKE-X system might make to the defense of our cities under two assumptions:

(1) That the Soviets do *not* react to such a deployment.

(2) That the Soviets do react in an attempt to preserve their "Assured Destruction" capability.

As you know, the major elements of the NIKE-X system are being developed in such a way as to permit a variety of deployments; two have been selected for the purposes of this analy-sis. The first, which I will call "Posture A," represents a light U.S. defense against a Soviet missile attack on our cities. It consists of an area defense of the entire continental United States, providing redundant (overlapping) coverage of key target areas; and, in addition, a relatively low-density SPRINT defense of a number of the largest cities to provide some protection against those warheads which get through the area defense. The second deployment, which I call "Posture B," is a heavier defense against a Soviet attack. With the same area coverage, it provides a higher-density SPRINT defense for twice the number of cities.

---

[1] Extract from Statement of Secretary of Defense Robert S. McNamara before the U.S. Senate Armed Services Committee, 90th Cong., 1st sess., January 25, 1967, p. 45 (Defense Department mimeograph).

Retitled by the editors, this reading is a series of extracted statements and analyses by Robert S. McNamara, the former Secretary of Defense, issued during 1962–1967 as indicated in specific footnotes.

Shown on the following table are the components and the costs (which, if past experience is any guide, may be understated by 50 to 100 percent for the systems as a whole) of Posture A and Posture B.

	Posture A Invest. Cost ($ billion)	Posture B Invest. Cost ($ billion)
Radars		
MAR		
TACMAR		
PAR		
MSR		
Invest. cost	$6.5	$12.6
Missiles		
SPARTAN		
SPRINT		
Invest. cost	$2.4	$4.8
DoD invest. cost	$8.9	$17.4
AEC invest. cost	1.0	2.0
Total invest. cost (ex-R&D)	$9.9	$19.4
Annual operating cost	$0.38	$0.72
No. of cities w/term. def:	X	2X

The Multi-function Array Radar (MAR) is a very powerful phased-array radar which can perform all the defense functions involved in engaging a large, sophisticated attack: central control and battle management, long-range search, acquisition of the target, discrimination of warheads from decoys or "spoofing" devices, precision tracking of the target, and control of the defense interceptor missiles.

The TACMAR Radar is a scaled down, slightly less complex and less powerful version of the MAR, which can perform all the basic defense functions in a smaller, less sophisticated attack.

The Perimeter Acquisition Radar (PAR) is a phased-array radar required for the very long-range search and acquisition functions involved in area defense. To achieve the full potential of the extended-range SPARTAN, the target must be picked up at much greater distances in order to compute its trajectory before the SPARTAN is fired.

The Missile Site Radar (MSR) is a much smaller, phased-array radar needed to control the SPRINT and SPARTAN interceptor missile during an engagement. It can also perform the functions of the TACMAR but on a considerably reduced scale. Actually, a number of different sizes are being studied. This "modular" approach will permit us to tailor the capacity of the radar to the particular needs of each defended area.

The SPARTAN is a three-stage missile with a nuclear warhead capable of intercepting incoming objects at relatively long range above the atmosphere.

The SPRINT is a shorter range, high-acceleration interceptor missile designed to make intercepts at lower altitudes.

The technical principles involved in the radars are now fairly well established. One R&D MAR-type radar has been constructed at the White Sands Missile Range. A contract has been let for the power plant of a second MAR-type radar, which is to be constructed on Kwajalein Atoll. The Missile Site Radar is well along in development and the construction of one of these radars on Kwajalein Atoll has also begun.

Testing of the SPRINT missile was started at White Sands in November 1965 and the tempo of testing will steadily increase during the current year. The SPARTAN is still on the drawing boards. It represents a very substantial redesign of the original ZEUS and we will not know until it is flight tested how well it will perform.

Facilities for testing both the SPRINT and the SPARTAN will be constructed on Kwajalein Atoll. These, together with the TACMAR and MSR and the programs for the computers will give us all of the major elements of the NIKE-X system which are essential to test its overall performance against reentry vehicles fired from Vandenberg Air Force Base in California. (We feel we know enough about the PAR technology to be able to use the mechanically steered radars already on Kwajalein as simulators.) The system will be tested in stages, starting with the MSR and SPRINT, then the SPARTAN missile and the TACMAR

radar. A large number of test shots will be launched from the west coast of the United States to Kwajalein to test the system thoroughly as a whole. The most important objective of this effort is to determine proper system integration and computer programming, since the individual components of the system will have already been tested.

But even after this elaborate test program is completed, some technical uncertainties will still remain unresolved; this is to be expected in a system designed for such a highly complex mission. Moreover, we have learned from bitter experience that even when the development problems have been solved, a system can run into trouble in production or when it is put into operation. All too often the development prototype cannot be produced in quantity without extensive re-engineering. Production delays are encountered and costs begin to spiral. Sometimes these problems are not discovered until the new system actually enters the inventory and has to function in an operation environment. The TERRIER, TALOS, and TARTAR ship-to-air missiles are a good example; after spending about $2 billion on development and production of these missiles, we had to spend another $350 million correcting the faults of those already installed, and we still plan to spend another $550 million modernizing these systems.

In this connection, it is worth noting that had we produced and deployed the NIKE-ZEUS system proposed by the Army in 1959 at an estimated cost of $13 to $14 billion, most of it would have had to be torn out and replaced, almost before it became operational, by the new missiles and radars of the

NIKE-X system. By the same token, other technological developments in offensive forces over the next seven years may make obsolete or drastically degrade the NIKE-X system as presently envisioned. We can predict with certainty that there will be substantial additional costs for updating any system we might consider installing at this time against the Soviet missile threat.

The deployment of a NIKE-X system would also require some improvement in our defense against manned bomber attack in order to preclude the Soviets from undercutting the NIKE-X defense; and we would want to expand and accelerate the fallout shelter program. The investment cost (including R&D) of the former is estimated at about $1.5 to $2.4 billion and would provide for a small force of F-111 or F-12 type interceptors and airborne warning and control aircraft (AWACS). The expanded fallout shelter program would cost about $800 million more than the one we are now pursuing. We would also need some of our anti-submarine warfare forces for use against Soviet missile submarines, but we are not yet clear whether these ASW forces would actually have to be increased over the currently planned levels. In any event, the "current" estimates of the investment cost of the total Damage Limiting package would amount to at least $12.2 billion for Posture A and at least $21.7 billion for Posture B.

To test the contribution that each of these NIKE-X deployments might make to our Damage Limiting objectives, we have projected both the U.S. and Soviet strategic nuclear forces (assuming no reaction by the Soviets to the U.S. ABM deployment) to the time when Posture B, the heavier defense, could be fully in place.

The fatalities which these Soviet forces could inflict upon the U.S. (with and without a U.S. ABM defense) and the fatalities which the U.S. forces could inflict on the Soviet Union (with a Soviet ABM defense) are shown on the table below:

NUMBER OF FATALITIES [a] IN AN ALL-OUT STRATEGIC EXCHANGE (IN MILLIONS) [b]
(ASSUMES NO SOVIET REACTION TO U.S. ABM DEPLOYMENT)

U.S. Programs	Soviets Strike First, U.S. Retaliates		U.S. Strikes First, Soviets Retaliate [c]	
	U.S. Fat.	Sov. Fat.	U.S. Fat.	Sov. Fat.
Approved	120	120+	100	70
Posture A	40	120+	30	70
Posture B	30	120+	20	70

[a] Fatality figures shown above represent deaths from blast and fallout; they do not include deaths resulting from fire storms, disease, and general disruption of everyday life.
[b] The data in this table are highly sensitive to small changes in the pattern of attack and small changes in force levels.
[c] Assumes U.S. minimizes U.S. fatalities by maximizing effectiveness of strike on Soviet offensive system.

The first case, "Soviets Strike First, U.S. Retaliates," is the threat against which our strategic forces must be designed. The second case, "U.S. Strikes First, Soviets Retaliate," is the case that would determine the size and character of the Soviet reaction to changes in our strategic forces, if they wish, as clearly they do, to maintain an Assured Destruction capability against us.

These calculations indicate that without NIKE-X and the other Damage Limiting programs discussed earlier, U.S. fatalities from a Soviet first strike could total about 120 million; even after absorbing that attack, we could inflict on the Soviet Union more than 120 million fatalities. Assuming the Soviets do not react to our deployment of an ABM defense against them, which is a most unrealistic assumption, Posture A might reduce our fatalities to 40 million and Posture B to about 30 million.

Although the fatality estimates shown for both the Soviet Union and the U.S. reflect some variations in the performance of their respective ABM systems, they are still based on the assumption that these systems will work at relatively high levels of effectiveness. If these ABM systems do not perform as well as our technical people postulate, fatalities on both sides could be considerably higher than shown in the table above, or the costs would be considerably higher if major improvements or additions had to be made in the systems to bring them up to the postulated level of performance.

If the Soviets are determined to maintain an Assured Destruction capability against us and they believe that our deployment of an ABM defense would reduce our fatalities in the "U.S. Strikes First, Soviets Retaliate" case to the levels shown in the table above, they would have no alternative but to increase the second strike damage potential of their offensive forces. They could do so in several different ways. Shown in the table below are the relative costs to the Soviet Union of responding to a U.S. ABM deployment in one of these possible ways:

Level of U.S. Fatalities Which Soviets Believe Will Provide Deterrence[a] (Millions)	Cost to the Soviets of Offsetting U.S. Cost to Deploy an ABM
40	$1 Soviet cost to $4 U.S. cost
60	$1 Soviet cost to $2 U.S. cost
90	$1 Soviet cost to $1 U.S. cost

[a] U.S. fatalities if U.S. strikes first and Soviets retaliate.

If the Soviets choose to respond in that way to our ABM deployment, the results would be as shown on next page.

In short, the Soviets have it within their technical and economic capacity to offset any further Damage Limiting measures we might undertake, provided they are determined to maintain their deterrent against us. *It is the virtual certainty that the Soviets will*

NUMBER OF FATALITIES IN AN ALL-OUT STRATEGIC EXCHANGE (IN MILLIONS)
(ASSUMES SOVIET REACTION TO U.S. ABM DEPLOYMENT)

U.S. Programs	Soviets Strike First, U.S. Retaliates		U.S. Strikes First, Soviets Retaliate	
	U.S. Fat.	Sov. Fat.	U.S. Fat.	Sov. Fat.
Approved (no response) ...	120	120+	100	70
Posture A	120	120+	90	70
Posture B	120	120+	90	70

act to maintain their deterrent which casts such grave doubts on the advisability of our deploying the NIKE-X system for the protection of our cities against the kind of heavy, sophisticated missile attack they could launch in the 1970s. In all probability, all we would accomplish would be to increase greatly both their defense expenditures and ours without any gain in real security to either side.

ALTERNATIVE DAMAGE LIMITING PROGRAM [2]

In order to assess the potentials of various Damage Limiting programs we have examined a number of "balanced" defense postures at different budget levels. These postures are designed to defend against the assumed threat in the early 1970s. To illustrate the critical nature of the timing of the attack, we used two limiting cases. First, we assumed that the enemy would initiate nuclear war with a simultaneous attack against our cities and military targets.

[2] Statement of Secretary of Defense Robert E. McNamara before U.S. Senate Armed Services Committee, 89th Cong., 1st sess., February 24, 1965, p. 47. (Defense Department mimeograph.)

Second, we assumed that the attack against our cities would be delayed long enough for us to retaliate against the aggressor's military targets with our missiles. In both cases, we assumed that all new systems will perform essentially as estimated since our main purpose here was to gain an insight into the overall problem of limiting damage. The results of this analysis are summarized in the table on page 174.

The $5 billion of additional investment (of which about $2 billion would come from non-Federal sources) would provide a full fallout shelter program for the entire population. The $15 billion level would add about $8½ billion for a limited deployment of a low cost configuration of a missile defense system, plus about $1½ billion for new manned bomber defenses. The $25 billion level would provide an additional $8½ billion for anti-missile defenses (for a total of about $17 billion) and another $1½ billion for improved manned bomber defenses (for a total of $3 billion).

The number of strategic missiles required to take full advantage of the possibility that the aggressor might

ESTIMATED EFFECT ON U.S. FATALITIES OF ADDITIONS TO THE APPROVED
DAMAGE LIMITING PROGRAM (BASED ON 1970 POPULATION OF 210 MILLION)

	Millions of U.S. Fatalities	
Additional Investment	Early Urban Attack	Delayed Urban Attack
$0 billion	149	122
5 billion	120	90
15 billion	96	59
25 billion	78	41

delay his attack on our cities is already included in the forces programmed through 1970.

The high utility of a full nation-wide fallout shelter program in the Damage Limiting role is apparent from the foregoing table—it would reduce fatalities by about 30 million compared with the present level of fallout protection. The following table shows that a transfer of resources from fallout shelters to other defensive systems would result in substantially less effective defense postures for any given budget level.

The figures indicate that in the case of an early attack on our urban centers, for the same level of survivors, any Damage Limiting program which excludes a complete fallout shelter system would cost at least twice as much as a program which includes such a system —even under the favorable assumption that the enemy would not exploit our lack of fallout protection by surface bursting his weapons upwind of the fallout areas. In addition, fallout shelters should have the highest priority of any defensive system because they decrease the vulnerability of the population to nuclear contamination under *all* types of attack. Since at the $15 and

$25 billion budget levels, the bulk of the additional funds would go to missile defense, a high confidence in the potential effectiveness of the system would have to be assured before commitment to such large expenditures would be justified. Furthermore, at these budget levels, missile defenses would also have to be interlocked with either local or area bomber defenses in order to avoid having one type of threat undercut a defense against the other.

Although missiles clearly have a better chance than bombers of destroying residual enemy offensive forces because they can reach them much sooner, we also examined the effectiveness of bombers in the Damage Limiting role. In one such analysis we compared a strategic aircraft—the AMSA—and two strategic missiles— MINUTEMAN II and an improved missile for the 1970s. (This improved missile could be developed and deployed within the same time frame as the AMSA.) Although there are many uncertainties with regard to both the assumptions and the planning factors used in this comparison, it did demonstrate clearly one important point, namely, that there are less costly ways

ESTIMATED EFFECT OF FALLOUT PROTECTION ON U.S. FATALITY LEVELS FOR SEVERAL DAMAGE LIMITING PROGRAMS (BASED ON 1970 TOTAL POPULATION OF 210 MILLION)

	Millions of U.S. Fatalities			
	Early Urban Attack		Delayed Urban Attack	
Additional Investment	Partial Protection	Full Protection	Partial Protection	Full Protection
$0 billion	149	149	122	122
5 billion	145	120	107	90
15 billion	121	96	79	59
25 billion	107	78	59	41

of destroying residual enemy missiles and aircraft than by developing and deploying a new AMSA—even ignoring the fact that enemy missile silos and bomber fields are far more likely to be empty by the time the bombers pass over than when the missiles arrive.

THE ROLE OF THE MANNED BOMBER FORCE [3]

Given current expectations of vulnerability to enemy attack (before and after launch), and simplicity and controllability of operation, missiles are preferred as the primary weapon for the Assured Destruction mission. Their ability to ride out even a heavy nuclear surprise attack and still remain available for retaliation at times of our own choosing weighs heavily in this preference. (We are quite confident that the Soviets do not now have, and are most unlikely to have during the next five years, the ability to inflict high levels of pre-launch attrition on our land-

[3] Statement of Secretary of Defense Robert S. McNamara before the U.S. Senate Armed Services Committee, 89th Cong., 2d sess., February 23, 1966, p. 49. (Defense Department mimeograph.)

based missiles, or any attrition on our submarine-based missiles at sea.)

However, in order to determine how best to hedge against the possibility that our missile forces may turn out to be less reliable and may suffer greater pre-launch attrition than currently estimated, we have analyzed alternative ways in which additional forces might be provided. To simplify the presentation, we show a hypothetical case in which our missile forces would be barely adequate for the Assured Destruction task, given the expected missile effectiveness and allowing no missiles for other tasks. (In fact, our approved missile forces are far larger than required for the Assured Destruction task and, therefore, already have built into them a large measure of insurance.) The table [below] shows the cost of insuring against various levels of unexpected missile degradation, by buying either additional missiles or bombers to attack the targets left uncovered as a result of the "assumed" lowered missile effectiveness. Against the current Soviet anti-bomber defenses, we have measured the cost to hedge with bombers in terms of B-52s armed with gravity bombs since the FB-111/SRAM would be a more expensive alternative. Conversely, against an improved Soviet anti-bomber defense, we have used the FB-111/SRAM since it would provide a less expensive hedge than the B-52 armed with either gravity bombs or SRAM.

Only when missile effectiveness falls to less than about 50 percent of what we *actually* expect are bombers less costly than missiles for insurance purposes. Against current Soviet defenses, the presently available B-52G-H force (255 aircraft) is adequate to hedge against complete failure of the missile force, insofar as our Assured Destruction objective is concerned. Against possible improved Soviet defenses, we must be willing to believe that our missile effectiveness could turn out to be lower than 30 percent of what we

expect before we would wish to insure with FB-111/SRAM aircraft rather than with missiles.

Similar arguments could be developed with respect to "greater-than-expected" Soviet ballistic missile defense effectiveness. I will discuss this and other "greater-than-expected" threats later in this statement.

In summary, for the Assured Destruction mission, manned bombers must be considered in a supplementary role. In that role they can force the enemy to provide defense against aircraft in addition to defense against missiles. This is particularly costly in the case of terminal defenses. The defender must make his allocation of forces in ignorance of the attacker's strategy, and must provide in advance for defenses against both types of attack at each of the targets. The attacker, however, can postpone his decision

COST TO HEDGE AGAINST LOWER THAN EXPECTED MISSILE EFFECTIVENESS
(TEN YEAR SYSTEMS COSTS IN BILLIONS OF DOLLARS) [a]

Assumed Degradation to Missile Effectiveness (Realized/Planned)	Additional Missiles	Cost to Hedge with:	
		B-52/Gravity Bombs (Against Current Soviet Anti-Bomber Defenses)	FB-111/SRAM (Against Improved Soviet Anti-Bomber Defenses) [b]
1.0			
.8	$ 0.8	$1.3	$ 5.4
.6	2.0	2.6	7.7
.5	3.0	3.3	8.7
.4	4.5	4.0	9.6
.3	7.0	4.7	10.6
.2	12.0	5.3	11.5

[a] Ten year systems costs include for missiles—operating costs plus procurement of missiles for replacement and testing; for bombers—operating costs of bombers/tankers, modification costs plus procurement of the FB-111.
[b] Assuming the Soviets were to deploy a force of new, improved interceptors in the western part of the Soviet Union.

until the time of the attack, then strike some targets with missiles alone and others with bombers alone, thereby forcing the defender, in effect, to "waste" a large part of his resources. In this role, however, large bomber forces are not needed. A few hundred aircraft can fulfill this function. Accordingly, as will be discussed later, we propose to maintain indefinitely an effective manned bomber capability in our Strategic Offensive Forces.

AIR LAUNCHED MISSILES [4]

Last year we initiated development of SRAM as an element of the four part AMSA program. Now, given the decision to proceed with the procurement and deployment of the FB-111/SRAM system, this development program must be reoriented to the FB-111 schedule. The cost to complete the SRAM development program is now estimated at $170 million, including the related B-52 and FB-111 avionics. Some $8 million was provided in prior years; about $40 million will be needed in FY 1967.

Although we do not now plan to deploy SRAM on the B-52G-Hs, we propose to undertake the necessary avionics development work to permit such a deployment if it should become desirable later. We would expect to keep the HOUND DOG missiles in the operational inventory through FY 1970 on the same schedule as envisioned a year ago. However, in 1971, with the completion of the phase-out of the

B-52C-Fs, the HOUND DOG force would be phased down accordingly. We also propose to undertake engineering development and test of a new terminal guidance system for HOUND DOG which gives promise of achieving a better overall system reliability. Total development cost is estimated at $20.5 million of which $6.6 million would be obtained by reprogramming presently available funds and $8.1 million is included in the FY 1967 Budget.

In summary, the objective of forcing the Soviets to split their defense resources between two types of threats could be performed adequately by B-52 bomber forces considerably smaller than those we now have, i.e., the B-52G-Hs alone. However, a mixed force of B-52G-Hs and FB-111/SRAM would force the Soviets to build expensive terminal bomber defenses or be vulnerable to low altitude attack. Even against very advanced terminal defenses, the small size and low weight of SRAM would allow the U.S. to saturate their defenses with large numbers.

The cost of the manned bomber force we now propose, compared with the cost of continuing the current forces, is shown in the table on page 178.

MANNED INTERCEPTORS [5]

The manned interceptor force consists of about 860 all-weather aircraft in active units committed to the defense of the North American continent— F-101's, F-102's, and F-106's. In addi-

---

[4] Statement of Secretary of Defense Robert S. McNamara before the U.S. Senate Armed Services Committee, 89th Cong., 2d sess., February 23, 1966, p. 62. (Defense Department mimeograph.)

[5] Secretary of Defense Robert S. McNamara's Posture Statement presented to the U.S. Senate Armed Services Committee, 88th Cong., 1st sess. February 19, 1962, p. 53. (Department of Defense mimeograph.)

	FY 1967	FY 1971	FY 1975
	(costs in billions of dollars)		
Current Force Extended			
Forces (# aircraft):			
B-52	600	600	600
B-58	80	70	64
Costs (Cumulative '67–)	.....	$8.6	$17
Proposed Bomber Force			
Forces (# aircraft):			
B-52	600	255	255
B-58	80	0	0
FB-111	0	210	210
Costs (Cumulative '67–)	.....	$8.4	$14

tion, there are about 500 Air National Guard aircraft, a few of which are maintained on runway alert, and a number of Canadian squadrons committed to NORAD.

One of the principal problems we encountered with the interceptor force was its concentration on a relatively few soft bases, many of which were shared with SAC units. Accordingly, our first effort to decrease the vulnerability of the force was devoted to dispersing the interceptors to additional bases. But even now one-half of the active interceptor squadrons are still co-located with SAC. We now propose to disperse these forces further in fiscal year 1964 by providing additional facilities at 21 existing United States interceptor dispersal bases. This action will permit the dispersed deployment of around 25 percent of the active interceptor force for extended periods of time. At the present time, these dispersal bases have only a limited capability for the support of interceptor aircraft. The initial cost of this program would be about $45 million with continuing annual operating costs estimated at $15 million.

We still plan to retain the existing interceptor aircraft in the force through the 1964–1968 period. As is shown in Table 3, the number of aircraft in the force, however, will decline gradually because of attrition. By the end of fiscal year 1968 the manned interceptor force would consist of about 750 active Air Force aircraft and 600 Air National Guard aircraft. We believe that this force will be adequate against what we presently foresee as a declining Soviet manned bomber threat. However, if the Soviets should deploy a new long-range bomber, which we do not now deem very likely, we would have to reconsider the size and character of our interceptor force and, particularly, the need for modernization. There are a number of aircraft already in production, under development or programmed which could be adapted to the interceptor role with only modest additional outlays for development costs.

First, there is the F-4, a high performance fighter-interceptor now being procured for both the Navy and the Air Force. A fire control system, the APG-59 and a missile, the SPARROW

III-6B, which would be suitable for this aircraft, are now under development by the Navy. An F-4 type interceptor, because of range and time-in-air limitations, may be the least effective of the alternatives open to us but it could be made available early.

Another possibility is the Navy A-5 (A3J) attack bomber which is already in operation. A fire control system, the ASG-18, and GAR-9 missile, now being developed and tested by the Air Force, would be suitable for this aircraft. The A-5 type interceptor would be somewhat slower and would cost considerably more than the F-4 but it would have a significantly longer range and "time-in-air"—attributes which are especially important in an interceptor— and it could be made available just as early.

A third possibility is the F-111 (TFX) which we have just started developing for the Air Force and the Navy in a tactical role. A suitable fire control system, the N-11, is now under development by the Navy and a long-range missile, HARPY, is being developed for this aircraft. The F-111 should make an excellent interceptor. Its short take-off and landing characteristics would permit dispersal to and recovery from a large number of airfields. Its very long-range and "time-in-air" would permit continuous air patrol during the probable duration of an air battle. The F-111, in an interceptor version would not, of course, become available until the 1968–1969 period, about two or three years later than either the F-4 or the A-5 (A3J).

A fourth possibility would be a completely new interceptor based upon some of the most recent work being done on airframes and engines. Such

an aircraft could use the Air Force-developed ASG-18 fire control system and GAR-9 air-to-air missile. It would be a very high performance, but also a very high cost aircraft. It would have a higher speed than the TFX but its range and "time-in-air" would be significantly less.

A fifth possibility would be the adaptation of a large transport aircraft such as the KC-135 or a C-141 as an air-to-air missile platform. Such an aircraft might use an advanced fire control system and a long-range missile like the "EAGLE" which the Navy had under study a few years ago. It would, of course, have a much lower speed than any of the others; i.e., below Mach 1, but it would have a much longer radius of action and "time-in-air" and could carry perhaps as many as 30 air-to-air missiles. The fire control system would be able to track a large number of objects out to long distances and could control a large number of simultaneous interceptions. Because of its size and endurance, the aircraft could also operate as an airborne control center together with shorter range high-speed interceptors. Such an interceptor system would also be less vulnerable to ballistic missile attack since it could take off immediately on warning, remain aloft during the initial missile bombardment, and still have sufficient endurance to engage the follow-on bomber attack.

Whether or not the Soviet Union actually deploys a new long-range bomber, we intend to make a thorough study of the entire problem of modernizing our manned interceptor force and we hope that next year we will be in a better position to make definite recommendations on this subject. I do not believe, in the light of presently available intelligence and the wide range of options still open to us, that the situation requires us to make a decision now.

AIRLIFT AIRCRAFT [6]

Even though the C-5A would be very expensive to acquire—$2.2 billion (including development and procurement) for a force of 48 operational aircraft, or $3.2 billion for a force of 96 aircraft —on a ten year systems cost basis (i.e., including the cost of development, procurement and ten years of operation), the C-5A would be a much better buy than additional C-141s.

Our calculations show that it would be desirable to reduce the tentatively planned 20 squadron (320 aircraft) C-141 force by seven squadrons (112 aircraft) and substitute 1½ squadrons (24 aircraft) of C-5As. The 1½ squadrons of C-5As would provide the same capability as seven to eight squadrons of C-141s. Further, it is tentatively estimated that the ten year systems cost would be the same, even including the high cost of developing and procuring the new aircraft. Beyond the "break even" point, the C-5A cost per ton delivered would be progressively less than that of the C-141, as shown on the following table:

Tons Delivered in 30 Days to SE Asia [a]	Number of aircraft		Tentative Estimates of 10-Year Systems Cost Per Ton Deliv. (000) [a]	
	C–141	C–5A	C–141	C–5A
X	29	6	$108	$223
2X	58	12	108	147
3X	86	18	106	119
4X	115	24	106	102
6X	172	36	105	84
8X	229	48	104	73
10X	286	60	104	69

[a] Real figures remain classified.

I have selected the figure of 13 squadrons of C-141s as the point of departure for this calculation for several reasons:

(1) The C-141 is already in production. A total of 145 aircraft have

[6] Secretary of Defense Robert S. McNamara's classified Posture Statement to the U.S. Senate Armed Services Committee, 89th Cong., 1st sess., February 24, 1965, p. 165. (Defense Department mimeograph.)

been placed in order through FY 1965 funding.

(2) Assuming we can start full scale development of the C-5A by about July 1, 1965, the first operational aircraft would not be available until late in FY 1969 and possibly not until the end of calendar year 1969. We should not halt the buildup of our airlift between now and then.

(3) A mixed force of C-141s and

C-5As would be desirable in any event since a variety of vehicles with different capacities more nearly produces a uniform matching of capabilities and requirements. The C-141 could carry the denser cargo, thus making fuller use of its payload potential, while the C-5A could carry the bulky cargo. Furthermore, there will always be trips which will not require the very large capacity of a C-5A.

For all of these reasons, a force of 13 squadrons (208 aircraft) of C-141s appears to be the best compromise.

Programs, Objectives and Decision Making

By
ARTHUR SMITHIES

This paper is designed mainly to introduce the use of an input-output matrix into program budgeting for systems analysis.

In much of the discussion of the subject it is implicitly or explicitly assumed that a given objective can be achieved in a number of alternative ways, and that analysis can reveal the mix of programs that will achieve the objective the most efficient way.

Virtually all practical situations are more complicated than that. Programs must be set up in terms of meaningful government activities that can be organized and administered effectively. Objectives, on the other hand, reflect the purposes of government action. There is no necessary correspondence between the structures of objectives and programs. In fact, most programs contribute to more than one objective, and it can be grossly misleading to ignore this fact. Consequently, an input-output approach is required, in which it is recognized that program inputs can yield a variety of outputs.

Another purpose is to emphasize the fact that objectives, themselves, are not clearly defined in advance. They become refined and amended in the course of the decision-making process. Ends and means are closely intertwined.

Finally, there is the question of quantitative measurement of outputs. When the government is producing non-marketable products, such as defense, dollar measurements of output are out of the question and other methods of quantification are imprecise. Yet decisions have to be made.

Rather than discuss these matters in a general way, I propose to outline a program approach to the problem of education. I have chosen this area because it brings out all the issues in-

Arthur Smithies is Nathaniel Ropes Professor of Political Economy, Harvard University.

volved and because it is less mysterious than areas such as defense or space. When the reader perceives how imprecise and speculative the analysis is, he should ask himself whether it is better to be unsystematic. He should also bear in mind that solutions to defense problems are much "softer" than the casual observer may think.

The analysis of education consists of the following components:

(a) Identification of the objectives to be pursued.
(b) Identification of system elements or programs.
(c) Identification of cost elements.
(d) Determination of relations between cost elements and system elements.
(e) Design of optimal system elements.
(f) Determination of relations between system elements and objectives.
(g) Selection of optimal systems at given levels of system cost.
(h) Selection of the optimal education system in the light of national objectives.

OBJECTIVES

The identification of objectives depends partly upon policy declaration contained in legislation, legislative histories, and Presidential announcements. It also depends upon established social values. For instance, the belief in universal literacy may be so well established that it is not declared to be an objective or any particular document. Furthermore, objectives in the field of education may depend upon the contribution that education can make to the attainment of other national objec-

tives, such as the desired increase in the productivity of labor.

As a tentative list of the educational objectives of the federal government, I suggest:

Cultural and Scientific

(1) Promotion of sciences and the arts.
(2) Presentation of cultural values.

Social and Political

(3) Achieving universal literacy.
(4) Promotion of effective citizenship.
(5) Maintaining effective military and civilian government services.

Economic

(6) Maintaining supplies of social and professional disciplines such as medicine, engineering, management, and business administration.
(7) Equipping the underprivileged for productive employment.
(8) Maintaining a satisfactory role of productivity increase.

Each of these objectives has an independent importance so far as education is concerned, but they may also compete with or complement each other. For instance, universal literacy is an end in itself, but it also contributes to effective citizenship and productivity. On the other hand, preservation of cultural values may interfere with productivity increase.

Before final decisions can be made, the decision maker must be able to assess the relative importance of the various objectives. A statement such as "improving literacy is more important than increasing scientific knowledge" has not much operational content. If it could be said that an additional billion dollars spent on improving literacy will contribute to social objectives more or less than a billion dollars spent on science, one has a basis for decision. But that statement cannot be made until it is known what an extra billion will do in either direction. In short, the relative importance of objectives is discovered in the course of the analysis of the entire system.

SYSTEM ELEMENTS

What are here called system elements are the various educational programs that appear in a program budget. Each of them relates directly to one or more of the policy objectives, and each of them can be analyzed in terms of meaningful cost elements. The system elements are also designed with due regard for the existing organizational structure. In some instances programs correspond with institutions; in others they cut across institutional lines in order to coordinate activities with a common purpose.

A preliminary list of system elements is:

(1) Primary education
   (a) Preschool
   (b) School
(2) Secondary education
   (a) College preparatory (high school)
   (b) Vocational (high school; other)
(3) Tertiary education
   (a) Liberal arts (B.A.)
   (b) Training for advanced scholarship (Ph.D.)
   (c) Professional training (M.D., LL.B., etc.)
(4) Military education
(5) Adult education
   (a) Educational TV
   (b) Public libraries and museums

COST ELEMENTS

Each system element or program depends on various cost elements. In broad categories these cost elements are: (1) teaching, (2) structures, (3) equipment and (4) subventions to students. The institution of a new program or the expansion of old ones should be thought of as time-phased operations: (1) the R&D phase; (2) the investment phase; (3) the operating phase. A continuing program will involve all of these elements simultaneously. Current operations will be accompanied by investment in structures and teacher training to provide for the expanding requirements of an expanding population.

PROGRAM OPTIMIZATION

The process of optimization of a program consists of determining the best way to spend, say, $1 billion on a particular program over, say, a 10-year future period. This involves highly complicated analysis of relating the numbers of students taught to quality of education provided, and the best mixes of teachers, structures and equipment that can attain prescribed educational standards at minimum cost. A closely related question is whether available funds should be put into enabling children to go to schools or providing better schools that a more limited number of children can go to.

To make matters more difficult the task cannot be regarded as one of suboptimization, as I am assuming for the sake of simplification. The composition of a program will affect its output and its contribution to educational objectives. From that point of view there is a qualitative, and not merely a quantitative, difference between having bad schools available to everyone and good schools available to a more limited number.

Nevertheless, for expository reasons, I shall assume that suboptimization is possible, and that in what follows we can speak of given amounts optimally spent on particular programs.

RELATION OF SYSTEM ELEMENTS TO OBJECTIVES

The next stage is to determine the contribution of expenditures of given amounts on particular programs that will contribute to the various education objectives. We are dealing with the federal government's activities, which are mainly subventions to state and local governments or private institutions. Consequently, it is necessary to estimate, first, the effect of a given amount of federal expenditure on total national program expenditure, and second, the effect of that latter increase on the attainment of objectives.

To carry out this task it is necessary to have quantitative indicators of the extent to which objectives are furthered by program expenditures. In the case of general productivity the objective can in principle be measured in GNP terms, leading to the familiar calculations of cost-benefit ratios. In some other cases single measures of output may suffice. For example, literacy may be measured by the increase in the number of children who attain prescribed reading standards.

In most cases, however, objectives or program outputs are characterized by vectors rather than single numbers; in some cases no quantitative indicators

may suffice. For instance, the beneficial or adverse social effects of changes in a liberal arts curriculum defy quantitative measurement. Yet for the analysis to proceed, some quantitative notion must be formed of the relative effects of expenditures on different programs on the attainment of objectives.

I shall therefore assume that research in all its aspects can yield such measures with a tolerable degree of reliability; that is, that it is possible to measure numerically the relative effectiveness of given expenditures on different programs in attaining program objectives.

This assumption can be conveniently represented by an input-output matrix. To simplify the exposition consider a simplified scheme with three programs: primary, secondary, and tertiary education; and three objectives: literacy, science and arts, and productivity increase. We then have the following matrix:

	Objectives		
Program	Literacy	Science and Arts	Productivity Increase
Primary	10	0	5
Secondary	0	3	9
Tertiary	0	10	4

The absolute numbers [1] are, of course, arbitrary; only relative magnitudes matter. Furthermore, only the columns have any significance. For the rows to be meaningful we would need to have measures of the relative social

---

[1] Sometimes even ordering in terms of a numerical scale may not be desirable, since it may imply more precision than the situation warrants. A letter grading system, A, B, C, D, and so on may be preferable in such cases. It may not be possible to go further than to use adjectives such as "good," "bad" or "indifferent."

importance of the objectives, which are yet to be determined.

SELECTION OF OPTIMAL SYSTEMS FOR GIVEN SYSTEMS COSTS

If weights could be given to the objectives and if they could be measured numerically, the problem would be a straightforward one of linear programming. The system could be found that would maximize "education" for a relevant planning period. But these requirements are not met. The final decision makers may have ideas of priorities among objectives at a particular time, and they may feel, for instance, that literacy has been reflected and, therefore, primary emphases should be placed on it. They may feel that as a result of a Sputnik incident more scientists should be brought into the world. They may be able to rank objectives—for instance science, literacy, productivity, and so on. But this is not enough.

If decision makers are to reach rational decisions by explicit rather than implicit processes, their evaluations of the relative merits of objectives must be more precise. The analyst can inform their judgment, but he cannot substitute for it. The process of choice among alternatives necessarily involves a large element of political judgment.

By studying the input-output table they can give concreteness to their thinking by becoming aware of the possibilities open to them. They can be aided in this process by examining a number of alternative systems which allocate a given system's cost in a variety of ways.

Consider in our simplified example the allocation of $3 billion among primary, secondary, and tertiary education in a variety of ways. From the output table we can then calculate the total contribution of each system to each objective. The results are summarized in the following table:

EFFECT OF VARIOUS ALLOCATIONS OF $3 BILLION ON EDUCATION OBJECTIVES

System	Allocation to Programs			Effect on Objectives		
	P	S	T	Literacy	Science	Productivity
a	1	1	1	10	13	18
b	0	1	2	0	23	17
c	0	2	1	0	16	22
d	0	0	3	0	30	12
e	1	0	2	10	20	13
f	2	0	1	20	10	14
g	3	0	0	30	0	15
h	2	1	0	20	3	19
i	1	2	0	10	6	23
j	0	3	0	0	9	27

Note: The rows again must not be added. The results show only the *relative* contributions of each system to each objective.

The range of alternative systems can be rapidly reduced by considering the urgencies of the moment. With a Sputnik challenge some combination of systems b, d, and e seems called for. If literacy needs attention, b, c, d, and j can probably be excluded. If productivity increase seems to be the most pressing need, there is a considerable range of choice which, however, becomes narrowed when the second priority objective is taken into account.

While the systems analyst cannot determine or discover the value judgments that enter into final decisions, he can do much to improve judgments by bringing relevant information to the attention of political decision makers. His research can point to changing trends in literacy levels, productivity, and research and can extrapolate these trends as to the future (although frequently he is wrong). He can, and I think should, express his views on what ought to be done. While I hold the view that the social scientist cannot be the final arbiter of values, that does not mean that he should not express his views on the subject in the light of his expertise—any more than a medical doctor should refrain from advising a patient to stop smoking or to reduce his weight.

It is not enough to optimize for one level of systems cost. The relative utilities of different programs may not be independent of their size, while on the production side, there may be increasing or diminishing returns to scale. Consequently, the analysis should be carried out for a number of different levels of systems cost.

All of this is complicated enough with three objectives and three programs. But we have already listed eight objectives and thirteen programs, and many will find even those listings inadequate. Clearly, to go through a complete analysis on that scale is out of the question.

The practical solution is not to reject the whole concept of systems analysis but to apply it partially rather than generally. Identify the areas where the need for change is most clearly demonstrated and work out from there in taking interdependencies into account. Ignore those segments of the matrix of possibilities where the need for change is of low importance.

In other words in practice one has to proceed by successive sub-optimizations and not by grand optimizations. While "zero-based" planning may be an ideal, it may not be a practical possibility. Economists will recognize a dilemma similar to that posed in economics by the relative merits of partial and general equilibrium analysis. With a partial approach one gets more useful results—and makes more mistakes. General equilibrium is a good thing to keep in the back of one's mind.

SELECTION OF THE OPTIMUM SYSTEM

Finally, the claimants of education must be considered in competition with other claimants on national resources: national security, health, and the private economy. Only in that context can the size of federal education expenditures be determined. Those concerned with education alone have not sufficient information.

CONCLUSION

This paper has attempted to set out what is involved in applying PPBS to a field such as education. It may provide a starting point for working out a satisfactory program of analysis. Or it may lead to the conclusion that PPBS cannot be applied comprehensively. The latter conclusion would leave one in the position that, while systematic analysis can be applied to lower-level, less important problems, more important questions are left to the law of the jungle. Why, then, disturb the jungle at all? An answer can be provided by experience elsewhere. Few would deny that it is a good thing to have safe cars and cool refrigerators, even though the purchase of cars and refrigerators is governed by highly irrational considerations.

The Interest Rate Applicable to Government Investment Projects

By
JACOB A. STOCKFISCH

This paper seeks to demonstrate that decision makers should apply to government investment projects an interest rate that equals the opportunity return on investment in the private sector of the economy. Moreover, it should be the rate of return that prevails *before* corporate taxes. Presently this rate is between 10 and 15 percent.

The use of a rate as high as 15 percent, as contrasted with one in the neighborhood of from 4 to 6 percent, is profound. Arnold Harberger, for example, stated that a majority of 53 Bureau of Reclamation and Corps of Engineers projects which he examined would have been rejected at a 10 percent rate.[1] Hirshleifer, DeHaven, and Milliman show that California's Feather River Project would be uneconomical at a 6 percent rate.[2] To employ a 15 percent rate would there-

Statement from *The Planning-Programming-Budgeting System: Progress and Potentials* (Hearings before the Subcommittee on Economy in Government of the Joint Economic Committee, Congress of the United States, 90th Congress, 1st Session, U.S. Government Printing Office, Washington, D.C., 1967). The author is a Senior Research Associate in the Institute for Defense Analyses. This paper had its origin in a study undertaken for Planning Research Corporation, Los Angeles, in the spring of 1960, on behalf of the Bureau of Supplies and Accounts, Department of the Navy, under contract No. NOnr-2713(00). The study received additional support through a research grant from the Division of Research of the UCLA Graduate School of Business Administration during the summer of 1960. Support from the Institute for Defense Analyses facilitated the final stage of gestation.

None of the above named institutions necessarily endorse or accept the views advanced in this paper.

[1] Arnold C. Harberger, "The Interest Rate in Cost-Benefit Analysis," *Federal Expenditure Policy for Economic Growth and Stability*, U.S. Govt. Printing Office, 1957, p. 241.

[2] Jack Hirshleifer, James C. DeHaven, and W. M. Milliman, *Water Supply: Economics, Technology, and Policy*, Chicago: 1960. pp. 341–346.

fore radically change government practices and operations. Current thinking in the government suggests that the proposed Supersonic Transport Program will be regarded a financial success or economically viable if the government can recover its outlay plus 6 percent. If a rate in the neighborhood of 15 percent is valid, it appears that present Government investment decision-making is extremely inefficient.

This paper consists of two parts. Part I develops the principle of why the opportunity rate of return on investment in the private sector should be used as the measure of capital cost in the public sector. Part II and Appendix A present a method to estimate that opportunity rate of return.

1. THE PRINCIPLE

The positive statement

Most resource using activities permit substitution between different kinds of resources. Often, it is possible to substitute larger initial investment outlays for smaller annual or periodic outlays, or vice versa, to achieve the given objective. For example, a large investment in spare parts can reduce the periodic maintenance and transportation costs necessary to support a weapon system during its life span. Or a law enforcement agency may acquire electronic data processing equipment in order to dispense with file clerks and thus reduce annual operating expenses. Possibilities such as these require that some interest rate be explicitly employed to make rational decisions.

There is a class of government resource-using activities which serve private ends by providing individuals instrumental services or products. For these activities it is often possible to identify the individuals or groups who benefit from the government operation. Government enterprises such as the Post Office Department, reclamation, conservation, and power projects are examples of such activities. It is also often possible for the government to employ prices to ration the service and to finance the operation. To determine the appropriate price, it is necessary to employ a cost of capital. The government may or may not use the price mechanism to ration the benefits or services the activity provides. To the extent that it does not price the service to cover the *full cost* of the project, including an appropriate interest cost, it provides private users a "subsidy in kind." Whether a subsidy should be provided is not a point at issue in a discussion of what the interest rate should be. An appropriate interest rate should nevertheless be applied to the project if only to determine the magnitude of the subsidy itself.

We may elaborate upon these points by an example which treats hypothetical alternative missile systems:

(In millions of dollars)

System	Initial Investment Cost	Annual Operating Cost
A	500	20
B	300	70
System life (years) .	5	....

For simplification we can assume that both systems have the same "kill potential."

It is unnecessary to be concerned with the question of whether the "product" is "worth" the cost of either system; this judgment may be a political-military one, not an economic one.[3] We may assume that the Strategic Air Command requires either system. Given agreement on this point the procurement decision can be approached in the same fashion as businessmen would evaluate two machine tools.

In the example of missile systems "A" and "B," one evaluation approach would be as follows: System "A" requires an incremental investment, as compared with System "B," of $200 million. System A relative to System B saves $50 million a year for five years. System A therefore enables the government to acquire a five-year annuity of $50 million a year. The internal rate return on the incremental $200 million investment is therefore 7.9%.

If the interest rate applicable to government investment projects is 15 percent, the government should not buy System A, since the incremental investment of $200 million in System A does not meet the 15 percent test, and System B is the preferred one. Stated another way, if the present costs of both systems were determined by applying a 15 percent discount rate, System B would be less costly: The present cost of System B is $534.6 million; System A's cost, $567 million.

Not to employ the same appropriate discount rate in the public sector that is encountered in the private sector can lead to many anomolies. A low discount rate "justifies" or signals the use of "capital intensive" production methods. As such, it would mean, for example, that a fork lift truck in a government warehouse or machine tools in a government arsenal would be more expensive and durable than are used in identical private operations. Government office buildings would be longer-lived than those in the private sector. More expensive automobiles, which would afford lower annual operation cost, would be called for. There appears to be no rational justification to promulgate such behavior.[4]

It should be noted that the level of the interest rate applicable to government operations has nothing to do with whether the total amount of government goods and services, or the magnitude of government activity as applied to meeting purely government ends, be large or small relative to the private sector of the economy. As exemplified by our weapon system example, the use of a 15 percent rate does not affect the decision of whether the government should procure a large or small quantity of weapons. Nor does it imply one way or the other whether we should have more "public goods" such as edu-

---

[3] It is possible, however, to address by analytical methods the question of whether the capability provided by either system is worth the cost. But this point takes us into other aspects of cost-effectiveness analysis, particularly the problem of identifying and measuring benefits. These problems should not be intertwined or confused with those of cost, which is what the discount rate treats.

[4] However, the point discussed above can help one understand the behavior of government agency and bureau heads to the extent that they do advocate the more "capital intensive" methods. To employ a less capital intensive technique necessitates higher annual outlays to maintain a given level of operations. Annual outlays can be (and are) controlled through the annual budget cycle. A capital intensive method, therefore, provides the agency a larger measure of protection against possible future control by higher decision makers, including Congress.

cation, national parks, space probes and ballistic missiles and fewer consumer goods, or vice versa. This issue is still to be determined by essentially political processes, to be hammered out by the liberal and conservative spenders. To follow the equalization principle is simply a means of maximizing the combined amount of both private and collective goods over whatever foreseeable future for which the appropriate rate of return will hold.

The social time preference school of thought

The "equalization principle" advocated here is not accepted by many students. Rather, they hold that the government employ some "social" rate of "time preference" for purposes of evaluating its investment projects. The main argument adopted by this group seems to run as follows: Investment decision-making in the private sector is governed by "time preference," which reflects the relative value that private individuals attach to present versus future consumption. The rate of return in the private sector reveals the "time preference" of private individuals who control resources. But there is no necessary reason, however, why the government should use the same rate. The private rate of time preference may be "too high" because private individuals are apt to be afflicted with "myopia," or possess a "defective telescopic facility," which causes them to save and invest less. The government should take a "longer view" since it has an obligation to promote the welfare of unborn generations. The appropriate social rate of time preference, there-

fore, should be lower than the "myopic" market rate.[5]

Such a line of argument is another way of saying that a larger capital stock is better than a smaller capital stock. The "optimum social rate of time preference" is therefore the opportunity return on the margin of investment that is consistent with some desired and larger total output goal. The assertion that the private rate of time preference is "too high" is therefore an assertion that the rate of capital formation will not be rapid enough, which is also an assertion that the national output at some future point in time should be higher than would result from spontaneous private investment and saving. The issue therefore becomes one of determining the rate of economic growth and net capital formation which assures that future generations will enjoy some policy-determined level of income.[6]

---

[5] See, e.g., Otto Eckstein, "A Survey of the Theory of Public Expenditure Criteria," *Public Finances: Needs, Sources and Utilization*, Princeton, 1961, p. 10; Stephen A. Marglin, "The Social Rate of Discount and the Optimal Rate of Investment," *The Quarterly Journal of Economics* (February 1963), pp. 95–111. This line of thinking has its intellectual foundation in the work of A. C. Pigou. See his *The Economics of Welfare*, 4th Ed. (London, 1949), p. 24. It was first published in 1912.
[6] At this point we must recognize that the "optimum" interest rate could be zero or even negative. For example, a per capita personal income of $50,000 a year by the year 2,000 might be attainable by utilizing all investment opportunities which at that time could offer any positive rate of return. Under such a condition the opportunity return would be zero. On the other hand, if we thought the per capita personal income should be $100,000 a year at that same point in time, an investment program that results in a negative opportunity return

Even if we grant that the over-all rate of growth of the economy and the rate of investment spending should be higher than what they would otherwise be, it does not follow that the government should employ, for evaluating its projects, an interest rate that is lower than the rate of return prevailing in the private sector of the economy. To the extent that a more rapid rate of capital accumulation promotes a higher rate of economic growth, it is simply sufficient that investment *per se* be increased, whether it be in the private sector of the economy or in government projects. In order to achieve a given growth objective most efficiently, we should still adhere to the equalization principle. By means of tax and subsidy devices, monetary policy, and possibly through other techniques, the opportunity return on *all* investment could be forced down from 15 percent to 10 percent, or even 3 percent. Whatever the rate of return might be, the same rate should also be employed for evaluating government projects. If the rates in the two sectors are not equalized, the policy of employing a lower rate for evaluating government projects will be an inefficient way of attaining the growth objective. It will also change the composition of output available to future generations. Moreover, it changes the product mix in an extremely inefficient manner. Let us demonstrate these points in connection with reclamation projects.

---

would have to be undertaken. Such a program, since all projects yielding positive returns would be exploited, would require that goods be stored for future generations. The cost of storing and deterioration would be responsible for the negative rate.

Let us assume that the going rate of return (before taxes) in the private sector of the economy is 15 percent. A proposed reclamation project that will provide water to irrigate land that can grow tomatoes is subjected to a cost benefit study. The study reveals that the internal rate of return on the tomato land reclamation project is 5 percent. In the cause of offsetting the "myopia" of the private sector of the economy, government policy-makers employ a 4 percent "social time preference" rate in their cost benefit analysis. On this basis the tomato-land reclamation project is undertaken. What are its consequences, and how does it benefit future generations?

Let us assume that the tomato land reclamation project costs $100,000,-000. In the cause of enhancing the welfare of future generations, steps are taken to insure that the resources diverted to the reclamation project come only out of private consumption. In this case future generations would enjoy a higher gross national product of $4,000,000 annually—the increment consisting solely of tomatoes. Should, however, $26.7 million of the resources required for the reclamation project be displaced from private investment, the future gross national product would be at the same level it would be if there had been no government project, although future generations would have more tomatoes but less consumer durables, entertainment, and other items normally produced in the private sector. Any larger displacement of resources from private investment into the tomato-land project would reduce the gross national product. For example, should the $100,000,000 project displace $40 million from private investment the future GNP will be $2 million less. Each year future generations would have $4 million more a year of tomatoes, but $6 million a year less of other goods. Thus the growth objective is defeated. For this happy outcome the present generation in addition sacrifices $60 million of consumption.

The operation is also an expensive way of getting additional tomatoes. If increasing tomato output is an important public goal, a more efficient way to attain it would be to subsidize tomato growing in the private sector of the economy that would cause some capital resources, which on the margin are yielding 15 percent, to be reallocated to tomato production and diverted from the production of other privately produced commodities.

Summary of the equalization principle

When we recognize that the government can attain any desired product mix by the use of selected excise taxes and subsidies, the use of an interest rate on government projects that supply private goods that is lower than the opportunity return in the private sector is an inefficient way of changing the composition of output. The use of a lower rate also leads to irrational decision-making within the government sector itself. For example, with the use of a zero rate, a $3 billion freeway system for a large metropolitan area would appear to have an annual opportunity cost of zero. At a 15 percent rate, the annual cost is $450 million. If we explicitly recognize the $450 million annual cost, the investment of say $1 billion in a rapid transit system with

an annual operating subsidy of $100 million a year and only $2 billion in freeways might provide an overall more effective urban transportation system. The use of low interest rates, or a zero rate, for evaluating government investments therefore seems almost certain to insure that the public goods and services we do get are likely to be the wrong kind.

Critics of the equalization principle (who generally are "low" interest rate advocates) usually criticize the position on the ground that it assumes that the level and structure of rates revealed in the private sector of the economy are optimal. They then correctly assert that optimality has not been proven. Therefore, the equalization principle should be rejected. Rejection of the equalization principle for this reason is a palpable *non sequitur*.

To invest resources purposefully in activities where the return is lower than the highest attainable is simply wasteful and inefficient, whether the highest rate of return is "optimal" or not. If we wish to attain a given growth objective, resources should be invested where the return is highest. If we want to change the composition of private goods, whether produced by government or private firms, the most efficient investment channels should be directed to that end by means of excise taxes and subsidies. If we want a given amount of government goods that meet "collective" wants, the investment policy that provides the highest GNP is the best means to get it. Even those who decry our nation's alleged "imbalance" between public and private goods (to say nothing of those who fly bombers or man submarines, or who teach school or supervise the national parks) can be motivated by offering them command over productive power, which includes the services of privately-created investment goods. If there is more such productive power, as contrasted with less, the burden of taxation or the inflationary incidence of deficit spending is less. The government can therefore proceed to divert more resources from the private sector to attain collective goals than it could if it caused resources to be invested in less productive channels. Thus, the assumption that the private opportunity rate of return is "optimal," in terms of some desired rate of economic growth, is not necessary to support the principle that the rates of return in the government and private sectors of investment be equalized.

ESTIMATING THE RATE OF RETURN

Ideally, we need a measure of the "marginal efficiency of investment." Moreover, it should be the rate of return before corporate and property taxes. Such a measure would enable us to address the following question: given an increment of new investment in the economy, what will be the resulting and permanent increase in the net national income and product? The reason we want the rate of return before taxes is because the government shares in the yield from private investment. This point is particularly germane with regard to treating government investment projects because the government experiences a loss of tax yields if it causes resources to be diverted from investment in the private sector. For example, an increment of private investment of, say, $100 million may increase the net national product by $15 million

annually. With a 50 percent profit tax, the government is able to extract $7.5 million of that increment. The overall social benefit of the private investment is thus 15 percent, and this should be the rate of return used to evaluate government investment projects.[7]

Such a rate of return concept also implies an equilibrium in the sense that rates of return are equal in all lines of activity. Actually, no such equality exists. The lack of equality between rates available on different margins of investment may be due to the fact that at any given time the economy is not in equilibrium.[8] It may also be due to the fact that investors have "tastes" for the differences in risk encountered with various types of physical assets. One is therefore forced to employ some average of marginal rates of return in order to get an overall measure of the social benefits of private investment.

Table 1 shows the average rates of return attributed to physical assets in major sectors of the American economy for selected periods. Column 1

------

[7] The overall impact of taxes on the earnings from all wealth—if one recognizes property, and corporate and personal income taxes—has been estimated by Arnold Harberger to be slightly under 50 percent, although the effective tax rates vary considerably as between sectors and activities. See Arnold Harberger, "Efficiency Effects of Taxes on Income From Capital," in *Effects of Corporation Income Tax,* ed. by Marian Krzyzaniak (Detroit, 1966), p. 110. Harberger's estimate is based on 1953–59 behavior, which may be mitigated somewhat by the Revenue Acts of 1962 and 1964. On the other hand, increases since that period in state income taxes and local property taxes will have worked in the opposite direction.
[8] However, there is nevertheless a strong tendency toward an equilibrium. See George J. Stigler, *Capital and Rates of Return In Manufacturing Industries* (Princeton, 1963), for a demonstration of this point.

shows total "earning assets" in 1965, to provide the reader a feeling for the relative importance of these sectors. Columns 2 and 3 show the average annual rates of return for the periods stated in Column 2. Column 5 presents

the average annual rates of return for the period 1961–65.

Before treating the behavior shown in Table 1, it is useful to describe the basis upon which the rates of return estimates were made.

TABLE 1

SUMMARY OF RATE OF RETURN BEHAVIOR FOR SELECTED MAJOR SECTORS [a]

Sector	Total Earning Assets, 1965 (billions of dollars)	Period	Annual Average Rate of Return (percent)	Annual Average Rate of Return 1961–65 (percent)
Manufacturing	274,574	1949–65	17.7	15.4
Electric utilities	53,534	1949–65	8.9	9.3
Gas pipelines	8,782	1955–65	8.5	8.6
Telephone	31,429	1949–65	10.6	11.9
Railroads	25,203	1956–65	4.8	4.1
Motor carriers	1,293	1958–64	13.0	14.7 [b]
Oil pipelines	2,793	1956–65	14.4	15.6
Airlines	4,384	1959–65	6.1	8.2

[a] Further detail, by year, is provided in appendix tables A–1 through A–8.
[b] Average of 1961–64 only.

Source: See appendix tables A–1 through A–8.

"Earning assets" in these calculations include inventory, net plant and equipment, and accounts receivable. Excluded from the asset base were cash and other short term liquid assets, and securities and long term debt that a company may hold as an investment. These adjustments warrant explanation.

From a firm's point of view, cash is necessary to provide liquidity. But, from the point of view of the overall economy, cash is not a "productive" resource. It yields no service or product in the same sense that workers or physical equipment create products. It is only a paper or legal claim against the government or a bank. The marginal cost of cash to society is zero, since the

supply of money can be increased or decreased by bookkeeping transactions and banking operations. As such, cash is not an asset the existence of which causes a displacement of real resources from the point of view of the economy as a whole, nor does cash create any real product in the economic system.

Other legal claims such as bonds and stocks are not physical, real resources; rather, they are claims against physical resources. Their creation, and their existence, therefore, do not involve the displacement of physical resources. Moreover, to the extent that a manufacturing or other operating enterprise owns them, that company is functioning as a portfolio investor, rather than a producer of economic goods and services. For these reasons such assets should not be considered part of the assets associated with the operations for which its physical investment is undertaken.[9]

The exclusion of these items from the estimate of a capital base, particularly the exclusion of cash and other short term financial assets, will cause the asset base to be smaller, and the derived rate of return to be higher, than those encountered in normal financial calculations.

In line with the same asset base, asset earnings were calculated to derive earnings before payment of interest on debt a company owes, before corporate taxes, and to exclude income not derived from operations, such as dividends or interest received from stocks or debt that a company owns.[10]

Table 1 indicates that in manufacturing the rate of return is around 15 percent; in the preponderance of the regulated sector it is around 10 percent, with the notable exception of the railroads. Examination of Appendix Tables A-1 through A-8 indicates that in manufacturing the rate of return has held fairly constant at around 15 percent after a leveling off from the Korean War induced highs. In the regulated sector, from the early and middle

1950's, the rate of return has tended to rise, to level off at around 10 percent. Railroads, however, have consistently done poorly, which reflects basic structural changes in our transportation sector. Until the last few years, airlines also fared poorly. However, since 1962 they have picked up dramatically, both in terms of rate of return performance as well as the absolute and relative allocation of investment to that sector.[11] Thus, a rate of return of 10 percent in the regulated sector and 15 percent in manufacturing —attributable to earning assets as defined above—appears to be a reasonable estimate of the opportunity cost of private investment in those sectors.

One may go a step further to ascertain the relative importance to attach to these rates. Table 2 shows the allocation of business investment on plant and equipment, by year, during the five year period of 1961–65. According to these data, about 70 percent of the total flows into the unregulated sector of manufacturing, mining, and commercial;[12] the remaining predominantly regulated sector absorbs 30 percent. If we assume that the revealed

[9] Accounts receivable are also legal claims, rather than physical assets; and one might contend that they, too, should not be part of the physical asset base. However, they constitute part of the "stock in trade" necessary for the conduct of business operations. They reflect displaced physical resources. They may be viewed as a "lending" or "renting" of goods or services for some specified period of time, with the firm receiving its earnings on its investment in the form of higher prices to customers.

[10] Further detail on the calculating methodology, including some discussion of the data sources, is presented in the Technical Notes in Appendix 1.

[11] The performance shown in Appendix Table A–8 for airlines has continued into 1966 when the rate of return was 12.5 percent, and the earning assets increased to $5.6 billion.

[12] The "commercial and other" category shown in Table 2 absorbs a large portion (24 percent) of the total. It includes trade and services. The preponderance of unincorporated businesses will be found in this sector, although it also contains large corporate activities—e.g., hotels, retail trade. Because of the diversity of activities and the importance of non-corporate firms in this sector, good data on investment and asset earnings are not readily available. For a discussion of some of the analytical and measurement problems of treating unincorporated businesses, see Stigler, *op. cit.*, pp. 114–118.

15 percent rate of return in manufacturing would also apply to the mining and commercial sectors, on the ground that competition within the unregulated sector would tend to promote equality in the rates of return, one could weight the 15 and 10 percent rates of return at the ratios of 70 and 30 percent, respectively. The overall rate of return is thus 13.5 percent.

TABLE 2

ALLOCATION OF BUSINESS INVESTMENT SPENDING ON PLANT AND EQUIPMENT, 1960–65

(billions of dollars)

	1961	1962	1963	1964	1965	5-Year Total	Percent
All industries	34.37	37.31	39.22	44.90	51.96	207.76	100
Manufacturing	13.68	14.68	15.69	18.58	22.45	85.08	41
Mining	.98	1.08	1.04	1.19	1.30	5.59	3
Commercial and other	8.46	9.52	10.03	10.83	11.79	50.63	24
Public utilities	5.25	5.48	5.65	6.22	6.94	29.54	14
Communications	3.22	3.63	3.79	4.30	4.94	19.88	10
Railroads	.67	.85	1.10	1.40	1.73	5.75	3
Transportation, other than railroads	1.85	2.07	1.92	2.38	2.18	11.03	5

Source: "Survey of Current Business," Apr. 1964, p. S–2; and Jan. 1967, p. S–2.

APPENDIX A

TABLE A–1—MANUFACTURING EARNING ASSETS, EARNINGS AND RATE OF RETURN
(BEFORE FEDERAL INCOME TAXES), 1949–65

(earnings and assets in millions of dollars)

Year	Earning Assets	Operating Profit [a]	Interest [b]	Earnings [c]	Rate of Return
1949	79,723	14,319	344	14,663	18.4
1950	84,061	22,651	340	22,992	27.4
1951	102,045	25,365	442	25,807	25.3
1952	122,780	22,456	624	23,080	18.8
1953	129,616	24,004	702	24,706	19.1
1954	132,092	20,541	663	21,204	16.1
1955	139,144	27,655	703	28,358	20.4
1956	159,043	28,742	932	29,674	18.7
1957	170,701	27,379	1,111	28,490	16.7
1958	175,341	21,926	1,173	23,099	13.2
1959	185,819	28,699	1,350	30,049	16.2
1960	198,713	26,486	1,538	28,024	14.1
1961	208,518	26,454	1,624	28,078	13.5
1962	222,624	30,819	1,822	32,641	14.7
1963	233,604	33,777	1,887	35,664	15.3
1964	248,896	38,416	2,143	40,559	16.3
1965	274,574	45,630	2,545	48,175	17.5

[a] Net operating profit as reported in source below.
[b] Estimated by method discussed below.
[c] Sum of "operating profit" and estimated "interest" costs.

Source: Quarterly financial report for manufacturing corporations, Federal Trade Commission, Securities Exchange Commission, 1949–66.

TABLE A–2—RATE OF RETURN, TOTAL AND SELECTED ASSETS, PRIVATELY OWNED ELECTRIC UTILITIES IN THE UNITED STATES, 1949–65

(assets and earnings in millions of dollars)

Year	Earning Assets	Earnings	Rate of Return on Earning Assets (percent)
1949	16,475	1,323	8.0
1950	18,150	1,519	8.4
1951	19,887	1,724	8.7
1952	21,954	1,985	9.0
1953	24,517	2,183	8.9
1954	26,716	2,371	8.9
1955	28,776	2,681	9.3
1956	31,127	2,888	9.3
1957	34,136	3,012	8.8
1958	37,012	3,212	8.7
1959	39,710	3,567	9.0
1960	42,241	3,828	9.1
1961	44,401	4,058	9.1
1962	46,403	4,372	9.4
1963	48,539	4,585	9.4
1964	50,770	4,753	9.4
1965	53,534	4,995	9.3

Source: "Statistics of Electric Utilities in the United States, Privately Owned," 1959 and 1965 volumes, Federal Power Commission.

TABLE A–3—NATURAL GAS PIPELINE COMPANY EARNING ASSETS, EARNINGS (BEFORE FEDERAL INCOME TAXES) AND RATE OF RETURN, 1955–65

(assets and earnings in millions of dollars)

Year	Earning Assets	Earnings	Rate of Return (percent)
1955	5,232	323	9.2
1956	5,789	359	9.0
1957	6,697	395	8.0
1958	7,270	427	8.0
1959	7,990	474	7.9
1960	8,718	549	8.6
1961	8,876	560	9.0
1962	9,356	605	8.6
1963	9,522	616	8.9
1964	9,397	586	8.3
1965	9,673	603	8.2

Source: "Statistics for Interstate Natural Gas Pipeline Companies," 1965, Federal Power Commission.

TABLE A–4—TELEPHONE COMMUNICATIONS EARNING ASSETS, INCOME, AND
RATE OF RETURN (BEFORE FEDERAL INCOME TAXES), 1949–65

(assets and earnings in millions of dollars)

Year	Earning Assets	Earnings	Rate of Return (percent)
1949	7,635	453	5.9
1950	8,239	709	8.6
1951	8,938	817	9.1
1952	9,801	915	9.3
1953	10,789	1,052	9.8
1954	11,729	1,184	10.0
1955	12,933	1,424	11.0
1956	14,685	1,572	10.7
1957	16,590	1,725	10.4
1958	18,015	2,085	11.6
1959	19,455	2,404	**12.4**
1960	21,108	2,601	12.3
1961	22,966	2,800	12.2
1962	24,861	3,030	12.2
1963	26,796	3,273	12.2
1964	28,964	3,377	11.7
1965	31,429	3,602	11.5

Source: "Statistics of Communications Common Carriers," Federal Communications Commission (annual reports).

TABLE A–5—RAILROAD EARNING ASSETS, EARNINGS, AND RATE OF RETURN
(BEFORE FEDERAL INCOME TAXES), 1956–65

(assets and earnings in millions of dollars)

Year	Earning Assets	Earnings	Rate of Return (percent)
1956	23,756	1,713	7.2
1957	24,034	1,515	6.3
1958	24,479	1,304	5.3
1959	24,469	1,340	5.4
1960	24,613	787	3.2
1961	24,496	1,167	4.7
1962	24,538	885	3.6
1963	24,593	970	3.9
1964	24,240	956	3.9
1965	25,203	1,126	4.5

Source: Transport Statistics in the United States (annual reports), pt. I, "Railroads," Bureau of Accounts, Interstate Commerce Commission.

TABLE A–6—OIL PIPELINES, EARNING ASSETS, INCOME, AND RATE OF RETURN
(BEFORE FEDERAL INCOME TAXES), 1956–65

(assets and earnings in millions of dollars)

Year	Earning Assets	Earnings	Rate of Return (percent)
1956	1,990	328	16.5
1957	2,048	291	14.2
1958	2,094	246	11.7
1959	2,253	259	11.5
1960	2,267	269	11.9
1961	2,316	326	14.1
1962	2,316	342	14.8
1963	2,718	358	13.2
1964	2,739	476	17.4
1965	2,793	521	18.7

Source: Transport Statistics in the United States (annual reports), pt. 6, "Oil Pipelines." Bureau of Accounts, Interstate Commerce Commission.

TABLE A–7—INTERCITY MOTOR CARRIER EARNING ASSETS, EARNINGS, AND
RATE OF RETURN (BEFORE FEDERAL INCOME TAXES), 1958–64

(assets and earnings in millions of dollars)

Year	Earning Assets	Earnings	Rate of Return (percent)
1958	844	95	11.2
1959	966	141	14.5
1960	991	66	6.7
1961	1,020	142	13.9
1962	1,104	164	14.9
1963	1,188	166	13.9
1964	1,293	208	16.1

Source: "Transport Statistics in the United States" (annual reports), "Part 7: Motor Carriers." Bureau of Accounts, Interstate Commerce Commission.

TABLE A–8—AIRLINES (CERTIFICATED AIR ROUTE CARRIERS) EARNING ASSETS, EARNINGS,
AND RATE OF RETURN (BEFORE FEDERAL INCOME TAXES AND SUBSIDIES), 1959–65

(assets and earnings in millions of dollars)

Year	Earning Assets	Earnings	Rate of Return (percent)
1959	2,114	75	3.5
1960	2,663	22	.8
1961	3,072	−58	—
1962	3,249	107	3.2
1963	3,236	197	6.0
1964	3,804	388	10.1
1965	4,384	593	13.5

Source: "Civil Aeronautics Board, Air Carrier Financial Statistics." (So-called Yellow Book, issued quarterly.)

TECHNICAL NOTES ON TABLES
A–1 THROUGH A–8

DERIVATION OF EARNING
ASSET ESTIMATES

Annual versus Quarterly Asset Values.
For all sectors, except manufacturing,
asset values were end of year (December
31) magnitudes. For manufacturing, the
average of end of quarter magnitudes
was employed. To the extent that an industry is growing, this difference will
tend to cause the asset base to be larger
when the end of year value is used than
when the average of the quarters is employed, with an opposite effect on the
rate of return calculation. Thus the rates
of return developed in this study on the
regulated industries will be slightly understated relative to those shown for manufacturing.

Elements of the Asset Base.
1. *Manufacturing.*—The items in the
Quarterly Financial Report (FTC–SEC)
"Total Receivables," "Inventories" and
"Total Property, Plant, and Equipment
(net)," were summed.
2. *Electric Utilities.*—The accounts labeled "net total utility plant," "notes and
accounts receivable less accumulated provisions for uncollected accounts" and
"materials and supplies" were summed.[1]
3. *Natural Gas Pipelines.*—"Net gas
utility plant," "gas stored underground—
non-current" accounts were summed to
derive long-term assets; "notes and accounts receivable, less accumulated provision for uncollected accounts," "materials and supplies" and "gas stored
underground—current" constituted short
term earning assets.
4. *Telephone Communications.*—"Total communications plant—net," "materials and supplies" and "accounts receivable
from customers, agents and others" were
summed.

---

[1] See references cited in Tables for source
documents.

5. *Railroads.*—"Total Properties less
recorded depreciation and amortization,"
"materials and supplies," "net balance
receivable from agents and conductors,"
"miscellaneous accounts receivable," and
"accrued accounts receivable" were
summed.
6. *Oil Pipelines.*—Only selected balance sheet data are provided in ICC reports treating this industry. Earning assets
were estimated as follows: "carrier property" less the sum of "accrued depreciation—property" and "accrued amortization—property" constituted estimate of
physical plant. "Total current assets" less
"cash" served as an estimate of receivables and inventory or supplies. This
method undoubtedly overestimates "earning assets" as defined in this study, and
will cause a slight underestimate of the
rate of return.
7. *Motor Carriers.*—"Net carrier operating property" plus 50 percent of
"Current assets—total" were summed.
The 50 percent factor was derived from
examination of more detailed statistics
for a subsample of the industry.
8. *Airlines.*—"Net value of operating
equipment," "materials," "net value of
spare parts" and "accounts receivable"
were summed. For the years 1959 and
1960, the above short term asset accounts
could not be clearly identified; hence, 50
percent of total short term assets was
employed.

EARNINGS

A. For each of the regulated industries, annual operating income (before
fixed charges, particularly interest) and
major tax components (including federal
income taxes) were readily identifiable.
For airlines, federal subsidies (which
mainly accrue to selected local route carriers) were *subtracted* from aggregate industry profits to derive before tax earnings. (In 1965, for example, the federal
subsidy was $79 million.) It is possible
that mail revenues may contain a subsidy

element; however, we had no way of estimating this for a fact.

B. *Manufacturing.*—The FTC–SEC definition of "Net profit from operations" *excludes* interest charges. That is, cost and expenses include interest on debt and bonds. Thus the "profit" figure (which compares with what corporate stockholders normally focus on) would understate asset earnings by the amount of interest payments. (The FTC–SEC reports, incidentally, follow the pattern employed in the Department of Commerce national income accounting methodology.) Nor do the FTC–SEC Quarterly Reports provide a separate interest cost component. It was therefore necessary to estimate interest charges. (This estimate is shown by year in Table A–1.)

The estimating method for interest was as follows: The FTC–SEC reports do pro-

vide balance sheet data on "short term loans from banks," (maturity of one year or less), "installments, due in one year or less, on long term debt," and "long term debt due in more than one year." For each year the quarterly average of these items was determined, the short term and the sum of the two long term items were multiplied by an appropriate interest rate. The sum of these products constitutes the estimated "interest" item shown in Table A–1.

The derivation of the interest rates was as follows: For long term debt, a 10 year moving average of Moody's composite yield on industrial bonds. For short term debt the arithmetic mean, for each year, of the rate on short term bank loans and the rate on 4 to 6 month prime paper. These rates are shown in Appendix Table A.

APPENDIX TABLE A—INTEREST RATES EMPLOYED TO ESTIMATE INTEREST COMPONENT OF MANUFACTURING ASSET EARNINGS, 1949–65

	Short-Term Rates			Moody's Composite Yield on Industrial Bonds (10-Year Moving Average)
Year	Short-Term Bank Loans	Prime Commercial Paper, 4 6 Months	Average	
1949	2.68	1.49	2.08	2.82
1950	2.69	1.45	2.07	2.78
1951	3.11	2.16	2.63	2.77
1952	3.49	2.33	2.91	2.77
1953	3.69	2.52	3.10	2.82
1954	3.61	1.58	2.59	2.85
1955	3.70	2.18	2.94	2.90
1956	4.20	3.31	3.75	2.99
1957	4.62	3.81	4.21	3.13
1958	4.34	2.46	3.40	3.25
1959	ª5.00	3.97	4.48	3.42
1960	5.16	3.85	4.50	3.62
1961	4.97	2.97	3.97	3.78
1962	5.00	3.26	4.13	3.93
1963	5.01	3.55	4.28	4.04
1964	4.99	3.97	4.48	4.18
1965	5.06	4.38	4.72	4.33

ª Beginning 1959, series revised to exclude loans to nonbank financial institutions.

Source: Short-term rates: Economic Report of the President, January 1967, p. 272. Long-term rate: Moody's Industrial Manual, 1965, p. a21.

On the Appropriate Discount Rate for Evaluation of Public Projects

By
WILLIAM J. BAUMOL

SIGNIFICANCE OF THE DISCOUNT RATE

It is generally recognized that the discount rate is a critical datum for the evaluation of any proposed government project. Even where there is little basic disagreement about the investment's prospective costs and benefits the choice of discount rate figure may make the difference between acceptance and rejection. A project which seems to yield substantial net benefits when evaluated at a 3 percent rate may well appear extremely wasteful if the rate is 5 percent.

Yet despite the critical nature of this parameter, in some calculations it is assigned a value almost cavalierly, with little attempt to show that the selected figure is not chosen arbitrarily and capriciously. In part this occurs because the choice of discount rate is a rather technical matter of economic analysis and it is not widely understood among nonspecialists. As a result, custom and convention become substitutes for careful analysis, and one sometimes encounters discount figures in cost-benefit calculations whose sole justification seems to be that similar figures were used in the past. Of course that can never be an acceptable argument,

first because the earlier figure may have had as little justification as the one presently employed and, second, because changing circumstances produce modifications in the appropriate value of the discount rate, as will be shown below.

At stake in the choice of an acceptable discount rate is no less than the allocation of resources between the private and the public sectors of the economy. The discount rate, by indicating what government projects should be undertaken, can determine the proportion of the economy's activity that is operated by governmental agencies, and hence, the proportion that remains in the hands of private enterprise. With so much at issue it is well worth the effort to explore in some detail the principles that should be employed in arriving at a discount figure, and the rationale that underlies those principles. This paper undertakes to

Statement from *The Planning–Programming–Budgeting System: Progress and Potentials* (Hearings before the Subcommittee on Economy in Government of the Joint Economic Committee, Congress of the United States, 90th Congress, 1st Session, U.S. Government Printing Office, Washington, D.C., 1967). William J. Baumol is Professor of Economics, Princeton University.

describe these principles extensively and carefully without heavy reliance on the jargon of technical economics.

THE BASIC CRITERION: OPPORTUNITY COST

The role of the discount rate as arbiter of the allocation of resources between private and public enterprise is critical. It serves to explain the grounds for our concern with the subject. This observation also proves to be the key to the principles which underly the choice of an acceptable discount figure. The right discount rate becomes that number which indicates correctly when resources should be transferred from one sector to another.

More specifically, suppose one is considering the construction of a dam which will employ x manhours of labor, y tons of cement and z kilowatt hours of electricity. In an economy in which the level of employment is high, if those resources are made available to the government they must be transferred out of the private sector. Just as in the guns vs. butter case, each item added to the public sector involves some corresponding reduction in the volume of resources in private hands.[1]

We may now establish a rather obvious criterion to test the desirability of the proposed resource transfer. If the resources in question produce a rate of return in the private sector which society evaluates at r percent,

then the resources should be transferred to the public project if that project yields a return greater than r percent. They should be left in private hands if their potential earnings in the proposed government investment is less than r percent. The logic of this criterion is self evident. It states no more than the minimal dictate of efficiency: Never take resources out of a use where they bring in (say) 9 percent in order to utilize them in a manner which yields only 6 percent!

The standard that has just been described is the concept economists call *opportunity cost*. (This is the only bit of jargon in which we shall indulge ourselves.) We have stated, in effect, that the proper standard on which to judge the desirability of a governmental project, from the point of view of the general welfare, is the value of the opportunities which the private sector must pass by when the resources are withdrawn from that sector. A government project is desirable if and only if the value of the net benefits which it promises exceeds the cost of the lost productive opportunities which that investment causes.

We are now in a position to define the standards for a correct discount rate figure to be used in evaluating government projects. *The correct discount rate is the percentage rate of return that the resources utilized would otherwise provide in the private sector.* That is, the correct discount rate is the opportunity cost potential rate of return on the resources that would be utilized by the project. An example will readily show why this must be so. Suppose these resources are capable of returning our hypothetical 9 percent in the private sector. Consider three proposed

---

[1] On the other hand, if any resources used by the government project would otherwise be totally unemployed, now and in the future, their use obviously incurs no opportunity cost in the private sector. In an economy such as that of the United States since World War II employment of resources has usually been so high that this consideration is quite irrelevant to the facts of the matter.

government projects: Project *A* which offers an average rate of return of 12 percent, Project *B* whose expected return is 9 percent and Project *C* whose anticipated yield is 7 percent. It should be obvious that if we discount the returns of Project *C* at the opportunity rate of 9 percent we will end up with a negative net present value figure (i.e., seven percent discounted at 9 percent comes out to less than the principal invested). If we discount Project *B*'s expected returns at 9 percent we will obtain a zero figure for the present value of net benefits (the returns will just cover the cost of the investment). Only Project *A* when discounted at 9 percent will receive a positive net benefit figure. Thus the discount rate calculated at the opportunity rate works just as it should: it passes projects whose yield is greater than its resources could earn in the private sector and turns down projects whose benefits are not equal to the earnings the resources could provide in private hands.

The same illustration also shows immediately how an incorrect choice of discount figure—one not equal to the opportunity rate—can result in decisions harmful to the general welfare. For example, consider two extreme possibilities in terms of our hypothetical figures—a discount rate that is much too high (say, 15 percent) and one that is much too low (say, 5 percent). At the excessive 15 percent figure the usual cost-benefit criterion would reject all three projects, even Project *A*. The government would then fail to undertake an investment that clearly represents an efficient use of society's resources. On the other hand, a 5 percent discount rate would, on a cost-benefit criterion, lead to the construction of all

three projects. Thus even investment *C* would be undertaken even though it uses resources that should better be left in private hands. For it takes resources from employments in which they return 9 percent and puts them into an occupation in which they bring in only 7 percent, a palpable two percent net loss to the community.

The upshot is perfectly clear. Any discount rate that is clearly above or clearly below the opportunity cost rate is indefensible because either of these will lead to decisions that reduce the general welfare. We must turn therefore to an investigation of the opportunity cost rate of resources, for once we have determined this we will have the requisite information for the choice of discount rate to be used in the evaluation of government projects.

THE OPPORTUNITY COST OF CONSUMER RESOURCES

When a government project withdraws resources from the private sector it must take them either from consumers or from business firms. A bag of cement used in constructing a dam might otherwise have been used to build a factory or in paving Sam Jones' driveway. The two sources need not always incur equal opportunity costs and they will therefore have to be examined separately. It will be seen presently that the opportunity cost of resources withdrawn from industry is relatively easy to explain and so, to get the more difficult matter out of the way first, we begin with the opportunity cost of consumer resources.

Since consumers' goods do not provide a rate of return that is measurable directly it is necessary to find some indirect means by which the opportunity cost can be inferred. Fortunately there is a straightforward way in which this can be done. When a consumer voluntarily purchases a bond which returns, say, 6 percent, he is indicating that this rate of return compensates him for giving up a dollar's worth of present consumption and hence deferring the consumption to the future. Put another way, if this consumption were worth more than 6 percent to him he would not buy the bond, while if the consumption were worth less than 6 percent to him he would purchase more bonds than he does. Thus without any conscious calculation on his part a consumer's security purchases reveal something about the rate of return his present consumption is worth to him— the opportunity cost incurred when a dollar's worth of consumption goods is prevented from going to him and is transferred to a government investment project. We can learn about this opportunity cost by observing the consumer's behavior exactly as in the physical sciences one learns about pressure, temperature, etc., by observation of items which themselves have knowledge of these magnitudes.

What about consumers who do not buy any bonds? It follows from the preceding discussion that their opportunity cost must be at least as high and probably higher than it is for bonds purchasers. To a man who chooses *not* to purchase bonds at 6 percent, the consumption for which he uses his money must by definition be worth more than 6 percent. This is no less true for a man who fails to purchase bonds because "he cannot afford them." That phrase merely implies that his consumption dollar means a

great deal to him—perhaps even survival itself, and is therefore certainly more valuable than 6 percent.

We may summarize by saying that the opportunity cost of present consumption to non-bondholders must be at least as great as the figure for bondholders and that to bondholders the opportunity cost of consumption is indicated by the rate of return on their bondholdings.

Here we are referring to the net rate of return after making allowance for risk. An 8 percent rate of return on a highly risky bond may be no greater than a 6 percent rate of return on a safe security because the additional two percent of the more speculative bond simply compensates the purchaser for the added risk it requires him to undertake. That two percent "risk premium" is therefore only a payment for the risk involved in holding an unsafe security and has nothing to do with the basic opportunity cost of deferred consumption which is incurred when resources are transferred from the consumer to the government. The criterion of bondholder's opportunity cost therefore is the rate of return on a riskless bond. For all practical purposes a government bond can be considered to be such a riskless security.

Moreover, what is relevant for this purpose is not the rate of return on short-term securities but the yield of long-term bonds. When cement is put into a dam that is expected to last for 50 years, these resources are taken out of the hands of consumers for such a long period, and the opportunity cost is the rate of return consumers expect when they voluntarily give up resources for a similar period, i.e., when they acquire long-term bonds.

We can now readily draw our conclusion about the opportunity cost of resources derived from consumers. Since in recent years government bonds with longer maturities have been returning between 4.75 and 5 percent one can be certain that the opportunity cost rate for consumers is at no lower than the smaller of these figures. For bondholders it may be taken to be somewhere in the 4.75 to 5 percent range while for individuals who do not purchase bonds deprivation of resources will incur an even higher opportunity cost. Hence on resources obtained from consumers there is no reason to utilize any discount rate lower than approximately 4.75 percent.

THE DISCOUNT RATE ON RESOURCES FROM THE BUSINESS SECTOR

Next we consider the opportunity cost of resources derived from business firms. Recent hearings on rate of return to various public utilities have suggested clearly that these are expected to provide a rate of return ranging from perhaps 5½ to 8½ percent *after taxes*. That is, the productivity of resources used by such companies is sufficient to return this much to company stockholders. Even those who have argued before the regulatory commissions for relatively low profit ceilings for such companies have not proposed that earnings be driven below this range. But with a corporation tax rate in the vicinity of 50 percent, in order to return say 6 percent to stockholders, the company must produce a product for which consumers are willing to pay approximately 12 percent! That is, one can state with some confidence that the resources used by firms in the private

sector characteristically produce returns in terms of value of output ranging from 11 to 17 percent. There is no need to enter here into the discussion of the proportion of this amount that should be ignored because of risk. The indisputable fact is that on any criterion the rate of return on resources transferred from business firms to government projects, i.e., their opportunity cost rate, is well in excess of the 4.75 to 5 percent that constitutes the minimum discount figure applicable to resources transferred from consumers to government projects.[2]

The upshot of the discussion is clear. No absolute and final figure has been suggested for the appropriate discount rate on government projects. However,

---

[2] A few remarks on the issue of risk may, however, be illuminating. It is true that in many firms new investments are highly risky —we cannot anticipate what future demands for their outputs will be. On the other hand, a government investment is also risky. For example, many abandoned canals were no doubt built in the anticipation that their use would continue much longer than it did in fact. Thus it cannot be argued that, e.g., a 9 percent return on a government project is perhaps the equivalent of a 15 percent return on a corporate investment, because both of them are subject to considerable risk. The treatment of risk has been the subject of considerable discussion by economists. Some highly reputable economists (e.g., Prof. P. A. Samuelson of the Mass. Institute of Technology and Prof. Kenneth Arrow of Stanford University) have argued that because there are so many investment projects undertaken in the economy overall they incur no risk on the same statistical principal (the law of large numbers) which largely eliminates the risk of life insurance companies who do not know when any individual policyholder is going to die. In any event it is quite certain that no economist of any substantial reputation, whatever his views of the risk issue in the calculation of the opportunity cost of resources transferred from private firms, would argue that this opportunity cost rate is below 4.75 percent.

it has been shown that on any standards, a figure below 4.75 percent is certainly too low and will lead to the wasteful transfer of resources from the private to the public sectors. For we have seen that for some resources (those transferred from consumer bondholders) the opportunity cost rate is at least 4.75 percent, while on resources which are kept from non-bondholding consumers or from business firms the opportunity cost is higher—probably in many cases by a considerable amount.

CHANGES IN RATES
ON GOVERNMENT BONDS

This completes the basic analysis of the determination of the appropriate rate of discount for use in a cost-benefit evaluation of government projects. However, a number of misconceptions have sometimes arisen in this area and it is therefore desirable to face up to them squarely. The next few sections address themselves to issues of this variety.

Thus, the preceding discussion may give rise to misunderstanding about the consequences of changes in the rates of interest which the federal government chooses to offer on its securities. Suppose the rate of interest on long-term bonds is initially five percent and the government decides to issue some bonds bearing a coupon of 4.5 percent. One may be tempted to question whether this automatically affects the desirability of a proposed government project. The answer is that this change *by itself* will have no such effect. For the real rate of return on government bonds is not necessarily equal to its coupon rate —the nominal percentage payment

which the treasury decides to assign to them; rather the real rate of return will be determined by the opportunity cost of money to bond purchasers. Suppose, for example, that the opportunity rate to consumers were 5 percent and (to take a ridiculous example for the sake of ease of arithmetic) the treasury decided to issue (perpetual) bonds offering only 2½ percent. The consequences would follow almost at once. Bonds with a face value of $100 could be sold for a market price of only $50 because no one would be willing to pay more for them.[3] And at that price the investor who put $100 into government bonds would obtain *two* bonds of face value of $100 for his money, bonds that would return to him $2.50 each, so that on his investment he would still obtain 5 percent. Hence the treasury decision to issue 2½ percent bonds would not in the slightest way change the fact that the effective yield on government bonds (and hence the opportunity cost of resources drawn from bondholding consumers) is 5 percent.

While the numbers in the preceding illustration are exaggerated, the situation it describes is very real. The effective yield on government bonds if often quite different from their nominal return. That is precisely what goes on whenever the price of such a security changes—its effective yield is affected

---

[3] An obvious exception is represented by the case of "E" and "H" bonds whose prices are fixed and yet continue to be sold when market rates of interest rise. However, the purchasers of these bonds are small investors who are not always fully informed of the alternative investment opportunities available to them and whole bond purchases are in part a response to patriotic appeals. The terms on which these securities are bought are therefore only distantly related to the opportunity cost of consumer resources.

by the market and investors' valuation of their money, even though the rate of return promised by the face value of the bond does not change.

It is true that the government can change the real rates of yields on bonds. It does so when it goes from an easy money policy to one involving tight money. But this it must accomplish through the use of much more powerful measures that do influence the opportunity cost of money itself.

Only by influencing GNP, or the supply of money or the supply of bonds, all of which affect the valuation which consumers place on their money, can the government institute a change in the real yields of its securities and really make it stick. Thus, when government policy does succeed in producing a change in the *effective* bond rate, the new bond rate does become a valid indicator of the correct rate of discount on government projects.

CALCULATION OF THE RATE OF RETURN ON LONG-TERM BONDS

The discussion of the preceding section has some clear implications about the manner on which the long-run bond rate of return should be calculated if it is to be used for the process of evaluation of the discount rate on government projects. There are two basic rules both fundamental and inviolable:

1. *The rate of discount should utilize in its calculation the market yield on government bonds not their fictitious coupon rate of return.* Consider again our previous example: a bond issue nominally designed to offer a (perpetual) return of 2½ percent (it yields a return of $2.50 and bears a face value of $100). If the market price of that bond falls to $50 the effective market rate will be five and not 2½ percent and it would be absurd to call the rate of interest anything but five percent.[4]

2. Suppose, for the sake of illustration, it is decided to call bonds "long term" only if the period they involve is in excess of ten years. *Then if a bond was originally issued for twenty years but currently has only one year left before it reaches maturity it must be considered a short-term (one year) bond and its interest rate must not be used in calculating an average rate of interest on long-term securities.* The reason for this rule should be clear on a moment's reflection. If I hold a bond which matures in one year, it makes no difference to me today whether it was originally issued for one or twenty or one hundred years. What is of importance to me (except as a matter of historical curiosity) is that the bond will return to me its face value in one year and pay me a certain amount in interest in the meantime. For precisely that reason the market prices of new one year bonds and of 20 year bonds with one year to run would behave in precisely the same ways provided their terms were the same—they would be

---

[4] This calculation and that in the previous section are somewhat oversimplified for purposes of exposition. The arithmetic is precisely accurate only for a perpetual bond such as the British consols in which no repayment of the principal is ever contemplated. If a bond matures in, say, 20 years the drop in current price does not affect its redemption value and this complicates the arithmetic slightly. The figure that is required in this case is what is called the yield to maturity which takes into account the present value of the amount the holder will receive when the security matures as well as the interest payments he receives in the interim.

priced to produce an identical effective rate of interest rate (yield to maturity), and hence both their interest rates would be *short-term* rates, irrelevant for the calculation of a long-term discount rate.

If it is true then, as I have been informed, that the rate of discount currently utilized in some cost-benefit calculations is obtained by averaging the *coupon rates* on all securities *whose original maturities were in excess of 15 years* one can only comment that the resulting figure has absolutely no relevance for the appropriate discount rate on public projects.

SUBSIDY FOR THE FUTURE?

Despite the firm economic grounds for our basic conclusion that there is no justification for a discount rate below the rate of interest on long-term government bonds, there may remain some who are tempted to argue for low rates of discount on what may be described as sentimental grounds. Such a view might rest its case on an appeal to the prospects for the nation's future—the argument that increased investment today is a contribution to the nation's welfare tomorrow. It would appear that this purpose can be served by a lower discount rate which would lead to approval of a larger number of governmental investment projects. The greater the number of investment projects that are put into effect the greater is the contribution to the nation's posterity.

Though such a position is likely to have considerable superficial appeal it can readily be shown to rest on a number of fallacies. First of all, there is no basis for the presumption that a

transfer of resources from the private to the public sector will necessarily produce a net increase in the amount of investment undertaken by the economy. The increase in the amount of governmental capital construction is very likely to be offset, at least in part, by a decline in private investments in plant and equipment.

Surely, if the nation's investment for the future is considered to be inadequate the appropriate remedy is to institute simultaneous inducements to both private and public capital formation.[5] As we have seen, an arbitrarily low discount rate on public projects certainly is not the instrument for that purpose. While it encourages government projects it discourages private investment by drawing resources away from industry and by providing disparate assistance to the competitors of those private firms who rely on no help from the government sector. Moreover, such arbitrarily low discount rates on public projects introduce serious inefficiencies into the investment process,

---

[5] There are of course important cases where it is considered socially desirable to stimulate governmental output of goods and services which cannot be provided effectively by the private sector. Education, elimination of pollution and national defense are all services whose supply, it is generally felt, should not be left exclusively in the hands of the private sector. In such cases government subsidy and, in some cases complete governmental financing, are entirely appropriate. But this does not justify a particularly low *discount rate* on the government projects which would distort the allocation of resources between short- and long-term investment. If we need more expenditure on education now—better books and better teachers—a reduction in the discount rate would not provide them. It would only stimulate the construction of durable school buildings, the long-term investment portion of educational expenditure.

by causing the withdrawal of resources from areas of use in which their yield is high and leading to their transfer to areas in which their return is low. This is a most peculiar way to encourage more effective investment for the future!

In any event, those who maintain that there is inadequate provision for the future draw incorrect general inferences from irrelevant particular cases. It is difficult to dispute the valid conservationist argument that the destruction of irreplaceable natural resources does indeed impose a heavy cost on our posterity. The destruction of a portion of a canyon, the extinction of a species of wildlife, the erosion of the soil all are matters of serious concern because once done they cannot be undone, and this is precisely the legitimate ground on which conservationists urge increased care in avoiding depletion of our natural resources.

But it is not legitimate to jump from the valid point that one generation has no right to use up wastefully the resources that cannot be replaced by its successors, to the groundless conclusion that each generation is constrained to engage in overall efforts to support its posterity beyond the level that is indicated by the free market. For that is precisely what is involved in a program of low discount rates or any other program of special inducements to investment. Any of these are, effectively, programs of subsidy in which society is committed to provide special assistance to governmental and other investment projects. And it is a commonplace of economic analysis that any act of real investment constitutes the transfer of resources from the present to the future. The construction of a durable dam amounts to the tying up of resources many of whose benefits will only become available to the community many years in the future.

The basic issue, then, is whether it is desirable to subsidize in this way the commitment to the future of resources which could otherwise serve society today. Considerable real investment is provided by the workings of free enterprise together with the program of government projects which can pass the standard cost-benefit test utilizing the discount rate that has already been described. Is there any justification for a program of subsidies designed to produce an even greater overall commitment of resources to the future?

A little thought shows that the grounds for such a program are highly tenuous at best. Our economy is characterized by a long run rate of growth of GNP of the order of 3 to 4 percent per year, compounded, and in recent years the growth rate has been even greater. Per capita income has risen persistently throughout our history and there is every reason to expect the rise to continue. We are therefore wealthier than our predecessors and it can quite safely be predicted that our successors will be richer than we. In effect, then, the artificial subsidization of a program of added investment amounts to an inducement for the transfer of additional resources from the poor to the rich. It would take inputs whose product would be available for consumption today and make them available tomorrow when the supply of consumer goods is likely to be so much more abundant than it is at present.

We see that there is no basis for the inference that because society should avoid the vandalism involved in the spoilation of irreplaceable resources, it should also subsidize the increased provision of resources of all sorts to future generations who are, even without this, so likely to be wealthier than we.

To summarize, there is no basis in terms of the welfare of society for a level of discount rate on government projects below the opportunity cost rate. A decision to utilize a low discount rate will, as we have seen, lead to three unfortunate consequences, all of them inimical to the welfare of the community.

First, insofar as it produces a net increase in investment by the economy, it will transfer resources from present consumption to future consumption even though future consumers are likely to be better supplied than those of today. Second, since such a low discount rate provides encouragement only to government investment, it will lead to the transfer of resources from the private to the public sectors of the economy and hence, very likely to a decrease in the level of investment undertaken by private enterprise as a whole. Third, and this is the most immediate issue, a low discount rate on government projects must lead to wasteful employment of these resources—it must induce their transfer from sectors of the economy in which their yield is high to other sectors in which their return is low, for that is precisely what is implied by a discount figure below the opportunity cost rate.

CONCLUDING COMMENTS: THE CONSENSUS OF PROFESSIONAL ECONOMISTS

The determination of the rate of discount is too important a matter to be left to casual calculation or the fortuitous practices that have developed over time. The literature of economics agrees both on the importance of a correct choice of discount rate and on the basic criterion which should be used in its determination. The logic of the issue dictates that opportunity cost is the relevant criterion and this conclusion is universally accepted by the profession.

It would, however, be misleading to pretend that economists are in complete agreement as to the precise magnitude this requires for the discount rate. Differences relating to the role of risk, the proportion of the relevant resources derived from consumers and from other business firms and other similar matters have led to divergences in the estimates of the appropriate discount rate figure. Precisely for that reason this paper has made no attempt to provide any single figure which purports to represent a uniquely correct rate of discount for government projects. A public forum has no special interest in the views of any single witness unless they have behind them the full weight of professional judgment and analysis.

But the writings of the leading authorities in the field do confirm the basic contention of this report, that there is no justification for the use in present circumstances of any discount figure significantly lower than 4.75 percent. By and large discussion in the literature centers about the amount by which the correct discount rate *exceeds* this order of magnitude. The reason is straightforward. We have seen that 4.75 percent is the lowest opportunity cost rate for any group from whom resources might be transferred to a government project. All that remains as a matter for further investigation is the proportion of these resources that would be drawn from other groups whose opportunity cost rate is higher. If, for example, the bulk of such resources is normally transferred from the corporate sector where they can earn far more than 4.75 percent it is obvious that a discount rate substantially higher than this figure would be required.

There can also be no doubt that no well-known economist would see any merit in a long-term discount rate on government projects obtained by averaging *coupon rates* on securities having more than 15 years to run *at time of issue*. For it is generally agreed among economists that it is the effective market yield and not the coupon rate that

has any relevance for consumer's discount rates, and it is also agreed that a security with six months to run is a short-term security whether it was originally issued for 9 months or 90 years.

Therefore, while there is not complete unanimity among economists on the precise number that should be used in discounting it would be misleading to infer that there is any disagreement on the basic point at issue. The profession speaks with one voice in asserting that a discount figure of 3.5 or 4 percent is too low in present circumstances, and warns us clearly of the misallocation of resources and inefficiencies that are likely to result from the use of such unjustifiable figures.

Survey of Use by Federal Agencies of the Discounting Technique in Evaluating Future Programs

By
ELMER B. STAATS

INTRODUCTION

The General Accounting Office has made a survey of the use by twenty-three selected federal agencies of the technique of discounting in making evaluations of future programs. The nature of the discounting technique is described in the background section of this report.

Our survey was made pursuant to the Budget and Accounting Act, 1921

(31 U.S.C. 53), and the Accounting and Auditing Act of 1950 (31 U.S.C. 67). The survey was performed in Washington, D.C., and was completed in December 1967.

We undertook this survey because of our belief that the rapid growth in program expenditures by the govern-

Edited excerpts from a Report to the Joint Economic Committee, U.S. Congress, January 29, 1968. Elmer B. Staats is Comptroller General of the United States.

ment and the increasing complexity of federal programs point up the need for responsible officials in the government to make effective use of objective aids to decision-making. This report discusses one such aid—the technique of discounting—and describes its use by the federal agencies included in our survey.

Our survey was directed primarily toward determining the extent to which the discounting technique is presently employed by federal agencies and the extent to which those agencies not employing this technique plan to do so and toward identifying the discount rates currently in use by the agencies. We did not evaluate the appropriateness of the agencies' stated policies and practices as they were revealed to us, neither did we examine into the actual discounting techniques and practices followed by the agencies or into other policies and practices used by them when evaluating Federal programs.

BACKGROUND

The theory underlying the discounting technique is that benefits from federal programs to be realized in the near future are valued more highly than benefits to be realized in the more distant future, and that costs which must be incurred in the near future loom larger than costs that will be incurred in the more distant future. The discounting of future benefits and costs makes them comparable to present benefits and costs, i.e., to the present values of benefits and costs. The numerical standard used in making these intertemporal comparisons is called the discount rate.

Federal agency programs, like other programs, generally involve a series of annual costs and a flow of benefits over time. Calculation of the present values of costs and benefits through discounting makes possible a comparison of costs and benefits, usually expressed in terms of a ratio of benefits to costs, which gives consideration to the time periods in which benefits will be realized and costs incurred. Such comparisons (or ratios) are useful in evaluating programs and in choosing between alternative programs. Furthermore, the discounting technique can be helpful to the decision maker in those cases in which the benefits associated with programs cannot be measured in dollars. Here, the present values of the costs of the programs can be presented to the decision maker for his decision as to whether the perhaps dimly perceived benefits are worth their costs. The technique can also be helpful in making comparisons of the costs of programs that have equal benefits.

The present values of program benefits and costs will not usually be the only information decision makers need concerning benefits and costs. For example, there may often be value in tables which show the time-phased undiscounted costs and benefits in a manner that enables the decision makers to see the full impact of benefits and costs in each fiscal year.

EXPLICIT AND IMPLICIT DISCOUNT RATES

Discount rates are often explicit, but in some cases they may be implicit. An explicit discount rate is a rate which is identified and used to calculate the present values of future benefits and costs. However, if in an analysis the assumed life of the program is different from the more probable life expected on the basis of experience or studies,

(millions)

	Undiscounted Amounts	Present Values	
		(A) Assumed 10-Year Life	(B) Most Probable Program Life—20 Years
Implicit discount rate			8.0%
Initial investment	$10	$10.0	$10.0
Annual operating costs	1	10.0	9.82
Annual benefits	3	30.0	29.45
Ratio of present value of benefits to present value of total costs (benefit-cost ratio), rounded		1.5	1.5

then an implicit discount rate is actually being used.

The meaning of such an implicit discount rate can be illustrated by the above example in which a ten-year program life is used in an evaluation study, but the most probable program life is twenty years. In order for the evaluation study based on ten years to lead to the same conclusion as one based on twenty years, the present values must be equal in both cases.

In this example the net annual program benefits will continue beyond the ten-year program life assumed in the study. Since the net annual benefits in the eleventh year through the twentieth year are not recognized in the ten-year study, an implicit discount rate is being used. In column A of the above table the total undiscounted values of program costs and benefits are shown for the assumed program life of ten years. In column B the program costs and benefits for the most probable program life of twenty years are shown discounted at 8 per cent—the discount rate that is required to equate the benefit-cost ratios in columns A and B. The implicit discount rate in this analysis which uses an assumed program life of ten years (column A) is thus 8 per cent.

Shown in the table below are the

IMPLICIT DISCOUNT RATES IN PERCENT

(in years)

Most Probable Program Life	Assumed Program Life					
	1	5	10	15	20	25
1	–	–	–	–	–	–
5	100	–	–	–	–	–
10	100	15	–	–	–	–
15	100	18	6	–	–	–
20	100	19	8	3	–	–
25	100	20	9	4	2	–

approximate discount rates, for a range of the most probable program lives, that would be implied by analyses in which explicit discounting is not used but in which the assumed program lives are shorter than the most probable program lives. The implicit discount rates in an actual case may be somewhat different, depending on the form of the cost or benefit streams over time.

Benefit-cost ratios may be very sensitive to the explicit discount rate used in calculating the present value of costs and benefits. As shown in the following example, which involves a program with a probable life of twenty-five years that requires an initial investment of $50 million, changes in the rate can turn what would appear to be an attractive program into an unattractive program and vice versa.

(millions)

| | | | Ratios of Benefits to Cost | | |
Initial Investment	Annual Operating Costs	Annual Benefits	Undiscounted	Discounted at 3 percent	Discounted at 7 percent
$50	$12	$16	1.14	1.08	0.98

EFFECT OF CHANGES IN DISCOUNT RATES ON BENEFIT-COST RATIOS

The chart on page 216 shows the inverse relationship between discount rates (shown on the horizontal axis) and benefit-cost ratios (shown on the vertical axis) for three different programs which have constant annual benefits and constant annual operating costs. The three curves illustrate the effect of discounting on the benefit-cost ratios of the three hypothetical programs with differing lives, each of which, if undiscounted, would reflect a benefit-cost ratio of 2; that is, total undiscounted benefits for each program would be double the total undiscounted costs. With discounting, the favorable benefit-cost ratios deteriorate as higher discount rates are applied. For example, Program A has a benefit-cost ratio

of about 1.7 at 3 per cent, but only about 1.1 at 10 per cent.

The curves drawn for these three hypothetical programs are probably typical of such curves for many programs; however, the curve for any particular program may be different because of the behavior of the program's benefits and costs. Such behavior would depend in part upon the assumed life of the program and the amount of initial investment cost relative to annual benefits and annual costs.

The chart also illustrates that changes in the higher discount rates have less relative effect on benefit-cost ratios than do changes in the lower discount rates. Therefore, a greater absolute error or wider range of uncertainty or variation may be tolerated in the higher discount rates than in the lower discount rates. For example, an

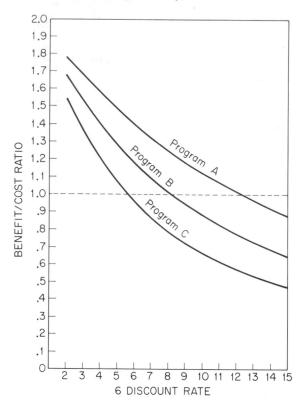

increase in the discount rate from 3 to 6 per cent reduces the program B benefit-cost ratio by about 23 per cent, whereas an increase from 10 to 13 per cent reduces the benefit-cost ratio by about 17 per cent.

DETERMINATION OF DISCOUNT RATE

With respect to determination of the rate, one school of thought holds that the rate should be determined by and be equal to the rate paid by the Treasury in borrowing money. Another school of thought holds that the rate should be determined by what is foregone, namely, the return that could have been earned in the private sector of the economy when the decision is made to commit resources to the public sector. Proponents of both views agree that the use of different discount rates has an effect on financial judgments which is similar to charging different prices for, say, identical labor in different programs.

Neither school of thought provides clear guidance on the specific discount rate that should be used. Cost to the Treasury, for example, will vary, depending upon the definition applied, from 3 to 8 per cent or more. The average rate of return in the private sector also varies depending upon historical periods selected and upon weighting of the various segments of the private sector which are used in computing an average.

A discount rate of about 3.2 per cent is the cost to the Treasury, if based upon the average rate payable on out-standing United States securities hav-ing a maturity of fifteen years or more, as prescribed by Senate Document 97 (discussed below).

The rate of return that can be earned in the private sector is estimated by most researchers to be significantly higher than the cost of Government borrowing based on Senate Document 97. According to one researcher, the average rate of return in the private sector amounted to 15.4 per cent for manufacturing companies and 4.1 per cent for railroads in the years 1961–65.[1] These and other estimates of the same researcher are shown in the following table.

Segment	Annual Average Rate of Return 1961–65 (percent)
Manufacturing	15.4
Electric utilities	9.3
Gas pipelines	8.6
Telephone	11.9
Railroads	4.1
Motor carriers [a]	14.7
Oil pipelines	15.6
Airlines	8.2

[a] Average for 1961–64 only.

Therefore, if Senate Document 97 is used as the basis for the cost of gov-ernment borrowing, the difference be-tween the two schools of thought is

[1] Prepared statement of Jacob A. Stockfisch, Hearings before the Senate Subcommittee on Economy in Government of the Joint Economic Committee, Ninetieth Congress, on the *Planning–Programming–Budgeting System: Progress and Potentials.*

quite significant. If, on the other hand, Treasury borrowing costs are calculated on the basis of total costs to the gov-ernment, including corporate and in-dividual income taxes foregone as a result of borrowing by the government to finance programs, an estimate of between 7 and 8 per cent results. (See illustrative calculation in Appendix III.) Thus, if government costs are calculated on this basis, the practical importance of the difference between the two schools of thought is greatly reduced.

DISCOUNT RATE FOR PLANNING WATER AND RELATED LAND RESOURCES PROJECTS

Senate Document 97 entitled "Poli-cies, Standards, and Procedures in the Formulation, Evaluation, and Review of Plans for Use and Development of Water and Related Land Resources" (87th Cong., 2d sess.), which provides congressional guidance on discount rates under certain circumstances, states that the discount rates "shall be based upon the average rate of interest payable by the Treasury on interest-bearing marketable securities of the United States outstanding at the end of the fiscal year preceding such computa-tion, which upon original issue, had terms to maturity of 15 years or more."

The document also states that "This procedure shall be subject to adjust-ment when and if this is found desirable as a result of continuing analysis of all factors pertinent to selection of a dis-count rate for these purposes."

Senate Document 97 was developed by the Secretary of the Army; the Sec-retary of Agriculture; the Secretary of Health, Education, and Welfare; and the Secretary of the Interior; and it was approved by President Kennedy on May 15, 1962. As indicated in the title, the document relates only to water and related land resources.

RESULTS OF SURVEY

Summary of agency practices

In our survey of the use of the discounting technique selected agencies were asked to respond to a questionnaire concerning the discount rates used, rationale for the rates chosen, and plans for future use by agencies which were not evaluating fiscal year 1969 programs on the basis of discounting.

The table below shows the agencies' plans for using the discounting technique.

As shown in the table, ten of the twenty-three agencies queried report that discounting is used in making decisions. An additional eight agencies do not now use discounting but report that they plan to do so in the future. The remaining five agencies do not use discounting at the present time and do not state that they plan to do so in the

AGENCY PLANS FOR USING THE DISCOUNTING TECHNIQUE

Agency	Discounting Used in Analysis of Fiscal Year 1969 Programs		Discounting Not Used But Plans Are to Use Discounting in Future	
	Yes	No	Yes	No
Tennessee Valley Authority	X			
General Services Administration	X			
Department of Agriculture	X			
Department of Defense	X			
Office of Economic Opportunity	X			
Department of Transportation (Federal Aviation Administration)	X			
Department of Health, Education, and Welfare	X			
Atomic Energy Commission	X			
Agency for International Development	X			
Department of the Interior	X			
Federal Communications Commission		X	X	
Department of Housing and Urban Development		X	X	
Interstate Commerce Commission		X		X
National Science Foundation		X	X	
Federal Power Commission		X	X	
Export-Import Bank of Washington		X		X
Department of Labor		X	X	
Peace Corps		X	X	
Veterans Administration		X		X
Department of the Treasury		X		X
Post Office Department		X	X	
National Aeronautics and Space Administration		X	X	
Department of Commerce		X		X

future. However, two—Department of Commerce and Veterans Administration—of these five agencies reported that some programs are evaluated in terms of periods of time which are shorter than the probable actual life of the programs—a procedure which involves implicit discounting. (See discussion of implicit discounting which begins on p. 213.)

Details of rates used by the agencies which use the discounting technique appear in Appendix I.

Explanations of the plans of agencies which do not use the discounting technique appear in Appendix II.

Divergent agency views on discount rates

A divergence of opinion on discounting is reflected in agency practices. Some agencies use the Treasury cost of borrowing money as the discount rate while others use a rate based on the return on investment in the private sector of the economy. Still others employ different criteria to determine the agency's discount rate including the Federal Reserve rediscount rate and agency borrowing cost. The agencies included in our survey use discount rates which vary over an extremely wide range—from about 3 per cent to 12 per cent.

Within each school of thought there are important differences of opinion. Of those agencies which tie the discount rate to Treasury borrowing costs, one uses the estimated cost of new money to the Treasury, another uses the average cost of money to the Treasury, others use the cost prescribed by Senate Document 97 (about 3.2 per cent at the time of our review).

One of those agencies which would tie the discount rate to the rate of return in the private sector uses a rate of return on a safe investment and a slightly higher rate (3 per cent and 5 per cent), while another uses for some programs the rate representative of average capital returns in the private sector (presumed to be 12 per cent) and for some programs permits the analyst to determine the rate on the basis of his judgment as to the nature of the program and the kind of analysis considered most meaningful.

Views are equally disparate in those agencies which report that discounting was not used in their analyses of individual programs for support of their fiscal year 1969 budget decisions. At one extreme is the view that decisions on programs should be made on the basis of first year costs and benefits—a procedure which implies a discount rate of 100 per cent, since the future is ignored. At the other extreme is the view that decisions should be based on total undiscounted costs and benefits—a procedure which implies a discount rate of zero, since costs and benefits applicable to, say, the twentieth year are treated as being as important as current costs and benefits.

Significance of differing practices

The fact that some agencies use discounting and some do not will tend to affect adversely the quality of decisions. This is illustrated in the following (hypothetical) cases.

Case A involves a program in an agency that *does* use discounting. Estimated costs and benefits of this program over its twenty-five-year life are:

Initial investment costs	$12,000,000
Annual operating costs	2,000,000
Annual benefits	3,000,000
Present value of total costs discounted at 4.5 percent	41,656,000
Present value of total benefits discounted at 4.5 percent	44,484,000
Benefit-cost ratio	1.07

Case B involves a program in a different agency which *does not* use discounting. Estimated costs and benefits of this program over its twenty-five-year life are:

Initial investment costs	$16,000,000
Annual operating costs	1,500,000
Annual benefits	2,500,000
Total costs	53,500,000
Total benefits	62,500,000
Benefit-cost ratio	1.17

On the basis of the benefit-cost ratio the net value of program A is marginal. To the extent that benefit-cost ratios are considered significant by the decision makers, there would be a tendency to prefer program B rather than program A because total undiscounted benefits exceed total costs by a relatively wide margin, even though if program B were subjected to the rate of discount (4.5 per cent) used for program A it would be much less attractive than program A (benefit-cost ratio of 0.97 compared with 1.07). Thus, the benefit-cost analyses for programs A and B would, if only the program A analysis used discounting, tend to bring about a misallocation of resources since the results of the analyses would favor program B.

In the above example the tendency

to misallocate will, of course, increase with higher discount rates. The following table illustrates this tendency as the discount rate increases from zero to 10 per cent.

Benefit-cost ratio	Program A	Program B	Difference
Undiscounted	1.21	1.17	.04
Discounted at 4½ percent	1.07	.97	.10
Discounted at 10 percent	.90	.77	.13

Differences in discounting practices (see Appendix I) in and among the agencies which *do use* discounting will tend to produce the same kind of misallocation. For example, a power-production program in the Tennessee Valley Authority (TVA) (life of fifty years) may have a benefit-cost ratio of 1.14 (if discounted at 4.5 per cent), while in the Department of the Interior the same flow of costs and benefits would yield a ratio of 0.96 (if discounted at 6 per cent) or only 0.58 if the project were felt to be risky (and for this reason discounted at 12 per cent). Thus, even though both agencies use discounting, the fact that different rates are used tends to favor programs of the agency using the lower discount rate and thus a misallocation of resources could be the result.

Similarly, interagency differences in implicit discount rates in agencies that do not use explicit discounting (see Appendix II) tend to produce misallocation. As shown in the table on page 214, the implicit discount rate increases as the difference between the most probable (longer) actual life of a program and the period of time considered in evaluating the program increases. The Veterans Administration (VA), for example, evaluates programs on the basis of a five-year period, while the most probable life of, say, a hospital is about twenty-five years. Thus, the implicit discount rate is about 20 per cent. The Department of Commerce, on the other hand, evaluates some programs having a most probable life of at least eleven years in terms of a seven-year period—a procedure which implies a discount rate of about 8 per cent. Under these conditions the benefit-cost ratio for a given stream of benefits and costs will be higher in the Department of Commerce than in the VA. To the extent that decisions turn on the relationship between costs and benefits, the VA will be inclined to reject projects which would be promoted under the standards employed in the Department of Commerce. Hence, resources will tend to flow from VA projects to Department of Commerce projects.

CONCLUSIONS

Federal agencies that use the explicit discounting technique may be making good use of this tool in evaluating individual projects. The analyst who examines a given project in detail, develops the discount rate which he considers appropriate, and calculates the present value of benefits and costs is in a better position to make defensible recommendations than if his analysis ignored the time periods over which benefits will be realized and costs incurred.

In our opinion, however, there is greater value for the discounting tech-

nique when the decision maker must choose between many competing projects and this calls for a common standard with justification for variations in the discount rate which may be appropriate in special circumstances. Although some agencies indicate that the discount rate is viewed as an aid in choosing between programs within an agency, there appears to be little recognition that the evaluation of federal programs calls for a common yardstick for use by all agencies.

In our opinion the general acceptance of the technique of discounting by federal agencies should be supplemented with improvements necessary to bring about consistency in and among agencies in discounting rates, techniques, and underlying concepts. We believe such improvements are needed if this aid is to be of most effective use to the agencies, the Bureau of the Budget, and the Congress in its evaluation of agency programs submitted for consideration.

Obstacles to reform in this important area are many and varied. For example, the specific nature of decisions that must be made needs to be examined in order that criteria for evaluating discounting techniques, discount rates, and underlying concepts can meet the needs of the various decision makers. It is clear to us that some measure of standardization is needed to enhance the quality and consistency of information presented to the various decision makers for their consideration.

MATTER FOR CONSIDERATION BY THE CONGRESS

Both the case for discounting and the choice of discount rates have been subjects of dispute for years. However, the results of our survey of federal agency practices suggest that the case for discounting is being accepted but that there is a significant difference of opinion among the agencies over discount rates. Because of the extreme variation in discount rates and techniques being used by the executive agencies for evaluating and justifying their programs and because there is strong impetus toward the use of the discounting technique provided by federal agency adoption of planning-programming-budgeting systems, the Congress may wish to provide guidance to the executive agencies on this important topic.

APPENDIX I

DISCOUNT RATES USED BY FEDERAL AGENCIES IN THE ANALYSIS OF INDIVIDUAL PROGRAMS IN FISCAL YEAR 1969

Agency	Programs	Rate (percent)	Rationale Treasury Borrowing Cost	Other
Tennessee Valley Authority	Fertilizer munitions and development	4.5	X	
	Power supply and use	4.5 to 5.5		Cost of money to TVA (note 1)
General Services Administration	Facilities program	4.5		Estimated productivity of capital (note 2)
Department of Agriculture	Housing loans	4.875	X	(note 3)
	Water and sewer loans and grants	4.875	X	
	Rural electrification loans	4.875	X	
	Rural telephone loans	4.875	X	
	Rural renewal district loans	4.875	X	
	Rural conservation and development loans	4.875	X	
	Farm operating loans	4.875	X	
	Farm real estate loans	4.875	X	
	Production efficiency	5.0	X	
Office of Economic Opportunity	Job corps	3.0 and 5.0		"Rate or return on a safe investment and a slightly higher rate" (note 4)
	Upward bound	3.0 " 5.0		Same
	Family planning program	5.0		Do.

APPENDIX I—*Continued*

Agency	Programs	Rate (percent)	Rationale — Treasury Borrowing Cost	Other
Department of Transportation (Federal Aviation Administration)	Facilities and basic systems	4.2		Federal Reserve rediscount rate
	Radar components	4.2		Same
	En route automation	4.2		Do.
Atomic Energy Commission	Enriched uranium production planning	5.0	X	
	Radioactive waste management planning	5.0	X	
	Value of special nuclear materials	5.0, 7.5, and 10.0	X	Use of 7.0 and 10.0 not explained
	Radiation pasteurization of meat	Government costs—5.0	X	
		Industry benefits—15.0		Rate used in industry
	Reactor development	5.0 to 9.0		6.0 and 7.0 typical of rate used by private utilities; 9.0 used to introduce a risk factor (note 5)
Department of Defense	41 shipyard projects	10.0		Time preference for current vs. future money sacrifices in private sector (note 6)
	14 air stations	10.0		Same
	18 other sations	10.0		Do.
Agency for International Development	Power plant in Afghanistan	8.0 (cost only)		Opportunity cost of money (note 7)
	Highway in Bolivia	12.0		Development on foreign exchange scarcity, opportunity costs, and other factors (note 8)
	Roads in Guyana	10.0		Same
	Roads in British Guiana	8.0		Do.
Department of the Interior	Utility program: Low risk	6.0		Representative returns on investment (note 9)
	Average	12.0		Average return in private sector (note 9)
	Energy and mineral development programs in which exploitation is a private function	12.0		Same (note 9)

APPENDIX I—*Continued*

Agency	Programs	Rate (percent)	Rationale — Treasury Borrowing Cost	Rationale — Other
	Aquatic living resources	3.1 and 6.0		No special explanation (note 10)
	Indian reservation resources development	3.1	X	Related to water or land resources, so S.D. 97 applies (note 11)
Department of Health, Education, and Welfare	Human investment programs (adult education, vocational rehabilitation, work experience)	0–8.0		(note 12)
	Individual diseases (tuberculosis, cancer, syphillis, arthritis, motor vehicle injury)	0–10.0		(note 12)
	Cost of illness	4.0 and 6.0		(note 12)
	Cancer control	4.0 " 6.0		(note 12)

Notes to Appendix I

1. The Tennessee Valley Authority (TVA) stated that its Power Supply and Use Program rates "are based on the expected costs of money which TVA must pay over the period of the evaluation. Since the power program is currently financed from earnings from the sale of power and from the sale of revenue bonds, the future cost of money varies with the proportion acquired from the different sources utilized as well as from changes in interest rates."

2. The General Services Administration (GSA) stated that in its facilities program the costs of alternatives were discounted to present value at 4.5 percent for 50 years, the estimated life of the buildings. GSA stated that the 4.5 percent rate was selected "as an estimate of the long term productivity value of capital" and was applied on the assumption that "the relationship between the costs of alternatives would hold over the life of the project under examination."

3. The Department of Agriculture stated that its analysts "often prefer to calculate internal rates of return for comparing investment-type programs, rather than use a benefit/cost ratio analysis which depends upon discounting." The "internal rate of return" is analogous to the "yields" of an investment. The procedure is to find the "internal rate" (the rate of discount) that equates the present value of the proceeds from an investment with the present value of the outlays on the investment.

4. The Office of Economic Opportunity advised us that the rates of 3 and 5 percent "were safely on the conservative side for estimates of this type," and that they represented a "rate of return on a safe investment and a slightly higher rate." The agency also advised us that these rates gave consideration to the secular growth in the price of quality-constant labor.

5. The Atomic Energy Commission stated that in its "reactor development studies, discount rates of 6 to 7 percent

are illustrative of those used by investor-owned utilities. (Companion studies employ appropriate discount rates based on data from the Federal Power Commission applicable to public power systems.)" The 5 and 9 percent rates were used to determine the sensitivity of the reference value of 7 percent.

6. The Department of Defense stated that all the programs to which it applied the 10 percent discount rate were related to its military construction program. The discount rate was selected "to reflect the amount of time preference for current versus future money sacrifices that the public exhibits in nongovernmental transactions. The 10 percent rate is considered to be the most representative point within a range of plausible rates obtained from considering this public time preference."

7. The Agency for International Development stated that the cost of its Afghanistan power plant project was discounted at 8 percent, assumed to be the opportunity cost of money in that country. Benefits were not discounted since "it is assumed that the expected demand for power must be met." The computations were for a useful life of 39 years.

8. The Agency for International Development (AID) stated that the three Latin American roads projects were discounted for 20 years at the rates shown in the rate column of Appendix I. Latin American roads projects, in general, are discounted to present value by AID at the opportunity cost of long-term capital "usually placed upwards of 8 percent and possibly ranging to 16 percent in some Latin American countries." AID analysts also compute the internal rate of return of such projects. The internal rate of return is described in note 3.

9. The Department of the Interior stated that no uniform or single discount rate had been applied in its major analyses outside the water and land resources area. The selection of the discount rate

generally had been left to the judgment of the analyst. But 6 percent, after taxes, is "considered to be representative of utility-type programs in which risk is relatively low; 12 percent presumed to be representative of average capital returns in the private sector, etc." The time frame for analysis is varied from a long-term useful life concept to shorter periods of 20 years or less for programs oriented to the private sector or to short-term objectives. In the mineral resource area, the Department's general approach is to identify and compare internal rates of return as a means for ranking or establishing program priorities. The internal rate of return is described in note 3.

10. The Department of the Interior stated that in its aquatic resources programs "Alternative program levels and mixes were subjected to benefit-cost analysis using discount rates of 3⅛ and 6 percent against benefit flows over 5, 10, and 15-year periods."

11. The Department of the Interior stated that, in its Indian-reservation resources development programs, comparative analyses of alternative programs "(irrigation, range development or livestock, dry-farming, timber production and industrial development) were based on an interest rate of 3⅛ percent; however, the periods of analysis necessarily varied because of distinct program characteristics." This discount rate was selected in accordance with Senate Document 97 since the programs were related to water and land resources.

12. The Department of Health, Education, and Welfare stated that "We feel that discounting a future stream of dollars to present value is helpful, but we are uncertain what rate to set. We (use) several to see whether the difference is critical, for the specific purpose of the study. If it does not seriously disturb relative rankings we note this. If it does have a significant effect, we wish to inform the reader of the study of this."

APPENDIX II

FEDERAL AGENCIES NOT USING DISCOUNTING
IN THE ANALYSIS OF INDIVIDUAL PROGRAMS IN FISCAL YEAR 1969

	Agency Comments
A. *Agencies that plan to use discounting in future*	
Department of Housing and Urban Development	Discounting used in appraisal of fiscal year 1968 programs, with the rate determined by then-current Treasury borrowing costs. Agency has a strong interest in the development of policies for measuring the costs and benefits applicable to Federal programs.
Federal Power Commission	Analyses of Federal Power Commission programs, other than those involving water resources, are still in a preliminary stage; decisions on appropriate discount rates must await completion.
Federal Communications Commission	Detailed cost-benefit analyses will be made in the future when additional staff capability is developed.
Peace Corps	The evolution of planning-programming-budgeting systems in the Peace Corps has not reached the stage where discount rates are applied to costs and benefits.
National Science Foundation	Analyses have not been so sophisticated as to require discounting.
National Aeronautics and Space Administration	Agency has not attempted to express in terms of percentage discounts, the effect of future (total) costs and benefits although these economic factors are implicit in consideration of alternative programs and the assessment of priorities.
Department of Labor	Agency has considered discounting at length. Would tend to use a projected rate of growth in Gross National Product as representing the opportunity cost of financing socio-economic programs, with sensitivity analysis to indicate the effects of different rates and different time horizons. Manpower development assistance program evaluated in terms of cost in the first year, while the program will continue for 5 to 20 years.
Post Office Department	Agency has used discounting in past in its facility modernization program and in its lease-purchase reports to the Congress. Currently studying the incorporation of discounting concepts and practices on a wider scale.
B. *Agencies that have no stated plans to use discounting or had no comments on their plans*	
Interstate Commerce Commission	Interstate Commerce Commission has no programs which lend themselves to the use of discount rates in measuring costs and benefits.
Veterans Administration	Useful life span of programs cannot be estimated in terms of duration based on a known or foreseeable termination point. Most programs, therefore, are evaluated on a 5-year projection basis.

Department of the Treasury	Programs are, in the main, continuing ones, and problems of efficiency relate primarily to the cost side; usually alternative costs for the same objective. This kind of comparison does not require use of a discount rate to evaluate future benefit streams. In those cases where procurement of capital equipment is involved, the benefits are generally large enough so that a simple payout period is all that is necessary.
Export-Import Bank of Washington	No comment.
Department of Commerce	Agency procedures involve appraisals of programs in terms of periods which are shorter than the estimated useful lives of the programs. The Economic Development Administration currently evaluates programs with 11 years' minimum lives in terms of the fiscal 1967–74 period. The Environmental Science Services Administration evaluates 10- to 50-year programs in terms of 5 years. The Bureau of Standards evaluates indefinite (continuing) programs in terms of 5 years.

APPENDIX III

ILLUSTRATION OF CALCULATION OF TOTAL COST
TO THE GOVERNMENT OF BORROWED FUNDS

Method I

The current interest cost of borrowing long-term money is approximately 5 percent. The moving average rate specified by Senate Document 97 is currently about 3.2 percent. Therefore, a rate of interest approximately halfway between 5.0 and 3.2 could be used for initial consideration as the Government cost of borrowed money.   4.0%

Add to this cost:

1. Corporate taxes foregone by the Government if the average corporate return on investment is 12 percent before taxes,[1] if the fraction of dollars borrowed by the Government which would have gone into corporate investment is 65 percent,[2] and if the marginal corporate tax rate is 40 percent.
   (.12) (.65) (.4)   3.1%

---

[1] Various economists have examined rates of return before taxes in the private sector. Stockfisch (see footnote on page 217), arrives at an average of 13.5 percent. Stiegler, National Bureau of Standards, determines a rate of 14 percent. Variations in this estimate result from consideration of differing time periods, weighting, etc. Our estimate of 12 percent used for this appendix is somewhat conservative in comparison with the recent experience noted by these economists.

[2] See Raymond Goldsmith's "Flow of Capital Funds in the Postwar Economy," National Bureau of Economic Research, 1965, where a table of gross capital consumption by major segments of the economy is shown. We are interested here in capital consumption for purposes of productive investment. Most household borrowing can be excluded as investment in consumption which would also result from payments by the Government to labor involved in Government programs. State and local capital consumption can be left out of this consideration. The corporate share of the remainder is approximately 65 percent.

2. Personal taxes foregone by the Government if the average return on propri-
   etorship, personal income-producing investments, etc., is such that the remaining 35 percent of money borrowed by the Government would have earned a
   10-percent return for the persons taxed, and if such return would be taxed at
   a composite marginal rate of 30 percent.[3]
   (.1) (.35) (.3)   1.0%

3. (a) Taxes foregone by the Government on dividends that would have been
       received by individuals from corporations if the composite marginal tax
       rate applicable to individuals is 30 percent, if the taxable dividends pay-
       out is 40 percent of corporate profits after taxes, and if the assumptions
       as to corporate earnings and the marginal tax rate shown above under
       (1) are applicable. The marginal corporate tax rate is assumed to be 40
       percent, therefore 60 percent of corporate earnings is assumed available
       to the corporation for payment of dividends.
       (.3) (.4) (.12) (.65) (.6) = .6%
   (b) Personal taxes foregone by the Government if the corporate investment
       is financed by bonds rather than by corporate earnings, if corporate
       bonds carry an interest rate of 5 percent, if the fraction of dollars bor-
       rowed by the Government which would have gone into corporate invest-
       ment is 65 percent, and if the composite marginal tax rate applicable to
       individuals is 30 percent.
       (.05) (.65) (.3) = 1.0%
   (c) Actual overall financing arrangements by corporations will generate tax
       revenues under both (a) and (b), therefore the cost to the Government
       may be assumed to be somewhere between .6 percent and 1.0 percent,
       say about   .8%

Subtract from this cost:
1. Income taxes collected on Government interest payments, if investments in
   bonds (see rate above of 4 percent) are divided between corporations and
   individuals in such a way that the tax rate is 35 percent.
   (.04) (.35)   −1.4%

   Cost to Government   7.5%

Method II

On an aggregate basis, a similar result may be computed assuming a composite corporate
and personal marginal tax rate of 50 percent [4] and a taxable return of 10 percent on any
money not borrowed by the Government.

(.5) (.1)   5.0%

Cost of Government borrowing (see explanation under Method I)   4.0%

Less taxes on Government bond interest (.04) (.35) (see explanation under
Method I)   −1.4%

Cost to Government   7.6%

---

[3] A table of marginal tax rates for various income levels is contained in a study done by the
Institute for Defense Analyses for the Office of Economic Opportunity, as summarized in
"R-116, Federal Poverty Program, Assessment and Recommendations," January 1966. This
document shows that the average marginal rate is approximately 30 percent for the higher
income levels, from which personal income-producing investments tend to originate.

[4] This is a rough composite marginal rate for corporate and personal taxpayers that provides
approximately for the separate estimates shown in 1, 2, and 3 for Method I.

C A S E

5

VETERANS ADMINISTRATION

HOSPITAL BOILER PLANT REPLACEMENT

In May of 1966, John Bernelli and Bill Simpson of the Heating and Steam Generation Division in the Office of the Assistant Administrator for Construction were asked to make an economic fuel analysis survey for a proposed boiler plant replacement project at the Veterans Administration Clear Springs Memorial Hospital. The data from this survey would then be analyzed to determine which of the feasible alternatives in providing the boiler plant replacement would be most economical.

The director of the hospital had transmitted a letter to the VA Central Office stating that there was an urgent need for the boiler plant to be replaced.

BACKGROUND

The Veterans Administration operates a large nationwide network of hospitals for the care and treatment of veterans. Besides operational responsibility the VA also constructs and maintains the physical plants used in the accomplishment of this mission.

One of the problems faced in the construction, maintenance, or modernization of such plants is to decide which type of boiler fuel system will most efficiently provide the required steam energy output for heating, laundry, and sterilization purposes at a given hospital.

RESULT OF PLANT INSPECTION

An on-site inspection of the existing coal-fired boiler plant produced the following observations:

The plant was originally built in the early 1900's and does not have proper headroom for modern equipment. There is some question concerning the ability of the floor and foundation to support new boilers and equipment, and some of the roof beams are charred from an old fire. In order to install new equipment,

This case was prepared by Kenneth L. McConoughey under the supervision of Graeme M. Taylor. The case is intended for class discussion only, and certain names and facts may have been changed which, while avoiding the disclosure of confidential information, do not materially lessen the value of the case for educational purposes. This case is not intended to represent either effective or ineffective handling of an administrative situation, nor does it purport to be a statement of policy by the agency involved.

access holes would have to be cut in existing walls and partitions.

The present boilers were installed in the early 1930's and are now obsolete. Much of the auxiliary equipment is also old and in need of repair.

Because of these general conditions an engineering recommendation was made to replace the entire plant with a new boiler plant building housing modern equipment. The cost of demolishing the old boiler plant would be almost a complete loss as the salvage value of the scrap steel and used brick was estimated to be only about $1,000.

ALTERNATIVES

Bernelli and Simpson finally selected three alternative proposals as being worthy of more intensive analysis. The three alternatives were as follows:

Alternative I — A new coal-fired boiler plant

Alternative II — A gas fired boiler plant with No. 6 (low sulphur) fuel oil as standby.

Alternative III — A gas fired boiler plant with No. 2 fuel oil standby.

As shown in Exhibit 1, the hospital's annual energy requirement, measured in terms of steam output, was approximately 145,000,000 lbs. of steam. Further analysis indicated that during the coldest day of the year in January, peak hourly demand was about 42,000 lbs. of steam.

As a rule of thumb for analysis, one pound of steam is approximately 1,000 BTU's, and one cubic foot of natural gas is approximately 1,000 BTU's. One pound of dry coal yields about 14,300 BTU's. To convert the 145,000,000 lbs. of steam energy to the common denominator of BTU's it is necessary, therefore, to multiply by 1,000. To find BTU input requirements it is necessary to divide by the relative boiler efficiency for each type of fuel. Exhibit 2 provides the computations for determining the amount of coal required and its cost.

For alternatives II and III two calculations are necessary. Since the gas supply would probably be interrupted for short intervals during peak demand periods, the total input consumption must be divided between the two fuels. Discussions with the gas company indicated interruptions would occur approximately 25 days per year with a 50 per cent reduction in the use of gas required. Exhibit 3 provides computations for the amount of fuel required and its cost for both alternatives II and III.

Manpower requirements also vary between the different types of plants. Annual labor costs are incurred for one supervisor and four plant operators in the gas-fired alternatives, whereas one supervisor, four operators, and three firemen are needed to handle the coal and ash of the coal-fired boilers. Exhibit 4 presents job descriptions and wages for the labor force involved. Electric power and maintenance costs would be about $5,000 less annually for the gas-fired alternatives compared with the coal-fired alternative because of the extra elevators, conveyors, ash unloaders, and other mechanical equipment needed for coal. These costs were estimated at $10,000 and $5,000 for the coal and gas alternatives respectively.

In addition to the annual operating costs described above, each alternative has a different capital investment cost.

The capital investment necessary to construct the three different plants are as follows:

Alternative I   — $1,770,300
Alternative II   —   889,200 [1]
Alternative III —   869,400

The two gas-fired plants are estimated to have a life of twenty-five years. The coal-fired boiler, because of its lower operating efficiency, was expected to last for twenty-eight years.

ADDITIONAL FACTORS

During the conversations between the analysts and the hospital director some additional points were brought to light. The coal supply for the existing boiler plant was delivered via a railway spur on an embankment which cut the hospital grounds in two and formed a barrier between the recreational buildings and the other hospital buildings. Patients traveling between these points were required either to climb and cross over the embankments, or walk through a single narrow vehicular underpass and be exposed to traffic. The director expressed a strong wish that something should be done to get rid of this railway embankment. The cost of removing the railway embankment would be approximately $2,500.

The analysts were also told that the local city government was concerned about air pollution, and the existing coal-fired boiler plant had been charged with being one of the prime causes of pollution. Whether this charge was true or not, any new boiler plant had to

meet the requirements for particulate emission from the chimney as set by the Department of Health, Education and Welfare. Gas-fired plants with No. 2 or No. 6 low sulphur oil would meet these requirements. A coal-fired boiler, even burning low sulphur coal, might need an electrostatic precipitator to meet the HEW standards. A complete engineering study would be required to determine the need for a precipitator. Such a study would involve about one man-month of time. A precipitator, if required, would cost approximately $47,000.

QUESTIONS

1. Which alternative would you recommend?
2. Is your recommended alternative sensitive to the choice of discount rate?
3. As an analyst employed by the Veterans Administration, what weight would you attach to such factors as the inconvenient railway embankment and the problem of air pollution?

EXHIBIT 1

VETERANS
ADMINISTRATION
Monthly Steam Consumption

Month	Lbs. of Steam
June	6,623,010
July	6,550,050
August	6,172,470
September	7,180,710
October	12,514,030
November	14,440,440
December	17,290,720
January	19,133,027
February	17,032,990
March	15,626,720
April	12,969,740
May	9,930,002
Annual Total	145,463,909

[1] The reason II is slightly higher than III is due to the heating capability needed in the storage tanks to keep the number 6 fuel oil warm in order to maintain its flashpoint and prevent coagulation.

EXHIBIT 2

VETERANS ADMINISTRATION

Alternative I—Annual Coal Requirements

BTU input = 145,000,000 Lbs x 1,000 BTU's
= 145,000,000,000 BTU

$$\frac{}{.75 \text{ Boiler eff.*}}$$
= 193,500,000,000 BTU input required
Approx. heating value = 14,300 BTU/lb.

$$\frac{193,500,000,000}{14,300 \times 2,000 \text{ BTU/ton}} = 6,770 \text{ tons coal}$$

Total Cost = 6,770 x $7.50 (average cost of coal incl. transp.)
= $50,700

* See text.

EXHIBIT 3

VETERANS ADMINISTRATION

Alternatives II & III—Annual Gas Requirements

Natural Gas Required

Annual steam production 145,000,000 lbs.

Maximum monthly steam produced = 19,100,000 lbs. in January.

Interruption of gas supply expected = 25 days at 50% decrease in usage. This occurs during periods of peak demand. (Since small household or commercial gas users who are entirely dependent on gas have priority, large plants must have oil switch over capability.) The Gas Company indicated that a 25 day reserve at a 50% reduction would be adequate.

$$\text{Maximum steam produced with oil} = \frac{25}{30} \times .50 \times 19,100,000 \text{ lbs.}$$

$$= 7,960,000 \text{ lbs. with oil}$$

$$145,000,000 - 7,960,000 = 137,040,000 \text{ lbs. with gas}$$

$$\text{BTU input (gas)} = \frac{137,040,000,000}{.78 *} = 176,000,000,000 \text{ BTU}$$

$$\text{BTU input (oil)} = \frac{7,960,000,000}{.81 *} = 9,820,000,000 \text{ BTU}$$

Gas Price

First 1000 cu. ft. per mo. @ $.50
Next 2000 cu. ft. per mo. @ .45
Over 3000 cu. ft. per mo. @ .40

Gas Costs

12,000 MCF × $.50 = $ 6,000
24,000 MCF × .45 = 10,800
140,000 MCF × .40 = 56,000

Est. total annual cost $72,800

No. 6 Fuel Oil Costs

$$\text{BTU input oil} \ \frac{7,960,000,000}{.81} = 9,820,000,000 \ \text{BTU}$$

Oil Required

$$\frac{9,820,000,000 \ \text{BTU}}{153,600\text{—BTU/gal.}} = 64,000 \ \text{gal.}$$

No. 6 Costs:

64,000 gal. @ $.1253/gal. = $8,020

No. 2 Fuel Oil Costs

Oil Required

$$\frac{9,820,000,000 \ \text{BTU}}{139,400 \ \text{BTU/gal.}} = 70,400 \ \text{gal.}$$

No. 2 Costs:

70,400 gal. @ $.1202/gal. = $8,460

---

* Relative fuel efficiency is the ratio of BTU output in steam to the BTU input of fuel. Fuels vary because of the difference in heat generated per unit consumed.

EXHIBIT 4

VETERANS ADMINISTRATION

Labor Costs

Job Description	Hourly Wages (inc. fringe benefits)
Plant Supervisor	$3.50
Operator	3.15
Operator	3.15
Operator	2.85
Operator	2.65
Fireman	3.15
Fireman	2.65
Fireman	2.50

C A S E

FEDERAL AVIATION AGENCY

PROPOSED REPLACEMENT OF AIR TRAFFIC
CONTROL RECEIVERS

In the early 1960's the Federal Aviation Agency (FAA) decided to standardize on 50 kc/s (kilocycles per second) channel spacing for their radio communications systems operating in the VHF (very high frequency) range for non-military air traffic control, because of an anticipated shortage of frequencies.

At that time the FAA operated many VHF tube-type radio receivers having 50 kc/s channel spacing; however, some of the older sets were of the 100 kc/s and 200 kc/s type. All UHF (ultra high frequency) receivers used for military air traffic control were of the 100 kc/s type. Narrow channel spacing would permit a larger number of assigned frequencies within a given section of the radio spectrum. Accordingly, in 1963 a contract was let for 3,210 tube-type VHF receivers at a cost of $319.70 per receiver.

During 1964 the Agency's Systems Research and Development Service (SRDS) completed development of specifications for 50 kc/s solid-state VHF and UHF receivers that would meet Agency requirements. The Agen-

cy's Installation and Materiel Service (IMS) proposed in early 1965 that all tube-type VHF receivers should be replaced by the solid-state type. Supporting this proposal was a brief cost-benefit analysis prepared by the Agency's Systems Maintenance Service (SMS) which indicated that the capital cost of the proposed procurement would be amortized in 3–4 years.

THE REVIEW PROCESS

The IMS proposal was included as a single-line item in the list of total

This case was prepared with the cooperation of the United States Federal Aviation Agency by Graeme M. Taylor under the supervision of Richard F. Vancil, Associate Professor of Business Administration, Harvard University, on behalf of the Office of Career Development, U.S. Civil Service Commission. The case is intended for class discussion only, and certain names and facts may have been changed which, while avoiding the disclosure of confidential information, do not materially lessen the value of the case for educational purposes. This case is not intended to represent either effective or ineffective handling of an administrative situation, nor does it purport to be a statement of policy by the agency involved.

Agency projects being considered for inclusion in the Agency's 5-year plan (FY 1966–1970) by the Agency Review Board (ARB). The ARB consisted of the Deputy Administrator and the four Associate Administrators, with the Director of the Office of Budget acting as secretary. The ARB discussed the IMS proposal in April 1965, and directed the Office of Budget's Requirements Analysis Staff (RAS) to validate the data prepared by SMS.

The RAS had been created within the Office of Budget to provide an independent analysis of major proposed projects. The ARB felt that, in order to be able to more properly evaluate the various proposals which came to its attention, it was necessary to have an independent staff group to assess the justifications accompanying these proposals. Most items proposed for inclusion in the 5-year plan did not go to RAS for evaluation. Many expenditure proposals fell into categories for which acceptability criteria had already been established and were thus included in the plan.

In the meantime the Agency's Air Traffic Service (ATS) had prepared a staff study to evaluate an IMS proposal to procure 5,100 kc/s UHF solid-state receivers to replace the existing 100 kc/s UHF tube-type receivers. In April, 1965 the RAS obtained this ATS study, and began to prepare their own evaluation of both the UHF and VHF solid-state receiver procurement proposals separately for presentation to the Agency Review Board. The remainder of this case is concerned only with the VHF solid-state receiver proposal.

MISSION OF THE FEDERAL AVIATION AGENCY

The Federal Airway System was established to increase the safety of aircraft traveling through the airspace over the United States. In 1965 it was the most extensive network of air navigation aids in the world, ranging from small location markers to complex radar systems. Most operate twenty-four hours a day. A large percentage of them are unattended but monitored and checked on a regular basis by technicians to assure proper operation.

In 1965 there were two FAA approved methods of flying; (1) visual flight rules (VFR), and (2) instrument flight rules (IFR). Many smaller aircraft were not equipped with the instrumentation necessary for flying by IFR; in 1965 there was no law that required an aircraft to have even a two-way radio, although almost all new planes were so equipped. As the number of aircraft and the sophistication of their navigation and communications equipment increased, there was an increasing utilization of FAA facilities and services. In 1965 there were 35.6 million aircraft operations (landing or take-off) recorded. By 1972 it is estimated that this activity will increase by 69%.

An aircraft flying IFR would be in VHF radio contact with two main types of FAA facilities: (1) airport towers, and (2) air traffic control centers with their attendant RCAGs (Remote Communications Air/Ground). In addition Flight Service Stations (FSS) would provide weather and other general information.

A pilot wishing to take off from, say, the Washington National Airport first received his taxiing instructions from ground control over one VHF frequency. When ready for take-off, he switched to clearance delivery on a second frequency to check his flight plan. Tower control then took over on a third frequency and gave him final take-off authorization. As soon as he was airborne, he switched to a fourth frequency to communicate with departure control. Once take-off procedures were completed, the Washington Center (Leesburg, Va.) took over on yet another frequency. As he traveled from Washington to, say, Boston, the pilot would be able to communicate with the Washington, New York, and Boston centers directly via RCAGs or individually through flight service stations located along his route.

Each VHF frequency used in this process involved a separate FAA receiver on the ground because most of the tube-type receivers in use, as well as all the proposed solid-state receivers, were of the fixed-tuned type.

THE REPLACEMENT PROPOSAL

The number and distribution of the tube-type receivers, as of December 31, 1964, were as follows:

Type of Facility	Number of VHF Receivers (tube-type)		
	Primary	Back-Up	Total
RCAG & Centers	1,165	1,165	2,330
FSS	955	—	955
Tower	3,220	510	3,730
Total	5,340	1,675	7,015

There were approximately 380 RCAG and centers, 350 FSS, and 300 towers in the FAA system.

Reliability

One of the questions to be resolved, if the tube-type receivers were replaced, was whether or not solid-state receivers would require the installation of back-up receivers to be available (in case of failure of the primary receiver) on a one-to-one basis, because of their much higher reliability. In preparing its specifications, the Systems Research and Development Service estimated the following "availability for use" of the equipment:

a. Solid-state with no back-up: 99.93%

b. Solid-state with back-up: 100.00% (virtually)

c. Tube-type with back-up: 99.85%

However, availability was also affected by control equipment and line [1] and power failures. Adjusted availability estimates including these factors were as follows:

a. 99.43%

b. 99.49%

c. 99.35%

Estimated cost

As part of the SRDS specifications contract cost data were estimated based on (a) replacing all 7,015 tube-type receivers, and (b) replacing only the 5,340 primary receivers. A contract to purchase 7,015 solid-state receivers was expected to result in an estimated unit cost of $340 per receiver; the cost

---

[1] For example, the microwave or leased telephone company cables connecting an RCAG with its center.

would be increased to $385 per receiver if only 5,340 were ordered. In both cases the installation cost was estimated at $75 per receiver. If a policy of piece-meal replacement were adopted, the smaller contracts involved would result in a unit cost of approximately $480. Delivery was estimated at 12 months following the letting of the contract, with delivery at the rate of 325 receivers per month.

Although SRDS specifications for solid-state receivers had been prepared by early 1965, no actual receivers had been purchased. Thus, the unit costs quoted above were estimates. Although transistors and other solid-state devices had been in use for almost twenty years for digital applications, the development of transistorized equipment for the analog applications involved in commercial radio receivers had proceeded much more slowly.

Operating savings

The proposal from the Installation and Materiel Service pointed out that the use of solid-state semiconductor devices, diodes, and transistors would result in an annual savings in power costs, maintenance, and tube replacement costs. Solid-state receivers were also more compact and thus would occupy less space in the facilities than the tube-type receivers. In addition the longer life expectancy and greatly reduced size of the semiconducting components would significantly reduce the quantity of spares stocked and the storage space required for a given quantity. Additional information about each of these potential savings is given below.

MAINTENANCE LABOR. Of the total of 7,015 tube-type receivers in use 620 were multi-channel receivers, involving different maintenance and utility costs from those for the 6,395 fixed-tuned receivers. The budgeted annual maintenance time for tube-type receivers was 39.6 man-hours per fixed-tuned receiver, and 55.4 man-hours per multi-channel receiver. The estimated annual maintenance time per solid-state receiver was 19.9 man-hours. This estimated time for the solid-state receivers represented a 50 per cent reduction from the fixed-tuned tube-type receivers; however, some FAA engineers felt that the potential reduction would possibly be closer to 75 per cent. Maintenance time, which included travel, was costed at $9,602 per man-year of 2,080 man-hours. Additional information about the maintenance activities provided by SMS is given in Exhibit 1.

REPLACEMENT PARTS. Annual cost of replacement parts per receiver was calculated at $17.95 for the fixed-tuned tube-type, $73.00 for the multi-channel tube-type, and was estimated at $1.95 for the solid-state type.

POWER COSTS. The fixed-tuned tube-type receiver was rated at 100 watts, the multi-channel tube-type at 265 watts, and the solid-state type at 40 watts. All receivers, whether primary or back-up, tube-type or solid-state, were operated continuously. The cost of electric power was 1 cent per kilowatt-hour.

SPACE UTILIZATION. Receivers were mounted in standard racks 83" high; each rack cost $100. The tube-type receivers occupied 8.75" of vertical rack space, while the solid-state receivers would require only 3.5".

The replacement cycle

The oldest tube-type receivers still in use in 1965 were approximately fifteen years old, while the average age was from six to eight years. The useful life of the tube-type receivers was estimated at from fifteen to twenty years. The life of the solid-state receivers would be at least twenty years.

As noted earlier, at the time of the IMS proposal, the Agency had already contracted for delivery of 3,210 tube-type receivers: 605 receivers had been delivered by early 1965, and an additional 1,083 were regarded as top priority and were being shipped directly to the regions to replace older receivers. Cancellation of this contract would be considered if the solid-state receiver procurement were approved; however, IMS indicated that little, if any, rebate could be expected.

The maximum salvage value for the tube-type receivers already in service was estimated at an average of 5 per cent of their original average purchase price of approximately $350 per receiver. It was anticipated, however, that these receivers would probably be turned over to AID or HEW, with no net return to the Government.

A future alternative would be to employ solid-state multi-channel combination transmitter/receiver units which would require even less maintenance than separate transmitters and solid-state receivers, would use common components, and would save considerably on space requirements. With these devices, known as transceivers, one compact package unit could suffice. However, availability was not expected prior to 1973. (Present multi-channel devices did not permit sufficiently rapid switching from one frequency to another; with solid-state this would become virtually instantaneous.) If these transceivers were installed, the solid-state receivers requested by IMS would have only limited use, primarily as back-up.

QUESTIONS

1. Calculate the estimated annual operating savings that would resul' from replacing tube-type receivers with solid-state receivers.

2. What action would you recommend regarding replacement in 1965?

EXHIBIT 1

FEDERAL AVIATION AGENCY
Notes on the FAA's System Maintenance Service

The SMS in FY 1965 spent $135,000,000, of which 70% was for personnel ($94 million), 10% for material ($13 million) and 20% for other ($28 million).

Of the $94 million for "personnel" expenses, 47% was direct labor, 16% was indirect, and 39% was for administrative and leave.

SMS divided the country into 550 sectors, each containing approximately from 5 to 30 "facilities," or functional groups of equipment requiring servicing. A typical sector may spend $160,000 per year on "personnel" expenses, employing 16 maintenance personnel of whom 14 might be electronic technicians.

Workload for a sector was determined by adding together the "point-counts" or man-hours per year estimated to maintain each individual component within the sector. For example, each receiver was "worth" approximately 50 man-hours per year, a transmitter was worth 100 man-hours per year and a VOR installation (Visual Omni-Range radio beacon) was worth 1500 man-hours per year. Each point-count figure included actual repair time, plus allowances for travel, training, leave, relief, etc.

The Corpus Christi, Texas, sector for example, embraced some 25 separate facilities, of which 8 involved receivers. For one typical month in early 1965, the actual breakdown of total maintenance time was as follows:

| | Electronic | | Plants & Structures | | | |
	Routine	Corrective	Routine	Corrective	Other	Total
Man-hours	1,467	421	112	67	473	2,540

The 8 facilities involving receivers consisted of 2 towers, 1 FSS, 2 RCAG, 1 RCO (Remote Communication Outlet—an unmanned satellite FSS) and 2 RTR (Remote Transmitter/Receiver, usually located close to a Tower).

Maintenance men typically had to travel anywhere from a few minutes to several hours to reach a remote receiver. Repair time can also vary from a few minutes to several hours.

Maintenance personnel were required to follow mandatory maintenance schedules for VHF receivers, as follows:

Weekly— Check aural quality of all receivers by listening to voice transmissions.

Monthly—Measure and record— sensitivity, signal-to-noise ratio, squelch differential and threshold, AVC (Automatic Volume Control) level control and threshold, maximum power output.

Annual— Check selectivity— bandwidth, symmetry and channel frequency.

For an average RCAG, total corrective maintenance time might be divided as follows:

Receivers   — 36%
Antennas   — 2%
Amplifiers   — 2%
Controls   — 11%
Transmitters — 49%

Other Notes

1. In case of a single receiver failure, the pilot might be instructed to switch to another frequency, if one is available. Emergency procedures also existed for the

EXHIBIT 1—*Continued*

use of radar transponder code signals, use of VOR, special pattern flying to be picked up on radar, etc., in case of voice communication failure.

2. Spare parts:
   a. Procurement of spare parts was handled centrally in Oklahoma City. When new equipment was to be installed, estimated spares for one year were normally obtained.

Thereafter, standard methods were used for determining minimum inventory levels of spares.
   b. Delivery time for spare tubes or transistors was approximately 2 months (average).
   c. Tubes may be expected to fail at the rate of 4 or 5 per tube-type receiver per year, while solid-state receivers were estimated at 1 failure per 10,000 hours.

CASE

DISEASE CONTROL PROGRAMS

BENEFIT-COST ANALYSIS OF PROGRAMS TO ENCOURAGE THE USE OF PROTECTIVE DEVICES BY MOTORCYCLISTS

In February, 1967, Mr. Harley Davidson, an analyst in the office of the Injury Control Program, Public Health Service (Department of Health, Education and Welfare) was reviewing DHEW's recently published Program Analysis 1966-1 titled *Disease Control Programs—Motor Vehicle Injury Prevention Program*. Mr. Davidson was a member of a task force established in DHEW to evaluate a series of benefit-cost analyses of various proposed disease control programs. In addition to motor vehicle injury prevention benefit-cost studies had been made of

This case was prepared with the cooperation of the United States Department of Health, Education and Welfare by Graeme M. Taylor under the supervision of Charles Christenson, Associate Professor of Business Administration, Harvard University, on behalf of the Bureau of Training, United States Civil Service Commission. The case is intended for class discussion only, and certain names and facts may have been changed programs dealing with control of arthritis, cancer, tuberculosis and syphilis. Mr. Davidson's specific responsibility was to review Program Unit No. 8 of the motor vehicle injury prevention program, *Increase Use of Improved Safety Devices by Motorcyclists,* in order to (a) evaluate the methodology and results of the benefit-cost analysis of Program Unit No. 8, and (b) recommend whether or not the analysis justified the level of funding contemplated in that program unit.

THE MOTORCYCLE PROGRAM UNIT

The following is the description of Program Unit No. 8 which appeared in Program Analysis 1966-1

Program Description—Increase Use of Improved Safety Devices by Motorcyclists

To prevent accidental deaths due to head injuries of motorcycle riders through appropriate public health activity at the National, State and local levels.

Approach

The Public Health Service approach to solving the motorcycle injury problem will involve four phases. Although each of the four phases of activity is identified separately, all will be closely coordinated and carried out simultaneously. The four phases of activity are:

1. A National education program on use of protective head gear aimed primarily at motorcycle users. It will also include efforts to prepare operators of other motor vehicles to share the road with motorcycles.

			(millions of dollars)		
	1968	1969	1970	1971	1972
Estimated Program Level	$1.679	$1.609	$1.575	$1.569	$1.567

2. A cooperative program with other National organizations and the motorcycle scooter industry to improve protective and safety devices.

3. Involvement of State and local health departments and medical organizations in programs and activities designed to minimize accidental injury in motorcycle accidents.

which, while avoiding the disclosure of confidential information, do not materially lessen the value of the case for educational purposes. This case is not intended to represent either effective or ineffective handling of an administrative situation, nor does it purport to be a statement of policy by the agency involved.

4. Conduct surveillance activity on appropriate aspects of the motorcycle accident and injury problem.

The program unit was estimated to require the above level of new funding during the 5-year planning period 1968–72:

Exhibit 1 gives a summary of the way in which the proposed funds would be spent.

The benefit-cost study estimated that the above program would result in the saving of 4,006 lives over the five-year period 1968–1972 (no reduction in injuries was considered). The cost of the program discounted at 4 per cent was $7,419,000; the benefits of the program, based on the lifetime earnings discounted at 3 per cent of those whose deaths would be averted, were estimated at $512,754,000.[1] Hence, the benefit-cost ratio equalled 69.1:1. Another measure of program effectiveness was the cost per death averted, $1,860. Exhibit 2 summarizes the benefit-cost ratios and the costs per death averted for all nine motor vehicle injury prevention program units and for the arthritis, cancer, tuberculosis, and syphilis programs. Exhibit 3 presents, for all programs, the estimated five-year reduction in numbers of injuries and deaths and the estimated discounted five-year program dollar costs and benefits.

OVERALL METHODOLOGY
OF THE BENEFIT-COST STUDIES

In describing the methodology used in the benefit-cost studies of the Motor Vehicle Injury Prevention Program, Program Analysis 1966-1 stated explicitly the constraints under which the analyses were performed.

Any methodology sets the parameters on how a problem will be managed and which of several possibly germane problem elements will receive attention. Consequently, much of this report deals with the mapping of boundaries. However, when presented under the guise of method, much of this limit-setting is implicit since attention is on the method of problem-solving rather than on the limits being placed on problem-solving by the method.

In this effort to apply benefit-cost

---

[1] Appendix II discusses the selection of the discount rates as well as the methodology used in determining lifetime earnings.

analysis to the domain of vehicular accidents, three major constraints were laid down. These constraints influence the entire analysis and warrant explicit attention.

1. The problem of motor vehicle accidents is examined exclusively in terms of public health concerns. This mandate focused on the role of human factors in vehicular accidents and the amelioration of injury caused by vehicular accidents. In adopting this posture, three major factors in the vehicular accident complex—law enforcement, road design and traffic engineering—were, for the most part, excluded. This constraint had the effect of limiting the problem to considerations traditionally within the purview of DHEW, while excluding those elements which are traditionally handled by the Department of Commerce and other Government agencies.

2. The problem of motor vehicle accidents is handled by nine programs which, in the opinion of Committee members, were feasible and realistic. Criteria for determining "feasible and realistic" were not made explicit. However, program proposals which were rejected, such as no person under 21 being allowed to drive, reduction of maximum speeds on all roads by 20 percent, the Federal Government paying for the installation of $100 worth of safety devices on all automobiles, indicate the cultural values and assumed cost factors which were two issues involved in judging "feasible and realistic." In Appendix D, "Lifting Constraints," the constraint of a program's being "feasible and realistic" was lifted and three potential program proposals, which were initially discarded because of this constraint, were examined.

3. The problem of motor vehicle accidents is handled by programs based on what is known today. This constraint ruled out dependence on new findings based on future research. Unlike the

other constraints, this ruling, in the minds of the Committee members, constituted a basic condition for undertaking a benefit-cost analysis of alternative program strategies. Unless the analysis was restricted to "what is known," the "need for more research would allow one partner in the dialogue to withdraw from the struggle without even having been engaged."

The report then went on to describe the rationale behind benefit-cost analysis.

The next step was to explore this area from two perspectives: (a) current program status and its apparent effect on the problem; (b) anticipated outcomes if the Federal Government does not increase its program effort beyond its present level.

The reasoning behind benefit-cost analysis is quite straightforward. The idea is to allow for a meaningful comparison of the change which results in a given situation as a result of applying alternative programs. In order to bring about this state of affairs, a measurable common denominator is useful for rating program outcome and program costs. This common denominator is dollars. Granting the existence of the common denominator, there must, in addition, be a point on which to take a "fix" in order to support the contention that change has, in fact, taken place. This point for fixing position and shifts in relation to change wrought by program is the baseline.

In this exercise the baseline was created by assessing past rates for motor vehicle and pedestrian deaths and injuries. The assumption was made that the current level of program effort in DHEW would remain constant through 1972 with the exception of increases for obligated administrative costs. The observed trend was then projected and applied to the anticipated population distribution for the years 1967–1972. Program costs and savings due to the introduction of the program were limited to the five-year period 1968–1972, although certain programs were just gathering momentum by the end of this period. . . . The required common denominator was incorporated into the baseline by converting fatalities into lost earnings and by translating lost work days, bed disability days, length of hospitalization, physician visits, and other medical services resulting from injuries into the direct and indirect costs represented by these statistical measures. . . . Throughout this analysis, the total dollar costs and benefit for the 5-year period are discounted to 1968, the base year, to convert the stream of costs and benefits into its worth in the base year . . .

With the baseline and common denominator established, the Committee was able to examine the potential payoff for a variety of program units even though these units differed with respect to such factors as cost of implementation, target group to be reached, method to be employed, and facet of the total program addressed by the proposed program.

With the establishment of the baseline and the development of techniques to convert all elements of the equation to a common denominator, the energies of the Committee were given over to the creation of program units. There are a number of variables which may contribute to the occurrence of a vehicular accident and its resultant injury or death. The skill of the driver, the condition of the road, the speed of the vehicle, the condition of the car, the failure to have or to use safety devices incorporated in the car are just a few of many that are mentioned in the literature. What we know about vehicular accidents is expressed in terms of these variables and as a consequence, program formulations are generally placed in the context of managing these variables, either singly or in combination. A program unit, as

TABLE 1

HISTORICAL DATA ON MOTORCYCLE REGISTRATIONS AND FATALITIES

Year	Total Number of Registered Motor-cycles in the U.S.	Number of Deaths from Motorcycle Accidents	Rate of Deaths per 100,000 Motorcycles
1959	565,352	752	133.0
1960	569,691	730	128.1
1961	595,669	697	117.0
1962	660,400	759	114.9
1963	786,318	882	112.2
1964	984,760	1,118	113.5

developed by the Committee, usually addressed a single variable.

The nine program units created by the Committee are briefly described in Appendix I.

There are two links needed to effect the benefit-cost analysis in vehicular accidents. The first link is associated with the estimate of reduction that could be realized if a given variable were addressed by a program of some sort. This link is supplied in vehicular accidents by the expertise of the Committee members and recourse to studies on the particular variable in question. The second link is associated with the effectiveness of the program proposed to bring about the estimated reduction. In vehicular accidents this is supplied by the experience with programs of the Committee members and the success in the past of programs, similar in content, devoted to public health problems. . . . Three assumptions must be made in working with the program units at this time:

1. Each program unit is independent. In combination with other program units the estimated impact will neither increase nor decrease.

2. Unless specified, a program unit will have an impact on the total target population, and its benefits, i.e., a reduction of fatality and injury, will be distributed in proportion to the occurrence of fatality and injury by age grouping among the baseline population. For example, if one percent of fatalities occur in the under-one-year-old age group, then one percent of the estimated reduction in fatality due to any program unit will be assigned to the under-one age group for the computation of benefits to the economy of the program unit.

3. Unless specified, the distribution of estimated injury benefits will be the same as with the fatality benefits. In addition, it is assumed that the reduction of injury estimates covers proportionally the same range of severity as is represented in the base-line figures.

ESTIMATE OF BENEFITS OF
THE MOTORCYCLE PROGRAM

As indicated in the previous section the benefit-cost studies of the motor vehicle injury prevention programs began with a stipulation of a baseline, or the number of deaths and injuries to be expected if the level of DHEW effort remained constant. Next, an estimate was made of the number of death and injuries which would be avoided if the proposed program unit were adopted. Finally, the reduction in deaths and injuries was translated into dollar terms. These three steps will now be described in further detail as they applied to Program Unit No. 8.

Baseline

The team working on the motorcycle unit had available the information given in [Table 1 on page 244].

The team estimated that (1) the number of registered motorcycles would continue to increase at an increasing rate, and (2) the death rate would decline in the absence of new safety programs to a level of 110 deaths per 100,000 registered motorcycles. Accordingly, the number of motorcycle accident deaths to be expected without the safety program was projected as shown in the following table:

TABLE 2

PROJECTED BASELINE CASE

Year	Projected Total Number of Registered Motor- cycles in the U.S.	Projected Number of Deaths from Motorcycle Accidents without Program (based on 110 deaths per 100,000 registered motorcycles)
1968	2,900,000	3,190
1969	3,500,000	3,850
1970	4,200,000	4,620
1971	5,000,000	5,500
1972	6,000,000	6,600

Effectiveness of the program unit

Calculation of the anticipated reduction in the number of deaths resulting from the proposed program unit involved two separate estimates: (1) the effectiveness of the program in persuading motorcyclists to wear helmets and protective eyeshields; and (2) the effectiveness of these devices in reducing deaths (injuries were not considered in the analysis of this program unit). The team's judgment was that the program would result in use of helmets and eyeshields to the degree shown in [Table 3 on page 246].

Regarding the second factor, the effectiveness of protective devices in reducing deaths, the team relied on a study entitled "Effect of Compulsory Safety Helmets on Motorcycle Accident Fatalities" which appeared in *Australian Road Research,* Vol. 2, No. 1, September, 1964. This study reported that the number of motorcycle fatalities occurring in the Australian state of Victoria in the two years following the effective date of a law requiring the wearing of helmets was only 31 while the number of fatalities projected on the basis of the experience of the two preceding years was 62.5,

TABLE 3

ESTIMATED EFFECTIVENESS OF PROGRAM
IN ENCOURAGING PROTECTIVE DEVICES

Year	Estimated Percentage of Motorcyclists Using Helmets and Eyeshields
1968	20%
1969	30%
1970	40%
1971	50%
1972	55%

for a reduction of about 50 per cent. Other states, which did not have such a law, had shown a reduction of about 12 per cent in the same period, a difference of 38 per cent. The committee concluded that 100 per cent usage of helmets and eyeshields by American motorcyclists would reduce the number of deaths by about 40 per cent.

Multiplication of the figures for projected usage of protective devices given in Table 3 by 40 per cent gave the estimated percentage reduction in deaths, and application of these percentages to the baseline data of Table 2 gave the estimated reduction in number of deaths. The results are summarized below.

Conversion to economic benefits

For the purpose of calculating the lifetime earnings lost in the event of a motorcycle fatality, it was necessary to estimate the distribution of fatalities by age and sex. In 1964 approximately 90 per cent of the victims of motorcycle accidents had been male and 10 per cent female; similarly, about 90 per cent had been in the age group 15–24 and 10 per cent in the age group 25–34. The data were not cross-classified, so it was considered necessary to assume that the sex distribution of fatalities in each age group was the same as the overall distribution, i.e., 90:10. Projecting these percentages into the future, it was calculated that of the 255 fatalities which the proposed program was expected to avoid in 1968, 207 would be males between 15 and 24 inclusive (i.e., .9 x .9 x 255). Combining this procedure for all categories and years resulted in the following estimates [in Table 5 on page 247] of the distribution of death reductions over the 5-year period.

The final step in calculating the expected benefits of the proposed program was to assign the appropriate dol-

TABLE 4

ESTIMATED REDUCTION IN DEATHS FROM PROPOSED PROGRAM

Year	Projected Number of Deaths from Motorcycle Accidents without Program	Estimated Percentage Reduction in Deaths with Program	Estimated Reduction in Number of Deaths with Program
1968	3,190	8%	255
1969	3,850	12%	462
1970	4,620	16%	739
1971	5,500	20%	1,100
1972	6,600	22%	1,450
5-year total	23,760	—	4,006

TABLE 5

ESTIMATED REDUCTION IN DEATHS BY AGE AND SEX

| | Death Reduction | | | | |
| | Age 15–24 | | Age 25–34 | | |
Year	Males	Females	Males	Females	Total
1968	207	23	22	3	255
1969	374	42	41	5	462
1970	598	67	67	7	739
1971	891	99	99	11	1,100
1972	1,174	131	130	15	1,450
Total	3,244	362	359	41	4,006

lar benefits to the above estimates of decreases in deaths by age group and sex. This was done by multiplying the decrease in deaths in each sex-age group "cell" in the above table by the applicable discounted lifetime earnings figure for that particular cell.

Table 6 shows lifetime earnings by age and sex, discounted at 3 per cent, used in computing the dollar benefits of reducing motorcycle accident fatalities.

The methodology used in deriving the figures in the table below is described in Appendix II.

The number of deaths saved in each cell of Table 5 was multiplied by the appropriate earnings figure from Table 6 and discounted at 3 per cent to the base year, 1968. For example, Table 5 indicates that it was estimated that in 1968 the lives of 3 females between the ages of 25 and 34 would be saved. The discounted lifetime earnings of females in this age group was found from Table 6 by averaging the discounted lifetime earnings for females 25–29 and 30–34, the average of $81,702 and $77,888 being $79,795. This was multiplied by 3 to give $239,385; using a present value factor of 1 (since 1968 was the base year), the figure derived was $239,385. Similarly, discounted

TABLE 6

DISCOUNTED LIFETIME EARNINGS BY AGE AND SEX

Age	Males	Females
Under 1	$ 84,371	$50,842
1–4	98,986	54,636
5–9	105,836	63,494
10–14	122,933	73,719
15–19	139,729	81,929
20–24	150,536	84,152
25–29	150,512	81,702
30–34	141,356	77,888

figures were obtained for each year by age group and sex; the results are shown below in Table 7.

Thus, over the five-year program period, 1968–1972, it was estimated that 4,006 deaths could be averted (Table 5), at a present-value cost of $7,419,000 (Exhibit 1). The present value of the lifetime earnings of the 4,006 persons whose lives would be saved during this period was shown in Table 7 to be $512,754,000.

These data were summarized in the form of two measures of program effectiveness:

(1) *Program Cost per Death Averted*
$$= \frac{\$7,419,000}{4,006} = \underline{\underline{\$1,860}}$$

(2) *Benefit/Cost Ratio*
$$= \frac{\$512,754,000}{\$7,419,000} = \underline{\underline{69.1}}$$

As noted earlier, Exhibits 2 and 3 summarize the results for all nine motor vehicle program units and also for the eight other disease control programs studied.

QUESTIONS

1. As Mr. Davidson, prepare a critique of the methodology and findings of the benefit-cost analysis of Program Unit No. 8.

2. Based on your evaluation of the analysis, would you recommend the level of funding proposed?

TABLE 7

DISCOUNTED SAVINGS RESULTING FROM PROGRAM TO PROMOTE
USE OF PROTECTIVE DEVICES BY MOTORCYCLISTS (000's)

Year	Total	Age 15–24		Age 25–34	
		Males	Females	Males	Females
TOTAL	$512,754	$434,002	$27,164	$48,714	$2,874
1968	36,140	30,347	1,976	3,578	239
1969	61,972	52,423	3,282	5,895	372
1970	97,152	82,363	5,059	9,248	482
1971	39,547	117,928	7,408	13,393	818
1972	177,943	150,941	9,439	16,600	963

EXHIBIT 1

DISEASE CONTROL PROGRAMS

Proposed Budget for Program to Increase Use of Protective Devices by Motorcyclists, 1968–1972
(costs in thousands)

	1968	1969	1970	1971	1972
Total Number of Persons	42	42	42	42	42
Total Costs	$1,679	$1,609	$1,575	$1,569	$1,569
Personnel	504	504	504	504	504
Program	1,175	1,105	1,070	1,065	1,065
Staff					
Central Office	13	13	13	13	13
Regional Office	9	9	9	9	9
State Assignees	20	20	20	20	20
Personnel	$ 504	$ 504	$ 504	$ 504	$ 504
Evaluation & Surveillance	300	300	300	300	300
State Projects [1]	500	500	500	500	500
National TV Spots	60	60	60	60	60
Educational TV Series	100	100	100	100	100
Safety Films	40	40	20	20	20
Publications	100	30	30	30	30
Exhibits	30	30	15	15	15
Community Projects	25	25	25	25	25
Campus Projects	20	20	20	15	15

[1] Ten projects at $50,000 per project.

EXHIBIT 2

DISEASE CONTROL PROGRAMS

Costs per Death Averted and Benefit/Cost Ratios for All Program Units Studied

Program	Program Cost per Death Averted	Benefit/Cost Ratio
Motor Vehicle Injury Prevention Programs		
Increase seat belt use	87	1,351.4:1
Use of improved restraint devices	100	1,117.1:1
Reduce pedestrian injury	600	144.3:1
Increase use of protective devices by motorcyclists	1,860	69.1:1
Improve driving environment	2,330	49.4:1
Reduce driver drinking	5,330	21.5:1
Improve driver licensing	13,800	3.8:1
Improve emergency medical services	45,000	2.4:1
Improve driver training	88,000	1.7:1
Other Disease Control Programs Studied		
Arthritis	N/A	42.5:1
Syphilis	22,252	16.7:1
Uterine Cervix Cancer	3,470	9.0:1
Lung Cancer	6,400	5.7:1
Breast Cancer	7,663	4.5:1
Tuberculosis	22,807	4.4:1
Head and Neck Cancer	29,100	1.1:1
Colon-Rectum Cancer	42,944	0.5:1

EXHIBIT 3

DISEASE CONTROL PROGRAMS

Reduction in Injuries and Deaths and Total Discounted Program Costs and Savings for All Program Units Studied, 1968–1972

Program Unit	Discounted Program Costs ($000's)	Discounted Program Savings ($000's)	Reduction in Injuries	Reduction in Deaths
Motor Vehicle Injury Prevention Programs				
Seat belts	2,019	2,728,374	1,904,000	22,930
Restraint devices	610	681,452	471,600	5,811
Pedestrian injury	1,061	153,110	142,700	1,650
Motorcyclists	7,419	512,754	——	4,006
Driving environment	28,545	1,409,891	1,015,500	12,250
Driver drinking	28,545	612,970	440,630	5,340
Driver licensing	6,113	22,938	23,200	442
Emergency medical services	721,478 [1]	1,726,000	[2]	16,000
Driver training	750,550	1,287,022	665,300	8,515
Other Disease Control Programs Studied				
Arthritis	35,000	1,489,000	N/A	N/A
Syphilis	179,300 [3]	2,993,000	N/A	11,590
Uterine Cervix Cancer	118,100 [3]	1,071,000	N/A	34,200
Lung Cancer	47,000 [3]	268,000	N/A	7,000
Breast Cancer	22,400	101,000	N/A	2,396
Tuberculosis	130,000	573,000	N/A	5,700
Head & Neck Cancer	7,800	9,000	N/A	268
Colon-Rectum Cancer	7,300	4,000	N/A	170

[1] Includes $300 million State matching funds.
[2] This program does not reduce injury; however, it is estimated to reduce hospital bed days by 2,401,000 and work loss days by 8,180,000.
[3] Funding shown used as basis for analysis—includes funds estimated to come from sources other than DHEW.

APPENDIX I

DISEASE CONTROL PROGRAMS

Brief Description of the Nine Motor Vehicle Injury Prevention Program Units

Program Unit 1—Improve Driver Licensing

This program will develop a selective licensing procedure in each State which will screen out the drivers unsafe because of medical conditions. In addition, the program's approach will help drivers with impairments through medical care, edu-cation, special devices, etc., so that they can continue to drive with reasonable safety.

Program Unit 2—Improve Driver Performance and Behavior by Upgrading Driving Skills, Knowledge and Attitude (Improve Driver Training)

An improved program of driver education and training, through classroom work on roads, cars, laws, and personal limitations and behind the wheel supervised driving experience, will help prevent accidental deaths and injuries. This program is aimed at the new driver. A program for retraining the experienced driver was considered to hold potential, but was not included.

Program Unit 3—Improve Driving Performance and Behavior by Decreasing Driving Exposure While Under the Influence of Alcohol and Drugs (Reduce Driver Drinking)

This program will include a National education program to inform school age children and adults about the effects of alcohol on body functions and driving, how it increases risk of accident, and how social drinking can be arranged so that the driving risk is significantly lowered.

Treatment and rehabilitation services for the chronic alcoholic will be supported as well as strict enforcement of the laws involving drivers with blood alcohol levels exceeding .10 percent.

Program Unit 4—Reduce the Exposure of Pedestrians to Injury (Reduce Pedestrian Injury)

A National education program will inform elderly persons of personal limitations, i.e., declining vision, and will inform the elderly and young children about traffic control devices, laws and characteristics of the modern automobile and motor vehicle traffic.

Program Unit 5—Increase Seat Belt Use

A National public education program will use all mass media and organizational approaches to inform individuals about the decrease in risk and other advantages involved in wearing seat belts

at all times. Opinion leaders such as clergy and the medical and legal professions will be utilized in transmitting the information.

Program Unit 6—Improve Driving Environment

A National education program will inform the general public about the desirability of changes in vehicle and road design, provide them with an understanding of their relationships to safer driving and create a readiness to accept instruction in their proper use.

Program Unit 7—Develop and Encourage Use of Improved Restraint Systems for Children and Adults (Use of Improved Restraint Systems)

Information on the development of restraining devices will be made available to manufacturers and others who can stimulate the production of the devices. A National public education program will use all mass media and organizational approaches, including opinion leaders, to inform individuals about the decrease in risk and other advantages of using the improved restraining systems at all times.

Program Unit 8—Increase Use of Helmets and Protective Eye Shields by Motorcyclists

Appropriate public health activity at all levels will prevent accidental deaths due to head injuries of motorcycle riders. A National education program includes the use of protective head gear and prepares operators of other motor vehicles to share the road with motorcycles. Other activities consist of a cooperative program with other National organizations and the motorcycle scooter industry to improve protective and safety devices and the involvement of State and local health departments and medical organizations in programs designed to minimize accidental injury in motorcycle accidents.

*Program Unit 9—Improve Emergency
Medical Services*

In order to assure adequate and timely
care for every injured person, a planned
approach must link the community ambu-
lance services and hospitals into an integrated system which includes: (1) the
setting and maintenance of standards;
(2) a communication system permitting
early accident detection and rapid dis-
patch of services; (3) a training program
for managing all patients; (4) public education on first aid; and (5) research on
better emergency care techniques.

Strategic pilot projects should be established in selected communities and should
include all elements of a total transportation program—land, air, and sea.

An extensive program of remodeling
of emergency departments in hospitals is
required to redesign, equip and staff them
adequately. Mobile emergency treatment
stations (Packaged Emergency Station—
PES) dispatched from the hospital to distant points of expected needs is suggested
for extending hospital capacity.

APPENDIX II

DISEASE CONTROL PROGRAMS

Some Methodological Problems

This appendix discusses briefly the
procedures used (1) to determine the
lifetime earning patterns of persons whose
deaths might be averted by a disease control program, and (2) to decide on appropriate discount rates to use in reducing
future benefits and costs to their present
values.

Lifetime Earnings Patterns

The calculation of lifetime earnings
figures used in DHEW'S 1966 series of
disease control program analyses was
based largely on methodology developed
by Mrs. Dorothy P. Rice of the Office of
Research and Statistics, Social Security
Administration, and reported by her in
Estimating the Cost of Illness.[1]

The appropriate measure of output
loss for individuals was considered to be
year-round, full-time earnings, including
wages and salaries before deductions plus
wage supplements such as employer contributions for social insurance and private pension and welfare funds. Unpublished mean earnings data for full-time
male workers in 1964 by 5-year age intervals were furnished by the Bureau of the
Census. Similar data were not available
for females, but the Bureau of the Census
published *median* incomes for year-round
full-time workers by sex and age. For
each age class, it was assumed that the
ratio of female to male *mean* income was
the same as the ratio of female to male
median income.

Each mean earnings figure was adjusted upwards to take account of wage
supplements by a factor of 1.08268, derived from data published by the Department of Commerce in *Survey of Current
Business.*

Although a relatively high proportion
of females are housewives and not in the
labor market, it was considered desirable
to impute a value to their services. For

---

[1] Health Economics Series No. 6, Public
Health Service Publication No. 947-6, May
1966.

this purpose the 1964 mean earnings of domestic servants, or $2,767, was used. It was recognized that the imputed value was "clearly on the low side," for it made no allowance for the housewife's longer work week and took no account of the size of the household cared for.

The following table presents 1964 mean earnings by age class, adjusted for wage supplements and including an imputed value for housewives' services.

Although Table A presents only cross-sectional data for a single year, 1964, it was assumed that it could also be used to represent the earnings pattern of an average individual over his working lifetime. In other words, an average 20 year-old male in the labor force could expect to earn $4,634 on the average for full-time work over the next five years, $6,373 for the five years after that, and so forth. It was recognized that this assumption might result in a downward bias in the estimate of discounted lifetime earnings because other data indicated that younger workers appeared to benefit more from economic growth than older workers. The evidence for this bias was considered inconclusive, however.

In converting the estimated mean earnings by year into lifetime earnings, several other factors had to be considered.

First, not everyone would have been working or productive had death from the cause under study not interfered. Some victims of fatal accidents would have been too old or too young or unwilling or unable to find a job. For the purpose of the disease control program analyses, it was assumed that if it were not for these illnesses or causes of death, persons stricken would have had the same employment experience as persons in the same age and sex groups. Accordingly, the 1964 labor force participation rates (proportion of all civilians who were employed or looking for a job) were applied and further adjustments were made for the number who would have been employed under conditions of full employment, defined as 4-percent unemployment. The unemployment rates for 1965 were used because 1965 was the most current year of full employment. Without the assumption of full employment, losses due to mortality and disability could not have been isolated from losses due to unemployment.

Table B [page 254] presents the data used for these adjustments.

TABLE A

ADJUSTED MEAN EARNINGS BY AGE AND SEX, 1964

Age Group	Male	Female
14–19	$2,829	$3,387
20–24	4,634	3,800
25–29	6,373	3,951
30–34	7,532	4,670
35–39	7,953	4,390
40–44	8,305	4,584
45–49	8,229	4,724
50–54	7,435	4,268
55–59	7,174	4,355
60–64	7,113	4,318
65–69	5,981	3,851
70 and over	5,887	3,790

TABLE B

LABOR FORCE PARTICIPATION AND UNEMPLOYMENT RATES BY AGE CLASS

Age Group	1964 Labor Force Participation Rates		1965 Unemployment Rates	
	Male	Female	Male	Female
14	17.7	9.9	6.8	5.2
15–19	44.8	31.9	13.7	14.8
20–24	85.6	49.1	6.3	7.3
25–29	94.7	37.9	3.3	5.7
30–34	96.4	36.2	2.6	5.2
35–39	95.8	41.7	2.6	4.8
40–44	95.4	47.7	2.5	4.4
45–49	95.2	51.4	2.5	3.6
50–54	93.3	50.5	2.6	2.8
55–59	89.6	45.9	3.2	2.9
60–64	77.4	32.7	3.4	2.7
65–69	41.7	17.2	4.2	3.1
70 and over	18.7	5.8	2.7	2.4

The second factor which had to be considered was mortality from causes other than the one under study. Even if a 16-year old motorcyclist is saved from fatal injury, he may succumb to some other cause before reaching normal retirement. To handle this factor, standard actuarial techniques were used; that is, mortality records were used to determine the proportion of males (females) of age a surviving to age n, and this proportion was then applied to the earnings in year n (adjusted as previously discussed) of any such male whose accidental death was prevented at age a.

The Discount Rate

Program Analysis 1966-1 stated that:

Although there is agreement among economists that comparison of streams of earnings over varying time spans should employ the process of discounting, there is no agreement on the discount rate to be used. For purposes of this cost-benefit analysis, a basic discount rate of 6 percent is used.

The basic discount rate was then adjusted to reflect anticipated differential changes in prices. Over the ten-year period 1955–65, for example, medical care prices increased at a rate of approximately 2% per year faster than consumer prices. It was assumed that this differential rate of increase would continue and that it would apply to program costs as well. To convert the program costs given in Exhibit 1 into terms comparable to consumer prices, therefore, the costs given should be increased by a factor of 2% per year before discounting. Essentially the same result would be obtained by subtracting the 2% from the basic discount rate of 6%, given an adjusted rate of 4% for discounting program costs.

In the case of lifetime earnings, it was assumed that worker productivity would continue to increase at a rate of about 3% per year as it had on the average from 1947 to 1965 and that wages would grow with productivity. The effect of increasing wages was taken into account by subtracting this 3% from the basic discount rate, giving an adjusted rate of 3% for discounting lifetime earnings.

CASE

DOWNTOWN PARKING AUTHORITY

PROPOSED MUNICIPAL PARKING FACILITY

In January, 1968 a meeting was held in the office of the Mayor of Oakmont to discuss a proposed municipal parking facility. The participants included the mayor, the traffic commissioner, the administrator of Oakmont's Downtown Parking Authority, the city planner, and the finance director. The purpose of the meeting was to consider a report by Richard Stockton, executive assistant to the Parking Authority's administrator, concerning estimated costs and revenues for the proposed facility.

Mr. Stockton's opening statement was as follows:

As you know, the Mayor proposed two months ago that we construct a multi-level parking garage on the Elm Street site. At that time, he asked the Parking Authority to assemble all pertinent information for consideration at our meeting today. I would like to summarize our findings briefly for you.

The Elm Street site is owned by the city. It is presently occupied by the remains of the old Embassy Cinema, which was gutted by fire last June. The proprietors of the cinema have since used the insurance proceeds to open a new theatre in the suburbs; their lease of the city-owned land on which the Embassy was built expired on December 31st.

We estimate that it would cost approximately $40,000 to demolish the old Embassy. A building contractor has estimated that a multi level structure, with space for 800 cars, could be built on the site at a cost of about $2 million. The useful life of the garage would probably be around forty years.

The city could finance construction of the garage through the sale of bonds. The Finance Director has informed me that we could probably float an issue of 20-year tax-exempts at 5% interest. Redemption would commence after three years, with one seventeenth of the original number of bonds being recalled in each succeeding year.

A parking management firm has al-

This case was prepared by Graeme M. Taylor under the supervision of Richard F. Vancil, Associate Professor of Business Administration, Harvard University, on behalf of the U.S. Bureau of the Budget. The case is intended for class discussion only, and certain names and facts may have been changed which, while avoiding the disclosure of confidential information, do not materially lessen the value of the case for educational purposes. This case is not intended to represent either effective or ineffective handling of an administrative situation, nor does it purport to be a statement of policy by the agency involved.

ready contacted us with a proposal to operate the garage for the city. They would require a management fee of $30,000 per year. Their proposal involves attendant parking, and they estimate that their costs, exclusive of the fee, would amount to $240,000 per year. Of this amount, $175,000 would be personnel costs; the remainder would include utilities, mechanical maintenance, insurance, etc. Any gross revenues in excess of $270,000 per year would be shared 90% by the city and 10% by the management firm. If total annual revenues are *less* than $270,000, the city would have to pay the difference.

I suggest we offer a management contract for bid, with renegotiations every three years.

The city would derive additional income of around $50,000 per year by renting the ground floor of the structure as retail space.

It's rather difficult for the Parking Authority to estimate revenues from the garage for, as you know, our operations to date have been confined to fringe-area parking-lots. However, we conducted a survey at a private parking garage only three blocks from the Elm Street site; perhaps that information will be helpful.

This private garage is open every day from 7 a.m. until midnight. Their rate schedule is as follows: 75¢ for the first hour; 50¢ for the second hour; and 25¢ for each subsequent hour, with a maximum rate of $2.00. Their capacity is 400 spaces. Our survey indicated that, during business hours, 75% of their spaces were occupied by "all-day parkers"—cars whose drivers and passengers work downtown. In addition, roughly 400 cars use the garage each weekday with an average stay of three hours. We did not take a survey on Saturday or Sunday, but the proprietor indicated that the garage is usually about 75% utilized by short-term parkers on Saturdays until 6 p.m., when the department stores close; the average

stay is about two hours. There's a lull until about 7 p.m., when the moviegoers start coming in; he says the garage is almost full from 8 p.m. until closing time at midnight. Sundays are usually very quiet until the evening, when he estimates that his garage is 60% utilized from 6 p.m. until midnight.

In addition to this survey, we studied a report issued by the City College Economics Department last year. This report estimated that we now have approximately 50,000 cars entering the central business district (CBD) every day from Monday through Saturday. Based on correlations with other cities of comparable size, the economists calculated that we need 30,000 parking spaces in the CBD. This agrees quite well with a block-by-block estimate made by the Traffic Commissioner's office last year, which indicated a total parking need in the CBD of 29,000 spaces. Right now we have 22,000 spaces in the CBD. Of these, 5% are curb spaces (half of which are metered, with a 2-hour maximum limit for 20 cents), 65% are in open lots, and 30% are in privately owned and operated garages.

Another study indicated that 60% of all auto passengers entering the CBD on a week-day were on their way to work; 20% were shoppers, and 20% were businessmen making calls. The average number of people per car was 1.75.

Unfortunately, we have not yet had time to use the data mentioned thus far to work up estimates of the revenues to be expected from the proposed garage.

The Elm Street site is strategically located in the heart of the CBD, near the major department stores and office buildings. It is five blocks from one of the access ramps to the new crosstown freeway which we expect will be open to traffic next year, and only three blocks from the Music Center which the Mayor dedicated last week.

As we all know, the parking situation

in that section of town has steadily worsened over the last few years, with no immediate prospect of improvement. The demand for parking is clearly there, and the Parking Authority therefore recommends that we go ahead and build the garage.

The Mayor thanked Mr. Stockton for his report and asked for comments. The following discussion took place:

Finance Director: I'm all in favor of relieving parking congestion downtown, but I think we have to consider alternative uses of the Elm Street site. For example, the city could sell that site to a private developer for at least $1 million. The site could support an office building from which the city would derive property taxes of around $200,000 per year at present rates. The office building would almost certainly incorporate an underground parking garage for the use of the tenants, and therefore we would not only improve our tax base and increase revenues but also increase the availability of parking at no cost to the city. Besides, an office building on that site would serve to improve the amenity of downtown. A multi-level garage built above ground, on the other hand, would reduce the amenity of the area.

Planning Director: I'm not sure I agree completely with the Finance Director. Within a certain range we can increase the value of downtown land by judicious provision of parking. Adequate, efficient parking facilities will encourage more intensive use of downtown traffic generators such as shops, offices, and places of entertainment, thus enhancing land values. A garage contained within an office building might, as the Finance Director suggests, provide more spaces, but I suspect these would be occupied almost exclusively by workers in the building and thus would not increase the total available supply.

I think long-term parking downtown should be discouraged by the city. We should attempt to encourage short-term parking—particularly among shoppers—in an effort to counteract the growth of business in the suburbs and the consequent stagnation of retail outlets downtown. The rate structure in effect at the privately operated garage quoted by Mr. Stockton clearly favors the long-term parker. I believe that, if the city constructs a garage on the Elm Street site, we should devise a rate structure which favors the short-term parker. People who work downtown should be encouraged to use our mass transit system.

Finance Director: I'm glad you mentioned mass transit, because this raises another issue. As you know, our subways are presently not used to capacity and are running at a substantial annual deficit which is borne by the city. We have just spent millions of dollars on the new subway station under the Music Center. Why build a city garage only three blocks away which will still farther increase the subway system's deficit? Each person who drives downtown instead of taking the subway represents a loss of 50 cents (the average round trip fare) to the subway system. I have read a report stating that approximately two-thirds of all persons entering the CBD by car would still have made the trip *by subway* if they had *not* been able to use their cars.

Mayor: On the other hand, I think shoppers prefer to drive rather than take the subway, particularly if they intend to make substantial purchases. No one likes to take the subway burdened down by packages and shopping bags. You know, the Downtown Merchants Association has informed me that they estimate that each new parking space in the CBD generates on average an additional $10,000 in annual retail sales. That represents substantial extra profit to retailers; I think retailing after-tax profits average about 3% of gross sales. Besides, the city treasury benefits directly from our 3% sales tax.

Traffic Commissioner: But what about some of the other costs of increasing parking downtown and therefore, presumably, the number of cars entering the CBD? I'm thinking of such costs as the increased wear and tear on city streets, the additional congestion produced with consequent delays and frustration for the drivers, the impeding of the movement of city vehicles, noise, air pollution, and so on. How do we weigh these costs in coming to a decision?

Parking Administrator: I don't think we can make a decision at this meeting. I suggest that Dick Stockton be asked to prepare an analysis of the proposed ga-

rage along the lines of the following questions:

(1) Using the information presented at this discussion, should the city of Oakton construct the proposed garage?

(2) What rates should be charged?

(3) What additional information, if any, should be obtained before we make a final decision?

Mayor: I agree. Dick, can you let us have your answers to these questions in time for consideration at our meeting next month?

QUESTION

As Mr. Stockton, prepare your response to the Mayor's request.

CASE

FOREST SERVICE

TIMBER SUPPLY/DEMAND PROJECTIONS

Forests cover one-third of the land in the fifty states. Two-thirds of the forest area is defined as commercial, i.e., suitable and available for the growing of continuous crops of industrial timber products. Over 70 per cent of commercial forest land is owned by private citizens.

The Forest Service of the U.S. Department of Agriculture was responsible in 1965 for managing, developing, and protecting 186 million acres of land and the associated natural re-

sources in the national forest system. This included 154 national forests in thirty-nine States and Puerto Rico con-

This case was prepared with the cooperation of the United States Department of Agriculture by Graeme M. Taylor under the supervision of Charles Christenson, Associate Professor of Business Administration, Harvard University, on behalf of the Office of Career Development, U.S. Civil Service Commission. The case is intended for class discussion only, and certain names and facts may have been changed which, while avoiding the disclosure of confidential information, do not materially lessen the value of

taining 182 million acres; 3.8 million acres of national grasslands and 160,000 acres of land utilization projects. About half of this total area was classified as commercial forest.

In addition to managing federally-owned forest land, the Forest Service cooperated with state agencies and private forest owners to protect 450 million acres of state and privately-owned forests and watersheds against fire, insects, and disease; to encourage better forest practices for conservation and profit on 367 million acres of private commercial forest land; to aid in distribution of planting stock for forests and shelterbelts; and to stimulate development and management of state, county and municipal forests.

Besides managing its own forests and cooperating with other forest owners, the Forest Service conducted research on the growth and harvesting of timber; protection of forests from fire, insects, and disease; management of rangelands and wildlife habitat; outdoor recreation; protection and management of watersheds; efficient and economical utilization of forest products; and forest economics.

In all its activities, but most particularly in its management of the national forest system, the Service was guided by the principles of multiple use and sustained yield. These deeply ingrained concepts were given statutory authority in 1960 by the passage of Public Law 86-517, which directed that "the national forests be managed under principles of multiple use and

the case for educational purposes. This case is not intended to represent either effective or ineffective handling of an administrative situation, nor does it purport to be a statement of policy by the agency involved.

to produce a sustained yield of products and services and for other purposes." This act, described in Forest Service literature as "highly significant and "masterfully brief," was considered basic to an understanding of Service activities; it is reproduced as Exhibit 1.

MANAGEMENT OF THE NATIONAL FOREST SYSTEM

For the purpose of administration the national forest system was divided into nine regions, each headed by a regional forester. Because of the vast areas and the varied land management problems involved, much of the responsibility for implementation of the Multiple Use-Sustained Yield Act was left to line managers in the regions. Activities in the national forests were coordinated for each region by a regional multiple use management guide, which took account of local conditions by designating various management zones, each with appropriate priorities and coordination among outdoor recreation, range, timber, watershed, and wildlife activities.

The Forest Service contained many men highly trained in the ecology of their regions and districts. The preservation of harmony within their areas of responsibility was stressed, and the complex interaction of the various material resources under their stewardship was a constant factor in their thinking and planning. Crest zones, or mountain ridges, were viewed not only as a source of water from winter snow packs but also in terms of their scenic beauty. Thinning a stand of timber had to be considered in relation to the effects this would have on the grazing of deer as well as on the productivity of the stand in annual timber growth. Building an access road to reach timber for cutting had to be thought of also in terms of the recreation areas this might open up or as to its effect on soil erosion.

Against this backdrop of respect for the natural environment, foresters had to determine from time to time specific policy on timber sales from national forests. To facilitate planning, the national forests were divided into areas known as working circles, each containing roughly 350,000 acres of commercial forest land. For each year certain portions of each working circle were designated for cutting; the total quantity of timber so designated was known as the annual allowable cut for that working circle. This figure, usually expressed in board feet, was regarded as an upper limit not to be exceeded on average over a ten-year period.

The figure set each year for the allowable cut in the national forests was not the annual incremental growth of timber as might be the case in private forests nor was it the maximum realizable growth of the area. Preservation of beauty and the many other factors involved in the multiple use-sustained yield principle prevented the application of a simple rule such as incremental growth for determining annual allowable cut. Achievement of maximum realizable growth depended on the application of intensive "silvi-culture" techniques such as pruning, thinning, and insect and disease control.

In 1965 93 per cent of the allowable cut of 12 billion board feet of timber for all national forests was in fact harvested, compared to 92 per cent in 1964 when the allowable cut was also set at 12 billion board feet. The percentage of allowable cut taken had been rising steadily since 1961, when only 81 per cent of the allowable cut of 10.4 billion board feet was actually harvested. During F. Y. 1965 receipts to the Treasury from the harvest of timber in national forests amounted to $138.8 million. A summary of all Forest Service receipts and expenditures for F. Y. 1965 is shown in Exhibit 2.

THE CHARACTERISTICS OF FOREST LAND

In 1965 the Forest Service published a report, *Timber Trends in the United States,* which projected the outlook for timber supply and demand through the year 2000. A principal conclusion of the study was that demand for timber would require a cut from growing stock of 21.6 billion cubic feet of roundwood in 2000, whereas supply in the same year was projected at only 18 billion cubic feet. Supply was defined as the sum of growth in the East, allowable cut on public lands in the West, and the prospective cut on private lands in the West.

As a base from which to appraise prospective trends in future timber supplies, *Timber Trends* first included a section on "Forest Land and Timber Resources." For purposes of this discussion, the United States was divided into four sections: Pacific Coast, Rocky Mountains, North, and South (see Exhibit 3).

Timber Trends noted that "the Nation's timber growing capacity is concentrated on a relatively small portion of the total forest land." About 31 per cent of all commercial forest land, to wit, that portion with a timber growth potential of 85 cubic feet per acre annually or higher, was capable of producing half of the potential growth (see

Exhibit 4). Productivity per acre was highest in the Pacific Coast states; these states, however, also had a relatively low fraction of the commercial forest land. The South also had relatively productive land and in addition a relatively high fraction of the total.

Nearly three-fourths of commercial forest area, or 367 million acres, was in private ownership on January 1, 1963 (see Exhibit 5). The largest class of industrial owners were the pulp and paper companies. Moreover, these companies had increased their acreage by 10 per cent between 1953 and 1963, particularly in the South. Farm and miscellaneous private owners held 59 per cent of the acreage on January 1, 1963, but this land held only 38 per cent of the growing stock (see Exhibit 6). Public lands, with slightly more than a quarter of the acreage, contained nearly half of the growing stock.

THE OUTLOOK FOR TIMBER SUPPLIES

The projections of timber growth contained in *Timber Trends* were made by a complex procedure which can be briefly described as follows.

First, an inventory of the timber stand and stock for each region as of January 1, 1963, was obtained from timber survey information. The inventory showed numbers and volumes of trees by 2-inch diameter classes, by softwoods and hardwoods in the East, and by ownership in the West.

Annual changes in numbers of trees by diameter classes were then computed for the period 1963–2000, taking into account growth rates, mortality rates, and cutting rates by diameter class.

In making the projections it was assumed that (a) gains and losses of

forest land would tend to balance during the projection period; (b) continued effectiveness of fire control would be maintained; (c) tree planting, stand improvement, and natural regeneration would continue at present rates.

Regarding the balance of gains and losses of forest land, it was suggested that diversion of forest land to other uses such as residential areas, industrial sites, highways, airports, reservoirs, and transmission lines would be balanced by such factors as, for example, the retirement of cropland from agricultural production.

In 1950 $74 million was spent on protecting 558 million acres of forest land against fire: 15.5 million acres burned. In 1962 $153 million was spent on protecting 754 million acres: only 4.1 million acres burned.

Tree-planting activities expanded rapidly during the 1950's from 0.5 million acres in 1950 to a peak of 2.1 million acres in 1959, followed by a decline to 1.4 million acres in 1962. It was assumed that planting would continue at the 1962 rate. It was also assumed that stand improvement work, such as thinnings and cull tree removal, would continue at the rate of 1.7 million acres per year (the 1962 figure).

A summary of the supply projections is contained in Exhibit 7.

RECOMMENDATIONS TO IMPROVE SUPPLY

After emphasizing trends toward poorer quality timber and the consequent need for improved technology to remedy this, the study suggested that overall growth could be improved "far above projected levels" by striving for the "realizable growth" potential of 27.5 billion cubic feet of growing stock. This "could be obtained in time if all the present area of commercial forest land in each region were managed as well as the better managed properties." The study again emphasized the importance of stand improvement and concluded with the following comments.

Increased Planting and Protection Also Would Increase Future Yields

Prompt establishment of vigorous young stands of desirable species following logging continues to be an important problem in the West and in many parts of the East as well. In addition, there are some 36 million acres of commercial forest lands presently nonstocked with growing stock trees, and 76 million acres of forest land that are poorly stocked.

Tree planting efforts in recent years have covered about 1.3 million acres annually, including considerable areas of abandoned farmlands. Expansion of planting on the more productive sites where prospective yields in volume and value are greatest would permit increases in timber harvests in the future, especially in the years after 2000. Shortening the regeneration period after logging by planting of desirable species also would make possible an immediate increase in allowable cut in some western forests.

Further reduction of mortality from fire, insects, and other destructive agents could likewise have a sizable effect on future wood supplies. Annual losses to these destructive agents in 1962 amounted to nearly 20 billion board feet, or the equivalent of about 36 per cent of the net growth of timber. Such losses could be reduced both through intensified fire and pest control programs and through more intensive timber management, including thinning and other measures to forestall mortality losses.

In all of these management activities —regeneration, protection, and cultural work—research will be necessary to pro-vide the knowledge needed for more efficient and abundant production of both timber and the related goods and services produced on forest lands.

Road Development Essential in the West

Much of the forest land in the West is still inaccessible for thinning or other management activities, and some mature timber resources will become economically available for harvesting only with completion of a major road system. Substantial investments in road construction will thus be necessary to permit closer utilization of available timber, more intensive cultural work, improved protection, and effective multiple-use management of timber and related resources.

Ownership of Major Significance in Forest Management

The extent to which timber management will be intensified in the future must depend in considerable part on the decisions of several million owners of farm and other non-industrial private forests. They own the major part of this Nation's commercial forest land—about 60 per cent of the total—and almost 40 per cent of the current inventory of growing stock. These lands also provide almost 40 per cent of all the roundwood products used by the forest industries.

Partly because of the uncertainty of intensified timber growing efforts on farm and miscellaneous holdings, relatively intensive management of the 28 per cent of the commercial forest land in national forests and other public holdings also appears necessary if projected demands are to be met. These public holdings contain nearly half the growing stock inventory and more than half of the sawtimber. They furnish about 25 per cent of the total cut.

Industrial holdings, which account for 13 per cent of the commercial forest, likewise play an especially important role in supplying timber products because of such considerations as the high productivity and relatively heavy stocking of these lands, and the availability of capital and management skills.

Future Consumption of Timber Dependent on Many Uncertain Supply and Demand Factors

Actual consumption of timber products in future years will depend both upon timber supplies forthcoming as a result of public and private forestry efforts, and the rate at which markets for timber products can be expanded. There are obviously many uncertainties in appraising long-range trends in both timber supplies and demands.

On the supply side, for example, losses of forest land to other uses may be considerable by the year 2000. In addition, an increasing portion of the area classed as commercial forest is also used for related or competing purposes such as recreation, wildlife habitat, or water protection as well as timber growing. Because of these impacts of competing uses, the supply of timber available for harvesting by the forest industries in the year 2000 may be significantly less than projected in this study. Intensification of forest management programs, on the other hand, could greatly increase future timber supplies.

On the demand side, it is possible that population and economic activity in the United States will expand more rapidly or more slowly than is assumed here, and that demands for timber and other raw materials will consequently differ from the projections developed in this study. New uses, new export or domestic markets for wood, and unforeseen changes in technology, also could materially change the outlook for timber demands.

Establishment of specific growth goals to achieve some ideal balance of timber supply and demand at future target dates thus must be largely a matter of judgment—both because of the many uncertainties in appraising distant markets for timber and competing materials, and current lack of information on the costs and responses of timber growing progress. It seems evident, however, that achievement of the levels of projected demand for timber around the end of this century will require some intensification of forest management and protection, as well as continuing technical adjustments in the forest industries to use the kind of timber prospectively available.

This analysis has been limited to a period ending in the year 2000, a relatively short time in the business of growing timber. With continued growth in numbers of people and economic output beyond the year 2000, the estimates of timber demands projected in this study may in time seem modest indeed. A long lead time is necessary in timber production. Hence judgments regarding such longer range market possibilities and prospective timber supply problems also must be considered in the formulation of today's forestry programs.

RELATION TO PPB SYSTEM

In February 1966 two members of the Forest Service concerned with the PPB system were discussing the format and content of their submissions for inclusion in the USDA's program memoranda. Preliminary crosswalk calculations performed within the Forest Service had allocated the majority of the Service's budget expenditures to USDA Program Categories I, VI, and VII. (Adequate Supply of Farm and Forest Products, Community Improvement, and Conservation of National Resources.) The discussion was, therefore, primarily concerned with the program memoranda for these categories.

Timber management was the first activity scheduled for discussion. The question immediately arose as to the type of multiyear analytical data to be included in the memorandum for Category I.

Taking part in the discussion were an economist, Robin Gourlay, who until recently had held a teaching post at a university, and John Macgregor, a veteran forester and graduate of one of the nation's leading schools of forestry.

Macgregor opened by suggesting that *Timber Trends* should be quoted or even read into the record, so to speak, as being the most comprehensive analytical effort to date on the future outlook for timber supply and demand. The analyses that had gone into producing the conclusions of *Timber Trends* were adequate, he felt, to justify and support the Service's timber management programs. "After all," he said "as *Timber Trends* pointed out, we have to start intensifying our efforts now to fill the projected gap of 3.6 billion cubic feet of growing stock which we'll be facing in the year 2000."

Gourlay disagreed emphatically. He felt that *Timber Trends* in itself would not be sufficient for top-level decision-making on the nation's timber goals and the role of the federal government. In his opinion the projected gap was somewhat illusory in that the market place would bring supply and demand together at an acceptable price level. The use of the assumption that timber prices would continue to maintain their present relationships with the prices of competing materials ignored this fundamental economic law.

Second, he felt that even if an adequate supply of timber could be produced at the relative price level, how

sure could one be of the demand projection of 21.6 billion cubic feet? "I know that 35 years is relatively short in the business of growing timber, but it's still a very long way into the future for an economic projection. I don't have to remind you of the constantly growing rate of change in technology, to mention only one major uncertainty. I would feel more comfortable with *Timber Trends* if we had more idea of the range of projections we'd get if we varied some of the basic assumptions."

Third, Gourlay stated that even the best supply/demand projections would still be inadequate for the program memoranda. "What we've been asked to do essentially is define goals, describe alternative means of achieving these goals, and prepare multiyear analyses of the costs and benefits of each alternative."

Macgregor replied that this was true, but these projections were certainly the best available at that time, and the Forest Service had to have such projections in view of the elementary fact of nature that a tree took a long time to grow.

"We'd be negligent," Macgregor continued, "if we didn't use the best available estimate we have in determining how much effort to put into stand improvement, new planting, and fire, disease, and pest control. I agree that a technological breakthrough some time in the future may even render wood obsolete, but we can't sit around and wait for that to happen. Besides, what about our obligations under other categories like community improvement? We have to plan so as to maintain stability of employment and the economy generally in the small communities dependent on Forest Service timber activities. Also, how about the conservationist aspects of our work?"

Gourlay replied that these were important factors, but that this work too would be helped by deeper analysis than that contained in *Timber Trends*. "However, this brings me to the subject of the concepts of the working circle and sustained yield. So long as we insist on a sort of natural balance within such small areas, how can we ever maximize nationally the return on our investment of timber dollars? We know that some of our forests simply are not as productive as others, and yet we sell regional timber from these lands barely covering the costs of administering the sale, when we could be investing in much more productive land, say in the Southeast, producing vigorous, healthy, growing stock for harvest later at a much greater return. Maybe," Gourlay concluded, "we should also be spending more money for fire control and so forth in cooperation with the private owners of productive forest land, rather than on our own marginal forests."

Macgregor said that he agreed that this was no doubt sound economics, but the Forest Service was obliged by law to observe the principles of sustained yield in managing its lands for multiple purposes. "We can't just be influenced purely by economic efficiency, nor can we ignore the non-timber aspects of our work. In any case maybe the question, as the Dean of the Forestry School at Michigan once wrote, 'is not whether economic analysis can, in a changing economy, give highly accurate forecasts on which to base plans. It is whether economics can give a better answer than would otherwise be obtainable.' [1] I think we do have a better answer as a result of the projections. At least we can be sure that demand for timber is certainly not going to decline over the next thirty-five years."

QUESTIONS

1. Develop an outline for the portion of the Program Memorandum on "Adequate Supply of Form and Forest Products."

2. How would you use *Timber Trends* in this memorandum?

3. What kind of role do you think the Forest Service should play in achieving the goals of this program category?

---

[1] S. T. Dana, "Functions of Forest Economics Research," *Research in the Economics of Forestry* (Washington, D.C.: Charles Lathrup Pack Forestry Foundation, 1953).

EXHIBIT 1

FOREST SERVICE

Public Law 86–517
86th Congress, H. R. 10572
June 12, 1960

AN ACT

To authorize and direct that the national forests be managed under principles of multiple use and to produce a sustained yield of products and services, and for other purposes.

Be it enacted by the Senate and House of Representatives of the United States of America in Congress assembled, That it is the policy of the Congress that the national forests are established and shall be administered for outdoor recreation, range, timber, watershed, and wildlife and fish purposes. The purposes of this Act are declared to be supplemental to, but not in derogation of, the purposes for which the national forests were established as set forth in the Act of June 4, 1897 (16 U.S.C. 475). Nothing herein shall be construed as affecting the jurisdiction or responsibilities of the several States with respect to wildlife and fish on the national forests. Nothing herein shall be construed so as to affect the use or administration of the mineral resources of national forest lands or to affect the use or administration of Federal lands not within national forests. — **National forests, managements.**

— **30 Stat. 34.**

SEC. 2. The Secretary of Agriculture is authorized and directed to develop and administer the renewable surface resources of the national forests for multiple use and sustained yield of the several products and services obtained therefrom. In the administration of the national forests due consideration shall be given to the relative values of the various resources in particular areas. The establishment and maintenance of areas of wilderness are consistent with the purposes and provisions of this Act. — **Multiple use; sustained yield.**

SEC. 3. In the effectuation of this Act the Secretary of Agriculture is authorized to cooperate with interested State and local governmental agencies and others in the development and management of the national forests.

SEC. 4. As used in this Act, the following terms shall have the following meanings:

(a) "Multiple use" means: The management of all the various renewable surface resources of the national forests so that they are utilized in the combination that will best meet the needs of the American people; making the most judicious use of the land for some or all of these resources or related services over areas large enough to provide sufficient latitude for periodic adjustments in use to conform to changing needs and conditions; that some land will be used for less than all of the resources; and harmonious and coordinated management of the various resources, each with the other, without impairment of the productivity of the land, with consideration being given to the relative values of the various resources, and not necessarily the combination of uses that will give the greatest dollar return or the greatest unit output. — **Definitions.**

(b) "Sustained yield of the several products and services" means the achievement and maintenance in perpetuity of a high-level annual or regular periodic output of the various renewable resources of the national forests without impairment of the productivity of the land.

EXHIBIT 2

FOREST SERVICE

Forest Service Receipts and Expenditures, All Programs and Sources, Fiscal Year 1965

Item	Receipts	Expenditures
National Forest Programs:		
Cash receipts and appropriation expenditures	$182,711,147	$302,046,658
Cash receipts from National Forest land collected by and deposited to accounts of other agencies (Federal Power Commission, Department of Interior)	18,114,194	
Noncash income and expense (roads built by timber purchases)	56,684,322	56,684,322
Total	$257,509,663	$358,730,980
Forest Research Programs:		
Forest Research appropriations		$ 30,179,038
Cooperative research work	$ 831,225	846,192
Total	$ 831,225	$ 31,025,230
State and Private Forestry Programs:		
Fire protection, tree distribution, and forest management cooperation		$16,942,294
Assistance to States for tree planting		998,058
Great Plains conservation program		20,105
Insect and disease control		1,834,802
Flood prevention and watershed protection		2,202,892
Forest fire prevention, "Smokey Bear"	$ 31,016	30,292
Cooperator funds	2,229,501	2,302,595
Total	$ 2,260,517	$ 24,331,038
Work for Other Government Agencies and Non-Government Persons and Firms:		
Economic Opportunity Program		$ 30,754,458
Insect and disease control (Interior Department lands)		48,975
Miscellaneous work for other government agencies	$ 3,397,278	5,589,544
Work performed for non-government persons, firms, etc. —cooperative work	2,588,231	2,255,629
Reimbursed	857,491	857,491
Total	6,843,000	39,508,097
Total Receipts and Expenditures	$267,444,495	$453,503,345
Cash Receipts Distributed to States, Counties, and Puerto Rico as Directed by Congress (receipts of fiscal year 1964 except as indicated):		
Payments to States and Puerto Rico (art. 5–23–08), National Forest Fund		[1] $ 32,837,416
Payments to School funds, Arizona and New Mexico (art. 6–20–10), National Forest Fund		108,205
Payment to Minnesota (Cook, Lake, and St. Louis Counties) (Superior National Forest) (art. 6–22–48), Forest fund		137,763
Payment to counties—National Grasslands and land utilization areas (art. 7–23–37) (receipts of calendar year 1964)		448,910
Total		$ 33,532,294
Internal Equipment and Supply Services (Working Capital Fund):		
Financed primarily by charges included above to Forest Service Programs	$ 25,831,518	$ 24,449,499

[1] Does not include approximately $3,116,025 due countries from fiscal year 1964 receipts on National Forest OAC lands. This amount was included in total receipts of $4,154,700 transferred to Interior for distribution under act of Aug. 28, 1937, 150 Stat: 8741, as amended.

Note: Expenditures are on an obligation basis except Working Capital Fund, which is on an accrual basis.

EXHIBIT 3

FOREST SERVICE (B)

Sections and Regions of the United States

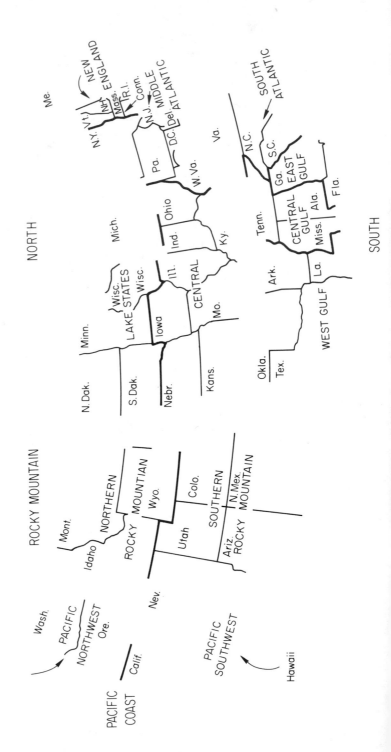

EXHIBIT 4

COMMERCIAL FOREST LAND IN THE UNITED STATES, BY PRODUCTIVITY CLASS AND BY SECTION, JANUARY 1, 1963

Productivity Class	Total U.S.[1]		North		South		Rocky Mountains		Pacific Coast	
	Million Acres	Percent	Million Acres	Percent	Million Acres	Percent	Million Acres	Percent	Million Acres	Percent
120 cu. ft. or more	43	8.5	1	1.2	16	8.0	1	1.5	24	34.3
85–120 cu. ft.	117	22.9	30	17.4	63	31.3	9	13.6	15	21.4
50–85 cu. ft.	232	45.6	95	55.2	93	46.3	20	30.3	24	34.3
25–50 cu. ft.	117	23.0	45	26.2	29	14.4	36	54.6	7	10.0
All classes	509	100.0	172	100.0	201	100.0	66	100.0	70	100.0

[1] Extrapolated from partial data for each section.

EXHIBIT 5

FOREST SERVICE

Commercial Forest Land in the United States, by Type of Ownership and Section, Jan. 1, 1963

Type of Ownership	Total U.S. Area (thousand acres)	Proportion (percent)	North (thousand acres)	South (thousand acres)	Rocky Mountains (thousand acres)	Pacific Coast (thousand acres)
Federal:						
National forest	96,804	19	10,265	10,476	43,398	32,665
Bureau of Land Management	5,426	1	81	27	2,076	3,242
Bureau of Indian Affairs	6,461	1	1,198	251	2,816	2,196
Other Federal	4,485	1	964	3,308	31	182
Total Federal	113,176	22	12,508	14,062	48,321	38,285
State	20,844	4	12,751	2,164	2,340	3,589
County and Municipal	7,848	2	6,748	656	83	361
Forest industry:						
Pulp and paper	35,022	7	10,797	21,614	. . . . .	2,611
Lumber	26,113	5	2,996	12,551	2,535	8,031
Other	5,493	1	523	3,257	. . . . .	1,713
Total industry	66,628	13	14,316	37,422	2,535	12,355
Farm	151,017	30	55,503	78,897	8,769	7,848
Miscellaneous private	149,332	29	69,963	67,868	3,575	7,926
All ownerships	508,845	100	171,789	201,069	65,623	70,364

EXHIBIT 6

FOREST SERVICE

Ownership of Growing Stock On Commercial Forest Land, by Type and Section, January 1, 1963

Type of Ownership	Total U.S.		North (million cu. ft.)	South (million cu. ft.)	Rocky Mountains (million cu. ft.)	Pacific Coast (million cu. ft.)
	Volume (million cu. ft.)	Proportion (%)				
National forest	234,284	37	8,696	10,212	72,007	143,369
Other public	62,506	10	14,683	4,046	9,347	34,430
Industrial	93,606	15	14,577	30,034	4,217	44,778
Farm & misc. private	237,486	38	98,513	89,794	13,153	36,026
Total	627,882	100	136,469	134,086	98,724	258,603

EXHIBIT 7

FOREST SERVICE

Timber Demand, Growth, Supply, and Inventories in the United States, 1952–2000
(billion cubic feet of growing stock)

	1952	1962	Projections			
			1970	1980	1990	2000
Demand	10.8	10.1	11.5	13.7	16.9	21.6
Growth	14.3	16.3	17.4	18.2	17.2	17.2
Supply [1]	—	17.2	18.2	18.8	17.8	18.0
Inventory	595.8	627.9	671.9	725.7	757.9	738.3

[1] Supply is defined as the sum of growth in the East, allowable cut on public lands in the West, and prospective cut on private lands in the West.

CASE

10

AGRICULTURAL STABILIZATION AND CONSERVATION SERVICE

PEANUT PROGRAM

The Agricultural Stabilization and Conservation Service has the responsibility for most of the existing farm programs designed to maintain farm income and to conserve agricultural resources.

The peanut crop has been designated a basic agricultural commodity by legislation. Although the peanut crop is restricted to certain geographical areas, it is an important source of farm income. The peanut crop is second in economic importance only to tobacco in Virginia and to cotton in Alabama. It is third, after cotton and tobacco, in Georgia and North Carolina and is an important cash crop in Texas and Oklahoma.

The peanut market is actually two markets. The domestic market, restricted to high quality nuts for human consumption, is confined to the United States and has no outside competition. Peanuts of lower quality are crushed for oil and meal and must compete in the world market with supplies from India and Africa.

PROGRAM OBJECTIVES

The objectives of the peanut program are:

1. To maintain farm income at a "reasonable" level. The Parity Index (i.e., that price which would be necessary to keep farm income on a "parity" with the non-farm sector of the economy) is used as the criteria of what is "reasonable."

2. To assure the market for peanuts a sufficient supply of high quality nuts at reasonable and stable prices (with emphasis on stable).

This case was prepared by Robert R. Stansberry, Jr., under the supervision of Graeme M. Taylor, with the cooperation of Joe F. Davis, U.S. Department of Agriculture. The case is intended for class discussion only, and certain names and facts may have been changed which, while avoiding the disclosure of confidential information, do not materially lessen the value of the case for educational purposes. This case is not intended to represent either effective or ineffective handling of an administrative situation, nor does it purport to be a statement of policy by the agency involved.

3. To keep program costs at a minimum, while assuring the continued growth and health of the industry.

THE ASCS PEANUT PROGRAM

The Agricultural Stabilization and Conservation Service (ASCS) program presently in effect for peanuts includes marketing quotas, acreage allotments, and price support. This program is carried out in the field by the state and county Agricultural Stabilization and Conservation (ASC) farmer-committees and peanut cooperative marketing associations.

State and county ASC committees handle marketing quotas and acreage allotments, while the farmer cooperatives, under agreement with ASCS, and the Commodity Credit Corporation (CCC) handle the price support operations.

Marketing quotas and acreage allotments

Marketing quotas must be proclaimed by the Secretary of Agriculture each year, without regard to the supply situation. Quotas may not go into effect, however, unless approved by at least two-thirds of the growers voting in a referendum. Peanut marketing quotas have been in effect since 1949.

The national marketing quota is converted into a national acreage allotment, which is divided among peanut producing states on the basis of a formula prescribed by law. The state ASC committees divide the acreage allotment among the counties while the county ASC committees apportion the allotment to individual peanut-producing farms. Under the present legisla-

tion the national acreage allotment cannot be less than 1,610,000 acres.

A farm marketing quota is the actual production on the acreage allotment. Thus, a producer who plants within his farm allotment may market all of his peanut production free of penalty and is eligible for the full level of price support. If he exceeds his acreage allotment, all the peanuts he markets will be subject to a marketing penalty and his crop will not be eligible for price support.

Price support

Price support for peanuts is mandatory, providing growers have not disapproved marketing quotas. The support may range from 75 to 90 per cent of parity, with the minimum depending on the level of supply at the beginning of the marketing year (August 1).

Price support on the 1967 crop of peanuts was available at a national average level of $227 per ton. This represents 75 per cent of the August 1967 parity price.

Price support is carried out primarily through non-recourse warehouse-stored loans to cooperatives acting for producer-members. Loans are available to individuals but are used very little. Loans may be made from time of harvest through January 31. They mature the following May 31. Price support rates are based on type, kernel content, and other quality factors.

In addition, CCC offers to buy peanuts from shellers who pay producers not less than the support price for peanuts bought for commercial uses and who participate in a quality control program. This quality control program was initiated to assure that only top grades and qualities were being marketed for food. Lower qualities are being diverted to uses for which they are suitable.

PROGRAM ALTERNATIVES

The majority of peanut farmers are strongly in favor of the present program. However, it is evident that increasing costs (see Exhibit 1), coupled with the prospect of continually rising future costs, are jeopardizing the program. As noted above, present legislation requires support at not less than 75 per cent of parity and limits national acreage allotments to a minimum of 1,610,000 acres (although some states do not use their allotment). The Parity Index has been increasing at a rate of about 2 per cent per year, while productivity (peanuts produced per acre) has increased at more than 5 per cent per year over the past five years.

Early in 1967 the Stabilization Advisory Committee on Peanuts, composed of farm leaders and department program specialists, met to discuss the peanut program. At that time a sub-committee was appointed and directed to seek alternatives to the present program within the guidelines of the program objectives: (1) maintain farm income, (2) reduce program costs, and (3) protect consumer interests while assuring the continued growth of the industry.

The sub-committee recommended that analysis be conducted along two broad approaches: (1) the acreage approach, and (2) the quantity approach. Based on these recommendations the program specialists in the department submitted four alternatives to the committee for their consideration. These were:

1. Voluntary diversion of a farm's entire peanut acreage with compensation. (Cropland Adjustment Program)

2. Mandatory diversion of a portion of a farm's peanut acreage without compensation, but with the option of using the diverted acreage for other crops.

3. A two-price system, with price support for the domestic quota as at present and lower (supported) prices for the remainder.

4. A certificate system, with price support equal to 50 per cent of parity and the certificate valued at the difference between the support price and the parity price as presently determined.

Discussion of Alternative No. 1

The mechanism for implementing this program would be the Cropland Adjustment Program (CAP), a program already in operation. Farmers who elect to participate would contract to divert their entire peanut acreage on a long-term basis (ten years or longer). In return, the farmer would be compensated for his loss of income, while the cropland would be planted to soil-building cover crops or allowed to revert to pasture. It is almost axiomatic that land can be diverted at less cost than a program supporting prices on excess production. For example, the estimated cost of producing an acre of peanuts is about $160. The present support price is $227, while the so-called world price is $100. The difference is $127 per ton, and is a program cost on excess production. On the other hand, it is estimated that farmers will participate in a diversion program for, at most, $80 per ton. Moreover, since the Parity Index is rising at about 2 per cent per year, the savings would be even greater in the tenth year of the contract.

However, there are disadvantages to a diversion program. There are strong feelings among both urban and rural people that there is something inherently immoral about being paid not to produce a crop. Neighbors resent tax expenditures for diversion payments, feeling that the participant is being paid for idleness while they continue to toil in the fields. In addition, if too many farmers in a single area decide to participate, allied processing industries (shellers, etc.) will be injured by less-than-economic volume. As this alternative is envisaged, producers would be encouraged to divert acreage to that point necessary to yield the edible requirement plus 20 per cent as a cushion.

Discussion of Alternative No. 2

This proposal, like Alternative No. 1, is an example of the acreage approach. The national acreage allotment would be established at that point needed to yield the domestic edible requirement plus 20 per cent to allow for crop failure and other contingencies. Farm allotments would be adjusted downward in proportion without compensation. However, the producer would be free to utilize the diverted acreage for the production of non-surplus crops, such as soybeans.

This alternative would reduce both program costs and farm income. But farm income would not be cut as much as program costs so long as the land is available to the farmer for alternate uses. Producers would save the variable costs (out-of-pocket expense) of producing the peanut crop on the diverted acreage (estimated at $160 per acre) while gaining whatever net income might accrue from the alternate crop (estimated at $10 per acre). Program costs would be reduced by the difference between the support price and $100 per ton on the acreage diverted.

Discussion of Alternative No. 3

This alternative is actually a price management approach. Domestic marketing quotas which would be supported as in the present program would be established for 75 per cent of the farm's acreage allotment. For the remaining 25 per cent of the farm's acreage allotment, the producer would have the option of producing peanuts on the land or diverting it with compensation. If he produces the extra acreage, prices on the over-quota peanuts would be supported at a lower level, say 60 per cent of parity. If he decides to divert, he would be compensated through the CAP program. Diversion would be voluntary.

This alternative would be less costly than the present program, while maintaining farm income. But the program would be difficult (but not impossible) to administer.

Discussion of Alternative No. 4

This program, utilizing certificates, would be similar to the present program for wheat. Peanuts produced on the national acreage allotment would be supported by CCC at 50 per cent of parity. This would place a floor under the domestic price. In addition, the producer would receive certificates on his share of the domestic quota, which would be set at 110 per cent of the edible requirement. The value of the certificate would be equated to the difference between the CCC loan level and the parity price as presently determined. The producer would receive payment through his county ASC office, and payment would be made even in the event of crop failure due to conditions beyond his control. At the same time shellers would be required to purchase certificates (at cost) for an amount equal to the total quantity of peanuts purchased and processed for edible consumption.

A producer would be permitted to produce peanuts in excess of his share of the domestic quota, up to the national acreage allotment providing he is willing to accept only the CCC support price (50 per cent of parity) and forego the value of the certificate on the extra acreage. It is estimated that enough low-cost producers would take advantage of this option to raise total production to about 120 per cent of the edible requirement.

This program has several advantages. First, it would permit a one-price market at the farm level. It would also permit a few very efficient producers to market peanuts in excess of their quota at the minimum support price. The program would be simple to administer and would reduce the cost of the peanut program. Farm income would be maintained near present levels, while consumer prices would

remain stable. On the other hand, this program would probably be harder to sell to producers (and Congress) than the other proposals.

ASSUMPTIONS

In order to maintain comparability and to simplify the arithmetic used in the projections and estimates, the following assumptions have been carried throughout the analysis and the projections which follow:

1. The variable cost of producing an acre of peanuts is estimated to be about $160.

2. Return (net) on diverted acreage utilized in the production of alternate crops is estimated at $10 per acre.

3. Productivity (pounds of peanuts produced per acre) will increase at the rate of 75 pounds per acre per year, using 1850 pounds per acre in 1968 as base.

4. Realized net loss by CCC (the bulk of program costs) is assumed to be the difference between the support price and $100 per ton.

5. The price elasticity of demand for peanuts is estimated to be 0.5 (i.e., an increase of 2 per cent in the support price will result in a 1 per cent decrease in edible requirements).

6. The cost of diverting an acre of peanuts is assumed to be 2.5 cents per pound of normal or projected yield.

7. The Parity Index will increase at an average rate of 2 per cent per year.

QUESTIONS

1. Develop measures of effectiveness appropriate for ranking the various alternative proposals mentioned.

2. Analyze the various programs as far as the data permit. Should one of

the alternative proposals be recom- analysis, it is suggested that you first
mended over the present program? clarify the objectives of the peanut
Note: Before proceeding with your program.
analysis, it is suggested that you first
program.

EXHIBIT 1 [1]

AGRICULTURAL STABILIZATION AND CONSERVATION SERVICE

Peanuts: Program Operations, Including Acreage, Costs, and Related Data, 1957–1967 [2]

Year	Acres Harvested (1,000)	Farm Value of Production (1,000 $)	Program Costs [3] (1,000 $)	Cost as per-cent of Value (Percent)
1957–1958	1,481	148,855	11,037	7.4
1958–1959	1,516	192,979	17,458	9.0
1959–1960	1,435	152,009	13,224	8.7
1960–1961	1,395	178,724	18,902	10.6
1961–1962	1,398	190,942	12,122	6.3
1962–1963	1,400	199,266	21,161	10.6
1963–1964	1,396	226,716	28,315	12.5
1964–1965	1,397	246,827	30,543	12.4
1965–1966	1,421	271,190	43,777	16.1
1966–1967 [4]	1,399	288,000	55,900	19.4

[1] The figures in this and subsequent exhibits were constructed for purposes of this case only.
[2] Fiscal year for data relating to the Commodity Credit Corporation; marketing year beginning August 1 otherwise.
[3] Commodity Credit Corporation net realized loss.
[4] Preliminary estimate.

EXHIBIT 2

AGRICULTURAL STABILIZATION AND CONSERVATION SERVICE

*Peanuts: Continuation of Present Program with Minimum Support and Minimum
Acreage Allotment, 1967–1971*

Item	Unit	1967	1968	1969	1970	1971
1. Acreage allotment	1,000 A	1,610	1,610	1,610	1,610	1,610
2. Acreage harvested	1,000 A	1,400	1,400	1,400	1,400	1,400
3. Yield per acre	Pounds	1,827	1,850	1,925	2,000	2,075
4. Production	1,000 T	1,278	1,295	1,348	1,400	1,453
5. Edible requirements	1,000 T	885	903	921	939	958
6. Surplus—to CCC	1,000 T	393	392	427	461	495
7. Parity price per ton	Dollars	302	308	314	320	326
8. Support price per ton	Dollars	227	231	236	240	245
9. Support—pct. of parity	Percent	75	75	75	75	75
10. Program cost (CCC loss)						
a. Per ton surplus [1]	Dollars	127	131	136	140	145
b. Total cost	Mil. dol.	50	51	58	64	72
11. Farm value of peanuts [2]	Mil. dol.	290	299	318	336	356

[1] At support price less $100 per ton.
[2] At support price.

EXHIBIT 3

AGRICULTURAL STABILIZATION AND CONSERVATION SERVICE

*Peanuts: Acreage Diversion with Compensation through the Cropland
Adjustment Program (CAP), 1967–1971*

Item	Unit	1967	1968	1969	1970	1971
1. Acreage allotment	1,000 A	1,610	1,610	1,610	1,610	1,610
2. Acreage diverted to CAP	1,000 A	—	270	299	321	341
3. Acreage harvested	1,000 A	1,400	1,143	1,121	1,100	1,081
4. Yield per acre	Pounds	1,827	1,850	1,925	2,000	2,075
5. Production	1,000 T	1,278	1,057	1,079	1,100	1,122
6. Edible requirements	1,000 T	885	881	899	917	935
7. Surplus—to CCC	1,000 T	393	176	180	183	187
8. Parity price per ton	Dollars	302	308	314	320	326
9. Support price per ton	Dollars	227	246	251	256	261
10. Support—pct. of parity	Percent	75	80	80	80	80
11. Program cost:						
a. Total CCC loss [1]	Mil. dol.	50	26	27	29	30
b. Diversion payments [2]	Mil. dol.	—	12	14	16	18
c. Total	Mil. dol.	50	38	41	45	48
12. Program benefit:						
a. Value of peanuts	Mil. dol.	290	260	271	282	293
b. Savings on production costs [3]	Mil. dol.	—	38	43	48	53
c. Diversion payment [2]	Mil. dol.	—	12	14	16	18
d. Total	Mil. dol.	290	310	328	346	364

[1] At support price less $100 per ton.
[2] At 2.5 cents per pound on projected yield.
[3] At 8.0 cents per pound on projected yield.

EXHIBIT 4

AGRICULTURAL STABILIZATION AND CONSERVATION SERVICE

Peanuts: Acreage Diversion without Compensation, but with Option of Planting Alternate Crop on Diverted Acreage, 1967–1971

Item	Unit	1967	1968	1969	1970	1971
1. Acreage allotment	1,000 A	1,610	1,336	1,313	1,291	1,271
2. Acreage harvested	1,000 A	1,400	1,143	1,121	1,100	1,081
3. Yield per acre	Pounds	1,827	1,850	1,925	2,000	2,075
4. Production	1,000 T	1,278	1,057	1,079	1,100	1,122
5. Edible requirements	1,000 T	885	881	899	917	935
6. Surplus—to CCC	1,000 T	393	176	180	183	187
7. Parity price per ton	Dollars	302	308	314	320	326
8. Support price per ton	Dollars	227	246	251	256	261
9. Support—pct. of parity	Percent	75	80	80	80	80
10. Program cost (CCC loss) [1]	Mil. dol.	50	26	27	29	30
11. Program benefit:						
a. Value of peanuts	Mil. dol.	290	260	271	282	293
b. Saving on production costs [2]	Mil. dol.	—	38	43	48	53
c. Return from other use of acreage [3]	Mil. dol.	—	3	3	3	3
d. Total	Mil. dol.	290	301	317	333	349

[1] At support price less $100 per ton.
[2] At 8.0 cents per pound on projected yield.
[3] At $10 per acre (net).

EXHIBIT 5

AGRICULTURAL STABILIZATION AND CONSERVATION SERVICE

*Peanuts: Two–Price Support Program with Option to Plant or
Divert Excess Acreage, 1967–1971*

Item	Unit	1967	1968	1969	1970	1971
1. Acreage harvested:						
a. Quota	1,000 A	—	1,117	1,089	1,064	1,041
b. Over-quota	1,000 A	—	48	47	46	45
c. Total	1,000 A	1,400	1,165	1,136	1,100	1,086
2. Yield per acre	Pounds	1,817	1,850	1,925	2,000	2,075
3. Production:						
a. Quota	1,000 T	—	1,033	1,048	1,064	1,080
b. Over-quota	1,000 T	—	45	45	46	47
c. Total	1,000 T	1,278	1,078	1,093	1,110	1,127
4. Edible requirements	1,000 T	885	898	911	925	939
5. Surplus—to CCC	1,000 T	393	180	182	185	188
6. Parity price per ton	Dollars	302	308	314	320	326
7. Support price per ton:						
a. Quota	Dollars	227	234	242	250	258
b. Over-quota	Dollars	—	185	188	192	196
8. Support—pct. of parity:						
a. Quota	Percent	75	76	77	78	79
b. Over-quota	Percent	—	60	60	60	60
9. Program cost:						
a. Total CCC loss [1]	Mil. dol.	50	22	23	25	27
b. Diversion payments [2]	Mil. dol.	—	12	14	16	18
c. Total	Mil. dol.	50	34	35	41	45
10. Program benefit:						
a. Value of peanuts:						
(1) Quota	Mil. dol.	290	242	254	266	279
(2) Over-quota	Mil. dol.	—	8	8	9	9
b. Saving on production costs [3]	Mil. dol.	—	35	41	46	52
c. Diversion payment [2]	Mil. dol.	—	12	14	16	18
d. Total	Mil. dol.	290	297	317	337	358

[1] At support price less $100 per ton.
[2] At 2.5 cents per pound on projected yield.
[3] At 8.0 cents per pound on projected yield.

EXHIBIT 6

AGRICULTURAL STABILIZATION AND CONSERVATION SERVICE

Peanuts: Certificate Program with Support at 50 Percent of Parity for Non-Certificate Production, 1967–1971

Item	Unit	1967	1968	1969	1970	1971
1. Acreage harvested:						
a. Certificate	1,000 A	—	1,068	1,041	1,018	996
b. Non-certificate	1,000 A	—	97	95	92	91
c. Total	1,000 A	1,400	1,165	1,136	1,110	1,087
2. Yield per acre	Pounds	1,827	1,850	1,925	2,000	2,075
3. Production:						
a. Certificate	1,000 T	—	988	1,002	1,018	1,033
b. Non-certificate	1,000 T	—	90	91	92	94
c. Total	1,000 T	1,278	1,078	1,093	1,110	1,127
4. Edible requirements	1,000 T	885	898	911	925	939
5. Surplus—to CCC	1,000 T	393	180	182	185	188
6. Parity price per ton	Dollars	302	308	314	320	326
7. Support price per ton:						
a. Certificate	Dollars	227*	234	242	250	258
b. Non-certificate	Dollars	—	154	157	160	163
8. Support—pct. of parity:						
a. Certificate	Percent	75*	76	77	78	79
b. Non-certificate	Percent	—	50	50	50	50
9. Program cost:						
a. Total CCC loss [1]	Mil. dol.	50	10	10	11	12
b. Cost of certificates	Mil. dol.	—	7	8	8	9
c. Total	Mil. dol.	50	17	18	19	21
10. Program benefit:						
a. Value of peanuts	Mil. dol.	290	166	172	178	184
b. Value of certificates	Mil. dol.	—	79	85	92	98
c. Saving on production cost plus other income [2]	Mil. dol.	—	39	45	51	57
d. Total	Mil. dol.	290	284	302	321	339

[1] At support price less $100 per ton.

[2] Savings on production costs estimated at 8.0 cents per pound on projected yield; income (net) from other use of remaining acreage estimated at $10 per acre.

* Under present program.

C A S E

11

NUTHATCH NATIONAL FOREST (A)

PROPOSED TIMBER SALE

In January, 1966 Mr. Lionel Ursus, the Supervisor of Nuthatch National Forest, was considering offering for sale federal timber from some 2,000 acres of choice old-growth stands. This particular area consisted of mixed conifers, mainly ponderosa pine (60 per cent), and true fir (40 per cent). The estimated amount involved was 50 million board feet of timber. The proposed timber sale area was located within the Willow Creek drainage.

Nuthatch National Forest occupied about 1,400,000 acres of rolling timberland in Nemorensis County, a remote section of one of the mountain states. The local economy was primarily dependent on the forest products industry, although for some time county and state officials had been attempting to devise means to exploit the undoubted recreational potential of their beautiful region. A constant concern was the steady loss of young people to the nearest large town, Inverness, located near an interstate highway 100 miles away.

Three sawmills were located in Blairgowrie, ten miles from the proposed timber sale area along Forest Highway 357. The Cameron mill, with a capacity of 75 million board feet per year, was a division of a nation-wide corporation, which owned several hundred thousand acres of timber-land adjacent to Nuthatch. The MacLeod and Affleck mills were each capable of handling 6 million board feet per year: neither owned any land. The 100 families dependent on the MacLeod and Affleck mills were all descendants of the original Scottish settlers of Nemorensis County.

Forest Service crews made a field survey of the timber in the Willow Creek drainage. They estimated timber

This case was prepared with the cooperation of the United States Department of Agriculture by Graeme M. Taylor under the supervision of Richard F. Vancil, Associate Professor of Business Administration, Harvard University, on behalf of the Office of Career Development, U.S. Civil Service Commission. The case is intended for class discussion only, and certain names and facts may have been changed which, while avoiding the disclosure of confidential information, do not materially lessen the value of the case for educational purposes. This case is not intended to represent either effective or ineffective handling of an administrative situation, nor does it purport to be a statement of policy by the agency involved.

volume, timber values, logging costs, roads needed to remove the timber, road costs, and probable timber stand improvement (e.g., reforestation) needed after logging. With this information a timber sale appraisal was made and an appraisal summary was completed. Advertised rates for each timber species were determined. The advertised rates would be the minimum amounts that could be accepted for the timber in the Willow Creek Timber Sale. Normally Mr. Ursus would advertise this sale and there would be competitive bidding—either sealed or oral. The timber sale contract would be awarded to the highest bidder. For the purposes of this case the exact prices each bidder would pay and how the logging would be done are given so that the student may consider the problems, alternatives, and decisions Mr. Ursus had before him.

Mr. Ursus had two alternative proposals before him.

SALE ALTERNATIVE 1

The Cameron mill had indicated that they would bid $43/Mbf (thousand board feet) for the ponderosa pine, and $2.00/Mbf for the true fir. They would build all roads involved (Roads A, B, C and D in Exhibit 1), to Forest Service standards for single lane unpaved roads, and would remove all timber during the first logging season (1967) after the roads were completed. If the Forest Service should decide that the main access road, Road A, should be double-lane and paved, and that they should therefore supplement Cameron's road building outlays to the extent of the necessary difference in construction costs, then Cameron's bid

would be $57.36/Mbf for ponderosa pine and $9/Mbf for the true fir. Cameron would pay the Forest Service for the timber in 7 monthly installments beginning April 1, 1967.

SALE ALTERNATIVE 2

The MacLeod and Affleck mills had submitted a joint proposal. Like Cameron, they too intended to build Roads A, B, C and D and commence logging operations by April 1, 1967. They intended to remove the timber according to the following schedule: 12,000 Mbf in 1967, 1968 and 1969, with the balance of 14,000 Mbf being removed by November 1, 1970. (The logging season in Nuthatch National Forest consisted of the seven months from April through October.)

Their bid was $45.33/Mbf for the ponderosa pine and $2/Mbf for the true fir. If Road A were paved, their bids would be $59.91/Mbf for the ponderosa pine, and $9.25/Mbf for the true fir. They proposed to pay for the timber in 28 equal installments, a payment to be made on the first of each month of logging operations.

The cost to the Forest Service of preparing for and administering the Cameron proposal was estimated at $20,000, whereas the second proposal would cost an estimated $30,000. (Assume that most of these costs would be incurred in the year the sale was offered for bid.)

The main access road (Road A) would be 8 miles long; spur roads B, C and D would be 2.5 miles, 2 miles, and 3 miles respectively. (See Exhibit 1.) Road construction costs were estimated at $15,000 per mile for single-lane unpaved roads, and $165,000 per mile for two-lane paved roads. All roads could be built within 12 months. Maintenance costs were estimated at $300 per mile per year for double-lane paved roads, $1,200 per mile per year for single lane unpaved roads during logging, and $200 per mile per year for single-lane unpaved roads when not used for logging.

Unpaved roads would be adequate for logging purposes only. However, should Mr. Ursus decide to open up this section of Nuthatch for recreational purposes, the 8-mile main access road would certainly have to be double lane and paved. Since prudent operator standards in Forest Service timber management regulations necessitated only that timber purchasers be required to build roads to meet logging needs, the Forest Service would have to supplement the timber operator's road-building outlays. Maintenance of the roads would be the responsibility of the timber operator until logging operations ceased; thereafter, the Forest Service would have to assume the maintenance costs for whichever roads it decided to keep open.

CALCULATION OF STUMPAGE PRICE

Stumpage price, the proceeds per thousand board feet of timber (Mbf) anticipated by the Forest Service from the sale, would be calculated in the following manner.

The timber in the section of Nuthatch under consideration had been appraised as likely to yield sawn lumber with an average value (selling price) of $140/Mbf for the ponderosa pine, and $90/Mbf for the true fir. From these figures, the mill's milling costs would be deducted (estimated at $15/Mbf). A profit margin of 10 per cent of the appraised selling price would also be allowed. Deduction of milling costs, including profit from the million portion, from the appraised selling price would give the estimated value of the logs as they arrived at the mill.

From this, transportation and logging costs would have to be deducted. Logging costs (consisting of costs of felling, limbing, bucking and skidding) were estimated at $14/Mbf. Road construction costs would be calculated per Mbf by dividing the timber operator's road-building costs (exclusive of any Forest Service supplement) by the amount of timber for which he had contracted. (In the case of the second alternative method of sale, should the MacLeod and Affleck mills be awarded the contract, these operators would pool their road-building resources and pro-rate their share of construction costs according to their share of the timber.) Road maintenance costs would be calculated and deducted in the same manner. Actual hauling costs from the stands to the mill were estimated at $4/Mbf per mile over unpaved roads and $2/Mbf per mile over paved roads. (For the purpose of calculation it may be assumed that one-third of all timber involved would travel over each of the 3 spur roads, and that the timber was evenly distributed along each spur road.)

As a final item, $2/Mbf would have to be deducted for deposit in funds under the K.V. Act[1] to provide minimum regeneration of the area logged. The Forest Service was authorized

---

[1] Knutson-Vandenberg Act, June 9, 1930 (46 Stat. 527; 16 U.S.C. 576).

to earmark a portion of stumpage receipts for retention in a special fund to be used to establish satisfactory stands of trees on cutover areas. Expenditure of these funds was not limited to the specific areas from which they were collected except that the funds had to be spent on the National Forest from which they were collected. Collections were to be made in amounts necessary to carry out the plan for a sale area but were not to exceed average experienced K.V. costs. In any event there was to be no change in the stumpage prices paid by the purchaser. The appraised stumpage value of a sale was not affected in any way by the rate of K.V. collections planned for the sale.

The balance would be the minimum stumpage price that Mr. Ursus would accept from bidders, with the proviso that, should the stumpage price calculated as above prove to be less than $20/Mbf for ponderosa pine or $2/Mbf for true fir, these latter prices would be the minimum acceptable. (The Forest Service required such minimum prices for each species and grade.) Of the stumpage price received by the Forest Service, 25 per cent would have to be turned over to Nemorensis County.

PROPOSED RECREATION AREA

In considering the possibility of opening up this section of the forest to recreational use, Mr. Ursus had on his desk a preliminary report outlining the recreational possibilities and planned facilities for the area, of which the Willow Creek timber sale area formed a small part.

The area contained four lakes and

fifty miles of excellent fishing streams, four sites for campgrounds, each with space for 200 family units, and two possible picnic areas with space for 100 family units each.

Campground construction costs were estimated at $1,000 per unit; picnic areas would cost $300 per unit to prepare.

In addition, a commercial developer proposed to build a lodge, parking lot, restaurant, and boat-launching ramp at a cost of $750,000. He estimated his gross revenue per season would amount to $1 million, on which he expected to make 15 per cent before federal and state taxes. Federal taxes would probably come to 30 per cent of his before-tax margin, and state taxes would be 2 per cent. County property taxes would amount to an additional $3,000 per year. His expected margin of 15 per cent before taxes had been calculated with the understanding that he would pay 3 per cent of his gross to the Forest Service for use of the area, and 1 per cent to the county.

Forest Service estimates of use of the proposed area ranged from 750 to 2,000 family automobiles per day during the tourist season, with an average of 3 persons per automobile. (The tourist season was expected to last from June 1st until Labor Day.) Ten per cent of the people visiting the area were expected to spend most of their time fishing, 10 per cent would be exclusively interested in camping and hiking. The remainder would probably want to picnic or bathe in the lakes besides using the other facilities from time to time.

It would cost the state $30,000 per year to keep the streams stocked with fish. A state fishing license cost $4 per year. Deer hunting would probably prove popular in season; up to 1,000 hunters were expected to pay the state $8 each for a license. Past experience in similar areas indicated that approximately 50 deer might be killed per season, thus relieving the state of a control program expense for that area amounting to $6,000 annually. A game warden would have to be hired, however, to patrol the area during the season; his salary and housing would cost the State an estimated $9,000 per year. The Wildlife Department at the state capital estimated that a deer carcass might be worth $200 commercially.

The area under consideration contained grazing land which could support up to 500 cattle for the four-month grazing season. The Forest Service would receive $1 per head per month for use of this land, of which 25 per cent would have to be turned over to the county, pursuant to the Act of May 23, 1908, as amended (35 Stat. 260, 16 U.S.C. 500).

Lightning fires were a constant problem in Nuthatch National Forest. In the area under consideration suppression costs had averaged $3,000 per year, with an annual loss of timber whose stumpage value was estimated approximately at $2,500. The road system contemplated would lower suppression costs by 50 per cent and would reduce timber losses from fire to negligible amounts. However, if the roads were open to recreationists, experience had shown that additional fire prevention measures would need to be taken costing an estimated $2,000 per month during the tourist season.

If the area was opened to recreation, the Forest Service would have to recruit additional staff to supervise the various facilities. It was estimated that 2 year-round men would be needed at a cost of $1,000 per man per year, including housing. During the tourist season six college students from the state university in Inverness could be hired at $700 per month each, including transportation and housing.

Mr. Ursus felt that he was faced with 3 interrelated decisions:

Which bid should he accept?

Should he have road A paved?

Should he authorize the proposed plans for development of the recreational facilities?

He was aware that building the recreational facilities could not commence until logging operations ceased. The developer and Forest Service officials felt that the area would be ready for the public 17 months after work began on the various facilities. Mr. Ursus had received a note from the regional forester pointing out that recreational facilities in the nearest national park, some 60 miles away in a neighboring state, were already overcrowded. He also had on his desk a letter from the Nemorensis County authorities advising him that the MacLeod and Affleck mills were running dangerously low on work in process. This letter also reminded Mr. Ursus that the county was hoping to use a portion of future timber receipts in a cooperative venture with the state university to retrain local high school dropouts.

QUESTION

1. What action should Mr. Ursus take on the three interrelated decisions listed above?

Note: The student should understand that in actual practice Mr. Ursus would not and could not make unilateral decisions of this type. However, for purposes of this case the student should proceed to define the specific problems facing Ursus, consider the various alternatives, predict the possible consequences of each, and choose the best alternative.

EXHIBIT 1

NUTHATCH NATIONAL FOREST (A)

Schematic of Proposed Road System for Timber Sale Area

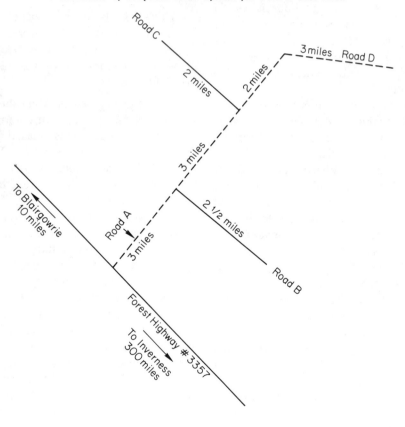

CASE

12

NUTHATCH NATIONAL FOREST (B)

FOREST MANAGEMENT ALTERNATIVES

Before making his final decision on the three interrelated issues described in the timber sale case, Mr. Ursus intended to consider the possible effects on his decision of two other factors:

1. allowing pre-logging operations *prior* to main harvest.
2. subjecting the Nuthatch timber sale area to management intensification *following* main harvest.

These two procedures are described in Exhibits 1 and 2.

Mr. Ursus was considering whether or not it might be better for the Forest Service itself to build all roads immediately to take advantage of the apparent additional gains of pre-logging. Of course, he realized that this would mean postponing the main harvest for at least 5 years. On the other hand the roads would be built immediately, and the area could be opened to the public for recreational use by June, 1967.

The decision regarding whether or not to apply management intensification over and above stand regeneration after the main harvest appeared at first sight to have no bearing on his most immediate problem, namely what action to take on the three interrelated decisions facing him as described in the timber sale case.

ASSIGNMENT

1. Using the estimate given in Exhibit 1, calculate the effect of conducting pre-logging on Mr. Ursus' approach to solving the three interrelated decisions as described in the timber sale case.

2. Using the data in Exhibit 2, evaluate the desirability of adopting the management intensification program.

This case was prepared with the cooperation of the United States Department of Agriculture by Graeme M. Taylor under the supervision of Richard F. Vancil, Associate Professor of Business Administration, Harvard University, on behalf of the Office of Career Development, U.S. Civil Service Commission. The case is intended for class discussion only, and certain names and facts may have been changed which, while avoiding the disclosure of confidential information, do not materially lessen the value of the case for educational purposes. This case is not intended to represent either effective or ineffective handling of an administrative situation, nor does it purport to be a statement of policy by the agency involved.

EXHIBIT 1

NUTHATCH NATIONAL FOREST (B)
Effect of Pre-Logging

---

1. Assume main harvest for virgin stands of mixed conifers (60% ponderosa pine, 40% true fir) would average 25,000 board feet per acre harvested.

2. *Pre-logging*

   If road systems were built by the Forest Service 5 years in advance of main harvest, in years 1 through 5 the forester would be able to do "pre-logging," without effecting the 25,000 board feet per acre available for main harvest in year 6.

   Pre-logging involves permitting small timber processors to remove from the projected sale area smaller diameter trees which would normally be damaged beyond salvage at the time of main harvest. This would yield some 10,000 board feet per acre with a weighted average stumpage price of $10 per Mbf. (This price is calculated assuming that (a) hauling costs for these small timber operators are independent of the type of road used and (b) no components of road building or maintenance costs are included, since this would be the responsibility of the Forest Service.) It would take the so-called "gypo-loggers" in the Nuthatch area a full 5 seasons to complete their pre-logging of the area. During this time, it would not be possible to conduct the main harvest. The gypo loggers would be able to work without disturbing the recreational use of the forest.

Sales administration costs for this type of sale would amount to $1.50 per Mbf, and would be incurred as the timber was removed.

During pre-logging operations, the Forest Service would be responsible for road maintenance. These costs would be $300 per mile per year for paved roads, $600 per mile per year for unpaved roads while used for logging operations, and $200 per mile per year for unpaved roads when not used for logging.

EXHIBIT 2

NUTHATCH NATIONAL FOREST (B)

Proposed Management Intensification Schedule for Nuthatch Timber Sale Area

The Nuthatch timber sale area would be regenerated by the Forest Service following the main harvest at a cost of $50 per acre.

Year 0 in the schedule below is the year of the first main harvest of the Nuthatch timber sale area.

Year	Operation	Cost per Acre	Yield in Mbf per Acre	Stumpage Price per Mbf per Acre	
				P. P.	True Fir
0	Stand regeneration	$50	—	—	—

MANAGEMENT INTENSIFICATION SCHEDULE

Year	Operation	Cost per Acre	Yield in Mbf per Acre	P. P.	True Fir
15	Pre-commercial thinning [1]	$ 9	—	—	—
30	1st commercial thinning [2]	$15(Admin.)	5	$25	$4
40	2nd commercial thinning	$15(Admin.)	6	$30	$5
50	3rd commercial thinning	$15(Admin.)	9	$30	$5
70	Main Harvest	$10(Admin.)	31	$40	$8

[1] See Note 5 below.
[2] See Note 6 below.

Notes:
1. Stumpage prices will vary from those calculated in (A) case because
   a. This is a new stand. Hence, even after 70 years, the average diameter of the trees will be less than when the stand was still a virgin, old-growth area. This will mean a lower stumpage price.
   b. Road maintenance costs are not reflected in the stumpage prices quoted in the table, since this will be assumed to be the responsibility of the F. S. throughout the period. Thus, these stumpage prices should be used as given.
2. However, for management intensification of the type outlined here, it must be assumed that Road A was paved at the time of the original main harvest in year 0 or before.
3. The stumpage prices are given in terms of 1966 dollars, as are all figures quoted. However, they are also based on 1966 timber values, and thus assume that 1966 price levels for timber will continue.
4. In the old-growth stands, the ratio of ponderosa pine to true fir was 60/40. With management intensification, it is estimated that this ratio will change to 80/20.
5. *Pre-commercial thinning:* removal of ill-formed and less vigorous saplings to permit the remaining saplings to continue maximum growth rate.
6. *Commercial thinning:* removal of inferior trees of commercial size to concentrate the growth of the stand on future crop trees; this would normally be done twice or more during the life of the stand. High-value species would normally be favored.

SCHEDULE WITHOUT MANAGEMENT INTENSIFICATION

Year	Operation	Cost per Acre	Yield in Mbf per Acre	Stumpage Price per Mbf per Acre	
				P. P.	True Fir
0	Stand regeneration	$50	—	—	—
75	Sanitation-salvage cut [3]	$15(Admin.)	10	$30 [4]	$5 [4]
90	Main harvest	$10(Admin.)	20	$37	$6

[3] Consists of removing dead, down and dying trees.
[4] These stumpage prices were calculated on the basis of the minimum road work necessary to remove the volumes involved.

CASE

13

BUREAU OF MINES

HELIUM CONSERVATION PROGRAM

In early summer, 1967, Mr. Frank Allen, a program analyst in the office of the Helium Activity Bureau of Mines, was considering how to respond to a request from the assistant director (helium) of the Bureau of Mines for a concise justification to support the program level requested by the Activity in its budget submission for fiscal 1969. The Activity had authority, under the terms of the Helium Act Amendments of 1960 (P. L. 86-777), to contract with private companies, up to an annual limit of $47.5 million, for the purchase of helium for storage in underground reservoirs. The assistant director (helium) planned to request that this contracting authority be increased to $60 million annually commencing in fiscal 1969. The proposed level of funding for the next five fiscal years is shown below:

This case was prepared with the cooperation of the United States Department of the Interior by Graeme M. Taylor under the supervision of Richard F. Vancil, Associate Professor of Business Administration, Harvard University on behalf of the Bureau of Training, United States Civil Service Commission. This case is intended for class discussion only, and certain names and facts may have been changed which, while avoiding the disclosure of confidential information, do not materially lessen the value of the case for educational purposes. This case is not intended to represent either effective or ineffective handling of an administrative situation, nor does it purport to be a statement of policy by the agency involved.

RECOMMENDED LEVEL OF FUNDING—PROPOSED PROGRAM

(dollars in millions and tenths)

	FY 1969	FY 1970	FY 1971	FY 1972	FY 1973
Total Cost	53.8	60.0	63.1	62.3	61.9
Less Receipts and Carryover Funds	34.6	35.0	38.1	42.3	44.9
New Borrowing Authority	19.2	25.0	25.0	20.0	17.0

OBJECTIVES OF THE HELIUM PROGRAM

The mission of the Helium Activity, the sole responsibility of one of the six assistant directors of the Bureau of Mines, was defined in a 1967 review draft of the fiscal 1969 Helium Program Memorandum as follows:

The objective of the helium program is to obtain maximum beneficial use of the natural helium resources of the United States.

The Bureau of Mines seeks to achieve the foregoing objective through the following functions:

1. Production and sale of helium for current use;

2. Acquisition and storage of helium that would otherwise be wasted in order that this helium may be used beneficially in the future; and

3. Research and development that will contribute to more effective use of our natural helium resources now and in the future.

EARLY HISTORY OF THE HELIUM PROGRAM

The element helium was discovered through observations of the surface of the sun in 1868. Its presence in the earth's atmosphere was first detected in 1895, and in 1905 helium was found to be contained in underground deposits of natural hydrocarbon gases. No more than laboratory scale production of helium was attempted prior to World War I when the use of lighter-than-air craft in military operations stimulated interest in its large-scale production as a nonflammable substitute for hydrogen. The Federal Government contracted with three private companies to design, construct, and operate experimental plants to produce

helium; the Bureau of Mines, which had been established in 1910, supervised the program. The first full-scale production plant, built by the Navy in 1921, was operated by a private company until 1925, when it and all other helium production activities were placed under the Bureau of Mines. From 1925 until 1960 virtually all helium production in the United States was conducted by the Bureau of Mines.

The Government's *de facto* monopoly of helium production during this period resulted from four factors:

(1) limited use of helium outside the military and Government

(2) widely fluctuating use volumes and the emergency character of demand expansion due to military contingencies

(3) rarity of occurrence

(4) lack of economic incentive to private industry because of low prices charged by the Government

As late as 1955, the largest single use of helium was still in Navy airships, the primary use during the entire period.

Beginning in 1945 the Bureau of Mines began to store helium to meet potential future mobilization needs. However, increasing demand, brought about by the discovery of new uses for helium following World War II, began by the 1950's to tax production capacity and erode the quantity of helium in storage. A major new plant was constructed by the Bureau in 1959, almost doubling production capacity, and the storage of significant quantities of helium became possible.

At the same time the rapid development of new helium applications in commercial and experimental work and in the missile program indicated the likelihood of long-term growth in demand (see Exhibit 1). The changing concept of war greatly reduced the possibility that large, sudden increases in demand for military purposes would occur. Thus, a *conservation* concept—production for storage on the assumption that future use values would outweigh current costs—was introduced into the helium program.

THE HELIUM CONSERVATION PROGRAM

Helium was clearly a depletable resource. It occurred in underground deposits as a constituent of either (1) combustible hydrocarbon gas (natural gas), or (2) noncombustible gas (generally nitrogen). In 1960 it was estimated that less than 5 per cent of domestic helium reserves occurred in non-combustible gas deposits, while over 95 per cent occurred in natural gas fields. Helium was present in almost all natural gas deposits, in concentrations varying from a trace up to approximately 8 per cent by volume, but it was not considered economically feasible to recover helium from deposits containing less than 0.3 per cent helium. High-grade helium-bearing natural gas deposits (i.e., with more than 0.3 per cent helium) constituted 15 per cent of total proven natural gas reserves in the United States and were estimated to contain some 196 billion cubic feet of economically recoverable helium. Nearly 95 per cent of recoverable helium reserves were located in an area north and northeast of Amarillo, Texas, and extending across the Oklahoma Panhandle and into Kansas. These reserves were largely associated with major natural gas fields owned by private parties and under active exploitation to supply commercial fuel markets.

If it were not extracted, helium would simply accompany the natural gas to its point of use, and be wasted by passing into the atmosphere. However, helium could be extracted from natural fuel gas at the surface by liquefying the hydrocarbon gases, drawing off the helium, and returning the hydrocarbons (once more in a gaseous state) to the commercial distribution channels.

One suggestion made during the late 1950's was that the Bureau of Mines itself should build and operate up to twelve plants for the extraction of helium from natural fuel gas. The capital investment required by this proposal would have been approximately $250 million. This approach was abandoned with the passage of the Helium Act Amendments of 1960 which gave authority to the Bureau of Mines to execute long-term contracts for the recovery of helium by private firms already engaged in the exploitation of high-grade helium-bearing natural gas deposits. These firms agreed to design and construct their own helium extraction facilities and to deliver crude helium to Government-owned pipelines; the Bureau of Mines would then place the helium in underground storage in the Government-owned field at Cliffside, Texas. The contracts, with four separate firms, were to run for twenty-two-year periods, commencing in 1961. The contract prices ranged from $10.30 to $11.78 per thousand cubic feet (Mcf), with an average of approximately $11 per Mcf. (It was anticipated that the unit cost of placing and maintaining helium in storage would be very small. The cost of extracting and purifying the stored helium prior to ultimate use would be approximately $2 per Mcf.)

The Bureau of Mines had originally requested annual contracting authority of up to $65 million to purchase helium for conservation purposes. Had this authority been granted in 1960, the Bureau estimated that it would have been able to purchase some 85 billion cubic feet between 1962 and 1985, the end of the contract period. Congress, however, authorized contracting authority of only $47.5 million annually; the Bureau of Mines anticipated that under such authority it would be able to purchase about 65 billion cubic feet between 1963 and 1984. However, it was estimated that annual demand for current consumption would by 1966 begin to exceed the combined annual production of the Bureau's own production plants and those of certain private producers of helium who, independently of the Government helium program, were planning to enter the market in the early 1960's (see Exhibit 2). Accordingly, the Bureau estimated that between 1966 and 1984 approximately 13 billion cubic feet of its contract purchases would have to be used to fill consumption needs and hence would not be available for conservation purposes. The amount of helium remaining in storage by 1984 under the $47.5 million program was, therefore, estimated at approximately 52 billion cubic feet, a twenty-six-year supply based upon demand projections.

With the $60 million annual contracting authority which the Bureau intended to request commencing in fiscal 1969, it was estimated that an incremental 21 billion cubic feet of helium could be purchased between 1970 and 1990. (See Exhibits 3, 4 and 5.) It was estimated that the contract prices per Mcf under the expanded program would be approximately the same as under the original $47.5 million program.

Under the $47.5 million program it was estimated that 2022 would be the last year in which recoverable resources of helium (helium in storage or still remaining in natural gas deposits) would be able to meet demand. It was estimated that the $60 million program would prolong the availability of helium by ten years, assuming that annual demand at that time would be 2 billion cubic feet. Without *any* conservation program, it had been estimated that helium available from natural gas sources would be insufficient to meet predicted demand commencing in 1988. (See Exhibit 3.)

Beyond the above dates the Bureau of Mines could foresee no alternate source of supply for significant quantities of helium other than extraction from the atmosphere. With 1967 technology the cost of extracting atmospheric helium had been variously estimated at between $1,000 and $2,000 per Mcf.

HELIUM PRICING

The price of helium, f.o.b. production plants, had varied considerably over the years. In 1921 the price was $525 per Mcf; it dropped sharply to $51 per Mcf by 1925, and reached a low level of $5.36 per Mcf in 1943. The price rose gradually after World War II and remained at $15.50 per Mcf between 1955 and 1961. The legislation of 1960, however, required that "Sales of helium . . . shall be at prices . . . which shall be adequate to cover all costs incurred . . . together with interest." Thus, the helium program, including the cost of acquiring helium for conservation purposes, was required to pay for itself; the time period within which any funds borrowed from the Treasury would have to be repaid (with accumulated interest at approximately 4 per cent per annum) was to be between twenty-five and thirty-five years from the date of passage of the Act (1960). Accordingly, in November, 1961 the Bureau of Mines established the price of helium, f.o.b. its plants, at $35 per Mcf. This price was calculated so that, over the life of the $47.5 million program contracts, revenues from sales of helium at $35 per Mcf would be sufficient to (1) repay net capital and retained earnings as of the date of passage of the Act (approximately $40 million), (2) defray operating expenditures, (3) purchase helium, primarily for storage, from the contract producers, and (4) repay with interest funds borrowed from the Treasury during the early years of the program.

In 1967 the pattern of sources and consumption of helium was expected to be as follows: The four contract producers under the $47.5 million program would produce approximately 3,795 million cubic feet of helium. All of this production with the exception of 76 million cubic feet would be placed in the Cliffside storage field. The Bureau of Mines' own plants would produce 724 million cubic feet; this, together with the 76 million cubic feet from the contractors, would result

in total sales by the Bureau of 800 million cubic feet. Of this amount 620 million cubic feet would be sold to other Federal Agencies, 120 million cubic feet to private firms working on government contracts, and 60 million cubic feet to other private consumers. In addition to the Bureau's activities three independent private producers of helium would sell 95 million cubic feet to private firms working on government contracts, and 105 million cubic feet to other private consumers. None of these three independent firms would place helium in storage.

Under the terms of the 1960 legislation Federal Agencies were required to purchase all their helium needs from the Bureau of Mines. The three independent producers were not bound by the Bureau's price of $35 per Mcf in making sales to their customers; Mr. Allen's information was that their f.o.b. prices were slightly less than the Bureau's price, and he expected that competition might in the future force the independents to reduce their prices as low as $20–$25 per Mcf.

USES AND PROPERTIES OF HELIUM

Helium was considered to be unique in its combination of unusual properties. Besides being light and inert helium had the lowest boiling point of all known substances—only 4 degrees above absolute zero, or −269 degrees centigrade. Liquid helium could thus be used to produce and maintain temperature conditions approaching absolute zero, and as such it was an invaluable tool in cryogenic research. In addition helium exhibited at these low temperatures some very remarkable properties of its own which were expected to give progressively greater understanding of the fundamental nature of matter. A comparative tabulation of some of the applications of the properties of helium and possible substitutes is presented in Exhibit 6.

The scientific community attached great importance to the continuing availability of helium. A former chairman of the National Science Foundation had stated prior to passage of the 1960 legislation: "Scientists are not particularly bothered by the possibility that the price they may have to pay for helium may rise substantially above its present level. They are seriously alarmed about the possibility that at some foreseeable time none will be available at any price."

QUESTIONS

(1) Based on the data available in the case, should the helium conservation program be expanded? (Support your answer with quantitative evidence.)

(2) Examine the stated objectives of the Helium Activity. How might you proceed to analyze alternative methods of attaining these objectives?

EXHIBIT 1

BUREAU OF MINES
Estimated Total Helium Demand FY 1950–1985

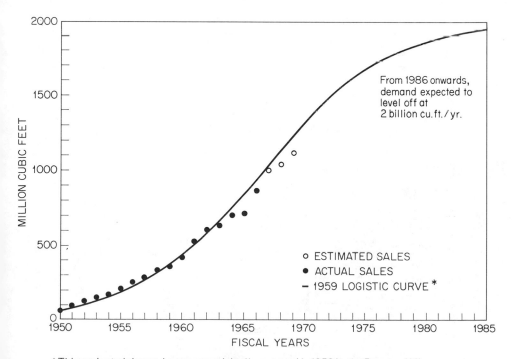

From 1986 onwards, demand expected to level off at 2 billion cu.ft./yr.

o ESTIMATED SALES
● ACTUAL SALES
— 1959 LOGISTIC CURVE *

*This projected demand curve was originally prepared in 1959 by the Bureau of Mines.

EXHIBIT 2

BUREAU OF MINES

Estimated U. S. Production of Helium
(not including production under conservation contracts)

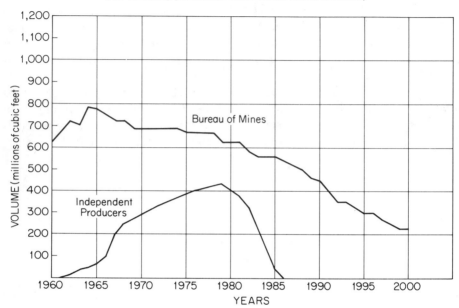

EXHIBIT 3

BUREAU OF MINES

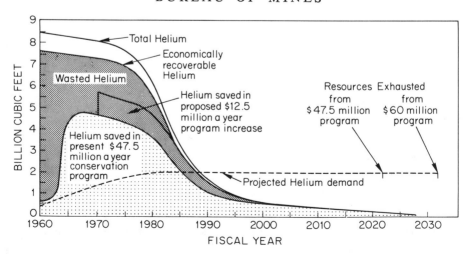

EXHIBIT 4

BUREAU OF MINES

Helium Resources

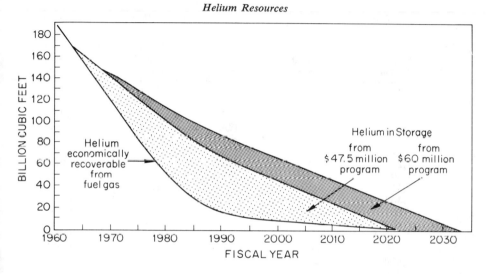

EXHIBIT 5

BUREAU   OF   MINES   (A)

Estimated Sales and Conservation of Helium 1968–1991
(all volume figures in millions of cubic feet)

	(2)	(3)	(4)	(5)	(6)
			\$47.5 million Program purchases from Contractors		\$60.0 million Program
	Sales of Helium				
Year	Bureau of Mines	Independent Producers	Volume sold for current consumption [1]	Volume placed in storage	Incremental volume purchased from contractors and placed in storage
1968	903	250	181	3,608 [2]	—
1969	977	270	295	3,497	—
1970	1,042	295	360	3,337	1,085
1971	1,106	315	424	3,207	1,085
1972	1,163	335	481	3,062	1,085
1973	1,218	350	536	2,954	1,085
1974	1,261	370	579	2,844	1,085
1975	1,301	385	635	2,746	1,050
1976	1,335	400	669	2,653	1,045
1977	1,367	410	701	2,295	1,030
1978	1,393	420	727	2,180	1,030
1979	1,414	430	801	2,025	1,010
1980	1,470	400	857	1,885	1,000
1981	1,520	380	907	1,743	1,000
1982	1,620	320	1,040	1,519	1,000
1983	1,710	250	1,150	1,329	1,000
1984	1,830	150	1,270 [3]	0	1,000
1985	1,960	40	1,400	0	950
1986	2,000	0	1,460	0	950
1987	2,000	0	1,480	0	950
1988	2,000	0	1,500	0	950
1989	2,000	0	1,540	0	950
1990	2,000	0	1,550	0	750
1991	2,000	0	1,600	0	0

[1] Volume figures in Column 4 are included in the sales figures in Column 2. For example, in 1968 the Bureau of Mines' own production was estimated to be 722 million cubic feet; this plus 181 million cubic feet from the contractors' production equals the total estimated sales of 903 million cubic feet in Column 2.

[2] It was estimated that there would be a total of 14.3 billion cubic feet already in storage at the end of 1967.

[3] Beginning in 1984 (with the expiration of the contracts under the \$47.5 million program) the helium volumes shown in the remainder of Column 4 would have to come from storage.

BUREAU OF MINES (A)

Helium Uses and Substitutes [1]

I. Properties of Helium	Molecular Structure	Low Temperature	Light Weight	Insoluble	Inert	No Radioactivity	Thermal Properties	Electrical Properties	
II. Uses of Helium	Lasers Leak detection Research	Masers Superconductors Cryopumping Cryobiology Computer elements Power generation & transmission Infrared detectors Free radicals Research	Liquid-fueled rockets	Breathing atmospheres Spaceships Sea labs Hospitals	Airships Balloons Research	Nuclear reactors Research	Chromatography Wind tunnels Research	Welding Aluminum Stainless steel Titanium et al.	Metallurgy Production of Titanium Zirconium Silicon Germanium Anesthetics
III. Substitutes	Neon Hydrogen	Nitrogen Hydrogen	Nitrogen	Nitrogen Oxygen Neon	Hydrogen	Carbon dioxide	Argon	Argon	Argon

[1] Although most of the individual properties of helium (except for molecular structure and low boiling temperature) can be obtained with some other gas, there is no other material which possesses the same combination of unique properties that serves as the basis for helium's usefulness. Hydrogen is lightweight and has a relatively low boiling point, but it is highly inflammable. Nitrogen also has a relatively low boiling point and is relatively inert, but it is relatively heavy. Argon is inert, but heavy; and it has different electrical properties useful in welding. Carbon dioxide will work in nuclear reactors, but it will become radioactive. Neon is very expensive.

Approximate comparative prices at points close to commercial distribution centers (1964 data):

(based on 20 Mcf quantities)

Helium:	$95 per Mcf [2]
Hydrogen:	$14 " "
Oxygen:	$16 " "
Nitrogen:	$16 " "
Argon:	$90 " "

[2] Note: This price is much higher than the *f.o.b.* price of $35 per Mcf, because of the considerable costs involved in (a) placing helium in containers, and (b) shipping.

C A S E

14

BUREAU OF NATIONAL CAPITAL AIRPORTS

RELIEVING CONGESTION AT
WASHINGTON NATIONAL AIRPORT

In June, 1967 Mr. Peter Delgado, a staff analyst in the Federal Aviation Administration's Bureau of National Capital Airports (BNCA), was studying a copy of Order Number E-25319 issued by the Civil Aeronautics Board (CAB), which instituted an investigation to

. . . determine what steps [the Board] should take through certificate amendment procedure or otherwise to improve the utilization of Washington National Airport, Dulles International Airport, and Friendship International Airport in order to improve air service to the Washington–Baltimore area, relieve congestion, and otherwise serve the public interest.

The Bureau of National Capital Airports, as operator of Washington National Airport and Dulles International Airport, would be expected to participate in the proceedings before the CAB. Mr. Delgado had been assigned to analyze some of the many solutions to the problem of congestion at National which had been proposed by various interested groups, other than the use of the regulatory powers vested in the CAB. Mr. Delgado was

to prepare his analysis in time for submission to the CAB during the course of its investigation. The remainder of this case outlines the information gathered by Mr. Delgado prior to commencing his analysis.

COMMERCIAL AIRPORTS IN THE WASHINGTON–BALTIMORE AREA

The Washington–Baltimore area was served by three major commercial airports. Two of these, Washington National Airport and Dulles International

This case was prepared with the cooperation of the Bureau of National Capital Airports, Federal Aviation Administration, U.S. Department of Transportation, by Graeme M. Taylor under the supervision of Charles Christenson, Associate Professor of Business Administration, Harvard University, on behalf of the Bureau of Training, U.S. Civil Service Commission. The case is intended for class discussion only, and certain names and facts may have been changed and certain hypothetical material included which, while avoiding the disclosure of confidential information, do not materially lessen the value of the case for educational purposes. This case is not intended to represent either effective or ineffective handling of an administration situation, nor does it purport to be a statement of policy by the agency involved.

Airport, were owned by the federal government and operated by the Bureau of National Capital Airports. The third, Friendship International Airport, was owned and operated by the City of Baltimore. Exhibit 1 gives the growth in passenger operations at the three fields for the fifteen-year period 1952–1966 inclusive.

Washington National Airport

National was located less than five miles from downtown Washington; driving time was approximately fifteen minutes. The fare by taxi was approximately $2.60 and by limousine $1.35.

National had been designed to handle a maximum of 4 million passengers per year. In 1966 8 million passengers used National and in 1967 the total was expected to be approximately 10 million. The North Terminal, which was built in 1958, alone handled approximately 200 passengers a year.

Approximately 75 per cent of the traffic using National was with cities within a radius of 500 miles of Washington. About another 15 per cent was with the seven major cities between 650 and 1,000 miles from National—Minneapolis, Miami, West Palm Beach, Tampa, Orlando, Memphis, and St. Louis.

Generally accepted airport design rules suggested that an airport should provide one daily parking space for every 1,000 of annual passenger volume. National, however, had available only 2,400 parking spaces. Parking rates were $2.50 per day.

Dulles International Airport

By general agreement Dulles was considered to be one of the most tech-

nically advanced airports in the world besides being of striking architectural beauty. Dulles occupied 10,000 acres; the passenger capacity of the original section of the terminal building was four million passengers annually.

When Dulles opened in November, 1962, it was anticipated that passenger volume would grow to ten million annually by 1975. Traffic growth had fallen far below expectations, however. Critics contended that the airport was too far from Washington—twenty-six miles to the west—and that the most convenient flights tended to be scheduled into Friendship Airport. For example, a would-be passenger to, say, Chicago would often find that he could fly from Dulles in the morning but that the return evening flight was scheduled into Friendship, thus preventing him from driving to Dulles and forcing him to rely on either expensive taxi rides (approximately $13 from downtown Washington to Dulles) or bus service (at a fare of $2.50). Buses left downtown Washington approximately one hour before each flight departure.

Dulles was served in 1967 by 14½ miles of four-lane divided limited-access road connecting with Interstate Route 495, the beltway surrounding Washington. The BNCA had resisted efforts to open this access road to local commuter traffic, believing that this would defeat the purpose for which the access road had been built. The capacity of the road was such that a speed of 60 to 65 miles per hour could be maintained by an automobile even under peak-hour traffic conditions until the annual passenger volume exceeded 5 million. Peak-hour speed would decline to 50 miles per hour at an annual passenger volume of 8 million. A proposed future expansion to six lanes would permit 60 to 65 mph peak hour speeds at the 8 million passenger level and 50 mph up to 12 million.

An advantage of Dulles was that it took an average of only ten minutes from the time a plane touched down to the time that the passengers were ready to board ground transportation. Congestion at National often resulted in disembarking times of twenty minutes or longer.

Dulles had 1,700 parking spaces in 1967, with ultimate expansion to 6,400 planned. Parking rates at Dulles were $1.50 per day.

Friendship International Airport

Friendship International Airport, owned and operated by the City of Baltimore, was located thirty-two miles northeast of Washington near the southern edge of Baltimore. Driving time was fifty minutes; the limousine fare was $3.50 one way.

Prior to the opening of Dulles in November, 1962 Friendship was the only airport serving the Washington area capable of handling four-engine jets. Even with the opening of Dulles Baltimore continued to be designated by the CAB as a co-terminal for the Washington area.

GROWTH OF CONGESTION AT WASHINGTON NATIONAL AIRPORT

On January 11, 1966 the FAA announced that Washington National Airport would be open to shorter-haul jets commencing on April 24, 1966. Extracts from a press release accompanying the announcement follow:

Washington National Airport will be opened to two and three-engine short-haul jets on April 24, shortening the flight time between the Nation's Capital and certain major cities in the eastern half of the United States by a significant margin, the Federal Aviation Agency announced today.

The airport, which was opened on June 16, 1941, has never previously accepted scheduled air carrier jets. The lifting of this prohibition will assure Washington that the airport will remain a close-in air carrier airport as the airlines replace their propeller-driven planes with pure jets. Prior to the development of the smaller two and three-engine jets, an FAA policy prohibited use of four-engine jets at Washington National. The introduction of such smaller jets as the Boeing 727, the Douglas DC-9, the BAC-111, and the Caravelle has altered the picture of air carrier service at Washington National since these newer, smaller airplanes can use the two longer runways regularly.

No consideration is being given to permitting the operation of big four-engine jets from Washington National.

The FAA noted that the opening of jet service at Washington National does not change the basic roles of the two federally-owned and operated airports serving the Washington area. Washington National will continue to serve the short and medium-haul markets while Dulles International will still perform the function for which it was designed—the service of long-haul domestic and international markets.

Airlines have agreed to limit non-stop jet operations from Washington National to a radius of approximately 650 miles, except that this limit will be extended as far as 1000 miles for scheduled service which was available from the airport in 1965. The jets will serve cities such as Miami, Memphis, St. Louis, Chicago, Cleveland, Detroit, Minneapolis, New York, and Boston.

The two and three-engine jets will cruise at approximately 550 miles per hour, nearly one-third faster than any propeller or turbo-prop aircraft.

The small and medium jets will climb out of the airport area more sharply and swiftly than propeller-driven aircraft, but otherwise they will use the same flight patterns now in effect at Washington National. Although the noise created by jet engines is different from that of piston engines, jet engine noise levels at Washington National are expected to be about the same as is now created by the piston aircraft.

The FAA decision was made after months of study devoted to the probable impact on air passenger traffic in the Washington area if jet restrictions at Washington National were modified. The most reliable data available indicate that the use of Washington National by short and medium-range jets will not prevent the continued growth of the other area airports, Dulles International and Friendship International.

With intermediate jet service, passenger traffic at Washington National is expected to rise from the current rate of 7 million persons per year to about 10 million within the next decade. Airlines are planning to enlarge their facilities at the airport, and the Federal Aviation Agency anticipates an eventual major modernization program for the terminal.

Traffic at Dulles International Airport is expected to rise from the 1965 total of one million passengers to about two million passengers a year by 1975. The airlines have agreed to maintain the daily schedule of flight service out of Dulles that was in effect on October 1, 1965, as a minimum—an average of 89 daily flights. Traffic at Friendship Airport also is expected to increase significantly during the next 10 years.

Following the introduction of jet service, congestion at WNA became even more serious than before. Accordingly, the FAA issued the following release on July 1, 1966:

An operating policy designed to emphasize the role of Washington National as a local service–commuter–general aviation airport, offering the most efficient service possible to commercial passengers and private users, was announced today by General William F. McKee, FAA Administrator, who predicted that the new policy would afford relief to the overcrowded terminal facilities of the Federally-owned airport.

Effective August 7, all scheduled nonstop air service between Washington, D.C., and cities more than 500 miles distant must originate from either Dulles International Airport or Friendship International Airport. Shifting these long-haul flights away from Washington National will reduce the number of daily airline operations by over 100 flights. The flow of passenger traffic through the terminal will drop from the present congested level, averaging 22,000 persons a day, to a level of about 18,000 persons a day.

It is tradition and policy to operate the air traffic control system on a "first-come, first-served" basis. However, the severe congestion at Washington National Airport requires a reduction in both air carrier and general aviation operations. It would be grossly unfair to the millions of passengers who will use the airport to severely restrict air carrier operations and then permit unrestricted general aviation operations to fill the void left by the air carriers to the extent that runway and airspace congestion thwarts the purpose of the air carrier restrictions.

The instrument flight capacity of the airport is approximately 60 operations per hour. Actual capacity varies from 30 to 100 depending upon wind, weather, and "mix" of traffic. The historical use has been 73% air carrier and 27% general aviation. It is intended to use the available capacity equitably between the competing classes by allocating 16 (27%) of the 60 to general aviation operations. All 60 operations will be handled under instrument flight rules (IFR) on a "first-come, first-served" basis regardless of actual weather conditions.

With the objective of optimum use of the runways, additional general aviation IFR flight plans will be accepted to the extent the air carriers do not use their hourly allocation. For example, if only 30 air carrier flights are scheduled in one hour, 30 general aviation IFR flights will be accepted.

Realizing that this method will still have unused capacity at certain times, visual flight rules (VFR) general aviation traffic will be accepted on a noninterference basis to the extent that capacity exists.

The new policy is expected to relieve crowded parking and passenger-handling facilities at Washington National Airport, especially during the early morning and later afternoon peak hours, by diverting both general aviation and air carriers to other area airports, where they can be handled more expediently.

As a local service–commuter airport, Washington National will provide swift, convenient flights to the entire Northeast, including New York, Hartford, Providence, Boston and other points to the North; Cleveland, Detroit, Indianapolis, Cincinnati and Louisville to the West; and Knoxville, Winston-Salem, Charlotte, Richmond and Norfolk to the South.

The policy adopted by FAA includes the following provisions:

1. Only flights to or from Washington National that stop within 500 miles are now approved to operate after August 7, 1966.

2. All changes or additions to schedules or type and model of aircraft after July 1 will require the written permission of the Director, Bureau of National Capital Airports.

3. Scheduled air taxi service may continue on the present basis. Any schedule changes or additions will require the written approval of the Director, Bureau of National Capital Airports. Non-scheduled air taxis fall into the category of general aviation.

4. The severe limitations on airline use of Washington National Airport require arrangements for use by other aircraft which will minimize interference with the scheduled movement of airline passengers.

5. The entire policy will be reviewed every 90 days and restrictions added or relaxed as required by the public interest.

The Federal Aviation Agency has agreed with the airlines to work through joint airline–FAA committees on other means of relieving congestion in the terminal vicinity and improving surface transportation between the three area airports.

Airport congestion has become a problem in the area because airline scheduling has been heavily concentrated at one airport, instead of being distributed evenly among the three available airports. The problem became more acute after the lifting of the jet ban at Washington National. With the use of jets, airline operations at this airport increased at a sharper rate than ever before in its history, rising from an average daily rate of 630 to 669 in less than two months.

Without the imposition of a restricting policy, the number of daily airline operations would soon have surpassed the all-time high of 700. With the greater seating capacity of present day aircraft, and with the increase in private flying, the number of persons using the airport has skyrocketed, resulting in delays, public inconvenience, and inefficient usage of facilities.

During the peak hours, the airport has

been handling as many as 53 airline operations per hour—nearly one a minute. The new policy will cut this number back to approximately 40 operations per hour.

The airport has had virtually no expansion of facilities since it opened 25 years ago, with the exception of the North Terminal, completed in 1958. During the decade of the Fifties, when the aviation industry was expanding rapidly, and traffic at Washington National increased from less than 2,000,000 passengers a year to nearly 5,000,000, the major concern of the Federal Government was with the planning and construction of a second National Capital Airport especially designed for long-range jet operations. A further concentration of traffic at Washington National would be not only undesirable, General McKee said, but also impossible without overstraining the present facilities of the airport.

Following the sharp increase in air traffic at the airport during May, the Federal Aviation Agency reached an agreement with the airlines using Washington National to "freeze" the number of daily schedules for a 60-day period beginning June 2, during which time better solutions to the problem of growing ground congestion can be determined. The problem was discussed individually and jointly with the airlines and with representatives of general aviation. After carefully reviewing all proposed solutions, the Federal Aviation Agency arrived at the present policy, with a distance restriction for air carriers, and a numerical limitation for other aircraft.

FAA expects to see an early improvement in the service at Washington National Airport and a better overall distribution of air traffic in the area.

While the 500-mile perimeter had been approved by ten of the thirteen airlines serving National, its announcement precipitated a storm of protest from the large number of travelers who frequently were required to fly to points beyond the perimeter. Accordingly, on July 27, 1966 the FAA issued a notice of proposed rule-making which would limit the airlines serving National to forty schedules per hour. Airlines were to be given their choice of scheduling operations within the forty-per-hour limit by cooperative action or being assigned individual quotas by BNCA. The effective date of the limitation was to be September 1, 1966.

Under the proposed rule the airlines could continue to serve within a non-stop radius of 650 miles. In addition, the airlines would be allowed to continue to provide non-stop service which was available in 1965 to a few points as far away as 1,000 miles.

It was hoped that the new hourly limitation would restrict total daily passengers at WNA to a more manageable level. It was also expected to halt the rise in operations at WNA; with no limitations daily operations at WNA would have risen to approximately 700 by the fall of 1966.

The airlines voluntarily agreed among themselves, with CAB approval, to limit schedules at WNA to 40 per hour, exclusive of extra sections (such as Eastern Air Lines' extra shuttle operations). While the formal agreement expired December 1, 1966 on an informal level, it was still in effect as of June, 1967. General aviation operators agreed to cooperate in limiting their operations as far as possible.

As of June, 1967 National was handling approximately 670 airline operations per day, while Dulles with a capacity of 80 instrument flight operations per hour was scheduled for a total of 130 air line flights per day.

PROPOSALS TO RELIEVE CONGESTION AT WASHINGTON NATIONAL AIRPORT

Modernization of the airport

Despite the limitations on aircraft operations described earlier, the number of passengers using National appeared likely to continue to rise. A primary reason for this expected rise was the fact that newer models of the short-haul jets were being built to accommodate larger numbers of passengers. For example, the existing version of the Boeing 727 had a capacity of 118 passengers, but the planned Boeing 727-200 model would carry up to 156 passengers.

As of June, 1967 the airlines had spent or intended to spend approximately $11 million on various improvements in their passenger handling facilities at National. In the meantime the FAA had contracted with a firm of architects to prepare a "reasonable and sensible" plan for the modernization of Washington National Airport. As of June, 1967 the architects had proposed some 15 design concepts; the FAA had selected four of these for further study. Although no details of these plans had been released, Mr. Delgado hypothesized for the purposes of his analysis that the eventual cost of any modernization of National would be approximately $50 million, and that this expenditure would result in facilities adequate to handle approximately 15 million passengers annually.

Speculation in the press, however, had placed a much higher cost on the modernization of National. An article appearing in *The Washingtonian,* for example, stated: [1]

To modernize a 25-year-old airport, everything must go. To increase efficiency, National must have parallel runways, a totally new system that would cost about $50 million plus an additional $30 million to align an alternate with the Anacostia River. This construction, in turn, would obliterate the present terminal, hangars, and auxiliary buildings, and so new ones would be needed. The new terminal would probably sit between the two runways, like the Saarinen terminal at Dulles. The balance of the $200 million would be consumed for much-needed additional parking facilities and roads.

Even the $200 million figure may be conservative, though, when one considers the problems of construction into the river and the problem of car access from a commuter road literally choked with increasing traffic, and considering the fact that the $110 million Dulles was originally projected to cost between $30 and $40 million.

Mr. Delgado estimated that a terminal modernization plan, such as he believed the FAA was contemplating, would have to be spaced over five years, with a resultant reduction in operations of 20 per cent each year; the modernization, if adopted, could begin no earlier than 1969.

Proposal to sell Washington National Airport

Mr. Delgado was aware that various groups had proposed that the site of Washington National Airport should be sold for housing development purposes. The claimed need for more

[1] *The Washingtonian,* Volume 2, No. 3, December 1966: "They're going to do what?" by Arthur Cotton Moore.

housing for residents of the District of Columbia was based on the fact that 269,000 people or 37 per cent of the District's population were living in substandard housing. National occupied a site of 680 acres close to the central city with all the scenic and recreational advantages of proximity to a river. Mr. Delgado realized it would be hard to estimate the market value of the National site but decided to use a conservative estimate of a minimum of $100,000 per acre.

Completion of Interstate Route 66

Most private motorists driving from Washington to Dulles preferred to follow the George Washington Memorial Parkway (four-lane highway with a speed limit of 50 mph) to the beltway, and then on to the Dulles access road. However, the Department of the Interior, which administered the parkway, required commercial vehicles taking passengers to Dulles to leave the parkway at State Route 123 near McLean, Virginia. If airline limousines were permitted to continue on the Parkway for a distance of about a mile and a half, they would run into the beltway and from there proceed to the Dulles access highway uninterrupted.

The Dulles access highway was originally intended to connect with Interstate Route 66 from Washington. Upon completion of Route 66, the BNCA intended to extend the access highway some 2½ miles to link up with Route 66. The cost of this extension including the necessary interchanges was estimated to be approximately $4.4 million. The necessary rights of way were already owned by the government.

Commenting on the status of the plans for completion of Route 66, the Fairfax County Globe reported on March 30, 1967:

At the present time, the completion of Route 66 is problematical, as the highway's right-of-way lies along the part of the recently abandoned Washington and Old Dominion Railroad, which is currently involved in court action to determine its ownership. . . . In 1965 . . . the chairman of Northern Virginia's Transportation Commission said in his annual report: 'Due to an untimely application of the Washington and Old Dominion Railroad to abandon its entire line between Alexandria and Purcellville, the NVTC diverted much of its resources to seek to preserve the railroad for rapid transit use by opposing abandonment. . . .'

Now, two years later, that case is still pocketed in the confines of the Interstate Commerce Commission and the courts. The rapid transit is at a standstill as is completion of Route 66. . . .

Mr. Delgado decided to assume that the earliest possible completion date for Route 66 and the extension of the Dulles access highway would be 1972. He estimated that upon its completion under favorable traffic conditions driving time from downtown Washington to Dulles would be approximately twenty-five minutes.

Proposed helicopter service

Mr. Delgado knew that the CAB was considering selection of a private company for certification to operate a helicopter service between downtown Washington and Dulles (and between National and Dulles). He thought that because of their limited carrying capacity helicopters would never provide mass transportation to Dulles. However, for the purposes of his analysis Mr. Delgado decided to assume that a twenty-five-passenger helicopter costing $1 million would be able to fly from downtown Washington to Dulles in ten minutes, with a one-way fare of $12.50.

Proposed rapid transit

Mr. Delgado knew that many proposals had been put forward for the construction of various forms of rapid transit systems to Dulles. One of the more futuristic of these was described in the *Washingtonian* article quoted above:

L. K. Edwards, former Assistant Chief of space at Lockheed, now president of Tube Transit, Inc., has developed a bored underground vacuum-tube train which runs on a combination of mechanical vacuum and gravity, and is capable of tremendous speeds with complete comfort. The train could travel from downtown Washington to Dulles in approximately six minutes. Because the system uses no fuel, it would allow a great frequency of trips at minimal cost, and in effect bring Dulles virtually into downtown Washington. The vacuum train would cost $80 to $90 million. If you apply realistic standards and double that, it's still cheaper than the National plan.

The article went on to describe some other rapid transit possibilities:

A cheaper and more conventional approach would be a souped-up surface train such as the Tokaido Line, a 120-m.p.h. train between Tokyo and Osaka, Japan. Variations such as air-suspension rides which may give higher speeds are being experimented with by the Ford Motor Company (Levacar) and also by the French (Aerotrain), whose designers hope for speeds of at least 250 m.p.h. If a Tokaido-type train, which is in daily operation in Japan, were built to Dulles, it would mean about a twelve-minute trip. Other types of rapid transit like the monorail might extend the time anywhere from fifteen to twenty minutes. Devices such as moving belts and automated highways are still in the future, but any of these other systems can be easily realized today. Any system could make several stops in central Washington, or could be tied in with the subway system, but certainly would serve a modern air terminal building with complete check-in facilities. The surrounding western and northwestern suburbs of Washington would probably continue to use the beltway and the new access highway to the airport in their favorite transport, the car. For a large portion of this area, Dulles is as close or closer than National.

Mr. Delgado estimated that a conventional, non-stop, highspeed train could make the trip in twenty minutes, with a capacity of 2,500 passengers per hour in each direction, and a one-way fare of less than $3.00. Such a system might cost upwards of $150 million to construct; the earliest possible completion date would be 1975.

Another possibility would be extend the subway system under consideration by the Washington Metropolitan Area Transit Authority from Falls Church, Virginia to Dulles. The extra cost of this extension would be approximately $30 million. The fare would probably be 75 cents one-way for the forty-five-minute trip from downtown Washington to Dulles. The earliest completion date would be 1976, and the peak hour capacity of the system would be 3,200 passengers per hour in each direction.

Miscellaneous proposals

Mr. Delgado also planned to consider other possibilities for relieving congestion at National such as building a completely new airport in the vicinity of Washington which would be used only by general aviation. The cost would be less than $10 million, and the new airport would be capable of handling up to ninety operations per hour.

A reduction in taxi fares was another possibility. Washington taxi drivers were not permitted to pick up passengers in Virginia, and Virginia drivers could not pick up passengers in Washington. Accordingly, the Washington/Dulles trip was a one-way fare proposition for all drivers. Mr. Delgado believed that if some agreement could be reached by the appropriate licensing authorities which would permit drivers to transport passengers in both directions, the one-way cab fare might conceivably fall from $13 to $6.50.

Political environment

Mr. Delgado realized that he could not ignore the effect of the influence of certain interest groups in making his analysis. He knew, for example, that Maryland's Congressional delegation strongly backed the promotion of Friendship as a major airport. Similarly, Virginia citizens' groups had recently begun to take a more active interest in promoting Dulles. Members of Congress liked the convenience of National's location; those members who lived in cities between 500 and 1,000 miles from National would be strongly opposed to any move to curtail flights to their cities.

In addition, Mr. Delgado felt that he must consider many other issues such as safety, noise levels near the airports, and the social cost of disrupting home owners whose property might stand in the way of any of the various proposed methods of surface transportation.

QUESTIONS

1. As Mr. Delgado, develop measures of cost and effectiveness appropriate for the purposes of ranking the various proposals mentioned in the case.

2. As far as data in the case permit, perform a systems analysis of the problem which Mr. Delgado has set himself.

EXHIBIT 1

BUREAU OF NATIONAL CAPITAL AIRPORTS

Number of Passengers Using the Washington Area Airports
(in thousands)

	National	Friendship	Dulles	Total
1952	2,492	235	—	2,727
1953	2,720	281		3,001
1954	3,103	306		3,409
1955	3,635	328		3,963
1956	3,964	344		4,308
1957	4,463	400		4,863
1958	4,534	388		4,922
1959	5,006	541		5,547
1960	4,726	747		5,473
1961	4,646	1,136		5,782
1962	4,837	1,436	53	6,326
1963	5,464	1,147	667	7,278
1964	6,188	1,459	782	8,429
1965	6,773	1,656	838	9,267
1966	7,920	2,001	1,175	11,096
1967 (estimated)	9,825	2,400	1,636	13,861

CASE

15

OFFICE OF ECONOMIC OPPORTUNITY

EVALUATION OF TRAINING PROGRAMS

In the summer of 1967 Mr. Tom O'Brien, an analyst in the Office of Research, Plans, Programs and Evaluation (RPP&E) in the Office of Economic Opportunity (OEO), was studying three papers dealing with the evaluation of anti-poverty programs. Mr. O'Brien had been given the task of evaluating the various approaches suggested by the three papers, particularly with reference to the Job Corps program. The three papers were:

1. "Evaluation of OEO Programs—A Progress Report"
2. "A Framework for the Evaluation of Training Programs"
3. "Benefit-Cost Study of Job Corps"

The remainder of this case discusses the three papers.

"EVALUATION OF OEO PROGRAMS— A PROGRESS REPORT"

In August, 1966 the assistant director of OEO for RPP&E presented a paper entitled "Evaluation of OEO Programs —A Progress Report" before a meeting of the American Statistical Associa-

tion. Some extracts from this paper follow.

The primary objective of the War On Poverty is to change people from 'poor' to "non-poor" *through their own efforts* —to enable them to support themselves above the poverty line through their own earnings. This is the meaning of an "opportunity program." Only secondarily should the objective be to change the state of the poor by giving them money, thus making them less poor or not poor at all. Let me make clear that the overall War on Poverty must do both. . . .

The objective of an opportunity program is to increase earnings, and the connection of vocational training to earnings is obvious and straightforward. To evalu-

This case was prepared with the cooperation of the Office of Economic Opportunity by Graeme M. Taylor under the supervision of Warren A. Law, Professor of Business Administration, Harvard University on behalf of the Bureau of the Budget. This case is intended for class discussion only, and certain names and facts may have been changed which, while avoiding the disclosure of confidential information, do not materially lessen the value of the case for educational purposes. This case is not intended to represent either effective or ineffective handling of an administrative situation, nor does it purport to be a statement of policy by the agency involved.

ate a training program our primary data needs are for characteristics of the trainee before entering the program and after passing through it. Such characteristics include both items of the demographic type such as age, race, and education as control variables; and also job-holding experience and earnings as variables of direct interest.

It is, of course, not proper to evaluate the effectiveness of a training program by comparing earnings after to earnings before, because change may be an effect of lapsed time or of other factors outside the program, as well as a direct effect of the program. Just as obviously, even though such before-after comparison is not really legitimate, we do it because we frequently have nothing else to fall back on. But the really important and legitimate form of evaluation compares the before-and-after experience of trainees to the similarly time-phased experience of non-trainees in a carefully selected control group. This makes things a lot less simple, particularly when we talk about youth training. Youth control groups are particularly difficult to come by, both because so many young people between the ages of 16 and 21 have passed through OEO programs, and because the self-selection process for our youth training programs means that the possible members of a control group may differ from the trainees in certain specific (but undefined) characteristics which led them to avoid the training program. Because of these difficulties we are proceeding rather carefully in setting up the youth control group which is vital to our program evaluation. We are, however, already collecting substantial data on the pre-training characteristics and some data on post-training characteristics of our program participants and are in the process of setting up a youth control sample.

A system has now been established for the collection of individual characteristic data for all enrollees in both Job Corps and Neighborhood Youth Corps. These data include information not only on the enrollees' own education and previous work experience, but also on family characteristics such as family size, number of working members, occupation and work status of family head, estimated family income plus a number of binary items on such things as housing and welfare. The Job Corps also regularly reports some initial aptitude and achievement level tests and the NYC is in the process of experimenting with such instruments.

There have been a few very small sample followups (about 200) of Job Corps graduates and a slightly larger sample followup is to be reported late this summer. There are presently no routine followups of NYC graduates, but a followup procedure is in the developmental stage.

A pilot study is now underway to determine the feasibility of setting up a large national sample of poor youth, 16–21, which could be tested and then reinterviewed and retested two or three years later. The objective is to create a sample which is large enough to allow the establishment of groups of youth which are statistically similar in terms of relevant socio-economic variables, some of whom have participated in training programs Job Corps, NYC and MDTA, and some of whom have not. Hopefully, such a sample would allow both cross-section and longitudinal comparisons which would provide some of the sort of evaluative information, admittedly crude, which is necessary for realistic judgments about reasonable program mix. Elements of this sample would serve as a control group so that program effects could be separated to some degree from effects due simply to growth of the youths and to changes in general economic and social conditions. In addition, it may be possible to determine which types of program are best suited for which types of poor youth and, within programs, which pro gram characteristics seem to be related with favorable results. We are fully aware of the limitations of such an approach to the problems of evaluation—and this is one of the reasons for proceeding first on a pilot basis—but it seems to us that the logic of the program evaluation effort leads inevitably to this type of an approach. If the limitations of this type of evaluative method prove too severe, I suppose we must re-examine the logic of program evaluation as it now stands.

Even lacking the control sample at this time, we already have some capability to do the less legitimate sort of before-and-after evaluation, and we have made some still quite hypothetical cost-effectiveness comparisons of our youth programs. It should be pointed out in discussing the cost and effectiveness of training programs, however, that we try to avoid the sort of cost-benefit analysis which states that a training program is justified if discounted future earnings are greater than costs. The program implication of such a cost-benefit calculation is that if discounted earnings are less than costs, transfer payments would be more economical than the training program, but given the hierarchy of objectives mentioned above—that it is more important to get people out of poverty through their own earnings than it is to give them money—War On Poverty training may be justified even if costs are higher than estimated benefits. For this reason, we avoid the sort of benefit calculation which compares something to nothing, and rather use such calculations to compare programs with some similarity.

Table 1 shows such a calculation—highly hypothetical, it should be reemphasized—comparing Job Corps and the out-of-school Neighborhood Youth Corps. [This table is presented as case Exhibit 1.] What was done was to estimate (on the basis of very sketchy data on before-and-after job-holding and earnings characteristics) the time period which it would take for Job Corpsmen to pay back to the economy with their increased earnings the cost of their Job Corps training. This came to about 5 years on the basis of these data plus some rather conservative assumptions, and the question was then asked what assumptions for the substantially cheaper Neighborhood Youth Corps program would equalize the payback period. We came to the obvious conclusion that it takes less change in earnings to pay back the NYC costs simply because these costs are lower than the Job Corps costs.

We also, however, came to the less obvious conclusion that for the higher costs of Job Corps to really justify themselves unambiguously, the Job Corps program should be capable of reaching and helping a group of hard core youth that Neighborhood Youth Corps cannot reach at all. If a group of youth does exist which cannot be helped by NYC then the payback period on NYC costs for them would be infinite; if Job Corps can help these youth with its more intensive programs, then its payback period would at any rate be less than infinite. It is this group which Job Corps is trying to reach. This example clearly illustrates the importance of making certain alterations in the conventional form of cost-benefit analysis when it is applied to poverty type programs.

It is our feeling that in the case of poverty programs the attempt to quantify benefits beyond those directly represented by changes in the lifetime income stream —sometimes called external or spillover benefits—is quite important. Most importantly, when looked at from the governmental decision point (where decisions are subject to the governmental budget constraint) the effects of the programs on other social expenditures need to be taken into account. If youth training programs not only raise incomes but also result in lower requirements for public expenditures for such things as welfare, unemployment compensation, health, crime prevention, then an attempt should be made to take these additional benefits into account in making program evaluations. We are currently attempting to develop some means of quantifying, at least in order of magnitude, these additional benefits.

"A FRAMEWORK FOR THE EVALUATION OF TRAINING PROGRAMS"

In September, 1966, a member of the staff of RPP&E published a staff paper entitled "A Framework for the Evaluation of Training Programs." The intention of the author was "to systematically set forth the current and projected costs of the different programs, examine the enrollee characteristics, compute expected yearly earnings flows, and then perform hypothetical calculations under different assumptions as to how much these earnings streams would need to be altered to justify the costs of the various programs."

The paper began with a discussion of the proper costs and benefits to be considered.

Considerable discussion has been focused on the inclusion criteria for costs and benefits in evaluating retraining programs. The basic area of conflict is between the *real resource* and *financial* approaches. An economist would consider only the real resources expended on a program as valid costs and real resources gained as benefits. Any transfer type expenditures or savings due to programs are merely of an offsetting nature, thus not suitable for inclusion in the benefit cost calculus.

Traditional economic theory is often inapplicable to a bureaucrat charged with

a specific object to be maximized subject to an externally imposed budget constraint. The decision regarding the proper cost and benefit elements to include is often highly dependent upon the point of reference of the analyst. The decision making criteria for bureaucrats operating from different perspectives will be briefly explored.

The first level is that of the Director of the Bureau of the Budget charged with maximizing social welfare subject to a budget constraint. In this case, financial and not real resource costs are the proper tool for analysis. Any financial (out-of-pocket) expenditure, be it a transfer or purchase of goods and services, reduces the amount of funds which may be allocated between competing alternative methods of pursuing the objective. By the same reasoning of two programs offering equal real returns, the one providing the greatest savings in transfer payments should be selected because it, in effect, provides a source of investible funds which mitigates the budget constraint. This is definitely a non-Musgravian world because the allocation and transfer branches are not watertight.

A second level of bureaucratic decision-making is the individual agency. Here the proper decision-making criteria depend upon the nature of the agency. On the cost side, it is apparently clear that an agency with a budget constraint and a specific mission should consider all financial costs of a program, which means it includes training allowances. The benefit picture is not nearly so clear. An agency should include savings in transfer payments as a benefit if, and only if, it has a means of capturing these benefits to reduce the constriction of its budget. Assume a training agency is given a fixed budget, charged with reducing unemployment and unable to collect any savings in unemployment compensation. Then the mix of programs that reduces unemployment the most, which is the agency's mission, will not necessarily be that mix which provides the greatest savings in unemployment compensation. The agency will have no incentive to include this savings unless it can employ them to further expand its programs.

Given the inconsistency of the various cases and the fact that this paper is written from a multi-agency viewpoint in a war against poverty, a real resource approach will be taken. This means that all trainee remuneration is considered as a transfer not a direct cost, and no estimate of reduced transfer payments is made in computing benefits. It also implies that an opportunity cost of removing the trainees from the labor force must be included based on expected trainee earnings over the period of program participation. Program costs, however, will be set forth in both real and financial terms for anyone desiring to perform computations on other bases.

The "Framework" paper presented a table summarizing projected program and real resource costs. (See Exhibit 2.) The Job Corps annual "program cost" of $5,625 per trainee was derived as follows:

1. A figure of $7,500 per "slot" was used as OEO's *projection* [1] of average annual costs for the Job Corps.
2. Assuming an average enrollee stay of 9 months, the Job Corps program cost per trainee was taken to be 75% of $7,500, or $5,625.

The opportunity costs shown in Exhibit 2 were for each program the "expected earnings of a trainee over a nine-month span, the usual expected program enrollment period . . . calculated from Census data," and repre-

sented the cost of removing the trainee from the labor force during the period of his enrollment.

The "Framework" paper recognized that "cost per enrollee data often do not give the most meaningful index to program impact." Accordingly, figures were derived for program costs for trainees, graduates, placements, and affectees. A summary of these costs is shown in Exhibit 3. The derivation of the costs per Job Corps graduate, placement, and affectee were explained in the paper as follows.

Job Corps assumes a steady state cost of $7,500/slot or $5,625/enrollee based on a nine month stay. Various completion assumptions are made with 75 percent completion factor being a rough median of the different estimates. The Program Memorandum assumes an 80 percent success rate for graduates, with success defined as a steady job, returning to school, more advanced training, or military service. An estimated 20 percent of nongraduates are assumed to be affected by the program. Quite clearly these figures are sensitive to the assumptions and a more thorough investigation will require additional and more complete data.

Turning to the discussion of *benefits* from the various training programs being considered, the "Framework" paper stated:

The benefits from any government program would be the discounted increase in the national product attributable to that program. In a manpower retraining program, the most obvious source of benefits is the differential earnings of the trainees after completion of a retraining program. Differential earnings of trainees are not, however, by any means a perfect measure of the benefits of a Federal retraining program.

---

[1] Historically, as of September, 1966 the Job Corps had spent $499,923,000 and "affected" 44,531 individuals at a cost of $11,226 per "affectee."

The most obvious concern is that training takes time (six months to two years), and that overall earnings presumably rise in both real and nominal terms in this period so that part of what shows up as an earnings differential may in reality be merely secular increase in earnings, thus not a program benefit.

A second problem relating to considering earnings differentials is that it implicitly assumes no impact on employment prospects for other members of the labor force. This is certainly not a valid assumption in its extreme form as the training program may . . . "merely shuffle the faces in the job queue." The other extreme (a complete shuffling) is not a likely solution, but it must be recognized that to some unknown extent, graduates from training programs do not obtain additional jobs, but simply take jobs away from other members of the labor force. For the present calculations, no estimates are made of the magnitude of this problem of reduced opportunities for the rest of labor force.

A third problem regarding pre- and post-earnings differentials results from the necessity of observing a pattern over a relatively short period (often less than one year) and then projecting it into the distant future. Are the differentials explosive in the sense of constantly widening or stagnating in the sense of having a brief life and then disappearing? This is the important question of whether the skills and experience acquired in the program will enhance the individual's expected earnings for the rest of his life, or whether it is merely a one shot benefit and he will be expected to return to his old earnings pattern.

Two sets of calculations will be made to account for this difficulty. The first set of calculations will take a relatively simple approach and assume that any earnings differentials that occur will be of a constant absolute amount over a finite time period. Using the various cost indices constructed in the previous section, the required absolute earnings differentials will be calculated. This approach will be labeled the simple *annuity* approach.

The second and more ambitious analysis will attempt to functionally relate education and the observed patterns of earnings streams, and then compute the degree to which the enrollee population's characteristics must be changed in order to enhance their expected time path of income in a manner great enough to justify the costs of the programs. This analysis will be labeled the *enhanced educational characteristics* approach.

It is hoped that both of these approaches will give future evaluators a set of criteria for program evaluation. In both sets of calculations a 5 percent social rate of discount is used. As yet, the determination of a proper social rate of discount is an unresolved matter and the selection of 5 percent can be justified on the grounds of reasonableness and workability. The conclusions of the analysis are sensitive to the choice of the discount rate.

The annuity approach consisted of finding that constant stream of differential earnings which, if discounted at 5 per cent, would be equal to the total cost of the program. The results of the "Framework" paper's calculations are shown in Exhibit 4. Two different time horizons were used—fifteen years and thirty years.

The enhanced educational characteristics approach resulted in, for each program, the derivation of the incremental number of years of educational achievement that the program would have to give the enrollee in order to justify the program's costs per enrollee. A summary of the "Framework" paper's findings is presented in Exhibit 5. A brief simplified outline of the paper's methodology follows.

Census data were obtained showing expected annual earnings by age and race for males aged eighteen to twenty-four through fifty-five to sixty-four, classified according to years of school. The paper stated:

The total expected earnings for someone with an 8th grade education were then subtracted from those of someone with a 12th grade education, and the remainder was divided by 4 to arrive at a rough approximation of the value (in terms of additional expected earnings) of a year's education at a given age level. The 1959 numbers were then inflated by the 1.22 coefficient to arrive at more realistic 1965 figures. Quite clearly other things such as intelligence, motivation, and family resources are interrelated with additional schooling so that it is unrealistic to attribute entire observed earnings differentials to education. At present, several attempts have been made to standardize for other characteristics and while precise calculations are clearly untenable for the present study, the Denison 60 percent factor will be used as the coefficient of adjustment for differences in education levels, meaning that 60 percent of the observed higher income differences by education is attributable to the education and the other 40 percent is explained by other factors.

The value of an additional year's schooling (at high school level) in terms of increased annual earnings power was then plotted against age for both whites and non-whites. Then, using statistical correlation techniques mathematical functions were found which would fit each of the observed plots. The value of an additional year's schooling was seen to be less at all ages for non-whites than for whites. The paper made the assumption that "nonwhites received a lower return on time spent in school due to inferior education and not economic discrimination." It was also assumed that identical training would be provided to all enrollees in a particular program, and that this training would have the same payoff as white education for all participants regardless of race. Accordingly, the mathematical function for whites was adopted.

This function was refined in several respects. For example, it was modified to recognize that the number of years elapsed from the time of receipt of education or training was a better predictor of an individual's differential earnings than his age *per se*. A function was then derived which would enable the analyst to compute the present value of an incremental year's education for an individual, given the individual's age and the age at which training occurred. This permitted the calculation of data such as the following.

Trained at age	Work till age	Present value of one year's education
18	65	$4,279
30	65	3,528
45	65	1,872
55	65	1,198

The final step was to divide the real resource program costs of the programs by the value of a year's education to arrive at an estimate of the degree to which enrollee characteristics would have to be changed to justify the costs of each program. For the purposes of calculation the average entrant into the Job Corps, NYC, and OJT-Youth programs was assumed to be eighteen years old; calculations were performed for the remaining adult programs assuming entry at thirty years and forty-five years. As noted above, the results are summarized in Exhibit 5.

"BENEFIT-COST STUDY OF JOB CORPS"

In May, 1967 a staff member of RPP&E completed a paper entitled "Benefit-Cost Study of Job Corps." This Job Corps Study resulted in benefit-cost ratios ranging from 0.58 to 1.88, with the interval from 1.05 to 1.69 suggested as "encompassing a set of ratios that are conservative and realistic." The study noted that "an important limitation of this study is that the sole measure of benefits is the improvement in labor market earnings of the Corpsmen. The measure of benefits should be considered, therefore, as a lower bound."

The overall methodology used in the Job Corps study may be summarized as follows.

The costs include an allowance for the overhead expenses of Job Corps and for the earnings foregone by the Corpsmen during the time spent in Job Corps. The appraised value of the work projects performed at the conservation centers are subtracted from the costs. Finally, the value of transfer payments made to the Corpsmen (and their parents) has been deducted from the costs. Transfer payments are not included because they do not require any net increase in resource use; rather they involve expenditures on consumption that would be spent if there were no program—the Corpsmen eat meals at the center (at the taxpayers' expense) instead of meals at home; they spend their allowance on various commodities and taxpayers buy fewer commodities; and so on. The transfer payments are highly relevant to the question of *who* is picking up the tab on the program, but not to the question of *what* is the rate of return on the program.

In computing benefits, two alternative measures of earnings improvements were used. One

. . . is based on the educational gains achieved in Job Corps in conjunction with the relations between education and lifetime earnings that have been estimated in the best statistical studies available. The second measure of earnings improvement is based on a direct comparison of wages currently earned by ex-Corpsmen with the wages of a comparable group of youth who had no Job Corps experience.

Costs

Exhibit 6 presents a summary of the study's calculation of the real resource costs of the Job Corps program per enrollee, for stays of five,[2] six, nine, and twelve months. Comments on the derivation of some of the figures in Exhibit 6 follow.

Column 1: This column shows $7,142 as the average center operating costs for a man-year in the Job Corps. The Job Corps operated four types of center with varying average annual man-year operating costs—Federal Conservation Centers ($6,016), State Conservation Centers ($5,088), Men's Urban Centers ($7,956), and Women's Urban Centers ($8,904). The average

---

[2] Recent data indicated the average length of stay in the Job Corps was 5 months.

man-year operating costs for the four types of centers were weighted by the number of man-years of use of each type, resulting in a weighted average Job Corps Center operating cost of $7,142 per man-year.

Average center variable costs of $2,520 per man-year were subtracted from $7,142 to give $4,622; this latter figure was regarded by the study as representing fixed costs per man-year. The figure of $2,520 comprised $1,220 for pay, allowance, and allotments to Job Corpsmen, and $1,320 for such items as clothing, subsistence, medical, education, and recreational supplies and services. Both variable and fixed costs were adjusted in the study to take account of less than 100 per cent capacity utilization of the centers. For example, assuming a 90 per cent utili-

zation for an average stay of six months, the figure for center operating costs per enrollee for a six-month stay in the Job Corps was calculated as follows.

Formula I

$$\$7,142 - (.50) \times (\$2,520) - (.90) \times (.50) \times (\$4,622) = \$3,802.$$

The figures in Column 1 for stays of nine months and five months were similarly derived.

Column 2: The capital costs per manyear were determined as follows. First, a total annual capital cost for all Job Corps centers was derived as shown in Table 1 below.

The figure of $17,719,000 was then divided by 24,348, the number of man-years in the Job Corps for the year ending April 1, 1967, to give an aver-

TABLE 1

CALCULATION OF TOTAL ANNUAL JOB CORPS CENTER CAPITAL COST
(FROM "BENEFIT-COST STUDY OF THE JOB CORPS")

	Type of Centers			
	Men's Urban	Women's Urban	Conservation	Total
Construction plus rehabilitation ($000)	$27,848	$3,926	$68,480	$100,254 (A)
Life of item (years)	20	7	15	—
Straight-line depreciation per year	1,392	561	4,565	6,518 (B)
Accountable equipment ($000)	13,363	3,101	17,691	35,360 (C)
Life of item (years)	8	8	8	—
Straight-line depreciation per year				4,420 (D)
Total capital investment costs ($000) (A) + (C)				135,614
Cost of capital at 5 percent ($000)				6,781 (E)
Straight-line depreciation of total (B) + (D) ($000)				10,938 (F)
Depreciation plus capital cost per year (E) + (F) ($000)				17,719

Source: Adapted from Job Corps Monthly Center Costs Reports, special property study and agency accounting records.

age capital cost per man-year of $700. This figure was then added to the average center operating costs of $7,142 from Column 1 to give $7,842 in Column 2. By using the procedure employed in Formula I above, the figure of $700 per man-year was modified for stays of nine, six, and five months, and the results subtracted from the appropriate figure in Column 1 to give the remaining figures in Column 2.

Column 3: Administrative costs included items such as enrollee recruitment, screening, placement, payroll administration, and central and regional headquarters expenses. They amounted to an average of $603 per man-year for the Job Corps as a whole. The corresponding amounts for stays of less than 12 months were calculated using the same method as in Formula I on page 319.

Column 4: Transfer payments included clothing, subsistence, and allowances, and amounted to $1,930 per man-year. Again, amounts corresponding to stays of less than twelve months were calculated using the method of Formula I.

Column 5: The method used to derive the earnings foregone by Job Corpsmen during their stay in the Job Corps is shown below in an excerpt from the study.

Basis for Estimating Foregone Earnings for Corpsmen While Enrolled in Job Corps

1. The pre-Job Corps median wage reported in surveys by Louis Harris, Inc., was $1.17 for all persons—graduates, drop-outs, discharged persons, and "No-Shows."

2. The median wage reported by all "No-Shows" after an average lapse of 16 months since their decision not to enter Job Corps was $1.42.

3. The median wage reported by late "No-Shows" after an average lapse of 7 months since their decision not to enter Job Corps was $1.31.

4. The wages reported in items 1. and 3. indicate the average gain in wages is 2 cents per hour per month.

5. The reported rate of "not-working" —approximately 40 percent —is equivalent to working an average of 24 hours a week (out of 40 hours).[3]

Items 4. and 5. lead to the following tabulations.

Months in Job Corps	Starting Wage	Predicted Ending Wage	Average Wage [a]	Average Weekly Wage (for 24 hours)	Average Total Earnings [b]
12	$1.17	$1.41	$1.29	$30.96	$1,610
9	1.17	1.35	1.26	30.24	1,179
6	1.17	1.29	1.23	29.52	768
5	1.17	1.27	1.22	29.28	644

[a] To derive the average, a straight-line interpolation was made between the starting and ending wages.
[b] The average total earnings are estimates of what the average Corpsman could have earned during the time he spent in Job Corps had he not entered Job Corps.

[3] The assumption of a 40% "not working" rate in Item 5 above was based on three factors:
(a) the unemployment rate reported among the Corpsmen before Job Corps was 42%;
(b) the unemployment rate among "no shows" in the post-Job Corps period was 40%;
(c) the unemployment rate among ex-Corpsmen in February 1967 was 36%.

Column 6: The study explained the derivation of the Column 6 figures [in Exhibit 6] as follows:

The appraised value of the work projects in conservation centers is $1,665 per manyear. Since about 38 percent of the Corpsmen were at conservation centers during the recent period, the value of the work projects distributed across all Corpsmen is $633 for a 12-month period. For periods less than 12 months, a proportionate reduction was used. It is worth noting that the implicit wage earned by the Corpsmen on these projects was only 80 cents an hour. Therefore, it is unlikely that the value of work projects are overstated.

Benefits

Exhibit 7 summarizes the study's estimates of benefits of Job Corps. Two different approaches are presented in Exhibit 7; the first was described in the study as follows:

Wage Gains. The measure of wage gains was derived from the data of two surveys by Louis Harris, Inc. One survey involved a sample of all types of terminations from Job Corps—graduates and dropouts. The other survey obtained data on "no shows"—youths who were scheduled to enroll in Job Corps but who did not. The pre and post wage rates of the ex-Corpsmen are determined and the difference is attributable to Job Corps after adjusting for an expected wage increase over the duration of the Job Corps period, using the wage data for the "no shows" to make the adjustment.

Exhibit 8 shows how the present value gains of $5,124 (3 per cent) and $3,666 (5 per cent) presented in Exhibit 7 were derived.

The second approach to estimating the benefits of the Job Corps relied on tests which had shown that a nine-month's stay in the Job Corps had the effect of increasing Corpsmen's skills in reading and mathematics by an amount equivalent to 1.625 years of schooling. The study then proceeded to relate this observed increase in Corpsmen's educational skills to an expected increase in the present value of their lifetime earnings. This process was described in the study as "an exceedingly complex task." Excerpts from the study describing the methodology employed are presented in Appendix A. A discussion of the choice of discount rates used in the study (3 per cent and 5 per cent) is presented in Appendix B.

Exhibit 9 presents the calculation of benefit-cost ratios performed by matching each cell in Exhibit 7 with the Column 6 cost estimates in Exhibit 6.

QUESTIONS

1. Evaluate the approaches used by the authors of the three papers described in the case, with particular reference to the Job Corps.

2. Tabulate the most significant methodological differences between the three papers.

3. Prepare to discuss how to improve the evaluation of anti-poverty programs such as Job Corps.

EXHIBIT 1

OFFICE OF ECONOMIC OPPORTUNITY

Comparison of Job Corps and Neighborhood Youth Corps Programs
(from August 1966 paper by Director of RPP&E)

	Job Corps*	Out-of-School Neighborhood Youth Corps
I. *Costs:*		
a. Steady State Costs Per Graduate	$6,980	$1,000†
b. Assumed Success‡ Rate Per Graduate	80%	50%
c. Cost Per Success		
(Cost per graduate ÷ success rate)	$8,725	$2,200
II. *Computation Equalizing Payback Period for These Costs:*		
d. Equalized Payback Period§	5.1 years	5.1 years
e. Annual Earnings Gain = Costs/Payback (Rounded)	$1,700	$ 430
f. Estimated Hourly Wage Gain	$ .60 =	$ .25 =
Due to Program	$ 1.60 − $1.00	$ 1.25 − $1.00
g. Assumed Annual Hours Worked Previous to Program	1,500 hours	1,500 hours
h. Annual Hours Worked After Program (Computed to equalize payback period)	2,000 hours	1,544 hours

* Job Corps data estimated from preliminary sample.
† Because NYC is a Work Experience Program rather than a training program like JC, it is assumed that all enrollees are graduates having received some benefit, therefore the costs per graduate are the same as the costs per enrollee.
‡ Success is defined as holding a good steady job. A good job is defined as semi-skilled or better.
§ Neighborhood Youth Corps payback period set equal to calculated Job Corps period.

EXHIBIT 2

OFFICE OF ECONOMIC OPPORTUNITY

Summary of Projected Program and Real Resource Costs from RPP&E Staff Paper:
"A Framework for Evaluation of Training Programs"

	MDTA				
	Institutional			OJT [4]	
	Full-Time		Upgrading		
	Adult	Youth		Adult	Youth
Program cost	2,630	1,994	708	1,719	1,396
Opportunity cost	1,808	1,831 [1]	[2]	907	611 [1]
Total cost	4,438	3,825	708	2,626	2,007
Less trainee remuneration	(2,160)	(1,350)	(468)	(1,008)	(630)
Real resource cost	2,278	2,475	240	1,618	1,377

	Adult Work Training	Rural Adult	NYC		Job Corps
			Out of School	In School	
Program cost	4,052	5,607	4,405	650	5,625
Opportunity cost	1,808 [3]	1,808 [3]	1,831	1,396	743
Total cost	5,860	7,415	6,236	2,046	6,368
Less trainee remuneration	(3,702)	(3,702)	(3,702)	(612)	(1,080)
Real resource cost	1,958	3,713	2,534	1,434	5,288

[1] Assumed equal to opportunity cost of NYC out of school.
[2] Assumed equal to zero since classes held at night.
[3] Assumed equal to opportunity cost of OJT individual.
[4] Opportunity cost equals only one-fourth of a year's expected income for an OJT trainee because 14 weeks are spent in training, and the remaining time is spent working with presumably no opportunity cost.

NOTE: The enrollee characteristics were often not displayed in a manner to compute opportunity costs of the various programs, primarily due to the detail of program mix for the future. Opportunity costs were assigned to taking the opportunity cost of the most likely population.

EXHIBIT 3

OFFICE OF ECONOMIC OPPORTUNITY

*Alternative Real Resource Cost * Indices of Federal Training Programs from RPP&E Staff Paper:
"A Framework for Evaluation of Training Programs"*

Program	Cost per Trainee	Cost per Graduate	Cost per Placement	Cost per Affectee
MDTA				
Institutional				
Full-time				
Adult	2,278	4,298	5,811	4,075
Youth	2,475	4,670	6,314	4,428
Upgrading	240	453	612	429
OJT				
Adult	1,618	2,697	3,249	2,564
Youth	1,377	2,295	2,765	2,182
Adult work training	1,958	3,906	5,221	3,133
Rural adult	3,713	7,426	9,901	5,936
NYC				
In-school	1,434	2,868	4,097	3,019
Out-of-school	2,534	3,620	5,631	3,334
Job Corps	5,288	7,051	8,813	8,135

* i.e., including the addition of opportunity costs of removing enrollees from the labor force and the subtraction of enrollee remuneration.

EXHIBIT 4

OFFICE OF ECONOMIC OPPORTUNITY

Required Additional Annual Earnings to Justify Program Resource Costs at 5% Discount Rate from RPP&E Staff Paper: "A Framework for Evaluation of Training Programs"

Program	15-Year Horizon				30-Year Horizon			
	Per Trainee	Per Graduate	Per Success	Per Affectee	Per Trainee	Per Graduate	Per Success	Per Affectee
MDTA								
Institutional								
Full-time								
Adult	$219	$414	$560	$393	$148	$280	$378	$266
Youth	238	450	608	427	161	304	411	289
Upgrading	23	44	59	41	16	30	40	28
OJT								
Adult	155	259	312	247	105	175	211	167
Youth	132	221	266	210	89	149	180	142
Adult work training	188	376	502	301	127	254	339	203
Rural adult	357	714	952	571	241	482	643	386
NYC								
In-school	138	276	394	290	93	186	266	196
Out-of-school	244	348	541	321	165	235	366	217
Job Corps	508	675	847	772	343	456	572	522

EXHIBIT 5

OFFICE OF ECONOMIC OPPORTUNITY

*Necessary Adjustment in Education Characteristics to Justify Program Real Resource Costs
(In Years of Educational Achievement) from RPP&E Staff Paper:
"A Framework for Evaluation of Training Programs"*

Program	Per Trainee		Per Graduate		Per Placement		Per Affectee	
	A*	B*	A*	B*	A*	B*	A*	B*
MDTA								
Institutional								
Full-time								
Adult	.65	1.22	1.22	2.30	1.65	3.10	1.16	2.18
Youth	.56	—	1.09	—	1.48	—	1.03	—
Upgrading	.07	.13	.13	.24	.17	.33	.12	.22
OJT								
Adult	.46	.86	.76	1.44	.92	1.74	.73	1.37
Youth	.32	—	.54	—	.65	—	.51	—
Adult work training	.55	1.05	1.11	2.09	1.48	2.79	.89	1.67
Rural adult	1.05	1.98	2.10	3.96	2.81	5.29	1.68	3.17
NYC								
In-school	.34	—	.68	—	.96	—	.71	—
Out-of-school	.59	—	.85	—	1.32	—	.78	—
Job Corps	1.24	—	1.65	—	2.06	—	1.90	—

* All adult programs are computed on the assumption of a 30 year old and 45 year old
input, corresponding to columns A and B.

EXHIBIT 6

OFFICE OF ECONOMIC OPPORTUNITY

Estimated Job Corps Costs from "Benefit-Cost Study of Job Corps"

Months in Job Corps	Reported Statutory Costs [a] (1)	Including Capital Costs [b] (2)	Including Administrative Costs Outside the Centers [c] (3)	Excluding Transfer Payments [d] (4)	Plus Foregone Earnings [e] (5)	Minus Value of Work Projects [f] (6)
12	$7,142	$7,842	$8,445	$6,515	$8,125	$7,492
9	5,414	5,948	6,408	4,960	6,139	5,664
6	3,802	4,187	4,519	3,554	4,332	4,005
5	3,300	3,641	3,934	3,130	3,774	3,510

[a] Costs of operating centers excluding capital costs.
[b] $700 per Corpsman for 12 months.
[c] $603 per Corpsman for 12 months.
[d] $1,930 per Corpsman for 12 months, which covers food, clothing, and allowances.
[e] $1,610 per Corpsman for 12 months. Estimates of the earnings the Corpsman *could have
made* during the time spent in Job Corps.
[f] $633 per Corpsmen for 12 months.

EXHIBIT 7

OFFICE OF ECONOMIC OPPORTUNITY

Estimates of Benefits from "Benefit-Cost Study of Job Corps"

Months in Job Corps and Discount Factor	Educational Gains [g]				Wage Gains [l]
	White/South Index [h]		Total Index [h]		All Corps-men Compared to the "Late" No-Show Group [m]
	Grade Level Basis				
	6–8 [i]	8–10 [i]	6–8 [i]	8–10 [i]	
9 months:					
3 percent [j]	$7,502	$10,655	$6,612	$8,073	
5 percent	4,769	7,447	3,971	5,570	
5 months:					
3 percent [j]	4,165	5,915	3,671	4,482	$5,124
5 percent	2,648	4,135	2,205	3,092	3,666

[g] Valuation of gains in Corpsmen's educational achievement.
[h] Index based on data for white Southern males or on all males.
[i] Assumed grade intervals over which the gains are made.
[j] Rate used to discount future earnings.
[l] Survey reported wage gains of Corpsmen.
[m] Late "No-Shows" are an assumed control group.

NOTE: In the original Benefit-Cost Study, the author also performed special calculations based on an exponential rate of educational achievement, i.e., starts slow and gains more rapidly in the final months.

EXHIBIT 8

OFFICE OF ECONOMIC OPPORTUNITY

Derivation of Present Value of Wage Gains Shown in Exhibit 7 from
"Benefit-Cost Study of Job Corps"

WAGE DATA FOR AUGUST 1966 TERMINEES FROM JOB CORPS AND "NO SHOWS" FROM 1966: PRE AND POST JOB CORPS EXPERIENCE

	Graduates	Dropouts	Late No-Shows
Pre Job Corps Wage	$1.14/hr	$1.19/hr	$1.17/hr
Wage in February 1967 (six months after leaving Job Corps)	1.48	1.40	1,31
Difference	+ .34	+ .21	+ .14
Net improvement allowing for the expected improvement shown by the "No-Shows"	+ .20	+ .07	
Weighted average of the improvement (using the proportion of graduates and dropouts as weights)	$0.12		

TRANSLATION OF WAGE GAIN TO ANNUAL AND LIFETIME-PRESENT-VALUE MEASURES

Assumed Unemployment Rate	Equivalent Hours per Week	Annual Earnings Differential (Hours × 12 cents × 52)	Present Value of Earnings Increase for 48 Years Discounted at:	
			3%	5%
25 percent	30	$187.20	$4,730	$3,384
18¾ percent	32.5	202.80	5,124*	3,666*
12½ percent	35	218.40	5,518	3,948
0 percent	30	259.60	6,559	4,693

* Values chosen as most appropriate and entered in Exhibit 7. An unemployment rate of 18¾ percent is probably less than that which will apply to the ex-Corpsmen in the first few years after leaving Job Corps, but is probably twice as high as the rate that will apply to the years between the ages of 25 and 50.

NOTE: The "Late No-Shows" were selected from all "No-Shows" to act as a control group because it was believed important to keep the time spent in the labor market approximately equal for the control group and the Corpsmen group.

EXHIBIT 9

OFFICE OF ECONOMIC OPPORTUNITY (A)

Summary of Benefit-Cost Ratios from "Benefit-Cost Study of Job Corps"

Row	Costs Basis, Months in Job Corps, and Discount Factor	Educational Gains				Wage Gains
		White/South		Total Index		
		6–8	8–10	6–8	8–10	
	9 months:					
1.	3 percent	1.32	1.88	1.17	1.43	
2.	5 percent	.84	1.31	.70	.98	
	5 months:					
3.	3 percent	1.18	1.69	1.05	1.28	1.45
4.	5 percent	.75	1.18	.63	.88	1.04

APPENDIX A

OFFICE OF ECONOMIC OPPORTUNITY

Calculation of Benefits Using Education Gains Approach (from "Benefit-Cost Study of Job Corps")

All the benefit calculations using educational data are based on data for males only. One justification for this simplification is that males accounted for over 90 percent of the Corpsmen man-months in the period analyzed in this study, and for 95 percent of the respondents in the Harris surveys. The assumption that the educational gains are the same for women as men is reasonable, although the translation to wage gains is somewhat ambiguous. On the one hand, the levels of earnings for working women are lower than those for men. On the other hand, the educational (and vocational) training may encourage the women to work more. But this overstates the benefits to the extent that more work really means more market work and less homework. The earnings ability of the women in Job Corps may be increased substantially in a relative sense but it is difficult to interpret this, given the difficulties in the meaning of work for women.

Estimating the increase in earnings that results from additional years of schooling is an exceedingly complex task. Simply to show the statistical association between education and earnings at a moment-in-time is difficult because of the many intervening variables which need to be 'held constant.' To draw inferences for the population on the basis of the sample evidence, which is the next step, is seriously hindered by the lack of experimental controls over the administration of 'treatments' (that is, education) and the operation of 'effects' (that is, earnings). Finally, the projection years hence of an education-earnings relation detected at one point in time—the assumption that the quantitative effects observed now will similarly hold in the future—is hazardous.

We believe, however, that previous studies have made sufficient progress in overcoming these difficulties to permit reasonably accurate estimates of the effects of educational attainment on earnings and employment in the labor market. The most recent and most thorough study is by Giora Hanoch.

The data source for Hanoch's study was the huge One-in-1,000 sample of the 1960 census. Briefly, the technique used by Hanoch involved measuring the earnings-education relationship for 28 groups of males (white, nonwhite, North, South, and seven age groups). Other variables controlled were the following: (a) age, (b) type of residence (urban, rural, etc.), (c) size of place of residence, (d) size of family, (e) presence of children, (f) mobility status, (g) marital status, (h) living alone, (i) foreign born, and (j) Southern born. For more details about the definitions of the variables used in the analysis and about the statistical procedures used, the interested reader is urged to examine Hanoch's study. The important point to be indicated here is that the analysis was a careful application of modern econometric techniques. Although there are a number of reasons why the estimated effect of education on earnings made by Hanoch may be biased, and anyone is free to speculate whether the upward biases do or do not cancel the downward biases, the results Hanoch obtained do give a reasonable basis for determining the gain in earnings that could be expected as a consequence of the gain in educational attainment achieved in Job Corps. See Table 2 for the basic age-education-earnings relations taken from Hanoch's thesis which are used in this paper.

White/South Index and Total Index. One set of tabulations in Hanoch's study consisted of four age-earning profiles for: white and nonwhite males, living in the South and North. Within each color-region group the age-earning profile was shown for eight educational levels. The

years-of-schooling categories range from 0–4 years to 17 years or more.

With these data we can determine the differences in lifetime earnings of, for example, white males living in the North with 5–7 years of schooling completed compared with those with 8 years of schooling completed. Let us examine the question of which region-color groups would best represent the Job Corps population.

The young men in the Job Corps are drawn from all over the country, although there is a slight overrepresentation of the South, which reflects the higher incidence of poverty in that region. The proportion nonwhite in the Corps has fluctuated around 40 to 50 percent during the past year, and 50 percent was assumed for calculations in this study. A simple unweighted average of the earnings gains from the selected educational levels across all four region-color groups gives us estimates that reflect the actual Job Corps population. This average is called the 'Total Index.'

Note that the Total Index gives a weight of 50 percent to the education-earnings estimates for nonwhites, even though the sample was only 10 percent as large as the white sample (since 10 percent is the population proportion of nonwhites). The relatively small sample size for the nonwhite estimates is one drawback to the 'Total Index.' Indeed, the conclusion reached by Hanoch in his study was that the nonwhite figures were unreliable for a number of subgroups because of several factors, including the smaller sample size, but also, and probably more importantly, because of greater response errors in the information on education and earnings. Another reason the nonwhite data is unsatisfactory for estimating an education-earnings relation is the likelihood that years-of-schooling completed is a weak measure of actual educational attainment because of the great variability in quality of nonwhite schooling. By contrast, the measure of years-of-schooling equivalency for the ed-ucational gains achieved in Job Corps is based on the hard evidence of actual tests. We would like to know the relation between actual educational achievement and earnings. But because years of school-ing, especially for nonwhite, inaccurately measures educational achievement, we will underestimate its quantitative effect on earnings when using the 'Total Index.'

These shortcomings of the Total Index prompted a search for alternative meas-ures of the education-earnings relation. The second basis for estimating the edu-cation-earnings relation was to use the data for white males living in the South, along with a downward adjustment to reflect the combined proportions of North-ern whites and nonwhites in Job Corps. (See Table 1.) The use of white data

TABLE 1—PROCEDURE FOR ADJUSTING THE EARNINGS OF WHITE/SOUTHERN MALES TO REPRESENT ALL MALES

I. BASIC EARNINGS DATA AS OF 1959

Years of Schooling Completed	8		9–11	
Region	North	South	North	South
Color and Age Group:				
White, 18–24	2,650	1,984	2,588	2,132
White, 25–64	4,731	3,857	5,341	4,556
Nonwhite, 18–24	2,352	1,171	2,139	1,256
Nonwhite, 25–64	3,802	2,437	4,042	2,587

II. EARNINGS OF AGE-COLOR-REGION GROUP AS A RATIO OF THE WHITE/SOUTH GROUP

(Earnings Ratios, with White/South in denominator)	8 years schooling	Average for all ages *	9–11 years schooling	Average for all ages *
North, White, 18–24	1.34	1.28	1.21	1.19
North, White, 25–64	1.23		1.17	
North, Nonwhite, 18–24	1.14	1.11	1.00	.94
North, Nonwhite, 25–64	.99		.89	
South, Nonwhite, 18–24	.59	.61	.59	.58
South, Nonwhite, 25–26	.63		.57	

III. COMPUTATION OF A SINGLE INDEX NUMBER USING THE RATIOS OF STEP II TO ADJUST THE WHITE/SOUTH EARNINGS

Average of ratios of all color-region-education groups, based on the ratios shown in Step II.

8 years measure

9–11 years measure

$$\frac{1.28 + 1.11 + .61 + 1.00 \dagger}{4} = 1.00 \quad \text{and} \quad \frac{1.19 + .94 + .58 + 1.00 \dagger}{4} = .9275$$

and averaging over both educational measures we have:

$$\frac{1.00 + .9275}{2} = .964$$

* The average gives almost equal weight to the age periods 18–24 and 25–64 to reflect the discount rate, which lessens the importance of earnings in the later ages and offsets the larger number of years.

† The ratio of White/South earnings to itself is, of course, unity.

TABLE 2—BASIC DATA FOR ESTIMATING THE PRESENT VALUE OF THE INCREASE IN EARNINGS FROM INCREASED EDUCATIONAL ATTAINMENT [1]

PANEL A: AGE-EARNINGS PROFILES

Net Earnings Differentials in 1959 of Males Whose Years of Schooling Completed are 6th, 8th, and 10th Grades, by Age, Color, and Region [8]

Age (1)	Age Interval (Number of Years in Parentheses) (2)	Years in the Future in Which Earnings Are Received [5] (3)	Whites in South		Whites in North		Nonwhites in South		Nonwhites in North	
			8–6 [9]	10–8 [9]	8–6	10–8	8–6	10–8	8–6	10–8
16		6	$−27 [10]	—	$91		$−194 [10]	—	$−591 [10]	—
18		7	−31	$225	101	$132	−216	$150	−692	$111
20	18–20 (2)	3	−31	229	103	135	−221	153	−752	140
22	20–22 (2)	5	83	224	170	218	−134	138	−646	207
24	22–24 (2)	7	197*	218*	237*	301*	−46*	122*	−537*	271*
27	24–26 (2)	9	367	211	338	426	84	99	−374	368
32	26–31 (5)	14	481	367	430	562	236	56	−183	452
37	31–36 (5)	19	339	776	412	589	289	7	−113	421
42	36–41 (5)	24	264	916	430	579	293	−34	−36	343
47	41–46 (5)	29	292	622	501	511	228	−63	50	196
52	46–51 (5)	34	385	428	506	561	269	−52	333	−120
57	51–56 (5)	39	573	375	414	786	474	16	911	−690
62	56–61 (5)	44	627	297	342	857	522	−2	1050	−743
67	61–66 (5)	49	185	185	299	697	335	−151	533	25

* The following figures show the actual estimated earnings given in Hanoch's study for 24 year-olds (as an illustration): actual estimated earnings at age 24 which lead to the differentials tabulated:

Years of School Completed	Whites in South	Whites in North	Nonwhites in South	Nonwhites in North
6th	$2,125	$2,610	$1,520	$2,483
8th	2,322	2,847	1,474	1,946
10th	2,540	3,148	1,596	2,217

Thus, the difference between 8th and 6th grade completers who are white Southerners is: 2,322–2,125 = 197.
[1] Numbered footnotes on page 333.

PANEL B: PRESENT VALUES OF INCREASES IN EARNINGS SHOWN IN PANEL A
FOR WHITE SOUTHERNERS AND FOR THE TOTAL

Discount Rate (percent)	White/South		Total (Unweighted Average of 4 Region-Color Groups)	
	6–8	8–10	6–8	8–10
1⅛ [11]	$11,989		11,042	
3	7,533	10,697	6,407	7,823
5	4,789	7,478	3,848	5,397

[2] The age listed in column (1) is the exact age at which the earnings were estimated. These earnings were assumed to apply to each year in the age interval given in column (2).

[3] For the earnings differential between 6th and 8th grade completers the age interval is the single year at age 17. No information is given for the earnings at age 16 for 10th grade completers.

[4] For the earnings differential between 6th and 8th grade completers the age interval is the single year at age 18. For the earnings differential between 8th and 10th grade completers the age interval is the two years over the ages 17 to18.

[5] The total amount of earnings in each interval was assumed to be received at the end of the interval, and, thus, the present value of earnings which would be received evenly over the interval is somewhat understated.

[6] One year hence for the 6–8th grade comparison.

[7] Two years hence for the 6–8th grade comparison; one year hence for the 8–10th grade comparison.

[8] The earnings differentials are shown for age, education, color, and region groups, and have been estimated holding constant (for "net of") the influences of: (a) age (by finer measures), (b) type of residence (urban, rural, etc.), (c) size of place of residence, (d) size of family, (e) presence of children, (f) mobility status, (g) marital status, (h) living alone, (i) foreign born, and (j) Southern born.

[9] Actual grade levels were 5–7 (instead of 6) and 9–11 (instead of 10).

[10] *All negative amounts in Panel A were changed to zero before computing the present values of the increased earnings from education.* Negative sums mean that for the age groups involved those with less education were making more than those with more education. There are several reasons for these anomalies—reasons which justify the procedure of substituting zero amounts for the negative amounts. In some instances, particularly at the youngest ages, a negative amount reflects the part-year earnings of the higher educated person which are due to leaving school during the year for which income is reported. Secondly, for young age groups, there may be some premium paid for the greater employment experience of the less educated person (who has left school earlier and worked longer). Finally, among older groups of nonwhites the anomaly may result from the combination of sampling variability, errors in reporting, and a low correlation between educational achievement and years of schooling completed. There may be instances, for example, in which a highly intelligent Negro recognizes that the school he attends is so bad that he is better off dropping out and working.

Since none of the reasons above are relevant to the educational achievement in Job Corps, there is no justification for using the negative amounts. Note that the use of zero amounts itself undoubtedly understates the earnings increases stemming from educational advances. Each time a zero is included, and for nonwhites in the North there are zeros for 24 years in the 8–6 comparison, we are assuming that *no* increase in earnings follows from an advance in education.

[11] The lowest rate of 1⅛ percent was used for calculating the benefit/cost ratios which were compared with water resource projects.

gives us the benefit of a much larger sample size, fewer response errors, and a more accurate estimate of the effect of *educational achievement* on earnings. The South was chosen to reflect generally lower paying labor markets (relative to the North) and a lower level of educational achievement for any given level of years of schooling completed (again, relative to the North). Both conditions apply to youth in Job Corps. Evidence for the lag in educational achievement of the South relative to the North, for both whites and nonwhites, is given in the "Coleman Report." The earnings computed on the basis of the White/South education-earnings relation were reduced by a factor of .964 to reflect the actual region-color composition of Job Corps— where, to simplify computations we use an unweighted average of the four region-color groups as the actual composition. This means, of course, that we assume the Job Corps has 25 percent each of the Northern nonwhites, Northern whites, Southern nonwhites, and Southern whites. It is likely that the average composition during the past year included more whites and more Northerners than these percentages provide. However, the correction would not make any significant change in the calculation of benefits—owing to a stronger relationship between education and earnings among Northerners and whites (compared to Southerners and nonwhites).

Grade Levels, 6–8 and 8–10. The incremental units of educational gains were applied over two intervals of completed years-of-schooling. The interval labeled '6–8' was between the category 5–7 years of school completed and the category 8 years of school completed. The second interval, '8–10' was from 8 years to the category 9–11 years-of-school completed. The average educational gain, translated into equivalent measures of years of schooling is, therefore, added to a base of either 6 years or 8 years.

The gain of 1.625 years which is achieved during the 9-months stay in Job Corps lifts the schooling of the Corpsmen to 7.625 or to 9.625 years, depending on the base chosen. In percentage terms the increase of 1.625 years amounts to 81.25 percent (1.625/2.00) of the gain in earnings associated with the intervals, 6–8 or 8–10.

The choice of the intervals, 6–8 and 9–10, was recommended by the two grade levels that characterize the entering Corpsmen: (1) an average of 9 years of school completed; (2) a level of reading and mathematics abilities at about the fifth grade.

If the trait of perseverance and the simple maturation that go with staying in school longer are the sources of the higher earnings that we see among higher educated youth (8th grade completers versus 6th, 10th grade completers versus 8th, etc.), then we should use the higher educational interval (8–10) for representing the Job Corps youth, since they have stayed in school 9 years. If, on the other hand, the earnings levels associated with different years-of-schooling reflect primarily educational achievement, then the lower interval (6–8) is appropriate. Our judgment is that the lower interval, 6–8, is a more realistic level over which to apply educational gains and to estimate earnings improvements for the Job Corps youth. Recall that the lower interval gave smaller gains on earnings and lower benefit/cost ratios. The tabulations of lifetime earnings differentials for the different educational groups are shown in Table 2 on pages 332–33.

Our reliance on the conservative estimates of gains from the 6–8 interval points up another reason for selecting the White/South group in the analysis. Individuals who have left school at the 6th grade are apt to be somewhat unusual, particularly those who have left in recent years. Using white Southerners instead of Northerners serves to minimize this disturbing element in the attempt to represent the Job Corps youth, since leaving school at an early age is more common in the South.

The present values shown in Panel B require three further steps to obtain the present values (used in the benefit cost calculations).

(1) Each amount was multiplied by 1.27 to allow for the average 27 percent increase in wages and salaries from 1959 to 1966. (See column 1, Table B-30, p. 248 of the *Economic Report of the President, 1967*.)

(2) Each amount was multiplied by the ratio of educational attainment in Job Corps to the 2-year interval of educational increase (between 6 and 8 or 8 and 10). Example: 5 months in Job Corps is expected to bring about an increase of .903 years of schooling (which is 5/9 of the 1.625 years gain reported for Corpsmen who stay 9 months). This leads to a factor of .4510 (= .903 divided by 2.000), which multiplies the present value sum.

(3) An additional adjustment factor for white/Southern earnings is .964 (see above).

APPENDIX B

OFFICE OF ECONOMIC OPPORTUNITY

Choice of Discount Rates (from "Benefit-Cost Study of Job Corps")

The interest rate used by government agencies in evaluating many of their investment projects is often between 3 and 4 percent; economists outside the government have more often used rates of 4–6 percent, although some cogent arguments have been made for rates as high as 9–10 percent. The investment in Job Corps is being evaluated in terms of the improvement in labor productivity of the Corpsmen, and I have argued that the rate used to discount future earnings from labor should allow for the secular (and, I would say, inevitable) growth in wage rates. For example, if earnings received 1 year hence are discounted by 5 percent *but* have increased in value by 2 percent, then the appropriate rate for discounting the future earnings is 3 percent.

A growth factor should not be attached to any set of prices measuring the benefits of the investment projects. Aside from the influences of inflation or deflation, product prices may rise or decline over time, and it is difficult to judge the expected long-run trend. As examples, the real prices of cars, TV's, and food have all moved both up and down over different extended periods of years, and it is likely that the secular trend of prices of these commodities (holding quality constant) is downward.

By contrast, when estimating future wages on the basis of current wages, a growth factor generally should be applied to the current wage levels. A secular rise in real wages deserves to be considered a sure bet over the near future in the United States. Rates of growth in output per employee (a measure of real wages) are listed below for several recent periods:

Years	1947–1965	1950–1965	1960–1965
Rate of growth of output per employee	2.5%	2.4%	3.1%

These growth rates are considerably higher than those that apply to longer time periods. The longest period for which data are available is 1909–1965, when the growth rate was 1.5 percent. For 1929–1965, the rate was 1.8 percent. However, periods that stretch further back in time are probably less reliable for projecting the near future, particularly since the earliest period includes the years of mass immigration to the United States and both periods include the catastrophic depression of the 1930's. Neither event is likely to be duplicated in the foreseeable future.

If we select a growth rate from the more recent periods, we might settle on 2.5 as an appropriate rate for projecting labor earnings. Using this rate, we need to make an additional adjustment before arriving at the 2 percent rate adopted in the analyses of the text. The need for the adjustment can be explained briefly. The growth rate of real wages is basically a composite of two ingredients: (a) the rise in the price of quality-constant labor (due in large part to a slower growth in the supply of labor than in the demand for labor); and (b) the increase in the quality of labor (due principally to increases in educational attainment). We want to allow for the secular growth stemming only from (a). Becker reduced the earnings growth rate by 25 percent, and I have used a 20 percent reduction factor to derive the growth rate of the price of labor of constant quality.

conclusion

John Haldi proposes some changes in emphasis and direction in the federal government's PPB system and discusses the program monitoring, evaluation, and control aspects of PPB. James R. Schlesinger considers the role of analysis in decision-making. Allen Schick examines the multiple purposes of budget systems (and suggests a role for PPB in the budget systems of the future) in a thought-provoking paper revised especially for this volume. The section concludes with excerpts from a brief report prepared by the Joint Economic Committee containing their evaluation of PPB, both its progress and its potentials.

Program Monitoring, Evaluation and Control

By
JOHN HALDI

On the basis of the experience gained through my personal involvement with the installation of PPB in the Government, I would like today to discuss what I consider to be the four most important points pertinent to the future development of the PPB system. Briefly, these are:

First, the PPB system should become a valuable aid for managerial control as well as for management decision-making; when fully developed, it is meant to be a complete system designed to help executives do a more effective job in managing their agencies or bureaus.

Second, given time to develop, the PPB system should produce more and better program information for Congress as well as for the executive branch.

Third, systematic program analysis will play two important roles in the PPB system: *evaluation* of existing, ongoing programs; and *appraisal* and development of new proposals.

Fourth, systematic program analysis, especially analysis of new programs and basic changes in existing programs, should and will become an increasingly valuable tool of Government decision-makers. As the capacity for good applied analysis develops, it will carry with it a considerable amount of initiative in both the legislative and budgetary processes.

Although full implementation of PPB throughout the Government is proceeding somewhat more slowly than I and others had hoped, we now have enough experience to see that the potential originally envisioned exists for all agencies. In fact, those agencies which are making the least progress with PPB probably have the most to gain from it. It should be understood that even today some of the details of PPB are not fully worked out; the total system is improving and evolving as we gain experience and learn from our mistakes. But as PPB continues to take root, it should play an increasingly important role in the budget process. Consequently, PPB should become in-

From *The Planning-Programming-Budgeting System: Progress and Potentials* (Hearings before the Subcommittee on Economy in Government of the Joint Economic Committee, Congress of the United States, 90th Congress, 1st Session, U.S. Government Printing Office, Washington, D.C., September 21, 1967).

creasingly important to Congress. Preparation for this hearing has forced me to collect my thoughts on the future and the potential congressional role more than in the past. There are several recommendations which the Joint Economic Committee and the Congress ought to consider. Briefly, they are:

First, Congress should consider adopting program budget structures for appropriations;

Second, Congress should consider holding budget hearings along program lines rather than strictly along bureau and appropriation lines;

Third, Congress should press agencies to develop better program control systems, with better information and better reports flowing to Congress;

Fourth, the Joint Economic Committee should consider holding hearings on the subject of national goals and objectives;

Fifth, Congress should create its own analytic staff which will be directly responsive to its own needs and which will act as a check on the quality of the analysis done by agencies; and

Sixth, Congress should become an important consumer of program analysis; competition in analysis should be encouraged and when differences emerge, as they almost invariably will, they should be aired before congressional committees.

Needless to say, these changes should be made judiciously, in some gradual fashion. For example, it is possible to start by having just one department present two budgets, one in PPB format and one in the customary appropriation, line-item format. When enough experience has been gained with the PPB format so that the two are equally familiar, the two can

then be compared on their merits. Similarly, it is possible to take one program area, and have each agency concerned with this area list its objectives, show what it is doing to achieve its stated objectives, and say how it thinks its efforts relate to those of other concerned agencies. The sample program area chosen for such an experiment could be large, such as "Health," or it could be smaller and somewhat more restricted, such as "Estuaries." [1]

Summing up my views about Congress and PPB:

Congress need have nothing to fear from adoption of the PPB system;

Congress should participate fully and demand that the PPB system be developed to the maximum extent possible; and

Congressional "participation" in PPB, to whatever extent it does materialize, should act as a healthy stimulant to development in the executive branch.

PPB SHOULD BECOME A VALUABLE AID FOR MANAGERIAL CONTROL AS WELL AS FOR DECISIONMAKING

The two primary goals of the PPB system are, in essence:

First, to help give the taxpayer the right Government programs; and

Second, to give him more from those programs—that is, more quantity or more quality of whatever the programs produce—for each dollar of taxes spent.

---

[1] The Interior Department admits to having more than five different bureaus concerned in one way or another with estuaries. Agriculture, the Corps of Engineers and perhaps other agencies are probably also concerned with some aspect of estuaries.

The Congress has often indicated its agreement with these general goals. But how can the PPB system achieve them? This is a fair question to ask, and the answer is: *By better management of Government programs.*

As used here, the term *management* is meant to be interpreted broadly. It includes, but goes far beyond, high-level decision-making. Our real interest lies in the end results achieved by our programs. Overall management and implementation are therefore important because, if the organization persists in carrying out badly all policies, decisions and strategies devised by top management, then even the best analysis and decisions will be somewhat thwarted. The PPB system has a great deal of potential for improving what might be called "managerial control"— the functions of budgeting, controlling, accounting, and information feedback —which affects considerably the way programs are executed. This potential tends to be frequently overlooked, however, as discussions about PPB often seem to narrow quickly to a debate over the role of analysis in governmental decision-making.

In any large organization, including Government agencies, the total management picture is a composite of the efforts of—

Executive management;

Line management; and

Staff:
Budget officers;
Financial managers;
Information managers; and
Planning groups.

Adoption of a program budget, which is one of the first steps in the installation of a PPB system, emphasizes the agency's major programs for reaching our national goals, such as Child Health Care, Crime Prevention, Outdoor Recreation, or Education for the Underprivileged. This emphasis on programs is important—more important than it may at first seem—because it provides a common ground for uniting and integrating the efforts of those who are trying, each in their own individual way, to contribute to better management. A common linkage via programs can greatly enhance the overall effectiveness of these complementary groups.[2] But, do not blow up this importance out of context, either. Let us all be clear that adoption of a program budget will not, by itself, result in any significant program changes. The definition of a program structure may be *necessary,* but is certainly *not sufficient* for achieving the desired end result—better design and execution of programs.

Thus a total PPB system should be viewed a tool, a device, a means, a system, or whatever you like to call it, for helping Government executives do a better job. In no sense does it replace either management or the decision-making function. Given time, as PPB develops into a complete system, it will offer the top executives of an agency:

---

[2] The emphasis on "programs" by a Government agency is analogous in many ways to the emphasis given "product lines" by many private firms. Thus program budgeting, program accounting, and program reporting are similar in many respects to product-line budgeting, product-line accounting, and product-line reporting, all of which are standard practices among many of our biggest and best managed corporations. PPB can be viewed simply as an attempt to get Government agencies to adopt the best management practices of our time.

Better program information and reports, including:

Better financial information;

Better statistical information; and

More integration of financial and statistical information.

Better methods of displaying comprehensively the program decisions which they make, including:

Estimates of program costs *and* program outputs; and

Making visible future implications of current decisions.

Better analyses of complex issues requiring top-level decisions and direction.

The relationship of these various components is shown somewhat more specifically in Figure 1, which indicates how the annual planning-programming-budgeting cycle should work in large Government agencies when the system is fully developed. As expected, the emphasis throughout Figure 1 is on programs. Moreover, although it is not clearly indicated in Figure 1, program evaluation and cost analysis are permanent, ongoing functions at all times, with information feedback and follow-up also on a recurrent basis. The view taken here, then, is that in its fully developed state PPB will become a *complete decision-making and control system* which includes analysis (systematic analysis, cost-effectiveness analysis, etc.), but it will be more than just analysis.

Proper installation of a complete PPB system in an agency will also help integrate the entire planning-budgeting progress reporting system in a much more meaningful way than has been achieved to date.[3] The purpose of this integration, of course, is to insure that (a) decisions to initiate or continue programs are based on meaningful evaluations of their costs and benefits, (b) the implications of program operations and costs in future years are considered along with annual budgets, and (c) provision is made for periodic reevaluation of programs in quantitative terms that can be compared with the stated program objectives.

Were it true that PPB is just analysis of selected issues, and no more, then PPB would not deserve to be labeled "A System." Moreover, there would have been no need for the Bureau of the Budget to require an investment of valuable time and resources by each agency to—

Define a program structure;

Define wherever possible measurable "outputs" for each element in the program structure;

See that good statistical data exist on these outputs;

Develop a multi-year Program and Financial Plan (PFP);

Display estimates of financial requirements *and* outputs for each program element for several years beyond the upcoming budget year;

Promulgate program change procedures,

Update and maintain the PFP on a current basis; and

Develop accounting backup and progress reporting support for the program structure adopted.

In short, a complete PPB approach is systematic in its treatment of each of these basic management functions:

Defining objectives;

Evaluating alternatives;

Developing plans; and

Maintaining control.

---

[3] A great deal of effort and cooperation from the people responsible for these functions is also required.

Obviously all of these functions have been performed in the past with varying degrees of success. The unique contribution of PPBS is welding these together in a consistent management framework.

For PPB to achieve its full potential as a management system will require a number of changes from the existing mode of operations. The Bureau of the Budget, for example, will need to—

First, require all budget submissions, including justification and backup material, to be submitted in program terms;

Second, conduct all budget reviews along program lines; and

Third, make its program decisions on the basis of the program submission and in terms of the program budget.

Figure 1. The Annual PPB Cycle in a Large Government Agency

1. *Do program analysis—*
   Evaluate existing programs (use progress reports—see step 5 below);
   Study new program proposals and alternatives; and
   Do analysis on a permanent, full-time, continuing basis.
2. *Agency management makes program recommendations or decisions:*
   Use studies from program evaluation and analysis (see step 1 above); and
   Obtain approval from Bureau of the Budget, the President, and Congress.
3. *Give budget allotments and directions to the "field organization"—both in program terms.*
4. *Programs are implemented by the field organization:*
   Each installation or "center"

should have financial responsibility for its activities;
Each center should be charged for all resources which it uses; and
The "system" should give field managers personal motivation to do the right thing.

5. *Progress reports (monthly or quarterly, say) on program performance flowback from the field organization:*
   Program costs;
   Program outputs; and
   Actual and planned program performance compared.
6. *Corrective top management action as necessary.*
7. *Agency management makes major program recommendations or decisions for the next year (that is, the budget cycle begins; evaluation and analysis are on a continuing basis).*

The Bureau of the Budget is moving more in this direction each year. Congress, too, has an important role to play. At a minimum, it should consider—

First, using the program budget structures for appropriations (after we have had another one to two years' experience with them); and

Second, conducting at least some of its hearings along program lines rather than strictly along bureau and appropriation account lines.

Since more than one agency or bureau is involved in many of our programs—major programs like health care, education, poverty or crime; and less major programs like outdoor recreation, estuaries, or water pollution—a systematic program approach should give congressional committees a much better perspective for considering appropriations requests. Undesirable duplication and overlap are more easily revealed in this way. Also, where agencies are involved in similar programs but, say, in different regions or areas, their performance can be more easily compared and they can be made to "compete" with one another in terms of vying to provide more value of output for each dollar of appropriations. In my opinion, this type of competition among Government agencies would be just as healthy a stimulant as is competition in the private sector of our economy.

PPB SHOULD PRODUCE BETTER PROGRAM INFORMATION

It was previously stated that a complete PPB system should lead to a substantial increase in more useful program information. I would like now to elaborate on this point.

I believe it is fair to say that in a number of Government agencies, perhaps most, financial records and statistical data are *not* now kept in ways that enable them to be brought together to assess the need for their programs, the results of their programs, or full program costs. This sort of information may seem rather basic, but when available such data are usually recorded separately and in non-comparable ways.

Often this sort of information is simply not available. Initiation of the PPB system, with its focus on "programs," has revealed extensive deficiencies in the data base of a number of agencies. For example, it would not be unusual to find financial records kept by appropriation account and by object class, with no explicit attempt to develop good program cost data at the field level (unless, when by purely fortuitous circumstances, appropriation and program accounts coincided). Moreover, in those agencies which do keep program cost records in field offices, it would not be unusual to find financial records collected along lines of the agency's districts and regions, whereas statistical information pertaining to the agency's programs may be recorded by county, along State lines, by standard metropolitan areas, or in some other way not at all consistent with the financial data which are available.

It may seem somewhat ironical that those Government agencies which spend much time recording and collecting statistical data cannot assemble consistent program information (costs related to other relevant measures) because the data are not in a useful form. However, this is a problem even in our more sophisticated agencies.

Other agencies have not had to worry about *comparability* because they simply lacked basic data. They have therefore had to start systematically collecting data rather than straightening out what they already had. The Bureau of Indian Affairs, for example, is now in the process of more accurately determining the number and economic characteristics of Indians living on the reservations; that is, BIA is taking a detailed census, reservation by reservation, for the first time.

Critics of PPB sometimes convey the impression that its practitioners are trying to put numbers on those intangible or imponderable elements which cannot be quantified, and which it is misleading to try and quantify. We are so far removed from this sort of thing, however, that such criticisms scarcely warrant response. As the example from the Bureau of Indian Affairs illustrates, initiation of the PPB system has encouraged agencies to do such fundamental things as count and describe their clientele groups and make a population forecast. Some professors have at times been surprised to discover that accurate population data were lacking for many foreign nations, and yet we are discovering similar "gaps" here at home.

It will take time to develop the data and the type of reports which a good PPB system should produce, but, as they evolve, such reports should be valuable aids to identification of program weaknesses and areas that can be improved. They should help managers at all levels do a better job and become more productive.

From the outset, it should be recognized that better information on program costs and outputs has important potential as a worthwhile control device. In time, such information should become an important supplement to the present controls on travel, personnel ceilings, vehicles, etc. Cost-output information will probably *not* replace these existing controls for some time to come, although conceivably it could.

The present system of controlling in some detail *inputs* or *object classes* without paying systematic attention to program *outputs* can lead to undesirable economic consequences. The present system does not provide a balanced picture. Even if tight controls on inputs

do force agencies to carry on their activities at minimum cost,[4] agencies are never forced to ask themselves whether they are pursuing the right activities, or the right *mix* of activities. Yet this is really a much more important question to ask. One of the ultimate paradoxes from our present approach usually occurs when Congress accuses an agency of not asking for sufficient money because some aspect of one of its programs is, by general agreement, lagging. It is quite possible, when this situation arises, that general priorities have shifted, but that the agency has not shifted its programs accordingly. The agency may be spending money elsewhere with virtually no results, or with relatively little effectiveness, and the resources represented by this money could, in theory at least, be transferred to the lagging part of the program. In fact, in this light the agency may already have too much money, rather than too little. But if tradition, political processes, or some other reason causes us to be absolutely wedded to the inefficient or inconsequential part of our programs, along with the more efficient and more important part, and if this *mix* cannot be changed, then of course the paradox is explained. The only way to get more of the desired result is by spending more total money, and of course the agency should have asked for more.

---

[4] Congressional controls on *inputs* usually do *not* achieve this result. And, moreover, the more individual inputs that are controlled, the more likely are we to get *less* economic efficiency.

Uses and Abuses of Analysis

By
JAMES R. SCHLESINGER

The Subcommittee's invitation to assess the role that analysis may play in governmental decisionmaking is gratifying for a number of reasons. In its current stocktaking, the Subcommittee is accomplishing something of a turnabout: the analysis of systems analysis. This evaluation takes place at a critical time. Like other offspring in American life, analysis has been absorbed into an environment which has been at once both too permissive and too resentful. There is ample evidence that such a pattern is beneficial to neither the offspring nor the environment. Currently there is a risk that reaction against what may be termed the exuberance of certain claims and activities of analysis could result in the discarding of the substantial benefits that analysis does offer. I shall be attempting to bring out the instances of undue gullibility as well as undue skepticism, but in so doing I should perhaps make my own position clear. My attitude has long been one of two-and-a-half cheers for systems analysis. I recognize—and have emphasized—its limitations. I will make no excuses for offenses committed in its name. But despite the limitations and distortions, I remain an unabashed, if qualified, defender of the value of analysis in policy formation.

In the pages that follow I shall deal with some salient issues regarding the role of analysis: its relation to decisions and decisionmakers, its functioning in a political environment where conflicting objectives exist, and its utility for improving the resource allocation process.

THE AUTHORITY OF ANALYSIS

Systems analysis has been variously defined. In the most ambitious formulation it has been described as "the application of scientific method, using that term in its broadest sense." Certain attributes of science—objectivity, openness, self-correctability, verifiability, etc.—are alleged to apply to systems analysis. Would that it were so, but realistically speaking such assertions must be rejected. Even for science—as those who are familiar with the history of scientific investigations will recognize—this represents a rather romanticized view. In science, however, competition takes the form of establishing hypotheses regarding the workings of the natural order. Evidence and experiments are reproducible, and institu-

Memorandum prepared for the Subcommittee on National Security and International Operations, Committee on Government Operations, United States Senate, April, 1968. James R. Schlesinger is a member of the Economics Department of the RAND Corporation.

tions and personalities consequently play a smaller long-run role. In scientific investigations the search for truth is by and large unfettered. By contrast, in the search for preferred policies such encumbrances as social values and goals, constraints, institutional requirements (both broad and narrow) pertain. Truth becomes only one of a number of conflicting objectives and, sad to relate, oftentimes a secondary one.

An alternative definition described systems analysis as "quantified common sense." By some expositors this definition has been treated as the equivalent of the earlier one, but is really quite distinct. However high the regard in which common sense, quantitative or otherwise, is held in the American community, it never has been regarded as synonymous with scientific method. Nonetheless, the definition is far more apt. Common sense, for example, will accept that within a complicated bureaucratic structure distortions inevitably creep into the process of acquiring and organizing evidence. What one sees depends upon where one sits —an earthy way of describing what is more elegantly referred to as cognitive limits. It may be inferred that a systems analysis shop attached to the Office of the Secretary of Defense will be quite responsive to the perceptions and prejudices of the Secretary and the institutional requirements of his Office. This should be no more surprising than that the Operations Analysis shop at Omaha will be influenced by the doctrine, present activities, and aspirations of the Strategic Air Command.

In the early years of the introduction of the PPB into the Department of Defense, faith in the ease with which scientific objectivity could be attained

tended to be high in OSD. For Service staffs, this was a rather painful period for rather invidious distinctions were drawn regarding *their* objectivity. In recent years an enormous change has taken place regarding the nature of the analytical dialogue. Undoubtedly this new attitude reflects experience and the growing awareness that past decisions and past commitments limit the openness and the freshness with which the OSD staff can address issues in controversy.

This new realism has been reflected in a number of ways. Especially in private appraisals analysis has been justified with increasing frequency and frankness as part of an adversary proceeding. But such an interpretation is symptomatic of a substantial change. Whatever the merits of an adversary procedure—and these are substantial where there exist clashes of interests and goals and where evidence is difficult to unearth—no one has ever suggested that adversaries seek to be wholly objective. One may hope that the result will be the elucidation of the best possible case for and the best possible case against. But, unfortunately, the emphasis tends to shift to a search for the winning argument as opposed to the correct conclusion. In view of the uneven distribution of debating skills, one cannot fail to have qualms about the probable outcomes. One senior official has observed, only half facetiously, that experience in debate is the most valuable training for analytical work.

Acceptance of the tug-of-war concept, as opposed to the objective-scholar concept, of analysis has coincided with recognition of an even greater limitation on analysis as a guide to policymaking. In recent years it has been recognized in public statements (as well as the textbooks) that analysis is not a scientific procedure for reaching decisions which avoid intuitive elements, but rather a mechanism for sharpening the intuitions of the decisionmaker. Once again this is right. No matter how large a contribution that analysis makes, the role of the subjective preferences of the decisionmaker remains imposing. Analysis is, in the end, a method of investigating rather than solving problems. The highest strategic objectives, the statement of preferences or utility, must in large part be imposed from outside. Poor or haphazard analysis may contribute to poor decisions, but good analysis by itself cannot insure correct decisions. This implies two things. First, whatever the complex of decisions, legitimate differences of opinion will persist. Second, disagreement with the decisions should not automatically cast doubt on either the role of analysis in general or on the quality of specific analyses. These must be examined in and of themselves.

To be sure, the judgment of the decisionmakers regarding major objectives and what is or is not important is likely to feed back and influence the analysis. This is not always true, but there are strong pressures to make it come true. Studies are driven by the underlying assumptions, and these may be imposed directly or indirectly from above. Specific terms of reference may indicate which scenarios are acceptable, which unacceptable, and which contingencies should or should not be considered. It is perfectly appropriate, if not obligatory, for the analyst to point out deficiencies in study assumptions or terms of reference. Yet, many will

lack the perception or the inclination, while others would regard such action as personally imprudent. In these cases the analysis will only play back to the decisionmaker a more sharply defined version of what was already implicit in his assumptions. The role of analysis then becomes not so much to *sharpen* the intuitions of the decisionmaker as to *confirm* them.

Under these circumstances analysis is not being used in its most fruitful form, that of raising questions. But analysis is a tool that can be used in a variety of ways. Much depends upon how the decisionmaker decides to employ it. Considerable fear has been expressed that analysis will usurp the decisionmaking role, that the decisionmaker will become passive, and let analysis (implicitly) make the decisions. This is possible; it is also improper. But whether the decisionmaker will control the tool rather than letting it run away with him strikes me as a less important question than whether he will employ it properly in another sense. Will the decisionmaker tolerate analysis—even when it is his own hobby horses which are under scrutiny?

How many hobby horses are there?
Are they off limits to the analysts?

Dr. Enthoven has quite properly objected to the canard that analysis is somehow responsible for what are regarded as the mishaps of the TFX decisions, pointing out that the new procedures were only tangentially involved. A more penetrating question, it seems to me, is: why did the analyst steer away from the issue?

A slightly different issue arises in the case of Vietnam. Numerous blunders are alleged to be chargeable to analytic errors. But analysis has been employed in the Vietnamese context in only the most cursory fashion. In this context neither the high-level civilian nor the military authorities have been eager to exploit the full potentials of analysis. Once again, rather than blaming analytic efforts for the failures, the appropriate question should be: why has analysis been so little employed?

An acquaintance, who has been deeply involved in analytic activities in one of the Departments, recently commented to me on his experiences. Analysis he felt had been relevant in only a small proportion of the decisions. Half the time a decision had been foreclosed by high-level political involvement: a call from the White House, interest expressed by key Congressmen or Committees. In an additional 30 percent of the cases, the careers of immediate supervisors were involved. Analysis could not influence the recommendations; it could serve only as an irritant. But, he argued, in something like 20 percent of the issues, analysis was unfettered and contributed to much improved overall results. This was only the experience of one individual. In other cases the proportions might be quite different. The point is that analysis should be judged on the basis of only the minority of cases in which its influence is in some sense instrumental. Analysis is a useful tool, but it is only a tool. It would be a mistake to turn over a new proverbial leaf—and generally find fault with tools rather than craftsmen.

PRACTITIONERS VERSUS INSTRUMENTS

Accepting that analysis only sharpens the intuitions of decisionmakers, that its powers may be curtailed by unquestioned (or question-begging) assumptions or by imposed terms of reference, and that it is increasingly viewed as a contest between adversaries permits us to be more realistic about analysis in a number of ways. The inflated claims, periodically made in its behalf, may be rejected—along with the misplaced criticisms made in response. Questioning of decisions is turned into questioning of decision-makers' judgments rather than the role of analysis. And analysis itself can be employed more effectively in clarifying the underpinnings of policies, thereby creating the potential for designing more effective ones. We should understand that analysis provides no formula for solving problems, no prescription for sensible policies. It cannot and should not be employed to "demonstrate" that one's own policies are so right and those of others, so wrong.

What analysis provides is an exercise in logical coherence, hopefully with knowledge of and respect for the underlying technical, economic, and organizational data. Coherence does not insure the "correctness" of policy. In fact, an incoherent policy will sometimes be closer to a correct than a coherent one. But the incoherence itself scarcely makes a contribution. It is almost invariably a source of waste, and typically of policy muddles.

Analysis may make a contribution, but we should be very clear what it cannot do. It does not provide an instant cure for pigheadedness. In fact, it does not provide an instant cure for anything—not because of its theoretical deficiencies, but because it has to be employed by people and by organizations with divergent goals and views and with stringently limited information about actual conditions.

It is a mistake to identify analysis with the particular judgments, prejudices or arguable decisions of some of its major proponents. Especially is this so when analysis has been employed as a weapon of political conflict. The political process being what it is, it is hardly advisable to admit error in public; that would prove too costly. Human emotions being what they are, it is also unlikely that error will be admitted in private. This does not gainsay the value of analysis before policy commitments are made—or when they are being seriously reconsidered. What it does say is that we should avoid tying analysis to the personal proclivities of the particular individuals who were instrumental in introducing it into government. To do so may be flattering to the individuals. Some may even be inclined to treat their own attitudes and commitments as synonymous with analysis. It would be a serious error for others to accept this view.

Disciplined, orderly thought is the characterization given to analysis, but disciplined, orderly thought suggests certain traits: reflectiveness, self-criticism, and the willingness to reconsider past commitments without self-justification. However rarely or frequently encountered in the general human population, these are not traits characteristic of the action-oriented, incisive individuals who reach policymaking positions. Questioning and self-doubt lead to Hamlet-like decisionmakers.

Analysts themselves may be self-doubting, bemused by uncertainties, frighteningly candid, but different tactics have been required of the missionaries who have proselytized in behalf of analysis. I do not need to develop this point at any length. It should be plain, for example, that the actual decision to introduce analysis on a government-wide basis (as previously within the DOD) required an act of judgment and courage passing beyond the confines of analysis. Some analysts found the manner in which analytical procedures were instituted disquieting. This no doubt reflects a certain naivete on their part regarding political processes. But analysis was introduced rather suddenly. There was little advance preparation, little attempt to assess resource availability or calculate short-run costs. There was no "program definition phase." What occurred was that the political conditions were ripe,[1] and the opportunity was seized—for analysis.

I have perhaps belabored the distinction between analysis and judgment and the fact that the act of deciding occurs in the non-analytical phase. These matters need to be emphasized right now. It is important that analytical procedures in the DOD or elsewhere *not* be identified with particular sets of policies, decisions, or individuals. If analysis comes to be confused with the idiosyncracies of a few dominant personalities, there is some risk that it will disappear along with its original proponents. Its potential benefits for U.S. policy would then be lost for some time to come.

Admittedly there have been overstated claims, planted stories, and an impression generated among the *cog-*

---

[1] This episode suggests why the politician in his role may find analysis both incomplete and frustrating. Analysis deals in a rather abstract way with resource usage and efficient allocations. It does not deal with the attitudinal issues of support-generation, coalition-gathering or with timing which are so important in the political context.

noscenti of a new, scientific means for grinding out decisions. Admittedly the limitations appeared in the footnotes and not in the fanfare. But these are just the accoutrements of attention-getting. Analysis itself should scarcely be discarded on these grounds. Even if some decisionmakers or analysts have failed to display the mental elasticity that analysis in principle demands, this is only a reflection of the human condition. Why throw the baby out with the bathwater?

PAYOFFS

What is the baby? I seem to have devoted most of my attention to the reasons for refraining from that last half cheer for analysis, and virtually no attention to the reasons for the two and one-half cheers. In part this is due to the excellent set of papers and comments that the Subcommittee has published. Therein the potential benefits of program budgeting and analysis are fully presented. Lengthy reiterations of either the potential advantages or the accomplishments seem unnecessary. However, there are some points on which I should like to add a few words.

First, analysis has great value in turning debates over resource allocation toward the realities and away from simple statements of noble purpose. Analysis is not scientific method. Neither will it necessarily be objective in an organizational context. Yet, within the adversary relationship, analysis at least focuses the debate on what particular systems can accomplish and what numbers are required. The emphasis is on the real rather than the symbolic function of weapon systems. Disappointed as many in the Services

have been with major policy decisions of the OSD, I believe most knowledgeable officers would agree that the new methods have been beneficial in this respect.

Second and closely related, analysis is oriented toward outputs rather than toward inputs. In this way expenditures can be tied to specific goals, and those expenditures which satisfy primarily the traditions or well-being of individual agencies are brought into question. There are difficulties with goal or output orientation, particularly since we so frequently lack complete understanding of the mechanism that ties inputs to outputs. But the orientation is correct. The government structure is subdivided into agencies that typically concentrate on inputs. Dams, warships, trees, post offices, bombers, nuclear power, supersonic transportation, and, I may add, research expenditures are often treated as ends in themselves—with little examination as to how these instruments serve public purposes. Conscious output orientation, with as much quantitative backup as possible, points in the right direction. It forces agencies to shift attention from their beloved instruments and to explain the goals they serve rather than the functions they perform—and this at a level more practical than the usual rhetoric of noble purpose.

Third, the attempt is made to design systems or policies with practical budgetary limits in mind. The time-honored gap between the planners and the budgeteers has been widely discussed, along with the difficulties it causes. There is little point in plans too costly to be implemented or systems too expensive to be bought in the requisite quantity—if some reduction in quality will provide a feasible and serviceable, if less ideal, posture. (Here we are discussing capabilities and postures which would be effective, if bought—keeping in mind that so many expensive proposals serve little purpose at all.)

Fourth, an attempt is made to take spillovers into account and to achieve better integration between the several Services and Commands. Once again, this is more easily said than done. For example, we are belatedly becoming aware of the spillovers and the integration problems between the strategic offensive force under Air Force management and the new Sentinel system under Army control. This indicates that the attempt to take spillovers into account has not been overwhelmingly successful, but the goal is a correct one. The nation would not wish to duplicate SAC's capabilities for SACEUR or the Polaris force for CINCSAC.

Fifth, the attempt is made to take into account the long-run cost implications of decisions. Perhaps, it is more appropriate to say . . . the attempt *should* be made. There has been a certain inconsistency on this account. The costs of some systems have been carefully investigated, before a choice is made. For other (preferred) systems this has not been the case. The Program Definition Phase was originally introduced to insure that technology was in hand and the long-run costs considered before force structure decisions were made. Yet, curiously, in the programmed forces for the '70s our strategic forces are scheduled to become increasingly dependent on MIRVed vehicles, even though the technology is not yet in hand and we have only an **inkling** of the ultimate costs. The appropriate review of alternatives and

hedges did not take place. But this represents, not a criticism of the objective, but a plea for more consistency in its pursuit. It hardly negates the desirability of the careful weighing of alternatives with the long-run cost implications taken into account.

These attributes and precepts of analysis seem unexceptionable.

They are.

An appropriate inference is that many of the complaints couched in terms of "too much analysis" or "the errors of analysis" should be altered into "better and more consistent analysis." In this connection, an editor and friend recently suggested a paper on the impact of systems analysis: "not the general appraisals, we've had enough of that; tell us whether systems analysis has ever really been employed in the Department of Defense." An exaggeration perhaps, but as the MIRVing case suggests, analytic techniques have not been consistently applied.

Bernard Shaw observed somewhere that the only trouble with Christianity was that it had never really been tried. An epigram is at best a half truth, designed as someone has commented to irritate anyone who believes the other half. In DOD systems analysis has at least been tried. But there is an element in Shaw's remark that needs to be taken into account. In assessing the success of analysis, both the incomplete implementation and the resistance should be kept in mind.

BUDGETS

Military posture is determined in large measure by the total volume of resources the society is willing to divert from non-defense to defense uses. Yet, understanding the determinants of this resource flow presents a most perplexing problem. No good mechanism or rationale exists for deciding what diversion is proper. Some analysts have shied away from the problem arguing that the main objective should be the efficient employment of whatever resources are provided. A limited feel for appropriate diversion may be obtained by asking such questions as how much more is needed for defense than is needed for other purposes. In principle, senior policymakers may find it no harder to decide on allocation between damage limiting and urban renewal than between damage limiting and assured destruction. They will certainly find it no easier. For a number of practical reasons, they may find it far harder actually to bring about such a resource shift.

The amorphousness of this decision area combined with the repudiation of what were regarded as the rigidities of the Eisenhower years led to some bold words in 1961: there would be no *arbitrary* budget limits; in addition, every proposal would be examined on its own merits. These guidelines have since been regularly reasserted—with perhaps somewhat falling conviction. Originally they might be attributed to sheer enthusiasm; now they can only be taken as either propaganda or self-deception.

However, no matter the source, they will not stand up to *analysis*.

At any time there exists a rough political limit on defense expenditures. For members of this Subcommittee—in fact for any practicing politician—such an assertion will seem like a truism. Something like a consensus develops regarding proper levels of defense expenditures—and in the absence of external shocks this sum will not be substantially augmented. Of course, the *arbitrary* limit is always the *other fellow's*. One's own limit is only proximate and is wholly reasonable. Yet, defense expenditures do tend to become stabilized for years within rather narrow limits. Inevitably, new pressure for funds leads to the sacrifice of programs previously desirable on their own merits. That is as simple as arithmetic.

The only time that budget limits are not pressing (and more or less arbitrary) is when, as during the early Kennedy years, a political decision has been made that much more can be spent on defense. After a brief period of exuberance, the old constraints reappear. The decision does not have to be announced by the President or the Budget Bureau. The Secretary of Defense may get a feel for what is feasible, or he may be trusted to bring in a reasonable figure. But within a rather narrow range he will face a limit, which he may not transcend without either creating a minor fiscal crisis or straining his own credit with the President of the United States.

Save in the rare periods of budgetary relaxation, this, rightly or wrongly, is the way the system works. There is no point in kidding oneself. One may erect a facade intended to demonstrate that there are no arbitrary budget limits and each proposal is examined on its own merits. The pretense can be partially successful, but only because the criteria for choice are so imprecise. Standards can be made increasingly stringent, yet no one can prove how large was the role of budgetary pressures.

Nonetheless, no one should be deceived. What happens is that various alternatives and hedges are discarded; programs become less pressing and are stretched out. The practices are well-known from the bad, old meat-axe days. Under budgetary pressure (arbitrary or not) it is truly remarkable how many options one discovers one can do without. Multiple options just become less multiple. Before uncertainties are resolved, commitments are made and hedge programs are terminated. In the well-advertised adversary relationship, the negotiator-analysts become much harder to persuade. If they are not directly instructed, *they know*.

These are not hypothetical possibilities. With the intensification of budgetary pressures stemming from the Vietnamese war, there has, for example, been a wholesale slaughter of programs in the strategic area. It is important not to be misled regarding the critical role of budgetary pressures—and thus come to believe that so many programs, previously regarded as merit-worthy, have suddenly lost their merit. Otherwise, we might gradually come to believe that we are doing far better than is actually the case. One should remain aware that the decimation of a program has long-run postural implications. That is, after all, the message that PPB attempts to convey.

These are elementary propositions. I do not dwell on certain theoretical problems and inconsistencies bearing on the relationship of overall defense spending to the optimality of programs. Suffice it to say that the *quality* of what one buys depends upon how much one wants to spend. This connection between level of demand and cost/effectiveness creates a dilemma in that *neither* the character of the programs nor the size of the budget can be determined initially. But that is a theoretical nicety, the direct consequences of which may not be of major importance.

The vital point is the way in which budgetary limits may control force posture and therefore strategy. Shifting sands seems the best way to characterize the strategic rationales of recent years. In 1961 the suicidal implications of massive retaliation were underscored: the United States would be faced with a choice between humiliation or holocaust. Interest then developed in damage-limiting and coercion. But there has been little willingness to invest money in either. Since 1965 the merits of Assured Destruction have been emphasized—with little attention paid to the suicidal implications found so distressing in prior years. The principal rationale for the current emphasis on Assured Destruction reflects certain recently-developed notions of arms control. It clearly falls within the province of the decisionmakers to adopt a strategy of measured response to any Soviet buildup with the long-term objective of preserving U.S. Assured Destruction capabilities. One should note, however, that to accept this particular guide to action implies that the buildup of the Minuteman force in 1961–62 was a mistake. These newer arms control criteria may be the preferred ones, but they rest on the judgments and intuitions of the decisionmakers. They certainly do not emerge by themselves from analysis.

May one infer that the oscillations in strategy have something to do with budget limits, or in this case something more specific: a preconception regarding how much this nation should spend on the strategic forces? I find the conclusion irresistible. The evidence antedates the current phase-down in the face of the Soviet buildup. Once again, these lie within the decisionmaker's prerogatives, but particular beliefs regarding budget limits or the "adequacy" of specific strategies should not be attributed to, much less blamed on, analysis.

A USEFUL IF OVERSOLD TOOL

Whatever resources are made available to defense (or any other mission), choices will have to be made.

Allocative decisions inevitably are painful; many claimants will be sorely disappointed.

Few will find fault with their own proposals, almost all with the machinery for selection.

Any procedures for allocation will be criticized—even in a hypothetical case in which the conceptual basis is unarguable and no errors are made. Analysis provides the backup for a selective process. What does it contribute? How does it compare with real-world alternatives—not with mythical alternatives in which all claimants get their requests and no one is disappointed?

It has been emphasized that analysis cannot determine the appropriate strategy. It can shed light on costs and tradeoffs. But the choice to press arms control or arms competition or to rely on tactical nuclears or nuclear firebreaks must be determined by the decisionmaker sustained primarily by hope, conviction, and prayer. Even if a decision could be demonstrated as correct at a given moment in time, there is the certainty that objectives will change over time. For these higher level problems analysis is an aid, but a limited aid. The toughest problems, dominated as they are by uncertainties and by differences in goals, do not yield to analysis.

Happily many problems are more mundane and more tractable. Where analysis has proved its highest value is in uncovering cases of gross waste: points at which substantial expenditures may contribute little to any stated objective. It might be thought that a problem of diminishing returns exists for analysis in that the cases of gross misuse of resources are likely to be uncovered at an early stage. Thus, as the opportunity for major savings through elimination of irrational forms of waste theoretically recedes, analysis would be forced into the more ambiguous areas in which strategic choices become intimately involved. In some cases, where information is readily available and objectives and conditions relatively unchanging, this could prove to be true. The very success of analysis would then undermine near-term expectations of additional returns. However, in defense this turns out to be irrelevant, since the problems are so volatile and information so difficult to unearth.

To say that analysis works best in cases of gross waste should not be taken to imply that analysis accomplishes little. The simple cases involving so-called dominant solutions may involve billions of dollars. The volume of government resources that may be lavished on the care and feeding of white elephants is simply staggering.

Here we have "quantified common sense" in its most direct form. In bureaucracies, units at all levels are concerned with organizational health. Rather than making the hard choices, the tendency is strong to maintain morale by paying off all parties. Analysis provides a means for coping with this problem. The big issues may not be directly involved, though they are likely to be dragged in by the proponents of particular programs.

Should the assessment of analysis be much influenced by the annoyance felt by those whose proposals have failed the tests? Certainly not in the general case. No more than should the decisionmakers be permitted to hide their judgments behind the camouflage of analysis, should the patrons of doubtful proposals be encouraged to argue that acceptance would and should have come—if *only* analysis had not been employed. Budgets are limited and hard choices must be made. If nobody were annoyed analysis would not be doing its job—of questioning both routinized practices and blue-sky propositions. Disappointment is unavoidable. The question is not the existence of annoyance, but to strive to annoy in the right way and for the right reasons.

In this light it may be desirable to examine the issue of the generalist versus the specialist which has been touched upon in the Hearings. In the nature of things specialists become committed to particulars: a piece of hardware, a technological criterion, a disciplinary blind spot. It is a case of suboptimization run wild. Proponents of specific capabilities or gadgets tend to become monomaniacs. In a sense that is the way they should be: totally dedicated to their tasks. But one does not turn to them for detached judgments. There is no substitute for the *informed* generalist. There is a recog-

nizable risk that the superficiality of the generalist may match the monomania of the specialist. However, that need not be the case. Although the generalist's knowledge cannot match that of the specialist in detail, analysis can once again play a useful role, by permitting the organization for the generalist of more specialized information than he alone could master.

How does this relate to the limits of the analyst's role? Two distinctions should be kept in mind: that between the technical specialist and the analytical generalist and that between the analyst and the decisionmaker. The analyst's tools are not circumscribed by discipline or even by subject matter. But general tools are not immediately convertible into broad policies. Many analysts are, in some sense, specialists in the use of general tools. Being a good analytical generalist does not necessarily imply possession of such additional qualities as breadth, judgment, and political attunement. These latter qualities are what many have in mind when they speak of the generalist as policymaker.

CONCLUSION

In closing I should like to underscore three points.

First, the position of the decisionmaker employing analysis is somewhat ambiguous. For tactical purposes this ambiguity may be deliberately augmented. Intermittently he may choose to stress *analysis* or *judgment,* and to shift hats according to the tactical requirements of the moment. His policy judgments may be obscured or defended by cryptic references to detailed analyses which allegedly force the policy conclusions. On the other hand, if any limitations or inadequacies in the analyses should come to light, these can be waved away with the reminder that all issues are ultimately matters for the decisionmaker's judgment.

Moreover, the pattern is in reality far more complicated than the standard exposition in which the analyst produces an *objective* study, and the decisionmaker's judgment enters at a later stage erected on the foundation of these objective results. That makes the analytical and judgmental stages seem clean-cut. Few studies are that pure. The decisionmaker's judgments quite typically are dumped in at an early stage in the form of guidance, assumptions, and terms of reference. The more political a study, the less likely is it to be pure. In fact, the process can be (and has been) far more corrupted, when questionable (phony) numbers are introduced. Since judgment and analysis are thoroughly intertwined in all but a few studies, the attempt of decisionmakers to shift roles by referring to fundamental analyses should be treated with some skepticism. The decisionmaker should not be permitted to escape the full burden of responsibility by the invocation of analysis.

The temptation for those who have introduced analytical techniques into the government to treat their own positions or careers as identical with analysis is understandable. No outsider should yield to the same temptation. The roles and even the temperaments of decisionmaker and analyst are quite distinct. The confusion tends to disguise the heavy personal burden borne by the decisionmaker. More important, if analysis is treated as synony-mous with particular decisions or personalities, there is a risk that it will be throttled or abandoned after their departure. From the standpoint of public policy this would be a major loss.

Second, we should avoid the erroneous belief that the performance or potential power of analysis will be uniform in all contexts. If a town is considering building a bridge, a number of difficult analytical problems must be addressed: does demand warrant construction, where should the bridge be built, what should be its capacity, and so on. But once these questions are resolved the engineer falls back on a solid technical base. By contrast, for such goals as deterrence, assured destruction, controlled nuclear warfare, damage limiting, to say nothing of welfare benefits, we fall back, not on a firm technical base, but on what may be scientific mush. The distinction is not always appreciated. The difficulty is sometimes dealt with by referring euphemistically to *the model problem*. But our ability to formulate models depends upon our knowledge of the mechanics of the real world. For many problems our knowledge is meager, and the proffered models are misleading or downright erroneous. The lack of good models in many problem areas simultaneously limits the power of analysis, while increasing the burden placed on judgment. In treating analysis as a uniformly efficient problem-solving technique, the variability of analysis, which reflects the variability of the knowledge base, is ignored.

Though analysis is a powerful tool, specific analyses vary greatly in quality. Some are little more than trash. But we need to discriminate, rather than to reject analysis *in toto*. At the present time there is some risk that we will do the latter. In an address some years ago Secretary Enthoven observed: "My general impression is that the art of systems analysis is in about the same stage now as medicine during the latter half of the 19th century; that is, it has just reached the point at which it can do more good than harm." That was a frank and realistic, if somewhat pessimistic, assessment of the state of the *art*. Scientifically speaking, there are numerous blind spots in medicine. Yet, most of us ultimately are inclined to accept the doctor's diagnosis, if not his advice. Quite plainly at the present time Congress and the public are having second thoughts regarding how much trust to put in systems analysis. No doubt it is necessary to develop a greater ability to discriminate. Nonetheless, I suggest that policy will bene-fit substantially from the analysts' diagnoses.

Third, there is little doubt that analysis has been oversold. That strikes me as a rather standard result in matters political. But the reaction against the overselling could be more costly than the over-selling itself. Analysis is a powerful instrument: with it our batting average has been far higher than without it. Analysis is also an adaptable instrument. The McNamara regime has in many respects been a highly personalized one. Its performance should not be taken as defining the limits of this flexible tool. Admittedly, analyses vary substantially in quality. Each should be taken with a large grain of salt. On the other hand, if one does not demand too much of it, analysis will prove to be a most serviceable instrument.

Multipurpose Budget Systems

By
ALLEN SCHICK

Under the Planning-Programming-Budgeting System introduced in 1965, federal agencies are required to reconcile their new program accounts with the existing appropriations structure. This crosswalk is necessary because PPBS has retained the traditional form of appropriation. As a result there is a disparity between the classification in the program structure and the object-organization classification in the appropriations.

Many people interpret crosswalking as a provisional arrangement that will be terminated once the appropriations are converted to a program basis. The Bureau of the Budget, according to

March, 1968; an earlier unpublished version of this paper was circulated in December, 1966 under the title, "Some Problems of Multipurpose Budget Systems." Allen Schick is with the Brookings Institution. He was formerly a member of the Department of Political Science, Tufts University, and a Consultant, Bureau of the Budget.

this view, has not tampered with the form of appropriation because of the risk of Congressional opposition to PPB. By restricting its innovations to those classifications completely within its jurisdiction, the Bureau has been able to introduce PPB unilaterally.[1] This view anticipates, however, that Congress ultimately will be weaned from its traditional proclivities and program classifications will be extended to the appropriations. During the interim crosswalking will be necessary as a data processing routine, but it will neither impair the effectiveness of PPB nor have any significant bearing on budgetary matters.

MULTI-PURPOSE BUDGET SYSTEMS

In contrast to the foregoing interpretation I regard crosswalking between the budget and appropriations as one technical manifestation of the broader problem of operating a budget system that performs a number of different functions. The *raison d'être* of crosswalking is the multiple purposes of a PPB system and the divergent informational and institutional requirements of each function. If budgeting were reduced to a single function, such as has been the case in the past, there would be no need for crosswalking. But under PPBS there will be a coexistence of several functions and, consequently, of several accounting structures. Crosswalking will be the process for linking them together. (Thus, I

define crosswalking as a process of reconciling the informational and institutional divergencies that spring from the multiple purposes of budgeting.)

In an earlier paper I identified three core functions of budgeting—control, management, and planning—and suggested that PPB, unlike previous systems, integrates all three functions into the budget process.[2] Because governments have had little experience with multi-functional budgeting and because of the tendency to compress all data into a single accounting frame, crosswalking may pose problems beyond the merely technical for the conduct of budgeting. In this regard business practices are a poor analogy, even though multiple accounting structures have been used successfully in business. Business budgeting has few of the functions associated with government budgeting. In government there is no substitute for the budget as the central financial apparatus; hence, most things that have fiscal implications are harnessed to it. This is the root of the multi-purpose budget problem.

The rudiments of multi-purpose budgeting were evident in Frederick Cleveland's seminal distinction between budgets and appropriations and in his abortive efforts to establish distinct informational criteria for each. This attempt was thwarted by the emphasis on using the budget to control certain administrative practices and the resulting insistence on a uniform set of accounts tied to the object and organization classifications. During the control era, all accounts—including

[1] For a discussion of how the Defense Department was able to introduce its budget reforms unilaterally, see Robert J. Massey, "Program Packages and the Program Budget in the Department of Defense," *Public Administration Review*, Vol. XXIII (1963), pp. 30–34.

[2] See Allen Schick, "The Road to PPB: The Stages of Budget Reform," *Public Administration Review*, Vol. XXVI, No. 4 (December, 1966).

agency estimates, the budget, appropriations, and apportionments—were classified according to organizations and objects. The linchpin of this control system was the appropriation which fixed statutory limits on spending units and on objects of expenditure. Since management and planning opportunities of budgeting were neglected, the types of classification needed for these functions were absent. Consequently, no reconciliation of accounts was required.

The conversion of budgeting to a management function opened the door to a host of problems. The emergence of management meant that budgeting now had a second central function in addition to control. The performance budgeting movement which brought the management ideal to fruition displayed considerable ambivalence and difficulty concerning the relationships between (1) objects and activities, (2) budgetary and organizational structures, and (3) control and management functions. These difficulties were resolved in ways that eliminated the need for a crosswalk.

Objects and activities

The first Hoover Commission, along with many of its early progeny in the United States, started with the assumption that objects and activities are competing bases of classification. Undergirding this assumption was the straightforward conviction that unless the objects are dislodged from their central position the addition of new activity classifications will be a pyrrhic accomplishment. Budget decisions will continue to be made in the old manner, according to objects and inspired by

control considerations. For this reason the Commission's recommendations implied the purging of object data from the budget and appropriations. But this aboriginal view depended on a radical transformation of the appropriations from a tool of legislative oversight and control over administration into a process for determining national programs and policies at the highest levels. Without this transformation the budget would have to continue producing the kinds of object data required for control. However, the traditional reliance on central and external controls and the corresponding lack of faith in internal controls made divestment of the appropriation's control function a difficult step. Consequently, there was a subtle modification in the performance budget concept to allow a hybridization of activities and objects. The prevailing *leitmotif* became: "A marriage of program, performance, and line-item budgets may and must be developed." [3] As things turned out, hybridization meant the continued predominance of object-organization categories. Performance budgeting introduced activity categories that served as intermediate classifications in the object-organization rubric; they furnished an additional way of reporting expenditures without disturbing the old ways. Sandwiched between the two pivots of central control, the new classifications had a very feeble impact on what participants did and decided. [4]

---

[3] Edward Hofgesang, quoted in David W. Minar *et al.* (eds.), *Problems and Prospects in Public Management: A Digest of ASPA Conferences 1956–57–58*, p. 113.

[4] The activity classification "provides information which has substantially more significance with regard to organization than finance. . . . It does not, in effect, provide an

Moreover, the lack of a real management base made it possible to get along without a reconciliation of control and management.

Budgeting and organizational structures

It was anticipated by the Hoover Commission that an activity classification would be equally useful for budgetary and organizational structures. But an activity classification, if it is strictly applied, may diverge from lines of responsibility within the organization. The Task Force of the Second Hoover Commission reported that in some instances it was "necessary to treat as separate programs activities for which there was not clear responsibility short of the agency head," and in others "it was impossible to provide adequate cost information to support many of the programs shown in the budget." [5] In view of these difficulties the Task Force concluded that "there are cases where the requirements of organization for good administration and those for good program budget presentation do not coincide. A program classification and an organizational unit classification both serve important but essentially different purposes." [6]

In his investigation of the early experiences with performance budgeting in the Department of Defense, Frederick Mosher pointed out that problems concerning the relationship of budget and organization structures *"must* occur in every organization which has regional and field offices having more than one major function. And the unifunctional field organization is the exception rather than the rule among Federal agencies." [7] Mosher hinted at the need for crosswalk techniques "to proceed from one type to the other and back again." Nevertheless, the second Hoover Commission brushed aside these difficulties and reaffirmed the orthodox view "that the agencies [should] take further steps to synchronize their organization structures, budget classifications, and accounting systems." [8] In the actual implementation of performance budgeting the dilemma was resolved by making the activity classifications in the budget dependent on the prevailing organizational structure. In many cases the activity designations were little more than new designations for identifiable organization sub-units; in almost none did they cut across organizational lines to facilitate choice among the expenditure proposals of competing organizational units. [9]

Control and management functions

Concerning the linkage of control and management functions, performance budgeting labored inventively but with

---

opportunity to select among alternatives in determining the type or level . . . services that shall be provided." John E. Briggs, *A Refined Program Budget for State Governments* (Washington: 1962), pp. 8, 10.
[5] Commission on Organization of the Executive Branch of the Government, *Task Force Report on Budget and Accounting* (June, 1955), p. 28.
[6] *Ibid.*

---

[7] Frederick C. Mosher, *Program Budgeting: Theory and Practice* (Chicago: 1954), p. 105.
[8] Commission on Organization of the Executive Branch of the Government, *Budget and Accounting* (June, 1955), p. 13.
[9] "If the objective of an accounting system is to produce data to be used in evaluating . . . a public . . . program, the accounts must reflect program elements regardless of organization." Association of Business Management in Public Health, *A Guide to Public Health Program Accounting* (December, 1958), p. 23.

little success. The problem boiled down to this: how to design a system that satisfies the requirements of control without driving out management. The proposed solution was predicated on a system that reduced central preoccupation with control by (1) removing central control over inputs (2) relying on internal rather than external controls, and (3) reducing itemized detail in the budget and appropriations. To compensate for the loss of traditional control devices, it proposed an alternative system based on (4) objective measurements of work and cost (5) performance audits and reports to check actual performance against budget projections, and (6) central intervention in case of serious deviations from original plans.

This scheme never was tried on a wide scale. There was an unwillingness to trade the old controls for new ones; consequently, the old controls weren't abandoned and the new controls weren't tried. As a practical matter, this left little room for the expansion of managerial aspects of budgeting. Control remained predominant, if not preemptive.

The past difficulties of crosswalking between management and control are germane to the current PPB movement. The injection of planning into the picture cannot help but complicate matters further, for management and control also will have to be served. It has been suggested that the three components of PPB—planning, programming, and budgeting—correspond to the three functions of budgeting. However, their combination into a three-letter byword for contemporary innovation does not mean that the reconciliation problem has been solved,

nor does the clichè that programming is the bridge between planning and budgeting show us how to translate from one process into the other. To be sure, we know a lot more today than we knew a decade ago about the techniques of reconciling different informational structures and we have a much more advanced data-processing capability. Nevertheless, there remains the basic crosswalk problem of how to reconcile the several budgetary functions in a way that gives primacy to planning. The survival of PPB is contingent on the development of a system that transfers control and management to lower levels. If this is not achieved, planning will be preempted by the routine immediate demands of control, and it will return to a state of dispersion and neglect. This is the principal lesson to be derived from the historical survey presented above. Objects-of-expenditure, after all, are indispensable for control and internal management. Hence, if there is to be a single "currency" in the classification of expenditures or a single ethic in budgeting it will be object- and control-oriented. Otherwise, the same thing that happened to performance budgeting some fifteen years ago will recur. There will be a grafting of the structural facade of PPB onto the old techniques and patterns. We will have structure but not analysis; the appearance but not the substance of PPB. Like the performance budget, we will have new-bottles-for-old-wine; agency justifications will be restyled into program memoranda; program categories will be refashioned from the existing organizational frame; agency projections will be stretched from single to multi-year lengths.

SPECIALIZED INFORMATION SYSTEM

To avert the preemption of planning by the routine will require a system that recognizes the multiple needs and diversities of budgeting, that is geared to the differential as well as the common needs of the participants, that does not force an absolute trade-off between the various types of data but relegates them to different purposes and levels. But the greatest threat to the maintenance of multi-purpose budgeting is the difficulty of maintaining a specialized and diversified informational system, not the problem of tying the diversities together. If there are several informational structures, it will be simple enough to develop an interface, but if there is only a single, homogeneous informational structure there will be nothing to reconcile.

PPB, then, requires a specialized and selective distribution and use of information. Specialization would be determined by the role and level of each participant. Ideally, the allocation of information under PPB would be dictated by an objective prescription of functions in contrast to the traditional "to each according to his wants" formula. Data would be packaged in one manner for policy-making and in another manner for agency administration. The information produced for legislators, agency heads, operating officials, and budget staff would vary in scope and focus. One type of information would be used for preparing estimates at the bureau level, another for department-wide review, still another for the Bureau of the Budget, and so on. Although PPB would mean an increase in the total supply of information, it would deprive Congressmen and other participants of some data they have traditionally received.

This sort of specialization would replace the relatively undifferentiated system under which the various participants receive roughly similar kinds and quanta of information. Although there always has been some informal specialization—Congressmen, for example, generally use less detailed data than operating officials—PPB would mark out clear-cut and fixed differentials in informational resources. In the psychology of PPB the link between informational resources and behavior is direct and significant. It is assumed that if the participants are "force fed" the right kinds of data, they will adopt the roles that are prescribed for themselves, and the whole budget system would achieve an optimal mix of planning, management, and control. Legislators who are denied information on the cost of typewriters, travel, and personnel and are furnished instead data on the costs and benefits of expenditure alternatives will cease meddling in administrative matters and embrace a policy role instead. Operating officials will take a vigorous interest in the efficiency of their activities if they are provided reliable cost data. The Bureau of the Budget will concentrate on formulating and reviewing comprehensive plans and programs instead of monitoring agency operations. In short, the roles of the participants would differ from one another, but they would be linked by a rationalized division of labor.

The specialized system just described requires a fixed delineation of roles and informational resources and represents an idealized version of PPB aspirations and potential. But the initial experiences with PPB, particularly in the federal government, have revealed certain problems with this specialized model. These problems cover vital aspects of budget life such as the classification and use of information, budgetary roles in a political context, the time dimension of budget decisions, and the staffing of budgetary institutions. Some of these problems also emerged during past efforts at budget reform; others derive from PPB's unique institutionalization of multi-purpose budgeting.

Multi-purpose problems cannot be solved by wishful recourse to the specialized model. What is required is a modification of the "pure" specialization ideal in which roles are exactly specified and differential informational resources allocated to each role are perfectly reconciled by means of a crosswalk. In the succeeding sections I discuss several of the more critical multi-purpose problems and propose a solution that accommodates the imperfect allocation of roles and the consequent tendency to homogenize informational resources. My solution allows "slack" in the operation of a multi-purpose budget system; that is, it permits imperfect integration of the several core functions of budgeting—control, management, and planning.

BUDGETARY ROLES

In the view of reformers a key stumbling block to rational resource allocation has been the malapportionment of roles resulting from the undifferentiated distribution and use of information. Because they have access to the wrong kinds of information, participants have been encouraged to neglect their proper spheres of responsibility and to trespass into areas beyond their jurisdiction. Congress generally is indicted as the most culpable participant. It has been castigated repeatedly for its preoccupation with administrative details and its failure to play a policy-making role. The solution proposed by reformers and embraced within PPB's multipurpose scheme is to divest Congress of its object-of-expenditure detail and to supply it with program data.

But the power to determine the distribution of information hinges on the power to prescribe roles. When that power is dispersed, it will be difficult to establish a fixed and specialized information structure. The actual distribution of information probably will be based on reciprocal arrangements among the participants rather than on a formula that carves out distinct domains for each. In a pluralistic political environment budgetary roles will tend to overlap and to be ambiguously defined with a resulting tendency to use similar data throughout the budget process. Moreover, the fragmented budget environment allows each player to call his own tune and to have considerable autonomy in responding to the tunes of others. The outcome often is an undifferentiated, unifunctional budget system.

Since multi-purpose budgeting presupposes some rational demarcation of roles, its success depends on the willingness of participants—legislators, administrators, central budget staff, and others—to conform to the prescribed roles and to work within a specialized informational framework. But if participants veto or circumvent changes in the form and use of information or otherwise refuse to play the assigned roles, there will be a tendency to retain central preoccupation with the control function and to continue the dispersion of planning among subordinate units. Even if PPB succeeds in introducing program structures and other formal changes, this will be a meaningless gesture because budgetary behavior will not be affected.

The history of previous reforms warns us that this is not an idle conjecture. Participants are capable of resisting or subverting the purposes of reform, even as they work within the new forms. Rather than take on unwanted roles, budget people may try to develop alternative informational resources to compensate for the loss of old ones. They may resist the foreclosure of traditional informational resources or reject the tender of new data. Still another option is to abandon the old role but also to spurn the proffered one—in other words, to withdraw from effective participation in budgeting. If they do not want to withdraw, participants may insist that program data supplement rather than replace the old data. In this way participants can continue their old roles and avoid the new ones.

All these possibilities are relevant to the treatment of the control function in terms of the roles of and the kinds of data made available to participants. Consider the position of Congress in the budget system. Multi-purpose budgeting, strictly applied, would force Congress to abandon its control role along with its extensive access to input (object-of-expenditure) data. In lieu of this Congress would receive program information and take on a more ex-

plicit and vigorous role in determining national goals and priorities. This expectation, however, fails to take into account the reasons for Congress' persistence with control and its unwillingness to yield object data. If current meddling in detail is as irrational as reformers claim, why doesn't Congress welcome the opportunity to play a more productive role in policy-making? A good part of the answer lies in the increasing importance of legislative oversight of administration as a congressional role. As the administrative state has grown, and as congressional grants of discretion to administrators have broadened, there has developed an understandable insistence on mechanisms to check and influence administrative performance. The increasing use of congressional investigations is one such mechanism. Another is the use of the appropriations power to maintain detailed surveillance over administrative practices. Congressional attention to the input side of the budget through the familiar object-organization classification has afforded a convenient, if not always effective, oversight procedure.

Despite the recent ferment for budgetary improvement Congress has not been offered an adequate substitute for its traditional control machinery. The alternatives suggested by reformers would mean the abandonment of congressional involvement in fiscal details in favor of concentration on the "big picture"—programs and policies. PPB would accomplish this shift by means of its program structure, a form of classification that is concerned with end-purposes rather than financial items. But Congress does not believe that it can effectively influence the whole unless it retains oversight of the details.

Moreover, for Congressmen (as well as for the other budget participants) individual items often have importance apart from the larger categories or purposes with which they may be associated. A particular project may be regarded as an end in itself, not merely as a link in the chain of resource utilization leading to the achievement of some overall mission. Consequently, they would not want the identity of this item—whether it be a project such as the operation of a veterans' hospital or an object-of-expenditure such as teachers' salaries—to be concealed in the mission-oriented program structure. This attitude must be reckoned with, even if it runs counter to the logic of rational resource allocation.

One could multiply examples and explanations concerning the entrenched position of the lines of input data in budgeting. The leading factor, I have suggested, is the role of the participants *as they see it,* not the roles as they are prescribed according to some *a priori* formula. Legislative oversight competes with legislative policy-making; the former invites congressional interest in spending details, the latter would rivet congressional attention on the goals of government spending. The administrator's role as a claimant for scarce funds is in tension with his role as the promoter and producer of public goals. While the claimant role influences the administrator to be concerned with the size of his staff, his travel funds, the availability of money to purchase desired equipment, and similar input matters, the goal-producer role demands attention to the end products. Even the central budget office is caught in

the web of contradictory roles. *De facto,* it serves as *budget cutter,* reducing agency estimates to manageable levels. Ideally, it would serve as *budget planner,* determining the overall course of government policy and formulating and evaluating programs to accomplish this policy. Budget cutting engenders a negativistic disposition that is effectively promoted by attention to the fine print of agency estimates. The budget examiner can reduce the estimates by cutting out discrete items without being explicitly concerned with the relation between the cuts and programs. Budget planning, by contrast, spawns an interest in the opportunities for spending funds and thus fits hand-in-glove with the program structure's focus on the end products.

All these real and potential incompatibilities call into question the existing multi-purpose budget strategy. As I understand it, the prevailing strategy is (1) to force a trade-off between the planning data provided by the program structure and the control data embedded in the object-organization classification, (2) to supply each budget participant with data objectively associated with his prescribed role, and (3) to tightly integrate the several data systems by means of a crosswalk.

Over the long run this strategy might be successful if it generates a reformulation of budget roles. Perhaps a decade or a generation from now a new breed of Congressmen will embrace a policy role and eschew the contemporary oversight role. In the near term, however, the strategy will thwart the progress of budget reform. The reason for this is that reform is presented as a threat: participants must surrender their traditional roles and data in order to benefit from the new wave. Faced with this forced trade-off participants will elect to retain their old data and roles and to disregard or subvert the new ones.

The solution I mentioned earlier allows slack in the definition of roles, the integration of data, and the allocation of budgetary functions. Rather than confronting Congress with an either-or situation, Congress should be permitted continuing access to control-object data while it is introduced to the potential uses of planning data. Rather than perfect integration of the several systems, there would be more casual integration, varying from one circumstance to another. Rather than being required to divest themselves of comfortable roles in favor of uncertain new ones, participants can make incremental adjustments in existing roles.

BUDGET CLASSIFICATIONS

What I have called slack or imperfect integration is manifested in the relationship among the several classification systems. The expectation that crosswalking among the budget, organization, and appropriation classifications will not be necessary once all three are placed on a program basis is probably erroneous. This expectation rests on the premise that organizational, budgetary, and appropriations structures have similar purposes. In fact, appropriations tend to have a control function; organizational structure is governed by management considerations; and the budget has a policy planning function. The primordial purpose of an appropriation is to place a limit on the executive's authority to spend money. Covertly, of course, and sometimes openly, the appropriation carries an expression of congressional policy, but its structure still will be devised to serve as an external, before-the-expenditure limitation on executive officials. Organizational structure is to facilitate the efficient utilization of resources for the accomplishment of authorized tasks or activities. The overriding consideration in the design of a program structure is decisional to facilitate rational choice among complementary and substitutive policies.

These three structures will be congruent and on a program footing only if the decisional structure (the budget) also is useful for the control and managerial functions of appropriations and organizations. In many instances congruence will be feasible and desirable. The ease with which appropriation and organizational units are allocated to programs in some sample program budgets suggests that there is much more congruence than is commonly supposed.[10] But there are many instances where perfect congruence would be dysfunctional.

Two aspects of the history of planning-programming-budgeting in the Defense Department illustrate this problem. Although it has had more than five years of experience with PPB, Defense has not completely realigned the appropriations and organizational structures to make them congruent with the program categories. As a matter of fact, what started as a necessity because of the inability to get Congress to go along with change now is inter-

---

[10] For one of many sample translations of the budget into program categories, see Werner Z. Hirsch, *Toward Federal Program Budgeting* (Rand Corporation, February, 1966), pp. 10–13.

preted as a virtue. In *Decision-Making for Defense* Charles Hitch avers that the existing appropriations structure in DOD (military personnel, operation and maintenance, procurement, and so on) "serves some very useful purposes":

This type of structure lends itself ideally to the manner in which the Defense Department actually manages its resources. Although military planning and the formulation of programs should logically be done in terms of missions and forces, the Department must be managed not only in those terms, but also in terms of resources. . . . This division of the budget by broad input or resources categories also provides needed flexibility for the adjustments in the program that are inevitably required in the course of the budget year. Program priorities and requirements always change in unanticipated ways even in the course of a single year as a result of international developments, technological breakthroughs (or disappointments), and all sorts of other events. It is important not to freeze programs in appropriation bills. . . . I now feel that the advantages of the existing budget structure far outweigh the disadvantages, which are principally mechanical, namely, the need to translate program categories into budget categories and vice versa. This is the sort of disadvantage that modern high-speed computers are well designed to overcome. Accordingly, we decided to leave the budget structure undisturbed and to span the gap between planning and budgeting with the new programming function.[11]

Another instructive feature of Defense's approach to PPB is "Project PRIME," an attempt by Robert An-

thony (the successor to Hitch as Assistant Secretary of Defense/Comptroller)

. . . to achieve a correspondence of operating costs among program, budget, accounting system, and reporting system. Such consistency would eliminate the necessity for the unrewarding "torque conversion," would lay the groundwork for budget submission to Congress in mission-oriented terms, and would create within the accounting system the capability for progress reporting back against the program.[12]

It is much too early to appraise the impact of PRIME on budget practices. (Fiscal 1969 is the first full year of implementation.) But several characteristics merit comment. First of all the attempt to integrate the various budget purposes and information systems has occurred some six to eight years *after* the advent of PPB. During these years there has been a modification of budget roles as a result of Secretary McNamara's strong leadership of the department. Had PRIME been attempted in 1961 when McNamara initiated his budgetary revolution, it probably would have stumbled because of confusion and resistance.

Second, even with PRIME Congress will retain the option of considering the budget on the old format. Congress is being invited, not compelled, to use the new format. Third, the organizational structure with Defense will not conform to the program structure. There still will be the need for a reconciliation of organizational and program accounts, despite claims to the contrary. Fourth,

---

[11] Charles Hitch, *Decision-Making for Defense* (University of California Press, 1966), pp. 29–30.

[12] Steven Lazarus, "Planning-Programming-Budgeting Systems and Project PRIME," *Defense Industry Bulletin,* January, 1967, p. S-18.

the implementation of PRIME has led to a reformulation of program structure in the Department of Defense. Like all program structures Defense's is supposed to be mission-oriented. But of the nine categories in the structure established in 1961, only one-third were framed in mission terms.

Under PRIME the concept of mission disappears almost entirely from the program structure of the Defense Department. Most of the categories (for example, Personnel Support, Logistics, and Administration) appear to have been designed with management and control purposes in mind.

Defense Department's Program Structure

Initial PPB	*PRIME*
Strategic Offensive Forces	Strategic Forces
Continental Air & Missile Defense Forces	General Purpose Forces
	Specialized Activities
General Purpose Forces	(Includes MAP)
Airlift/Sealift Forces	Airlift and Sealift
Reserve and Guard Forces	Guard and Reserve Forces
Research and Development	Research and Development
General Support	Logistics
Retired Pay	Personnel Support
Military Assistance	Administration

In an integrated system when a choice has to be made between planning and the other functions, planning often loses out. To protect planning from the requirements of control and management, a safer course might be to tolerate some measure of slack.

TIME DIMENSIONS

One of the crucial reasons for urging slack in the integration of budget systems pertains to the time frames of budgeting. The conventional cycle of budgetary routines and deadlines is geared to a control function. The lengthy and detailed preparation of estimates demands a strict sequence of repetitive steps and techniques. All this is appropriate for the kind of accuracy-in-details sought for purposes of control. Real planning is destroyed by fixed routines and omnipresent deadlines. Planning is opportunistic and

episodic, taking advantage of circumstance and need. This problem was one of the factors that led Frederick Mosher to propose, more than a decade ago, a bifurcation between the program budget and the administrative budget.

While the management and control functions of budgeting invite a retrospective focus, planning is always a prospective exercise. For management and control purposes one is likely to be interested in how this year's spending compares with last year's or with the comparison of anticipated and actual performance. Accordingly, the information systems of control and management will have to provide detailed data on the spending history of past years. Informational systems for planning, however, deal with a different universe of concerns. The emphasis shifts from past spending to future state of affairs, from past commitments to future goals.

Necessarily, control and management are bounded by the beginning and ending of the fiscal year. It is vital to know how much was spent during some uniform time period. Planning, by contrast, uses a multi-year time frame, and the duration of the planning span will vary from one area to another. Viewed from the planning perspective, the fiscal year is an artificial and possibly obstructive boundary.

If the several purposes were closely integrated, planning inevitably would be forced into the time cycle of management and control and would be subjected to the same routines and deadlines that are appropriate for them. As a matter of fact, this has been the story of PPB thus far. Planning has been crowded into the limits of the fiscal year, with the result that it has not produced much for resource allocation policy. If a more leisurely course were followed and planning were allowed some freedom from the pressures of the next deadline or the next budget, it would have a greater impact on budget decisions.

It would be possible to cite other reasons for suggesting a partial divorcement of planning from the more routine sides of budgeting, but I think a satisfactory case has already been made. Perhaps I have belabored the obvious, but the fact is that thus far the practice and theory of PPB have operated on the assumption that anything less than perfect integration is undesirable.

STAFFING AND DATA PROBLEMS

Despite the advantage of slack in multi-purpose budgeting, there are two prob-lems which deserve consideration be-cause they are partly related to the multi-purpose character of PPB.

One apprehension expressed by budget people pertains to the estab-lishment of a two-track budget system in which separate budgets are prepared by the budget and PPB staffs. Undoubt-edly, this concern has been inflated by the ordinary interpersonal difficulties that accompany institutional change. In the long run each agency will have to decide for itself whether to retain separate staffs or to combine them into a single budget unit. But the budget of the future will be a joint product of men with different backgrounds and perspectives. There will be a persisting need for satisfactory working relation-ships among men who are separated institutionally or vocationally.

It is understandable that during the installation stage of PPB each agency was instructed to establish a separate analytic staff. Without this protection PPB might have withered because of a lack of bureaucratic support and ca-pability. At the present time, however, agencies should be encouraged to ex-periment with a variety of staffing arrangements. I happen to believe that multi-purpose budgeting requires a two-track system and some separation of the budget and planning staffs. The history of budget reform recounted earlier indicates that planning will be swallowed by the control and manage-ment functions if it is not insulated from them. But this is a conclusion that agencies will have to learn by trial and error, not by Bureau of the Budget fiat.

Of course, something that is taken apart must be reunited again. If plan-ning is foreclosed from influencing budgeting by virtue of its isolated status, it will be a meaningless function. At least at the level of the department secretary or his deputy, the various functions must be brought together. Regardless of the particular staffing arrangement used, the crucial integration of the multiple purposes of budgeting must occur at that level.

Historically, changes in budget procedure have resulted in increased informational burdens. The tendency has been to add the new information to the old, not to substitute. In PPB this tendency will be sharpened by the multiple needs to be served by the informational system. Budget people have expressed the fear that they will be inundated by the sheer mass of data pouring in from the Program Memoranda, A-11 submissions, and a hundred other sources.

If multi-purpose budgeting is to work, it will be essential to review all the existing informational requirements and outputs of the budget system and to remove from the informational stream, particularly at central levels, those data that are not absolutely necessary for the conduct of budgeting. To take a conspicuous case, Circular A-11 (the annual "call for estimates" issued by the Bureau of the Budget) must be purged of the peripheral information it has accumulated over many years.

The full resources of ADP (Automatic Data Processing) must be applied to the production and distribution of a variety of budgetary data. It should be possible to look at the budget in a number of ways, without time consuming manual operations. There is also a need to develop accounting support for the various informational requirements. At the present time many budget systems are not geared to produce routinely and accurately the kinds

of information needed for policy choices, though they perform more satisfactorily with regard to control and managerial data.

The complexity of data required for PPB far surpasses the data requirements of performance budgeting. Yet it is a fact that the activity and work accounts associated with performance budgeting are maintained in only a small number of jurisdictions. PPB, therefore, demands a quantum jump in the data capabilities of governments. As I have already said, automated data processing is a *sine qua non* for multipurpose budgeting. Governments will have to surrender their reluctance to automate the budget system.

There is one data-related problem that cannot be resolved by data processing but by human skill. If the appropriation and program structures diverge, it will be necessary to decide the budget in one informational context and to defend it in another. There is ample evidence of this difficulty in the confrontations between Secretary McNamara and congressional committees. A decision which is rational in terms of end purposes will not always appear to be sensible if it is appraised in terms of inputs. Administrators, like machines, will have to master the arts and sciences of multi-purpose budgeting if PPB is to succeed.

CONCLUSION

Multi-purpose budget systems are a vital part of the future of budgeting. Although many of the problems have not been solved or even recognized, budgeting in the future will not be able to neglect its planning role or abandon its investment in control and management. Those who are responsible for the current infusion of planning purposes into budgeting must give consideration to the other needs of budgeting, and they must design a system which qualifies on all counts.

As we have suggested, the main problem is not technical. Rather, it is the sheer lack of experience with a budget system that serves several purposes. Virtually all the experience of governmental budgeting has been with single-purpose systems. Lacking previous experience and unable to imitate business practices, we must probe and adjust until satisfactory procedures and practices are developed.

At this time it is premature to forecast the exact relationships among the various purposes that will exist in the future. While I have recommended "imperfect integration," this does not provide a precise indicator of the optimal level of integration. The optimum will emerge from experimentation and certainly will vary among programs.

The Planning-Programming-Budgeting System: Progress and Potentials

BY
THE SUBCOMMITTEE ON ECONOMY IN GOVERNMENT
OF THE
JOINT ECONOMIC COMMITTEE,
CONGRESS OF THE UNITED STATES

GENERAL PERSPECTIVE

PPBS is one of the more recent attempts to achieve a more systematic and rational approach to decisionmaking in respect to Government programs. It undertakes to assess costs of achieving objectives against the benefits to be expected therefrom, and in this way makes possible a more intelligent use of resources by the public sector.

The effort is by no means free of handicap. Unquestionably, it is easier to measure costs and benefits that are amenable to marketplace assessment than it is to measure the true costs or true value of those more intangible effects of Government activity that are not solely subject to market determination. In assessing the cost-benefit relationship of a proposed dam, for example, it is far easier to measure benefits in terms of water supply, power supply, and navigation than it is to measure the many other incidental effects, such

The conclusion, "General Perspective," of a Report of the Subcommittee on Economy in Government (Senator William Proxmire, Chairman) of the Joint Economic Committee, U.S. Congress, U.S. Government Printing Office, Washington, D.C., December, 1967.

as redistribution of income, esthetic improvement, effects on long-term population movements, and the like.

There is a tendency to exaggerate both the potential and the progress of PPBS. Judging from the brief hearings held, it is the subcommittee's conclusion that some progress has been made in bringing a more rational means of decisionmaking into the public sector, but that this is only a beginning. The Government has a long way to go in applying PPBS or any similar system of program management on any kind of comprehensive basis.

Likewise, there is considerable confusion about the role of PPBS in making basic decisions. Public economic policy questions, by their very nature, often involve decisions which affect people as to burdens and benefits. In other words, a public policy decision may increase the burdens of one group and raise the benefits of another, or effect resource transfers between regions. These decisions are frequently made now, particularly by legislatures, but on a judgmental and necessarily subjective basis. PPBS can help to provide a more rational and coherent basis for judgment. But many decisions will remain beyond the reach of quantitative analysis.

In addition, PPBS does not help us much in deciding on ultimate goals for public policy or in deciding between alternative goals. Our knowledge is not sufficiently advanced to answer definitively such questions as whether we ought to put more money into housing or welfare, whether to emphasize decentralization of our cities or not. Such basic choices are far beyond the reach of quantitative measure. Given determined objectives, cost-benefit analysis or any other systems approach can help us in deciding which alternative would provide the most effective means of achieving an objective. But we should not expect it to go beyond this. The choice of goals is a basic political decision, arrived at democratically; we should not rely on budgetary techniques to eliminate the hard problem of choice that now confronts both the Congress and the executive branch.

The subcommittee is of the firm opinion that PPBS represents a substantial forward step in budgetary techniques. At the same time, it is our opinion that much more work is needed in the definition of national objectives and the determination of priorities in the allocation of public funds. If the Nation had a little clearer notion of its goals and national priorities (bearing in mind that they are apt to be continuously shifting in a society like ours), it would ease the task of PPBS inasmuch as it would give rise to definable objective programs which could then be subjected to a systems approach.

This subcommittee recommends to the Joint Economic Committee that the full committee conduct an inquiry into the possibilities for a clearer definition of Federal program objectives than now exists and develop information on possible conflicts, overlaps, or lack of coordination in our present goals and on ways of setting priorities in the allocation of Federal funds.

As a general guide to improved budgeting, the subcommittee feels it appropriate to restate some of the proposals set down by the committee previously which emphasize basic economic principles. Among the recommendations made in the 1957 report of the Subcommittee on Fiscal Policy entitled "Federal Expenditure Policy for Economic Growth and Stability," and in the 1963 report of the Subcommittee on Economic Statistics entitled "The Federal Budget as an Economic Document," the following have particular relevance to this study:

(1) Economy in Government should be measured by the relative benefits and costs of each program. While quantitative evaluation of many Federal programs directed at social problems is admittedly difficult, the priority of these programs must be weighed by careful consideration of their relative costs.

(2) Federal programs aimed at supporting or improving the economic position of particular groups or industries should be constantly reevaluated in light of changing circumstances.

(3) The alternative-resource-use test also should be applied to Federal programs which involve no significant Federal expenditures. Federal enterprise activities and programs for insurance and guarantee of private loans may involve only small net budget expenditures, but exert a powerful influence on the allocation of resources.

(4) Recognizing that economic considerations may not always prevail in determining Federal expenditure programs emphasizes the need for carrying out these programs at minimum real cost.

(5) Federal expenditure policies closely geared to the Nation's economic growth objectives must provide for as rapid adjustment as possible in spending programs in response to changing demand and supply. Rigidities in Federal spending programs may limit significantly the economy's growth potential.

(6) The scope and character of Federal spending programs should reflect, wherever possible, the comparative economic advantages of the Federal, State, and local governments and of private enterprise in achieving program objectives.

(7) Federal participation in activities shared by State and local governments and private enterprise should be aimed primarily at improving the effectiveness of these activities and should avoid merely transferring responsibility for them to the Federal Government.

(8) The budgetary process should show how the various activities of the Federal Government are related to each other on a program basis, and how these programs are related to similar activities outside of the Federal Government.

(9) Budget decisions should be based upon a clear recognition of the longer range prospects for Government programs in terms of their costs and benefits. Specifically, the budget for each year should be presented in the context of a longer run set of budgetary projections, probably covering a 5-year period; and regular periodic revisions of budgetary estimates should be provided, on at least a quarterly basis

appendices

APPENDIX 1

TABLE A

PRESENT VALUE OF $1

Years Hence	1%	2%	4%	6%	8%	10%	12%	14%	15%	16%	18%	20%	22%	24%	25%	26%	28%	30%	35%	40%	45%	50%
1	0.990	0.980	0.962	0.943	0.926	0.909	0.893	0.877	0.870	0.862	0.847	0.833	0.820	0.806	0.800	0.794	0.781	0.769	0.741	0.714	0.690	0.667
2	0.980	0.961	0.925	0.890	0.857	0.826	0.797	0.769	0.756	0.743	0.718	0.694	0.672	0.650	0.640	0.630	0.610	0.592	0.549	0.510	0.476	0.444
3	0.971	0.942	0.889	0.840	0.794	0.751	0.712	0.675	0.658	0.641	0.609	0.579	0.551	0.524	0.512	0.500	0.477	0.455	0.406	0.364	0.328	0.296
4	0.961	0.924	0.855	0.792	0.735	0.683	0.636	0.592	0.572	0.552	0.516	0.482	0.451	0.423	0.410	0.397	0.373	0.350	0.301	0.260	0.226	0.198
5	0.951	0.906	0.822	0.747	0.681	0.621	0.567	0.519	0.497	0.476	0.437	0.402	0.370	0.341	0.328	0.315	0.291	0.269	0.223	0.186	0.156	0.132
6	0.942	0.888	0.790	0.705	0.630	0.564	0.507	0.456	0.432	0.410	0.370	0.335	0.303	0.275	0.262	0.250	0.227	0.207	0.165	0.133	0.108	0.088
7	0.933	0.871	0.760	0.665	0.583	0.513	0.452	0.400	0.376	0.354	0.314	0.279	0.249	0.222	0.210	0.198	0.178	0.159	0.122	0.095	0.074	0.059
8	0.923	0.853	0.731	0.627	0.540	0.467	0.404	0.351	0.327	0.305	0.266	0.233	0.204	0.179	0.168	0.157	0.139	0.123	0.091	0.068	0.051	0.039
9	0.914	0.837	0.703	0.592	0.500	0.424	0.361	0.308	0.284	0.263	0.225	0.194	0.167	0.144	0.134	0.125	0.108	0.094	0.067	0.048	0.035	0.026
10	0.905	0.820	0.676	0.558	0.463	0.386	0.322	0.270	0.247	0.227	0.191	0.162	0.137	0.116	0.107	0.099	0.085	0.073	0.050	0.035	0.024	0.017
11	0.896	0.804	0.650	0.527	0.429	0.350	0.287	0.237	0.215	0.195	0.162	0.135	0.112	0.094	0.086	0.079	0.066	0.056	0.037	0.025	0.017	0.012
12	0.887	0.788	0.625	0.497	0.397	0.319	0.257	0.208	0.187	0.168	0.137	0.112	0.092	0.076	0.069	0.062	0.052	0.043	0.027	0.018	0.012	0.008
13	0.879	0.773	0.601	0.469	0.368	0.290	0.229	0.182	0.163	0.145	0.116	0.093	0.075	0.061	0.055	0.050	0.040	0.033	0.020	0.013	0.008	0.005
14	0.870	0.758	0.577	0.442	0.340	0.263	0.205	0.160	0.141	0.125	0.099	0.078	0.062	0.049	0.044	0.039	0.032	0.025	0.015	0.009	0.006	0.003
15	0.861	0.743	0.555	0.417	0.315	0.239	0.183	0.140	0.123	0.108	0.084	0.065	0.051	0.040	0.035	0.031	0.025	0.020	0.011	0.006	0.004	0.002
16	0.853	0.728	0.534	0.394	0.292	0.218	0.163	0.123	0.107	0.093	0.071	0.054	0.042	0.032	0.028	0.025	0.019	0.015	0.008	0.005	0.003	0.002
17	0.844	0.714	0.513	0.371	0.270	0.198	0.146	0.108	0.093	0.080	0.060	0.045	0.034	0.026	0.023	0.020	0.015	0.012	0.006	0.003	0.002	0.001
18	0.836	0.700	0.494	0.350	0.250	0.180	0.130	0.095	0.081	0.069	0.051	0.038	0.028	0.021	0.018	0.016	0.012	0.009	0.005	0.002	0.001	0.001
19	0.828	0.686	0.475	0.331	0.232	0.164	0.116	0.083	0.070	0.060	0.043	0.031	0.023	0.017	0.014	0.012	0.009	0.007	0.003	0.002	0.001	0.001
20	0.820	0.673	0.456	0.312	0.215	0.149	0.104	0.073	0.061	0.051	0.037	0.026	0.019	0.014	0.012	0.010	0.007	0.005	0.002	0.001	0.001	0.001
21	0.811	0.660	0.439	0.294	0.199	0.135	0.093	0.064	0.053	0.044	0.031	0.022	0.015	0.011	0.009	0.008	0.006	0.004	0.002	0.001		
22	0.803	0.647	0.422	0.278	0.184	0.123	0.083	0.056	0.046	0.038	0.026	0.018	0.013	0.009	0.007	0.006	0.004	0.003	0.001	0.001		
23	0.795	0.634	0.406	0.262	0.170	0.112	0.074	0.049	0.040	0.033	0.022	0.015	0.010	0.007	0.006	0.005	0.003	0.002	0.001			
24	0.788	0.622	0.390	0.247	0.158	0.102	0.066	0.043	0.035	0.028	0.019	0.013	0.008	0.006	0.005	0.004	0.003	0.002	0.001			
25	0.780	0.610	0.375	0.233	0.146	0.092	0.059	0.038	0.030	0.024	0.016	0.010	0.007	0.005	0.004	0.003	0.002	0.001	0.001			
26	0.772	0.598	0.361	0.220	0.135	0.084	0.053	0.033	0.026	0.021	0.014	0.009	0.006	0.004	0.003	0.002	0.002	0.001				
27	0.764	0.586	0.347	0.207	0.125	0.076	0.047	0.029	0.023	0.018	0.011	0.007	0.005	0.003	0.002	0.002	0.001	0.001				
28	0.757	0.574	0.333	0.196	0.116	0.069	0.042	0.026	0.020	0.016	0.010	0.006	0.004	0.002	0.002	0.002	0.001	0.001				
29	0.749	0.563	0.321	0.185	0.107	0.063	0.037	0.022	0.017	0.014	0.008	0.005	0.003	0.002	0.001	0.001	0.001	0.001				
30	0.742	0.552	0.308	0.174	0.099	0.057	0.033	0.020	0.015	0.012	0.007	0.004	0.003	0.002	0.001	0.001	0.001					
40	0.672	0.453	0.208	0.097	0.046	0.022	0.011	0.005	0.004	0.003	0.001	0.001										
50	0.608	0.372	0.141	0.054	0.021	0.009	0.003	0.001	0.001	0.001												

TABLE B

PRESENT VALUE OF $1 RECEIVED ANNUALLY FOR N YEARS

Years (N)	1%	2%	4%	6%	8%	10%	12%	14%	15%	16%	18%	20%	22%	24%	25%	26%	28%	30%	35%	40%	45%	50%
1	0.990	0.980	0.962	0.943	0.926	0.909	0.893	0.877	0.870	0.862	0.847	0.833	0.820	0.806	0.800	0.794	0.781	0.769	0.741	0.714	0.690	0.667
2	1.970	1.942	1.886	1.833	1.783	1.736	1.690	1.647	1.626	1.605	1.566	1.528	1.492	1.457	1.440	1.424	1.392	1.361	1.289	1.224	1.165	1.111
3	2.941	2.884	2.775	2.673	2.577	2.487	2.402	2.322	2.283	2.246	2.174	2.106	2.042	1.981	1.952	1.923	1.868	1.816	1.696	1.589	1.493	1.407
4	3.902	3.808	3.630	3.465	3.312	3.170	3.037	2.914	2.855	2.798	2.690	2.589	2.494	2.404	2.362	2.320	2.241	2.166	1.997	1.849	1.720	1.605
5	4.853	4.713	4.452	4.212	3.993	3.791	3.605	3.433	3.352	3.274	3.127	2.991	2.864	2.745	2.689	2.635	2.532	2.436	2.220	2.035	1.876	1.737
6	5.795	5.601	5.242	4.917	4.623	4.355	4.111	3.889	3.784	3.685	3.498	3.326	3.167	3.020	2.951	2.885	2.759	2.643	2.385	2.168	1.983	1.824
7	6.728	6.472	6.002	5.582	5.206	4.868	4.564	4.288	4.160	4.039	3.812	3.605	3.416	3.242	3.161	3.083	2.937	2.802	2.508	2.263	2.057	1.883
8	7.652	7.325	6.733	6.210	5.747	5.335	4.968	4.639	4.487	4.344	4.078	3.837	3.619	3.421	3.329	3.241	3.076	2.925	2.598	2.331	2.108	1.922
9	8.566	8.162	7.435	6.802	6.247	5.759	5.328	4.946	4.772	4.607	4.303	4.031	3.786	3.566	3.463	3.366	3.184	3.019	2.665	2.379	2.144	1.948
10	9.471	8.983	8.111	7.360	6.710	6.145	5.650	5.216	5.019	4.833	4.494	4.192	3.923	3.682	3.571	3.465	3.269	3.092	2.715	2.414	2.168	1.965
11	10.368	9.787	8.760	7.887	7.139	6.495	5.937	5.453	5.234	5.029	4.656	4.327	4.035	3.776	3.656	3.544	3.335	3.147	2.752	2.438	2.185	1.977
12	11.255	10.575	9.385	8.384	7.536	6.814	6.194	5.660	5.421	5.197	4.793	4.439	4.127	3.851	3.725	3.606	3.387	3.190	2.779	2.456	2.196	1.985
13	12.134	11.343	9.986	8.853	7.904	7.103	6.424	5.842	5.583	5.342	4.910	4.533	4.203	3.912	3.780	3.656	3.427	3.223	2.799	2.468	2.204	1.990
14	13.004	12.106	10.563	9.295	8.244	7.367	6.628	6.002	5.724	5.468	5.008	4.611	4.265	3.962	3.824	3.695	3.459	3.249	2.814	2.477	2.210	1.993
15	13.865	12.849	11.118	9.712	8.559	7.606	6.811	6.142	5.847	5.575	5.092	4.675	4.315	4.001	3.859	3.726	3.483	3.268	2.825	2.484	2.214	1.995
16	14.718	13.578	11.652	10.106	8.851	7.824	6.974	6.265	5.954	5.669	5.162	4.730	4.357	4.033	3.887	3.751	3.503	3.283	2.834	2.489	2.216	1.997
17	15.562	14.292	12.166	10.477	9.122	8.022	7.120	6.373	6.047	5.749	5.222	4.775	4.391	4.059	3.910	3.771	3.518	3.295	2.840	2.492	2.218	1.998
18	16.398	14.992	12.659	10.828	9.372	8.201	7.250	6.467	6.128	5.818	5.273	4.812	4.419	4.080	3.928	3.786	3.529	3.304	2.844	2.494	2.219	1.999
19	17.226	15.678	13.134	11.158	9.604	8.365	7.366	6.550	6.198	5.877	5.316	4.844	4.442	4.097	3.942	3.799	3.539	3.311	2.848	2.496	2.220	1.999
20	18.046	16.351	13.590	11.470	9.818	8.514	7.469	6.623	6.259	5.929	5.353	4.870	4.460	4.110	3.954	3.808	3.546	3.316	2.850	2.497	2.221	1.999
21	18.857	17.011	14.029	11.764	10.017	8.649	7.562	6.687	6.312	5.973	5.384	4.891	4.476	4.121	3.963	3.816	3.551	3.320	2.852	2.498	2.221	2.000
22	19.660	17.658	14.451	12.042	10.201	8.772	7.645	6.743	6.359	6.011	5.410	4.909	4.488	4.130	3.970	3.822	3.556	3.323	2.853	2.498	2.222	2.000
23	20.456	18.292	14.857	12.303	10.371	8.883	7.718	6.792	6.399	6.044	5.432	4.925	4.499	4.137	3.976	3.827	3.559	3.325	2.854	2.499	2.222	2.000
24	21.243	18.914	15.247	12.550	10.529	8.985	7.784	6.835	6.434	6.073	5.451	4.937	4.507	4.143	3.981	3.831	3.562	3.327	2.855	2.499	2.222	2.000
25	22.023	19.523	15.622	12.783	10.675	9.077	7.843	6.873	6.464	6.097	5.467	4.948	4.514	4.147	3.985	3.834	3.564	3.329	2.856	2.499	2.222	2.000
26	22.795	20.121	15.983	13.003	10.810	9.161	7.896	6.906	6.491	6.118	5.480	4.956	4.520	4.151	3.988	3.837	3.566	3.330	2.856	2.500	2.222	2.000
27	23.560	20.707	16.330	13.211	10.935	9.237	7.943	6.935	6.514	6.136	5.492	4.964	4.524	4.154	3.990	3.839	3.567	3.331	2.856	2.500	2.222	2.000
28	24.316	21.281	16.663	13.406	11.051	9.307	7.984	6.961	6.534	6.152	5.502	4.970	4.528	4.157	3.992	3.840	3.568	3.331	2.857	2.500	2.222	2.000
29	25.066	21.844	16.984	13.591	11.158	9.370	8.022	6.983	6.551	6.166	5.510	4.975	4.531	4.159	3.994	3.841	3.569	3.332	2.857	2.500	2.222	2.000
30	25.808	22.396	17.292	13.765	11.258	9.427	8.055	7.003	6.566	6.177	5.517	4.979	4.534	4.160	3.995	3.842	3.569	3.332	2.857	2.500	2.222	2.000
40	32.835	27.355	19.793	15.046	11.925	9.779	8.244	7.105	6.642	6.234	5.548	4.997	4.544	4.166	3.999	3.846	3.571	3.333	2.857	2.500	2.222	2.000
50	39,196	31.424	21.482	15.762	12.234	9.915	8.304	7.133	6.661	6.246	5.554	4.999	4.545	4.167	4.000	3.846	3.571	3.333	2.857	2.500	2.222	2.000

Bibliography

This bibliography is arranged in two parts. Part I contains a brief list of references which are virtually essential reading for students wishing to investigate further the subject of benefit-cost analysis and its impact on public decision making. Part II presents an extensive list of references to aid the student who wishes to study in depth the application of benefit-cost analysis in particular fields.

Part II is arranged under the following headings:

Bibliographies
Background Material
General
Community Development and Services
Health, Education, and Welfare
Highways
National Defense
Research and Development
Resource Development
Transportation

The references in Part II, with some modifications and additions, are largely drawn from *Program Analysis Techniques: A Selected Bibliography (Revised)*, prepared in 1966 by the Bureau of the Budget Library, and from the Supplement issued by the Library in July, 1967. The editors wish to acknowledge their debt to the compilers of these extensive bibliographies.

PART I

American Economic Association and the Royal Economic Society. "Resource Allocation," *Surveys of Economic Theory,* III. New York: St. Martin's Press, 1966.

Dorfman, Robert, ed. "Measuring benefits of Government Investments." Papers presented at a conference, November 1963. Washington, D.C.: Brookings Institution—Studies of Government Finance, 1965.

Eckstein, Otto. *Water Resource Development; the Economics of Project Evaluation.* Cambridge, Harvard University Press, 1958.

Enke, Stephen, ed. *Defense Management.* Englewood Cliffs, N.J.: Prentice-Hall, Inc., 1967.

Hatry, Harry P., and John F. Cotton. *Program Planning for State, County, City.* Washington, D.C.: State–Local Finances Project, The George Washington University, 1967.

Hitch, Charles J., and Roland N. McKean. *The Economics of Defense in the Nuclear Age.* Cambridge: Harvard University Press, 1965.

McKean, Roland N. *Efficiency in Government through Systems Analysis, with Emphasis on Water Resource Development.* New York: John Wiley & Sons, Inc., 1958.

National Bureau of Economic Research. *Public Finances: Needs, Sources, and Utilization.* Princeton, N.J.: Princeton University Press, 1961.

Novick, David, ed. *Program Budgeting: Program Analysis and the Federal Government.* Cambridge: Harvard University Press, 1965.

Quirin, G. David. *The Capital Expenditure Decision.* Homewood, Illinois: Richard D. Irwin, Inc., 1967.

Schick, Allen. "The Road to PPB: the Stages of Budget Reform," *Public Administration Review,* XXVI, 4, 1966.

State–Local Finances Project, The George Washington University. *PPB Note 5:* Development of output-oriented program structure. *PPB Note 6:* Role and nature of cost analysis in a PPB system. *PPB Note 7:* Output measures for a PPB system multi-year program and financial plan. *PPB Note 8:* The multi-year program and financial plan. *PPB Note 9:* Demographic and economic data guide lines for a PPB system. *PPB Note 10:* Program objectives, effectiveness criteria and program structure—an illustration for highway safety. *PPB Note 11:* A first step to analysis: the issue paper.

U.S. Congress Subcommittee on Economy in Government of the Joint Economic Committee, "The Planning-Programming-Budgeting System: Progress and Potentials." *Hearings,* Washington, D.C.: Government Printing Office, 1967.

U.S. Senate; Subcommittee on National Security and International Operations, Committee on Government Operations.
  - Official Documents; Memorandum, July 1967
  - Selected Comment; Memorandum, July 1967
  - Hearings on PPB; Part 1; Charles L. Schultze, August 1967
  - Hearings on PPB, Part 2; Alain C. Enthoven, October 1967
  - PPBS and Foreign Affairs, Memorandum by
      Thomas C. Schelling, January 1968.
  - Hearings on PPB, Part 3; Elmer B. Staats, March 1968

PART II

Bibliographies

Blaug, Mark. *Economics of Education: A Selected Annotated Bibliography.* New York: Pergamon, 1966.

Don Vito, P.A. *Annotated Bibliography on Systems Cost Analysis* (rev. ed.). Santa Monica, Calif.: RAND Corporation, Memorandum RM4848-1-PR, 1967. 80 p.

Pearman, Elizabeth H. *Bibliography on Cost-Benefit Analysis and Planning-Programming-Budgeting.* McLean, Va.: Research Analysis Corporation, 1966. 44 p.

Prest, A. R., and Ralph Turvey. "Cost-Benefit Analysis: A Survey," *Economic Journal,* 1965, 75, 683–730, Bibliography 731–35.

U.S. Defense Documentation Center. "Cost: Analysis and Methodology, A Report Bibliography," Alexandria, Va.: Operations Research Series, I, 1967.

U.S. Industrial College of the Armed Forces. *Defense Oriented Cost Analysis.* Washington, D.C.: Government Printing Office, 1965. Pp. 11–18. 64 p.

U.S. Library of Congress, Legislative Reference Service. *The Planning-Programming-Budgeting System: An Annotated Bibliography* (rev. ed.), Robert L. Chartrand and Dennis W. Brezina. Washington, D.C.: Government Printing Office, 1967.

Background Material

Baumol, William J. "Informed Judgment, Rigorous Theory, and Public Policy," *Southern Economic Journal,* 1966, 32, 137–45.

————, *Welfare Economics and the Theory of the State* (2nd ed.). Cambridge: Harvard University Press, 1965. See especially "Cost-Benefit Analysis," 22–24.

Buchanan, James M. "Positive Economics, Welfare Economics, and Political Economy," *Journal of Law and Economics,* 1959, 2, 124–38.

Coase, R. H. "The Problem of Social Cost," *Journal of Law and Economics,* 1960, 3, 1–44.

Davis, Otto A., and Andrew B. Whinston. "Some Notes on Equating Private and Social Cost," *Southern Economic Journal,* 1965, 32, 113–26. See also Carnegie Institute of Technology, Pittsburgh, Penn.: Graduate School of Industrial Administration, Reprint No. 215.

————, "Welfare Economics and the Theory of Second Best," *Review of Economic Studies,* 1965, 32, 1–14. See also Carnegie Institute of Technology, Pittsburgh, Penn.: Graduate School of Industrial Administration, Reprint No. 194.

Eckstein, Otto. "A Survey of the Theory of Public Expenditure Criteria," *Public Finances: Needs, Sources, Utilization; A Conference. . . ,* Universities–National Bureau Committee for Economic Research. Princeton: Princeton University Press, 1961. Pp. 438–504.

Foley, Duncan K. "Resource Allocation and the Public Sector," *Yale Economic Essays,* 1967, 7, 45–98.

Hirshleifer, Jack. "Investment Decision under Uncertainty: Applications of the State-Preference Approach," *Quarterly Journal of Economics,* 1966, 80, 252–77.

————, "Investment Decision under Uncertainty: Choice-Criteria Approach," *Quarterly Journal of Economics,* 1965, 79, 509–36.

————, "On the Theory of Optimal Investment Decisions," *Journal of Political Economy,* 1958, 66, 329–52. Compares the present value and internal rate of return approaches to the problem of arriving at optimal investment decisions.

Mishan, E. J. "A Survey of Welfare Economics, 1939–1959," *Surveys of Economic Theory, I.* Prepared for the American Economic Association and the Royal Economic Society. New York: St. Martin's Press, 1965. Pp. 154–222. Also in *Economic Journal,* 1969, 70, 197–265.

Musgrave, Richard A. *The Theory of Public Finance: A Study in Public Economy.* New York: McGraw-Hill Book Company, 1959.

Rothenberg, Jerome. *The Measurement of Social Welfare.* Englewood Cliffs, N.J.: Prentice-Hall, Inc., 1961. 357 p. Focuses on the nature of the fundamental criterion needed for analysis relevant to public policy decisions.

Samuelson, Paul A. "Aspects of Public Expenditure Theories," *Review of Economics and Statistics,* 1958, 40, 332–38. Considers some of the difficulties of expenditure theory and political decision making.

————, "Diagrammatic Expansion of a Theory of Public Expenditure," *Review of Economics and Statistics,* 1955, 37, 350–56.

————, "The Pure Theory of Public Expenditure," *Review of Economics and Statistics,* 1954, 36, 387–89. See also "Comment," by Julius Margolis, *Review of Economics and Statistics,* 1955, 37, 347–49. Explains "the basic philosophy and concepts that underlie" this technique and outlines the necessary steps for adapting this system for non-defense purposes.

Turvey, Ralph. "On Divergences between Social Cost and Private Cost," *Economica,* 1963, 30, 309–13. Illustrates the uselessness of a general prescription of a tax as a means of dealing with external diseconomies.

————, "Present Value versus Internal Rate of Return—An Essay in the theory of Third Best," *Economic Journal,* 1963, 73, 92–98.

General

American Economic Association. "Resource allocation," *Surveys of Economic Theory,* III. New York: St. Martin's Press, 1966. See pp. 155–207 for reprint of "Cost-Benefit Analysis: A Survey," by A. R. Prest and R. Turvey, previously published in *Economic Journal,* 1965, 75, 683–735.

American Political Association, Papers delivered at the 1966 annual meeting. Washington, D.C.: 1966. Partial contents: No. 3, "The Impact of Analysis on Bargaining in Government," by William M. Capron; No. 11, "Data Requirements for Testing Systems Theories: Problems in the Measurement of Output Allocations," by William C. Mitchell; No. 14, "Bargaining and Analysis in Government," by Henry S. Rowen.

Arrow, Kenneth J. "Criteria for Social Investment," *Water Resources Research,* First quarter 1965, 1, 1–8. An exposition of criteria for choosing social investments.

Bell, Chauncey F. *Cost—Effectiveness Analysis as a Management Tool.* RAND Corporation, Santa Monica, Calif.: paper, 1964. 52 p. Defines cost-effectiveness analysis, considers its strengths and weaknesses and demonstrates the construction of cost-effectiveness models.

Black, Guy. *The Application of Systems Analysis to Government Operations.* Washington, D.C.: National Institute of Public Affairs, 1966. 35 pp.

Bryk, Oliver. "Models in Cost-Effectiveness Analysis: An Example," rev. ed. McLean, Va:, Research Analysis Corporation, RAC Paper RAC-P-2, 1965. 29 pp. Describes a set of models designed for a cost-effectiveness analysis of alternative aircraft systems.

——————, "Aspects of Cost and Utility Analysis in Planning," McLean, Va.: Research Analysis Corporation, RAC Paper RAC-P-8, 1965. 9 pp.

Capron, William M. "The Potential Role of Cost Effectiveness Analysis for Evaluation of Government Domestic Programs," *Address . . . before the Symposium on Cost Effectiveness Analysis, Institute for Defense Analyses, June 15, 1965.* Washington, D.C.: Bureau of the Budget, 1965. 15 pp.

Chamberlain, Neil W. "Government Investment: How Scientific Can It Be?" *Challenge,* 1966, 14, 32–35.

Committee for Economic Development. "Budgeting for National Objectives; Executive and Congressional Roles in Program Planning and Performance," A Statement on National Policy by the Research and Policy Committee. New York: 1966. 65 pp.

Dorfman, Robert, ed. "Measuring Benefits of Government Investments," paper presented at a conference of experts held Nov. 7–9, 1963. Washington, D.C.: Brookings Institution, *Studies of Government Finance,* 1965.

Dunn, Robert M. "A Problem of Bias in Benefit-Cost Analysis: A Consumer Surplus Reconsidered," *Southern Economic Journal,* 1967, 33, 337–42. Argues that "the current market values of the resources to be used in a project may not be an accurate measure of their cost to society."

Eckstein, Otto. *Public Finance.* "Efficiency in Government Expenditures," Englewood Cliffs, N.J.: Prentice-Hall, Inc., 1964, 20–36.

English, J. M. and R. H. Haase. "Economic Selection of Alternative Risk Investments," Santa Monica, Calif.: RAND Corporation, Paper P-2869, 1964. 16 pp. Develops a technique for making investment decisions in situations involving different levels of risk.

Feldstein, Martin S. "Opportunity Cost Calculations in Cost-Benefit Analysis," *Public Finance,* 1964, 19, 117–139. Investigates various concepts of the social opportunity cost rate proposed in discussions of cost-benefit analysis.

——————, "The Social Time Preference Discount Rate in Cost Benefit Analysis," *Economic Journal,* 1964, 74, 360–79.

Fields, Davis S. "Cost/Effectiveness Analysis: Its Tasks and Their Inter-relation," *Operations Research,* 1966, 14, 515–27.

Fisher, G. H. "The Role of Cost-Utility Analysis in Program Budgeting." Santa Monica, Calif.: RAND Corporation, Research Memorandum RM-4279-RC, 1964. 39 pp.

————, "What is Resource Analysis?" Santa Monica, Calif.: RAND Corporation, Paper P-2688, 1963, 14 pp. Defines the concept of resource analysis and outlines the characteristics of resource analysis techniques for use in long-range planning.

————, "The World of Program Budgeting," Santa Monica, Calif.: RAND Corporation, Paper P-3361, 1966. Discusses the role of analysis in program budgeting.

Geisler, Murray A. and Wilbur A. Steger. "The Combination of Alternative Research Techniques in Logistics Systems Analysis," Santa Monica, Calif.: RAND Corporation, Paper P-2660, 1962. 19 pp. Considers the problem of selecting techniques to use in a systems analysis, drawing examples from supply and inventory systems problems.

George Washington University. "Planning, Programming, Budgeting for City, State, County Objectives." Washington, D.C.: State-Local Finance Project, PPB Notes, 1967–1968. 8 Vols.

Contents: Note 1—"Answering the Question: Is An Integrated Planning, Programming, Budgeting System Useful for our Jurisdiction?"; Note 2—"Administrative Framework for Establishing Planning-Programming-Budgeting Systems in States, Cities, and Counties: Some Considerations and Suggested Possibilities"; Note 3—"Development of Initial Instructions to Inaugurate a Planning-Programming-Budgeting System: Some Preliminary Considerations and Model Instruction to be Adapted for Local Use"; Note 4—"Problems of Staffing and Training for a PPB System in State and Local Governments"; Note 5—"Development of Output-Oriented Program Structure"; Note 6—"Role and Nature of Cost Analysis in a PPB System"; Note 7—"Output Measures for a PPB System Multi-Year Program and Financial Plan"; Note 8—"The Multi-Year Program and Financial Plan"; Note 9—"Demographic and Economic Data Guidelines for a PPB System"; Note 10—"Program Objectives, Effectiveness Criteria, and Program Structure—An Illustration for Highway Safety"; Note 11—"A First Step to Analysis: The Issue Paper."

Goldman, Thomas A., ed. *Cost-Effectiveness Analysis: New Approaches in Decision-Making.* New York: Frederick A. Praeger, 1966.

Greenhouse, Samuel M. "A 'Distributed Output' Concept for the Planning-Programming-Budgeting System," *Personnel Administration,* 1967, 30, 35–41. Suggests that "Departmental and Presidential decision making can be aided immeasurably by PPBS" only when "Federally produced goods and services that reach the public have been identified. Once that has been done, the PPBS budget can be structured on an output basis—with each distributed end-product considered to represent a separate program."

Gross, Bertram M., ed. *Action under Planning: The Guidance of Economic Development.* New York: McGraw-Hill Book Co., 1967.

Partial contents: "Planning the Improbable," by Bertram M. Gross; "Economic Activation, Planning, and the Social Order," Peter J. D. Wiles; "Activating National Plans," by Bertram M. Gross; "What is National Planning?" by Robert J. Schaefer *et al;* "Some Fundamental Questions on National Planning," by Peter J. D. Wiles *et al.*

————, *The Managing of Organizations: The Administrative Struggle,* I, II, New York: The Free Press of Glencoe, 1964.

Partial contents: II, 467–804: "The Matrix of Purposes"; "Satisfaction of Interests"; "Output: Services and Goods"; "Output: Quantity and Quality"; "Output: Operations and Functions"; "Efficiency or Profitability"; "Investment in Organizational Viability"; "Mobilization of Resources"; "Observance of Codes"; "Rationality: Satisfactory Action Patterns"; "Rationality: Administrative Processes."

————, "The State of the Nation: Social Systems Accounting," *Social Indicators,* Raymond Bauer, ed., Cambridge: The M.I.T. Press, 1966. Contents: "A Social Systems Model"; "States of a Nation"; "System Structure"; "System Performance"; Toward Social Indicators."

————, "What are your Organization's Objectives? A General-Systems Approach to Planning," *Human Relations,* 1965, 18, 195–216.

Gross, Robert N. "An Introduction to Cost-Effectiveness Analysis," McLean, Va.: Research Analysis Corporation, RAC Paper RAC-P-5, 1965, 27 pp. Explains the theory underlying cost-effectiveness analysis and provides a basis for developing greater understanding of the applications of this analytic technique.

————, *Principles of Cost Effectiveness Analysis.* Washington, D.C.: U.S. Industrial College of the Armed Forces, publication No. L66-24, 1966. 75 pp.

Haldi, John. "Issues of Analysis in Cost-Effectiveness Studies for Civilian Agencies of the Federal Government," paper presented at the Institute of Management Sciences, Philadelphia, Pa.: Sept. 7, 1966. Washington, D.C.: Bureau of the Budget, 1966. 22 pp.

————, "Criteria for Definition of Program Categories and Program Elements," *Remarks . . . before the U.S. Naval Post Graduate School,* Defense Management Systems Course, Monterey, Calif., Nov. 9, 1965. Washington, D.C.: Bureau of the Budget, 1965. 25 pp.

Hammond, Richard J. "Convention and Limitation in Benefit-Cost Analysis," *Natural Resources Journal,* 1966, 6, 195–222. A critical appraisal of the present application of cost-benefit analysis techniques.

Hatry, Harry P. and John F. Cotton. "Program Planning for State, County, City," Washington, D.C.: 1967. 72 pp.

Henderson ,William M. "The Analysis Mystique," *Air University Review,* 1967, 18, 34–45. A layman's guide to systems analysis.

Heymont, I. *et al.* "Guide for Reviewers of Studies Containing Cost-Effectiveness Analysis," McLean, Va.: Research Analysis Corporation, Study 63.2, 1965. 67 pp. Presents a series of "key questions" as an aid in evaluating military cost-effectiveness analysis.

Hines, Lawrence G. "The Hazards of Benefit-Cost Analysis as a Guide to Public Investment Policy," *Public Finance,* 1962, 7, 101–117. Criticizes the application of cost-benefit analysis to water resource development projects.

Hirsch, Werner Z. "Integrating View of Federal Program Budgeting." Santa Monica, Calif.: 1965. RAND Corporation. Research memorandum RM-4799-RC. 27 p.

————, "Toward Federal Program Budgeting." Santa Monica, Calif.: 1966. RAND Corporation. Paper P-3306, 27 p. Presents "some basic concepts of program budgeting," develops "an example of a Federal program budget," and discusses "its applications, and problems and prospects of implementation."

International Congress of Administrative Sciences. 13th, Paris, 1965. "New Techniques of Budget Preparation and Management." General report by H. J. Hofstra, Netherlands. Brussels, International Institute of Administrative Sciences, 1965, 112 p. (2 Reports.) Part II of the discussion deals with several techniques including long term planning and methods of evaluating costs and benefits.

Kahn, Herman and Irwin Mann. "Techniques of Systems Analysis." Santa Monica, Calif.: 1957. RAND Corporation. Research memorandum RM-1829-I, 161 p.

Kantorovich, Leonid V. *The Best Use of Economic Resources.* Cambridge, Harvard University Press, 1965. Sums up the extensive researches of the author, a member of the Academy of Sciences of the U.S.S.R., in developing methods of linear programming which can be used for quantitative analysis of economic questions—providing proofs and illustrations in the solution of specific technical-economic and planning problems especially concerned with evaluation of alternative allocation of factors of production.

Karmiloff, G. "Soviet Economic Models, Investment Criteria, and Prices: An Analytical Review," *Kyklos,* 1963, 16, fasc. 1, 83–109 (Brookings Lib.) "Investment criteria," pp. 96–101; "The Effects of Mathematical Analysis on Economic Theory," pp. 101–106.

Kendrick, John W. "Summary and Evaluation of Recent Work in Measuring the Productivity of Federal Government Agencies," *Management Science,* December 1965, 12, B120–B134.

Krutilla, John V. "Welfare Aspects of Benefit-cost Analysis," *Journal of Political Economy,* June 1961, 69, 226–235. Reprint no. 29. Also available as *Resources for the Future.*

Maass, Arthur. "Benefit-cost Analysis: Its Relevance to Public Expenditure Decisions," *Quarterly Journal of Economics,* May 1966, 80, 208–226. Examines and evaluates cost-benefit analysis, suggesting ways to improve it to make it more "applicable to the real issues of public investment."

McCullough, J.D. "Cost Effectiveness: Estimating Systems Costs." Bethesda, Md.: RAND Corporation. 1965. Paper P-3229. 26 p. A discussion of the important aspects and general techniques of systems analysis for the users of cost estimates.

————, "Cost Analysis for Planning-Programming-Budgeting Cost-Benefit Studies." Santa Monica, Calif.: RAND Corporation 1966. 64 p. Paper P3479. One of a series of seminar lectures sponsored by the Civil Service Commission at the University of Maryland, this article uses a simplified, hypothetical cost-benefit analysis in the field of education to illustrate the chief feature of cost analysis.

McKean, Roland N. "Evaluating Alternative Expenditure Programs." Universities-National Bureau Committee for Economic Research. *Public Finances: Needs, Sources, and Utilization; a Conference . . .* Princeton: Princeton University Press, 1961, pp. 337–364.

Marglin, Stephen A. *Public Investment Criteria; Benefit-Cost Analysis for Planned Economic Growth.* Cambridge: M.I.T. Press 1967. Explores some of the problems of formulating investment criteria for the public sector of a mixed-enterprise, underdeveloped economy.

————, "The Opportunity Costs of Public Investment," *Quarterly Journal of Economics,* May 1963, 77, 274–289. Discusses the problems of measuring opportunity costs in order to arrive at the optimal rate of investment.

————, *Public Investment Criteria.* Cambridge, Mass.: In. Te. Press, 1966.

————, "The Social Rate of Discount and the Optimal Rate of Investment," *Quarterly Journal of Economics,* February 1963, 77, 95–111. Considers the question of a social rate of time preference.

Margolis, Julius. "Secondary Benefits, External Economies, and the Justification of Public Investment," *Review of Economics and Statistics,* Aug. 1957, 39, 284–291. Discusses the measure of indirect or secondary benefits used by the Bureau of Reclamation, arguing that a different framework would be more relevant.

Margolis, M. A. "Cost Analysis: Concepts and Methods Outline." Santa Monica, Calif.: 1966 LV. RAND Corporation. Paper P-3344. Outline of a talk given in April, 1966, as part of a lecture series sponsored by the American Institute of Aeronautics and Astronautics.

Mishan, E. J. "Criteria For Public Investment: Some Simplifying Suggestions," *Journal of Political Economy,* Apr. 1967, 75, 139–146. Criticizes certain characteristics of the formulation of public investment criteria proposed by Marglin and Feldstein.

Mushkin, Selma J. "State Programming and Economic Development" (and comments by W. Lee Hansen). Chicago: 1965. 45 p. Council of State Governments. Publication *RM-379.* Defines the purposes of State economic programming and describes the tools available to carry out these purposes.

Mushkin, Selma J. and Robert F. Adams. "Emerging Patterns of Federalism," *National Tax Journal,* Sept. 1966, 19, 225–247. Discusses criteria for evaluating the structure of Federal aid to State and local governments.

National Industrial Conference Board. *The Federal Budget; Its Impact on the Economy.* Fiscal 1968 ed. New York: 1967. 41 p. See "Planning-programming-budgeting," pp. 25–29. Also published in Conference Board *Record,* May 1967, 4, 41–43.

Novick, David. "Origin and History of Program Budgeting." Santa Monica, Calif.: 1966, RAND Corporation. Paper P3427. 11 p. Transcript of a talk filmed in August 1966 for use in PPBS training courses sponsored by the Budget Bureau and the Civil Service Commission.

Novick, David, ed. *"Program Budgeting: Program Analysis and the Federal Budget."* Cambridge: Harvard University Press, 1965. Also available in an abridged version published by the Government Printing Office, 1965.

————, "Resource Analysis and Long-range Planning." Santa Monica, Calif.: 1963. RAND Corporation. Research memorandum RM-3658-PR, 22 p. Discusses the terms "program budgeting," "cost-effectiveness," and "cost analysis" and shows their importance for long-range planning in the Air Force.

Operations Research, Inc. "Description and Evaluation of Current SBA Program Formulation and Control (PFC) System." Prepared for the Bureau of the Budget [and the] Small Business Administration. Silver Spring, Md.: 1966. Technical report 395. 89 p.

————, "SBA Goals and Objectives in the Context of Program Budgeting and Analysis (Phase I)." Technical report 394. Prepared . . . for the Bureau of the Budget [and the] Small Business Administration. Silver Spring, Md.: 1966.

Pardee, F. S. "The Financial Portion of a Management Information System." Santa Monica, Calif.: 1961. RAND Corporation. Research memorandum RM-2836-PR. 45 p. Discusses the requirements of a financial system designed to provide military planners with the data necessary for evaluating cost implications of alternatives.

Peacock, Alan T. and D. J. Robertson, eds. *Public Expenditures: Appraisal and Control.* Edinburgh: Oliver and Boyd, 1963.

Peterson, Robert L. "The Use and Misuse of Cost Effectiveness," *Air University review,* March–April 1966 17, 81–84. Illustrates the effect of different viewpoints in drawing conclusions from a cost-effectiveness analysis.

"Planning-Programming-Budgeting System: A Symposium," *Public Administration Review,* Dec. 1966, 26, 243–292.
Contents.—"The road to PPB: the stages of budget reform," by Allen Schick.—"Toward Federal program budgeting," by Werner Z. Hirsch.—"The Planning-Programming-Budgeting System: Rationale, Language, and Idea-Relationships," by Samuel M. Greenhouse.—"A Management Accounts Structure," by Francis E. McGilvery.—"The Program Budget and Interest Rate for Public Investment," by Robert L. Banks and Arnold Kotz.—"The Political Economy of Efficiency: Cost-benefit Analysis, Systems Analysis, and Program Budgeting," by Aaron Wildavsky.

Posner, Ben. "Planning-Programming-Budgeting," *Federal Accountant,* Summer 1966, 15, 9–21. Discusses the actual and potential impact of PPBS on financial management in Federal civilian agencies.

Quade, E. S. "Systems Analysis Techniques for Planning-Programming-Budgeting." Santa Monica, Calif.: 1966. RAND Corporation. Paper P-3322. 31 p. Discusses the extension of military systems analysis to civilian activities of Government, points out some of the limitations of this approach, and calls attention to promising techniques.

Rowen, Henry S. "Improving Decision Making in Government." Talk . . . at at a meeting of the Budget Bureau's Summer Seminar on Systems Analysis and Program Evaluation, August 19, 1965. Washington, Bureau of the Budget, 1965. 28 p.

————, "Statement . . . before the Special Subcommittee on Scientific Manpower Utilization of the Senate Labor and Public Welfare Committee," May 17, 1966. Washington, Bureau of the Budget, 1966. 16 p. Discusses the present and future uses of systems analysis in connection with the Planning-Programming-Budgeting System.

Schick, Allen. "Introducing PPBS at the State and Local Level," "C–E Cost Effectiveness Section, Operations Research Society of America," *Newsletter,* May 1967, 2, 4–5. Suggests ways in which State and local governments should adapt the PPBS techniques developed by the Federal Government to their particular needs.

————, "The Road to PPB: The Stages of Budget Reform," *Public Administration Review,* XXVI, No. 4, December 1966.

Smithies, Arthur, "A Conceptual Framework for the Program Budget." Santa

Monica, Calif.: 1964. RAND Corporation. Research memorandum RM-4271-RC. 41 p. See also Novick, David, ed. "Program Budgeting: Program Analysis and the Federal Budget," p. 24–60.

————, "Government Decision-Making and the Theory of Choice." Santa Monica, Calif.: 1964. RAND Corporation. Paper P-2960. 11 p. Using the allocation of a given defense budget as an example, examines "the nature of decision-making in terms of standard economic theory."

Steiner, George. "Program Budgeting: Business Contribution to Government Management," *Business Horizons,* Spring 1965, 8, 43–52. Brief, non-technical survey of the elements of the program budget and the analytical approach to choosing among alternative courses of action.

Stohler, Jacques. "Zur Methode und Technik der Cost-Benefit Analyse," *Kyklos,* 1967, 20, fasc. 1, 218–245.

Terleckyj, Nestor E. "The Analytical Staff Assistance to Agency Management Under the Planning-Programming-Budgeting System." Talk given . . . at the Institute for Budget and Management Training, National Association of State Budget Officers, Lexington, Ky., Sept. 30, 1966. Washington, Bureau of the Budget, 1966. 36 p.

————, "Measurement of Output of Federal Government Programs." Lecture . . . at the U.S. Naval Postgraduate School, Monterey, Calif.: Oct. 29, 1965. Washington, Bureau of the Budget [1965] 16 p.

Tweeten, Luther G. and Fred H. Tyner. "The Utility Concept of Net Social Cost—A Criterion for Public Policy," *Agricultural Economics Research,* April 1966, 18, 33–42.

U.S. Bureau of the Budget. "Planning-Programming-Budgeting (PPB)." Washington, July 18, 1967. (Bulletin no. 68-2) 14 p. Contains current guidelines for the continued development of integrated Planning-Programming-Budgeting systems. Replaces Bulletin no. 66-3 and supplement thereto.

————, *Program Evaluation Checklist.* Washington 1966. 7 p.

————, *Measuring Productivity of Federal Government Organizations.* Washington, D.C.: Government Printing Office, 1964. 370 p.

U.S. Congress. House Committee on Appropriations. Department of Agriculture and related agencies appropriations for 1968. Hearings before a subcommittee . . . 90th Cong., 1st sess. Washington, D.C.: Government Printing Office, 1967. Status report on program planning, evaluation, and programming activities, pt. 3, pp. 612–621.

U.S. Congress. Joint Committee on the Organization of Congress. Hearings . . . 89th Cong., 1st sess. Washington, D.C.: Government Printing Office, 1965. pp. 1775–1873. Budget Director Schultze presents his views on the Planning-Programming-Budgeting System.

U.S. Congress. Joint Economic Committee. "Fiscal Policy Issues of the Coming Decade." Hearings . . . 89th Cong., 1st sess. Washington, D.C.: Government Printing Office, 1965. 105 p. Testimony of Budget Director Schultze, pp. 62–87.

U.S. Public Health Service. "The Plan for Implementing a Planning-Programming-Budgeting System in the Public Health Service. Washington, D.C.: 1965. 38 p.

Universities-National Bureau Committee for Economic Research. "National Economic Planning; a Conference." Max F. Millikan, ed. New York,

Distributed by Columbia University Press for National Bureau of Economic Research, 1967. 413 p. "Techniques for Project Appraisal," by Arnold C. Harberger, pp. 131–152; "Planning Public Expenditure," by W. Arthur Lewis, pp. 201–229.

Ward, J. T. "Cost-benefit Analysis," *Journal of Public Administration.* New Zealand, March 1967, 29, 18–30. A general introduction outlining the nature of the concept, discussing some of its basic principles, and indicating problems which can arise in applying it.

Weidenbaum, Murray L. "Innovations in State and Local Government Finance." St. Louis: 1967. Washington University. Institute for Urban and Regional Studies. Working paper EDA 1 21 p. "Analyzes alternative methods of reallocating public resources from national to State and local levels," and discusses the possibility of applying "the newer techniques of program budgeting" to improve the allocation of local government resources.

Weidenbaum, Murray L. "Program Budgeting: Applying Economic Analysis to Government Expenditure Decisions." St. Louis: 1966. 24 p. (Washington University, Dept. of Economics. Working papers).
Also in *Business and Government Review,* July–Aug. 1966, 7, 22–31.

Williams, B. R. "Economics in Unwonted Places," *Economic Journal,* March 1965, 75 20–30. Indicates the consequences of neglecting cost-benefit analysis in British public investment decision making.

Wise, Harold F. Planning-Programming-Budgeting Systems and the Planning Role. Government Relations and Planning Policy Conference, 4th. Washington, D.C.: 1967. "Planning and the Federal Establishment, Proceedings of AIP Fourth Biennial . . . Conference [Washington]" *American Institute of Planners,* 1967, p. 35–40.
Also in *Congressional Record,* Feb. 15, 1967, 113 (temp.) S1975–S1978.

Community development and services

Bloom, Max R. "Fiscal Productivity and the Pure Theory of Urban Renewal," *Land Economics,* May 1962, 38, 134–144. Discusses the criteria used to evaluate the impact of land use changes resulting from urban redevelopment, pointing out the shortcomings of the fiscal productivity approach and the need for a more inclusive conceptual framework in formulating criteria for project selection.

Burns, Leland S. "Cost-benefit Analysis of Improved Housing: A Case Study." Los Angeles, Graduate School of Business Administration, University of Calif.: 1956. 29 p. Prepared for the Meeting of Experts on Cost-Benefit Analysis of Social Projects, United Nations Research Institute for Social Development, Rennes, France, September 26–October 2, 1965. (International Housing Productivity Study, Graduate School of Business Administration. University of Calif., Los Angeles.)

Conference on Public Expenditure Decisions in the Urban Community, Washington, D.C., 1962. Public expenditure decisions in the urban community. Papers presented at a conference, May 14–15, 1962, under the sponsorship of the Committee on Urban Economics of Resources for the Future, Inc. Howard G. Schaller, ed. Washington, D.C.: *Resources for the Future.* Baltimore, Md.: distributed by the Johns Hopkins Press, 1963, 198 p.

Conference on Urban Public Expenditures, 2d, New York, 1964. "The Public

Economy of Urban Communities." Papers presented at the second Conference on Urban Public Expenditures, held February 21–22, 1964, under the sponsorship of the Committee on Urban Economics of Resources for the Future, Inc. Julius Margolis, ed. Washington, D.C.: *Resources for the Future*. Baltimore, Md.: distributed by the Johns Hopkins Press, 1965, 264 p.

Davis, Otto A. "A Pure Theory of Urban Renewal," *Land Economics,* May 1960, 36, 220–226. Discusses the application of the cost-benefit criteria to enable cities to base urban renewal projects on their "profitability." See also comments by Morton Schussheim (*Land Economics,* November 1960, 36, 395–396), and Nathaniel Lichfield (*Land Economics,* February 1963, 39, 99–103), and the reply by Otto Davis (*Land Economics,* February 1963, 39, 103–108).

Davis, Otto A. and Andrew B. Whinston. "Economic Problems in Urban Renewal." (Phelps, Edmund S., ed. *Private Wants and Public Needs: Issues Surrounding the Size and Scope of Government Expenditure.* (Rev. ed.) New York: W. W. Norton 1965 pp. 140–153).
Appeared originally in *Law and Contemporary Problems,* Winter 1961, 26, 105–117.

Gallaway, Lowell E. "An Economic Analysis of Public Policy for Depressed Areas," *Industrial and Labor Relations Review,* July 1962, 15, 500–509. Discusses criteria justifying Federal aid to depressed areas, giving particular attention to the problem of "establishing the existence of inequities in the distribution of benefits and costs of economic growth, as between depressed areas and the rest of the economy."

Gruen, Claude. "Systems Analysis Applied to the Problems of Local Urban Governments." Paper presented at the session on "Local Government" at the 1966 meeting of the Institute of Management Sciences, Dallas, Tex., Pleasantville, N.Y., 1966 15 p.

Hamburg, Morris and Thomas W. Langford. "Selected Methods of Analysis for Urban Economic Planning and Development in Pennsylvania," commentary on regional economic accounting systems, benefit-cost analysis and statistical decision theory. Harrisburg, Commonwealth of Pennsylvania, Dept. of Internal Affairs, 1964. 65 p. "Benefit-cost Analysis and Statistical Decision Theory," pp. 36–65.

Hansen, Niles M. "Some Neglected Factors in American Regional Development Policy: the Case of Appalachia," *Land Economics,* February 1966, 42, 1–9. Argues that the Appalachian Regional Development plan overemphasizes expenditures on economic overhead capital, since considerations of opportunity cost and labor mobility have been neglected.

Hirsch, Werner Z. "Cost Functions of an Urban Government Service: Refuse Collection," *Review of Economics and Statistics,* February 1965, 47, pp. 87–92. Attempts to relate the cost of a municipal service to the variables of quality and condition of the service.

————, "Local Versus Areawide Government Services," *National Tax Journal,* December 1964, 17, 331–339. Discusses the formulation of criteria to determine which government services are better performed on a local and which on an areawide basis and which of the services that favor local operations should be given subsidies by higher levels of government.

——————, "Regional Accounts for Policy Decisions," Conference of Regional Accounts, Miami Beach, Fla., 1964. Resources for the Future, Inc. Baltimore, Md.: Johns Hopkins Press, 1966.

Institute for Defense Analyses. "Science and Technology; Task Force Report." A report to the President's Commission on Law Enforcement and Administration of Justice. Washington, D.C.: Government Printing Office, 1967. 228 p. Considers the application of systems analysis to the design of some operations in police departments, courts, and agencies of correction.

Kelnhofer, Guy J. "Slum Clearance—its Costs and Benefits," *Tennessee Planner*, April 1955, 15, 153–158. Discusses the distortion of cost-benefit analyses of slum clearance projects resulting from the inadequate statistical measures of the comparative consumption of municipal services among various sections of a city.

Lichfield, Nathaniel. "Cost-benefit Analysis in City Planning," *American Institute of Planners Journal*, November 1960, 26, 273–279.

——————, "Cost-benefit Analysis in Urban Redevelopment." University of California at Berkeley, 1962. Real Estate Research Program. Report No. 20. 52 p. Discusses the techniques of cost-benefit analysis and then applies them to three case studies of urban redevelopment in San Francisco.

——————, and Julius Margolis. *Benefit-Cost Analysis as a Tool in Urban Government Decision Making*, pp. 11–146.

Mc Kean, Roland N. *Costs and Benefits from Different Viewpoints*, pp. 147–162.

Mao, James C. T. "Efficiency in Public Urban Renewal Expenditure through Capital Budgeting." Berkeley, 1965. 118 p. Center for Real Estate and Urban Economics, Institute of Urban and Regional Development, University of California. Research report 27. Suggests using capital budgeting techniques to measure costs and benefits of public expenditure for urban renewal. See also *American Institute of Planners Journal*, 32, March 1966, 95–107 and September 1966, 297–299.

Nourse, Hugh O. "The Economics of Urban Renewal," *Land Economics*, February 1966, 42, 65–74. Demonstrates that current slum clearance and neighborhood rehabilitation policies do not usually produce increased property values.

Page, David A. "Urban Renewal." A paper presented to the Bureau of the Budget [Summer Seminar on Systems Analysis and Program Evaluation] August 10, 1965. 47 p. Discusses the objectives of the urban renewal program, analyzes two projects in the light of these objectives, and discusses the application of the cost-benefit technique to urban renewal.

Regional Science Association. Papers, European Congress, Cracow, 1965. [Philadelphia] Published in cooperation with the Department of Regional Science, Wharton School, University of Pennsylvania [1966] 171 p. Papers, 16, 1966. See also "Data Collection Systems for Metropolitan Planning," by L. S. Jay, p. 77–92; "Cost-Benefit Analysis in Urban Redevelopment— A Case Study: Swanley," by Nathaniel Lichfield, p. 129–153; "Cost-Benefit Analysis of a Social Overhead Project for Regional Development," by Leland S. Burns, pp. 155–161.

——————, Papers, the Philadelphia meeting, November 1965 and 1966. 224 p. Papers, 17, 1966. "Policy Aspects," pp. 163–224.

Ross, William B. "A Proposed Methodology for Comparing Federally Assisted Housing Programs," *American Economic Review,* May 1967, 57, 91–100.

Rothenberg, Jerome. "Urban Renewal Programs." Robert Dorfman, ed. *Measuring Benefits of Government Investments.* Papers presented at a conference of experts, November 7–9, 1963. Washington, D.C.: Brookings Institution, 1965, p. 292–366.

Schaff, A. H. "Public Policies in Urban Renewal: An Economic Analysis of Justifications and Effects," *Land Economics,* February 1964, 40, 67–78.

Stone, P. A. "The Economics of Housing and Urban Development." *Royal Statistical Society Journal,* Series A, 1959, 122, pt. 4, 417–483. Discusses techniques for deriving comparative costs of different types of development to determine the impact of the development on the national economy "and the total real cost to the community."

Thompson, Wilbur R. *A Preface to Urban Economics.* Published for Resources for the Future, Baltimore, Md.: Johns Hopkins Press, 1965.

U.S. Advisory Commission on Intergovernmental Relations. "Metropolitan Social and Economic Disparities: Implications for Intergovernmental Relations in Central Cities and Suburbs." Washington, D.C.: Government Printing Office, 1965. Report A-25, 253 p. "Costs and Benefits of Metropolitan Wide Services," pp. 56–84; "Use of Cost-Benefit Studies in Allocating Costs for Areawide Services," pp. 129–131; "State and Federal Standards of Measurement of Costs and Benefits and Assignment of Costs among Local Jurisdictions," pp. 131–133.

————, "Performance of Urban Functions: Local and Areawide." Washington, D.C.: U.S. Government Printing Office, 1963. Information report M-21, 281 p.

————, "Economic Criteria for Allocation of Urban Functions," pp. 42–50.

U.S. President's Commission on Law Enforcement and the Administration of Justice. "The Challenge of Crime in a Free Society, a Report . . . ," Washington, D.C.: Government Printing Office, 1967. "Science and technology," pp. 245–271.

Weisbrod, Burton A. "Investing in Human Capital," *Journal of Human Resources,* Summer 1966, 1, 5–21. "Analyzes private and social, monetary and non-monetary benefits from health and educational investments in human capital," and examines some implications of this analysis for "overall public policy with respect to investments in people, and particularly for investments in education."

Williams, Alan. "The Optimal Provision of Public Goods in a System of Local Government," *Journal of Political Economy,* February 1966, 74, 18–33. Develops a model illustrating the interdependence among decision making sectors of governmental units and concludes that "the complex interactions that occur even in highly simplified situations make it impossible to predict a priori whether oversupply or undersupply will generally result."

Foreign aid

Aharoni, Yair. "The Foreign Investment Decision Process." Boston, Mass.: Division of Research, Graduate School of Business Administration, Harvard University, 1966.

Chenery, Hollis B. and A. M. Strout. "Foreign Assistance and Economic Development," *American Economic Review,* September 1966, 56, 679–733. Using a model, the authors demonstrate the "conditions under which external assistance" can result in notable acceleration of economic development, and consider the implications of this analysis for questions of effectiveness and allocation of foreign assistance.

Enke, Stephen. "The Economic Aspects of Slowing Population Growth," *Economic Journal,* March 1966, 76, 44–56. Argues that economic resources devoted to reducing population growth are more effective in raising per capita income in underdeveloped areas than are the same resources applied to accelerating production, and estimates the cost of an adequate birth control program.

Farmer, J. "Applying Analytic Methods to Problems of Development Assistance." Santa Monica, Calif.: 1966. RAND Corporation. Paper P3384. 15 p.

Jacoby, Neil H. "Foreign Aid as a Problem of Resource Management: the Case of Free China," *California Management Review,* Fall 1966, 9, 3–10.

Kravis, Irving B. and Michael S. Davenport. "Political Arithmetic of International Burden Sharing," *Journal of Political Economy,* August 1963, 71, 309–326.

Nye, J. S. "Corruption and Political Development: a Cost-benefit Analysis," *American Political Science Review,* June 1967, 61, 417–427.

Olson, Mancur and Richard Zeckhauser. "An Economic Theory of Alliances." Santa Monica, Calif.: 1966. RAND Corporation. Memorandum RM4297-ISA, 38 p. Develops a model to aid in determining the allocation of costs of international cooperative ventures among participating nations.

Pincus, John A. "Economic Aid and International Cost Sharing." A report prepared for the Office of Assistant Secretary of Defense, International Security Affairs. Santa Monica, Calif.: 1965. RAND Corporation. Report R-431-ISA. 221 p. Analyzes the issues related to "sharing the costs of internationally financed activities" and suggests ways to deal with some of these problems.

Tweeten, Luther G. "A Proposed Allocative Mechanism for U.S. Food Aid," *Journal of Farm Economics,* November 1966, 48, 803–809. Suggests a way of coordinating foreign aid and U.S. food production control programs and supplies guidelines to aid in determining the real costs and benefits in uses of American food output.

Health, education, and welfare

Andersen, Bent R. "Work or Support: an Economic and Social Analysis of Substitute Permanent Employment." Paris: Organization for Economic Cooperation and Development, 1966. 122 p. A cost-benefit analysis and evaluation of human and social gains provided by sheltered workshops as compared to cash benefits, based on careful observation of these programs in six countries.

Bateman, Worth. "An Application of Cost-benefit Analysis to the Work-experience Program," *American Economic Review,* May 1967, 57, 80–90.

Becker, Gary S. "Human Capital; a Theoretical and Empirical Analysis, With Special Reference to Education." New York: distributed by Columbia University Press, 1964. National Bureau of Economic Research. General series, No. 80. 187 p.

Blaug, Mark. "Approaches to Educational Planning," *Economic Journal,* June 1967, 77, 262–287.

Bortnick, Paul J. "Breaking the Cycle of Despair: the Need for a System Analysis in Welfare," *SDC* (System Development Corporation) *Magazine,* May 1966, 9, 2–15.

Borus, Michael E. "The Economic Effectiveness of Retraining the Unemployed; a Study of the Benefits and Costs of Retraining the Unemployed Based on the Experience of Workers in Connecticut." Boston: 1964. Research report to the Federal Reserve Bank of Boston, No. 35, 219 p.
Also in Yale Economic Essays, Fall 1964, 4, 371–429.

Bowen, William G. "Economic Aspects of Education, Three Essays." Princeton: 1964. Princeton University. Industrial Relations Section. Research report No. 104, 122 p. "Assessing the Economic Contribution of Education," pp. 3–40.

Bowen, William G. and T. Aldrich Finegan. "Educational Attainment and Labor Force Participation," *American Economic Review,* May 1966, 56, 567–582.

Burkhead, Jesse, *et al. Input and Output in Large-city High Schools.* Syracuse University Press: 1967 110 p. "Education in large cities," 2. Examines "the allocation of resources within large-city school systems," traces "relationships between allocational levels and patterns and the resulting outputs of the schools," and explores "the complex of factors . . . that affect the output of public education."

Campbell, Robert and Barry N. Siegel "The Demand for Higher Education in the United States, 1919–1964," *American Economic Review,* June 1967, 57, 482–494. Postulates a model of educational demand and uses aggregate enrollment data since World War I to test the validity of the model, concluding that the results substantiate it "at least in part."

Carroll, Adger B. and Loren A. Ihnen. "Costs and Returns of Technical Education; a Pilot Study." Prepared . . . for Office of Manpower Policy, Evaluation and Research, Department of Labor. Raleigh: Department of Economics, North Carolina State University, 1966. 52 p. Presents data from a study designed to measure "costs and returns of human capital created by investments in two years of post-high school technical education."

Chance, W. A. "Long-term Labor Requirements and Output of the Educational System," *Southern Economic Journal,* April 1966, 32, 417–428. Offers a method of projecting future labor requirements and relating them to the output of the educational system to help decide "what alternatives in educational policy will allow the system to meet these requirements."

Conference on Policies Affecting Rural People, Raleigh, 1965. Papers presented at the . . . conference . . . held in Raleigh, N.C., December 2–3, 1965. Sponsored by the Agricultural Policy Institute, North Carolina State University, and the Center for Agricultural and Economic Development, Iowa State University. Raleigh 1966. 84 p. "Costs and Benefits of

Past Agricultural Programs," by J. C. Williamson, p. 29–49; "Evaluating the Costs and Benefits of Past Farm Programs," by Donald C. Horton, p. 51–57.

Conference on the Economics of Health and Medical Care, University of Michigan, 1962. *The Economics of Health and Medical Care: Proceedings.* Ann Arbor: University of Michigan, 1964. 321 p.
Contents: "The Role of the Economist in the Health Services Industry"; "Organization and Financing of Health Services"; "Demand, Costs, and Prices of Health Care"; "Investment in Health"; "Agenda for Research"; "Microeconomics of Health Care."

Conley, Ronald W. "The Economics of Vocational Rehabilitation." Baltimore, Md.: Johns Hopkins Press, 1965. 177 p. Investigates selected aspects of the economic problems caused by physical and mental disability and of the economic benefits of vocational rehabilitation.

Coulson, John E. and John F. Cogswell. "Systems Analysis in Education." Santa Monica, Calif.: 1965. Systems Development Corporation. Paper SP-1863. 14 p. Discusses methods and procedures of a systems analysis and some possible implications of this technique for educational data banks.

Diehl, William D. "Farm-nonfarm Migration in the Southeast: A Costs-returns Analysis," *Journal of Farm Economics,* February 1966, 48, 1–11.

"Economics of Education," *American Economic Review,* May 1966, 56, p. 358–400.
Contents: "Education and the Distribution of Earnings," by Gary S. Becker and Barry R. Chiswick; "Investment in the Education of the Poor: a Pessimistic Report," by Eugene Smolensky; "Measurement of the Quality of Schooling," by Finnis Welch; "Discussion," by Alice M. Rivlin, Lee R. Martin, and Andre Daniere.

"Economics of Education," *International Social Science Journal,* 1962, 14, 619–718.
Partial contents: "Social Returns to Education," by Mary Jean Bowman; "Teaching Methods and their Costs," by Charles Benson.

"Economics of Health," *American Economic Review,* May 1967, 57, 109–157.
Contents: "The Allocation of Biomedical Research," by Simon Rottenberg; "Economics of Hospital Systems: Peak Loads and Regional Coordination," by Millard F. Long and Paul J. Feldstein; "The Economic Effects of Malaria Eradication," by Robin Barlow.

Farm Policy Review Conference, Raleigh, 1964. "Rural America Looks to the Future." Papers Co-sponsored by the Agricultural Policy Institute, North Carolina State University and the Center for Agricultural and Economic Development, Iowa State University. Raleigh 1964. 152 p. See also, "Projections of Farm Income and Public Costs under Several Farm Program Alternatives," by Leo V. Mayer, Earl O. Heady, and Luther G. Tweeten, pp. 59–86.

Feldstein, Martin S. "Economic Analysis, Operational Research, and the National Health Service," *Oxford Economic Papers,* March 1963, 15, 19–31. Reviews some applications of economic analysis to public expenditures, discusses the concern over efficiency in the National Health Service, and considers the value of operations research for the NHS.

Gorham, William. "Allocating Federal Resources among Competing Social

Needs," *Health, Education, and Welfare Indicators,* August 1966, 1–13. The Assistant Secretary for Program Coordination, Department of Health, Education, and Welfare, discusses the problems of measuring and evaluating the output of HEW programs.

Harbison, Frederick and Charles A. Myers. *Education, Manpower and Economic Growth, Strategies of Human Resource Development.* New York: McGraw-Hill, 1964.

Hirsch, Werner Z. *et al.* "Spillovers of Public Education Costs and Benefits." Los Angeles, Institute of Government and Public Affairs, University of California, 1964.

Hirsch, Werner Z. and Elbert W. Segelhorst. "Incremental Income Benefits of Public Education," *Review of Economics and Statistics,* November 1965, 17, 392–399. Attempts to estimate the increase in income associated with a given increase in education, taking other factors into account, as an aid to determining the rate of return on educational investments.

Jahn, Julius A. "The Statistical Design and Analysis of an Experiment to Measure the Effectiveness and Costs of a Health and Welfare Program," American Statistical Association. *Proceedings of the Social Statistics Section,* Washington, D.C.: 1965, pp. 42–50.

Kershaw, Joseph A. and Roland N. McKean. "Systems Analysis and Education." Santa Monica, Calif.: 1959. RAND Corporation. Research memorandum RM-2473-FF, 64 p.

Klarman, Herbert E. *The Economics of Health.* New York: Columbia University Press, 1965. See also, "Selected Problems," pp. 149–176.

Klarman, Herbert E. "Syphilis Control Program," *Measuring Benefits of Government Investments.* Robert Dorfman, ed. Papers presented at a conference of experts, November 7–9, 1963. Washington, Brookings Institution 1965, pp. 367–414.

Levine, Abraham S. "Cost-Benefit Analysis and Social Welfare," *Welfare in Review,* February 1966, 4, 1–11. Explores possible applications of cost-benefit analysis in evaluating social welfare program expenditures.

—————, "Cost-Benefit Analysis of the Work Experience Program," *Welfare in Review,* August–September 1966, 4, 1–9. Outlines the "basic principles underlying an optimal research strategy" for a cost-benefit analysis of the Aid to Families with Dependent Children program.

Linnenberg, Clem C. "Economics in Program Planning for Health," *Public Health Reports.* December 1966, 81, 1085–1091. Discusses some of the applications and limitations of economic analysis of health programs.

"Manpower and Welfare Programs: Benefit-cost Analysis," Industrial Relations Association. Procedings of the 17th annual meeting, Chicago, December 28–29, 1964. Madison, Wis.: 1965, pp. 171–214.
Contents: "Benefit-cost Analysis of Manpower Retraining," by Gerald G. Somers and Ernst Stromsdorfer; "Benefit-cost Analysis of Welfare Programs," by John S. MacDonald: "Capital-output Analysis of Housing Programs for Developing Nations," by Leland Burns; "Discussion," by Juanita Kreps, Selma Mushkin, and Benson Soffer.

Marshall, A. W. "Cost/benefit Analysis in Health." Santa Monica, Calif.: 1965. 18 p. RAND Corporation. Paper P-3274. Reviews some of the previous work on measuring health costs and benefits, examines a sample program budget for HEW-administered programs, and discusses some of the problems and opportunities for cost-benefit analysis in the health area.

Merrett, Stephen. "The Rate of Return to Education: a Critique," *Oxford Economic Papers,* November 1966, 18, 289–303. Concludes that "research into the rate of return on education should be discontinued."

————, "Student Finances in Higher Education," *Economic Journal,* June 1967, 77, 288–302. Derives "a set of principles for governments to adopt in directing the money flows reciprocating the cost and benefit streams of higher education."

Miner, Jerry. "Social and Economic Factors in Spending for Public Education." Syracuse University Press, 1963. pp. 7–36.

Mood, Alexander M. "Operations Analysis of American Education," Paper delivered at the 1966 annual meeting of the American Political Science Association, New York City, September 6–10, 1966. Washington, D.C.: American Political Science Association, 1966, 12 p. Discusses the goals and methods of the Office of Education program of operations analysis.

Mushkin, Selma J., ed. "Economics of Higher Education." Washington, D.C.: Government Printing Office, 1962, pp. 69–169. U.S. Office of Education. Bulletin, 1962, No. 5.

Nicol, Helen O. "Guaranteed Income Maintenance, a Public Welfare Systems Model," *Welfare in Review,* November 1966, 4, 1–12. Uses systems analysis to "design a public welfare model which fulfills the requirements of a broadened public welfare mechanism as envisaged by both the Council of Economic Advisers and the Advisory Council on Public Welfare."

Page, David A. "Retraining under the Manpower Development Act: A Cost-benefit Analysis," *Public Policy, 1964.* Cambridge, Mass.: Harvard University Press 1964, pp. 257–267. See also, Brookings Institution, Washington. Reprint No. 86.

"Problems of Planning," *Public Policy, 1965.* Cambridge, Mass.: Harvard University Press 1965, pp. 161–235.
   Contents: "Rate of Return vs. Manpower Approach in Educational Planning," by Andre Daniere; "Recent Discussion of the Problems of Higher Education in Great Britain," by Lord Robbins; "Some Economic Problems of Education Expenditures on Education and Income Levels," by Seymour E. Harris.

"Public Finance and Education," *Public Finance,* 1966, 21, No. 1–2, 1–324.
   Partial contents: "The Theory of Spillovers and its Connection with Education," by Maurice Peston; "The Planning of Budgetary Expenditures on Education on the Basis of a Mathematical Model—the Method Employed in Hungary," by Lajos Faluvegi; "Comment," by Alan T. Peacock; "Public Finance and Education: a Summary of the Issues," by Jack Wiseman.

Robinson, E. A. G. and J. E. Vaizey, eds. "The Economics of Education," Proceedings of a Conference held by the International Economic Association. New York: St. Martin's Press, 1966. 782 p.
   Contents: "General Problems of Education," "Education and Economic Progress," "Demand and Supply," "The Cost and Financing of Education," "Balance between Different Forms of Education," "International Aid in Education," "Summary Record of the Discussions."

Ross, Arthur M., ed. "Employment Policy and the Labor Market." Papers presented at the Research Conference on Unemployment at Boulder, Colorado, June 1964. Berkeley: University of California Press, 1965. 406 p. "Retraining: an evaluation of gains and costs," by Gerald G. Somers, p. 271–298.

Schultz, Theodore W. *The Economic Value of Education*. New York: Columbia University Press, 1963. 92 p.

————, "Education and Economic Growth," National Society for the Study of Education, *Social Forces Influencing American Education, The Sixtieth Yearbook* . . . Chicago: University of Chicago Press, 1961, pt. 2, p. 46–88.

Seminar on the Economics of Higher Education, Harvard University, 1958–1959. *Higher Education in the United States: The Economic Problems*, Edited with an introd. by Seymour E. Harris, *et al.*, Cambridge: Harvard University Press, 1960. 252 p. See also, "Some Observations on the Allocation of Resources in Higher Education," by Kenneth Deitch, pp. 192–198. *Review of Economics and Statistics,* August 1960, supp., 42, 192–198.

Smith, A. D. "Active Manpower and Redundancy Policies: Their Costs and Benefits," *International Labour Review,* January–February 1967, 95, 49–60. Examines the interrelationship and importance of these two types of policies, the facts which must be taken into account when comparing the costs and benefits of each type of policy, and the principles on which such costs should be allocated.

Stone, Richard. "Input-output and Demographic Accounting: a Tool for Educational Planning," *Minerva,* Spring 1966, 4, 365–380. Describes the techniques developed by the author to provide a dynamic accounting structure for building a model of an educational system.

————, "A Model of the Educational System," *Minerva,* Winter 1965, 3, 172–186. Outlines a model of the British educational system "designed to work out the present implications of future levels of educational activity as determined by the evolution of the demand for places . . . and the economic demand for the products of education."

Swift, William J. and Burton A. Weisbrod. "On the Monetary Value of Education's Intergeneration Effects," *Journal of Political Economy,* December 1965, 73, 643–649. Presents "an empirical model for placing a monetary value on the influence of education in one generation [upon] . . . attitudes and educational attainments in the next generation." Rates of return are estimated from two viewpoints: the actual money expenditures and the actual expenditures on education per student plus earnings foregone.

United Nations. Research Institute for Social Development and Office of Social Affairs. "Cost-benefit Analysis of Social Projects," report of a meeting of experts held in Rennes, France, September 27–October 2, 1965; Geneva, 1966. United Nations. Research Institute for Social Development. Report No. 7, 129 p.
Partial contents: "Account of Proceedings," by Norman Scott; "Some Problems of Cost-benefit Analysis of Social Investment," by Norman Scott; "Costs and Efficiency of Health and Social Welfare Institutions," by J. Arnion; "Analysis of the Economic Effects of Housing Investment," by Edward Kuminek.

U.S. Dept. of Health, Education, and Welfare. *Program Analysis.* Washington: 1966. 5 nos.

Contents: "Disease Control Programs: Motor Vehicle Injury Prevention Program, 1966–1; Cancer, 1966–3; Arthritis, 1966–4; Selected Disease Control Programs, 1966–5; "Maternal and Child Health Care Programs, 1966–6."

U.S. Public Health Service. *The Principles of Program Packaging in the Division of Indian Health.* Silver Spring, Md., 1966. 39 p.

U.S. Public Health Service. *Economic Benefits from Public Health Services; Objectives, Benefits, and Examples of Measurement.* Washington, D.C.: Government Printing Office, 1964. 31 p. Publication No. 1178.

Universities-National Bureau Committee for Economic Research. *Investment in Human Beings.* Papers presented before the Exploratory Conference on Capital Investment in Human Beings held at the Carnegie Endowment International Center, New York, 1961. Chicago: University of Chicago Press, 1962. 157 p. *Journal of Political Economy,* 70, No. 5, pt. 2, supp., October 1962. See also, "Investment in Human Capital: a Theoretical Analysis," by Gary S. Becker, pp. 9–49, "Education and Investment in Human Capital," by Burton A. Weisbrod, pp. 106–123; "Health as an Investment," by Selma J. Mushkin, pp. 129–157.

Weisbrod, Burton A. *Economics of Public Health; Measuring the Economic Impact of Diseases.* Philadelphia: University of Pennsylvania Press, 1961, 127 p.

Weisbrod, Burton A. *External Benefits of Public Education: An Economic Analysis.* Princeton: Princeton University Press, 1964. 143 p. Industrial Relations Section. Research report No. 105.

————, "Preventing High School Dropouts," *Measuring Benefits of Government Investments.* Robert Dorfman, ed. Papers presented at a conference of experts, November 7–9, 1963. Washington, D.C.: Brookings Institution 1965, pp. 117–171.

West Virginia University Conference on Poverty Amid Affluence, 1965. *Poverty Amid Affluence.* Leo Fishman, ed. New Haven: Yale University Press, 1966. 246 p. See also, "Public Approaches to Minimize Poverty," by Theodore W. Schultz, pp. 165–181; "Strategies in the War Against Povery," by Otto Eckstein, pp. 200–211; "Ends and Means in the War against Poverty," by Robert J. Lampman, p. 212–230.

Wiseman, Jack. "Cost-benefit Analysis and Health Service Policy," *Public Expenditure: Appraisal and Control.* Peacock, Alan T. and D. J. Robertson, eds. Edinburgh: Oliver and Boyd, 1963, pp. 128–145.

————, "Cost-Benefit Analysis in Education." *Southern Economic Journal,* July 1965, supp., 32, 1–14.

Highways

American Association of State Highway Officials. Committee on Planning and Design Policies. "Road User Benefit Analysis for Highway Improvements, a Report . . . ," Washington, D.C.: 1960. 152 p.

Friedlaender, Ann F. "The Interstate Highway System, a Study in Public Investment." Amsterdam: North-Holland Publishing Co., 1965. 178 p. "Contributions to economic analysis," 38. Aims to provide a "general framework for evaluating any large highway investment program," and, in particular, to evaluate the costs and benefits of the Interstate Highway System.

Kafgolis, Milton Z. "Highway policy and External Economies," *National Tax Journal,* March 1963, 16, 68–80. Considers the concept of external benefits of highway investment as reflected in the problems of subsidy and determination of the non-user costs and benefits.

LeBaron, A.D. "Theory of Highway Finance: Roots, Aims, and Accomplishments," *National Tax Journal,* September 1963, 16, 307–319. Examines the effectiveness of suggested tax plans for narrowing the gap between the costs of investments in highways and benefits to users.

Mohring, Herbert. "Urban Highway Investments," *Measuring Benefits of Government Investments.* Robert Dorfman, ed. Papers presented at a conference of experts, November 7–9, 1963. Washington, D.C.: Brookings Institution 1965, pp. 231–291.

Mohring, Herbert and Mitchell Harwitz. "Highway Benefits, an Analytical Framework," Evanston, Ill.: Published for the Transportation Center at Northwestern University by the Northwestern University Press, 1962. 209 p.

National Research Council, Highway Research Board. "Highway Finance and Benefits, Four Reports." Washington, D.C.: 1966. 64 p. *Highway Research Record,* No. 138; National Research Council. Publication 1382. See also, Partial contents: "The Measurement of Vehicular Benefits," by G. P. St. Clair, *et al.;* "New Approach to Benefit Cost Analysis," by Robinson Newcomb.

————, "Benefits to Utilities from Highway Locations," Washington, D.C.: 1962. 59 p. Special report 75.

————, "Highway Economics," seven reports presented at the 42nd annual meeting, Committee on Highway Engineering Economy, January 7–11, 1963. Washington, D.C.: 1963. 148 p. Highway Research Record No. 12; National Research Council. Publication 1109.

————, *Studies in Highway Engineering Economy.* Papers presented at the 40th annual meeting, January 9–13, 1961. Washington, D.C.: 1961. 121 p. Highway Research Board Bulletin 306, National Research Council. Publication 935. See also, "Economy Studies for Highways," by E. L. Grant and C. H. Oglesby, pp. 23–38; "Economic Evaluation of Traffic Networks," by George Haikalis and Hyman Joseph, pp. 39–63; "Economic Aspects of Highway Planning," by Tillo E. Kuhn, pp. 81–121.

U.S. Bureau of Public Roads. Final Report on the Highway Cost Allocation Study. Letter from Secretary of Commerce transmitting . . . pursuant to Section 210 of the Highway Revenue Act of 1956. Washington, D.C.: United States Government Printing Office, 1961. 2 nos. 87th Cong., 1st sess. House. Doc. 54; 72. See, Pts. 1–5: "Summary of Findings," pp. 3–14; "General Discussion of the Study," pp. 29–32; "Available Concepts and their Relevance," pp. 63–75; "Comparable Costs and Benefits," pp. 100–111; "The Cost-Function Study, pp. 188–200; "The Differential Benefit Study," pp. 200–224, Pt. 6: "Data Concerning the Economic and Social Effects of Highway Improvements."

————, Progress report of the highway cost allocation study. Washington, United States Government Printing Office, 1957. 131 p. (85th Cong., 1st sess. House. Doc. 106.) "Methods of Attack on the Tax-Allocation Problem," p. 62–116.

————, Supplementary report on the highway cost allocation study. Washington, United States Government Printing Office, 1965. 367 p. (89th Cong. 1st sess. House. Doc 124.) "The Differential Benefit Study," pp. 212–234.

Witheford, David K. "Investigation and Description of Benefit-cost Analysis Procedures." Pittsburgh Area Transportation Study 1962. Technical paper No. 32. 12 p. Discusses the application of evaluation techniques for highway systems developed by the Chicago Area Transportation Study.

Workshop Conference on Economic Analysis, Washington, D.C., 1959. "Economic Analysis in Highway Programming, Location and Design"; proceedings. Washington, D.C.: 1960. 187 p. Highway Research Board. Special report 56.

National defense

Bowman, Richard C. "Analysis in War Planning," *Air University Review*, March–April 1966, 17, 40–48.

Bradley, B. D. "Building a New Force Structure Cost Analysis Model." Prepared for U.S. Air Force Project RAND. Santa Monica, Calif.: 1965. 20 p. RAND Corporation. Memorandum RM4764-PR. Describes the concepts underlying the model, explains the framework devised for it, and describes the development of submodels for the use of the cost analyst.

Carlson, Jack W. "Improving Efficiency in the Use of Manpower Resources." Delivered at the twenty-fifth anniversary symposium on personnel research and systems advancement, San Antonio, Tex.: November 3, 1966. Washington, D.C.: Council of Economic Advisers, 1966, 26 p. Identifies areas for analysis and improvement in Air Force and Defense Department manpower management.

Clark, John J. "The Economics of Systems Analysis," *Military Review*, April 1964, 44, 25–31. Points out the values and the weaknesses of weapons systems analysis.

————, "The Management of National Defense by Systems Analysis: An Evaluation," Royal United Service Institute. *Journal*, November 1964, 109, 298–308.

————, *The New Economics of National Defense*. New York: Random House, 1966. "The Management of National Defense by Systems Analysis," pp. 39–73.

Curry, David A. "Costing Concepts for the Defense Programs Management System." Memorandum report prepared for [the] Deputy Assistant Secretary of Defense (Programming). Menlo Park, Calif.: Stanford Research Institute, 1962. 58 p. SRI Project No. IMU-3683.

"Defense Economics: Applying Economic Criteria," *American Economic Review*, May 1965, 55, 416–438.

Contents: "Using Costs to Select Weapons," by Stephen Enke; "Military Cost Analysis," by Robert N. Grosse and Arnold Proschan; "Discussion," by James R. Schlesinger and Rolf N. Piekarz.

Enke, Stephen, ed. *Defense Management*. Englewood Cliffs, N.J.: Prentice-Hall, Inc. 1967. Each chapter explains or assesses some aspect of cost-benefit analysis as it is currently being carried on in the Department of Defense.

Enthoven, Alain C. "Decision Theory and Systems Analysis." Lecture . . . sponsored by the Metropolitan Washington Board of Trade, Science Bureau . . . December 5, 1963. Washington, D.C.: Department of Defense, 1964. 23 p.

——, "Economic Analysis in the Department of Defense." Address by the Deputy Assistant Secretary of Defense (Systems Analysis) before the American Economic Association, Pittsburgh, Pa.: December 29, 1962. Washington, D.C.: Department of Defense, 1962, 17 p. Also in *American Economic Review,* May 1963, 53, 413–423.

——, "Systems Analysis and Military Decision Making," *Military review,* January 1963, 43, 10–17.

——, "Systems Analysis and the Navy." Annapolis, Md.: U.S. Naval Institute, 1964. 25 p. *Naval Review,* 1965, reprint. Discusses the concept of systems analysis, examines its relationship to operations research, considers its strengths and limitations, and demonstrates its application to problems of determining the nature and size of naval forces.

Enthoven, Alain C. and Henry S. Rowen. "Defense Planning and Organization," Universities-National Bureau Committee for Economic Research, *Public Finances, Needs, Sources and Utilization; a Conference* . . . Princeton: Princeton University Press, 1961, p. 365–417. Also available as RAND Corporation. [Paper] P-1640.

Fisher, Franklin M. and Anton S. Morton. "The Costs and Effectiveness of Reenlistment Incentives in the Navy," *Operations Research,* May–June 1967, 15, 373–387. Develops a nonlinear dynamic model "to investigate trade-offs between costs and effectiveness of raising the first-term rate."

Fisher, G. H. "A Discussion on Uncertainty in Cost Analysis." A lecture for the AFSC cost analysis course. Santa Monica, Calif.: 1962. RAND Corporation. Research memorandum RM-3071-PR, 28 p.

——, "The New OASD (Comptroller) Programming/Budgeting Process." A lecture for the AFSC cost analysis course. Santa Monica, Calif.: 1962. RAND Corporation. Research memorandum RM-3048-PR, 16 p. Discusses the structure, operation, and objectives of the programming/budgeting system introduced into the Department of Defense in 1961.

Fox, Peter D. "A Theory of Cost-Effectiveness Analysis for Military Systems Analysis," *Operations Research,* March–April 1965, 13, 191–201. Examines the differences between military systems analysis and other economic analysis, considers the derivation of the cost-effectiveness schedule where cost or effectiveness is a random variable, and presents some general observations relating to military systems selection.

Hayes, James H. "Basic Concepts of Systems Analysis," *Military Review,* April 1965, 45, 4–13. Clear explanation of the principles underlying systems analysis.

Hitch, Charles J. "Decision-Making for Defense." Berkeley: University of California Press, 1965. 83 p. Traces the historical evolution of defense management, describes the purpose and function of the programming system installed in 1961, and explains the application of systems analysis techniques to the problems of defense.

————, "Economics and Military Operations Research," *Review of Economics and Statistics*, August 1958, 40, 199–209.

Hitch, Charles J. "Plans, Programs, and Budgets in the Department of Defense," *Operations Research*, January–February 1963, 11, 1–17.

Hitch, Charles J. and Roland N. McKean. "The Economics of Defense in the Nuclear Age." Cambridge, Mass.: Harvard University Press, 1960. Basic work in the problems of allocating resources for national defense so as to produce "that strategy . . . [which] maximizes the attainment of the objective with the given resources . . . [or] minimizes the cost of achieving the given objective . . ."

Hoch, Saul. "Cost Criteria in Weapons Systems Analysis and Force Studies." Washington, D.C.: Dept. of Defense, 1965. 35 p. Deals with the manner in which costs are used in studies comparing "the relative merits of systems to perform a particular mission," the relative merits of dynamic and static studies, and "the problems involved in the initial estimation of systems costs."

Hoffman, Fred S. "The Economic Analysis of Defense: Choice Without Markets," *American Economic Review*, May 1959, 49, 368–379.

Jones, M. V. "System Cost Analysis: a Management Tool for Decision Making." Prepared for the Comptroller (Programs Division) Electrical Systems Division, Air Force Systems Command . . . Bedford, Mass.: 1965. (Mitre Corporation. Technical report No. ESD-TR-405) 178 p. "Presents a generalized, integrated conceptual approach to the major steps involved in estimating the costs of a military system."

Kahn, Herman and Irwin Mann. "Techniques of Systems Analysis." Santa Monica, Calif.: 1957. RAND Corporation. Research memorandum RM-1829-I, 161 p.

McKean, Roland N. "Cost-Benefit Analysis and British Defence Expenditures." Peacock, Alan T. and D. J. Robertson, eds. *Public Expenditure: Appraisal and Control.* Edinburgh: Oliver and Boyd, 1963, pp. 17–35.

————, "The Economics of Defense," Santa Monica, Calif.: 1964. RAND Corporation. Paper P-2926. 26 p. Prepared for the International Encyclopedia of Social Sciences.

Martino, Joseph P. "Systems Analysis and Counterinsurgency," *Air University Review*, September–October 1966, 17, 23–33. Develops a model to illustrate the possible applications of systems analysis to problems of counterinsurgency.

"Military Manpower Procurement," *American Economic Review*, May 1967, 57, 19–70.
Contents: "The Supply of Military Personnel in the Absence of a Draft," by Stuart H. Altman and Alan E. Fechter; "Reenlistments in the U.S. Navy: A Cost Effectiveness Study," by Franklin M. Fisher and Anton S. Morton; "The Economic Cost of the Draft," by Walter Y. Oi.

Noah, J. W. "Concepts and Techniques for Summarizing Defense System Costs." Washington, D.C.: Franklin Institute, 1965. Center for Naval Analyses. Systems Evaluation Group. Research contribution No. 1, 40 p.

Discusses five separate methods for summarizing total system costs; i.e., five-year system cost, net cost, period outlay, present cost, and annual cost.

————, "Identifying and Estimating R&D Costs." Santa Monica, Calif.: 1962. RAND Corporation. Research memorandum RM-3067-PR, 65 p. "Intended primarily as a textbook for persons who may be faced with the problem of estimating research and development costs, particularly for ballistic missile or launch vehicle systems."

Novick, David. "Costing Tomorrow's Weapon Systems." Santa Monica, Calif.: 1962. RAND Corporation. Research memorandum RM-3170-PR, 12 p. Discusses the problems involved in establishing cost estimates for projected weapons systems upon which a realistic cost-benefit calculation can be made.

————, "System and Total Force Cost Analysis." Santa Monica, Calif.: 1961. RAND Corporation. Research memorandum RM-2695, 141 p. "Describes the aims, concepts, and methods of military cost analysis as developed by the Cost Analysis Department of the Rand Corporation."

Proschan, Arnold. "Programming System of the Department of Defense," *Armed Forces Comptroller,* September 1963, 8, 14–21.

Quade, E. S. "Analysis for Military Decisions." A report prepared for the United States Air Force Project RAND. Santa Monica, Calif.: 1964. RAND Corporation. Report R-387-PR, 382 p. Treats the origin and development of systems analysis and its application to national security planning, presents the basic techniques and methods, and deals also with special aspects of the systems analysis approach.

————, "Military Systems Analysis." Santa Monica, Calif.: 1963. RAND Corporation. Research memorandum RM-3452-PR, 29 p. Describes systems analysis and explains the stages of the analysis, taking examples from the area of national defense problems.

Sobin, B. "Some Interest Rate Aspects of Weapons Systems Investment Policy." Arlington, Va.: Institute for Defense Analyses, 1965. Research paper P-171, 70 p. "Presents a formal examination of the theoretical basis for the use of interest rates in weapons systems evaluations and an analysis of economic data that yield a numerical estimate of a suggested rate of interest."

Symposium on the Methodology of Weapons Systems Decision, San Francisco, 1962 [Proceedings] Sponsored by the Systems Requirements Committee of the Electronic Industries Association, San Francisco, Calif., November 26, 1962. Washington, D.C.: Electronic Industries Association, 1962, 33 p.

U.S. Air Force, Systems Command, Weapons System Effectiveness Industry Advisory Committee. Final report of Task Group IV. *Cost-effectiveness Optimization.* Washington, D.C.: 1965. 3 Vols.
Contents: Vol. 1: "Summary Conclusions and Recommendations"; Vol. 2: "Tasks and Analysis Methodology"; Vol. 3: "Technical Supplement."

U.S. Congress, House Committee on Government Operations. "Systems Development and Management, Hearings before a Subcommittee . . . ," 87th Cong., 2d sess. Washington, D.C.: Government Printing Office, 1962. 5 pts. See also, Testimony of Charles J. Hitch, Assistant Secretary of Defense, *Comptroller,* pp. 513–547; Appx. IV(b), pp. 643–644.

U.S. Industrial College of the Armed Forces. *A Modern Design for Defense*

Decision; a McNamara-Hitch-Enthoven Anthology. Edited by Samuel A. Tucker. Washington, D.C.: 1966.

U.S. Office of the Chief of Naval Operations. *Navy Programming Manual.* Washington, D.C.: 1965. v.p. OPNAV 90P-1. Standard reference for the operation of the Department of Defense programming system in the Navy.

"The United States Department of Defense Planning-Programming-Budgeting Systems," presented by W. Lynn Johnson. Washington, D.C.: Dept. of Defense, 1965, 55 p.

Wohlstetter, Albert J. *et al.* "Selection and Use of Strategic Air Bases, April 1954." A report prepared for U.S. Air Force Project RAND. Santa Monica, Calif.: 1963. RAND Corporation. Report R-266. An example of a systems analysis.

Research and development

Barro, S. M. "Economic Impact of Space Expenditures." Santa Monica, Calif.: 1966. RAND Corporation. Paper P3386, 15 p. Discusses the fiscal aspects of space spending.

Brandenburg, R. G. and A. C. Stedry. "Planning and Budgeting in a Multiphase R&D Process." Pittsburgh, Pa.: 1966. Carnegie Institute of Technology. Graduate School of Industrial Administration. Management Sciences Research Report, No. 87, 40 p.

Brooks, Harvey. "Science and the Allocation of Resources." Paper delivered at the 1966 annual meeting of the American Political Science Association, New York City, September 6–10. Washington, D.C.: American Political Science Association, 1966. 22 p. "Stresses the viewpoint that the problem of 'scientific choice' involves simultaneous trade-offs in many different dimensions and not the simple choice between fields of science or of priorities internal to science which some recent discussions seem to imply."

Brunner, E. D. "The Cost of Basic Research Effort: Air Force Experience, 1954–1964." Prepared for United States Air Force Project RAND. Santa Monica, Calif.: 1965. RAND Corporation. Research memorandum RM-4250-PR, 52 p.

Carey, William D. "Decision on Research and Development: Viewpoint From the Bureau of the Budget," National Conference on the Administration of Research, Newport Beach, Calif.: 1965, *Proceedings* . . . Denver: Denver Research Institute, University of Denver, 1966. Pp. 107–110.

Conference on Research Program Effectiveness, Washington, D.C., 1965. *Research Program Effectiveness; Proceedings of the Conference Sponsored by the Office of Naval Research* . . . Edited by M. C. Yovits *et al.* New York: Gordon and Breach, Science Publishers, Inc. [1966] 542 p.

Enke, Stephen. "Government-industry Development of a Commercial Supersonic Transport," *American Economic Review,* May 1967, 57, 71–79.

Glennan, Thomas K. "Issues in the Choice of Development Policies." Santa Monica, Calif.: 1965. RAND Corporation. Paper P-3153, 49 p. "Describes the development process and identifies important elements of development decisions."

Griliches, Zvi. "Research Costs and Social Returns: Hybrid Corn and Related

Innovations," *Journal of Political Economy,* October 1958, 56, 419–431. Estimates the "realized social rate of return" on investments in hybrid corn research.

Grossfield, K. and J. B. Heath. "The Benefit and Cost of Government Support for Research and Development: A Case Study," *Economic Journal,* September 1966, 76, 537–549. An attempt to develop a quantitative assessment of prospective social benefits of Government support of innovation, using as an example the support given by the National Research Development Corporation to the development of a potato harvester.

Hohenemser, Kurt H. "The Supersonic Transport," *Scientist and Citizen,* April 1966, 8, 1–10. Discusses some of the unanswered questions relevant to a cost-benefit analysis of the proposed supersonic transport plane.

Intriligator, Michael and Bruce L. R. Smith. "Some Aspects of the Allocation of Scientific Effort Between Teaching and Research," *American Economic Review,* May 1966, 56, 494–507. Develops a model for the allocation of new scientists and identifies optimum allocations of such scientists in the light of certain science policy objectives.

Knorr, Klaus. "On the Cost-effectiveness Approach to Military R&D: A Critique." Santa Monica, Calif.: 1966. RAND Corporation. Paper P3390, 10 p. See also *Bulletin of the Atomic Scientists,* November 1966, 22, 11–14.

Lipetz, Ben-ami. "The Measurement of Efficiency of Scientific Research," *Intermedia,* Carlisle, Mass.: 1965. 262 p. Aims "to clarify the meaning of efficiency as applied to scientific research activity" and "to indicate some specific approaches by which objective efficiency measurements might be applied to scientific research for the purpose of improving productivity."

Martino, Joseph P. "A Method for Balanced Allocation of Resources among R&D Projects." Alexandria, Va.: Processed for Defense Documentation Center by Clearinghouse for Federal Scientific and Technical Information, Air Force Office of Scientific Research, Technical report, AFOSR-67-0326, 1967. 30 p. "AD 648 649."

National Academy of Science. "Basic Research and National Goals; a Report to the Committee on Science and Astronautics," U.S. House of Representatives. Washington, D.C.: Government Printing Office, 1965. 336 p. Fifteen papers consider two issues: "the allocation of resources between science and other activities" and "the allocation of resources within science."

Nelson, Richard R. "The Efficient Achievement of Rapid Technological Progress: A Major New Problem in Public Finance," *American Economic Review,* May 1966, 56, 232–241.

————, "The Simple Economics of Basic Scientific Research," *Journal of Political Economy,* June 1959, 67, 297–306.

Nelson, Richard R. and others. "Technology, Economic Growth, and Public Policy." Washington, D.C.: Brookings Institution 1967, 238 p. See "Public Policy Proposals," pp. 171–211.

Ohio State University Conference on Economics of Research and Development, Columbus, 1962. *Economics of Research and Development,* edited by Richard A. Tybout. Columbus: Ohio State University Press, 1965. 458 p. "Classification of Social Costs and Social Benefits in Research and Development," by Bruno Fritsch and others, p. 258–267; "The Allocation of Research and Development Resources: Some Problems of Public Policy," by Richard R. Nelson, p. 288–306.

Reagan, Michael D. "R&D: Suggestions for an Allocations Framework," *Public Administration Review,* June 1967, 27, 104–111. Attempts "to sketch a rationale for research support allocation and to indicate some of the criteria inputs and practical institutional complications involved in practising any allocational system."

Renshaw, Edward F. "Atomic Power: Research Costs and Social Returns," *Land Economics,* August 1959, 35, 222–231. Holds that it is possible to estimate not only the *ex post* returns from public and private investment in research but also to make *ex ante* estimates of returns from research not yet completed.

Robbins, C. K. "A Management System for Exploratory Development." Prepared for Air Force Flight Dynamics Laboratory, Research & Technology Division, Wright-Patterson AFB, Ohio. Processed for Defense Documentation Center by Clearinghouse for Federal Scientific and Technical Information, Alexandria, Va.: 1967, 23 p. "AD 648 699" "Describes one approach to the evaluation of research tasks and the efficient allocation of exploratory development dollars and manpower" to such tasks.

Scherer, Frederick M. "Government Research and Development Programs," Robert Dorfman, ed. *Measuring Benefits of Government Investments.* Papers presented at a conference of experts, November 7–9, 1963. Washington, D.C.: Brookings Institution [1965] pp. 12–70.

Smith, Bruce L. R. "The Concept of Scientific Choice: a Brief Review of the Literature," *American Behavioral Scientist,* May 1966, 9, 27–36. Also available as RAND Corporation. Paper P-3156.

Solo, Robert. "A Critical Evaluation of the National Academy of Science's Cost-benefit Analysis for Oceanographic Research," *Land Economics,* November 1966, 42, 527–531.

Stoodley, Francis H. "A Study of Methods Which Could Improve the Relevance of Naval Applied Research and Exploratory Development." Washington, DC.: Office of Naval Research, 1966. 132 p.

U.S. Congress, Senate. Committee on Labor and Public Welfare. "Scientific Manpower Utilization, 1965–66." Hearings before the Special Subcommittee on the Utilization of Scientific Manpower . . . 89th Cong., 1st–2d sess. on S.2662 . . . Washington, D.C.: Government Printing Office, 1967. 213 p.

————, "Scientific Manpower Utilization, 1967." Hearings before the Special Subcommittee on the Utilization of Scientific Manpower, 90th Cong., 1st sess. on S.430—S.467. Washington, D.C.: Government Printing Office, 1967. 377 p.

U.S. Congress, House, Committee on Government Operations. "The Federal Research and Development Programs: the Decision Making Process." Hearings before a subcommittee . . . 89th Cong., 2d sess. Washington, D.C.: Government Printing Office, 1966. 212 p.

Universities-National Bureau Committee for Economic Research. "The Rate and Direction of Inventive Activity: Economic and Social Factors," a conference of the Universities-National Bureau Committee for Economic

Research and the Committee on Economic Growth of the Social Science
Research Council. Princeton: Princeton University Press, 1962. 635 p.
See also, "The Decision Making Problem in Development," by Burton H.
Klein, p. 477–508.

Weinberg, Alvin M. "The Choices of Big Science," *Reflections on Big Science*.
Cambridge, Mass.: M.I.T. Press 1967. 65–122.

Weinberg, Alvin M. "Criteria for Scientific Choice," *Minerva*, Winter 1963, 1,
159–171. Proposes guidelines for Government allocation of resources to
competing fields of basic science.

Resource development

Bain, Joe S. "Criteria for Undertaking Water-Resource Developments," *American Economic Review*, May 1960, 50, 310–320. See also, discussion by
Otto Eckstein, p. 335–337.

Bain, Joe S. *et al.* "Northern California's Water Industry; the Comparative
Efficiency of Public Enterprise in Developing a Scarce Natural Resource."
Baltimore, Md.: Johns Hopkins Press. Published for *Resources for the
Future*, 1966, 766 p. See Pt. 3: "Performance," p. 529–636; Pt. 4: "Summary and Policy Proposals," pp. 639–672; "Appendices," p. 675–729.

Barber, C. L. "Water Resource Development," *Canadian Journal of Economics
and Political Science*, November 1961, 27, 533–540.

Bramhall, David F. and Edwin S. Mills. "Alternative Methods of Improving
Stream Quality: An Economic and Policy Analysis." *Water Resources Research*, Third quarter, 1966, 2, 355–363.

Brooks, David B. "Strip Mine Reclamation and Economic Analysis," *Natural
Resources Journal*, January 1966, 6, 13–44.

Brown, Gardner and C. B. McGuire. "A Socially Optimum Pricing Policy for
a Public Water Agency," *Water Resources Research*, First quarter 1967,
3, 33–43. Develops "a simple model for determining the socially optimum
price to charge locationally differentiated irrigation districts for both
surface and groundwater supplies."

Castle, Emery *et al.* "Water Resources Development: A Review of the New
Federal Evaluation Procedures," *Journal of Farm Economics*, November
1963, 45, 693–704. Examines the economic rationale underlying the statement of policy superseding Bureau of the Budget Circular A-47.

Ciriacy-Wantrup, S. V. "Conservation and Resource Programming," *Land
Economics*, May 1961, 37, 105–111.

————, *Resource Conservation, Economics and Policies*. Rev. ed. Berkeley,
University of California at Division of Agricultural Sciences, Agricultural
Experiment Station, 1963. pp. 230–250.

Clawson, Marion and Jack L. Knetsch. *Economics of Outdoor Recreation*.
Baltimore, Md.: Published for *Resources for the Future* by the Johns
Hopkins Press, 1966, pp. 209–285, 287–317.

Clawson, Marion. "Methods of Measuring the Demand for and Value of Outdoor Recreation." Washington, D.C.: 1959. 36 p. *Resources for the Future*.
Reprint No. 10. A paper presented at a meeting of the Taylor-Hibbard
Club, University of Wisconsin, January 13, 1959.

Conference on Water Resources and Economic Development in the South,

Atlanta, 1965. [Papers presented at the conference . . . held at the Atlanta-Biltmore Hotel, Atlanta, Ga., March 1965] Sponsored by the Council of State Governments, Southern Land Economics Research Committee and the Agricultural Policy Institute. [Raleigh] 1965. 179 p.

Partial contents: "Water Resources and Economic Development: the Challenge to Knowledge," by S. V. Ciriacy-Wantrup. "Systems Analysis," by Maynard Hufschmidt. "Economics of Pollution Control," by Allen V. Kneese. "Government and Water Resources Development," by Stephen C. Smith.

Crutchfield, James A. "Valuation of Fishery Resources," *Land Economics,* May 1962, 38, 145–154.

Daiute, Robert J. "Methods for Determination of Demand for Outdoor Recreation." *Land Economics,* August, 1966, 42, 327–338. "Reports the results of a survey of methods for determining demand . . . to show the relevance of previously-designed methods both as individual techniques and as parts of a battery of instruments for ascertaining demand for outdoor recreation."

Darling, F. Fraser and John P. Milton, eds. *Future Environments of North America.* The record of a conference convened by the Conservation Foundation in April 1965 at Airlie House, Warrenton, Va. Garden City, N.Y., Natural History Press, 1966. See "Standards and Techniques of Evaluating Economic Choices in Environmental Resource Development," by Ayers Brinser, pp. 235–245; "Natural Resources and Economic Development: the Web of Events, Policies and Policy Objectives," by Joseph L. Fisher, pp. 261–276.

Design of Water-Resource Systems; New Techniques for Relating Economic Objectives, Engineering Analysis and Governmental Planning, Arthur Maass *et al.* Cambridge, Mass.: Harvard University Press, 1962.

Eckstein, Otto. *Water Resource Development; the Economics of Project Evaluation.* Cambridge: Harvard University Press, 1958.

"Economic Analysis of Water Resource Problems," *American Economic Review,* May 1967, 57, 158–196.

Contents: "Nonmarket Values and Efficiency of Public Investments in Water Resources," by A. Allen Schmid. "Urban Water Supply: A Second Look," by Jack Hirshleifer and J. W. Milliman. "Water Policy and Economic Optimizing: Some Conceptual Problems in Water Research," by S. V. Ciriacy-Wantrup.

"Economics of Water-Resource Use," *American Economic Review,* May 1962, 52, 450–473.

Contents: "Political Economy of Water Development," by Vincent Ostrom. "Extensions of Benefit-Cost Analysis," by George S. Tolley and Cleon Harrell.

Fox, Irving K. and Orris C. Herfindahl. "Attainment of Efficiency in Satisfying Demands for Water Resources," *American Economic Review,* May 1964, 54, 200–206.

Also available as *Resources for the Future.* Reprint No. 46.

Freeman, A. Myrick. "Adjusted Benefit-cost Ratios for Six Recent Reclamation Projects," *Journal of Farm Economics,* Nov. 1966, 48, 1002–1012. Reviews Reclamation Bureau cost-benefit estimates for six projects, points out the chief sources of bias, and concludes that, although benefit estimates are overgenerous, the comparison of estimated and actual costs is favorable.

————, "Income Distribution and Planning for Public Investment," *American Economic Review,* June 1967, 57, 495–508. Examines "the implications of introducing income redistribution as a policy goal in public investment planning and project selection." The model was initially applied to water projects, but may be made applicable "to any federal investment where benefits and costs are tangible and beneficiaries do not bear the full cost of the project."

————, "Six Federal reclamation Projects and the Distribution of Income," *Water Resources Research,* Second quarter 1967, 3, 319–332. An application of project evaluation techniques with distribution of income as a criterion.

Gertel, Carl. "Recent Suggestions for Cost Allocation of Multiple-purpose Projects in the Light of Public Interest," *Journal of Farm Economics,* February 1951, 33, 130–134.

Gramm, Warren S. "Water Resource Analysis: Private Investment Criteria and Social Priorities," *Journal of Farm Economics,* November 1963, 45, 705–712. A critical appraisal of the techniques for analysis of investment in water resource development advanced by Hirshleifer and other economists.

Hammond, Richard J. "Benefit-cost Analysis and Water Pollution Control." Stanford, Calif.: 1960 (Stanford University. Food Research Institute. Miscellaneous publication No. 13) 95 p.

Hartman, L. M. and D. A. Seastone. "Welfare Goals and Organization of Decision-Making for the Allocation of Water Resources," *Land Economics,* February 1965, 41, 21–30. Identifies, describes, and appraises institutional arrangements for transferring water among users "in terms of an efficiency model of water use with special reference to external economies."

Haveman, Robert H. "Water Resource Investment and the Public Interest, an Analysis of Federal Expenditures in Ten Southern States." Nashville, Tenn.: Vanderbilt University Press, 1965. Examines the benefit-cost ratios problem with a series of concrete criteria and formulae and demonstrates that the present system of computing benefit-cost ratios is inaccurate and misleading.

Herfindahl, Orris C. and Allen V. Kneese. "Quality of the Environment: An Economic Approach to Some Problems in Using Land, Water, and Air." Baltimore, Md.: Distributed by the Johns Hopkins Press for *Resources for the Future* 1965, 96 p.

Hirshleifer, Jack, *et al. Water Supply: Economics, Technology, and Policy.* Chicago, Ill.: University of Chicago Press, 1960.

Howe, Charles W. "Methods for Equipment Selection and Benefit Evaluation in Inland Waterway Transportation," *Water Resources Research,* First quarter 1965, 1, 25–39.

Hufschmidt, Maynard M. "Field Level Planning of Water Resource Systems." *Water Resources Research,* Second quarter, 1965, 1, 147–163. "Examines the process of comprehensive water resources planning . . . to determine ways in which new knowledge and techniques can be applied to major planning tasks now under way."

Hufschmidt, Maynard M. and Myron B. Fiering. *Simulation Techniques for*

Design of Water Resource Systems. Cambridge, Mass.: Harvard University Press, 1966. 212 p. Develops the methodology for constructing decision models, using as an example a simulation program for the Lehigh River Basin.

James, Douglas L. "Economic Analysis of Alternative Flood Control Measures," *Water Resources Research,* Second quarter 1967, 3, 333–357. Develops a digital computer program to determine "the optimum combination of structural and nonstructural measures for flood control according to the criterion of economic efficiency."

Jarrett, Henry, ed. "Environmental Quality in a Growing Economy," *Resources for the Future.* Essays from the Sixth RFF Forum. Baltimore, Md.: Johns Hopkins Press, 1966. See "Beyond the Market Mechanism," pp. 47–65; "Economic Research in Problems of Environment," pp. 69–101.

Johnson, Edwin L. "A Study in the Economics of Water Quality Management," *Water Resources Research,* Second quarter 1967, 3, 291–305. Studies the effluent charge scheme as a means of allocating waste reduction among dischargers.

Johnson, Hugh A. and Judith M. Huff. "Toward Measuring the Intangible Values of Natural Beauty." Paper presented at annual meeting, Soil Conservation Society of America, Albuquerque, N.M., August 14–17, 1966. Washington, Economic Research Service, Department of Agriculture 1966, 19 p. Surveys some of the problems involved and questions to be answered in measuring the costs and benefits of resource management for natural beauty.

Kindsvater, C. E., ed. "Organization and Methodology for River Basin Planning," proceedings of a seminar based on the U.S. Study Commission, Southeast River Basins. Georgia Institute of Technology, Atlanta. Water Resources Center. Atlanta, 1964.

Kneese, Allen V. "The Economics of Regional Water Quality Management," *Resources for the Future,* Baltimore, Md.: Johns Hopkins Press, 1964.

————, "Water Pollution: Economic Aspects and Research Needs," *Resources for the Future,* Washington, D.C.: 1962. "Evaluation—Determination and Integration of Individual and Social Values—Focus of Public Policy," pp. 29–42; "Benefit-Cost Analysis and the 'Constrained Cost Minimization' Framework," pp. 42–44.

Knetsch, Jack L. "Land Values and Parks in Urban Fringe Areas," *Journal of Farm Economics,* December 1962, 44, 1718–1729. Discusses the need to consider the social value of land used for community purposes and means of arriving at measures which will provide the basis for optimal allocation of land.

————, "Outdoor Recreation Demands and Benefits," *Land Economics,* November 1963, 39, 387–396. Examines various promising approaches to the problem of providing "information on demand relationships and values, useful for decision purposes."

Kohn, Robert E. "Leaf Burning—an Economic Case Study," *Scientist and Citizen,* April 1967, 9, 71–75. Demonstrates the application of cost-benefit analysis to problems of air pollution abatement.

Krutilla, John V. "The Columbia River Treaty; the Economics of an International River Basin Development," *Resources for the Future.* Baltimore,

Md.: Johns Hopkins Press, 1967. This case study of the potentialities and limitations of an international river basin development considers two broad questions: "what was the basis for the selection of projects . . . and how closely did the selection adhere to economic criteria," and "how does the division of the benefits from the cooperative venture affect each party."

————, "Criteria for Evaluating Regional Development Programs," *American Economic Review*, May 1955, 45, 120–132.

————, "An Economic Approach to Coping with Flood Damage," *Water Resources Research*, Second quarter, 1966. 2, 183–190. Demonstrates that "a compulsory flood use insurance scheme is one means of achieving efficient use of flood plain lands."

————, "Is Public Intervention in Water Resources Conducive to Economic Efficiency?" *Natural Resources Journal*, 6, 60–75, January 1966. Considers certain problems in cost-benefit techniques as presently applied and certain deficiencies in the institutional mechanism for Federal planning of water resources development.

————, and Otto Eckstein. "Multiple Purpose River Development: Studies in Applied Economic Analysis," *Resources for the Future*. Baltimore, Md.: Johns Hopkins Press, 1958.

————, "Some Recent Developments in River Basin Planning and Evaluation," *Journal of Farm Economics*, December 1958, 50, 1674–1687. Also available as *Resources for the Future*. Reprint No. 11.

Kuiper, Edward. *Water Resources Development; Planning, Engineering, and Economics*. London, Butterworth's 1965. See "Economic analysis," p. 405–436.

Lind, Robert C. "The Nature of Flood Control Benefits and the Economics of Flood Protection." Prepared . . . for [the] Office of Naval Research. Stanford, Calif., 1966. Stanford University. Institute for Mathematical Studies in the Social Sciences. Technical report No. 145.

Mack, Ruth P. and Sumner Myers. "Outdoor Recreation," Robert Dorfman, ed. *Measuring Benefits of Government Investments*. Papers presented at a conference of experts, November 7–9, 1963. Washington, D.C.: Brookings Institution 1965, pp. 71–101.

McKean, Roland N. *Efficiency in Government Through Systems Analysis, with Emphasis on Water Resource Development*. New York: John Wiley, 1958.

————, "Operations Research and Government budgets." Santa Monica, Calif.: 1957. RAND Corporation. Paper P-999-C, 19 p. "The techniques of operations research may be employed to seek an improved allocation of funds among programs or to seek the best size of particular programs; [i.e.] to compare, not only alternative ways to carry out a specified activity, but also alternative scales of that activity or alternative allocations of resources among activities." Uses the program of the Forest Service as an example.

Margolis, Julius. "The Economic Evaluation of Federal Water Resource Development," *American Economic Review*, March 1959, 49, 96–111. Lengthy discussion of cost-benefit procedures of Eckstein, Krutilla, and McKean.

Marts, M. E. and W. R. D. Sewell. "The Application of Benefit-cost Analysis to Fish Preservation Expenditures: a neglected aspect of river basin investment decisions," *Land Economics*, February 1959, 35, 48–55.

Meek, Ronald L. "The Allocation of Expenditure in the Electrical Supply Industry: Some Methodological Problems," Alan T. Peacock and D. J. Robertson, eds. *Public Expenditures: Appraisal and Control.* Edinburgh: Oliver and Boyd 1963, pp. 36–60.

Michelson, Irving and Boris Tourin. "Comparative Method For Studying Costs of Air Pollution," *Public Health Reports,* June 1966, 81, 505–511. Reports the methodology of a 1960 study of air pollution costs in the Upper Ohio Valley.

National Research Council. Committee on Oceanography. "Economic Benefits from Oceanographic Research." Washington, D.C.: 1964. Publication 1228, 50 p.

Ogden, Delbert C. "Economic Analysis of Air Pollution," *Land Economics,* May 1966, 42, 137–147. Develops a model approximating "the total cost of air pollution and the cost of specific pollutants to an air shed."

Renshaw, Edward F. "Toward Responsible Government; An Economic Appraisal of Federal Investment in Water Resource Programs." Chicago, Ill.: Idyia Press, 1957.

Resources for Tomorrow Conference, Montreal, 1961. *Resources for Tomorrow.* Extracts. Ottawa, R. Duhamel, Queen's Printer 1961. 2 Nos. "Benefit-cost Analysis and Project Evaluation," by R. A. Spargo, 1, 299–310; "Water Workshop B, Benefit-cost Analysis," 3, 145–159.

Richards, Allen B. "Some Economic Considerations of the Multiple Use of Forest Land." *Land Economics,* August 1958, 34, 263–268.

Ridker, Ronald G. *Economic Costs of Air Pollution; Studies in Measurement.* New York: Praeger 1967. Develops and tests three methods of measuring the economic effects of air pollution and applies the methods in six studies.

Robinson, K. L. "Cost and Effectiveness in Recent Government Land Retirement Programs in the United States," *Journal of Farm Economics,* February 1966, 48, 22–30. Analyzes the success of land retirement programs in reducing grain surpluses and points out alternative courses of action that would achieve the same objective at a lower unit cost.

Ruttan, Vernon W. "The Economic Demand for Irrigated Acreage; New Methodology and Some Preliminary Projects, 1954–1980." *Resources for the Future.* Baltimore, Md.: Johns Hopkins Press 1965. A significant departure from traditional efforts to project long-range water requirements, "bringing into play the possibilities for substitution among resources and regions."

Seckler, David W. "On the Uses and Abuses of Economic Science in Evaluating Public Outdoor Recreation," *Land economics,* November 1966, 42, 485–494. Criticizes some of the present methods of appraising recreation costs and benefits and suggests improvements in recreation evaluation procedures.

Sewell, W. R. D. *et al. Guide to Benefit-cost Analysis.* Ottawa: R. Duhamel, Queen's Printer, 1965.

Sewell, W. R. D. and M. E. Marts. "The Nez Perce Dam and the Value of a Fishery," *Land Economics,* August 1961, 37, 257–260.

Smith, Stephen C. and Emery N. Castle, eds. "Economics and Public Policy in Watery Resources Development." Ames: Iowa State University Press, 1964.

Stade, Marinus. "Cost Effectiveness of Water Bombers in Forest Fire Control," *Canadian Operational Research Society Journal*, March 1967, 5, 1–18.

Steiner, Peter O. "Choosing Among Alternative Public Investments in the Water Resource Field," *American Economic Review*, December 1959, 49, 893–916.

————, "The Role of Alternative Cost in Project Design and Selection," *Quarterly Journal of Economics*, August 1966, 79, 416–430. Develops a model to answer the question, "When and to what extent can the cost of an alternative project substitute for or provide limits to benefit measurement.?"

Stevens, Joe B. "Recreation Benefits from Water Pollution Control," *Water Resources Research*, Second quarter 1966, 2, 167–182. Develops a model of "biological and behavioral relationships involved in sports angling" as a means of estimating direct recreational benefits from pollution control.

———— , "Recreation Benefits from Water Pollution Control: a Further Note on Benefit Evaluation," *Water Resources Research*, First quarter 1967, 3, 63–64. Corrects a nomenclatural error in article cited above.

Symposium on the Economic and Social Aspects of Weather Modification, National Center for Atmospheric Research, 1965. "Human Dimensions of Weather Modification." Chicago, Ill.: 1966. 423 p. University of Chicago. Dept. of Geography. Research papers No. 105. "Evaluation of Benefit-cost Analysis as Applied to Weather and Climate Modification," by Ivars Gutmanis and Lester Goldner, pp. 111–125; "Public Policy Issues Raised by Weather Modification: Possible Alternative Strategies for Government Action," by Fremont J. Lyden and George A. Shipman, pp. 289–303.

Symposium: "Water Resources Research," *National Resources Journal*, October 1965, 5, 218–297. "Research on Comprehensive Planning of Water-resource Systems," by Maynard M. Hufschmidt; "Economic and Related Problems in Contemporary Water Resources Management," by Allen V. Kneese.

Thomas, Harold A. "The Animal Farm: a Mathematical Model for the Discussion of Social Standards for Control of the Environment," *Quarterly Journal of Economics*, February 1963, 77, 143–148.

Timmons, John F. "Economic Framework for Watershed Development," *Journal of Farm Economics*, December 1954, 34, 1170–1183.

Tolley, George S. and F. E. Riggs, eds. "Economics of Watershed Planning." A Symposium on the Economics of Watershed Planning held in Knoxville, June 1959. Sponsored by the Southeast Land Tenure Research Committee, the Farm Foundation, and the Tennessee Valley Authority. Ames: Iowa State University Press, 1961, 339 p. See "Philosophy and Objectives of Watershed Policy," p. 1–14; "Benefits from Watershed Development," pp. 27–41; "State of the Economic Data," pp. 111–126; "Applying Economic Principles in Watershed Planning," pp. 151–166.

Trice, Andrew H. and Samuel E. Wood. "Measurement of Recreation Benefits," *Land Economics*, August 1958, 34, 195–207. See also discussion in *Land Economics*, November 1958, 34, 365–370.

Turvey, Ralph. "On Investment Choices in Electricity Generation," *Oxford Economic Papers*, November 1963, 15, 278–286. Illustrates the nature of complications in determining costs and benefits of one component in a system, using as an example the Mackenzie report on "Electricity in Scotland."

U.S. Bureau of Reclamation. "Report of Panel of Consultants on Secondary or Indirect Benefits of Water-Use Projects . . ." June 26, 1952. Washington, D.C.: 1952. 63 p. Panel: John M. Clark, Eugene L. Grant, Maurice M. Kelso.

U.S. Bureau of the Budget. "Standards and Criteria for Formulating and Evaluating Federal Water Resources Development, Report of a Panel of Consultants . . . ," Washington, D.C.: Government Printing Office, 1961. 71 p.

U.S. Congress, House, Committee on Interior and Insular Affairs. Lower Colorado River Basin Project. Hearing before the Subcommittee on Irrigation and Reclamation . . . 89th Cong., 1st sess. on H.R.4671 [etc.] Washington, D.C.: Government Printing Office, 1965, pt. 2, pp. 1493–1539.

————, Recreation Allocation Policy. Hearings . . . 88th Cong., 1st sess. on H.R.9032. Washington, D.C.: Government Printing Office, 1964. 126 p.

————, "Water Project Planning Policy," Hearings before the Subcommittee on Irrigation and Reclamation . . . on policies and procedures applicable to the planning of water resource development projects, 88th Cong., 1st sess. Washington, D.C.: Government Printing Office, 1963. 191 p. Serial No. 2.

U.S. Congress, Senate, Committee on Interior and Insular Affairs. Water Project Recreation Act. Hearings . . . 89th Cong., 1st sess. on S.1229 . . . Washington, D.C.: Government Printing Office, 1965. 66 p.

U.S. Interagency Committee on Water Resources. "Proposed Practices for Economic Analysis of River Basin Projects; Report . . . by the Subcommittee on Evaluation Standards," Rev. May 1958. Washington, D.C.: 1959, 56 p.

U.S. Outdoor Recreation Resources Review Commission. "Economic Studies of Outdoor Recreation; Reports . . . by Commission Staff . . . ," Marion Clawson et al. Washington, D.C.: Government Printing Office, 1962. 166 p. ORRRC study report No. 24. See also "Economic Analysis Bearing upon Outdoor Recreation," by Ivan M. Lee, pp. 1–44; "Economic Evaluation of Outdoor Recreation Benefits," by the Commission staff, pp. 45–69.

U.S. President's Water Resources Council. "Policies, Standards, and Procedures in the Formulation, Evaluation, and Review of Plans for Use and Development of Water and Related Land Resources." Prepared under the direction of the . . . Council, together with a statement by Senator Clinton P. Anderson. Washington, D.C: Government Printing Office, 1962. 13 p. (87th Cong., 2d sess. Senate Doc. 97) Supersedes Bureau of the Budget Circular A-47.

Wennergren, E. Boyd and N. Keith Roberts. "Managing State Lands: Some Legal-Economic Considerations," Natural Resources Journal, April, 1967, 7, 252–265. Develops an analytical framework to provide a logical procedure for analyzing State land management alternatives.

Western Agricultural Economics Research Council. "Water Resources and Economic Development of the West; Proceedings of the Water Resources Development Committee . . . ," Report No. 0: "Direct and Indirect Benefits." Berkeley, Calif., 1951. 89 p.

————, "Water Resources and Economic Development of the West; Proceedings of the Water Resources Development Committee . . . , Report

No. 1: Research needs and problems." Berkeley, Calif., 1953. 131 p. See "Economic Analysis of Water Resource Policies," pp. 21–48; "Evaluation of Secondary Benefits of Water-Use Projects," pp. 49–62.

——————, "Water Resources and Economic Development of the West; Proceedings of the Water Resources Development Committee . . . Report No. 3: Benefit-cost analysis." Berkeley, Calif., 1954. 35 p.
Contents: "Current Concepts and Practices in Benefit-cost Analysis of Natural Resource Development," by Mark M. Regan and John F. Timmons. "The Role of Benefit-cost Analysis in Public Resource Development," by S. V. Ciriacy-Wantrup. "Discussion," by William E. Folz and Eugene L. Grant.

——————, "Water Resources and Economic Development of the West; Proceedings of the Water Resources Development Committee . . . , Report No. 13: Economics in the Decision Making Process; Economics of Water-Based Outdoor Recreation." Berkeley, Calif., 1964. 149 p.

Western Resources Conference. 7th, Colorado State University, 1965. "Water Research . . . ," Allen V. Kneese and Stephen C. Smith, ed. Published for *Resources for the Future,* Baltimore, Md.: Johns Hopkins Press, 1966. Partial contents: "Issues in Theoretical Economic Analysis"; "Case Studies of Water Management"; "Research on Evaluation Problems"; "Political and Administrative Studies."

Western Resources Conference. 6th, Colorado School of Mines, 1964. "New Horizons for Resources Research: Issues and Methodology." Boulder: University of Colorado Press, 1965. See "The Demand-value Structure of Recreation," by Lionel J. Lerner, pp. 21–27; "Use of Systems Analysis in Estaurine Water Pollution Control," by Robert V. Thomann, pp. 47–59; "Systems Analysis Approach to Water Quality Prediction in a Complex River Basin," by J. L. Worley and F. J. Burgess, pp. 61–86.

Western Resources Conference. 3d, Colorado State University, 1961. "Land and Water: Planning for Economic Growth," Harold L. Amoss and Roma K. McNickle, eds. Boulder, University of Colorado Press, 1962. See "Welfare Economics and Resource Development," pp. 177–204.

Whipple, William. "Economic Basis for Effluent Charges and Subsidies," *Water Resources Research,* First quarter 1966, 2, 159–164.

——————, "Economic Feasibility of Federal Power Projects," *Land Economics,* August 1962, 38, 219–230. Reviews progress in developing analytical principles for Federal hydro-electric projects and suggests further steps needed.

White, Gilbert F. "Choice of Adjustments to Floods." Chicago, Ill.: 1964. 150 p. University of Chicago, Dept. of Geography. Research paper No. 90. See "Problems of Comparing Adjustments," pp. 83–92; "Judging Alternative Investments," pp. 93–105; "Economic Effect of Local Flood Protection Measures," pp. 127–149.

Whittlesey, Norman K. "Cost and Efficiency of Alternative Land-Retirement Programs," *Journal of Farm Economics,* May 1967, 43, 351–359. Estimates the costs of land-retirement programs by the application of "interregional competition linear programming models to problems of production allocation under conditions of production capacity" greater than that needed to meet given levels of demand.

Wolozin, Harold, ed. "The Economics of Air pollution," a symposium. New
      York: W. C. Norton, 1966.
      Partial contents: "Air Pollution—General Background," by Allen V.
      Kneese; "Economic Incentives in Air Pollution Control," by Edwin S.
      Mills; "Strategies for Measuring the Cost of Air Pollution," by Ronald G.
      Ridker; "The Use of Government Statistics in Air Pollution Control," by
      Edward T. Crowder; "Setting Criteria for Public Expenditures on Air-
      Pollution Abatement: Theoretical Foundations and Limitations," by Harold
      Wolozin.

Transportation

Berkley, George. "Municipal Garages in Boston: A Cost-benefit Analysis,"
      Traffic Quarterly, April 1965, 19, 213–228.
Bruck, H. W. *et al.* "Evaluation of Alternative Transportation Proposals: The
      Northeast Corridor," *American Institute of Planners Journal,* November
      1966, 32, 322–333. "Deals with the nature and strategy of the impact
      modelling and with the problems of developing measures to evaluate in-
      direct consequences of changes in the transportation network."
Committee for Economic Development. "Developing Metropolitan Transporta-
      tion Policies: A Guide for Local Leadership. A Statement on National
      Policy by the Research and Policy Committee . . ." Washington, D.C.:
      1965. 100 p. See "Principles for Government Decisions on Transporta-
      tion," pp. 35–45.
Crumlish, Joseph D. "Notes on the State-of-the-Art of Benefit-Cost Analysis as
      Related to Transportation Systems." Washington, D.C.: Government Print-
      ing Office, 1966. 41 p. (U.S. National Bureau of Standards. Technical note
      294.)
Ferguson, Allen R. *et al. The Economic Value of the United States Merchant
      Marine.* Evanston: Transportation Center at Northwestern University,
      1961. 545 p.
Fort, Donald M. "Systems Analysis as an Aid in Air Transportation Planning."
      Santa Monica, Calif., 1966. RAND Corporation. Paper P-3293-1, 42 p.
Foster, C. D. "The Transport Problem." London: Blackie & Son 1963. See
      "The Social Surplus Criterion," pp. 62–68; "The Consumers' Surplus
      Criterion for Railways," pp. 117–150; "The Consumers' Surplus Criterion
      for Investment in Roads," pp. 254–279; "Coordination of Investment,"
      pp. 298–300; "Summary of Conclusions," pp. 307–309; "Opportunity Cost
      and Time Preference Rates," pp. 321–322.
Foster, C. D. and M. E. Beesley. "Estimating the Social Benefits of Construct-
      ing an Underground Railway in London," *Royal Statistical Society Journal,*
      Series A, 1963, 126, pt. 1, 46–93.
Fromm, Gary. "Civil Aviation Expenditures," Robert Dorfman, ed. *Measuring
      Benefits of Government Investments.* Papers presented at a conference of
      experts, November 7–9, 1963. Washington, D.C.: Brookings Institution
      1965 pp. 172–230.
————, "Economic Criteria for Federal Aviation Agency Expenditures."
      Prepared for Aviation Research and Development Service, Federal Avia-

tion Agency, June 1962 . . . Cambridge, Mass.: United Research, Inc., 1962. v. p.

———, "Transport Investment and Economic Development." Washington, D.C.: Brookings Institution, Transport Research Program 1965, 314 p. See "Design of the Transport Sector," by Gary Fromm, pp. 90–94; "Evaluation of Transport Projects," by Hans A. Adler, pp. 170–194.

Haikalis, George and E. W. Campbell. "Evaluating Urban Transportation Systems," ASCE (American Society of Civil Engineers) Proceedings. *Journal of the City Planning Division,* Sept. 1963, 89, No. CP1, Paper 3626, pp. 1–15. Uses the development of highway and transit plans by the Chicago Area Transportation Study to demonstrate the applications of cost-benefit analysis techniques.

Harral, Clell G. "Preparation and Appraisal of Transport Projects." Washington, D.C.: Transportation Research Project, Brookings Institution, 1965. 142 p.

Institute of Public Administration, New York. "Urban Transportation and Public Policy." Report prepared for U.S. Department of Commerce and Housing and Home Finance Agency. New York, 1961. See "Cost-Benefit Analysis and Expansion of Transportation Facilities," pp. 58–61.

Kuhn, Tillo E. *Public Enterprise Economics and Transport Problems.* Berkeley: University of California Press, 1962. Discusses the problems of evaluating public enterprise actions, proceeding from "definitions to analysis from the detailed to the general, from the individual project to processes in the economy at large."

Meyer, John R., J. F. Kain, and M. Wohl. *The Urban Transportation Problem.* Cambridge, Mass.: Harvard University Press, 1965. Pt. II discusses methods to "determine the costs of providing various services at different volume levels, for different route lengths and under specified conditions of speed, frequency, convenience, and comfort."

Pittsburgh area transportation study, final report in two parts . . . Study conducted under the sponsorship of the Commonwealth of Pennsylvania, County of Allegheny, City of Pittsburgh . . . U.S. Bureau of Public Roads. Pittsburgh 1961, 2 Vols. See "Techniques of transportation planning," 2, 80–103.

Swaine, Harold R. "A Proposal for Control of Local Service Subsidies." Santa Monica, Calif.: 1965. RAND Corporation. Paper P-3184, 24 p. Evaluates various procedures for efficient use of funds in Federal subsidies for local air service. Also in *Journal of Air Law and Commerce,* Summer 1965, 31, 181–197.

Universities-National Bureau Committee for Economic Research. "Transportation Economics," a conference sponsored by the Committee. New York: Distributed by Columbia University Press for National Bureau of Economic Research, 1965. 464 p. National Bureau of Economic Research. Special Conference series, No. 17. See "The Uses and Measurement of Costs for Transport Policy," pp. 1–165; "Urban Transportation," pp. 245–348.

Witheford, David K. "Economic Analysis of Freeway Lighting," *Traffic Quarterly,* April 1967, 21, 289–303.

Zwick, Charles J. Session II—"Urban Transportation Problems: Evaluating

Alternative Systems." Remarks . . . before the Symposium on "Science, Engineering and the City" sponsored by [the] National Academy of Sciences [and the] National Academy of Engineering, Washington, D.C.: April 26–27, 1967. Bureau of the Budget 1967. 8 p.